Advance Comments

"This is more than a handbook for investigators in tracking down computer crime–it also tells you how to respond to threats and ways to avoid problems. This book shows where computing meets law enforcement."

> — Cliff Stoll, author of *The Cuckoo's Egg* and
> *Silicon Snake Oil*

"This book provides an excellent primer for both the network security professional and the criminal investigator...The authors assisted in the successful conclusion of several federal investigations."

> — James C. Settle, I-NET and former FBI agent

"...a very helpful and interesting book. I'm going to make sure all of the Secret Service new Electronic Crimes Special Agents get a copy to assist them."

> — Bob Friel, Financial Crimes Division, Electronic Crime Branch,
> *U.S. Secret Service*

"This is an excellent and worthwhile handbook for both the novice and experienced computer crime investigator. I will recommend it to my computer crime classes."

> — Detective Robert M. Snyder, Intelligence Bureau, Computer Crime Unit,
> Columbus Ohio Police Department

"Any organization that is worried about attacks on their computer systems, especially those attached to the Internet, should run to the bookstore to pick up a copy of Computer Crime. It's one-stop shopping for system administrators and law enforcers, with plenty of pointers to additional resources if needed."

> — Lance J. Hoffman, Director, Institute for Computer and
> Telecommunications Systems Policy, School of Engineering, The
> George Washington University

Computer Crime
A Crimefighter's Handbook

Computer Crime

A Crimefighter's Handbook

David Icove, Karl Seger, and William VonStorch

O'Reilly & Associates, Inc.
103 Morris Street, Suite A
Sebastopol, CA 95472

Computer Crime: A Crimefighter's Handbook
by David Icove, Karl Seger, and William VonStorch

Editor: Deborah Russell

Consulting Editor: Eugene H. Spafford

Production Editor: Ralph Pescatore

Printing History:

August 1995:   First Edition.

ISBN: 1-56592-086-4   [1/96]

Table of Contents

Foreword

Daily, huge amounts of society's assets are being developed, stored, transmitted, and manipulated using computers and their associated data networks. The U.S. financial industry alone transmits trillions of dollars of transactions per day over computer networks. Information relating to the design of new industrial products, medicine, insurance, scientific research, social policy, law enforcement, and national defense has all been moving from file cabinets and desktops to the virtual workplace presented by computers and computer networks. Soon, high-speed computing may also support critical components of our daily commerce, entertainment, and news media. If some peoples' visions are correct, we may soon exercise our right to vote through a computer link; we can already communicate with many of our elected representatives via computer. Computer networks, email, and similar linkage is already becoming a tool of politics: both the president and vice president have widely known (and heavily used) electronic mail addresses, as do many members of Congress. State and local government are also "coming online."

Some current growth projections suggest that every person in the world may have access to global networks by early in the next century. Those estimates are already reflected in actual usage. At the time this book went to press, the Internet, the largest computer network in the world, was estimated to reach over 25 million people in more than 100 counties on all seven continents. Those numbers are increasing at the rate of as much as 15 percent per month.

Other projections have estimated that not only will the number of users grow, but so will the number of computers per person. By the end of the century, each person in industrialized society may own and use scores (or hundreds) of networked computers. We will have computers in our home appliances, phones, televisions, offices, and automobiles. Those computers will share information to optimize our use of resources and provide convenience in our everyday lives. "Smart" houses and cars will adjust themselves to level of use, schedule, season, and situation using computers. We will be able to query and adjust their settings from anywhere we may be. These capabilities should enable us to conserve vital resources and at the same time enhance our quality of life. Industry, academia, and government may all be impacted in similar dramatic ways.

This brave new world is not without its dark side, however. Most of these applications are likely targets for traditional crimes, including theft, fraud, vandalism, extortion, and espionage. They are also susceptible to new threats specific to computers and networks, such as computer viruses. Currently, there are insufficient obstacles to the commission of these crimes: the people computerizing these resources have failed to consider the security requirements necessary to properly safeguard them, or their managers don't understand the risks well enough to fund the efforts. Insufficient training in security, buggy software, and inadequate software engineering methods all may contribute significant flaws to the installed protection mechanisms. Our more traditional systems of ledger and file have protection methods developed over decades (sometimes centuries) of experience. They are not perfect; however, they have known risks and failure modes. We do not yet have such experience with computer systems and networks. Unfortunately, the rush to massive computerization and networking has not given us sufficient time to develop and test workable defenses before they are needed.

It is in this new arena that law enforcement will need to adapt and to operate, for it is here that major crimes will be (and are now being) committed. Investigators will need to gain an understanding of new criminal methods, different investigative techniques, and some new approaches to law enforcement. Investigators will need to become comfortable with the investigation of computer crimes, not only to protect the interests and resources of society as a whole but also to protect many of the freedoms and rights we all desire as individual citizens. Political corruption, economic oppression, invasion of privacy, and terrorism can all be conducted by computer, too.

Investigators will also need to become comfortable enough with computers to provide protection during investigations. Agents of the law must strive to avoid damage to the property, livelihood, and rights of bystanders and suspect users of computers in an investigation. Experience has already shown how easy it is to cause incidental damage when conducting a computer crime investigation, and how important proper training and knowledge are to conducting an effective investigation. Excesses and damage caused during an investigation, whether accidental or not, may lead to dismissal of charges against suspects. Worse, each such incident may serve to alienate and injure the citizens that the investigator is charged with protecting.

This book is directed to these goals of effective law enforcement: detecting criminal activity, gathering evidence, conducting an investigation, and protecting victims, bystanders, and suspects alike. The book is not intended to make computer experts out of law enforcement personnel (and neither will it enable computer specialists to become expert investigators). Instead, the authors present a comprehensive introduction to basic computing terminology and computer security as appropriate for a nonspecialist investigator.

After studying this book, you will have a good understanding of how computers are protected against criminal activities and how those controls may be circumvented. You will also be able to gain an understanding of applicable laws (mainly in the United States), characteristics of likely perpetrators, and common motives for computer crimes. You will also gain some understanding of when an outside expert may be needed, both to aid in the investigation and to protect the rights and property of the suspects and victims. For most law enforcement personnel, that is all that is really necessary; investigators are not generally experts in fields such as telephony, counter-espionage, or toxicology. However, when crimes occur involving components in those areas, a good investigator should be able to recognize the basic elements of the crime, conduct a preliminary investigation, and preserve volatile evidence. Then, the investigator will know to consult with subject-area experts for a more comprehensive investigation.

The challenge to law enforcement with computing is basically the same as with any new technology: keeping a delicate balance between society's needs and individual rights. For the protection of society, law enforcement must develop new techniques that allow for investigation and countering criminal behavior, undoubtedly including new methods of monitoring communications and searching large collections of data. Society cannot allow antisocial or injurious behavior simply because it occurs in the intangible realm of "cyberspace." At the same time, law enforcement personnel must help prevent the curtailment of vital rights of individuals, including the rights to privacy, to free speech, and to publication. Because a message is composed of electrons through a wire rather than ink on paper does not make the right of free expression any less cherished. Because records stored on disk can be easily read and indexed does not mean they should be without just cause. If the future of computing is as we envision, it will be *our* future, and we all should be concerned that it becomes one we wish to embrace.

As you read this book, you will gain some insight into this challenge. You will recognize that computers and networks are really not so radically different from other technologies. The challenge appears more complex because of the fleeting nature of the communications, the (potential) international scope of the parties, and the technical sophistication of the perpetrators. However, similar challenges have been faced with the automobile, the airplane, the telephone, and the fax: we now take those for granted and make accommodations for them if they are components of an investigation. Within a short time, you may be as comfortable with investigations that involve computers and networks. Unfortunately, it appears certain there will be no shortage (in the near term, at least) of opportunities to demonstrate this newfound ease. There is little time to waste: the highwaymen are already lurking on the Information Superhighway.

Professor Eugene H. Spafford
COAST Laboratory Director
Purdue University
West Lafayette, Indiana
May 1995

A Message from the Other Side . . .

In the last 15 years I have approached computer security from several directions. As a hacker, I've moved unnoticed through the world's computer networks, right under the noses of their administrators. As a consultant, I've worked with those same administrators to protect from unauthorized access. As a journalist, I've followed the culture of the international computer underground, reporting on tips and techniques of use to both hackers and administrators. As an individual, I've had my phones tapped, my credit file browsed, my relatives harassed, and been forced to contact federal law enforcement for assistance.

Having been able to view security from so many perspectives, one fact keeps shining out with amazing clarity: law enforcement professionals are grossly unprepared and undereducated when dealing with crimes of a high-tech nature.

In 1990, I was a target in a federal investigation on computer crime. During the course of this investigation, the United States Secret Service executed a search warrant on my residence in Austin, Texas. Not only was I notified several months in advance of an investigation through a poorly executed subpoena, but once the special agents finally arrived at my apartment, their lack of information astounded me. Not only was it glaringly obvious that the agents executing the raid had done only minimal preliminary investigations, but once on-site they didn't even know what to look for. One over-zealous agent wanted to confiscate my arcade-size Pac Man machine, while another took a bag of stereo cable into evidence. Other agents scoured my house for illegal drugs and street signs, and spent a good deal of time perusing my collection of *Playboy* magazines. It was only upon their exit that one eagle-eyed individual remarked, "Why is that video game attached to the phone line?" It was then that they confiscated my only piece of computer equipment: a 300-baud dumb terminal.

In the years since that raid, it would appear that law enforcement has been making some progress in learning how to effectively prepare cases against computer criminals. This progress can best be described as baby-steps rather than lengthy strides towards the ultimate goal of "understanding the enemy." Raids are still bungled, unnecessary equipment is still seized while leaving important evidence behind, and innocents are still targeted while true criminals roam free.

On the federal level, training is still behind the times, and may never catch the state of the art. Inter-agency (and intra-agency) squabbling keeps important information out of the hands of investigators, sometimes causing investigations to be hindered or even ruined. Agents are also often kept from receiving necessary training due to lack of funds budgeted for continuing education.

On a local or city level, most police detectives don't even know where to begin when investigating computer-related crimes. In many instances, the cases are shuffled off to "the computer guy," namely the officer or officers who have let it be known that they are not intimidated by a personal computer, and whose experience with them usually doesn't go much further than Microsoft Excel or, for the more advanced, the ability to navigate CompuServe.

As the criminal element becomes far more computer-literate, and computers begin to play a much more prevalent role in more traditional crimes, law enforcement professionals must become computer experts, or at a minimum possess some level of computer literacy beyond that of the ordinary citizen. Advanced computer training should be as much of a necessity among cadets as weapons training or investigations if law enforcement is to have any hope in coping with the 21st century.

Will this book ultimately provide any true assistance to law enforcement professionals?

It is certainly a start.

Chris Goggans
Austin, Texas
February 1995

Preface

*October 13, 1991. At 9:15 yesterday morning, our bomb went off in
the FBI's national headquarters building. Our worries about the
relatively small size of the bomb were unfounded; the damage is
immense. We have certainly disrupted a major portion of the FBI's
headquarters operations for at least the next several weeks, and it
looks like we have also achieved our goal of wrecking their new
computer complex.*
—Andrew MacDonald*

*Federal officials say Mr. Mitnick's motives have always been murky.
He was recently found to have stashed thousands of credit card
numbers on computers in the San Francisco Bay area—including
the card numbers of some of the best-known millionaires in Silicon
Valley. But there is no evidence yet that Mr. Mitnick had attempted to
use those credit card numbers. Indeed, frequently ignoring the
possibility of straightforward financial gain from the information he
has stolen, Mr. Mitnick has often seemed more concerned with
proving that his technical skills are better than those whose job it is to
protect the computer networks he has attacked.*
—John Markoff†

Throughout history, each technological advance has inevitably become the target
of those who seek to subvert it or use it for their own purposes. Outlaws used to
have to ride into town to rob the local bank and terrorize the citizenry. With the
onset of the telephone, crimes could be planned and in some cases (with extortion and blackmail, for example) even committed by phone. Telephone wiretaps
became a tool of law enforcement, but the technology also allowed criminals to
tap their victims' lines. With the dawn of the computer age, both the good guys
and the bad guys had a new technology to use and abuse. These days, many crim-

---

* *The Turner Diaries*, National Alliance, Washington DC, 1980. This is a work of fiction, but it has been
widely circulated among, and is much admired by, extremist groups in the United States.
† *The New York Times,* February 16, 1995.

inals are computer-literate. They keep their records in handy databases; they use email to plan and sometimes carry out their crimes; they monitor network traffic and use it to steal credit card numbers, telephone access card numbers, and passwords; and they steal billions of dollars a year by illegally transferring funds, diverting payments, and shaving pennies off other people's earnings.

Just as each new technology opens the door to new kinds of criminal activity, each new crime requires that new safeguards be adopted and new law enforcement skills be learned. Technology, the criminal, and law enforcement are continually leapfrogging each other, as the race continues to build better tools, commit bigger crimes, and develop more effective law enforcement.

This book is an introduction to the crimes, the criminals, the safeguards, and the law enforcement responsibilities of the computer age.

About This Book

This book started as a training manual for the Federal Bureau of Investigation, where it was developed by the National Center for the Analysis of Violent Crime. Although this group is best known for its profiling of major criminals, such as serial killers (as seen in the 1991 movie, *Silence of the Lambs*), it is also known in government and computer security circles for its responsibility for profiling computer criminals and developing tools for investigation of computer crimes. FBI agents were increasingly being asked to investigate, or advise in, computer crime cases, and few investigators had the technical background to do the job. To meet this need, FBI agents and contractors developed a book called *The Prevention and Investigation of Computer Crime: A Training Manual*. Over time, the book was also used in the training of other law enforcement personnel—local police forces, state police, prosecutors, and others—at FBI Headquarters. We started getting requests for the book from people outside the Bureau and the law enforcement community.

We decided that the book merited a wider audience. Although it is not highly technical, we thought that a publisher of computer books might be interested in it. We contacted O'Reilly & Associates because they were known for their publishing of computer security books. After a good deal of discussion about how the book might be made more accessible to the larger community outside the FBI, we decided to proceed.

This book is intended mainly as an introductory book on computer crime for those who need to deal, firsthand, with such crimes. This includes:

• Investigators from the law enforcement community who are brought in to investigate computer crimes.

- Judges seeking to understand better the technical details of cases before them.

- Prosecutors who may be evaluating evidence, presenting technical details to a nontechnical judge and jury, and prosecuting computer criminals.

- People from organizations who use computers and risk computer crimes—managers, administrators, legal staff, physical security staff, and computing staff. This includes anyone who may become involved with a computer crime investigation within his or her own organization, and who needs to know how to proceed if such a crime does occur. It also potentially includes anyone who uses computers (particularly those connected to the Internet or even to a local network) who wants to reduce the chances that he or she will be the target of a computer crime.

- People who want to learn about the current legal situation in cyberspace—for example, their rights and responsibilities and the current laws.

Although this book contains a number of technical hints and summaries of security procedures, it is not intended to be in any way a computer security textbook: there are a number of good books on this topic; see Appendix A, *Resource Summary,* for suggestions.

Scope of the Book

This book is divided into five parts:

Part I, *Overview.* This part introduces the problem of computer crime, outlines the major types of computer crimes and computer criminals, and summarizes the main U.S. laws that are used to prosecute computer crimes.

Chapter 1, *Introduction to Computer Crime,* describes a number of different types of attacks on government and corporate sites and provides an overview of the risks to computer systems.

Chapter 2, *What Are the Crimes?,* describes the categories of computer crimes, from masquerading, to war dialing, to dumpster diving, to planting viruses and worms.

Chapter 3, *Who Commits Computer Crimes?,* profiles the different categories of computer criminals.

Chapter 4, *What Are the Laws?,* provides an overview of the major laws that prohibit computer crime.

Part II, *Preventing Computer Crime.* This part looks at ways of preventing computer crime—identifying the risks to computer systems and implementing various security measures that can protect those systems.

Chapter 5, *What Is at Risk?*, identifies the assets of a computer site and system and outlines computer security threats, vulnerabilities, and countermeasures.

Chapter 6, *Physical Security*, describes the threats to physical security (natural and environmental disasters, physical break-ins) and presents measures for countering these threats.

Chapter 7, *Personnel Security*, discusses briefly the important components of a personnel security program for various types of people, including employees, vendors and contractors, and others.

Chapter 8, *Communications Security*, describes the threats to networked systems and the techniques (e.g., password controls, encryption, firewalls) for countering these threats.

Chapter 9, *Operations Security*, discusses how operations security works with other types of security measures. Operations security includes ways of increasing awareness of possible computer crimes, ways of actually preventing such crimes, and ways of finding out that they have occurred.

Part III, *Handling Computer Crime*. This part describes how to plan for, detect, investigate, and prosecute a computer crime.

Chapter 10, *Planning How to Handle a Computer Crime*, discusses ways of detecting computer crimes, assembling a crisis management team, and sensitive issues (e.g., should you bait a trap for a computer criminal?) to consider before a computer crime actually occurs.

Chapter 11, *Investigating a Computer Crime*, outlines procedures to follow in investigating a computer crime, describes the investigative team, discusses the preparation of a search warrant, and describes rules for collecting and protecting evidence.

Chapter 12, *Prosecuting a Computer Crime*, discusses the special problems involved in describing computer crimes in the courtroom, issues such as the hearsay problem, and suggestions for testifying about computer crimes.

Part IV, *Computer Crime Laws*. This part contains a complete listing of the text of the major U.S. laws that prohibit computer crime, as well as the relevant state laws and some international laws, as of the time this book went to press.

Part V, *Appendices*. This part contains a resource summary and several articles that expand on topics introduced in earlier chapters.

Appendix A, *Resource Summary*, contains a listing of resources that may be helpful to you in preventing, investigating, and prosecuting computer crimes. It includes books, periodicals, and online resources relevant to computer crime.

Appendix B, *Raiding the Computer Room,* is an article by John Gales Sauls about seizing computer crime evidence and Fourth Amendment considerations.

Appendix C, *The Microcomputer as Evidence,* is an article by Michael G. Noblett about examining computer crime evidence.

Appendix D, *A Sample Search Warrant,* contains an actual search warrant used in an investigation of a computer crime at a university; only certain identifying information has been changed.

The *Glossary* defines the special terms used in this book.

Comments and Questions

Please address comments and questions concerning this book to the publisher:

O'Reilly & Associates
103 Morris Street, Suite A
Sebastopol, CA 95472
1-800-998-9938 (in the U.S. or Canada)
1-707-829-0515 (international or local)
1-707-829-0104 (FAX)

You can also send us messages electronically. To ask technical questions or to comment on the book, send email to:

bookquestions@ora.com (via the Internet)

For complete information on our online resources (FTP, World Wide Web page, and more), see the insert at the end of this book.

Acknowledgments

Many thanks to Gene Spafford, the consulting editor for this book, who edited the book and added explanatory information from his years of teaching, writing, and consulting in the computer security field. We are particularly indebted to Spaf for writing the foreword to this book. Our thanks as well to Shabbir Safdar, a computer security professional employed by a major financial services firm, who also read this book and provided edits to generalize some of the FBI-specific portions of it.

Thanks to all those who reviewed drafts of the book before publication and who made helpful suggestions: Scott Charney, Chief of the Computer Crime Unit at the U.S. Department of Justice Criminal Division, and Alex White, an attorney from that unit; Bryn Dole, Christoph Schuba, and Mark Joseph Crosbie in the COAST group at Purdue University; James C. Settle of I-NET; Detective Robert M. Snyder of the Intelligence Bureau in the Computer Crime Section at the Columbus Ohio Police Department; Bob Friel of the Financial Crimes Division in the Electronic Crime Branch at the U.S. Secret Service; Harry Onderwater of CRI-ACC in the Netherlands; William Hugh Murray, consultant to Deloitte and Touche; and John Smith, Senior Investigator of the Computer/High Tech Crime Unit at the Santa Clara County District Attorney's Office. John was especially helpful in gathering the text of laws and search warrants. Thanks as well to Jonathan Byers of the North Dakota Office of the Attorney General, to Chris Goggans for his comments, to Bradley Ross, who translated the French laws for us, and to Kevin J. O'Leary, of Peabody & Arnold, who helped us to find and understand various laws.

Special acknowledgments from the authors to the following persons; without their support and guidance, the original FBI book would not have become a reality:

At the Department of Defense (DOD), present and former employees: Lt. Commander David G. Vaurio (USN, retired). Harriet Roberts (former employee), Frank L. Wladkowski, and Rebecca G. Bace. Research for the original FBI training manual, *The Prevention and Investigation of Computer Crime: A Training Manual,* was supported in part under DOD interagency agreement MOD 5087.89.

At the Advanced Research Projects Agency (ARPA): Teresa F. Lunt.

At the Federal Bureau of Investigation (FBI), present and former members of the National Computer Crimes Squad: Beth D. Babyak, Beth E. Barnett, Levord M. Burns, Carol A. Covert, Jolene S. Jameson, James L. Kolouch (retired), William Maxberry, Jr., Richard A. Ress, James C. Settle (retired), Kenneth L. Welch. At FBI Headquarters: Paul FitzGerald, Joseph K. Kielman, Harold M. "Hal" Hendershot, and J. Michael Gibbons. At the FBI Academy, Quantico: Steven Band, John E. Douglas (retired), Timothy G. Huff, Roger L. Depue (retired), Richard L. Ault (retired), and James A. O'Connor (retired). At the FBI San Francisco Office: William L. Tafoya. At the FBI Baltimore Office: Mark M. Pollitt. At the FBI Atlanta Office: Sharon A. Kelley. Many thanks to the FBI for allowing us to use the FBI training manual as the basis for this book.

At the National Institute of Standards and Technology (NIST): Timothy Grance.

At the Tennessee Valley Authority (TVA): Robert G. Carter and Robert L. Thompson.

Many thanks as well to Chuck Bushey of Digital Equipment Corporation; Dan Farmer and Harry J. Foxwell of Sun Microsystems; Peter G. Neumann of SRI; Steve Smaha of Haystack Labs; Tsutomu Shimomura of the University of California-San Diego; John Markoff of *The New York Times*; and Cliff Stoll.

A very special thanks to Donn B. Parker of SRI, a long-time expert in the field of computer crime. His work inspired our own. Many sections of the original FBI book were based on Donn's research and writing, particularly in *Computer Crime: Criminal Justice Resource Manual,* a book that he developed for the National Institutes of Justice and which we heartily recommend that you read.

Thanks to everyone at O'Reilly & Associates who made this published work a reality: Deborah Russell, the acquisitions editor, who worked with us from beginning to end; Stephen Spainhour, the production editor; Nancy Priest, who designed the interior format; Edie Freedman, who designed the cover; Chris Reilley, who created the figures; and Clairemarie Fisher O'Leary, who tracked down numerous computer crime statutes.

Overview

This part of the book introduces the problem of computer crime, outlines the major types of computer crimes and computer criminals, and summarizes the main U.S. laws that are used to prosecute computer crimes.

Chapter 1, *Introduction to Computer Crime,* describes a number of different types of attacks on government and corporate sites and provides an overview of the threats to computer systems.

Chapter 2, *What Are the Crimes?,* describes various types of computer crimes in four major categories: breaches of physical security, personnel security, communications security, and operations security.

Chapter 3, *Who Commits Computer Crimes?,* profiles the different categories of computer criminals.

Chapter 4, *What Are the Laws?,* provides an overview of the major laws that prohibit computer crime.

1

Introduction to Computer Crime

Computer crimes are increasingly in the news. And why not? When Willie Sutton was asked why he robbed banks, he replied, "Because that's where the money is." Today's criminals have learned where the money is. Instead of settling for a few thousand dollars in a bank robbery, those with enough expertise can walk away from a computer crime with a good deal more (for some of them, many millions). And they do walk away—far too often. The FBI's National Computer Crimes Squad estimates that between 85 and 97 percent of computer intrusions are not even detected. In a recent test sponsored by the Department of Defense, the statistics were startling. Attempts were made to attack a total of 8932 systems participating in the test. 7860 of those systems were successfully penetrated. The management of only 390 of those 7860 systems detected the attacks, and only 19 of the managers reported the attacks.[*] Why are so few attacks detected? Although there are detection tools available, too few systems use them. And why are so few attacks reported? Mainly because organizations frequently fear that their employees, clients, and stockholders will lose faith in them if they admit that their computers have been attacked. Of the computer crimes that *are* reported, few are ever solved.

Worse still, in the courts and in the media, computer criminals are rarely treated with the severity meted out to more conventional types of criminals. Indeed, they are sometimes turned into heroes. When Kevin Mitnick (see the sidebar) was taken into custody, "Free Mitnick," "Mitnick for President," and other slogans were broadcast on online newsgroups and bulletin boards. When juveniles commit crimes, sometimes at the urging of their older comrades, there are other complications. Too often, young offenders are considered simply to be misguided, and the

---

[*] Richard Power, *Current and Future Danger: A CSI Primer on Computer Crime and Information Warfare,* Computer Security Institute, 1995.

federal court system is less and less likely to take on cases in which a juvenile is the perpetrator.

Over the past several decades, the amount of financial, military, and intelligence information, proprietary business data, and even personal communications stored on and transmitted by computers has increased beyond anyone's imaginings. Governments, the military, and the world's economy couldn't operate without computer automation. Increasingly, the computers that transact this huge amount of business are linked to each other via the Internet or various military or financial networks. The numbers are staggering. More than a hundred million electronic messages traverse the world's networks every day. Banking networks transfer trillions of dollars daily.

And all that information being stored and transmitted is vulnerable to attack. Nobody knows the true scope of computer crime, but it is informally estimated to be in the billions of dollars stolen or lost. Almost every organization has been affected in some way by computer crime. The British National Computer Centre reported that more than 80 percent of British organizations suffered a security breach in the last two years. The increasing use of interconnected networks makes these crimes easier than ever. Four out of every five computer crimes investigated by the FBI in 1993 involved unauthorized access to computers via the Internet.

This chapter introduces you to the problem of computer crime. We'll look briefly at the questions the rest of this book attempts to answer:

 What types of computer crimes are there?

 Who commits computer crimes?

 What laws prohibit computer crime?

 What is at risk in a computer crime?

 How can you keep computer crimes from occurring?

 How do you detect that a computer crime has occurred?

 How do you handle a computer crime?

 How do you investigate a computer crime?

 How do you prosecute a computer crime?

This chapter outlines a number of different types of attacks on computers and the data they store and transmit. We'll use these cases to introduce you to the vulnerabilities of computer systems, the threats to these systems, and the need for effective computer security.

Types of Attacks

In this age of automation and connectivity, almost no organization is exempt from computer crime. This section outlines the most common targets for computer crimes:

- Military and intelligence computers may be targeted by espionage agents.

- Businesses may be targeted by their competitors.

- Banks and other financial organizations may be targeted by professional criminals.

- Any organization but especially government and utility company computers, may be the target of terrorists.

- Any company may be the target of employees or ex-employees. Similarly, universities may be the target of students and former students.

- Any organization may be the target of crackers—sometimes they're in it for the intellectual challenge, and sometimes they are professionals who may do it for hire.

Chapter 2 looks at the many different types of computer attacks, from stealing login accounts to eavesdropping on communications to programming viruses to dumpster diving.

Military and Intelligence Attacks

National security is increasingly in the hands of computers. Computers store information ranging from the positioning of Air Force satellites to plans for troop deployment throughout the world. Just as common criminals have learned that computers are where the money is, espionage agents have learned that computers are where the intelligence information is. More and more, espionage is becoming a game of computer break-ins, computer-based cryptography, and message traffic analysis. The cloak and dagger have become virtual.

In his book, *The Cuckoo's Egg*, Cliff Stoll describes in fascinating detail how a 75-cent accounting imbalance in California led him to the discovery of a West German cracker who was extracting information from defense computers in more than 10 nations. The information was then reportedly sold to the Soviet KGB.

The cracker in Stoll's book is not a lone phenomenon. In June 1988, computer cracker Kevin Mitnick (code-named "Condor") broke in remotely to a Defense Department network. He allegedly stole a pre-release version of Digital Equipment Corporation's VMS V5.0 Operating System software, and temporarily stored the software on a Navy computer at the Patuxent Naval Air Station. Officials say that no classified information was obtained during the incident—this time! (As this book was going to press, Mitnick was arrested after an intensive manhunt; see the sidebar for details of the case that led to his downfall.)

Intrusion into U.S. government computers is common, despite the best efforts to enforce computer security. In January 1990, three Silicon Valley workers were arrested for breaking into government and telephone company computers. They allegedly broke into systems that provided them with information on military exercises, flight orders, FBI investigations into associates of the late Philippine President Ferdinand Marcos, and instructions on how to eavesdrop on private telephone conversations. Some of the military information that was compromised as a result of the intrusions was previously classified SECRET.

Department of Energy facilities were targeted by attackers in March 1990. The intruders were prevented from obtaining classified information, and an investigation was initiated immediately to identify the source of the attempted intrusions. Several weeks later, they were located and identified. They were attempting to break in to the computers from outside the United States. Many such attempts and attacks have been reported in the intervening years. It is clear that military and government systems continue to be attractive targets for computer criminals, whatever their motivation.

Business Attacks

Just as the Cold War seems to be ending, a new era of worldwide economic competition has begun. Increasingly, rivalries among national economies make industrial espionage a growing threat. Even "friendly" nations have become our economic enemies. In a recent case, Boeing Aircraft accused the French company, Airbus, of bugging Boeing employees' hotel rooms and airline seats, and tapping their phone lines, to get secret corporate information.

An Ernst and Young/Information Week survey (reported in the *Toronto Financial Post*, December 15, 1994) found that 54 percent of companies reported some type of financial loss over the past two years as the result of computer problems—some crashes and internal problems, but many of them were the result of malicious damage.

Businesses are increasingly the target of both competitors and the curious, although most business crimes are still committed by employees. Even computer companies such as Apple Computer are not immune to attacks by computer criminals. In December 1987, Apple Computer found a virus in its electronic mail system. The virus succeeded in shutting down the system and erasing all of Apple's voice-mail. Apple also reported that computer criminals may have reverse-engineered the highly secret code that underlies its Macintosh computers. This copyrighted and seemingly highly protected code could be used to build a clone of the Macintosh computer.

Shimomura vs. Mitnick:
The Computer Crime of the Year?

The story of the Christmas Day, 1994, attack on Tsutomu Shimomura and the events that unfolded following that attack may provide a behind-the-scenes look at an Internet-based computer crime—known as IP spoofing—unfortunately, the type of crime we can expect to see more and more in the future. Just as this crime shows how today's technologies can be used to commit a crime, it also shows how such technologies can be used to catch the criminal.

Tsutomu Shimomura, a computational physicist at the San Diego Supercomputer Center, is known for his interest in computer security—in particular, methods of preventing intrusion into systems. For years, he has collected information about security holes in various systems and tools for exploiting these holes. He has also developed many tools for preventing intrusion and tracking system intruders. On Christmas Day, while Shimomura was en route to a ski vacation at Lake Tahoe, an intruder broke in, remotely, to his highly secured home computer at Solana Beach, California, and began copying his files—tens of thousands of them.

A graduate student at the Supercomputer Center noticed alterations in system log files at a computer there, and caught on to what was happening. (Shimomura had installed on his computer a program that automatically copied logging records to a backup computer at the San Diego site.) The student notified Shimomura, who rushed home to inspect the damage. In the days after the attack, as Shimomura was inventorying what had been stolen, the attacker added insult to injury. In a December 27 voice-mail message (disguised by computer alteration), he told Shimomura, "Damn you. My technique is the best...Don't you know who I am? Me and my friends, we'll kill you."

Far from frightening Shimomura away, the message further strengthened his resolve. He wouldn't leave this investigation exclusively to law enforcement. This one was personal.

Few victims of computer crime have the technical knowledge—or the determination—of Shimomura. Right from the start, he went public with news of the break-in, announcing it at a conference in Sonoma, California, and publishing the technical details of the attack so others on the Internet could protect themselves from similar attacks.

Shimomura has long been known as someone who believes in free discussions about system vulnerabilities. Where some people in the computing community feel that publicizing security holes aids and abets intruders, Shimomura believes in revealing these holes—so everyone will know about them and fix them. He set out to understand exactly what happened and why, and to see if he could use the electronic traces the intruder left behind to track him down.

What was to blame for the attack on Shimomura's system? The attack was based on the intruder's ability to fake the source address of the packets that are sent to a system. Some systems and applications decide whether to trust another system to send it commands by looking at the source address on the incoming packets. That was the case with Shimomura's otherwise well-protected system. The intruder got access by making it appear that the packets came from a system other than the one they were really coming from.

What are packets and how do they work? Packets are the messages, or sections of messages, that are sent from one computer to another. Rather than being transmitted directly from one computer to another, these packets bounce from system to system to system, using the best route available on the Internet's huge collection of interconnected networks. Addresses attached to the packets are interpreted by the protocols that make the Internet work. One of these, called the Internet Protocol, or IP, was the source of the attack on Shimomura. What the intruder did was to send file transfer commands to Shimomura's computer that looked like they came from a computer that was authorized to read these files.

The attack was a particularly tricky one. Computers don't simply listen to instructions and obey them. When a packet is received by a system, that system sends back a reply to the originating computer, confirming receipt of the packet. In this way, the two computers synchronize their transmissions using sequence numbers associated with the packets. Without being able to see the acknowledgments being sent back by Shimomura's system (those acknowledgments were going to the computer the attacker was pretending to be), the attacker was nevertheless able to guess the sequence numbers being passed, and thereby associate appropriate numbers with future packets he sent.

Once Shimomura figured out how the intruder gained access, he publicized the method.[1] The CERT (Computer Emergency Response Team) Coordination Center (see sidebar later in this chapter), sent out an advisory to Internet users, warning them that the same thing could happen to them. Shimomura now turned his attention to finding out who attacked his system by monitoring all further packets sent to his computer.

Shimomura's willingness to share the details of the attack with the world worked to his advantage. A month after the break-in, something odd happened at the Well, a commercial online service used by many in the San Francisco Bay area. The Well's system administrator had noticed a huge flooding of files in an area of the Well's disk storage designated for use by the Computers, Freedom, and Privacy (CFP) group. Because the group used the Well only occasionally, this didn't make any sense. Bruce Koball, a programmer who helps

---

[1] Actually, this method was first published by Robert T. Morris in February, 1985.

run CFP, had read about the Shimomura break-in, and when he looked through the mystery files, he saw immediately that these were the same files stolen from Shimomura.

When Shimomura learned that his intruder had used the Well, he set up software there that monitored Well operations to see what else the intruder might do. By examining packets coming into the Well, the intruder's keystrokes could be recorded. Watching the intruder's electronic activities might provide clues about who he was and where he could be found. Had the intruder laid low for a while, he might never have been found. But he couldn't stop cracking systems. He wanted to try out the new tools he'd stolen from Shimomura. And this proved to be his undoing.

In short order, the intruder had broken into Motorola as well. This made sense. Cellular telephones are a prime tool for crackers, and Motorola is a major manufacturer. In fact, along with Shimomura's files on the Well, investigators found a copy of Motorola's cellular phone control software. Next, the intruder moved to Netcom, another large West Coast online service. There, he hit the jackpot. He managed to copy the credit card numbers of nearly 20,000 Netcom subscribers. Other computer companies and online services also fell victim to his cracking skills.

When the intruder hit Netcom, law enforcement got busy. Sensitive files are valuable, but credit cards are big business that any investigator can understand. The FBI was involved from the start, but now Kent Walker, at the time the Assistant United States Attorney from the San Francisco area, obtained subpoenas, allowing them to wiretap calls to Netcom. Initially, this didn't help much. Netcom provides many dial-in lines from all over the country. The intruder had manipulated a switching center so his calls would look as if they originated in Colorado and Minnesota. Did they? It was too early to tell.

The more Shimomura watched the intruder's activities, the more suspicious he became. The intruder was leaving his fingerprints at the scene. They might be electronic ones, but like the smudges found around doorjambs and on wall safes, they were there. As time went on, they became clearer and clearer.

Shimomura began to suspect that everything pointed to Kevin Mitnick as being the intruder.

Who is Kevin Mitnick? At age 31, he's older than many computer crackers, and he has spent half his life breaking into systems, starting with the computer system that ran the Los Angeles Unified School District's attendance, grade reporting, and scheduling applications. During those early years, a là *War Games,* he also broke in remotely to a computer at the North American Air Defense Command in Colorado Springs and attacked a number of telephone company computers in New York and California. Mitnick was always attracted by telephone company computers; the lure of free telephone calls, the ability to route his calls through switches that disguised his whereabouts, and the technology that let him play pranks on friends and enemies was too powerful to resist.

A few years later, Mitnick, who had come to be known as "Condor" in the computer cracking community, was sentenced to probation for stealing technical manuals from Pacific Bell. In the years since, he's served a few jail terms for stealing a million dollars worth of software from Digital Equipment Corporation and for violating parole. Eventually, Mitnick's lawyer saved him from a hefty jail term by convincing a judge to place Mitnick in a Los Angeles treatment program; his love of computer cracking was an addiction, like drugs or alcohol, the lawyer declared. Three years ago, Mitnick took off after the FBI started suspecting he had been involved in several Pac Bell cases. Since his flight was a federal parole violation, federal authorities have been looking for him ever since. Mitnick has also been the target of a state probe. After he wiretapped the FBI's own calls to the California Department of Motor Vehicles—and thereby got access to the California drivers' license database—the California State Police issued a warrant for his arrest as well.

Although, over the years, Mitnick had stolen credit card numbers, telephone access numbers, and all kinds of valuable software and documents, he has never appeared to be motivated primarily by financial gain. In the Shimomura case, for example, he apparently didn't sell the cracking tools he stole (although one can assume that, by now, the tools have been widely distributed to the computer underground), nor did he appear to use or distribute the credit card numbers taken from Netcom. Cracking was its own reward.

Mitnick's continued cracking activities did suggest a kind of addiction. It appears that he couldn't bring himself to stop, even though his best bet would have been to lay low until Shimomura and law enforcement lost interest in him. The more he prowled through the Internet, the more opportunities they had to follow his trail. Eventually, the trail of telephone calls into Netcom started to bear fruit. It became apparent that the calls came from a cellular telephone modem, a favorite tool of Mitnick's. Although the calls moved through a GTE local switching office, they actually were looping through a cellular phone switch operated by Sprint in Raleigh, North Carolina. Careful comparison of Sprint's records with Netcom's tracked Mitnick to Raleigh. Law enforcement officials then used cellular phone tracking equipment to trace him to the Players Court apartment complex. The FBI made the final determination of which apartment was Mitnick's.

In the middle of the night on February 16, less than two months after the Christmas Day break-in, Shimomura had tracked the person he believed to be the attacker to his lair. At the time of this writing, Mitnick awaits trial on a variety of charges.

IBM has also been the target of computer abuse. One example occurred in December 1987, when a creative West German programmer managed to plant a Trojan horse program (many incorrectly labeled it a virus) in the IBM electronic mail systems on five continents. Anytime someone on an affected system typed "Christmas" on his or her computer, the program displayed a holiday message, shown in Figure 1–1. It then sent a copy of itself to other network addresses kept

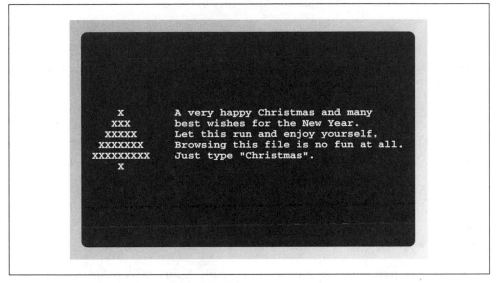

Figure 1-1. The IBM Christmas Trojan horse program

in that user's electronic mail file. Anyone who tried to stop the message lost electronic mail and other information that had not been saved. The incident was so severe that IBM had to shut down the system for 72 hours while it purged the message.

Financial Attacks

These days, our money may seem to be nothing but bits in a computer, numbers on a screen, and ink on an occasional bank statement. Our paychecks are deposited electronically. Our bills may be paid electronically; when we write checks, the dollar amounts get subtracted electronically. It's only fitting that the biggest theft and fraud cases are electronic as well.

Banks are always a tempting target for computer criminals. Back in 1988, seven not-quite-clever-enough criminals hatched a plot against the First National Bank of Chicago. The group used a wire transfer scheme to move $25.37 million belonging to Merrill Lynch and Company, $25 million belonging to United

Airlines, and $19.75 million belonging to the Brown-Forman Corporation to a New York bank and then to two separate banks in Vienna. The transfers were authorized over the telephone, and follow-up calls were made by the bank to verify the requests. All of the follow-up calls were routed to the residence of one of the suspects. On Monday morning, the three companies called the bank to find out what happened to their deposits. Investigators used the telephone records of the verification calls to trace the crime to the suspects. Had these criminals been a little more clever or a little quicker, they may have gotten away with over $70 million.

Financial attacks are often perpetrated by insiders who know the technical ropes. In 1994, an MCI switch technician was arrested for allegedly selling thousands of credit card numbers. The total cost was estimated at $50 million.

Incarcerating criminals doesn't always prevent computer crime. Toll fraud is one of the oldest forms of computer crime and continues to be a concern to the communications industry. Fifteen inmates at the Metro jails in Davidson County in Nashville, Tennessee, were charged in February 1989 with accessing long-distance telephone accounts and charging over $2,000 in long-distance charges in just one weekend. Inmates who had access to the codes sold them to others in jail for $5.00 or more, or sold individual calls for $1.25 each.

Terrorist Attacks

Even terrorists have gone high-tech. In the early hours of September 2, 1985, a bomb detonated in front of the Hamburg office of the West German software developer, Scientific Control Systems. Within seconds, another explosion occurred at the offices of Mathematischer Beratungs und Programmierungsdienst, another software firm. Terrorists were striking at the computer industry, but not for the first time. The Italian Red Brigade had launched attacks against more than 25 computer and electronics firms in Italy back in the 1970s. Other attacks against computer facilities and high-technology firms have taken place in South America and other parts of Europe. And recently, terrorists have targeted U.S. facilities as well.

Think about it from the terrorist's point of view: Why blow up a single utility tower—causing a rather unmemorable blackout—when you can crack the utilities system and turn out the lights in the northeastern United States for a whole day? How about the anti-tax group that decides to go to the source, attacking the computers of the Bureau of Engraving and Printing, which prints money, and the Internal Revenue Service, which collects taxes on it?

Paranoia? Not really. Among the ranks of today's criminals, spies, and terrorists are plenty of computer-literate individuals. And, although the IRS and the Bureau of Engraving and Printing have taken elaborate measures to protect their systems, there are plenty of other targets in the U.S. and abroad.

Grudge Attacks

Not all computer criminals are seeking information. Some simply want to wreak damage and destruction. One of the better-known cases in this category is that of a Texas insurance company employee, Donald Gene Burleson. Burleson was a systems security analyst who worked for his employer for more than two years before being fired. After he left the firm, its IBM System/38 crashed, and the company suffered a major loss of commission records used to prepare the monthly payroll. The program responsible for the problem was traced to Burleson's terminal and his account. Investigators were able to show that he had planted a "logic bomb" in the program while he was still with the company. (Chapter 2 describes logic bombs and other types of attacks.)

In fall of 1994, two computer writers, Michelle Slatalla and Josh Quittner, were the target of an "electronic mail bomb" (reported by *Time* magazine, December 12, 1994). Apparently in retaliation against articles the victims had written about the cracker underground, someone broke into computers at the writers' Internet service provider, IBM, and Sprint. Their home computer mailbox was clogged with thousands of pieces of electronic mail. Their Internet connection was then shut down. Their telephone was reprogrammed so calls were forwarded to an out-of-state number; when callers reached that number, they heard an obscene recording.

"Fun" Attacks

In some ways, computer crime is a logical extension of other types of crimes; it simply represents a bigger, faster, and more anonymous way to accomplish the same results—espionage, attacks on competitors, bank fraud, and terrorism. But, in other ways, computer crime is very different. It's full of variants and seeming contradictions. At one extreme, computer crime can be much more profitable than other forms of larceny or fraud, so it has a clear attraction to financial criminals. At the other extreme, computer crimes are often perpetrated as intellectual challenges without any profit motive at all.

A lot of computer criminals aren't in it for the money at all. Except for the fact that what they do breaks the law, they don't fit the stereotype of criminals. The criminals in this category wouldn't dream of holding up the corner convenience store or writing graffiti on bathroom walls, but here they are breaking into military bases, universities, banks, and businesses large and small.

> ## *The CERT Coordination Center*
>
> After the Internet worm incident in 1988, the computer community came to-
> gether to found an organization that would be able to respond quickly to future
> Internet security attacks. Under the auspices of the Defense Advanced Re-
> search Projects Agency (DARPA), the Department of Defense established the
> Computer Emergency Response Team (CERT) Coordination Center.
>
> Located at Carnegie-Mellon University's Software Engineering Institute in Pitts-
> burgh, the CERT, in cooperation with public and private computer networks,
> serves as a clearinghouse, helping organizations respond to attacks and to
> share information about them.
>
> Since the CERT was first established, the organization has reported more com-
> puter security incidents each year—less than 200 in 1989, about 400 in 1991,
> 1,400 in 1993, and around 2,000 in 1994. And the sites reporting break-ins are
> only a small percentage of those affected.
>
> Appendix A, *Resource Summary,* tells you how you can contact the CERT if
> you have an Internet security problem.

Many of them are kids, sometimes quite young ones, who think of their
computers as the next step up from a video game. In June 1989, a 14-year-old
Kansas boy used a small home Apple computer to crack the code of an Air Force
satellite-positioning system. The teenager, who reportedly began his career as a
cracker at age 8, specialized in breaking into Hewlett-Packard's HP3000 minicomputers that were used by businesses and a number of government agencies.

They may be kids, and bright ones at that, but they are breaking the law, endan-
gering both people and businesses, and they need to be stopped from expressing
their creativity and spirit of adventure in this way.

The worm that made its way into the Internet in November of 1988 showed the
computer world, for perhaps the first time, how dangerous an experiment on the
Internet can be. Robert T. Morris, at the time a Cornell University graduate
student, says that he planted the worm as a network experiment, but, because of
a bug in the program, the worm quickly raged out of control. Once installed, it
multiplied across network links, creating processes that rapidly clogged the individual computers' available space until other work on the affected machines
virtually ground to a halt. The worm exploited several UNIX security holes.
Although it didn't damage data, the worm created havoc on the systems it
invaded. Many system administrators had to shut down computers and network
connections. Other work was halted, electronic mail was lost, and research and
other business was delayed. Estimates of the cost of testing and repair exceed $5

million. (Nobody knows for sure because there has been no formal accounting of the repair and lost work time.)

Criminal Automation

Even when they aren't directly targeting computers or electronic data, criminals– like so many other people in our technological society–are automating their operations. Extremist groups like the Aryan Nation have established computer networks to communicate their messages of hate and violence. Drug dealers use computers to store records of transactions and financial dealings. In at least one case, an organized crime group used computers to store intelligence information on local vice and narcotics officers. This information was then sold to other criminals and criminal organizations.

Criminals are learning to take advantage of the latest advances. There have been recent reports that drug dealers, pedophiles, and other types of criminals are using various encryption programs to keep their communications secret from prying eyes even if their files are seized.

What Does It Mean to You?

Computer crime and the use of computers by criminal enterprises is a serious problem. It threatens national security and creates opportunities for modern criminals beyond anything we've previously experienced. Although improvements in computer security are helping to control the computer crime problem, the problem continues to keep pace with technology.

How do all these technological horror stories affect you?

If you are a manager or an owner of a business, you must realize that computer crime can undermine everything you have worked so hard to accomplish within your organization. Computer criminals masquerading as authorized users may be able to figure out how to log in and steal the business plans you've labored over. Secret information about the product you're about to release may help your competitor beat you to market. Disclosure of confidential material may also lead to loss of trade secret status.

If you are involved in any type of law enforcement—as an investigator or a prosecutor, for example— you can expect at some point to deal with either a computer crime investigation or an investigation where computers have been used by those responsible for other crimes. You may have to assist in the preparation of a subpoena for computer crime evidence, participate in the collection of computers and computer media during an arrest or during the execution of a search warrant, or be called on to conduct a major investigation of a computer crime.

If you are the victim of a computer crime, you may be asked by law enforcement to assist investigators in tracking a computer trespasser or putting together data that will later serve as evidence in the investigation and prosecution of a suspected computer criminal.

If you are just an ordinary computer user, realize that you too are vulnerable. If you don't protect your login ID, your files, your disks and tapes, and other computer equipment and data, they might be subject to attack. Even if what you have is not confidential in any way, having to reconstruct what has been lost will cost you hours, days, or longer in productivity and annoyance. And even if you're not worried about your own data, you have a responsibility, in this era of internet-worked computers, to provide some protection for others. Someone who breaks into your account could use your account to become a privileged user at your site. If you are connected to other machines, someone could use your system's networking facilities to connect to other machines that may contain even more vulnerable information.

What Laws Prohibit Computer Crime?

In the United States, a number of federal laws protect against attacks on computers, misuse of passwords, electronic invasions of privacy, and other trans-gressions. The Computer Fraud and Abuse Act of 1986 (it's been amended several times) is the main piece of legislation that governs most common computer crimes, although many other laws may be used to prosecute different types of computer crime.

In addition to federal laws, most of the states have adopted their own computer crime laws. A number of countries outside the United States have also passed legislation defining and prohibiting computer crime. Chapter 4, *What Are the Laws?*, introduces the major laws that govern computer crime. Part IV of this book contains the actual language of the various laws.

In addition to the explicit violations covered by these specific laws, there may also be many other crimes in which computers are not the target but are simply used in the commission of the crime. For example, drug dealers may keep their records on computers, and terrorists and criminal organizations may transmit messages via the Internet. (In general, this book doesn't focus on crimes of these kinds.)

Where Are the Vulnerabilities?

Computer crime encompasses a wide range of offenses, from the physical theft and destruction of equipment, to the electronic sabotage and misappropriation of data and systems, to the outright theft of money—which, these days, is largely electronic. This section summarizes the major points of vulnerability in any computer system: its hardware, software, data, and communications.

Hardware

> Hardware is what most people think of as "the computer." It includes the basic computer, computer terminals, and other components such as printers, external modems, and disk and tape drives.

Software

> Software is what people use to do their work. It's what causes instructions and information to appear on the screen, and what makes the computer work. There are two basic categories of software: operating system software and application programs.

> Most users never have to worry about the operating system's software. It's usually already programmed into the machine when the user turns it on. The operating system consists of the instructions that tell the computer to check itself every time it is turned on, to respond to initial commands from the keyboard, and to provide the system with the information needed to use the other levels of software.

> The second type of software includes the application programs—word processing programs (e.g., Microsoft Word, WordPerfect), spreadsheets (e.g., Lotus 1-2-3, Excel), and other application programs ranging from graphics to games to educational and scientific packages. These programs are usually purchased from a software supplier, but many organizations also develop their own proprietary application programs to perform such business operations as accounting, inventory, and order entry.

Data

> Data are the lifeblood of most organizations. Hardware and software are replaceable, though they may be expensive, but the information gathered in the course of doing business may well be irreplaceable. Data are generated from everything your organization does—taking orders, writing documents, processing money, or performing engineering operations. When people steal data, they are stealing an asset, just as they do when they steal money or equipment.

> Data files may be stored on a number of different types of media—disk, CD-ROM, magnetic tape, diskette, even paper. There are many different ways to steal data files—walking out of a building with a disk, a tape, or a piece of

paper, exporting files over phone lines, or printing data at a remote site. Paper is a form of data few people take seriously; although security guards might notice tapes and disks leaving a building, most will overlook a few sheets of paper.

Communications

Communications take place on a network. A *network* is essentially a wire that connects two or more computers together. An *internetwork* is a wire between two or more networks; it's a network of networks. The Internet is a global interconnection of a variety of national networks. (Chapter 8, *Communications Security*, describes networks.) Connecting a computer to any kind of network inevitably increases the vulnerability of the information stored on it. The Internet and the other large international interconnected networks pose a special problem. Crackers can use one machine on a network to connect to another machine, perhaps one on another network entirely, often without leaving a trail. Because so many networks are interconnected, crackers who get into one system have a golden opportunity to crack other systems and networks as well. Cracker will often jump from network to network, making it difficult to detect intrusions or to trace their whereabouts. Intruders' movements from one local phone exchange to another further improves their ability to elude detection, because different phone exchanges don't readily exchange information and tracing becomes more difficult.

Networks also permit users to access a number of different services including bulletin board services (BBSs). Bulletin boards are places where computer users can exchange information, leave messages, or get new programs that are in the public domain. They are also places where crackers may trade access secrets.

Hardware, software, data, and communications are at risk in a variety of ways, as we'll describe in the following sections. See Chapter 5, *What Is at Risk?*, for a more complete discussion of risks to computer sites and systems.

Destruction of Hardware

Terrorists have been known to bomb computer facilities. Current employees have gone berserk and taken hammers or axes to computers, thrown PCs out of windows, and flung fragile disks against the walls of their offices. Ex-employees have avenged some real or imagined grudge against their former employers by setting the place on fire. It doesn't happen often, but it does happen. And whenever equipment is damaged, there is usually an accompanying, and even more expensive, loss of software and data.

Theft of Hardware

Computer hardware is an attractive target for thieves because components can be resold. In our computerized society, there is little difficulty selling hot hardware of any kind—everyone is looking for a bargain. Theft not only disables processing until replacements are found but it also may result in an unrecoverable loss of critical data stored on stolen storage devices.

Theft of Software

Computer software can be stolen, either as part of a computer theft (the software may be on the hard disk) or in its own right. Thieves may take disks or tapes containing copies of commercial software or, more destructively, they may steal copies of an organization's own privately developed software. Software is intellectual property, and it may have an enormous, if less tangible, value. If competitors get hold of a fully developed and working system, they may not need to invest their own time and money in developing such a program on their own.

There are other types of software theft that may not be immediately obvious. Consider the employee who copies commercial software at work to use at home for personal reasons. The software the employee duplicates is copyrighted and, in most cases, has been licensed only for use on the employer's computer. In a case like this, the terms of the license are crucial in determining whether a crime or violation has taken place. Software developers use a number of different approaches to prevent thieves from duplicating their products, but the theft of software remains a multibillion-dollar international crime problem. Indeed, the duties on China that President Clinton put into place in 1995 are in part the result of the out-of-control pirating of U.S. software.

Most employers take only minor disciplinary action against their employees when such violations occur. Very few respond by requiring the employee to pay the software developer for the stolen software. Sadly, there are some employers who even encourage their employees to copy software so they won't have to buy multiple licenses. (In general, we don't discuss violations of this kind in this book.)

Sabotage by Computer

Computers control national defense information, the transfer of trillions of dollars daily on fund transfer networks, medical procedures, airline navigation, and virtually everything else these days. Someone who gains control of these systems can do an enormous amount of damage, both to the systems themselves and to the people whose lives and finances may depend on them.

Some sabotage is obvious. In January of 1995, someone shut down the computers that controlled life support for more than a dozen patients in Guy's Hospital in London; they were saved only by the heroic efforts of medical staff who kept them alive manually while the computers were put back online.

Some sabotage is more subtle. Consider how easy it is to plant a virus in an organization's computer. An unsuspecting employee accesses a bulletin board from her home computer; there, she finds a new public domain software package that she thinks might make her job easier (or maybe it's a game she'd like to play while allegedly working). She has no idea that hiding inside that seemingly useful program is a dangerous virus. Our unsuspecting employee downloads the software onto a diskette, and the next day she loads it into her workstation at the office. In no time, the virus spreads to all of the computers on the local area network, potentially causing the loss of valuable files and other assets.

Forgery of email messages falls into the sabotage category as well. It's all too easy to fake email, pretending either that you're sending a message from someone else or that you've received one. Such antics can wreak havoc with business and personal communications. (Imagine a "Dear John" letter, signed by Jane, that really came from rival Tom!) Digital signatures provided by encryption packages are an excellent way to protect against such forgeries, as we'll describe later in this book.

We've described an electronic "mail bomb" that flooded two writers' Internet mailbox and the Internet worm that did its damage by filling up affected computers with more and more processes demanding memory. *Denial of service* is the term given to such attacks because, although they don't necessarily damage data directly, they deny service to the victims and often to anyone else on the affected machine. In general, computer hardware, software, and data must be kept available to users. When denial of service occurs in any of these areas (e.g., because a disk is full or has been damaged, or because software has been subverted), people can't be productive. Even if nothing has been damaged, computer "uptime" is affected, and people can't get their work done.

Theft of Assets

As we've seen earlier in this chapter, professional criminals—and a good many amateur ones—are finding that computer crime can be financially rewarding and much safer than holding up banks or mugging people on the street. Billions of dollars a year are stolen by diverting electronic funds transfers, directly stealing from bank, stock, and pension accounts, and committing various other types of online fraud.

Theft of Output

Computer criminals don't always need to commit highly sophisticated online crimes. Some computer crimes simply involve picking up valuable data on disk, tape, or paper and walking away with it. Even a few sheets of paper may contain vital military information, a company's sensitive financial records, medical records, academic transcripts, and much more. Even discarded output can be valuable to computer criminals, as we'll see in Chapter 2 when we discuss the art of dumpster diving.

Unauthorized Use

There are several types of unauthorized use. First is the use of a computer system by people who aren't authorized to use it—for example, crackers who steal passwords or figure out how to bypass system access controls. They may do damage to your system or they may simply browse through your files; they'll probably also use your system as a base for connecting to other networks or host systems on the Internet. At the very least, they're using your system for free.

Second is the use of a computer system by employees for nonwork activities. Employees often use company computers for their own purposes—to balance their checkbooks, to keep personal telephone lists, to keep rosters of teams they coach, to prepare reports for night school, to send email to their friends and their kids at college. This type of usage is epidemic. Although most organizations don't object to an employee's occasional use of a system for strictly personal reasons, some do. And some draw the line when employees start using the organization's computer to keep the books for the business they run on the weekend. Things can easily get out of hand. Every time a computer is turned on and an employee spends time on nonwork purposes, it may cost an organization money; if the system is being used without the organization's permission, a theft is theoretically occurring. The other problem is that such offenses can escalate into copying company software, taking disks and other media for personal use, and borrowing company laptops for use at home.

Using an employer's computer and other resources for personal reasons is not necessarily "criminal." Whether an offense is a crime depends on the nature of the business, the jurisdiction, the nature of the use, the organization's guidelines, and the contract an employee signed with the organization. Because the total loss to the organization from any single offense is usually small, few incidents of unauthorized use are investigated or prosecuted. (In general, we don't focus on these types of crimes in this book.)

Who Commits Computer Crimes?

The previous sections have alluded to a number of different kinds of attacks and different kinds of computer criminals—for example, the espionage agent, the defrauder, the cracker. The link between type of crime and type of offender isn't always a direct one. For example, professional espionage agents might try to obtain secret military and intelligence information—but so might young crackers. The target, and even the methods, may be similar, but the motivations are very different, as we'll see in later chapters.

Although in discussions of computer security we tend to focus on outside attackers, in fact the vast majority of computer crimes and security incidents are the result of insider error or intentional attack. Figure 1-2 shows a set of thought-provoking statistics.*

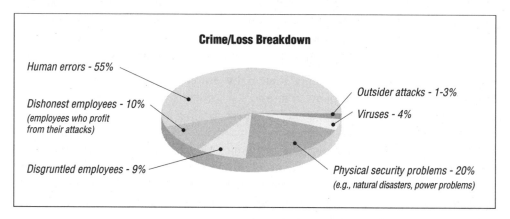

Figure 1-2. Types of computer crime and other losses—estimated breakdown

Regardless of who commits computer crimes—and why—good security practices and good investigative techniques will help in prevention and detection. Part II of this book summarizes the kinds of controls that you should use within your organizations, both to prevent and to detect computer crime. Part III discusses how to handle computer crimes if they do occur.

Chapter 3, *Who Commits Computer Crimes?*, lists a number of different types of computer criminals that the FBI has identified. It includes a Computer Crime Adversarial Matrix that summarizes a variety of characteristics of each type. You may find this summary helpful if you are trying to track down or prosecute an intruder in your own system.

---

* *Source*: Computer Security Institute.

How Can Computer Crime Be Prevented?

So far in this book, it may appear that computer criminals are so powerful, and computer systems are so vulnerable, that there is nothing to do but give in to these threats. Not so! There are many approaches to protecting computer systems from attack. As with all crimes, combating computer crime begins with prevention. In the next few sections, we briefly describe ways of preventing computer crime, which are elaborated in Part II of this book. Part II describes the process of identifying the assets—and the risks—associated with a computer or a site, and the various types of security that can protect the assets you've identified: physical security, personnel security, communications security, and operations security. The goal of all of these types of security is to make it harder for computer criminals to get to your computer systems—and to make it easier for you to detect those criminals if they do.

None of these different security solutions and procedures can solve the problem of computer crime in isolation. Together, they can make a big difference. For example, physical security procedures may be state-of-the-art, but if they are predictable, then they can be compromised. By combining physical security with operations security, as we describe in later chapters, physical security becomes less predictable and, as a result, more effective. Similarly, communications security methods may be highly effective, yet if people don't take threats seriously, they won't use these methods. An important part of personnel security is training in security threats, so the people who use systems will be sensitive to the risks to them.

Identifying Risks

Computer crime is a tradeoff. Absolute security is a near impossible goal for most organizations; they simply can't afford the price tag. More commonly, you'll need to balance the costs of various types of protection against the risks of doing without them. When it's formalized, this process of analysis and decision making is called *risk analysis*. Risk analysis involves identifying the threats to a system, the vulnerabilities of that system, and the measures that can be taken to protect the system. Identifying the risks to a system is the first step in establishing an appropriate computer security program for that system—and in fighting computer crime. Chapter 5, *What Is at Risk?*, describes the process of risk analysis in greater detail.

Physical Security

Physical security protects a physical computer facility (the building, the computer room, the computer and associated equipment, and its disks, tapes, printouts, and documentation). Physical security measures can help prevent the theft or damage of this equipment. They can also help protect you against natural disasters (e.g., fire, flood, lightning, earthquakes) and environmental disasters (e.g., problems with electricity, heating, and air conditioning systems). Chapter 6, *Physical Security,* describes this type of security in greater detail.

Personnel Security

Personnel security is a broad field, and preventing computer crimes is only one aspect of it. (Preventing employee theft and workplace violence are also in this category.) A personnel security program must cover threats by a variety of different types of people, including employees, vendors and contractors, professional criminals, and others. Background checks and careful monitoring on the job are important components of personnel security. Chapter 7, *Personnel Security*, describes this type of security in greater detail.

Communications Security

Like personnel security, communications security is a broad field in which computer crime prevention is only one component. Communications security includes the protection of mail, fax, telephone, and voice-mail communications, as well as the protection of data transmitted from one computer to another across a network connection. In these days of Internet connectivity, communications security is particularly important. It encompasses a variety of methods and devices, including the use of good passwords and other, more secure authentication devices (e.g., smart cards and one-time passwords), the physical protection and shielding of network cabling, encryption of transmitted data, and the building of firewalls that protect internal systems and networks from other networks. Chapter 8, *Communications Security*, describes this type of security in greater detail.

Operations Security

Operations security includes two major aspects of computer security:

- Ways you can increase awareness among potential victims of possible computer crimes

- Ways you can keep computer criminals from actually committing a computer crime

Operations security is effective only when it is integrated into an organization's physical, personnel, and communications security programs, as we describe in Chapter 9, *Operations Security.*

Handling Computer Crime

Computer crimes do occur, try as we do to prevent them. Planning for a computer crime doesn't mean giving up on preventing such crimes. It *does* mean being prepared for the worst—knowing how to spring into action if one does occur. Unfortunately, these days, organizations that use computers and electronic data, as well as the law enforcement community, need to develop skills in detecting, investigating, and prosecuting computer crimes. Part III of this book focuses on these needs.

The FBI uses the model shown in Figure 1-3 in discussions of how to fight computer crime. This model incorporates stages of prevention (the types of risk ~~~~~~~~~~ discussed in the previous section), investigation, ~~~~~~~~~~ ne.

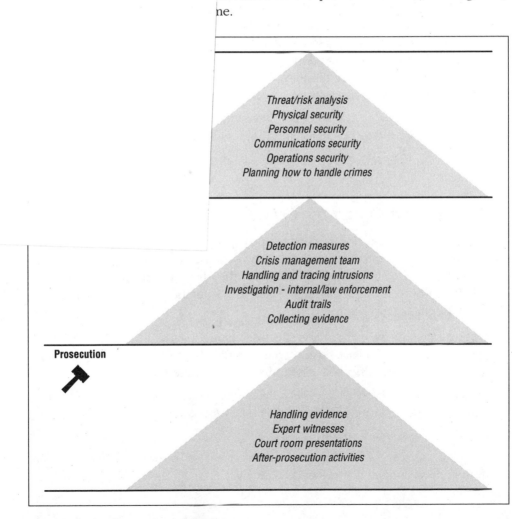

Figure 1-3. Computer crime model

Planning for and Detecting Computer Crime

Contingency planning encompasses many activities, from fire prevention to fraud detection. Today, planning how to prevent and detect a computer crime is an important part of any organization's contingency planning.

There are four main components to a computer crime contingency plan:

- Putting detection measures in place. With these measures, you'll be able to tell as quickly as possible when a computer crime does occur. Too often, computer crimes are detected only by auditors, after the fact, when information has already been compromised or money stolen.

- Assembling a team of people who will respond to a computer security incident.

- Figuring out how that team should respond to different types of situations, from the least to the most serious. For example, they'll need to know who to contact, whether to shut down the system and network connections completely (or try to trace the intruder), and how to document their activities for legal and financial use later on.

- Making sure that you'll be able to change your plans over time, to respond to changing times and technologies and to throw attackers off guard.

Chapter 10, *Planning How to Handle Computer Crime*, describes these activities in greater detail.

Investigating a Computer Crime

Computer crime investigation is new to most people—both the victims and the law enforcement investigators. In many ways, computer crime investigations are like other types of criminal investigations, but they have the potential to become a tangled web of technical challenges. There are a number of key components to a computer crime investigation:

- Putting together the proper investigative team. It's vital to include technical advisers who can understand the technical details of the crime and can help to keep evidence, particularly electronic evidence, safe from harm.

- Investigating the incident by checking records, interviewing informants, and performing surveillance of suspects and bulletin board activity.

- Preparing the search warrant.

- Studying the scene of the crime, knowing what to seize, collecting evidence from it, and handling that evidence securely.

Chapter 11, *Investigating a Computer Crime*, describes these activities in greater detail.

Prosecuting a Computer Crime

Prosecuting a computer crime is often more complex and demanding than prosecuting most other types of crimes. Like computer crime investigations, computer crime prosecutions are often new territory for prosecutors, judge, and jury. Prosecution requires:

- Doing special technical preparation.

- Dealing with special evidence problems because of the electronic (and "hearsay") nature of most computer evidence.

- Testifying about technical matters before a nontechnical judge and jury. Trying to convey technical information to a judge and jury—sometimes, even trying to convince them that a crime has actually occurred when no physical equipment has been stolen—may be a challenge.

- Using expert witnesses who can explain highly technical concepts in lay terms.

Chapter 12, *Prosecuting a Computer Crime*, describes these activities in greater detail.

2

What Are the Crimes?

Computer crimes range from the catastrophic to the merely annoying. A case of computer-driven espionage might wreak devastating losses to national security. A case of commercial computer theft might drive a company out of business. A cracker's prank might not actually cause damage at all—but might cause a video game company or another computer user some annoyance. Some computer crimes are perpetrated for kicks, and some for social or political causes; others are the serious business of professional criminals. There is perhaps no other form of crime that cuts so broadly across the types of criminals and the severity of their offenses.

This chapter touches on a wide range of computer attacks.[*] Some are truly crimes, and others are not. Whether a particular attack is viewed as being a full-fledged crime or is simply dismissed as being a prank will depend upon the motives of the attacker, the type of organization and data attacked, and other aspects of the situation that can't be neatly summarized in a chapter of this kind.

The attacks discussed in this chapter are those in which the computer itself—or, more likely, the information it stores—is the target of the crime. We do not cover crimes in which the computer is simply used by the perpetrators in their criminal enterprises (for example, drug deals in which a syndicate keeps computerized records). We also do not cover the larceny of computers and computer components.

There are many ways to categorize computer crimes. You might divide them according to who commits them and what their motivation might be (e.g., profes-

---

[*] Some of the types of attacks described in this chapter were originally categorized by Donn B. Parker in *Computer Crime: Criminal Justice Resource Manual* . That manual is a valuable reference for any investigator involved in computer crime investigations.

sional criminals looking for financial gain, angry ex-employees looking for revenge, crackers looking for intellectual challenge). Or, you might divide these crimes by how they are perpetrated (e.g., by physical means such as arson, by software modifications, etc.). In this chapter, we have chosen to divide computer attacks (remember that some of these attacks are not crimes in the legal sense, but annoyances) by the types of computer security that ought to prevent them— the same types of security we explain in Part II of this book:

Physical security

> Protection of the physical building, computer, related equipment, and media (e.g., disks and tapes).

Personnel security

> Protection of the people who work in any organization, and protection of computer equipment and data from these people and others outside the organization.

Communications security

> Protection of software and data, especially as it passes from computer to computer.

Operations security

> Protection of the procedures used to prevent and detect security breaches, and the development of methods of prevention and detection.

In some cases, the boundaries between these categories may be rather fuzzy, and some attacks may overlap several categories.

NOTE

Many of the attacks we describe in this chapter are technically complex, and we can't explain them in detail in an introductory book of this kind. In this chapter, we are simply outlining the various types of attacks that you are likely to see when you investigate a computer crime so that you will have some familiarity with the concepts and the terminology. If you need to know the details of any particular type of attack, consult your technical advisors and the technical references listed in Appendix A, *Resource Summary*.

Breaches of Physical Security

As we describe in Chapter 6, physical security is concerned with physical protection of the computer, computer equipment, computer media, and the overall physical facility from natural disasters, accidents of various kinds, and intentional attacks. That chapter describes the basics of what is being protected, and provides guidelines that will help keep your facility physically secure.

We've already discussed some obvious breaches of physical security in Chapter 1. Terrorist bombings on buildings housing computer equipment, arson, and theft and destruction of computer equipment fall into this category. You may not realize that less obvious attacks, like turning off the electricity in a computer room, spilling soda on a keyboard, and throwing sensitive papers in the trash may also invite disaster. This section describes some of these less obvious breaches.

Dumpster Diving

Dumpster diving, or *trashing*, is a name given to a very simple type of security attack—scavenging through materials that have been thrown away, as shown in Figure 2-1. This type of attack isn't illegal in any obvious way. If papers are thrown away, nobody wants them—right? Dumpster diving also isn't unique to computer facilities. All kinds of sensitive information turns up in the trash, and industrial spies through the years have used this method to get information about their competitors.

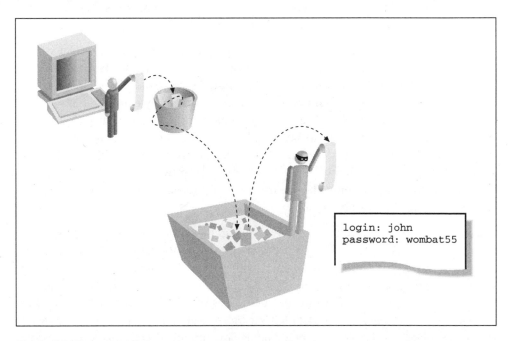

```
login: john
password: wombat55
```

Figure 2-1. Dumpster diving

Computer facilities are especially good places for scavengers who are looking around for information that might help them penetrate a system (People often write down information that they shouldn't). Around the offices and in the trash, crackers can find used disks and tapes, discarded printouts, and handwritten notes of all kinds. Crackers have been known to literally dive into the dumpsters outside telephone companies and network providers, searching for passwords and access codes. They may also retrieve printouts, computer manuals, and other documents from which they extract information needed to crack the system. They'll often share this information with other crackers by posting it to BBSs or in publications of various kinds. The trash of computer and telephone companies is of special interest to trashers because it's usually a rich source of helpful information.

There is another type of computer-related "trash" that you might not consider. In the system itself are files that have been deleted, but that haven't actually been erased from the system. Computers and computer operators are oriented towards saving data, not destroying it, and sometimes data is saved that shouldn't be. Remember the last time the system crashed while you were working on a project? Even though you might have lost some data, you were probably able to recover using a backup that you or your system operator or administrator made. If backups aren't made regularly—and your data loss is greater than it might be— you'd complain bitterly. But, when is the last time you complained because data you thought was erased was still in the computer?

Electronic trashing is easy because of the way that systems typically delete data. Usually, "deleting" a file, a disk, or a tape doesn't actually delete data, but simply rewrites a header record. If you are running MS-DOS, for example, you can delete a file via the DEL command; however, someone can retrieve the contents of the file simply by running UNDELETE. System utilities are available that make it easy to retrieve files that may seem to be completely gone. This is sometimes a source of embarrassment. Lieutenant Colonel Oliver North discovered to his dismay that erasing sensitive Iran-Contra email didn't really remove the files, but simply removed references to them. The files were easily retrieved and used during the hearings into the Iran-Contra affair.

Although there are methods for truly erasing files and magnetic media, most computer operators who work on large systems do not take the time to erase disks and tapes when they are finished with them. They may discard old disks and tapes with data still on them. They simply write the new data over the old data already on the tape. Because the new data may not be the same length as the old, there may be sensitive data left for those skilled enough to find it. It is far safer to explicitly write over storage media and memory contents with random data and to degauss magnetic tapes.

One computer company in Texas that does business with a number of oil companies noticed that whenever a certain company asked them to mount a temporary storage (scratch) tape on the tape drive, the read-tape light would always come on before the write-tape light. The ingenious oil company was scavenging the tape for information that might have been put on it by competitors that used the tape before them.

Trashing can have deadly consequences. When some old Department of Justice computers were sold off, they had on their disks information on the whereabouts of witnesses in the Federal Witness Protection Program. Although the data had been deleted, it had not been completely erased from the disk. The DOJ was able to get back some of the computers, but not all, and was forced to relocate the compromised families as a result.

Wiretapping

There are a number of ways that physical methods can breach networks and communications. Some of the offenses we discuss below overlap with those described in "Breaches of Communications Security," later in this chapter. Telephone and network wiring is often not protected as well as it should be, both from intruders who can physically damage it and from wiretaps that can pick up the data flowing across the wires.

Criminals sometimes use *wiretapping* methods to eavesdrop on communications. It's unfortunately quite easy to tap many types of network cabling. For example, a simple induction loop coiled around a terminal wire can pick up most voice and RS232 communications. More complex types of eavesdropping can be set up as well. As we describe in Chapter 8, *Communications Security*, it's important to physically secure all network cabling to protect it both from interception and from vandalism.

Telephone fraud has always been a problem among crackers, but with the increasing use of cellular phones, phone calling cards, and the ordering of merchandise over the phone using credit cards, this problem has increased dramatically in recent years.

Eavesdropping on Emanations

Electronic emanations from computer equipment is a risk you need to be aware of, although this is mainly a concern for military and intelligence data. Computer equipment, like every other type of electrical equipment from hairdryers to stereos, emits electromagnetic impulses. Whenever you strike a computer key, an electronic impulse is sent into the immediate area. Foreign intelligence services, commercial enterprises, and sometimes even teenage crackers may take advantage of these electronic emanations by monitoring, intercepting, and decoding them. This may sound highly sophisticated, but there have been some embarrassingly easy cases. The original HeathKit H19 terminals transmitted radio signals that were so strong that they could be picked up by placing an ordinary television set beside the terminal. As characters were typed on the terminal screen, a distinctive pattern appeared on the TV screen and could be decoded, as shown in Figure 2-2.

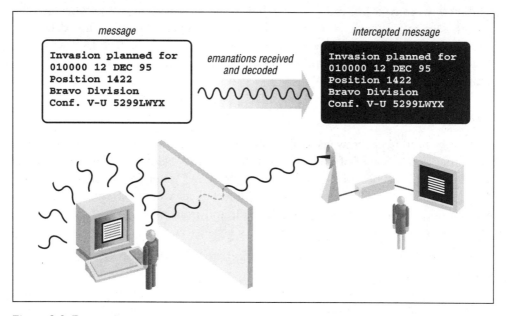

Figure 2-2. Emanations

Because of the emanation threat, government computers that are used to store and process classified information require special physical shielding. The U.S. federal TEMPEST program is designed to develop, test, and certify specially shielded computer equipment from mainframes to terminals to cabling.

There are other types of emissions as well. Criminals have even recorded the noise from a computer printer (the key-and-ribbon variety; it can't be done with laser printers) and then play the recording later to determine which keys were active.

Denial or Degradation of Service

A few security breaches span most of the categories discussed in this chapter. How these breaches are categorized depends largely on the methods used to prevent or detect them. In security terms, *availability* means that the computer facility, the computer itself, and the software and data users need are all working and available for use. Someone who shuts down service or slows it to a snail's pace is committing an offense known as *denial of service* or *degradation of service*. There are many ways to disrupt service, including such physical means as arson or explosions; shutting off power, air conditioning, or water (needed by air conditioning systems); or performing various kinds of electromagnetic distur-bances. Natural disasters, like lightning and earthquakes, can also disrupt service. Chapter 6, *Physical Security*, describes these physical disruptions in some detail.

Actually, there are two quite different types of attacks in this category. Some cases of electronic sabotage involve the actual destruction or disabling of equipment or data. Turning off power or sending messages to system software telling it to stop processing are examples of the first type of attack—a classic denial of service.

The other type of attack, known as *flooding* (or sometimes *wedging* or *spam-ming*) is the type we saw with the Internet worm. As the worm spread across systems and networks, it kept creating new processes that so clogged the affected systems that other work couldn't get done. In this type of attack, instead of shut-ting down service, the attacker puts more and more of a strain on the systems' ability to service requests, so eventually they can't function at all. Another example of a flooding attack was the "electronic mail bomb" that victimized writers Michelle Slatalla and Josh Quittner, as we described in Chapter 1.

Denial of service doesn't have to be a complex technical attack. Sometimes, it even occurs by accident. Suppose all of your system administrators get (or are given) food poisoning at a company lunch. Suppose a determined fax machine ties up your own machine by continuing to dial it. Suppose a new user starts printing a PostScript file as text on the company's only printer, and doesn't know how to stop the job. There are many examples of accidental denial of service.

Breaches of Personnel Security

To some extent, nearly all of the attacks we discuss in this chapter could be considered in the realm of personnel security—after all, people commit the offenses and people ultimately detect them. In fact, many of the crimes we talk about in terms of computer security happen whether or not computers are involves—bribery, subversion, extortion, and malicious mischief of all kinds. Only the targets and the media may differ.

There are a few particular security breaches that merit special discussion here.

Masquerading

Masquerading occurs when one person uses the identity of another to gain access to a computer. This may be done in person or remotely. We describe basic masquerading in this section, but masquerading is an attack that spans the bound-aries of the categories we've identified in this chapter. Because operations security methods should be in place to prevent and detect masquerading, that category is also relevant. In fact, we discuss some technically complex forms of masquerading in the section called "Breaches of Operations Security" later in this chapter.

There are both physical and electronic forms of masquerading. In person, a criminal may use an authorized user's identity or access card to get into restricted areas where he will have access to computers and data. This may be as simple as signing someone else's name to a signin sheet at the door of a building. It may be as complex as playing back a voice recording of someone else to gain entry via a voice recognition system. (The 1992 U.S. movie, *Sneakers,* had some nice scenes showing how this could work—at least how it could work in Hollywood!)

A related attack, sometimes called *piggybacking*, involves following an authorized person into a restricted area—a building or a computer room. For example, someone who wants to gain access to a restricted area might show up at a secured door, carrying a heavy armload of computer equipment, at the same time as an authorized employee arrives, and looking as if they belong. The authorized employee kindly holds the door open, and the intruder tags along into the area. Of course, there is nothing high-tech about this; it's the same principle burglars follow to gain entry to apartment houses. It's easy enough to prevent piggybacking: guards and access methods like turnstiles and mantraps (which allow only one user to enter at a time) usually do the job. User education is also a very important deterrent.

Electronically, an unauthorized person will use an authorized user's logon ID, password, personal identification number (PIN), or telephone access code to gain access to a computer or to a particular set of sensitive data files. There are many ways to obtain this information, some of them quite simple and others quite complex. For example, they might have obtained this information by theft (if the authorized user has written down these numbers and codes), eavesdropping electronically (via password sniffers or other types of monitoring programs), or simply looking over the shoulder of the user while he or she types. In fact, one gang of juvenile crackers in Atlanta obtained passwords by using binoculars to look across a street into windows where users were typing their passwords.

Unauthorized password use is the most common type of electronic masquerading, and it's a very effective one. If an outsider steals or figures out a password, there is no easy way for the system to tell whether the person who enters the password is the legitimate, authorized user, or an outsider. Unfortunately, passwords are often far too easy to crack. People are very likely to pick passwords that can be easily guessed by intruders or can be cracked by password cracking or dictionary programs. They pick the names of their spouses, children, or pets, their birthdates or license plates or astrological signs, or the names of sports teams or fictional characters. (Chapter 8 provides some good hints for selecting sound passwords.)

To understand how masquerading works, you need to know a few basics about how users gain access to shared systems via a two-step process known as identification and authentication.

Identification is the way you tell the system who you are. For example, you enter your user account name in response to a "login" prompt, or you enter your bank account number at an ATM machine. *Authentication* is how you prove to the system that you are who you say you are. There are three classic ways in which you can prove yourself:

Something you know
> The most common example is a password or a PIN. The theory is that if you know the password or PIN for an account, you must be the owner of it.

Something you have
> Examples are keys, tokens, badges, and smart cards that you use to "unlock" a building, a door, a computer, or an account.

Something you are or do
> Examples are physiological traits, like your fingerprint or voiceprint, or behavioral traits, like your signature or keystroke pattern.

It's unfortunately very common for computer criminals to steal, guess, or otherwise obtain account names and passwords. And, once someone is masquerading as you, he can do virtually everything you can do. Not only can he steal your files (breaching their confidentiality), he can also modify them (destroying their integrity) or perhaps even delete them completely. Figure 2-3 shows a simple case of masquerading.

Most damaging of all, a masquerader can pretend to the outside world that he is you, thus damaging your reputation as well as your data. A few years ago, a Dartmouth student sent forged electronic mail, supposedly from a professor at the college, saying that a midterm exam had been canceled because of a family emergency. Half the class believed the email and didn't show up for the exam. In another case, someone masquerading as a Texas A&M professor sent out many thousands of electronic copies of racist hate mail; a year later, the victim of this forgery is still dealing with the consequences.

The principle of *repudiation* comes into play here. There are ways in software of ensuring that someone who does something in a system—sends a message, changes a file, etc.—is held accountable and cannot claim later that he did not do what he did. To make this work—to keep masquerading from being a problem in your system—your system needs methods of strong authentication, as well as excellent operations security. (These concepts are beyond the scope of this book. The references in Appendix A provide sources of additional information.)

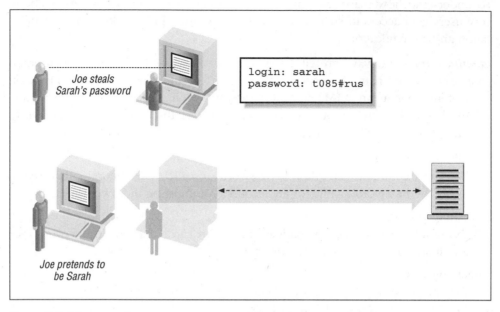

```
login: sarah
password: t085#rus
```

Joe steals
Sarah's password

Joe pretends to
be Sarah

Figure 2-3. Masquerading

Social Engineering

Social engineering is the name given a category of attacks in which someone manipulates others into revealing information that can be used to steal data or subvert systems. Such attacks can be very simple or very complex. In one low-tech case we know about, a man posing as a magazine writer was able to get valuable information over the telephone from the telephone company simply by asking for it—supposedly for his story. He then used that information to steal more than a million dollars in telephone company equipment.

An old trick is to make a few phone calls to find out the names of certain key machines in an organization. (With most operating systems, the appropriate networking programs let you find this information online, with no need for human contact.) The attacker can then stroll into the building (perhaps he's timed his visit for the system administrator's lunch hour) and tell the receptionist he's there to service the "SPIRIT" machine, for example. He'll probably be convincing enough that he'll be given free rein of the system.

Harassment

A particularly nasty kind of personnel breach we've seen lately is *harassment* on the Internet. Sending threatening email messages and slandering people on bulletin board systems and newsgroups is all too common. In a recent harassment

Special Problems with Masquerading

Skilled intruders may even hide their identities by manipulating telephone and telecommunications systems. Keep in mind, when you are investigating intrusions, that the phone numbers you uncover during an investigation may, in fact, not be the ones used directly by the intruders.

Masquerading is one of the most frequently used methods of gaining criminal access to a computer system. Unfortunately, should the case ever come to trial, masquerading is also one of the hardest to prove. By the very nature of the crime, the records (e.g., system logins, signin sheets, etc.) erroneously show that the authorized person—not the criminal—was using the computer during the time that it was penetrated. Some cases have been successfully prosecuted when eyewitnesses are able to place the suspect at the terminal used to connect to the computer at the time the crime took place. The next best thing is to show that the authorized user was somewhere else during this period. Also, be ready to demonstrate, when possible, how the suspect gained access to the password, personal identification number, or other access code.

case, a student from the University of Michigan was indicted for posting a particularly graphic story about a sex murder on an Internet newsgroup. Because he used the name of an actual female student at Michigan, his activities were initially considered to be harassment. (The case was eventually dismissed.)

These kinds of attacks are not new, and personally threatening remarks can as easily be sent by letter or posted on a wall, as they can be sent over the Internet. But the electronic audience is a much larger one, and such messages, sent out from an organization's network domain, may damage the reputation of the organization as well as that of the particular perpetrator.

Software Piracy

Software piracy is an issue that spans the category boundaries and may be enforced in some organizations and not in others. Pirated computer programs are big business. Copying and selling off-the-shelf application programs in violation of the copyrights costs software vendors many millions of dollars. The problem is an international one, reaching epidemic proportions in some countries. (As we've said, software piracy was a major issue in the 1995 Clinton trade agreement with China.) Too many people don't take copyrights seriously. Law-abiding people everywhere think nothing of copying games to share with friends, or office software for home use.

Bulletin board systems often make pirated software available for downloading or swapping. In a recent case, an MIT student was accused of running a BBS that was used in this way. Charges against him were eventually dropped, however, on the theory that the federal wire fraud statute did not apply to a case involving copyright infringements. Only the copyright statute would apply, and it was not applicable where the infringing person did not intend to profit from his conduct.

The stealing of proprietary programs is also a major business problem. A company may spend millions of dollars to develop a specialized program, only to find that its competitor has the same program—and the competitor hasn't had to invest in the development costs! Remember from Chapter 1 the fear that Apple Computer had that the source code for its Macintosh computers may have been compromised. Had this happened, then Macintosh clones could be manufactured anywhere in the world.

Employees need to be educated about the legalities, ethics, and company policies relating to software piracy and other forms of unauthorized copying of information. Some breaches of personnel security occur because procedures have broken down—either the procedures for training employees or the procedures for dealing with the system and the data after these employees leave an organization. (In Chapter 7, we'll summarize these procedures.) Some breaches really come down to policy and policy enforcement. What might be considered a crime in some organizations might be a minor infraction, or even legitimate, in another. For example, does an organization allow employees to carry sensitive data outside the office? Can the employee use company software and databases from a home computer?

Sometimes, policy enforcement is spotty. For example, some organizations that work with sensitive information prohibit employees from carrying paper copies or disks and tapes home from work. On the other hand, they encourage those same employees to work from home by giving them modems to use in accessing company databases. They forget that data can as easily be downloaded to a home computer as carried out the office door.

Breaches of Communications and Data Security

In this category we include attacks on computer software and on the data itself. The other categories we've discussed in this chapter are more focused on physical equipment, people, and procedures.

Data Attacks

There are many types of attacks on the confidentiality, integrity, and availability of data. *Confidentiality* keeps data secret from those not authorized to see it. *Integrity* keeps data safe from modification by those not authorized to change it. *Availability*, as we discussed under "Denial or Degradation of Service" above, keeps data available for use.

The theft, or unauthorized copying, of confidential data is an obvious attack that falls into this category. Espionage agents steal national defense information. Industrial spies steal their competitors' product information. Crackers steal passwords or other kinds of information on breaking into systems.

Two terms you'll hear in the context of data attacks are *inference* and *leakage*. With inference, a user legitimately views a number of small pieces of data, but by putting those small pieces together is able to deduce some piece of non-obvious and secret data. With leakage, a user gains access to a flow of data via an unauthorized access route (e.g., through eavesdropping).

We've talked about wiretapping and monitoring electronic emanations in "Breaches of Physical Security" above. In this section, we discuss attacks on the integrity of the data itself.

Unauthorized Copying of Data

Software piracy, which we discussed in "Breaches of Personnel Security" above, is another attack that spans the categories we've identified in this chapter. In some sense, piracy is just another example of the *unauthorized copying* of data. The methods for detecting and preventing such a crime are the same whether the copied data is national defense plans, commercial software, or sensitive corporate or personal data.

Preventing and detecting this type of attack requires coordinated policies among the different categories of computer security. In terms of personnel security, user education is vital. In terms of operations security, automated logging and auditing software can play a part as well.

Traffic Analysis

Sometimes, the attacks on data might not be so obvious. Even data that appears quite ordinary may be valuable to a foreign or industrial spy. For example, travel itineraries for generals and other dignitaries help terrorists plan attacks against their victims. Accounts payable files tell outsiders what an organization has been purchasing and suggest what its future plans for expansion may be. Even the fact that two people are communicating—never mind what they are saying to each other—may give away a secret. *Traffic analysis* is the name given to this type of analysis of communications.

In one industrial espionage case, a competitor monitored a company's use of online data services to find out what questions it had and what information it was collecting on certain types of metallurgy. The information allowed the competitor to monitor the company's progress on a research and development project and to use this information in developing its own similar product. That product reached the market several weeks before the original developer was able to. The original company's research and development investment and its potential share of the market—many millions—were all but lost.

This kind of analysis isn't confined to sophisticated computer methods. It's an issue whenever anyone tries to keep a secret. During the U.S. Desert Storm crisis, a number of people in Washington DC correctly concluded, in the absence of any actual announcement by the White House, that the United States was about to mount a military operation. How? Government officials were meeting far into the night to plan their strategy. To fortify themselves, they kept calling a nearby pizza parlor for provisions. The pizza makers knew something was up—and when the press corps saw those pies being carried in, they also knew that something big was happening at the White House.

Covert Channels

One somewhat obscure type of data leakage is called a *covert channel*. A clever insider can hide stolen data in otherwise innocent output. For example, a file-name or the contents of a report could be changed slightly to include secret information that is obvious only to someone who is looking for it. A password, a launch code, or the location of sensitive information might be conveyed in this way. Even more obscure are the covert channels that convey information based on a system clock or other timed event. Information could, in theory, be conveyed by someone who controls system processing in such a way that the elapsed time of an event itself conveys secret information.

Software Attacks

We've talked so far in this section about attacks on data. There are also attacks that subvert software.

Trap Doors

One classic software attack is the *trap door* or *back door*. A trap door is a quick way into a program; it allows program developers to bypass all of the security built into the program now or in the future.

To a programmer, trap doors make sense. If a programmer needs to modify the program sometime in the future, he can use the trap door instead of having to go through all of the normal, customer-directed protocols just to make the change. Trap doors of course should be closed or eliminated in the final version of the program after all testing is complete, but, intentionally or unintentionally, some are left in place. Other trap doors may be introduced by error and only later discovered by crackers who are roaming around, looking for a way into system programs and files. Typical trap doors use such system features as debugging tools, program exits that transfer control to privileged areas of memory, undocumented application calls and parameters, and many others.

Trap doors make obvious sense to expert computer criminals as well, whether they are malicious programmers or crackers. Trap doors are a nifty way to get into a system or to gain access to privileged information or to introduce viruses or other unauthorized programs into the system.

For example, in 1993 and 1994, an unknown group of computer criminals repetitively broke into systems on the Internet using passwords captured by password sniffers. Once on the system, they exploited software flaws to gain privileged access. They installed modified login and network programs that allowed them reentry even if the original passwords were changed.

The detection of trap doors is an operations security problem—checking to see if the trap doors are there in the first place, and whether they exist and operations are correct on an ongoing basis.

Session Hijacking

Session hijacking is a relatively new type of attack in the communications category. Some types of hijacking have been around a long time. In the simplest type, an unauthorized user gets up from his terminal to go get a cup of coffee. Someone lurking nearby—probably a coworker who isn't authorized to use this particular system—sits down to read or change files that he wouldn't ordinarily be able to access.

Some systems don't disconnect immediately when a session is terminated. Instead, they allow a user to re-access the interrupted program for a short period. A cracker with a good knowledge of telephone and telecommunications operations can take advantage of this fact to reconnect to the terminated session.

Sometimes, an attacker will connect a covert computer terminal to a line between the authorized terminal and the computer. The criminal waits until the authorized terminal is on line but not in use, and then switches control to the covert terminal. The computer thinks it is still connected to the authorized user, and the criminal has access to the same files and data as the authorized user. Other types of hijacking occur when an authorized user doesn't log out properly so the computer still expects a terminal to be connected. Call forwarding from an authorized number to an unauthorized number is another method of getting access.

Tunneling

Technically sophisticated *tunneling* attacks fall into this category as well. Tunneling uses one data transfer method to carry data for another method. Tunneling is an often legitimate way to transfer data over incompatible networks, but it is illegitimate when it is used to carry unauthorized data in legitimate data packets.

Timing Attacks

Timing attacks are another technically complex way to get unauthorized access to software or data. These include the abuse of race conditions and asynchronous attacks. In *race conditions,* there is a race between two processes operating on a system; the outcome depends on who wins the race. Although such conditions may sound theoretical, they can be abused in very real ways by attackers who know what they're doing. On certain types of UNIX systems,[*] for example, attackers could exploit a problem with files known as setuid shell files to gain superuser privileges. They did this by establishing links to a setuid shell file, then deleting the links quickly and pointing them at some other file of their own. If the operation is done quickly enough, the system can be made to run the attacker's file, not the real file.

Asynchronous attacks are another way of taking advantage of dynamic system activity to get access. Computer systems are often called upon to do many things at the same time. They may, for example, be asked by different users to analyze data using an application program that can work with only one set of data at a time. Or they may be told to print data by more users than they can handle at once. In these cases, the operating system simply places user requests into a queue, then satisfies them according to a predetermined set of criteria; for example, certain users may always take precedence, or certain types of tasks may come before others. "Asynchronous" means that the computer doesn't simply satisfy requests in the order in which they were performed, but according to some other scheme.

A skilled programmer can figure out how to penetrate the queue and modify the data that is waiting to be processed or printed. He might use his knowledge of the criteria to place his request in front of others waiting in the queue. He might change a queue entry to replace someone else's name or data with his own, or to

---

[*] System V-based systems prior to Release 4 and systems derived from BSD UNIX.

subvert that user's data by replacing it. Or he could disrupt the entire system by changing commands so that data is lost, programs crash, or information from different programs is mixed as the data is analyzed or printed.

Trojan Horses

Trojan horses, viruses, worms, and their kin are all attacks on the integrity of the data that is stored in systems and communicated across networks. Because there should be procedures in place for preventing and detecting these menaces, they overlap with the operations security category as well.

During the Trojan War, the Greeks hid soldiers inside a large hollow wooden horse designed by Odysseus. When the Trojans were persuaded to bring the horse inside the gates of the city, the hidden soldiers emerged and opened the gates to allow their own soldiers to attack the enemy.

In the computer world, *Trojan horses* are still used to sneak in where they're not expected. A Trojan horse is a method for inserting instructions in a program so that program performs an unauthorized function while apparently performing a useful one. Trojan horses are a common technique for planting other problems in computers, including viruses, worms, logic bombs, and salami attacks (more about these later). Trojan horses are a commonly used method for committing computer-based fraud and are very hard to detect.

Consider this typical situation: A Trojan horse is hidden in an application program that a user is eager to try—something like a new game or a program that promises to increase efficiency. Inside the horse is a logic bomb that will cause the entire system to crash the third time the user runs the new program. If he's lucky, the user will thoroughly enjoy the program the first two times it's run, because when he tries to use it the third time, the program he was eager to try will disable his whole system.

Viruses and Worms

People often confuse *viruses* and *worms*, so we try to differentiate them in this section. Indeed, they have many similarities, and both can be introduced into systems via Trojan horses.

The easiest way to think of a computer virus is in terms of a biological virus. A biological virus is not strictly alive in its own right, at least in the sense that lay people usually view life. It needs a living host in order to operate. Viruses infect healthy living cells and cause them to replicate the virus. In this way, the virus spreads to other cells. Without the living cell, a virus cannot replicate.

In a computer, a virus is a program which modifies other programs so they replicate the virus. In other words, the healthy living cell becomes the original program, and the virus affects the way the program operates. How? It inserts a copy of itself in the code. Thus, when the program runs, it makes a copy of the virus. This happens only on a single system. (Viruses don't infect networks in the way worms do, as we'll explain below.) However, if a virus infects a program which is copied to a disk and transferred to another computer, it could also infect programs on that computer. This is how a computer virus spreads.

The spread of a virus is simple and predictable—and it can be prevented. Viruses are mainly a problem with PCs and Macintoshes. Virus infection is fortunately hard to accomplish on UNIX systems and mainframes.

Unlike a virus, a worm is a standalone program in its own right. It exists independently of any other programs. To run, it does not need other programs. A worm simply replicates itself on one computer and tries to infect other computers that may be attached to the same network.

NOTE

> An important distinction between worms and viruses: A worm operates over a network, but in order to infect a machine, a virus must be physically copied.

Some viruses and worms are nondestructive (comparatively speaking), while others are extremely malevolent. Many common PC viruses, such as Michaelangelo, cause machine crashes or data loss as a result of bugs or other unexpected interactions with existing code. The Christmas Tree worm program which attacked IBM systems started out as nondestructive. But, as it spread itself to other computers, it became destructive when it proliferated into the system to such a degree that no other work could be done and the entire network had to be shut down to purge the infection.

The 1988 Internet Worm didn't actually destroy data, but shutting systems and networks down to clean up after it required a vast amount of system administration time and lost productivity among users.

A malevolent virus is meant to do damage. Such viruses are sometimes designed to crash an entire system on a certain date or after so many iterations of self-replication. They may be written to destroy specific application programs or data. The potential impact of a virus is limited only by the imagination of the criminal who writes it. Some government people are concerned that viruses could infect our defense system computers, causing weapons systems to malfunction or become inoperative. Viruses could also be used to crash law enforcement computers, destroying intelligence and investigative information. It would be naive not to believe that our adversaries, both domestic and international, haven't considered these possibilities.

Some crackers see viruses as intellectual challenges. With the advent of freedom in Eastern Europe, there has been an outbreak of computer viruses apparently planted by individuals who believe that in one fell swoop they can express their freedom and also strike back at a government that has oppressed them for years. In Hungary, "Yankee Doodle," "Ivan the Terrible," and "Ping Pong" are all appearing on computer screens across the country. The "Yankee Doodle" virus plays that familiar tune when the computer is turned on. The "Ping Pong" virus attacks the computer when it is turned on but not in use. A ball appears on the screen and bounces back and forth between letters. "Ivan the Terrible" gets into the system and destroys files.

The best ways to prevent viruses and worms from invading a system are:

- Be vigilant about introducing new and untrusted software into a system.
- Use virus scanning software to check for viruses.
- Do frequent and careful backups.

Employees who bring software to the office from their home machines (usually free software they have downloaded from bulletin board systems) are the greatest threat.

Salamis

The Trojan horse is also a technique for creating an automated form of computer abuse called the *salami* attack, which works on financial data. This technique causes small amounts of assets to be removed from a larger pool. The stolen assets are removed one slice at a time (hence the name salami). Usually, the amount stolen each time is so small that the victim of the salami fraud never even notices.

One theoretical financial salami attack (it's assumed the status of an urban accounting legend and has never actually been known to have been attempted) involves rounding off balances, crediting the rounded off amount to a specific account. Suppose that savings accounts in a bank earn 2.3%. Obviously, not all of the computations result in two-place decimals. In most cases, the new balance, after the interest is added, extends out to three, four, or five decimals. What happens to the remainders? Consider a bank account containing $22,500 at the beginning of the year. A year's worth of interest at 2.3% is $517.50, but after the first month the accumulated interest is $43.125. Is the customer credited with $43.12 or $43.13? Would most customers notice the difference? What if someone were funneling off this extra tenth of a penny from thousands of accounts every month? Although this particular salami hasn't to our knowledge been attempted, salamis that shave a quarter on up *have* been tried.

A clever thief can use a Trojan horse to hide a salami program that puts all of the rounded off values into his account. A tiny percentage of pennies may not sound like much until you add up thousands of accounts, month after month. Criminals using this scheme have been able to steal many thousands of dollars. They are sometimes discovered by a bank audit. More often, they are detected only when they use their new-found gains to entertain a life style that is not supported by their legitimate income.

Logic Bombs

Logic bombs may also find their way into computer systems by way of Trojan horses. A typical logic bomb tells the computer to execute a set of instructions at a certain date and time or under certain specified conditions. The instructions may tell the computer to display "I gotcha" on the screen, or it may tell the entire system to start erasing itself. Logic bombs often work in tandem with viruses. Whereas a simple virus infects a program and then replicates when the program starts to run, the logic bomb does not replicate – it merely waits for some pre-specified event or time to do its damage.

Time is not the only criterion used to set off logic bombs. Some bombs do their damage after a particular program is run a certain number of times. Others are more creative. In several cases we've heard about, a programmer told the logic bomb to destroy data if the company payroll is run and his name is not on it.; this is a sure-fire way to get back at the company if he is fired! The employee is fired, or may leave on his own, but does not remove the logic bomb. The next time the payroll is run and the computer searches for but doesn't find the employee's name, it crashes, destroying not only all of the employee payroll records, but the payroll application program as well.

Trojan horses present a major threat to computer systems, not just because of the damage they themselves can do, but because they provide a technique to facilitate more devastating crimes.

Breaches of Operations Security

Because operations security includes the setting up of procedures to prevent and detect all type of attacks on systems and personnel, we've discusses elements of operations security in most of the other preceding sections. Here, we describe a few special kinds of breaches of operations security.

Data Diddling

Data diddling, sometimes called *false data entry*, involves modifying data before or after it is entered into the computer. Consider situations in which employees are able to falsify time cards before the data contained on the cards is entered into the computer for payroll computation. A timekeeping clerk in a 300-person company noticed that, although the data entered into the company's timekeeping and payroll systems included both the name and the employee number of each worker, the payroll system used only the employee's number to process payroll checks. There were no external safeguards or checks to audit the integrity of the data. She took advantage of this vulnerability and filled out forms for overtime hours for employees who usually worked overtime. The cards had the hardworking employees' names, but the time clerk's number. Payment for the overtime was credited to her, as illustrated in Figure 2-4.

In another case, two employees of a utility company found that there was a time lapse of several days between when meter readings were entered into the computer and when the bills were printed. By changing the reading during this period, they were able to substantially reduce their electric bills and the bills of some of their friends and neighbors.

Why do we discuss these very simple attacks in the context of operations security? Because these attacks should not occur. Operations should be set up in any organization to prevent and detect this type of crime—safeguards on data modification, audits of changed data to be sure it was modified with authorization, and so on.

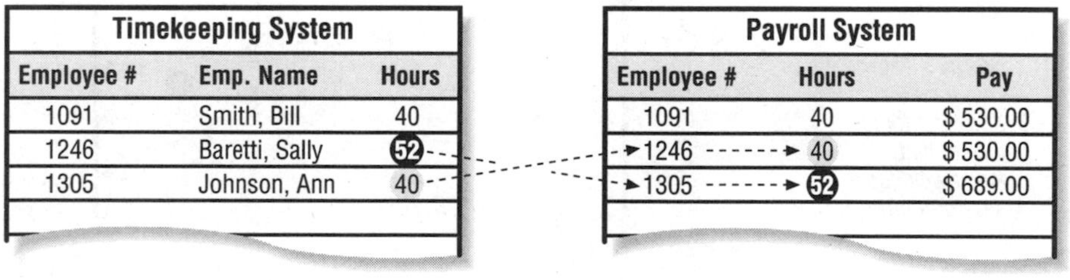

Timekeeping System				Payroll System		
Employee #	Emp. Name	Hours		Employee #	Hours	Pay
1091	Smith, Bill	40		1091	40	$ 530.00
1246	Baretti, Sally	52		1246	40	$ 530.00
1305	Johnson, Ann	40		1305	52	$ 689.00

Employee numbers were switched so overtime was credited to wrong employee.

Figure 2-4. Data diddling

IP Spoofing

In "Breaches of Personnel Security" above, we introduced masquerading attacks, particularly those involving one person pretending to be another. But there are some more complex masquerading attacks that can be prevented only by strong operations security.

A method of masquerading that we're seeing in various Internet attacks today is known as *IP spoofing* (IP stands for Internet Protocol, one of the communications protocols that underlies the Internet). Certain UNIX programs grant access based on IP addresses; essentially, the system running the program is authenticated, rather than the individual user. The attacker forges the addresses on the data packets he sends so they look as if they came from inside a network on which systems trust each other. Because the attacker's system looks like an inside system, he is never asked for a password or any other type of authentication. In fact, the attacker is using this method to penetrate the system from the outside. (This is the method used in the attack on Tsutomu Shimomura's system, which we describe in Chapter 1.)

Figure 2-5 illustrates a particular type of IP spoofing, an IP sequence number attack.

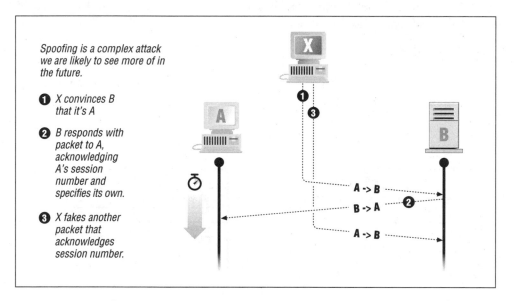

Figure 2-5. IP spoofing

How can an operations security program prevent IP spoofing attacks. Two good ways are to require passwords in all cases and to prevent trust relationships among systems.

Password Sniffing

Earlier in this chapter, we introduced the use of passwords and the way they can be compromised in masquerading attacks. Chapter 8 will summarize what makes a good password, and what types of passwords you should avoid. However, a relatively new type of attack on the Internet is putting even the most carefully chosen passwords at risk.

Password sniffers are able to monitor all traffic on areas of a network. Crackers have installed them on networks used by systems that they especially want to penetrate, like telephone systems and network providers. Password sniffers are programs that simply collect the first 128 or more bytes of each network connection on the network that's being monitored. When a user types in a user name and a password—as required when using certain common Internet services like FTP (which is used to transfer files from one machine to another) or Telnet (which lets the user log in remotely to another machine)—the sniffer collects that information. Additional programs sift through the collected information, pull out the important pieces (e.g., the user names and passwords), and cover up the existence of the sniffers in an automated way. Best estimates are that in 1994 as many as 100,000 sites were affected by sniffer attacks.

Figure 2-6 shows password sniffing.

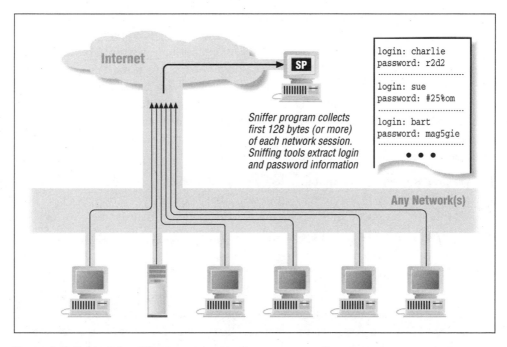

Figure 2-6. Password sniffing

One-time passwords and encrypted passwords are good ways to keep password sniffing attacks from compromising systems.

Scanning

A technique often used by novice crackers, called *scanning* or *war dialing*, also is one that ought to be prevented by good operations security. Remember the 1983 movie *War Games*, in which the high school cracker programmed his computer to dial telephone number after telephone number until it found one that connected to a modem?

With scanning, a program known as a war dialer or demon dialer processes a series of sequentially changing information, such as a list of telephone numbers, passwords, or telephone calling card numbers. It tries each one in turn to see which ones succeed in getting a positive response, as shown in Figure 2-7. In *War Games*, for example, the program dialed all of the telephone numbers in a particular region sequentially; if the number was answered by a tone, it was recorded for later experimentation. The computer doing the calling can make hundreds of telephone calls within several hours.

Suppose that a computer criminal looks in the telephone book and finds that the telephone numbers for the Fourth National Bank range from 791-0000 to 791-5578. Before he goes to bed one night, he programs his computer to call all of the numbers in this range and to record the ones that are answered by a modem. In the morning, he prints out the successful numbers. He now has a list of the telephone numbers that are most likely to give him access to the bank's computers. The next evening, he dials those numbers and tests his skills as a cracker. With skill, determination, and a little luck, he may eventually use these phone numbers as the opening wedge into a bank computer—and eventually into some accounts from which he can transfer funds.

The programs used for scanning, called war dialers or demon dialer programs, are available from many bulletin board systems (BBSs). Successful scanners often post the telephone numbers they've identified on bulletin boards and in cracker publications.

Excess Privileges

If a cracker breaks into one user's account, he can compromise and damage that user's files, but he can't ordinarily get beyond the boundaries of the user's account to damage the rest of the system. Or can he? Sometimes, the answer is yes, and the reason is that, too often, users in a system have *excess privileges*—more privileges than they ought to have. An ordinary user on an ordinary system doesn't need to be able to modify all of the files on that system. And yet, in many systems, a user has the system privileges that entitle him to do just that. The user may never actually want to change anyone else's files—he may not even know

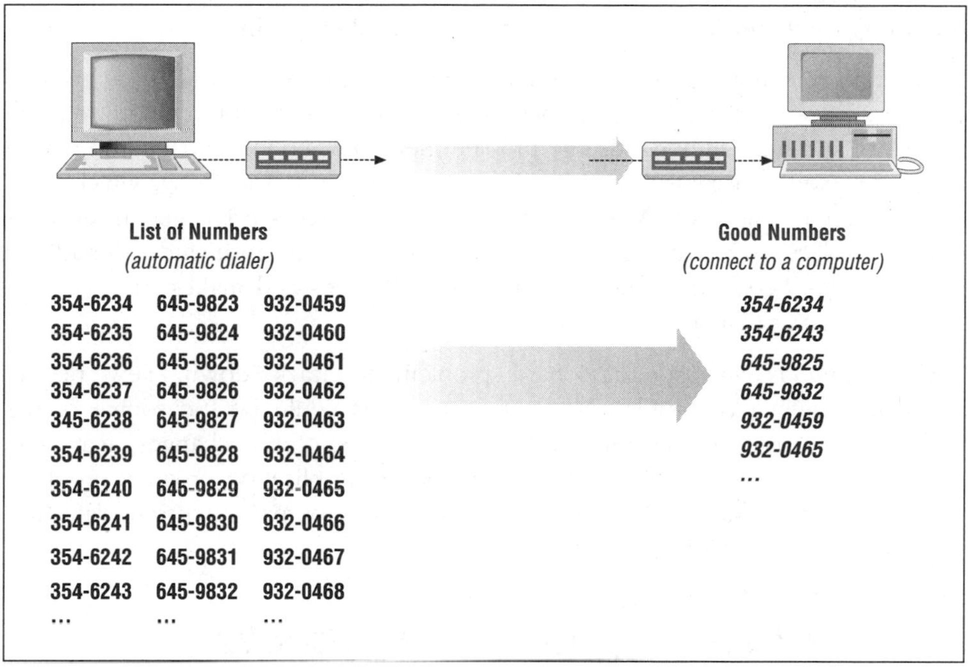

List of Numbers			Good Numbers
(automatic dialer)			*(connect to a computer)*
354-6234	645-9823	932-0459	*354-6234*
354-6235	645-9824	932-0460	*354-6243*
354-6236	645-9825	932-0461	*645-9825*
354-6237	645-9826	932-0462	*645-9832*
345-6238	645-9827	932-0463	*932-0459*
354-6239	645-9828	932-0464	*932-0465*
354-6240	645-9829	932-0465	*...*
354-6241	645-9830	932-0466	
354-6242	645-9831	932-0467	
354-6243	645-9832	932-0468	
...	...	...	

Figure 2-7. Scanning

that he is allowed to—but nevertheless the privileges are there. If an intruder gets access to the system through the user's account, he can exploit this weakness.

In UNIX environments, intruders who manage to get "root" or "superuser" privileges can play havoc with the system. In mainframe systems, abuse of privileges is sometimes called *superzapping*. The term comes from Superzap, the name of a utility program that is used in most IBM mainframes. Superzap lets system administrators or other highly trusted individuals override system security to quickly repair or regenerate the system, especially in an emergency. Similar utilities are found on many other types of computer systems. Programs of this kind can be thought of as the master key to the system. They unlock most other safeguards and controls. In the wrong hands, their use can be devastating.

In one case of superzapping, the manager of computer operations in a bank was told by his boss to correct a problem affecting account balances. The problem was originally caused by unanticipated problems in the changeover of the bank's computer system. While working on the project, the manager found that he could use the Superzap program to make other account changes as well, without having to deal with the usual controls, audits, or documentation. He moved funds from various accounts into the accounts of several friends, netting about $128,000 in all. He was detected only when a customer complained about a shortage in his account. Because the Superzap program left no evidence of data file changes, the fraud was highly unlikely to be discovered by any other means.

Superzapping is not intrinsically a crime or even a misdeed. Use of supervisor or root privileges, or the running of programs that bypass security checks, may be necessary and fully authorized. The problem here is in how it is used and why it is not detected and controlled through system logging and auditing, which we'll discuss later in this book. We discuss the abuse of excess privileges in terms of operations security because good operations security ought to include an auditing capability that keeps track of who has what privileges—and makes sure they are needed in each situation.

Superzapping is an especially hard problem to track down. Few people confronted with a computer crime expect that this could be the source of the problem. Because superzapping leaves no evidence of file changes, managers may assume that the loss of funds is a data entry or application program problem. The only reliable way to detect this technique is by comparing current data files with previous generations of the same files.

Ways of Detecting Common Attacks

This section provides a quick summary of how you might be able to anticipate or detect the most common types of attacks we've discussed in this chapter. Note that this listing is not exhaustive; too many of the attacks don't fall into neat categories, and too many require a good deal of technical understanding to anticipate and detect. However, this information will give you some guidance in analyzing types of computer crimes and in better understanding the material presented in Part III of this book.

This section briefly summarizes:

- Potential offenders—what type of individual (e.g., a programmer, a spy) might commit a crime of this type.

- Methods of detection—how such crimes are found out (e.g., tracing equipment of various kinds, analyzing log files).

- Evidence—trails that might be left by the intruders and that might help in detection (e.g., system logs, telephone company records).

Dumpster Diving

Potential Offenders

1. System users.

2. Anyone able to access the trash area.

3. Anyone who has access to computer areas or areas used to store backups.

Methods of Detection

1. Tracing proprietary information back to its source (e.g., memos with company names or logos).

2. Observation (guards may actually see intruders in action).

3. Testing an operating system to discover data left over after job execution.

Evidence

1. Computer output media (e.g., may contain vendor name or identifying page numbers).

2. Similar information produced in suspected ways in the same form.

3. Characteristics of printout or other media (e.g., type fonts or logos).

Wiretapping and Eavesdropping

Potential Offenders

1. Communications technicians and engineers.

2. Agents for competitors.

3. Communications employees, former employees, vendors, and contractors.

4. Agents for foreign intelligence services.

Methods of Detection

1. Voice wiretapping methods.

2. Tracing where the equipment used in the crime came from (e.g., monitoring equipment).

3. Tracing computer output (e.g., disks and tapes) to their source.

4. Observation.

5. Discovery of stolen information.

Evidence

1. Voice wiretapping as evidence.

2. Computer output forms.

3. Computer audit logs.

4. Computer storage media.

5. Characteristics of printout or other media (e.g., type fonts or logos).

6. Manual after-hours signin/signout sheets.

Masquerading

Potential Offenders

1. Potentially everyone.

Methods of Detection

1. Analysis of audit logs and journals (e.g., a log shows that an authorized user apparently logged in, but it is known that the person was away at that time).

2. Observation (e.g., an eyewitness saw an intruder at an authorized user's terminal).

3. Password violations (e.g., a log shows repeated failed attempts to use an invalid password).

4. Report by the person who has been impersonated (e.g., the authorized person logs in, and the system tells him that he has had six unsuccessful logins since the last time he knows he actually logged in).

Evidence

1. Backups.

2. System audit logs.

3. Telephone company records (pen register and dialed number recorder (DNR) records).

4. Violation reports from access control packages.

5. Notes and documents found in the possession of suspects.

6. Witnesses.

7. Excessively large phone bills (excessive message units may indicate that someone is using resources).

Software Piracy

Potential Offenders

1. Purchasers and users of commercial software.

2. Software pirates.

3. Employees who steal proprietary software.

Methods of Detection

1. Observation.

2. Testimony of legitimate purchasers of software.

3. Search of users' facilities and computers.

Evidence

1. Pictures of computer screens where pirated software is being executed.

2. The contents of memory in computers containing pirated software.

3. Copies of media on which pirated software is found.

4. Printouts produced by pirated software.

Trap Doors

Potential Offenders

1. Systems programmers.

2. Applications programmers.

Methods of Detection

1. Exhaustive testing.

2. Specific testing based on evidence.

3. Comparison of specifications to performance.

Evidence

1. Programs that perform tasks not specified for them.

2. Output reports that indicate that programs are performing tasks not specified for them.

Timing Attacks

Potential Offenders

1. Advanced system analysts.

2. Advanced computer programmers.

Methods of Detection

1. System testing of suspected attack methods.

2. Complaints from system users that their jobs are not being performed efficiently.

3. Repeat execution of a job under normal and safe conditions.

Evidence

1. Output that deviates from normally expected output of logs.

2. Computer operations logs.

Trojan Horses, Viruses, Worms, Salamis, and Logic Bombs

Potential Offenders

1. Programmers who have detailed knowledge of a program.

2. Employees or former employees.

3. Vendor or contractor programmers.

4. Financial system programmers.

5. Computer users.

6. Computer operators.

7. Crackers.

Methods of Detection

1. Comparison of program code with backup copies of the program.

2. Tracing of unexpected events of possible gain from the act to suspected perpetrators.

3. Detailed data analysis, including analysis of program code (e.g., you may detect a virus because a file increases in size when it is modified or because disk space decreases).

4. Observation of financial activities of possible suspects (especially for salami attacks).

5. Testing of suspect programs.

6. Examination of computer audit logs for suspicious programs or pertinent entries (e.g., log entries that show that many programs were updated at the same time) (especially for viruses).

7. Transaction audits.

Evidence

1. Output reports.

2. Unexpected results of running programs.

3. Computer usage and file request journals.

4. Undocumented transactions.

5. Analysis test program results.

6. Audit logs.

Data Diddling

Potential Offenders

1. Participants in transactions being entered or updated.

2. Suppliers of source data.

3. Preparers of data.

4. Nonparticipants with access.

Methods of Detection

1. Comparison of data.

2. Manual controls.

3. Analysis of computer validation reports.

4. Integrity tests.

5. Validation of documents.

6. Analysis of audit logs.

7. Analysis of computer output.

Evidence

1. Data documents for source data, transactions, etc.

2. Manual logs, audit logs, journals, etc.

3. Backups and other computer media (e.g., tapes and disks).

4. Incorrect computer output control violation alarms.

Scanning

Potential Offenders

1. Malicious intruders.

2. Spies attempting to access systems for targeted data.

3. Criminals intent on committing fraud.

Methods of Detection

1. Computer logs that show when telephone calls were received by the computer and when attempts were made.

2. Loss of data or transfer of funds or other assets.

3. Telephone company records.

Evidence

1. Telephone company records (pen register and dialed number recorder (DNR) records).

2. Possession of war dialing programs.

3. Computer logs.

4. Possession of information compromised as a result of scanning, including lists of telephone numbers.

Excess Privileges

Potential Offenders

1. Programmers with access to Superzap-type programs.

2. Computer operations staff.

Methods of Detection

1. Comparison of files with historical copies.

2. Examination of computer usage logs.

3. Discrepancies noted by those who receive reports.

Evidence

1. Discrepancies in output reports.

2. Computer usage and file request journals.

3. Undocumented transactions.

3

Who Commits Computer Crimes?

In Chapter 2, we discussed a number of different types of computer crimes. Just as these crimes vary widely in their severity, their targets, and their motivations, so too do the people who commit these crimes. At one extreme there are the teenage "joyriders," playing around with their computers and modems. At the other extreme are ultra-dangerous criminals who break into classified military systems or corporate databases, for reasons of terrorism or military or corporate espionage. In the middle are disgruntled or fired employees, looking to wreak revenge on an employer, as well as hired crackers who break into systems under contract. This chapter explores the motivations and characteristics of these various categories of computer criminals.

Some law enforcement agencies have developed personality profiles of computer criminals. In this chapter, we introduce you to one specific criminal profiling tool—the Computer Crime Adversarial Matrix. The matrix outlines three general categories of computer criminals and their organizational, operational, behavioral, and resource characteristics. If you use the matrix as a guide, it can be a valuable investigative tool. Remember, though, that criminal profiling is not an exact science. It can be, and has been, misused a good deal in the media. Be sure to temper all discussions of profiling—including this one—with a liberal amount of common sense.

Types of Offenders

Many different ways of describing and categorizing computer criminals exist. It is not a simple taxonomy. There is a continuum of offenders and crimes, ranging from pranks to acts of international terrorism. There are numerous ways to categorize computer criminals; we divide them into three categories:

- Crackers[*]
- Criminals
- Vandals

These categories overlap substantially. To some extent, they are best differentiated by motivation: The main motivation of a cracker is *access* to a system or data; the main motivation of a criminal is *gain*; the main motivation of a vandal is *damage*.

In the following discussion, we divide only the third category—vandals—into two distinct groups: authorized users of the system being attacked, and strangers to that system. Each of the categories could, in theory, include both groups, although such a division is far more likely in the vandal category where the motivation and resources of users and strangers are quite different.

Please note that in trying to neatly summarize the characteristics of different types of computer criminals, we are necessarily presenting stereotypes. In actual cases, individuals and circumstances will potentially be quite different. View this presentation only as a starting point in understanding computer crimes and those who commit them.

Crackers

Although perpetrators in any of the three categories may engage in the act of cracking, crackers themselves are a unique group. Historically, they've been attracted to their calling by boredom and the intellectual challenge it presents. They may see themselves as pitted against the establishment. They may operate in the dead of night, often because they are in school or at a less than exciting job during the day. Remember, though, that while most crackers operate at night, they may often break into computers in many different time zones.

Many of these perpetrators are teenagers; despite their tender years, they have been successful at breaking into all kinds of systems—banks, companies that manufacture games, traditional corporate machines, and military machines. In one case, a 14-year-old broke into the computer that positions Air Force satellites.

Some crackers operate in groups, but many are loners. Despite their intelligence, many do poorly in school, or don't attend at all. Some have few friends, aside from their cracker buddies. Their major form of human interaction may be computer bulletin boards where they can interact with other crackers without actually having to be together. Although some are motivated by personal gain, many

---

[*] Although it is customary to call people who break into computers *hackers*, this is a term that has been misapplied by the press; the word *hacker* also refers, in many cases, to talented and legitimate programmers. In this book, we use the term *cracker* to describe people who break into computers.

others are looking for intellectual challenge or a way to attack the system. Their activities may take some to a fantasy world where they can pretend they are a Robin Hood type of character, fighting for truth, justice, and freedom against the system of the evil King John.

Cracker groups tend to be very informal, springing up in an ad hoc way to discuss or collaborate on projects. In 1990 the first organized cracker international convention was held in Europe. Crackers from all over the world gathered to share ideas, learn how to break into computers in other countries, and practice their skills. Since that time, additional conferences have been held in the United States and abroad.

To some extent, this stereotype presented here is accurate; a lot of crackers do still fit this profile. But in recent years, many crackers have become a good deal more professional. Frequently, they'll work for hire or will offer, to the highest bidder, the information they've been able to acquire from military or corporate targets. The theft of credit card numbers transmitted over the Internet, as well as stolen numbers from telephone calling cards, is becoming big business in the cracker community.

Computer Criminals

Although perpetrators in all three of the groups we are discussing can be considered criminals, the typical "criminal" category focuses on two main types of criminal behavior: espionage and fraud and abuse.

Espionage

This nation's government—indeed, our entire society—is heavily reliant on computers. Computer systems store and process our most sensitive national and industrial secrets. Computer-related espionage is the espionage of the 1990s and beyond. This category of computer crime includes international spies and their contractors who steal secrets from defense, academic, and laboratory research facility computers. It includes criminals who steal information and intelligence from law enforcement computers. It also encompasses industrial espionage agents who operate for competitive companies or for foreign governments who are willing to pay for information.

Fraud and Abuse

Computerized fraud and abuse is a major growth industry. Both individuals and criminal organizations are hard at work in this area. On the largest scale, major organized crime groups—both domestic and international—are moving into computer crime as a direct source of illegal income and as a means of laundering drug money. As we pointed out in Chapter 1, criminals have come to realize that they can make a lot more money committing fraud by computer, and a lot more safely, than they can in other ways.

Smaller criminal organizations and individuals have manipulated money transfers and used other schemes to further their own economic gain. They add phantom workers to payrolls and cash the checks themselves. They retire nonexistent people from retirement systems and take their lump-sum retirement payments. They double pay on invoices and split the difference with the vendors. There is no end to the number of schemes hatched by such computer criminals.

Vandals

Computer criminals in the vandal category do not usually commit their crimes for intellectual stimulation (as do the crackers) or for financial or political gain (as do true computer criminals). Often, the people in this category are angry—most often at a particular organization, but sometimes at life in general. Vandals can be roughly divided into two groups, which we call users and strangers. Users are those who are authorized to use the system they abuse, although they are likely to have extended their privileges. Strangers are those who are not authorized to use the system in any way.

Users

In this group are authorized users who perform unauthorized actions. An example is the employee who figures out how to get "root" or "superuser" access in a UNIX system and is then able to browse through payroll files, password files, and other highly confidential files. Users in this group may be just looking or they may damage files as they go. Perhaps they have been fired or have received a pay cut or a bad review. Perhaps they feel wronged in some way. So they react by attacking a company asset. Instead of taking an ax to the copying machine, they use their skills to do more hidden, but often more critical, damage. They wipe out files, scramble data, insert logic bombs in code, and so on.

Strangers

In this group are unauthorized users who access a system, to which they have no rights at all, to do damage. Outside vandals are relatively rare. Most often, the strangers who break into systems aren't vandals; they are either crackers, looking for fun or intellectual stimulation, or they are true criminals, trying to steal or change data for their own financial gain or the gain of others. Most acts of vandalism are perpetrated by insiders who are angry at some particular offense.

There are a variety of ways in which a stranger can gain access, ranging from some type of masquerading, to the use of password sniffers or other technical attacks, to outright extortion or bribery of authorized users.

Characteristics of Computer Criminals

The Computer Crime Adversarial Matrix, first developed for the FBI, describes a number of different types of computer criminals and, for each, summarizes certain characteristics in four categories:

- Organizational characteristics
- Operational characteristics
- Behavioral characteristics
- Resource characteristics

Organizational Characteristics

Organizational characteristics describe the ways in which computer criminals group themselves. Is there a group structure? What attracts the criminal to the group? Does the group operate internationally or only domestically? Let's look at each element of this part of the matrix:

Organization

Spies and organized crime obviously have tightly structured organizations. In other cases, computer criminals most often operate as loners or in very loosely structured groups. While three or four crackers might hang out together, exchange techniques, and applaud each other's efforts, even such a structured entity as the Computer Crime Adversarial Matrix will have a hard time calling this a "group" in any real sense of the word.

Recruitment/Attraction

More so than with most types of crimes, computer crime offers a myriad of attractions and inducements, ranging from pure greed to intellectual challenge. In some respects, perpetrators of computer crimes are not that different from perpetrators of other types of fraud. In general, though, perpetrators of fraud crimes tend to be older, more mature, and better educated than other types of criminals. Crackers, on the other hand, are often attracted much more by the intellectual challenge or peer group prestige of the break-in and much less by the potential for making money.

International Connections

Both crackers and espionage agents may have international connections. To the cracker, these connections are like-minded thinkers with whom he or she shares the intellectual challenge of beating the system. To the espionage agent, the international connection is his employer. And with today's computer network systems, neither the cracker nor the agent needs to leave home to break into computer systems on the other side of the world.

Operational Characteristics

Operational characteristics describe the ways in which computer criminals actually carry out their crimes. How carefully do they plan their crimes? What is their level of skill? How do they actually do what they do? Let's look at each element of this part of the matrix:

Planning

> In many cases, computer crimes are planned meticulously. In other cases (for example, in crimes of vandalism), opportunities present themselves because organizations have failed to take the proper precautions, and the criminals simply take advantage of the situation.

Level of Expertise

> Although the level of expertise varies, many computer criminals are highly skilled and very knowledgeable. They spend a great deal of time researching and preparing to commit their crimes. Countering this threat requires computer and security experts who are equally adept at their jobs.

Tactics/Methods Used

> Tactics vary according to the motive and the level of expertise. The matrix summarizes tactics and methods, but these are explained in greater detail in Chapter 2.

Behavioral Characteristics

Behavioral characteristics describe the computer criminals themselves. What motivates them? What are they like? What weakness do they have that might be exploited by those who investigate their crimes? Let's look at each element of this part of the matrix:

Motivation

> Motivation ranges from money to fun, from economic gain to intellectual challenge, from revenge to "why not?" In some cases, there may be more than one motivational factor. An angry employee might decide to get even with an employer and, while doing so, contribute to his or her own economic well-being. In a good many cases, particularly among authorized users of a system, the overriding motivation may be the perceived need to solve a problem of some kind. This is personal gain in a larger sense than pure financial gain; the criminal may feel that he has such a driving motive (e.g., the need to pay off a debt, the need to funnel money to a cause, or the need to avenge himself) that the rules simply don't apply.

Personal Characteristics

This is not a detailed personality profile, but merely some notes about what type of intelligence or other traits computer criminals in different categories might possess.

Potential Weaknesses

How can you catch a computer criminal? Look to the potential weaknesses of each type of criminal. Remember that some crackers don't even consider their acts a crime; in fact, in some countries, what they do is, in fact, not a crime. The view of these criminals is simple: if the system doesn't protect itself, then it's not our fault if we break in. Some crackers even consider themselves heroes for helping society to identify its vulnerabilities. Computer criminals, like other types of criminals, typically get caught when they become greedy or sloppy. Their self-confidence gets in the way, and they start leaving clues, either by bragging or by living a more extravagant lifestyle.

Resource Characteristics

Resource characteristics describe what resources the computer criminals have or need. What training do they need to do their deeds? What equipment do they need? Who is available to help them? Let's look at each element of this part of the matrix:

Training

Training skills range from formal training to on-the-job experience. The higher the level of training, the greater the expertise.

Minimum Equipment Required

In most cases, computer crimes can be committed with the most basic computer equipment: a personal computer and a modem. If the criminal has direct access to the target computer system, then no additional equipment may be needed. Of course, in extreme cases, more sophisticated equipment may be required—for example, for maintaining and intercepting electronic communications.

Support Structure

What support does the criminal or criminal organization receive? Crackers receive peer group support from other crackers. Espionage agents receive support from their supporting governments. Many computer criminals simply operate on their own, with no support structure at all.

Computer Crime Adversarial Matrix

Remember, the Computer Crime Adversarial Matrix is meant to be used as an investigative tool, not as a definitive descriptive-or predictive weapon.

Table 3-1. Computer Crime Adversarial Matrix

ORGANIZATIONAL CHARACTERISTICS			
Categories of Offenders	**Organization**	**Recruitment/Attraction**	**International Connections**
Crackers			
Groups	Unstructured organization with counterculture orientation.	Peer group attraction.	Interact and correspond with other groups around the world.
Individuals	None; these people are true loners.	Attracted by intellectual challenge.	Subscribe to cracker journals and may interact on cracker bulletin boards.
Criminals			
Espionage	Supported by hostile intelligence services.	In most cases, money; some cases of ideological attraction; attention.	Use computer networks to break into target computers around the world.
Fraud/Abuse	May operate as small organized crime group or as a loner.	Money; power.	Use wire services to transfer money internationally.
Vandals			
Strangers	Loner or small group. May be quite young.	Revenge; intellectual challenge; money.	Use of computer networks and phone systems to break into target computers.
Users	Often employee or former employee.	Revenge; power; intellectual challenge; disgruntlement.	None.

OPERATIONAL CHARACTERISTICS			
Categories of Offenders	**Planning**	**Level of Expertise**	**Tactics/Methods Used**
Crackers			
Groups	May involve detailed planning.	High.	Enter target computers via computer networks. Exchange information with other crackers and groups.
Individuals	Study networks before attempts are made.	Medium to high. Experience gained through social networks.	Use networks but more likely to use trial and error online than to do careful research and planning. Use BBSs to share accounts on other systems
Criminals			
Espionage	Same characteristics as crackers.	High.	May contract with crackers to conduct information and data collection.
Fraud/Abuse	Careful planning prior to crime.	Medium to high, although is typically more experienced at fraud than at computer programming.	May use more traditional intrusion methods such as wiretapping and trap doors. Will break into systems using basic methods.
Vandals			
Strangers	Not much planning. More a crime of opportunity.	Varies.	Looks around until able to gain access to system.
Users	May involve detailed planning and execution.	Varies. May have high level of expertise.	Trap doors and Trojan horse programs. Data modification.

Table 3-1. Computer Crime Adversarial Matrix (Continued)

BEHAVIORAL CHARACTERISTICS			
Categories of Offenders	**Motivation**	**Personal Characteristics**	**Potential Weaknesses**
Crackers			
Groups	Intellectual challenge; peer group fun; in support of a cause.	Highly intelligent individuals. Counterculture orientation.	Do not consider offenses crimes. Talk freely about actions.
Individuals	Intellectual challenge; problem solving; power; money; in support of a cause.	Moderately to highly intelligent.	May keep notes and other documentation on actions.
Criminals			
Espionage	Money and a chance to attack the system.	May be crackers operating in groups or as individuals.	Becomes greedy for more information and then becomes careless.
Fraud/Abuse	Money or other personal gain; power.	Same personal characteristics as other fraud offenders.	Becomes greedy and makes mistakes.
Vandals			
Strangers	Intellectual challenge; money; power.	Same characteristics as crackers.	May become too brazen and make mistakes.
Users	Revenge against organization; problem solving; money.	Usually has some computer expertise.	May leave audit trail in computer logs.

RESOURCE CHARACTERISTICS			
Categories of Offenders	**Training Skills**	**Minimum Equipment Needed**	**Support Structure**
Crackers			
Groups	High level of informal training.	Basic computer equipment with modem.	Peer group support.
Individuals	Expertise gained through experience.	Basic computer equipment with modem.	BBS; information exchanges.
Criminals			
Espionage	Various levels of expertise.	Basic computer equipment with modem. In some cases, uses more sophisticated devices.	Support may come from sponsoring intelligence agency.
Fraud/Abuse	Some programming experience.	Computer with modem or access to target computer.	Peer group; possible organized crime enterprise
Vandals			
Strangers	Range from basic to highly skilled.	Basic computer equipment with modem.	Peer group support.
Users	Some computer expertise. Knowledge of programming ranges from basic to advanced.	Access to targeted computer.	None.

4

What Are the Laws?

There are several United States laws or sections of laws that apply specifically to computers and computer-related crimes. There are others in which certain sections have been interpreted to cover computer technology. In addition to these U.S. federal laws, many states have adopted their own computer crime laws. This chapter provides an introduction to the major laws covering computers and computer crime. Part IV of this book contains the actual language of the federal and state laws that are most often used to prosecute computer crime. In that part of the book we have also included a number of computer crime laws from other countries.

NOTE

The laws included in Part IV and described below were in place at the time this book went to press. However, the field of computer crime is an active one, and there is a good deal of legislative review going on at this time. Make sure to get up-to-date legal advice about the current laws and interpretations before proceeding with any investigation.

In addition to the explicit violations mentioned below, there are many crimes in which computers are not the focus, but are simply used in the commission of the crime. For example, drug dealers may keep their records on computers, and terrorists and criminal organizations may transmit electronic mail messages via the Internet. In such crimes, the computer isn't intrinsic to the crime, but is in the category of a car, a telephone, or some other tool. In general, this book doesn't address such crimes.

Table 4-1 summarizes the major U.S. federal statutes that directly concern computer crime, or that have been used in the prosecution of computer crimes.

Table 4-3 summarizes the statutes from the states that have adopted computer crime laws.

Who Has Jurisdiction?

When is a computer crime a federal crime, subject to the federal laws described in this chapter? When is it a crime only in the state in which it occurred? For federal crimes, what agency has jurisdiction in particular cases? You don't want to have to figure out the answers to these questions after a computer crime has occurred. Make sure you have an understanding, in advance, of who's in charge, and whom you should call if an incident does take place.

In general, a computer crime breaks federal laws when it falls into one of these categories:

- It involves the theft or compromise of national defense, foreign relations, atomic energy, or other restricted information.

- It involves a computer owned by a U.S. government department or agency.

- It involves a bank or most other types of financial institutions. (See the detailed list later in this chapter.)

- It involves interstate or foreign communications.

- It involves people or computers in other states or countries.

Of these offenses, the FBI ordinarily has jurisdiction over cases involving national security, terrorism, banking, and organized crime. The U.S. Secret Service has jurisdiction whenever the Treasury Department is victimized or whenever computers are attacked that are not under FBI or U.S. Selective Service jurisdiction (e.g., in cases of password or access code theft). In certain federal cases, the Customs Department, the Commerce Department, or a military organization, such as the Air Force Office of Investigations, may have jurisdiction.

To be sure, contact the FBI or the U.S. Secret Service directly, or call the U.S. Attorney in your region.

NOTE

If a computer criminal has stolen or compromised classified or highly sensitive military or intelligence information, notify agents from the FBI's National Security Division.

For crimes not falling under Federal jurisdiction, contact your local police department or state Attorney-General. The U.S. Attorney for your region may also be able to recommend specific local law enforcement to contact.

Note that jurisdiction is only one factor determining who will handle and prosecute a case of computer crime. Jurisdiction, the nature and severity of the offense, and the resources of the agency at the time are all contributing factors.

U.S. Federal Laws

This section summarizes the U.S. federal statutes that are most often used to prosecute computer crime, and provides fuller descriptions of two particularly important computer crime statutes—18 USC, Chapter 47, Sections 1029 and 1030.

Please note that the descriptions below are brief, lay summaries of the laws, not legal descriptions. For the full text, see Part IV of this book.

Table 4-1. Federal Computer Laws

15 USC	**Commerce and Trade**
Chapter 41	Consumer Credit Protection
Section 1644	Fraudulent use of credit cards; penalties
	Prohibits any use, attempt, or conspiracy to use credit cards in transactions affecting interstate or foreign commerce. Also covers the transport of cards, the receipt or concealment of goods and tickets, and the furnishing of money through the use of credit cards. This section may be used in cases involving the posting or exchange of credit cards on computer bulletin board systems. It may also be extended to cover other types of codes and account numbers used to obtain goods and services; for example, computer user IDs, passwords, computer account numbers, personal identification numbers (PINs), banking account numbers, telephone credit cards, smart cards, and cryptographic keys may all fall in this category.
17 USC	**Copyrights**
Chapter 1	Subject Matter and Scope of Copyrights
Section 101	Definitions
	Defines terms used in copyright law.
Section 102	Subject matter of copyrights; In general

Table 4-1. Federal Computer Laws (Continued)

	Defines the subject matter of copyrights: literary works; musical works; dramatic works; pantomimes and choreographic works; pictorial, graphic, and sculptural works; motion pictures and other audiovisual works; sound recordings; and architectural works. States that copyright protection does not extend to ideas, procedures, concepts, and so on. This section may be used in cases of copyright infringement on computer programs.
Section 117	Limitations on exclusive rights; Computer programs
	States that it is not an infringement for the owner of a copy of a computer program to make or authorize the making of another copy or adaptation of a computer program as long as certain criteria are met.
Chapter 5	Copyright Infringement and Remedies
Section 501	Infringement of copyright
	Defines infringers and specifies procedures to be followed if copyright violations occur.
18 USC	**Crimes and Criminal Procedure**
Chapter 5	Arson
Section 81	Arson within special maritime and territorial jurisdiction
	States the penalties for arson; this section may be used in cases of destruction of computer facilities and equipment.
Chapter 31	Embezzlement and Theft
Section 641	Public money, property or records
	States the penalties for embezzling or otherwise stealing money or other things of value to the United States or any government department or agency. This section may be used in cases of the theft of computers or information from U.S. facilities.
Section 659	Interstate or foreign shipments by carrier; State prosecutions
	States the penalties for embezzling or otherwise stealing, concealing, or obtaining any goods conveyed by interstate or foreign commerce. This section may be used in cases of the shipment of computer equipment or information.
Chapter 37	Espionage and Censorship
Section 793	Gathering, transmitting, or losing defense information

Table 4-1. Federal Computer Laws (Continued)

	States the penalties for getting or losing documents or any other information that may injure the United States or be to the advantage of any foreign nation. Unlike Section 794, this section does not require that the information actually be transmitted to a foreign nation. This section may be used in cases of the theft of computer-based information.
Section 794	Gathering or delivering defense information to aid foreign government
	States the penalties for communicating or transmitting to any foreign government documents or any other information that may injure the United States or be to the advantage of any foreign nation. This section may be used in cases of the theft of computer-based information.
Chapter 47	Fraud and False Statements
Section 1001	Statements or entries generally
	States the penalties for falsifying or concealing any scheme, or making any false statements, in any matters under the jurisdiction of any United States department or agency.
Section 1029	Fraud and related activity in connection with access devices
	Defines access devices and states the penalties for producing or using counterfeit access devices. Access devices are defined as any card, plate, code, account number, electronic serial number, mobile identification number, personal identification number (PIN), or other telecommunications service, equipment, or instrument identifier, or other means of account access that can be used to obtain money, services, or anything else of value. (For additional details, see the section below.)
Section 1030	Fraud and related activity in connection with computers
	States the penalties for accessing computers without authorization, exceeding authorization, or trafficking in passwords or similar access information. This section prohibits access with the intent to defraud, as well as trespassing. Specific penalties depend on what type of computer is accessed (e.g., national defense, government, financial) and on whether access is intended to cause harm or is simply done with "reckless disregard of a substantial and unjustifiable risk." It covers a range of activities, from stealing databases containing atomic energy information to

Table 4-1. Federal Computer Laws (Continued)

	posting federal computer passwords on pirate bulletin boards. This section, passed into law as part of the Computer Fraud and Abuse Act of 1986, was first used to prosecute an offense in the case of Robert T. Morris, author of the Internet worm. Morris was convicted of a felony under 18 USC 1030 (a)(5). (For additional details, see the section below.)
Chapter 63	Mail Fraud
Section 1341	Frauds and swindles
	States the penalties for fraud committed via the U.S. mail.
Section 1343	Fraud by wire, radio, or television
	States the penalties for fraud committed via other media besides conventional mail in interstate or foreign commerce. This section may be used in cases of furthering a fraud scheme using computers and computer networks—for example, when terminals used in furthering a fraud scheme communicate across state lines.
Chapter 65	Malicious Mischief
Section 1361	Government property or contracts
	States the penalties for attacks on any U.S government department or agency property. This section may be used in attacks on government computers or information.
Chapter 101	Records and Reports
Section 2071	Concealment, removal, or mutilation generally
	States the penalties for concealing, removing, or destroying any documents or other things filed or deposited with U.S. officials. This section may be used in attacks on government computer-based information.
Chapter 105	Sabotage
Section 2155	Destruction of national defense materials, national defense premises, or national defense utilities
	States the penalties for injuring or obstructing any national defense facilities or materials. This section may be used in attacks on national defense computers or information.
Chapter 113	Stolen Property
Section 2314	Transportation of stolen goods, securities, moneys, fraudulent State tax stamps, or articles used in counterfeiting

Table 4-1. Federal Computer Laws (Continued)

	States the penalties for transporting in interstate or foreign commerce any stolen or counterfeited goods. This section may be used in the transport of documents or other information forged or modified without authorization by computer.
Chapter 119	Wire and Electronic Communications Interception and Interception of Oral Communications
Section 2510	Definitions
	Defines the terms used in this chapter.
Section 2511	Interception and disclosure of wire, oral, or electronic communications prohibited
	This section, passed into law as part of the Electronic Communications Privacy Act of 1986, expands the traditional coverage of telephone communications to protect all private communications, regardless of how they are transmitted. For example, cellular telephones, satellites, paging devices, and electronic mail are covered by the new law.
Section 2522	Enforcement of the Communications Assistance for Law Enforcement Act
	States penalties and other enforcement activities for the Communications Assistance for Law Enforcement Act (popularly known as the Digital Telephony Bill), which effectively requires telecommunications carriers to build in capabilities for surveillance of electronic communications for use with properly authorized court orders.
Chapter 206	Pen Registers and Trap and Trace Devices
Section 3121	General prohibition on pen register and trap and trace device use; exception
	Defines exceptions to the general prohibition on the use of pen register and trap and trace devices. In general, these devices may not be used without a court order. However, under this section, a provider of electronic or wire communication services may install such a device to test the service, to protect the rights or property of the provider or its users from unlawful use, or to record the fact that a communication was initiated or completed.
42 USC	**The Public Health and Welfare**
Chapter 21A	Privacy Protection

Table 4-1. Federal Computer Laws (Continued)

Section 2000aa	Searches and seizures by government officers and employees in connection with investigation or prosecution of criminal offenses
	States that it is unlawful for government officials to search for or seize any work product materials possessed by someone engaged in publishing the material or engaged in interstate or foreign commerce unless there is probable cause to believe that the person has committed or is committing a crime to which the materials relate. There is also an exception if there is reason to believe that immediate seizure will prevent the death of or serious injury to a person. These two exceptions apply to other materials as well; for other than work product materials, there are additional exceptions if there is reason to believe that giving notice will cause destruction of the materials or that the materials have not been produced in response to a court order.
47 USC	**Telegraphs, Telephones, and Radiotelegraphs**
Chapter 5	Wire or Radio Communication
Section 226	Telephone operator services
	States the penalties for telegraph, telephone, and radiotelegraph carriers who abuse billing or customer notification requirements.

Section 1029

18 USC, Chapter 47, Section 1029 prohibits fraud and related activity that is made possible by counterfeit access devices such as PINs, credit cards, account numbers, and various types of electronic identifiers. The nine areas of criminal activity covered by Section 1029 are listed below. All require that the offense involve interstate or foreign commerce.

1. Producing, using, or trafficking in counterfeit access devices. (The offense must be committed knowingly and with intent to defraud.)

   Penalty: Fine of $50,000 or twice the value of the crime and/or up to 15 years in prison, $100,000 and/or up to 20 years if repeat offense.

2. Using or obtaining unauthorized access devices to obtain anything of value totaling $1000 or more during a one-year period. (The offense must be committed knowingly and with intent to defraud.)

Penalty: Fine of $10,000 or twice the value of the crime and/or up to 10 years in prison, $100,000 and/or up to 20 years if repeat offense.

3. Possessing 15 or more counterfeit or unauthorized access devices. (The offense must be committed knowingly and with intent to defraud.)

   Penalty: Fine of $10,000 or twice the value of the crime and/or up to 10 years in prison, $100,000 and/or up to 20 years if repeat offense.

4. Producing, trafficking in, or having device-making equipment. (The offense must be committed knowingly and with intent to defraud.)

   Penalty: Fine of $50,000 or twice the value of the crime and/or up to 15 years in prison, $100,000 and/or up to 20 years if repeat offense.

5. Effecting transactions with access devices issued to another person in order to receive payment or anything of value totaling $1000 or more during a one-year period. (The offense must be committed knowingly and with intent to defraud.)

   Penalty: Fine of $10,000 or twice the value of the crime and/or up to 10 years in prison, $100,000 and/or up to 20 years if repeat offense.

6. Soliciting a person for the purpose of offering an access device or selling information that can be used to obtain an access device. (The offense must be committed knowingly and with intent to defraud, and without the authorization of the issuer of the access device.)

   Penalty: Fine of $10,000 or twice the value of the crime and/or up to 10 years in prison, $100,000 and/or up to 20 years if repeat offense.

7. Using, producing, trafficking in, or having a telecommunications instrument that has been modified or altered to obtain unauthorized use of telecommunications services. (The offense must be committed knowingly and with intent to defraud.)

   Penalty: Fine of $50,000 or twice the value of the crime and/or up to 15 years in prison, $100,000 and/or up to 20 years if repeat offense.

8. Using, producing, trafficking in, or having a scanning receiver or hardware or software used to alter or modify telecommunications instruments to obtain unauthorized access to telecommunications services.

   Penalty: Fine of $50,000 or twice the value of the crime and/or up to 15 years in prison, $100,000 and/or up to 20 years if repeat offense.

9. Causing or arranging for a person to present, to a credit card system member or its agent for payment, records of transactions made by an access device. (The offense must be committed knowingly and with intent to defraud, and without the authorization of the credit card system member or its agent.)

Penalty: Fine of $10,000 or twice the value of the crime and/or up to 10 years in prison, $100,000 and/or up to 20 years if repeat offense.

Section 1030

18 USC, Chapter 47, Section 1030, enacted as part of the Computer Fraud and Abuse Act of 1986, prohibits unauthorized or fraudulent access to government computers, and establishes penalties for such access. This act is one of the few pieces of federal legislation solely concerned with computers. Under the Computer Fraud and Abuse Act, the U.S. Secret Service and the FBI explicitly have been given jurisdiction to investigate the offenses defined under this act, as summarized in Table 4-2.

The six areas of criminal activity covered by Section 1030 are:

1. Acquiring national defense, foreign relations, or restricted atomic energy information with the intent or reason to believe that the information can be used to injure the United States or to the advantage of any foreign nation. (The offense must be committed knowingly by accessing a computer without authorization or exceeding authorized access.)

   Penalty: Fine and/or up to 10 years in prison, up to 20 years if repeat offense.

2. Obtaining information in a financial record of a financial institution or a card issuer, or information on a consumer in a file of a consumer reporting agency. (The offense must be committed intentionally by accessing a computer without authorization or exceeding authorized access.)

   Penalty: Fine and/or up to 1 year in prison, up to 10 years if repeat offense.

3. Affecting a computer exclusively for the use of a U.S. government department or agency or, if it is not exclusive, one used for the government where the offense adversely affects the use of the government's operation of the computer. (The offense must be committed intentionally by accessing a computer without authorization.)

   Penalty: Fine and/or up to 1 year in prison, up to 10 years if repeat offense.

4. Furthering a fraud by accessing a federal interest computer (see the definition below) and obtaining anything of value, unless the fraud and the thing obtained consists only of the use of the computer. (The offense must be committed knowingly, with intent to defraud, and without authorization or exceeding authorization.)

   Penalty: Fine and/or up to 5 years in prison, up to 10 years if repeat offense.

5. Through use of a computer used in interstate commerce, knowingly causing the transmission of a program, information, code, or command to a computer system. There are two separate scenarios:

a. In this scenario, (i) the person causing the transmission intends it to damage the computer or deny use to it; and (ii) the transmission occurs without the authorization of the computer owners or operators, and causes $1000 or more in loss or damage, or modifies or impairs, or potentially modifies or impairs, a medical treatment or examination.

Penalty with intent to harm: Fine and/or up to 5 years in prison, up to 10 years if repeat offense.

b. In this scenario, (i) the person causing the transmission does not intend the damage but operates with reckless disregard of the risk that the transmission will cause damage to the computer or deny use to it; and (ii) the transmission occurs without the authorization of the computer owners or operators, and causes $1000 or more in loss or damage, or modifies or impairs, or potentially modifies or impairs, a medical treatment or examination.

Penalty with reckless disregard: Fine and/or up to 1 year in prison.

6. Furthering a fraud by trafficking in passwords or similar information which will allow a computer to be accessed without authorization, if the trafficking affects interstate or foreign commerce or if the computer affected is used by or for the government. (The offense must be committed knowingly and with intent to defraud.)

Penalty: Fine and/or up to 1 year in prison, up to 10 years if repeat offense.

Section 1030 defines a federal interest computer as follows:

1. A computer that is exclusively for use of a financial institution or the U.S. government or, if it is not exclusive, one used for a financial institution or the U.S. government where the offense adversely affects the use of the financial institution's or government's operation of the computer; or

2. A computer that is one of two or more computers used to commit the offense, not all of which are located in the same state.

This section defines a financial institution as follows:

1. An institution with deposits insured by the Federal Deposit Insurance Corporation (FDIC).

2. The Federal Reserve or a member of the Federal Reserve, including any Federal Reserve bank.

3. A credit union with accounts insured by the National Credit Union Administration.

4. A member of the federal home loan bank system and any home loan bank.

5. Any institution of the Farm Credit System under the Farm Credit Act of 1971.

6. A broker-dealer registered with the Securities and Exchange Commission (SEC) pursuant to section 15 of the SEC Act of 1934.

7. The Securities Investor Protection Corporation.

8. A branch or agency of a foreign bank (as defined in the International Banking Act of 1978).

9. An organization operating under section 25 or 25(a) of the Federal Reserve Act.

Table 4-2 summarizes the likely division of jurisdiction (FBI, U.S. Secret Service, or joint jurisdiction) under Section 1030. Note, however, that as we discuss in "Who Has Jurisdiction?" above, jurisdiction may differ from that shown below and may even include the Customs Department, the Department of Commerce, military organizations such as the Air Force Office of Investigations, or other federal agencies.

Table 4-2. Section 1030 Offenses and Jurisdiction

Section of Law	Type of Information	Jurisdiction		
		FBI	USSS	Joint
1030 (a)(1)	**National security:**			
	National defense	X		
	Foreign relations	X		
	Restricted atomic energy	X		
1030 (a)(2)	**Financial or consumer:**[1]			
	Financial records of banks and other financial institutions	X		
	Financial records of card issuers		X	
	Information on consumers in files of a consumer reporting agency		X	
	Non-bank financial institutions			X
1030 (a)(3)	**Government computers:** [2]			
	National defense	X		
	Foreign relations	X		
	Restricted data	X		
	White House			X
	All other government computers		X	

Table 4-2. Section 1030 Offenses and Jurisdiction (Continued)

Section of Law	Type of Information	Jurisdiction		
		FBI	USSS	Joint
1030 (a)(4)	**Federal interest computers:**			
	Intent to defraud			X
1030 (a)(5)(A)	**Transmission of programs, commands:**			
	Intent to damage or deny use			X
1030 (a)(5)(B)	**Transmission of programs, commands:**			
	Reckless disregard			X
1030 (a)(6)	**Trafficking in passwords:**			
	Interstate or foreign commerce			X
	Computers used by or for the government			X

[1] The FBI has jurisdiction over bank fraud violations, which include categories (1) through (5) in the list of financial institutions defined above. The Secret Service and FBI share joint jurisdiction over non-bank financial institutions defined in categories (6) and (7) in the list of financial institutions defined above.

[2] The FBI is the primary investigative agency for violations of this section when it involves national defense, information pertaining to foreign relations, and other restricted data. Unauthorized access to other information in government computers falls under the primary jurisdiction of the Secret Service.

State Laws

In addition to the federal laws applying to computer crime, many states have their own computer crime laws. Investigators need to be aware of the particular laws that govern computer crimes in the state in which the crime occurs. Table 4-3 summarizes the computer crime statutes for each state. Part IV of this book contains the complete text of these statutes.

Table 4-3. State Computer Laws

Alabama	13A-8-10; 13A-8-100, 102, 103	Maine	17-A-2-15-357
Alaska	11.46.200, 484, 740, 985, 990; 11.81-900	Maryland	27-I-145, 146, 340, 45A
Arizona	13-2301, 2316, 3016	Massachusetts	266-12E, 33-A, 127; 233-58A 1/2, 79K
Arkansas	5.41-100 through 107	Michigan	752.791 through 797
California	13-5-484j, 499c, 502, 502.01,502.07,1203.047, 1203.048, 2702	Minnesota	609.87, 88, 89, 891, 892; 626A-27
Colorado	18-5.5-101, 102	Mississippi	97-45-1, 3, 7, 9, 11, 13
Connecticut	52-570b; 53a-250 through 261	Missouri	569.093, 095, 097, 099
Delaware	11-5-931 through 930	Montana	45-6-310, 311
Florida	46-815.01 through 07; 847.0135	Nebraska	28-1343 through 1348
Georgia	16-9-90 through 95	Nevada	15-205-473 through 477
Hawaii	37-708-890 through 896	New Hampshire	62-638:16 through 19
Idaho	18-2201 through 2202; 48-801	New Jersey	2A:38A-1 though 6; 638:19; 2C:20-1; 2C:20-23 through 34,
Illinois	3-15-1, 2; 16D-1 through 7	New Mexico	15-1-9; 30-45-1 through 7
Indiana	35-43-1-4, 35-43-2-3	New York	J-155.00; 156.00 through 50; 165.15; K-170.00; N-250.30
Iowa	35-716A.1 through 16	North Carolina	14-453 through 457
Kansas	21-3704, 3745, 3755	North Dakota	12.1-06.1-08, 12.1-32-01
Kentucky	40-434.840 through 860	Ohio	2913.01, 04, 42, 81
Louisiana	14-73.1 through 5	Oklahoma	21-1953 through 1956

Table 4-3. State Computer Laws (Continued)

Oregon	16-164-125, 377	Utah	76-6-701 through 705
Pennsylvania	18-3933	Vermont	No known statutes
Rhode Island	11-52-1 through 5	Virginia	18.2-152.1 through 14; 8.01-40-1
South Carolina	16-16-10 through 40	Washington	9A.48.100 through 130; 9A.52.010
South Dakota	43-43B-1 through 8	West Virginia	61-3C-1 through 21
Tennessee	39-14-601, 602, 105, 603	Wisconsin	943.70; 939.50; 939.51
Texas	7-33.01 through 05; 13.24	Wyoming	6-3-501 through 505

International Laws

Part IV of this book also includes the text of a number of laws of other countries regulating computer crime. We have collected statutes from Australia, Canada, France, the United Kingdom, and a bill that has been proposed (but at the time we went to press had not yet been passed) in Ghana.

Preventing Computer Crime

This part of the book looks at ways of preventing computer crime—identifying the risks to computer systems and implementing various security measures that can protect those systems.

Chapter 5, *What is at Risk?*, identifies the assets of a computer site and system and outlines computer security threats, vulnerabilities, and countermeasures.

Chapter 6, *Physical Security*, describes briefly the threats to physical security (natural and environmental disasters, physical break-ins) and presents measures for countering these threats.

Chapter 7, *Personnel Security*, summarizes the important components of a personnel security program for various types of people, including employees, vendors, contractors, and others.

Chapter 8, *Communications Security*, discusses briefly the threats to networked systems and the techniques (e.g., access control, cryptographic methods, firewall technology) for countering these threats.

Chapter 9, *Operations Security*, summarizes ways in which operations security works with other types of security measures. Operations security includes methods of increasing awareness of possible computer crimes and methods of actually preventing such crimes.

5

What Is at Risk?

All computer security is a tradeoff. Few organizations can afford to pay the price necessary to completely protect their assets against all risks (if such protection is even possible!). Instead, they balance the cost of various types of protection against the risks of doing without them. This process of analysis and decision is called *risk analysis*. The level at which the organization agrees that it can operate is called *acceptable risk*.

Threats, Vulnerabilities, and Countermeasures

Three words come up in every risk analysis: *threats, vulnerabilities*, and *countermeasures*:

Threat

A possible danger to your system; the danger might be a person (a spy, a professional criminal, or a cracker), a thing (faulty hardware or software), or an event (a fire, a lightning strike, or an earthquake) that might attack the system.

Vulnerability

A point where a system is susceptible to attack—for example, the people who operate and use your system (are they properly trained?), your system's connections to the Internet (are your communications encrypted?), and the fact that your facility is in a flood zone (is your system on the bottom floor of the building?). A threat is a concrete intention of exploiting the vulnerabilities in a system.

Countermeasure

A technique for protecting a system—for example, password controls, network cable shielding, and locks on doors.

A risk analysis is really a process of asking questions—first, about threats, next, about vulnerabilities, and finally, about what countermeasures might be appropriate to handle the threats and vulnerabilities you've identified. Here are a few of the initial questions you'll ask:

Who is most likely to attack your particular site or system, and why?

What particular information, money, or other assets will they find there?

To answer these questions, you need to ask some additional questions:

Does your system or network contain sensitive government, industrial, or scientific information that would prove valuable to an espionage agent working for a foreign government?

Does it contain financial information that a professional criminal would find interesting?

Does it contain information that might be particularly appealing to crackers (e.g., new computer games)?

How well is your system protected against such attacks?

What are its vulnerabilities?

What security countermeasures do you have in place?

Based on the answers to these questions:

What is the probability that someone will target your particular computer system?

How likely is each of the particular threats you've identified?

Here are a few examples. Suppose that your site has military information, and suppose that your system is networked to others outside the organization. Let's look at a few likely threats, vulnerabilities, and countermeasures (and note that these are only a few examples of the actual threats, vulnerabilities, and countermeasures you'd identify in a real risk analysis):

Threats

The type of information on your system suggests that it might be of interest to industrial espionage agents whom your competitors might hire to steal data or sabotage your system.

Vulnerabilities

Your site's physical security is not terrific. There are many doors into the facility, and there is a somewhat primitive alarm system. Only some of your communications are encrypted, and your physical network cabling is not shielded against radio frequency (RF) emanations.

Countermeasures

You do have guards at the main doors, but some doors are simply locked. Your software includes some encryption facilities, but encryption is not routine. Your risk assessment will probably result in a strong recommendation that you improve both physical security and communications security.

Risk analysis also involves evaluating how well an organization plans for the worst—sometimes called contingency planning or crisis management. We'll examine that type of planning in Chapter 10.

When you are conducting a risk analysis, be creative! Don't limit yourself to traditional threats. Consider every possible threat to your system, even types of attacks that haven't occurred in the past. Rest assured that your adversaries are at work, dreaming up new approaches to attack your data. By being equally creative, you may be able to stay one step ahead of them.

Proactive and Reactive Assessments

There are two distinct types of risk analysis:

* *Proactive assessment:* You perform this type of assessment *before* an incident occurs. What are the possible threats to the system you are attempting to protect? What are the possible vulnerabilities? Given these threats and vulnerabilities, what countermeasures might be needed to provide acceptable security for the system?

* *Reactive assessment:* You perform this type of assessment *after* you've already had an incident. What were the actual threats to the system that was attacked? What vulnerabilities were exploited? What countermeasures were inadequate, and what countermeasures are now needed to keep this type of incident from happening again?

Static and Dynamic Threats and Vulnerabilities

The vulnerabilities of your system, and the threats that may exploit these vulnerabilities, may be categorized as either static or dynamic. Whatever risk analysis you perform, remember that it will need to be monitored and updated as time goes on and as changes occur, both inside and outside your organization.

Static threats and vulnerabilities remain relatively the same over time. The physical location of your computer system and the surrounding buildings or terrain are examples of static vulnerabilities. The building is not likely to move. If the computer is located in the basement of a flood-prone area, this is a static threat.

Dynamic threats and vulnerabilities are those that may change at any time or are constantly changing. Changes may be within your organization, in technology, or in the world at large (see sidebar). For dynamic threats and vulnerabilities, you'll need sufficiently dynamic countermeasures—those that can respond to changing events. Developing static contingency plans to address dynamic threats is a sure road to failure. Your organization must be flexible enough to be able to respond quickly to a crisis, whatever it might be.

Stay Alert

Make sure that you redo your risk analysis if events such as these occur:

- The staff turnover is high within your organization. You will need to conduct additional background checks to keep up with the flow of new personnel.

- Your organization is awarded a new government contract that requires the handling of sensitive government information.

- Your organization merges with another organization, is sold, or otherwise becomes visible in the news.

- A computer crime occurs within your organization.

- A terrorist group or militants of some kind make your organization, or its parent organization, a target.

- A new virus or some other type of vulnerability is discovered in equipment or software of the kind you are using in your organization.

- Political events occur that have repercussions for your organization or for organizations within your area or country.

Steps in Risk Analysis

A typical risk analysis breaks down into five specific steps:

1. Ask the questions.

2. Apply intelligence reports.

3. Conduct a vulnerability analysis.

4. Develop security countermeasures.

5. Document your findings and decisions.

Ask the Questions

Begin every risk analysis by asking a series of questions of the type asked in previous sections. For example:

Who would target this system?

What techniques would they use in the attack?

What resources or assets of the system would they attempt to steal or disrupt?

This step in risk analysis is a theoretical one. You're trying to figure out all of the possible attacks that *might* take place. In one case, you might envision a vandal who plants a virus simply to create malicious mischief. In another case, the likely attacker might be an expert spy who is going after classified military information. In a third case, thieves for hire might be out to steal actual hardware and software. In a final case, the threat might be nature itself—fire, flood, or lightning.

Apply Intelligence Reports

This step is more specific. By adding both criminal intelligence and foreign counterintelligence to our theory, we make the theoretical risks from step 1 come alive. For example, intelligence might tell us that a criminal organization is laundering drug money through banks via computer/wire transfer systems. Or an informant may have revealed that the organization intends to fraudulently obtain assets belonging to a legitimate company via a computer fraud scheme. Foreign counterintelligence information may suggest that agents of a foreign government are seeking to hire crackers who can access the computers of the Department of Defense or its contractors. If we're conducting a risk analysis for a system that fits the profile of those suggested by this intelligence, then we need to make sure that our security countermeasures are adequate to counter these very real threats.

Conduct a Vulnerability Analysis

The next step in the risk analysis is also highly specific. Given the threats you've identified, where are the particular vulnerabilities in your own system? Even if the threats appear to be minor ones, you'll need to identify all possible vulnerabilities; minor threats can become major ones, and threats you never thought were likely ones may suddenly materialize. How you decide to deal with those vulnerabilities is a separate question. At this point, your goal is simply to itemize them. If you've done a good job of analyzing all possible vulnerabilities, you'll be in a better position to take quick action to install new or enhanced security in case of an emergency.

See the section called "Identifying Vulnerabilities and Countermeasures," and Table 5-2, later in this chapter, which contains a summary of possible vulnerabilities and countermeasures.

Develop Security Countermeasures

Now that you know about your system's vulnerabilities and the threats that may exploit those vulnerabilities, what are you going to do about them? What security countermeasures are already in place at your site, and what more can you do?

Sometimes, simple and inexpensive measures are sufficient to give your system a reasonable level of security. Sometimes, you'll find that to truly secure your site and system, you'll need to spend some serious money. Now is the time to find out.

Your own organization will have to assess how serious the threats are to your system, how vulnerable your system seems to be, and what your resources really are. Obviously, the degree to which you are going to plug your system's own holes will depend on how deep the holes—and your pockets—are. Sometimes, in risk analysis, you will hear the term *threat level*. If the threat level is minimal, expenditures and efforts to address the vulnerabilities will also be minimal. If the threat level is high, then the expenditures and efforts will be a good deal more substantial.

Now is also the time to set priorities for future purchases. Divide your needs for security countermeasures into these categories:

- Immediate needs are exactly that. These are needs that must be addressed now! Broken locks, employees who circumvent the system, and holes in the fence are examples of immediate needs.

- Midrange needs are changes to be made in this budget year. These might include making changes to existing problems (to increase their security) or upgrading current security equipment.

- Long-range needs are those that will be added into future budgets. These usually address complete system upgrades and anticipated future needs (perhaps a more sophisticated access control system more suitable to a larger organization), rather than current requirements. Such needs may also anticipate changes in technology—for example, the availability of new smart card technology.

You need to plan for the future, but you need to be able to respond to present events as well. Regardless of what you decide to do about buying new equipment and adopting new policies for the future, you also need to build in some plan for responding quickly in case of an emergency. If a computer criminal actually does break into your system, you will need to quickly find the resources to shut the barn door and clean up the stable.

Document Your Findings and Decisions

It's a good idea to put all your findings and decisions in writing. You may need no more than a single-page summary showing the current threats to your system, the potential vulnerabilities there, and the security countermeasures currently available and being adopted to bring the risk down to an acceptable level. Remember that this document, sometimes called a *threat statement*, contains extremely sensitive material. Protect it carefully, and don't distribute it to anyone who does not have an obvious need to see it.

Identifying Threats

As we've mentioned, there are many different types of threats, ranging from spies to criminals to teenage crackers to angry employees to fire, flood, and other acts of nature.

People

People—users and strangers—are the biggest threat to computer security. Computers don't write their own viruses, dump or change their data, or steal sensitive information while committing espionage. Obviously, people are responsible for these actions. As we've discussed, these people may be employees of the organization that is being attacked or individuals who have gained access to the system from down the block or around the world.

Your own employees are the greatest threat of all, sometimes because of grudges and more often because of human error. It's apparently the case that most computer crimes are committed by inside users, just as most murders are committed by family members.

When you are thinking about the kinds of people who may threaten your system, you may find the Computer Crime Adversarial Matrix in Chapter 3 helpful. That matrix helps identify the types of attackers, their likely level of expertise, and their typical modus operandi.

Hardware

What are the threats to your hardware? Millions of dollars in computer equipment are stolen every year. Huge amounts are destroyed by protesters, vandals, and angry employees and customers. Fire, floods, earthquakes, and explosions can ruin a computer center in a matter of seconds.

Software

What are the threats to your software? Could programs be modified by professional criminals, looking to defraud your organization? Could they be compromised by employees or by those outside the organization? Could someone plant a virus in your software? Are employees stealing copies of proprietary software or software purchased and licensed for use by the company?

Natural and Environmental Disasters

Natural disasters—such as fire, floods, lightning, and earthquakes—represent threats to your computer facility and systems. This is also true for environmental threats, such as the climate, your heating and air conditioning systems, and electrical service.

Chapter 6 lists many suggestions for protecting your site against natural and environmental disasters, and for minimizing the effects of them, should they occur. See also the list of physical security countermeasures in Table 5–2.

Identifying Assets

As part of a risk assessment, you will need to catalog all of the assets that you are trying to protect at your site and within your system. These range from people to physical hardware to data. Table 5–1 contains a sampling of assets; you will need to modify this list to suit your own site.

Table 5-1. Sample Assets

SOFTWARE	HARDWARE
• Operating system	• Central machine
• Programs	CPU
Application	Main memory
Standard application	I/O channels
and operating programs	Operator's console
System utilities	• Storage medium
Communications	Magnetic media

Table 5-1. Sample Assets (Continued)

Disk pack
Magnetic tape
CD/ROM
Diskettes (floppies)
Cassettes
Drums
Nonmagnetic media
Punched cards
Paper tape
Paper printout
- Special interface equipment
  Network front ends
  Data base machines
  Intelligent controllers
- I/O Devices
  User-directed I/O devices
  Printers
  Card readers
  Card punch
  OCR readers
  Paper tape reader
  Terminals—local and remote
  Storage I/O devices
  Disk drives
  Tape drives

DATA
- Sensitive
- Classified
- Operations
- Tactical
- Planning
- Financial
- Statistical
- Personal
- Personnel
- Logistic
- Other

ADMINISTRATIVE
- Documentation
  Software
  Hardware
  File
  Program
  Application
  JCL
  System
- Operations
  Schedules
  Operating guidelines and manuals
  Audit documents
- Procedures
  Emergency plans
  Security procedures
  I/O procedures
  Integrity controls
- Inventory records
- Operational procedures
  Vital records
  Priority-run schedule
  Production procedures

COMMUNICATIONS
- Communications
  Communications equipment
  Communications lines
  Communications procedures
  Multiplexors
  Switching devices
  Telephones
  Modems
  Cables

HUMAN RESOURCES
- Computer personnel
  Supervisory personnel
  Systems analysts

Table 5-1. Sample Assets (Continued)

Programmers
Applications programmers
System programmers
Operators
Librarians
Security officer
Maintenance personnel
Temporary employees and
contractors
System evaluators and auditors
Clerical personnel
• Building personnel
Janitors
Guards
Facility engineers
• Installation management
PHYSICAL
• Environmental systems
Air conditioning
Power

Water
Lighting
• Building
• Computer facility
Computer room
Data reception
Tape and disk library
Customer engineer room
Patch and test facility
I/O area
Data preparation area
Physical plant room
• Backup equipment
Auxiliary power
Auxiliary environmental controls
Auxiliary supplies
• Supplies
Magnetic media
Paper
Ribbon

Identifying Vulnerabilities and Countermeasures

There are widely differing vulnerabilities, ranging from natural and environmental hazards, to personnel problems, to specific hardware and software problems. For each, you will need to develop appropriate countermeasures. But first, you need to identify them all. Table 5–2 is a matrix showing a wide variety of vulnerabilities and suggested countermeasures for each. Use this matrix as a starting point for your own vulnerability assessment. Every site differs, so your own set of vulnerabilities and countermeasures may not match this one.

Table 5-2. Sample Vulnerabilities and Countermeasures

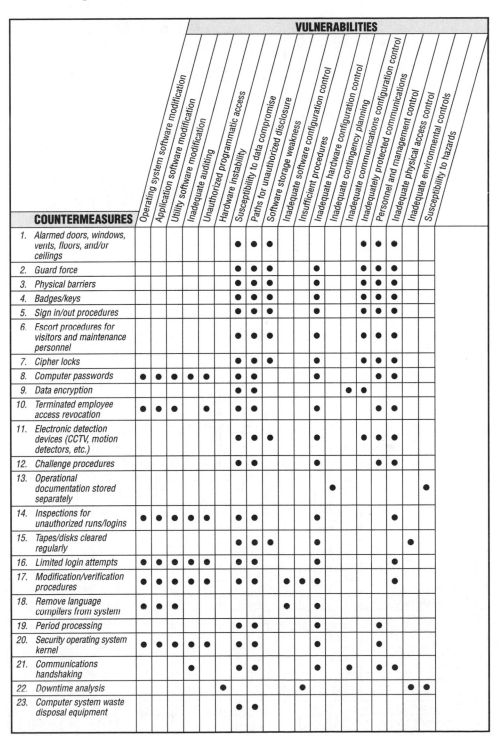

VULNERABILITIES

Vulnerability columns (left to right):
1. Operating system software modification
2. Application software modification
3. Utility software modification
4. Inadequate auditing
5. Unauthorized auditing
6. Hardware instability
7. Unauthorized programmatic access
8. Susceptibility to data compromise
9. Paths for unauthorized disclosure
10. Software storage weakness
11. Inadequate software configuration control
12. Insufficient procedures
13. Inadequate hardware configuration control
14. Inadequate contingency planning
15. Inadequate communications configuration control
16. Inadequately protected communications
17. Personnel and management control
18. Inadequate physical access control
19. Inadequate environmental controls
20. Susceptibility to hazards

COUNTERMEASURES	1	2	3	4	5	6	7	8	9	10	11	12	13	14	15	16	17	18	19	20
1. Alarmed doors, windows, vents, floors, and/or ceilings							•	•	•							•	•	•		
2. Guard force							•	•	•			•				•	•	•		
3. Physical barriers							•	•	•			•				•	•	•		
4. Badges/keys							•	•	•			•				•	•	•		
5. Sign in/out procedures							•	•	•			•				•	•	•		
6. Escort procedures for visitors and maintenance personnel							•	•	•			•				•	•	•		
7. Cipher locks							•	•	•			•				•	•	•		
8. Computer passwords	•	•	•	•	•		•	•				•					•	•		
9. Data encryption							•	•						•	•					
10. Terminated employee access revocation	•	•	•		•		•	•				•					•	•		
11. Electronic detection devices (CCTV, motion detectors, etc.)							•	•	•			•				•	•	•		
12. Challenge procedures							•	•				•					•	•		
13. Operational documentation stored separately													•							•
14. Inspections for unauthorized runs/logins	•	•	•	•	•		•	•				•						•		
15. Tapes/disks cleared regularly							•	•	•			•							•	
16. Limited login attempts	•	•	•	•	•		•	•				•						•		
17. Modification/verification procedures	•	•	•	•	•		•	•		•	•	•						•		
18. Remove language compilers from system	•	•	•							•		•								
19. Period processing							•	•				•					•			
20. Security operating system kernel	•	•	•	•	•		•	•				•					•			
21. Communications handshaking			•				•	•				•		•		•	•			
22. Downtime analysis						•				•									•	•
23. Computer system waste disposal equipment							•	•												

Table 5-2. Sample Vulnerabilities and Countermeasures (Continued)

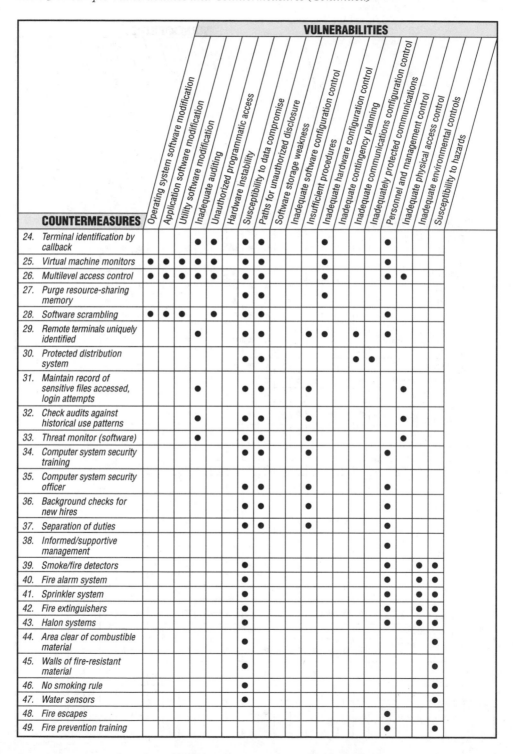

VULNERABILITIES

COUNTERMEASURES	Operating system software modification	Application software modification	Utility software modification	Inadequate auditing	Unauthorized modification	Hardware instability	Unauthorized programmatic access	Susceptibility to data compromise	Paths for unauthorized disclosure	Software storage weakness	Inadequate software configuration control	Insufficient procedures	Inadequate hardware configuration control	Inadequate contingency planning	Inadequate communications configuration control	Inadequately protected communications	Personnel and management control	Inadequate physical access control	Inadequate environmental controls	Susceptibility to hazards
24. Terminal identification by callback				●	●		●	●				●					●			
25. Virtual machine monitors	●	●	●	●	●		●	●				●					●			
26. Multilevel access control	●	●	●	●	●		●	●				●					●	●		
27. Purge resource-sharing memory							●	●				●								
28. Software scrambling	●	●	●		●		●	●									●			
29. Remote terminals uniquely identified				●			●	●			●	●		●			●			
30. Protected distribution system							●	●							●	●				
31. Maintain record of sensitive files accessed, login attempts				●			●	●				●						●		
32. Check audits against historical use patterns				●			●	●				●						●		
33. Threat monitor (software)				●			●	●				●						●		
34. Computer system security training							●	●				●					●			
35. Computer system security officer							●	●				●					●			
36. Background checks for new hires							●	●				●					●			
37. Separation of duties							●	●				●					●			
38. Informed/supportive management																	●			
39. Smoke/fire detectors						●											●		●	●
40. Fire alarm system						●											●		●	●
41. Sprinkler system						●											●		●	●
42. Fire extinguishers						●											●		●	●
43. Halon systems						●											●		●	●
44. Area clear of combustible material						●											●			●
45. Walls of fire-resistant material						●											●			●
46. No smoking rule						●											●			●
47. Water sensors						●											●			●
48. Fire escapes																		●		
49. Fire prevention training																		●		●

Table 5-2. Sample Vulnerabilities and Countermeasures (Continued)

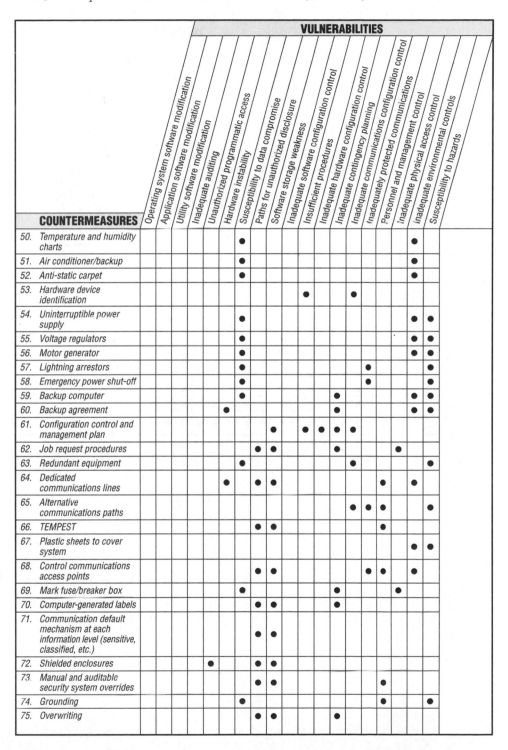

COUNTERMEASURES	Operating system software modification	Application software modification	Utility software modification	Inadequate auditing	Unauthorized programmatic access	Hardware instability	Susceptibility to data compromise	Paths for unauthorized disclosure	Software storage weakness	Inadequate software configuration control	Insufficient procedures	Inadequate hardware configuration control	Inadequate contingency planning	Inadequate communications configuration control	Inadequately protected communications	Personnel and management communications	Inadequate physical access control	Inadequate environmental controls	Susceptibility to hazards
50. Temperature and humidity charts						●												●	
51. Air conditioner/backup						●												●	
52. Anti-static carpet						●												●	
53. Hardware device identification									●			●							
54. Uninterruptible power supply						●												●	●
55. Voltage regulators						●												●	●
56. Motor generator						●												●	●
57. Lightning arrestors						●							●						●
58. Emergency power shut-off						●							●						●
59. Backup computer						●							●					●	●
60. Backup agreement					●								●					●	●
61. Configuration control and management plan									●		●	●	●	●					
62. Job request procedures							●	●				●				●			
63. Redundant equipment						●							●						●
64. Dedicated communications lines					●		●	●							●		●		
65. Alternative communications paths														●	●	●			●
66. TEMPEST							●	●								●			
67. Plastic sheets to cover system																		●	●
68. Control communications access points							●	●							●	●	●		
69. Mark fuse/breaker box						●							●				●		
70. Computer-generated labels							●	●					●						
71. Communication default mechanism at each information level (sensitive, classified, etc.)							●	●											
72. Shielded enclosures					●		●	●											
73. Manual and auditable security system overrides							●	●								●			
74. Grounding						●										●			●
75. Overwriting							●	●					●						

Table 5-2. Sample Vulnerabilities and Countermeasures (Continued)

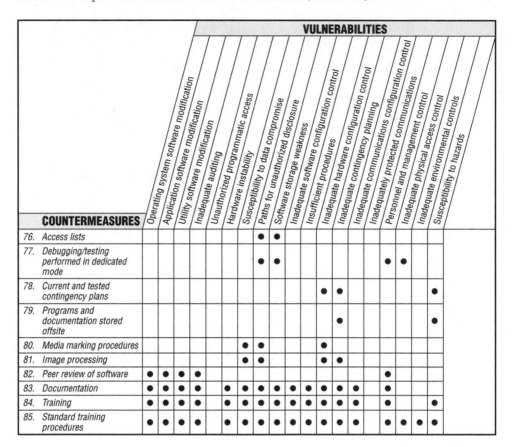

COUNTERMEASURES	Operating system software modification	Application software modification	Utility software modification	Inadequate auditing	Unauthorized programmatic access	Hardware instability	Susceptibility to data compromise	Paths for unauthorized disclosure	Software storage weakness	Inadequate software configuration control	Insufficient procedures	Inadequate hardware configuration control	Inadequate contingency planning	Inadequate communications	Inadequately protected communications	Personnel and management configuration control	Inadequate physical access control	Inadequate environmental controls	Susceptibility to hazards
76. Access lists							●	●											
77. Debugging/testing performed in dedicated mode							●	●								●	●		
78. Current and tested contingency plans													●	●					●
79. Programs and documentation stored offsite														●					●
80. Media marking procedures						●	●			●									
81. Image processing						●	●			●	●								
82. Peer review of software	●	●	●	●												●			
83. Documentation	●	●	●	●		●	●	●	●	●	●	●	●	●		●			
84. Training	●	●	●	●		●	●	●	●	●	●	●	●	●		●		●	
85. Standard training procedures	●	●	●	●		●	●	●	●	●	●	●	●	●		●	●	●	●

6

Physical Security

Physical security protects a physical computer facility—the building, the computer room, the computer itself, associated equipment (e.g., disk and tape drives and printers), storage media (e.g., disks, tapes, and printouts), and communications media (e.g., fiber optic cable, twisted pair cable). Physical security measures are tangible defenses that you can take to protect a facility from natural disasters, environmental problems, accidents, and intentional damage.

Unquestionably, physical security is a vital part of any computer crime defense. You can't always see a particular crime coming, so you must have programs in place that make such crimes extremely difficult to perform. For example, the best way to prevent someone from bombing a computer facility is simply to deny the would-be bomber access. You can do this consistently, over time, only if you have a good physical security program at your site. How can you keep an employee from going berserk and damaging computer equipment? You can't control the person's sanity, but you can make it less likely that he will do serious damage if he runs amok. One way to do this is to establish a policy that keeps at least the most powerful and expensive hardware in locked areas of your building.

Your site's physical security is a concrete signal to employees and clients that you take security seriously. Regardless of how sophisticated and high-tech the automated forms of computer security you have in place may be, physical security remains essential. Building, computer room, computer, and media protection provide an important outer physical perimeter of security. Within the perimeter, computer passwords, network authentication systems, and other online forms of security provide finer-grained protection of information.

The physical security measures you can take to prevent disasters—or at least to minimize the effects of them—range from the simple to the complex: installing fire suppression systems, adopting earthquake countermeasures, controlling access to the building and computer room, and much more.

Although natural and environmental dangers are a serious threat to any computer facility, they generally become the concern of the computer crime investigator only if they are used to do intentional damage. For example, someone bent on sabotage might start a fire or a flood or might turn off the electricity or air conditioning.

This chapter introduces you to the field of physical security and gives you enough information so you will be able to understand the different areas of physical security. This summary only skims the surface. If you are installing security measures, or if you need to investigate physical security problems in depth, you should arrange fo assistance from a physical security expert.

When Investigating. . .

If the computer crime was committed at the site, rather than by remote cracking of system security, then it is clear that physical security and the access controls to the system have been compromised—either that or there were no controls in the first place.

In either case, you'll need to figure out exactly where and how physical security was breached if you're going to solve the case and successfully prosecute it.

You may need help. If the intruders bypassed highly technical physical security procedures, then you're going to need expert advice. If you find that the perpetrator also must have had expertise in this area, this information may help to narrow down your list of potential suspects.

Basic Physical Security

At one extreme, physical security is simply good common sense. Common sense tells us to lock doors to keep strangers out of sensitive areas of a building and to install the computer center somewhere other than in the basement of a building located on a flood plain or next to a room where explosives are stored. At the other extreme, physical security can encompass almost futuristic technology. For example, the systems used for intrusion detection and access control are highly sophisticated and state of the art.

Although we provide information about controlling natural and environmental disasters in the following sections, this is done mainly as background. The details of such controls are usually not important to the criminal investigator unless the environment was intentionally manipulated by vandals to cause damage to the equipment.

Locks and Keys

The first line of defense against intruders is to keep them out of your building or computer room. This isn't as easy as it used to be in the days when most organizations had a single mainframe computer in one locked room. In most organizations these days, every employee has a PC, a workstation, or at least a terminal, and printers are distributed around the office. It's hard in this type of environment to lock up. But, it's still a good idea to centralize the most expensive and vulnerable computer equipment—for example, to keep large shared systems, central disk or tape drives, and precious disks and tapes in a locked computer room. (Ideally, the disks and tapes will be in a room other than that occupied by the computers, so that a natural or human disaster that imperils one will spare the other.)

To gain access to a building or to a locked computer room, a user should have to pass an authentication test of some kind. The convention in computer security is to speak of three classic ways in which you authenticate yourself (i.e., prove that you are who you say you are):

- Something you know—for example, a password

- Something you have—for example, a key, a badge, or a smart card

- Something you are—for example, the fingerprint on your finger (which matches the print on file)

All of these authentication techniques can be used for physical security. (Authentication in general, and various techniques and products used to authenticate, are described in detail in some of the references included in Appendix A.)

Physical security is measured in *penetration time*—how long it would take for an intruder to break your physical defenses. Your objective is to slow down that intruder to give law enforcement, security, or automated detection procedures time to kick in.

Natural Disasters

Computer facilities are subject to the same kinds of dangers that imperil any other facilities. Natural disasters—such as fire, flood, lightning, and earthquakes—are risks for all types of facilities. Many natural dangers are actually more of an issue for computers than for other types of equipment because computers are particularly sensitive to smoke, dust, vibration, water damage, and other such threats. The risks are also greater for computers because, unlike buildings and office equipment, computer loss or damage involves the loss of information as well as equipment. Unlike equipment, information is not interchangeable; it may be irreplaceable—or its replacement may be so costly and disruptive as to put an organization out of business.

Some natural disasters are more likely than others. Consider your own geography when you make your physical security plans. In areas where earthquakes are a threat, for example, computers, consoles, printers, and other equipment should be secured to the ceiling and the floor. If floods are a concern, equipment should not be installed on the lower levels of the building.

Environmental Threats

Environmental threats, such as electricity and heating and air conditioning systems, must also be part of a physical security plan. Electricity is a special threat for computer systems. Computer equipment is highly sensitive to any disruption of electrical service or its quality. If there are peaks or surges in the service, information can be lost and equipment may be damaged. In 1990, the New York and American Stock Exchanges had to be closed three times because of electrical power failures, resulting in major upheavals to members and investors. You will also need to worry about controlling the temperature and humidity of any areas in which computer equipment is kept. Static electricity is yet another concern.

The Concentric Circle Approach

When you assess the physical security of any facility, including computers, use a concentric circle approach. Start with the circle farthest from the point of interest, perhaps at the edge of a parking lot or even down the street, and systematically move closer to that point. Are there natural barriers between the edge of each circle and the target? Are there human-made barriers? Are there access controls? Answer these questions for each point within each circle. If one of your concentric circles is around the building from the parking lot to the outer wall, and if you have a guard at the entrance to the parking lot, then the guard is one of the access control points that a criminal would have to pass through.

The next concentric circle is the outer wall itself. If the doors and windows are locked or ingress is limited to specific locations, then this is the next layer of access control. Performing a systematic concentric circle survey may show you how the criminal gained access to the facility and to the location of the crime.

When you are evaluating the physical security of computer systems, you will find that some vulnerable points are inevitably located away from the computer room, CRTs, or other obvious locations. Systems are subject to compromise via remote telephone junctions or controls. The electric system can be "spiked" from a point near the electric meters or from other junctions. There are other wires and cables throughout the building that link local computers together. In a large facility, these wires and cables have been added over time, and no one may actually know what goes where. (That's when the investigator puts on old clothes and starts crawling around ceilings, storerooms, and basements.)

As we mentioned earlier, in most modern organizations, computing facilities are so distributed that it is difficult to secure a "computer room." However, it is a good idea to try to centralize whatever equipment can be handled in that way in order to provide extra security for it.

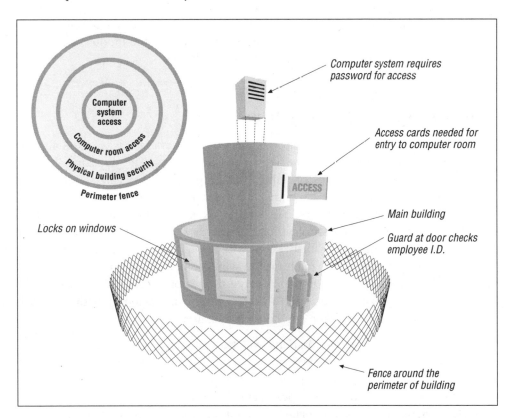

Figure 6-1. The concentric circle approach

Testing Physical Security Programs

Other than waiting for a crime to occur, there are at least three types of tests you can perform to examine and validate a physical security program:

1. Conduct systematic physical security inspections on a regular basis.

2. Conduct random checks to make sure employees don't bypass physical security measures when they think no one is watching.

3. At high-risk sites, conduct penetration tests.

When Investigating. . .

If you are called to investigate or respond to a computer crime, ask for copies of the organization's physical security test results, and check over the organization's contingency plans. Find out if the plans were, or are being, followed. Locating physical security breaches may provide clues to the modus operandi of the intrusion, and may help lead you to the suspect.

Regular Physical Security Inspections

Physical security surveys are usually conducted by personnel who work for the agency or company, using previously prepared checklists. The checklists help to ensure that all potential points of vulnerability are inspected. This system seems to work best when the people conducting the survey do not work in the area being surveyed. For example, people who work on the fifth floor of a federal building might conduct the survey for the fourth floor. This is to counter the sensory accommodation effect that occurs when you are in the same location day after day. You get used to the latch on the window being broken and may fail to report it during the survey. Or it may have been your responsibility to fix the latch and you forgot. In either case, a person from outside the immediate area is more likely to report the broken latch during the survey.

Occasionally, physical security experts will be contracted to conduct the survey. This is likely to happen at sensitive sites, wherever a major loss has just occurred, or where major changes in the physical security are being planned. The professional team's report is more technical than the home team's and it may include specific recommendations that relate to federal requirements or guidelines.

The information obtained during the security survey is then used to develop recommendations for short- and long-term improvements. Future needs may also be anticipated so they can be included in next year's budget. After the survey is completed, previous surveys are reviewed to determine if some of the problems had been identified earlier but had not been corrected. Criminals would love to get their hands on a physical security survey that outlines all of the organization's vulnerable points, so this should be treated as sensitive, if not classified, information.

Random Checks

As good as security surveys are, they are also predictable. Spot checks introduce an element of randomization into any program. With spot checks, you can find out how—or whether—people are actually using security features. For example, access control systems may be very sophisticated at your site, but if the local employees consider them a pain in the neck and prop open all the doors, the system is useless.

There may be less obvious problems than propped-open doors. As we mentioned in Chapter 2, watch out for piggybacking—where an employee or other person who is not authorized to be in a sensitive area hangs around an access control point holding printouts and computer media until an authorized person passes through. The piggybacking unauthorized person then follows the authorized person into the sensitive area.

Penetration Tests

Penetration tests are generally performed by professional teams at such high-risk sites as sensitive military installations, nuclear facilities, and Internal Revenue Service offices. Penetration testers include covert operation teams who crawl on their bellies in the dead of night, bypassing supposedly impenetrable barriers and gaining access to restricted areas. Penetration tests may also be conducted by harmless-looking people in the bright light of day. In any case, the objective of penetration testing is to find the vulnerable points and prove that the physical security can be breached.

More than Logic Bombs. . .

There are some threats that are even more dangerous than the theft of proprietary data or the invasion of payroll files. Bombers, arsonists, extortionists, and various types of extremists present special risks because the damage they can wreak is so severe. A bomb or an incendiary device could literally destroy your computer center. An extremist could attack your computer system with a sledge hammer. An extortionist could plant a virus or other command that might shut down or otherwise damage the system if his demands are not met.

How can you protect against such people? If other offices and facilities of the organization have been targeted by any of these people, then the security at computer locations should be increased. If the organization has just been the brunt of a lot of negative media coverage that might inspire these people to action, the physical security of computers should be reviewed and contingency plans put into place to upgrade that security.

Threats of this kind are dangers to all organizations, not just those whose business involves computers. In general, you'll deal with these threats just as you would if you worked at a bookstore or a restaurant. Your computing power does add a new dimension to the threat, though, because of the potential damage not only to your own site and data but also to client data you might be managing.

How, specifically, do you handle bomb threats in the context of computer crime? It's no different from bomb threats at any other site. Your receptionists and secretaries must be trained to handle telephoned threats. You must know how to reach bomb threat response teams, which have training in searching for suspicious devices. You will also need to know how to contact negotiators who are trained to deal with the extortionist.

Suppose the threat is a programmed one—suppose that an extortionist warns that he has planted a virus or other peril in your system, and that he will cause it to "explode" if you do not meet his demands. Your systems personnel or consultants must be prepared to go into action immediately to find the virus or other programmed threat in your system.

Along with all of these other responses, you'll need to do a careful check of all of your physical security to see if you can determine whether, in fact, it has been breached. Many threats are fakes.

Natural Disaster Checklists

This section includes checklists[*] of items that may help you to avert or prepare for natural disasters.

Fire and Smoke

- Use masonry wall construction whenever possible.

- Install fire barriers to piping, cabling, and other openings to computer rooms.

- Install smoke detectors near your equipment—and check them periodically. The toxic particles in smoke can do a great deal of damage, even if a fire turns out to be a minor one.

- Make sure that your smoke-activated fire alarm system automatically shuts down the computer system and air conditioning.

---

[*] Many of the suggestions in the checklists in this chapter are extracted from *Computer Security Basics* by Deborah Russell and G. T. Gangemi, Sr. (O'Reilly & Associates, 1991).

- Keep portable water and carbon dioxide fire extinguishers in and near your computer rooms, and be sure everyone knows they are there and how to use them.

- Enforce no-smoking policies—both to keep smoke away from computer equipment and to avoid fire danger.

- Although computer centers frequently use carbon dioxide and gases such as Halon, which smother fires without causing water damage, the dangers from these gases are now better understood. (The Montreal Protocol Treaty limits the use of Halon.) Most experts now recommend sprinkler systems, even in computer rooms.

- Use noncombustible furniture, approved trash containers, and nonflammable cleaning solvents.

- Avoid or minimize the use of cellular plastics in computer rooms. Such plastics generate hazardous fumes and smoke particles when they burn.

- Keep computer media in fireproof containers when they aren't being used.

Earthquakes and Vibration

- Keep computers away from glass windows and high surfaces, particularly if you're in a high-risk area.

- In earthquake areas, secure computers, consoles, printers, and other equipment to the floor.

- Be sure that if strong vibration occurs, other objects won't easily fall on your computer equipment.

Water

- Keep computers out of basement areas. (In addition to water, hazardous pollutants may leak in.) Install computers on higher levels of the building if it's located in flood areas.

- Install under-floor drainage.

- Install a water sensor on the floor near your computer systems. If you have a raised floor, install one on the raised floor and one beneath it.

- If your computer does get wet, let it dry thoroughly before you attempt to turn it on again, and contact your service representative and system administrators.

Lightning

- If a lightning storm hits, try to turn off your computer and unplug it. Lightning generates an enormous power surge; it's a danger—particularly to your disks—even if you have a surge protector on your computer and even if your computer is turned off.

- To protect your backup tapes from the magnetic field created if lightning strikes your building, store the tapes as far away as possible from the building's steel supports. Even metal shelving may pose a hazard.

Environmental Disaster Checklists

This section includes checklists of items that may help you to avert or prepare for environmental disasters.

Heating and Air Conditioning

- Keep all rooms containing computers at reasonable temperatures (approximately 50–80 degrees Fahrenheit or 10–26 degrees Celsius).
- Keep the humidity at 35–50 percent.
- Install separate air conditioning systems for computer rooms.
- Install gauges and alarms that warn you if the temperature and humidity are getting out of range.
- Equip your heating and cooling systems with air filters to protect against dust—another peril to computers and especially to disks.

Electricity

- Your computer will suffer if it gets too much or too little electricity. Blackouts, brownouts, and fluctuations in power can all damage your equipment. Make sure that you have good electrical service.
- Install an uninterruptible power supply (UPS). It will absorb surges, will provide extra voltage during brownouts, and, if power fails completely, will provide power until you're able to shut down the system. An unprotected power loss can result in serious damage. Note that surge protection won't work unless your electrical system is well grounded.
- Install a voltage regulator or line filter on your computer's power supply; a voltage spike can destroy your computer's power supply.
- If you can, install a special electrical circuit with an isolated ground for each of your systems.

- Avoid locating electrical transformer equipment inside computer rooms.

- Install anti-static carpeting in your facility. This carpeting contains special filaments that dissipate static electricity.

Intruder Checklists

This section includes checklists of items that may help you to keep intruders out—and detect when they've broken in.

Intruder Prevention

There may be many ways into your facility. Be careful about the following:

- Take special precautions at doors to computer rooms and rooms where media and manuals are stored. (See the Intruder Alert checklist for possible ways of preventing access.)

- Be sure the walls extend above any dropped ceilings so that intruders can't climb over the walls.

- Be sure the walls extend down beyond any raised floors so that intruders can't crawl under the raised floor.

- Be sure the air ducts are small enough so intruders can't crawl through them.

- Keep computers away from windows. They're too easy to break, and if an intruder does break in, the glass itself can cause a lot of damage. (People can also look through glass walls into computer rooms and conference rooms and potentially get access to sensitive information that way.)

- Intruders can't sneak in over communications lines (not literally, at least), but they can cause a lot of damage by unplugging or cutting cables. Keep unauthorized people away from telephone controls, junction boxes, and all cabling. Physical access to cabling also opens up the possibility of wiretapping. (See Chapter 8, *Communications Security,* for more information.)

- Few people think about what they throw away, but someone who gets hold of your trash can often learn passwords, system names and filenames, and other sensitive information that can help him or her attack your computer or site. (See the section called "Dumpster Diving" in Chapter 2.)

Intruder Alerts

Consider installing such intrusion detection devices as the following:

- Guards at critical points, such as the entrance (possibly supplemented by physical controls such as "mantraps;" with these, if you fail an access control test after entering a facility, you are trapped between double doors until a guard investigates), at loading docks, and at outlying warehouses.

- Access control systems using such devices as smart cards that may use challenge-response technology.

- Access control systems using biometric devices (devices that compare such physical characteristics as fingerprints, retina patterns, handprints, or voice patterns, or such behavioral characteristics as signatures and keystroke patterns).

- Standard burglar alarms.

- Surveillance equipment such as closed circuit television.

7

Personnel Security

The biggest vulnerability in any computer system—and the biggest threat to computer security—is people. Some people may simply be untrained; they may unwittingly destroy important information that is stored in the system or may interfere with system operations. Other people may deliberately violate rules and use the system for personal business or pleasure. Still others are outright criminals who steal data—or the computers themselves—or may vandalize computer facilities.

Personnel security is a broad issue that encompasses far more than computer crime prevention. This chapter focuses only on those aspects of personnel security that touch on computer crime. An organization's overall program will have to include measures for dealing with violence and harassment in the workplace, kidnapping, and other such threats.

There are many types of people who imperil computers and information, ranging from novice computer users to disgruntled employees to professional criminals to espionage agents. Read this chapter in conjunction with Chapter 3, *Who Commits Computer Crimes?* That chapter talks about the general categories of computer criminals and explores what motivates them. This chapter further breaks down the categories and discusses possible ways of setting up organizational policies to contain these people.

Will you prosecute the crimes you uncover through your personnel security program? Some organizations do; it's particularly important to do so when professional criminals are involved. Some organizations prefer not to prosecute their own employees, who may be reacting to some personal problems. In any case, you will want to check out Part III of this book, particularly the discussions of documenting events and gathering evidence for investigation and prosecution.

Developing a Personnel Security Program

Most detected computer crime is committed by employees, whether they are motivated by grudges, greed, or simple boredom. However, because the computer provides a way to attack a site remotely, personnel security programs must also address threats from outsiders: vendors, contractors, even people on the other side of the world who have never directly interacted with the organization before, cracking its computer systems.

Every organization needs to begin with good physical security. One way to keep unauthorized people from getting into your computer system is to keep them out of the building. Next, work on tightening your communications security so they will have a harder time cracking your system from a remote location.

Now, look carefully at your own employees. Are you screening them appropriately before you hire? Hiring a payroll clerk without conducting a background check, at least a credit check, is inviting trouble, yet it happens all the time. Do you have good managers who are monitoring employee performance and morale? Are you training employees so they won't make foolish mistakes that will damage files and programs? Do you have counseling programs to help out if things go wrong? We'll touch on each of these areas in later sections in this chapter and in Chapter 9, *Operations Security*.

Be aware that the real world has an effect on your personnel security program. Monitor events inside and outside the organization so you can beef up security when certain types of problems arise. For example, an organization that is about to experience serious labor problems could be targeted for a computer attack by employees—or by outsiders who are sympathetic to the employees' cause. A company that just landed a major sensitive defense contract could be targeted by crackers for industrial or international espionage. An agency or company that has been receiving extensive negative publicity could become the victim of an ideological terrorist group or an emotionally disturbed person. Whenever an organization is in the news—for either positive or negative reasons—it can become an attractive target.

Types of Threats

The threat that any one individual presents to a computer system depends on several factors:

- Type of access
- Level of expertise
- Motivation

Type of Access

The amount of damage someone can do to a computer system depends in large part on the level of access they have. First, consider hardware access. Does the person have access to the main computer itself or only to terminals at remote locations? If she has direct access to the system, then the threat she represents is a much greater one. Not only can the individual potentially break into the system from a terminal, she might also be able to change the system from the system console, to implant a virus, to do physical damage to the system, or to steal the equipment.

Next, consider software access. System administrators, managers, and analysts are likely to need access to the operating system itself. Programmers will probably need access to proprietary programs under development, but perhaps not to the operating system. Users will typically need access only to the specific files and data with which they are working. Do your customer service representatives need access to payroll records? Of course not. Nor do they need access to most other types of business records. It's important to limit access to the resources people actually need to do their jobs effectively—and no more. In the military, such a limitation is called *need to know*. By limiting access in this way, you'll not only protect against deliberate theft, sabotage, or viewing of confidential or valuable information but you'll also keep employees from accidentally damaging other files—a more likely threat.

Level of Expertise

What is the person's level of expertise? The greater the expertise, the wider the range of threats. Programming a virus requires a greater knowledge of computing than most data-entry clerks possess. A system operator, analyst, or programmer could plant a virus or another programmed threat that could damage the system extensively at some time in the future.

On the other hand, ignorance can also expose a system to great danger. For example, an employee who doesn't know enough not to download virus-infected software from a BBS to his home computer—and then use it at work—represents a major risk to system security.

Motivation

What motivates the person? Employees who like their jobs and feel appreciated by their employers are not likely to commit acts of vandalism or sabotage against employers. On the other hand, employees who have just been passed over for a promotion, have been reprimanded for poor performance, or are about to be fired may have a very different attitude. Obviously, the second category of employees represents more of a threat.

Not all computer crime is motivated by a negative attitude toward a particular organization. Some computer criminals are simply motivated by the "intellectual challenge" or a sense of power. Others see it as a means of striking back at the system, a few are in it for the money, and a few are simply disturbed persons who happen to be computer-literate.

Different People/Different Threats

In Chapter 2, we divided computer criminals into three basic categories: crackers, professional criminals, and vandals. With this approach, we looked mainly at what the attackers do. In this chapter, we take a different cut at the population of attackers; here, we focus on who they are from an organizational point of view. Do they work for you? What are they trying to get from you? And why?

In the next sections, we examine each of the following categories and suggest some possible countermeasures.

- Employees

- Vendors and contractors

- Professional criminals

- Professional espionage agents

- Untrained or careless users

Employees

We've already mentioned that employees are the greatest threat to any computer system. They have access to the system, they know the physical layout, and they may hold a grudge. Do you know who your employees are? Do you hire people who will have access to the inner sanctum of a computer system without conducting at least a cursory background investigation? If so, you're almost sure to be targeted sooner or later.

Background Investigations

Background investigations are the first line of defense in any personnel security program. The types of background checks are likely to vary widely from organization to organization. Some may conduct detailed checks on all employees, and may even administer drug and lie detector tests. Most organizations do more informal checks. The degree to which employees are checked depends mainly on the type of job that person will hold and the type of data to which they may be exposed. Obviously, someone handling highly sensitive data needs special qualifications. The Department of Defense formalizes this process by classifying certain kinds of data as confidential, secret, and top secret, and by assigning security clearances (after doing extensive and rigorous background checks) to people who will be handling these types of data. For example, only someone with a secret clearance will be allowed to handle secret data.

Background checks may help you determine whether employees got into trouble before joining you. But what about employees who run into trouble after they come to work for you? There are many kinds of trouble: a serious life crisis such as a death in the family or a divorce, a substance abuse problem, gambling debts, and so on. Some employees just seem to go bad, with no apparent reason or provocation. What can you do?

Monitoring

Your second line of defense is to monitor employee behavior. The closer employees are to the operation of the system or to sensitive data, the more important it becomes to monitor their behavior. There is a fine line between monitoring employees and invading their privacy. You don't have to spy on your employees, but you do need to watch out for truly suspicious behavior—behavior that might indicate either that an individual has embarked on a computer crime or that he is at risk of being involved in one. Some organizations feel uncomfortable about doing this. You will have to make your own decision about whether the value of your computer systems and data outweigh your feelings, and your employees' feelings, about such investigations.

There are various types of monitoring. Some organizations conduct a randomly selected update of the background investigation on a certain percentage of their employees each year. Because employees never know who will be selected for the update investigation, the kind of unpredictability we discuss in Chapter 9 in terms of operations security becomes part of your personnel security program.

Supervisors play an important role in monitoring employee behavior by trying to be aware of employees who are experiencing personal problems. Not only is this smart security but it is also humane. Supervisors can, when appropriate, help employees find the professional help that may be needed to deal with their problems, whether they are substance abuse problems, psychiatric problems, or logistics issues that are causing them great stress—such as finding day care for their children or elder care for their parents. Usually, referring an employee to your organization's employee assistance program is the first step.

A change in behavior is one important sign that an employee may need help. A change in financial situation is another. Supervisors must be alert to employees who suddenly exhibit a period of conspicuous spending that goes far beyond their known resources. Watch out, too, for employees who are receiving telephone calls at work from collection agencies or other creditors or those who are constantly borrowing money from other employees.

Sometimes, an employee's problem becomes so severe that the organization must take steps to protect itself. If the risk appears to be minimal, counseling and monitoring may be sufficient. (However, you may want to take some proactive measures like doing extra system backups and limiting the employee's ability to modify files, just as a precaution.) If the threat appears to be a greater one, you may have to remove the employee from his position.

Employee security goes beyond just watching your employees for signs of criminal behavior. The best security—and the best productivity—comes from employees who like their work and feel responsible for it. Don't just enforce security within your organization; explain the reasons for it.

Training and Accountability

Employees need training both in the use of the system and in taking responsibility for that system. Train employees first in basic system operation. Not all security incidents are the result of malice; many are caused by simple human error. Employees who work in a sloppy or inefficient way may incorrectly enter sensitive data or may make mistakes updating or exporting it.

Employees also need to be clear about the security policy of their organization. For example, what is company policy on using company computers for personal business, as we describe in Chapter 1? (Most companies take a fairly lenient view of this offense, as long as the use is minor, does not interfere with work, and does not use too many resources.) How about taking licensed software home for personal use? (Most companies come down hard on such violations; this is a crime.)

How about bringing in software from home? Consider the danger of virus contamination that we discussed in Chapter 2. Some organizations completely prohibit employees from bringing programs from an outside source to work. No exceptions. Other organizations may insist that all such programs be evaluated and tested before they can be used. The testing is typically conducted at a stand-alone workstation (one that is not connected to a network) so that if the program does cause damage, the damage will affect only a single workstation. Most organizations also insist that all outside programs be tested using anti-virus tools.

Employees need to know that they are accountable for their actions and for any use of their organization's computing resources, such as terminals, accounts, and passwords. They need to understand that they are responsible not only for using these resources with care but for protecting them against intruders to the best of

Telephone and Keystroke Monitoring

One type of monitoring that has gained recent attention—both pro and con—is the monitoring of employee phone calls and keystrokes. The organizations that do this are primarily interested in employee productivity: How long does it take a directory assistance operator to serve each caller? How long does it take an airline reservation agent to book a flight? Is an employee making personal phone calls on company time? The same techniques, however, can be used to monitor and enforce personnel security.

Under the Electronic Communications Privacy Act,[1] all monitoring of wire, oral, and electronic communications is prohibited, unless a specific statutory exception applies. With a search warrant aimed at protecting against abuse of a communications system, certain recording devices can be used in specific cases. These include pen registers, which record the telephone numbers received by a specific telephone, or dialed number recorders (DNRs), which record the telephone numbers dialed from a specific telephone. In the text of statutes and search warrants, the term "trap and trace device" sometimes encompasses both types of recorders.

It is not entirely clear whether companies can use these same techniques to monitor their own employees. In one case in California, the monitoring of telephone calls was ruled illegal. In Pennsylvania, the Supreme Court even ruled against the CALLER*ID feature offered by many local telephone companies. An incident early in 1995, in which a McDonald's manager monitored the voice-mail boxes of two employees who were having an affair (and then played the messages for the employee's wife!) may result in an interesting case.

What about the electronic monitoring of the keystrokes entered on a keyboard? Some observers think that the courts are more likely to allow such monitoring, especially of employees, on the principle that the computer programs and files being used and accessed are the property of the organization. Others say that, unless your system displays a warning banner or unless the user of an account has been warned that the account will be monitored and has signed an appropriate agreement, then the system administrator who looks through email or runs the monitoring software could be guilty of a crime and liable for civil penalties.

Stay tuned. . .

---

[1] See the text of the Electronic Communications Privacy Act (18 USC. 2510/2511 et seq) and the Digital Telephony Act (Public Law 103-414) in Part IV of this book.

their ability. Accountability means that when a violation of the rules is found in the logs or other documentation, the responsible employee can be identified. Even if the employee claims that someone stole her password or used her terminal when she was at lunch, there must still be a degree of accountability. Did the employee do everything possible to keep this from happening—for example, log out during lunch, not write the password down, pick a hard-to-guess password? (See Chapter 8 for a discussion of login and password security that employees should be aware of.)

Accountability extends to management as well. In any personnel security program, managers need to keep their eyes open and to take action when necessary. There are a lot of common-sense factors at play, and they are too frequently violated. For example, an employer does not fire an employee who is in a sensitive position and give that individual the opportunity to get back on the computer. Sounds obvious? We've seen it happen. Accountability must begin with management and be woven into the fabric of the entire organization.

Auditing

Most computer crimes involving the false entry or the modification of data in an organization's databases are committed by employees. Consider the data-entry clerk who changes the social security numbers on payroll records to add someone's pay (perhaps that of a nonexistent person) to his own, or to shift a portion of his taxes to another employee. Auditing is an important way to verify the integrity of data as they are entered, while they are stored in the database, and when they are being retried.

There are a number of ways to enforce auditing, such as:

- Make sure that all employees check data as they are being entered and retrieved, and set up procedures for periodically checking stored data. Notify the system operator if anything doesn't match up.

- Periodically hire contractors who specialize in auditing computerized information to do a thorough check of all system data and controls.

- Consider investing in software that audits the system in automated fashion on a day-by-day basis.

Vendors and Contractors

Vendors and contractors present a unique threat to computer security. They probably know more than anyone in your own organization about systems they have installed or that they maintain. Yet, they often are not subject to the same regulations and discipline as those governing your own employees. Programmers from the vendor company that sold and installed the system have been known to leave back doors that allow them to access the system remotely to make future modifications or updates. Although the motives of the original programmers may be benign, such back doors are extremely dangerous because they can be used by criminals to steal information and plant viruses.

Vendor and contractor employees are subject to the same problems and challenges as those confronting employees. They may develop substance abuse, financial problems, or other problems that could potentially lead them to commit criminal acts.

Just as you must know who your employees are, you must also know who your vendors and contractors are. Carefully check the history of any firm with which you do business, and find out whether it conducts background checks on its employees. Determine what measures the vendor takes to monitor employee behavior and to identify and assist problem employees. Verify the information you receive, too: some computer criminals have become "computer security consultants," and these people may be less than candid about their personal histories.

Periodically, review all contracts and other vendor agreements to determine the vendor's liability in case one of its employees intentionally or unintentionally causes damage to your system. Remember that there are several different types of damage. Physical damage to the hardware, or an incident that results in changes in the software, can be expensive. But the loss of information in the system could put a company out of business.

To protect your organization, closely monitor the activities of vendors and contractors when they are on site. If possible, make sure that one of your own employees remains with the vendor or contractor at all times. You must also monitor the vendor organization itself. Remember that businesses don't always remain static. You may trust an organization completely, but what if it merges with a competitor? What if it is purchased by foreign investors? What if new management decides that employee background checks are a waste of money because the company has had no problems in the past? Any of these changes would increase the risk to your own organization. When such changes occur, discuss the increased risk with the vendor company. If you don't get the cooperation you need, it may be time to change vendors, however disruptive that might seem to be.

Professional Criminals

Professional criminals may target your system—to commit fraud either to benefit themselves directly, under contract to others, or on speculation (e.g., to crack your system to get proprietary or military information that they can later sell). How can you prevent fraud attacks by the professional criminal, and how can you detect such crimes if they do occur? The same kinds of computer and communications security measures (e.g., strong passwords, encryption) that you use against other types of crackers are your best bet for keeping professionals out. Logs and audit trails help to identify fraud if it does take place.

Identify those files and programs that are particularly enticing, and take special precautions to keep them safe. If checks are prepared by computer, for example, make sure that audit procedures monitor the programs that instigate the writing of checks, and make sure to severely limit access to these programs. We've often seen accounts payable programs being compromised, resulting in organizations paying for goods that were never received or paying twice for goods they did receive.

As with most forms of fraud, an auditor will find and follow the paper trail once a computer-related fraud is detected. The trail will usually lead to the perpetrator.

If a professional criminal cracks your system remotely, your problem is a somewhat different one, especially if the motive is something other than fraud. The evidence trail may be a maze of interconnected networks that could lead almost anywhere, and the motive of the crime is not always as obvious as money or hard goods. In some cases, crackers may extract information from the system, and you may never be the wiser. Or crackers may modify information, and you may not notice the modifications until after they're out of the system, leaving extensive damage behind.

Some crackers are after specific information (for example, there have been cases of crackers who stole defense information and sold it to the KGB); others are simply malicious. Some skilled criminals don't even view their actions as a crime; rather, they see their actions as an intellectual challenge or as a Robin Hood type of gesture. If these criminals are careful, their trails may be very difficult to follow. Despite the nonmonetary nature of these attacks, perpetrators are indeed professional in their outlook and expertise, and they're difficult to track down. They are typically caught only when they become brazen and careless (for example, when they brag to others or post advice for breaking into your system on bulletin board systems). And sometimes they are found when their friends inform on them or when we just get lucky.

Professional Espionage Agents

The Department of Defense, every major law enforcement agency, and government contractors around the world rely on computers. Quite simply, they couldn't do their jobs without them. They also find it absolutely necessary for certain systems to be connected by networks. Most of the classified information in these systems is well guarded, but there is a great deal of other information that may not be classified and yet is highly sensitive. Such information is constantly under attack by crackers, and there have been many successful compromises of data.

Such espionage is very likely to increase in the decades to come. Hostile intelligence services (and even some services of "friendly" nations) are increasing their efforts to gain military information and also sensitive industrial information. Why bother to develop a new microchip if someone else already has it and you can steal the design by breaking into their computer system?

Computer systems that contain information sensitive to the national interests of the United States must comply with certain strictly defined and enforced security requirements. (The Trusted Computer System Evaluation Criteria [TCSEC], known as the "Orange Book," is one of these.) Although compliance with these regulations is constantly monitored, problems can occur. If you become aware that sensitive or classified information has been targeted or compromised, notify agents from the FBI's National Security Division.

Some states, such as California and Illinois, have specific laws that prohibit the theft of trade secrets (proprietary commercial information). At this time, there are no comparable federal regulations.

Espionage agents come in all flavors. At one extreme are professional agents who may be highly skilled and difficult to detect, regardless of whether they're going after national defense or competitive business information. At the other end are terrorists and other militants who may appear to you to be acting irrationally. Terrorists include such groups as the Neo-Nazi or Red Brigade groups, which have been successful at entering computer facilities and damaging hardware. Individuals in this category are typically interested in destruction, not data theft or compromise. Such groups don't usually break into systems, steal information, plant viruses, or change programs. Their approach is more direct; they are much more likely to vandalize computer rooms and systems.

Untrained or Careless Users

We talk in this book about intelligent attacks on computer systems, perhaps giving the impression that the crackers among us possess virtually superhuman intelligence. But a greater threat may come from those who are ignorant about computer operation and procedures.

Organizations must make sure that everyone who is given access to the computer room or any computer equipment is trained in its use and understands the importance of being careful with equipment and data. Teach users how to use any hardware and software they will have responsibility for, and make sure they understand the organization's security policy. An untrained data-entry clerk could potentially blow away important files. An incompetent system administrator could do untold damage to your system. Limit the exposure of your system by limiting the privileges each user has. If someone doesn't need access to a computer or a file, don't give it to them.

Personnel Security Checklist

Here is a summary of specific steps that can be taken to improve personnel security

1. Conduct preemployment background investigations.

2. Update the information for these checks on a random basis.

3. Check all vendor agreements to determine if vendors conduct checks of their employees and if vendor liability is clearly stated in the agreement.

4. Publicize the security philosophy of the organization. Put all policies in writing. Make sure that management accepts and enforces it, and employees understand it.

5. Train employees to be alert and to report suspicious activity.

6. Establish a buddy system to prevent individuals from having access to the equipment or files when they are alone.

7. Train supervisors to identify and respond to potential employee problems. Responses may range from getting psychiatric help for employees to taking specific measures to protect computer systems, such as locking rooms and doing extra backups.

8. Separate authorization and operational functions.

9. Establish security audit procedures.

10. Expect "revenge" from disgruntled employees, ex-employees, or customers.

11. Make all regulations and requirements regarding the use of the system, the software, and other restrictions explicit. Take action whenever these regulations are violated.

12. Enforce vacation policies and rotate assignments. Some security attacks may take a long time to complete (e.g., salami attacks on bank accounts) or may require monitoring on a daily basis. If you shake up staffing assignments every once in a while, you may uncover long-term attacks.

13. Don't grant privileges automatically. Limit access to highly sensitive systems and data—if someone doesn't need access to a particular computer, computer room, or set of files, don't allow that person access.

14. When an employee leaves, even voluntarily:

- Review that employee's obligations with him or her.

- Don't allow that employee any further access to the computer systems. Delete his or her computer accounts and all passwords.

- Get back any keys,

- smart cards, and so on.

- Check the employee's files and save them in a secure location in case you need them at some future time.

- If the employee had superuser or other supervisory status, change *all* passwords on the system..

When Investigating. . .

If you are investigating a computer crime, you may find it valuable to determine which of the steps in the Personnel Security Checklist were in place and which were ignored. It might help you determine the modus operandi and to identify suspects. It may also help the organization to improve its policies in the future.

8

Communications Security

Communication between computers vastly increases their power. But the more a computer system communicates—with other systems within a building, with other systems in branch offices, and with other systems, both domestic and international—the more vulnerable an organization may be to having those communications channels used for nefarious purposes. As we mentioned earlier in this book, four out of five of the computer crimes investigated by the FBI over the past few years were aided by Internet access.

Data communications is only one aspect of the broad field of communications security. The field also includes the protection of mail, fax, telephone, and voice-mail communications, which are outside the scope of this book.

This chapter describes, at a very basic level, how computers communicate and how communications security can reduce threats to computer systems, and it touches on more general issues of data security. Network and communications security are complex topics, and even among computer security practitioners, there is disagreement about the precise definition of these terms. This chapter skims the surface. For those who need more technical information, we've included some references in Appendix A.

Types of Networks

There are three basic types of computer networks, each with its own technical characteristics and security risks:

- Local area networks (LANs)

- Wide area networks (WANs)

- Internetworks

Local Area Networks

Local area networks are designed to connect computers that are located in the same geographic area and that belong to the same administrative domain. Such networks are typically found in small companies or agencies where employees share computer services—both hardware services such as printers and software services such as regular file backups—and also have a need to communicate with each other. A typical LAN usually connects several dozen workstations (terminals or CRTs), is usually limited to a single building, and includes services such as electronic mail, file transfer, and backup and recovery of files. Each workstation on the LAN must have special software that allows it to communicate with the other workstations on the system. LANs usually connect PCs or workstations via network media such as twisted pair, coaxial, or fiber optic cable.

Crimes committed on a LAN are usually perpetrated by an employee, a vendor, or someone else who has access to the physical facilities where the workstations are located.

LANs become more vulnerable to outside attack when they have gateways to larger regional, national, and international networks, usually called wide area networks (WANs). When LANs are connected beyond their original boundaries in this way, an attacker becomes much more difficult to track.

Wide Area Networks

Wide area networks are large networks that span a large geographic area, usually larger than a single city or a metropolitan area. Worldwide military networks, public utility networks, large funds transfer networks, and major corporate networks are examples of WANs. Computers on a WAN are usually connected by leased, high-speed, long-distance data circuits. WANs that are relatively small in size (sometimes called metropolitan area networks, or MANs) are more likely to be connected by coaxial cable, microwave, or fiber.

Internetworks

Networks can be linked together to allow users on one network to communicate with users on another. A common method of connecting networks is via a gateway—a system that is part of two or more networks. Communications from one network to another pass through the gateway that is attached to both of them.

The growth of large international networks in recent years is astounding. Look at BITNET as an example. BITNET was originally chartered in 1981 to service IBM computers at the City University of New York (CUNY). It has since expanded to a worldwide network that links computers across North America, Europe, the Far

East, the Middle East, and the various republics of the former Soviet Union. User support services are provided by BITNET administration, as well as by individuals throughout the network. BITNET provides electronic access that allows computers at Brookhaven National Laboratory to communicate, virtually instantaneously, with computers located at the Illinois Institute of Technology, computers located in Stuttgart, Germany, and computers located in Rehovot, Israel. BITNET makes it possible for researchers and academicians around the world to share ideas, papers, and research findings. They can collaborate over long distances—distances that would have made collaboration prohibitively difficult and expensive in the past, before computer networks were in place.

Like all such networks, BITNET serves a valuable function, but there is a dark side to this connectivity as well. BITNET also provides a potential channel for crackers to access computer systems they might not otherwise have been able to access. To counter this threat, BITNET uses a series of monitoring procedures and basic communications security approaches. Individuals on the system take measures to prevent others who access their computers using BITNET to then access more sensitive or restricted computers or files. Of course, the challenge to crackers is to discover ways of circumventing these controls, and many are very good at what they do.

The Internet, the largest interconnected computer network in operation, is the premier example of an internetwork. It is composed of thousands of interconnected WANs and LANs. By mid-1994, the Internet had reached 100 countries and all seven continents, with about 600,000 host machines connected, and a user population in the multi-millions. The Internet is now doubling in size every 9 to 10 months. This phenomenal growth obviously presents both interesting technological challenges and significant law enforcement challenges.

In *The Cuckoo's Egg*, Cliff Stoll describes how a German hacker located in Hannover, Germany, broke into a succession of computer networks on the Internet. Once he'd broken into a few sites, the cracker was able to use these sites, and their network connections, to break into additional systems and networks. Eventually, he made his way to a number of sensitive military and commercial sites, including the U.S. Navy Coastal Systems computer in Panama City, the Air Force Systems Command in El Segundo, the Anniston Army Depot in Alabama, and the Fort Buckner Army Base in Japan.

One of the networks that has been repeatedly targeted is the U.S. Defense Data Network, MILNET. This is an unclassified military network that has nearly 200 authorized systems in the United States and more than 50 more in Europe and the Pacific. Intruders have been able to compromise unclassified but highly sensitive data from this network. Even more frightening, they have also used MILNET as a gateway to other, more sensitive networks.

When Investigating. . .

If an incident occurs at a system that is on line with external networks, make sure that you identify all of the networks to which that computer has direct and indirect access. It may not be at all obvious at first how wide a net you'll need to catch the intruder. The technical experts working with you will help to determine if there have been intrusions, viruses, or other problems elsewhere on the network that are similar in any way to the one you've experienced. (The organizations in the Forum of Incident Response and Security Teams [FIRST] are excellent sources of help when doing investigations of this kind.) This information may help lead to the culprit, even if that person is halfway around the world. See Appendix A for how to contact these organizations.

Network Communications

As we've described, there may be one or many computers in a network. In a small local area network, there may be only a single computer to which an organization's terminals or workstations are attached. On a larger network, computers communicate with other computers.

When you send a message from your workstation to someone on another computer on the network, hundreds or even thousands of miles away, it may appear that you are communicating directly with that person. In fact, though, you send your message from your computer to your local network, from which it usually travels through many other computers across a series of network connections to the network used by the message recipient. The recipient retrieves the information from the network and ultimately reads it on his or her own local computer, as shown in Figure 8–1.

This network connectivity makes your messages all the more vulnerable. Each of the computers through which you are communicating may have hundreds of other users and may be connected to numerous other networks. At any point, there is a possibility that an eavesdropper may tap into your message.

Types of Terminals

There are several different types of terminals used for network communication. In the past, typewriter-like terminals were used; teletypes were the earliest devices of this kind. Such systems included a keyboard and a printing device, and few of them are still in use.

The display terminal (CRT or VDT) includes a keyboard and a screen for displaying information. These are reasonably fast and easy to use. Newer models

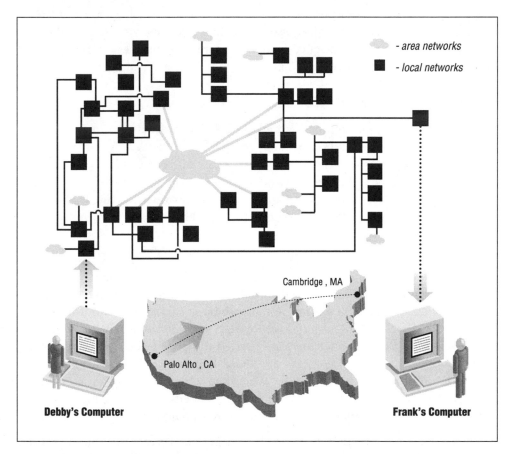

Figure 8-1. Network communications

of display terminals incorporate high-resolution color graphics capabilities, sound processing, and additional input devices (e.g., a mouse or a tablet). These newer displays are often network devices themselves, and are capable of opening "windows" connected to multiple computer systems at once.

Both low-end personal computers and high-powered workstations may be used as intelligent terminals. Not only can they send and receive information, but they are also fully functional computers in their own right. They can also be connected to individual or shared printers so that information being transmitted or received can also be printed.

Remote job entry (RJE) terminals, once quite common, are now used only in some mainframe environments. These terminals usually consist of a card, tape, or cassette reader and a high-speed line printer. Terminals of this kind are typically used when high volumes of information must be transmitted or received.

Numerous types of special-purpose and usually quite expensive terminals are in use today. These include machines used for airline reservation systems, CAD/CAM graphics workstations for science and engineering, consumer cash-dispensing machines, and many other types of devices.

Types of Communications

There are a number of communication carriers that the network may use. The best known are the telephone operating companies of the AT&T system and the regional Bell operating companies. Other U.S. carriers include Sprint, MCI, Western Union, and GTE. The networks contract with the carriers to connect computers on the net across the country, as well as overseas. The U.S. Department of Defense also maintains its own network, which may be involved in some communications.

Two types of data transmission circuits exist: analog and digital. Voice transmission networks typically use analog circuits capable of transmitting a range of sounds. Digital communications circuits use the binary on-off principle to communicate information in a digital form. Because computers communicate using digital circuits, but their communications are often carried along analog channels, modems (MOdulator-DEModulators) are needed to perform the necessary conversion. A modem at one end converts the digital information from the computer to analog information for transmission. When the communication is received, a modem at the other end of the communication converts the analog message back into its digital format so that it can be received by a computer.

The discussion of communications in this chapter is a simplistic one; there are many other technical complexities involved in computer communications. However, it is not necessary to understand all of these complexities to detect and investigate computer crime. You will find, though, that getting a technical expert to help, especially in investigations involving communications, is an absolute must. Consult the references in Appendix A for additional communications information.

Protecting Your Network Communications

There are many different ways to protect communications, including access control, cryptographic methods, firewall technology, and various physical measures.

Access Control

Access control is crucial to enforcing computer security in networked environments. Many systems use passwords as a means of access control. The model is simple: whoever presents the correct password in the correct context is granted access. It is therefore important that the knowledge of the correct password remains limited to the authorized user and the access control system.

Here are some basic rules for taking care of passwords:

- Don't ever write down your password and leave it near the computer or terminal.

- Don't create passwords that use your name or any other easy-to-guess information (see the sidebar for specific suggestions and warnings).

- Don't ever share your password with anyone, even once.

- Don't store passwords in your computer files.

If you are scrupulous about following these rules, password controls will work well. Unfortunately, too few people are careful enough about selecting difficult-to-crack passwords and protecting them.

Although most sites let users select their own passwords, many sites impose additional controls on these passwords. For example:

- *System-generated passwords.* Some systems require users to use passwords generated randomly by the system, rather than relying on user-selected ones. Although system software usually ensures that such passwords are at least pronounceable, they are usually hard to remember. Unfortunately, that causes many users to write them down, defeating the whole purpose of the approach.

- *Password length.* In general, longer passwords are more secure than shorter ones because they are harder to guess and because it takes longer to crack them. Many systems and sites impose a minimum length on passwords.

- *Password aging and expiration.* At many sites, users must change their passwords on a regular basis—perhaps once a month. This limits the vulnerability of any one password. If a user doesn't change his or her password after some warning, the password may expire.

- *Limited login attempts.* Most systems limit the number of times users can try to log in. A user can mistype the user ID or password a couple of times, but after that, the system may log the user (or the cracker) out.

- *Last login messages.* When users log in, many systems display the time of the last login—or the last unsuccessful login attempt. If a user hasn't logged in for

Good and Bad Passwords[1]

Do *not* choose any of the following as passwords:

- Your name or the name of your spouse, parent, pet, child, close friends, coworkers, favorite fantasy characters, boss, or anybody's name

- The name of the operating system you're using

- The hostname of your computer

- Your phone number

- Your license plate number

- Any part of your social security number

- Anybody's birth date

- Other information that is easily obtained about you

- Words such as wizard, guru, gandalf, and so on

- Any user name on the computer in any form (as is, capitalized, doubled, etc.)

- A word in an English or foreign dictionary

- A place

- A proper noun

- Passwords of all the same letter

- Simple patterns of letters on the keyboard, like "asdfgh"

- Any of the above spelled backwards

- Any of the above followed or prepended by a single digit

Do choose passwords that:

- Have both uppercase and lowercase letters

- Have digits and/or special characters as well as letters

- Are easy to remember, so they do not have to be written down

- Are at least eight characters long, and preferably longer

- Can be typed quickly, so somebody cannot follow what you type by looking over your shoulder

---

[1] These suggestions are from *Practical UNIX Security* by Simson Garfinkel and Gene Spafford, 2nd edition, (O'Reilly & Associates, 1995).

a while and sees a recent attempt, she will be tipped off that someone has been trying to crack the account.

- *Encrypted and shadow password files.* Most systems encrypt files containing passwords and keep these passwords in well-secured locations within the system, available only to system administrators and the password system itself.

- *Password locks.* System administrators can use locks to restrict certain users from logging in to certain systems (perhaps the user is under investigation), to lock accounts that haven't been used for an extended period of time, to restrict users to certain terminals, or to lock users out except during regular business hours.

- *Additional passwords.* For certain types of systems, users may need to enter both a "system" password and their own password. A second password may also be required for dial-in access. In some highly sensitive systems, two users may both need to enter their passwords before the system will allow entry.

- *Smart cards.* Some systems will require users to gain access to the system via smart cards that necessitate the use of a personal identification number (PIN) before being allowed to access their traditional passwords.

- *One-time (non-reusable) passwords.* A one-time password is used only once. Because it isn't stored for future use, it's very hard to steal. The S/Key system provides a freely available method that's very helpful for people who need to log in remotely to their systems. Using a cryptographically secure algorithm, the system generates a series of login sequences (perhaps 20 at a time), which it encodes as short words. These can be printed and carried by the user. The first time the user logs in, the first of the words is used to authenticate the user; the second time, the second word is used, and so on.

- *Time-based passwords.* With certain kinds of authentication systems (e.g., the SecureID by Security Dynamics), the password varies every minute or so. A smart card displays some function of the current time and the user's secret key. To get access, the user must enter a number based on her own key and the current time.

- *Challenge-response.* A number of systems support challenge-response systems in which the system generates a random challenge. Using a smart card (e.g., the ones manufactured by Digital Pathways or Enigma Logic), the user unlocks the card with her personal identification number and keys in this challenge. The card encrypts the challenge and displays the encrypted result. (See the discussion of encryption.) The user sends the result back to the system as a response. The system compares that response to the one it has calculated to see if the user will be allowed access. Figure 8-2 shows an example of how this works.

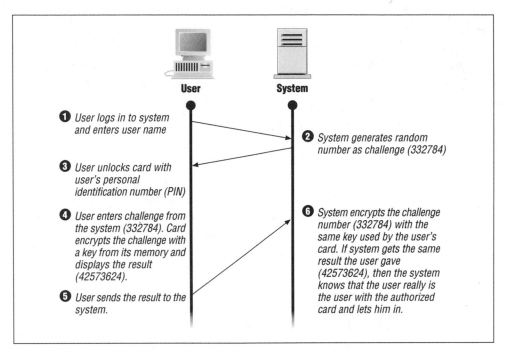

Figure 8-2. How a challenge-response system works

Cryptographic Methods

Scrambling or encrypting data is another approach to limiting access to sensitive information. Encryption is especially important when information is being transmitted across a network. Encryption transforms original information, called *plaintext*, into scrambled information, called *ciphertext*. The technique or rules selected for encryption—known as the *encryption algorithm*—determines how simple or how complex the process of transformation will be.

The Dangers of Password Sniffers

Although passwords work well within your local area network, even the most carefully chosen and protected passwords put you at risk on the Internet. Although you may never share your password, and although your local machine never displays it, your password may unfortunately be transmitted across networks when you use certain common Internet services, such as FTP (to transfer files) and Telnet (to log in remotely to another machine).

Password sniffer programs are able to monitor all traffic on certain parts of a network. Sniffer programs collect the start of each network connection (usually the first 128 bytes, but sometimes as much as the first 2048), and look for the unencrypted account names and passwords being transmitted as part of this traffic. Additional programs hide the existence of the sniffers.

With conventional encryption techniques (private key cryptography), a secret value called a *key* is used to encrypt a message before it is transmitted. Once data are encrypted, they can be decrypted only by someone who has the same key. With newer public key cryptography, two mathematically related keys are used to encrypt and decrypt a message. Public key cryptography also allows messages to be "signed" so the receiver will know, without question, who sent them.

Encryption has traditionally been used only in the military, in intelligence agencies, in federal law enforcement agencies, among defense contractors, and in the financial industry, although private citizens have recently begun to use encryption in greater numbers. The availability of free encryption packages, such as PGP, accounts for much of this increased usage.[*]

Cryptography is a complex topic, and we can't cover it in any detail in a book of this kind. Appendix A provides some references for further reading.

Protecting Network Cabling

Enforcing communications security requires physical measures, as well as the password controls and other online technologies discussed in this chapter. (Chapter 6 describes physical security in detail.) The cables that carry data are very vulnerable to intruders. It is a relatively simple matter to tap into cabling, and it is trivial to vandalize it. A vandal can disable a whole section of a network simply by cutting an Ethernet wire. Fiber optic cable is harder to cut but is more difficult to repair.

---

[*] Unfortunately, current Federal export regulations discourage other businesses and private individuals from using good encryption, thus depriving them of this strong protection.

Be sure to protect cables that carry data. One simple, though expensive, way to do this with a local area network is to run the network cable through physically secure locations. Instead of suspending Ethernet cable from the ceiling, you might run it through steel conduit. Some high-security installations use double-walled shielded conduits with pressurized gas between the layers; if the pressure drops (as a result of someone intruding on the pipe), a warning alarm goes off.

Shielding

All electrical equipment, from hair dryers to computers, emits electromagnetic radiation. As we discussed in Chapter 2, in "Eavesdropping on Emanations," one way to eavesdrop on a system or a communication is to intercept and decipher these emissions. With relatively inexpensive equipment, eavesdroppers are able to pick up signals every time a user strikes a computer key and, with a little work, figure out what data are being displayed or transmitted.

Radio frequency (RF) shielding can protect against the interception of electromagnetic emissions. Typically, a shield attenuates electromagnetic signals, conducting them to ground before they can escape. Shielding can protect computers, cabling, or even whole buildings. Shields are made of materials that are especially conductive—for example, copper. By shielding your cabling, you can greatly increase the security of your communications. The U.S. TEMPEST program tests such shielding and mandates its use for certain classified and sensitive government systems. In some circumstances, defense installations and contractors may be required to design whole buildings to be TEMPEST-certified.

Firewall Technology

A potentially effective way to protect a site from attackers while allowing its users some access to Internet services is to build a firewall. To be truly effective, a firewall must be configured, installed, and maintained with great care.

A firewall is a hardware/software approach that restricts access by forcing all network communications—those traveling from the internal network to the Internet and those traveling from the Internet to the internal network—to pass through the firewall. A firewall might also protect one part of your internal network from the rest of it. The hardware and software that makes up the firewall screens all traffic; it makes decisions about whether this traffic—email, file transfers, remote logins, and other such operations—may pass through. A simple firewall is illustrated in Figure 8-3.

Organizations configure their firewalls in a variety of ways. Some sites might use a firewall to completely block all access to and from the Internet. Others might limit access so only one particular machine or user can connect via the Internet to

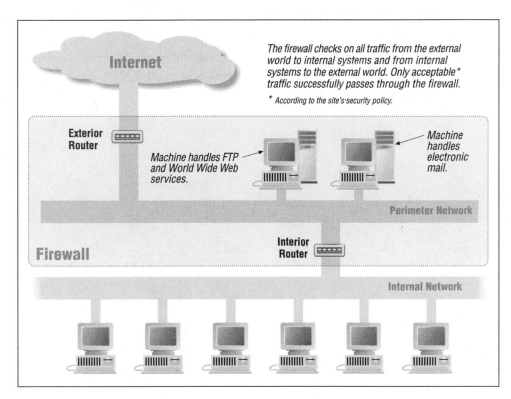

Figure 8-3. A firewall

machines outside the internal network. Some might enforce more elaborate rules that involve examining every message or communication that passes from inside to outside, or vice versa, to make sure that it matches the site's particular security policy. Despite its overall effectiveness, a firewall provides no protection from insiders or from an attacker who has already penetrated the firewall.

For more information on firewalls, see the references in Appendix A.

Communications Security Checklist

Here is a summary of specific steps that can be taken to improve communications security:

1. Use password controls.

2. Consider using additional authentication devices such as smart cards and one-time passwords.

3. Encrypt data, particularly data that are being transmitted across networks.

4. Know what networks your site may be connected to.

5. Protect your physical network cabling.

6. Shield cables.

7. Consider building a firewall to protect your site from the Internet, to separate two or more parts of your internal network, or to filter incoming and outgoing requests.

9

Operations Security

Operations security encompasses two aspects of computer security:

- Ways you can increase awareness of possible crimes among potential victims

- Ways you can keep a computer criminal from actually committing a crime

How do you increase awareness? In whatever ways possible, try to engage your employees and contract staff in your security program. Let them know that there are threats to security and that everyone shares the risk and the responsibility. Once you've analyzed the risks and vulnerabilities of your own site and systems, you'll have to determine how much information ought to be shared with employees. Obviously, certain classified and sensitive information has to be restricted, and this information will be shared only on a need-to-know basis. But, in general, there is a lot you can do to increase awareness and encourage reporting. We'll explore some of these ways later in this chapter. (See also the discussion of personnel security in Chapter 7.)

Operations security cannot exist in a vacuum. The only way it can be effective is if it is integrated into an organization's physical, personnel, and communications security programs. In fact, operations security is used to help make those programs more productive. Let's look at some examples.

Suppose that your physical security program includes strict procedures for controlling access to the building and the computer room. A clever and determined criminal could study that program and, in most cases, figure a way to defeat it. However, if the program also includes having security officers or management check on the building, the computer room, and the access control procedures themselves at unpredictable times, then the attacker won't be able to predict whether his intrusion will be successful.

Here are some simple ways that operations security can work with your other security procedures:

- Change the passwords for your computer system frequently, but change them according to an unpredictable schedule, not simply once a month.

- If your building is normally an open one, control access to it for several hours a week—and don't let anyone know in advance when those hours will be.

- Disguise operational patterns so they are difficult to predict. For example, instead of running a program to check for unauthorized programs each night at 2:00 A.M., run it at random times during each 24-hour period, and give the program a different name each time.

- Take active measures to protect the information needed by computer criminals to plan a crime. (See the discussion of computer and communications security approaches in Chapter 8.)

- Formulate ways to detect that computer crimes have occurred or are likely to occur.

Here, operations security reinforces the system and physical security measures in place, and it increases the risk to the computer criminal. Unless the criminal is targeting your site in particular, he is likely to go down the street and look for a different target—one that is more predictable and therefore represents less of a risk.

Let's put this advice in the context of network security. If an intruder knows when the system operator is monitoring a computer system, then he will obviously attempt to break in at other times. But if the system operator directly monitors the system on a random basis, the cracker won't be able to tell if the attempted intrusion is being watched. What about a system that is electronically monitored 24 hours a day? Wouldn't such a system catch the cracker anyway? Unfortunately, no. By the time the intrusion is noted by someone reading the daily logs, the intruder may be long gone and the damage done. Also, the audit trail may be so out of date or complex by now that the intruder will never be identified.

NOTE
There are some systems that have both ongoing electronic monitoring and software alarms. These alarms alert system managers and system operators in the event of attempts to thwart access controls.

Planning Operations Security

What are the key elements of an operations security program?

1. Identify the information a computer criminal would like to get from your particular system. What is the special value of your system or its data? For example, computer game manufacturers know that early versions of new games are especially attractive targets.

2. Determine the methods the computer criminal could use to get that information. Does the criminal need to physically break into the building? Can he get the data via a network? What kinds of special privileges would he need to access the data?

3. Develop operations procedures to counter the computer criminal's methods, prevent his access to that information, and detect any breaches of security.

4. Engage employees in the program. Your employees need to know that operations security—and computer security in general—is an important part of their jobs.

Thinking Like a Computer Criminal

To develop an effective operations security program, you must first learn to think like a computer criminal:

> What are your motives in attacking this particular target?
>
> How skilled do you need to be to be successful in this attack?
>
> What information are you after?
>
> How will you try to get that information?

The Adversarial Computer Crime Matrix included in Chapter 3 can help suggest answers to these questions.

Developing Employee Awareness

As mentioned in Chapter 7, *Personnel Security*, an essential part of operations security is that the people who work with systems need to understand why such security is necessary, what the methods are that allow computer criminals to break into sites and systems, and what they personally can do to prevent such break-ins.

There are two reasons why employee awareness is important. First, there are ways in which employees can take action to keep intruders out of a system; for example, they can be careful not to write down passwords and not to throw sensitive paper reports in the trash. Second, if they are alert, employees may be able to recognize when people are trying to compromise information.

How would your employees know if someone were attacking the site or the computer? Make sure they watch out for oddities in their own accounts and files. Does the system report unsuccessful logins to users? Here's an example:

```
Sun OS UNIX (kirby)
login: joe
Password:
Last login: Mon Feb 27 08:18:30 from 140.186.64.147
Last unsuccessful login: Mon Feb 27 11:16:42 from 140.186.82.132
```

Encourage employees to check to be sure that such messages accurately reflect their own use of the system. For example, if they were away for the weekend, but the system reported that the last login was Saturday, something is wrong. Likewise, if the system reports a series of unsuccessful logins, and the employees are sure this didn't happen to them, something is wrong. Employees need to know that such information is important and that it suggests a possible attack on the system; they also need to know who to tell about problems of this kind.

Where Do Computer Criminals Get Information?

There are five basic ways that computer criminals get the information they need to commit their crimes:

1. Simply observing equipment and events

2. Using information that is openly available

3. Dumpster diving (also called trashing or scavenging)

4. Compromising systems

5. Compromising people

In the following sections, we'll outline the actions of the computer criminal and then note what the good guys should look for.

Simple Observation

Computer criminals have been known to simply walk through work areas, noting passwords taped to the sides of desks, the locations of computers or CRTs that are left on but unattended, and the procedures or protocols used to access different programs. Sometimes, computer criminals pretend to be repair or maintenance people, or pretend to be delivering a package to the office. In one case we know about, a group of young delinquents used binoculars to spy on an organization from across the street. In another case, they simply walked, unchallenged, into a room where a good deal of computer equipment was located and copied the telephone numbers that were clearly written on the lines where they came into the modem. Nothing fancy.

What to Do . . .

There are two ways to counter this threat. First, look around. Check out what an intruder could see, and then take pains to better protect the equipment and information. Make sure that system users don't leave passwords, telephone numbers, and other information where it is readily visible. In some organizations, this common-sense rule is violated all the time—typically because employees don't understand its importance and because managers don't enforce it until after they've suffered a major loss. Keep in mind that criminals may go to great lengths to observe operational patterns and to gain access to sensitive information.

Second, as we've said before, include your employees in the program. Encourage all staff to make suggestions about operational patterns that could be observed by unauthorized personnel. Motivate them to be alert to persons who are too inquisitive or nosy, people wandering in areas where they do not have any business, and especially to individuals who are obviously observing operations patterns or other potentially valuable information. Generally, employees should not confront potential perpetrators in a hostile way. A friendly "Can I help you?" or "How are you today?" will let people know that they have been noticed. As soon as possible, employees should report suspicious situations to a supervisor or to the organization's security department.

Using Openly Available Information

The cracker community is an active one, and its members are known for sharing information and tools with each other. Cracker bulletin boards, Internet Relay Chat (IRC), and online newsgroups, conference groups, and forums are some ways crackers share passwords, telephone credit card numbers, specific operating system bugs and vulnerabilities, and actual cracking programs. There are also some publications (both online and offline), such as *Phrack* and *2600*, that crackers use to keep each other up to date. These publications are often read by others in the computer security and law enforcement communities. Be aware that, although you may find useful information in these publications, they often contain incorrect and misleading information—sometimes on purpose. Be cautious in using these publications as sources.

Many of the online sources used by crackers are the same sources used by others in the computer and computer security communities. There are many legitimate and very helpful technical newsgroups and archives of tools, documents, and information of all kinds which technical people publish in an effort to inform their peers and stimulate discussion. Online newsgroups like *comp.risks* and *alt.secu-*

rity.cu-digest contain useful information for computer security practitioners which can, naturally enough, be used by crackers as well.

In addition to these online sources, there is a tremendous amount of relevant information available through openly available print publications. Some suspected cases of espionage, both industrial and international, have turned out to be the result of criminals simply finding things out, about systems and organizations, from newspaper clippings. A good deal of useful information is available to those who want it and can interpret it. Computer criminals know how to seek this information and how to make valuable use of it.

Documentation for computer systems contains a good deal of information that may be of use to computer criminals, who are usually able to buy computer manuals for different systems and use them to identify system vulnerabilities. Espionage agents also often use openly available information to identify target organizations that may have information of value to them and then to learn all they can about these organizations, so they can penetrate them.

There are several books on the market that tell you how to use computer databases and search techniques to identify and learn about organizations you may be interested in. A recent computer magazine included an article called "Get the Goods on Competitors, It's All On-Line." What we used to refer to as *industrial espionage* is now called *competitor intelligence*. The more openly available information people collect, the better able they will be to figure out how to get more sensitive information.

Remember these two rules of information analysis:

- Often, the combination of unimportant pieces of data leads to valuable information. (See the discussion of data inference in Chapter 2.)

- With the use of computers, the collection of inferential processes is considerably faster than with conventional methods.

What to Do . . .

In an open society, it is difficult to keep secrets, and yet the most effective way to counter this threat is to minimize the amount of sensitive information that is released into the public domain. You might also keep your own file on the information you know has been made publicly available. At least this way, you will know exactly what information is available to the public and may then be able to instigate security measures, such as random checks and inspection, to minimize the potential use of openly available information.

Again, employee awareness is an important countermeasure. All of the employees should keep an eye out for news in the press about their own organization. Make sure they know to let supervisors and security staff know if they see anything in the press that they think might be used by a criminal.

Dumpster Diving

As we've discussed, *dumpster diving*, also called *trashing* or *scavenging*, is an activity that has special significance to computer criminals and law enforcement officers. It is exactly what is sounds like: going through someone's trash. Because the courts have ruled that individuals lose their expectation of privacy once trash is placed at the street, going through a suspect's trash for evidence has proven to

fective for computer
curb. They simply
ften find computer
and other valuable

Tom Sorauf

PROXY

Extension x4727

nformation before it
verything before it
ffices do not have
er meant to handle
uter manual with a
at a time.)

dumpster or trash
on may prevent a
y guards may even
a secure location.

system to find the
alk freely around
tecting passwords,
s, all contribute to
iscussed examples

urity measures we
assword and other
fficult for intruders

to penetrate a system. If such measures are not in place, the cracker will have a field day.

Compromising People

Often, the easiest way for a computer criminal to obtain information about a system is to get it from someone who has access to that system: no time-consuming hacking activity, no messy diving through dumpsters—just a small bribe or piece of coercion.

Your employees must be aware that such overtures are a possibility; sometimes, they will be overt. Recall the case of the Eastern Bloc diplomat who openly recruited a cracker to break into a system, bribed trash collectors to deliver materials discarded by a defense contractor, and tried to get cooperation from employees. Usually, such contacts are more discreet. The overture may come from anyone—another employee who is already on the payroll of an outside organization or who is looking to pay back the company for some real or imagined offense, a contractor, a vendor, or a complete stranger.

What to Do . . .

Warn your employees to be alert to outsiders—both old friends and new—who ask about the intricacies of their organization's computer system and computer security policies. Employees should know that they must not respond to these questions and that they must report such attempts to obtain information to their supervisor or security department. (See the section on "Social Engineering" in Chapter 2.)

Make sure that your employees know that they must also be alert to unusual activity on the system—for example, the computer takes longer than usual to respond to commands, or programs don't seem to be running properly. They should also immediately report any suspicious problems.

Developing an Operations Security Program

One reason that we recommend that you adopt an operations security program is that it can be implemented for a very small investment. Time is needed, but not expensive equipment or consultants. As mentioned earlier, there are three steps to establishing an initial operations security program:

1. Identify the information the computer criminal might want from your particular computer system.
2. Determine what methods the criminal might use to get that information.

3. Develop countermeasures to prevent these methods from being effective.

You will sometimes see more complex operations security models with many more steps, but they all boil down to these three.

What Is the Information?

In law enforcement circles, the information that a computer criminal would want to compromise is referred to as the *essential elements of information*. We have acronyms for everything in the computer security business, so we call this the EEI.

Let's assume we have to develop an operations security program for a government office with an IBM mainframe system and a number of CRT terminals. The system is on line with other systems around the United States. A good way to begin developing the program is to involve your key managers and operations staff in the process. It is also helpful to include representatives from the various user communities that your organization serves. Get these people together and brainstorm about exactly what a computer criminal would like to get from your organization. Spend one whole morning talking together, listing all the EEI that participants can think of. Remember that in brainstorming sessions there is no evaluation and there are no bad ideas. Write everything down, preferably on chart paper, and tape it to the walls where everybody can see it and think further about it.

Next, break for lunch. After lunch, refine the EEI list. Eliminate duplications, add things that were not mentioned during the morning, and so on. By the end of the day, you should have a comprehensive list of the information a criminal would like to have. Now do two things. First, secure the list as you would any classified document. Second, forget about what you just did for the next week.

A week later, pick up the project again. Conduct a second brainstorming session. Here, the focus is figuring out how a computer criminal could gain access to your site and data. First, ask if anyone has additional EEI he or she thought of after the last session. Usually, there will be a couple of valuable additions.

How Can an Intruder Get In?

During the second brainstorming session, the objective is to identify methods the bad guys could use to get the information on the EEI list. Spend the morning talking together, and then break for lunch. During the afternoon session, refine your list of potential methods. Now secure both lists and spend another week away from this process.

The reason a week is allowed between brainstorming sessions is to permit the brain to incubate on the process. When you return for the second session, someone is bound to have thought of something important that was left out during the first session. The same thing will happen when you return for the third session.

How Can You Prevent It?

During the third brainstorming session, the objective is to develop a list of countermeasures that may eliminate or decrease the effectiveness of the methods listed during the second session. Brainstorm all morning and then break for lunch. After lunch, refine your list of countermeasures.

Putting the Plan into Action

Now that you have the raw material, appoint an operations security committee within the organization. It will be the responsibility of this committee to take the lists to management and to put the suggestions into action. When recommending countermeasures, remember the value of randomness and unpredictability.

Remember: Operations security is, by its very nature, dynamic. The whole point is to change your methods and approaches so to keep your opponents off balance. For this reason, your EEI, your methods of compromise, and your countermeasures will have to change constantly. Make sure you build in systems to monitor the effectiveness of your operations security measures and to make adjustments when necessary. At the very least, reevaluate the entire program once a year, or whenever a major change occurs within the organization.

When Investigating . . .

Operations security is a simple, yet effective, add-on to other types of computer security. Without operations security, everything else you do becomes predictable and therefore subject to compromise.

If you are investigating a computer crime, it's important to assess the operations security measures that were, or were not, in place when the crime was committed. For one thing, assessing these measures may yield information on the methods used by the perpetrators. For another, you may be able to advise the victim organization on how it can improve its crime prevention efforts for little, if any, financial investment.

Ongoing Operations Security

A key part of operations security involves keeping the program going. Don't formulate a plan, train employees, and then think you're done. Security is an ongoing process. You need to continue watching for breaches in security, continue improving your methods of prevention and detection, and continue training employees and system users. The next chapter, *Planning How to Handle a Computer Crime*, describes detection measures.

Handling Computer Crime

This part of the book describes how to plan for, detect, investigate, and prosecute a computer crime.

Chapter 10, *Planning How to Handle a Computer Crime,* discusses ways of detecting computer crimes, assembling a crisis management team, and considering sensitive issues (e.g., should you bait a trap for a computer criminal?) before a computer crime actually occurs.

Chapter 11, *Investigating a Computer Crime,* outlines procedures to follow in investigating a computer crime, describes the investigative team, discusses the preparation of a search warrant, and states rules for collecting and protecting evidence.

Chapter 12, *Prosecuting a Computer Crime,* profiles the special problems involved in describing computer crimes in the courtroom, summarizes issues such as the the best evidence rule, discovery, and protective orders, and suggestions for testifying about computer crimes.

10

Planning How to Handle a Computer Crime

The title for this chapter sounds pretty negative, doesn't it? But computer crimes do occur, try as we do to prevent them. How will you know if a crime does occur? Because computer crimes don't always result in obvious physical destruction, it may take a while for your organization even to realize that it's been attacked—and by the time you find out, it may be too late to learn anything about the intruder. And what will you do when you *do* find out? If information has been stolen and programs compromised, it's critical that your system and data be examined immediately, and measures taken to restore backups. Are you prepared to spring into action?

When a computer crime does occur, it's too late to do a good job of managing the crisis that has occurred—especially a crisis as devastating and far-reaching as many computer crimes can be. Remember this adage? "When unsure and filled with doubt, run in circles, scream, and shout." The time for planning is *before* the crisis occurs. If you have a plan in place and a team that is ready to respond, handling the crisis will be far easier and the overall damage will be far less.

Contingency planning, crisis management, and *disaster recovery* are the various names given to this process of planning for, detecting, and cleaning up after a disaster of some kind. Although your organization ought to have plans for a wider range of contingencies and disasters, ranging from fires to kidnappings to computer fraud, this chapter focuses on planning for and responding to computer crime.

Planning for a computer crime involves a number of different activities:

- Put various types of detection measures in place so you will be able to tell as quickly as possible when a computer crime does occur.

- Assemble a team of people who will respond to any incidents.

- Figure out how that team will respond to different types of situations. Some computer crimes are major and some are not. Many organizations establish plans for different "threat levels." Threat level 1 might be a massive attack on a computer site or system—for example, a bombing, a deletion of system files, or a major shutdown or slowdown of all system activities. Threat level 4 might be a pattern of random snooping on the system—unsuccessful attempts to log in, for example. Threat levels 2 and 3 might be somewhere in the middle. In theory, everyone on the team knows ahead of time how and when to respond to each type of threat level.

- Whatever plans are put into place, be sure that they will change from time to time. As we describe in Chapter 9, *Operations Security,* it's important to keep possible intruders off guard by doing spot checks, changing the pattern of security audits, and otherwise shaking things up. This way, computer criminals won't be able to predict whether and how their actions will be monitored as they try to break into the system.

Every computer crime is different. Although we provide some guidance in Chapters 11 and 12, there is no formula for investigation and prosecution. However, there is one piece of advice that applies in every single case: document what is happening. Write down everything the perpetrator did, everything that is done during the investigation—by every person on the team, and everything else that remotely touches on the incident. You'll need this information to prosecute the crime, to figure out if you did the best you could during this crisis, and to guide your actions during future incidents.

NOTE

Do not document your findings and activities on the system that has been attacked or on any networked system. People often make this mistake. In many investigations, system managers send each other email comparing notes and exchanging information about the ongoing incident. Sometimes, they also collect system log files into their home directories for analysis. Unfortunately, the same crackers who broke into the system in the first place can often read this email and potentially modify the log files.

Finding Out About a Computer Crime

There is rarely a "smoking gun" with computer crimes; in other words, the crimes are not always obvious. How can you tell if a computer crime has occurred?

- You might catch the suspect in the act. In the simplest case, a burglar alarm goes off, and you catch someone breaking into your building or computer room. In other cases, you might detect someone breaking into your system. Here's a simple case. Suppose that you're the system operator and the only one who has rights to a certain privileged account on the system (e.g., the UNIX superuser), but you notice that someone else is logged in to that account from a dial-up terminal. Clearly, there is an unauthorized user on the system.

- You might deduce that a crime has occurred because of evidence left behind. If a physical break-in has occurred, equipment might be damaged or missing. If a system has been cracked, you might find that files have been damaged or that new and unauthorized passwords have been added to the system. Your system's log files may show that an intruder has accessed systems or data.

- You might be informed that a crime has occurred. Sometimes, crackers will tell you themselves that they have broken into your system. Often, they will brag to their friends or describe their exploits on bulletin board systems. In cases involving spies and professional criminals, informants may offer to finger the intruders for a payoff or leniency in another case. Sometimes, you'll be told that a break-in has occurred, but not who did it. You may find out that someone has broken into your system only after the perpetrator has used your system as a gateway to some other system; your first alert may be a message (perhaps a rather nasty one) from the system operator of that other system. Sometimes, police or other law enforcement officials may inform you that, during their investigation of a case, they've found passwords or other access codes for your system. Although there may be no evidence yet that your system has been attacked, this is certainly a tipoff that you are vulnerable.

In some of these cases, it will be all too obvious that a computer crime has occurred or is in progress; in other cases, you will know only if you have set up appropriate detection measures.

Do You Know Who's Watching You?

Several recent tests have shown how rarely attacked sites even know they've been attacked. The CERT Coordination Center conducted an experiment[1] in which they probed a number of sites connected to the Internet (with the permission of the sites). These probes were experimental intrusions into an internal network in which activity was observed, but no data were damaged or stolen. Only about 2 percent of the sites probed were capable of detecting the intrusion. The DoD test we cited at the beginning of Chapter 1 showed a similar result: Only about 5 percent of attacked sites detected intrusion.

---

[1] Reported in *Computerworld*, January 30, 1995, page 12.

Setting Up Detection Measures

Various types of measures can be set up to detect computer crimes at your site and in your system; some are expensive and high-tech, and others are inexpensive and very simple. Detection measures fall into two general categories: proactive and reactive.

Proactive Measures

Proactive measures detect crimes before or as they are being committed. To protect your physical facility, you will need standard equipment such as burglar alarms. You will also need software that works in a similar way. Just as a burglar alarm goes off as a thief first enters a building, detecting the attempted crime before the burglar has even stolen anything, this software detects intruders roaming around your system.

You can get intrusion-detection software that notifies the system operator or security officer that an intrusion into the system is being attempted (e.g., by sounding an alarm and displaying a message on that person's terminal or workstation). Such software may also notify the appropriate people when someone within the system tries to access information that he is not authorized to access—for example, payroll files, classified data, or sensitive company planning documents. Many systems keep track of all login attempts—successful and unsuccessful; some also notify the operator or security officer when someone attempts to enter the system but repeatedly enters the wrong password; usually, systems allow up to three tries before automatically disconnecting.

Remember, though, none of these measures will work against a cracker who is using a valid account—one that he obtained, for example, by cracking your password file. (He might have been able to do this by exploiting system bugs in ways that didn't set off alarms.)

Reactive Measures

Reactive measures are designed to detect ongoing crimes and crimes that have already been committed. Such measures include performing regular audits of the system and checking the system logs generated automatically by the system. Of course, you might also stumble on a computer crime simply by discovering that equipment, disks and tapes, printouts, and actual money are missing as a result of a computer crime. See the discussion of system logs in "Examining Log Files and Other Evidence" later in this chapter.

Forming a Crisis Management Team

When a computer crime occurs, the first thing to do is to call your organization's crisis management team together. A crisis is no time to form this team. You will need to figure out who should be on this team—and how they will work together—before any incidents occur.

You can't handle a computer crime with one or two people. You need technical help, law enforcement assistance, and auditing expertise. Although organizations differ in the number of people they can commit to a project, we recommend that the following members make up any crisis management team—each plays a particular role in managing, investigating, and understanding the crime.

- Manager
- System operator (may also be a system manager or system programmer)
- Auditor
- Investigator
- Technical adviser

Additional team members may be needed in certain situations. For example, if classified information has been compromised, then your team will be joined by someone from the FBI's National Security Division. If your organization has a security officer, that officer will help identify where and how security was breached.

Who Are You Going to Call?

At least one member of the crisis management team is from a law enforcement agency. But which agency? With a computer crime, it's not always clear. Possible players include the FBI, the U.S. Secret Service, several other federal agencies, and local law enforcement agencies such as a police department, sheriff's office, district attorney/prosecutor, or state attorney's office. Check out the section in Chapter 4 called "Who Has Jurisdiction?" For a brief summary of this issue. Call your U.S. Attorney if you need more information. But do it before you are in the middle of a crisis. Make sure you know which law enforcement agency has jurisdiction over your organization or the different types of incidents that may occur there, so you won't waste valuable time when one does occur.

Once you have a team in place, don't wait for an emergency to find out how well it works. You can put together some training exercises that will test the team's ability to cope with computer crimes. Give them a scenario of a typical computer crime and let them work out how they would handle the crime on their own system.

NOTE

A response team generally needs very clear authority allowing them to act and specifying exactly who should report to whom. During a security incident, actual management decisions are often made in a crisis environment in which every last detail can't be cleared with upper management. The members of the team must be able to make these decisions, and upper management must be willing to stick with them.

Manager

The manager leads the crisis management team and decides how to respond to the incident. This person is someone who can assess both the value of the compromised information and the potential impact of the loss on the organization. This individual also takes responsibility for documenting all of the events that have taken place.

System Operator

The system operator (this person could also be a system manager or a system programmer) must know his or her way around the system better than anyone else. For crimes in progress, this person will try to track the criminal through the maze of events or system connections and will monitor all system activity. For crimes that have already taken place, the system operator will try to reconstruct the crime. Whether these efforts are successful or unsuccessful, this person must take responsibility for documenting everything that has happened.

Auditor

The auditor has two main functions. First, he or she helps the system operator follow the trail of the crime. Because this person has the background to know how to use the audit trails and logs built into the system, he or she may be able to use these tools to find out more about the crime and the criminal.

Second, the auditor takes responsibility for determining the economic impact of the incident. Exactly what is the loss in dollars to the organization? It's important, for legal reasons, to know. Remember that the loss encompasses more than just tangible losses of equipment or software. The auditor needs to put a value on the information that has been stolen, lost, or damaged, on the productive time lost on the system, and on the time needed to figure out the extent of the loss and repair the damage.

In most small businesses, research labs, and educational institutions, there is no separate auditor; the manager and the system operator share this function.

Investigator

The criminal investigator comes from the law enforcement agency that has jurisdiction over the crime. This person makes sure that all evidence is collected and documented in accordance with legal requirements. The investigator also makes sure that none of the actions taken after the break-in compromise the investigation or hinder prosecution. For example, he or she checks that all evidence is labeled properly, that witnesses are identified, and so on. As we discuss in Chapter 11, in certain types of crimes, the "investigator" may actually be an entire team of investigators.

Technical Advisor

The technical advisor typically comes from the same law enforcement agency as the investigator. This person knows both technology and criminal investigation. As we discuss in Chapter 11, investigating a computer crime is new to many investigators. It may not be at all obvious to them that turning off a computer may cause all evidence to be lost, that disks and tapes can be damaged simply by heat or cold, and that it may be possible to find the criminal by engaging him in an online conversation. This is where the technical advisor comes in. This person takes responsibility for collecting evidence in a way that ensures its safety, and advises on whether equipment can be turned off, moved, and shipped. The technical advisor will also work closely with the system operator on examining system logs and other system activity that may help explain the crime and lead to a suspect.

What to Do If the Intruder Is on the System

There is a big difference between a computer crime that is over and done with and one that is continuing. You will have a decision to make if you find that someone is actually still on the system at the time you discover evidence of intrusion. Plan ahead of time what response makes sense for your organization for different types of incidents. If you have a plan for how to proceed at such a chaotic time, your system operator or whoever else finds the intruder will have some guidelines for what to do next.

If you find out that an intruder is loose in your system, what are your choices?

1. *Disconnect.* You could immediately break the connection by disconnecting the modem or network connection or by simply turning off the computer.

2. *Trace.* You could try to trace the connection, perhaps even trying to keep the intruder on the line to give you a better chance to track him down. (It's much easier to trace an active connection than one that has been disconnected. It's also easier to clean up after an intruder if you have some idea of what he's been doing.) There may be a safe way that you can covertly monitor the intruder's actions without the intruder knowing that he has been detected and that you can keep his intrusion from doing serious damage to your system or data.

3. *Talk.* You could actually engage the intruder in conversation; some systems give you the ability to do this with system functions like UNIX's *write* and *talk* commands. This may sound foolish, but some intrusions are casual explorations. If you feel confident that this intrusion falls into that category, you might want to take this approach. But you should also be aware that a direct threat of this kind might simply egg on the intruder to further attacks. In any case, before you confront an intruder, make sure that you have protected your system from the intruder's return.

4. *Ignore.* You could ignore the situation and hope it never happens again. Obviously, we don't recommend this choice, but it's surprising how many organizations go this route.

NOTE

This discussion of what to do if an intruder is still on the system demonstrates the value of calling in an investigator as early as possible. Sometimes, system administrators may do a lot of leg work, collecting information and even tracking down intruders, only to find that their evidence can't be used in court. They may even land *themselves* in court! A trained investigator can advise how to proceed.

Shut Down or Stay Connected?

There is a good deal of controversy over whether it is better to shut down the connection or try to trace the intruder. This is an issue you will have to explore with your management, system staff, law enforcement agency, and legal advisors.

Briefly, here are the practical pros and cons. If you shut down the system, the criminal will know he has been detected. Thus, he may disappear before you will have any chance of tracing the connection and possibly identifying him. On the other hand, you will have saved your system from any further damage—this time. If you allow the intruder to stay on the system, he may do further damage or may succeed in getting valuable information, money, or other assets.

There is a legal side to this as well. There is genuine disagreement in the computing and legal communities about what the appropriate response should be. Not enough cases have yet gone to court. If you know that an intruder is on your system, and yet allow him to stay, might your organization be liable for further losses of data? Even if you think keeping the intruder on-line represents your best shot at catching him, can you risk the loss of your users' and clients' data? And what about other systems that the intruder might be able to access through your system? Can you make a decision that might result in losses not only to your own organization but to other organizations as well?

On the other side of this, might you actually have a responsibility to do everything in your power to catch the intruder—not only for your own organization's sake but for the sake of others who might be attacked? After all, if you kick the intruder off your system, he is unlikely to give up completely. Remember that an attacker may have compromised many accounts on your system; he might just move on to another account. If you lock him out completely, he'll probably just move on to another system. Shouldn't you do all you can to stop him now?

These thorny issues have not yet been resolved—inside or outside the courts.

NOTE

The most conservative approach, from a legal point of view, is probably to shut down the system. It is possible that a system administrator who knows about and allows an intruder on a pirate site to stay up and running for any substantial amount of time might incur civil liability.

Tracing an Intruder

There are various approaches to tracing intruders. Your log files may indicate the terminal and line numbers from which the intruder is connecting to your system. By finding out what system the intruder is coming from, you have a chance of being able to find him.

Remember, though, most intruders are wily enough to cover their tracks. You may indignantly call the system administrator at the college computer center in your town—your logs and on-line monitoring programs may clearly indicate that the cracker is connecting from their machines—only to find that they've been attacked, just as you have. The cracker may actually be a continent away, hopping from site to site and masquerading as he travels electronically. Figure 8-1 illustrates the many connections there may be between you and the cracker.

Many standard features in most operating systems (e.g., *finger* in UNIX) allow you to discover information about the users who are logged into your system— what terminal number they are logged in from, what system and/or network connection they are using, what programs they are running, what files they are accessing, and so on. There are also software products, some commercial and some public domain, that let you find out additional information. These may be helpful in discovering what account your intruder is using, and what he is doing.

There is also some equipment that can help you monitor and trace the intruders. Some of this equipment simply records the session so you can monitor an intruder's activities; the output provides evidence in the event that the case is ever prosecuted. For example, by installing serial line analyzers, recorders, and printers on all incoming ports and by installing software such as MILTEN Spy—and then using PCs to monitor this equipment—you will be able to capture every one of the intruder's keystrokes, including passwords, filenames, and the rest of it.

NOTE

Monitor the line, and print everything that takes place on it, but be sure to set up the monitoring and printing in a way that is not visible from the system itself so the intruder won't be alerted to the fact that he has been detected.

Other equipment, such as the pen registers, dialed number recorders, and trap and trace devices we described in Chapter 7 can actually be used to trace the physical connection. Source address loggers are software versions of these devices, which log the network addresses of originating communications.

The federal Electronic Communications Privacy Act (ECPA),[*] prohibits all monitoring of wire, oral, and electronic communications unless specific statutory exceptions apply. To wiretap a telephone call, you must show that you need to protect against abuse of a communications system. After you've filed a crime report with law enforcement, the prosecutor's or U.S. Attorney's office will have to approve the telephone trap request (similar to a search warrant) before it goes to a judge for a signature.

System administrators must be very careful not to listen in on lines or to monitor email in violation of the ECPA. If they do, they could incur criminal or civil liability.

NOTE

Consult your legal advisor for detailed information. This area is a complex and frequently changing one.

When you try to trace an intruder via a network, be aware that he may be using many other computers on the network as well. One computer may be a gateway

---

[*] See the text of the Electronic Communications Privacy Act (18 USC, Chapter 119, Section 2510/2511 et seq.) and the Digital Telephony Act (Public Law 103-414) in Part IV of this book.

to another computer or to another whole network. You will probably want to work with the system administrators of these other computers. By better understanding what kind of data the intruder is looking for on these different machines, you may better understand the intruder's motivation and level of expertise. By pooling your knowledge and resources with other people—system administrators, network providers, and perhaps a network specialist who can help you navigate the networks—you may together succeed in tracking down the intruder.

Tracing the intruder across computer networks can be a major challenge. You will need to plan well ahead of time so that when the time comes, you will know who to contact and how. Because wiretap equipment may need to be used, you must obtain the appropriate court orders. You will also need the cooperation of the carrier and the network provider. And, because the criminal may be operating across national borders, you may even have to obtain court orders and cooperation on more than one continent. It may seem a daunting prospect, but as more and more computer crime takes place, the people you'll be contacting are probably growing more sympathetic with the issue and more willing and able to cooperate quickly.

When Investigating. . .

To successfully prosecute a computer crime, you may need physical evidence, such as telephone bills, printouts of information, or actual stolen data that have been found on the person of the perpetrator, or some other type of physical evidence. The computers themselves, and any witnesses who observed the break-in or the effects of the break-in, will also be useful evidence. Chapters 11 and 12 discuss the specifics of evidence gathering and the use of the evidence at prosecution time.

Baiting a Trap

Should you ever bait a trap for an intruder—either to keep one on the line or to attract one in the first place? You may find that the same intruder breaks into your system time after time, looking through files, possibly in search for particular types of information. You may be able to use this pattern to your advantage. If your intruder appears to be interested in defense files, for example, perhaps you can entice him to look at files labeled Star Wars Status or Doomsday Response Plan. (OK, be a little more subtle). This is one way that Cliff Stoll tracked his wily hacker in *The Cuckoo's Egg*.

You might be able to use the enticement of your phony files to keep the intruder connected long enough for you to find out more about him. If you've obtained the appropriate court orders and permissions, you may be able to actually trace the connection using equipment that has been installed for the purpose. Using phony data in this way may serve another purpose as well; if you have contrived certain information and the suspect is later found in possession of it, you have strong evidence that he has stolen it.

NOTE

The use of bait and the tracing of connections in general have legal implications. We advise you to talk to a lawyer or to your law enforcement representatives before you take any actions such as these. You want whatever evidence you obtain in this way to hold up in court.

Examining Log Files and Other Evidence

Most systems produce log files as part of their everyday operation. Whenever a certain type of event occurs in the system, information about the event (including who initiated it, what the date and time are, and what files, if any, were affected) is logged to these files. The purpose of these logs is not to catch criminals—they are simply a record of system activity. However, the information they contain can be very helpful in figuring out the extent of a computer crime. They can also be used as evidence in computer crime cases. For example, an entry is made in a log file whenever:

- A user logs into the system or attempts to log in.

- A user opens a file or attempts to open one for which he does not have the necessary authorization.

- A user runs a program—for example, one that changes privileges on the system or exports data to an off-site device.

The format and quantity of data in log files differ widely from system to system, depending on the operating system and network connections. Highly secure systems may include a good deal of additional information in the logs. Many systems let you customize the logs—to turn various types of logging on and off, to specify the type of information you want logged (e.g., you might want to log information only for certain users, who you may suspect of wrongdoing, or only certain files, which contain highly sensitive information), and to specify the device on which you want the log files to reside. Plan ahead of time how you will use these log files in the event of a computer crime.

Figure 10-1 shows an excerpt from a log file.

System Log
Events Logged on May 10, 1995

Time	Subject		Event (* = Violation)	Data	Recorder	
	Jobname	UID @WS			Jobname	UID @WS
16:02:08.2		SRH 84	CHANGE ACCESS LISTS CHANGE ACL	File: @1602079 Lib: WPPSRH Vol: SYS400 Owner: SRH Fileclass: New: ( ) PART 1 OF 1		SRH 84
16:02:08.9		SRH 84	CHANGE FILE ATTRIBUTES	File: @1602079 Lib: WPPSRH Vol: SYS400 Owner: SRH Fileclass: Attribute: EXPIRATIONDATE Old: 91130 New: 91129		SRH 84
16:02:09.0		SRH 84	OPEN FOR POSSIBLE MOD	File: @1602079 Lib: WPPSRH Vol: SYS400 Owner: SRH Fileclass: Device: DISK Open Mode: OPEN FOR IO MODE		SRH 84
16:02:20.6		SRH 84	RENAME	OFile: @1602079 OLib: WPPSRH OVol: SYS400 NFile: AF010838 NLib: WPPSRH Owner: SRH Fileclass: Type: RENAME OF A FILE		SRH 84
16:02:20.7		SRH 84	CLOSE	File: AF010838 Lib: WPPSRH Vol: SYS400 Device: DISK 257 I/O cnt: 2 Open Mode: OPEN FOR IO MODE		SRH 84
16:02:39.5		SRH 84	SCRATCH	File: @160237 Lib: #027000W Vol: SYSCAP Owner: SRH Fileclass:		SRH 84
16:02:42.4		SRH 84	PROGRAM INVOCATION	File: WPEMUSSL Lib: @SYSTEM@ Vol: SYSCAP Owner: WJT Fileclass:		SRH 84
16:02:42.8		SRH 84	OPEN FOR POSSIBLE MOD	File: @1602414 Lib: WPPSRH Vol: SYS400 Owner: SRH Fileclass: Device: DISK Open Mode: OPEN FOR IO MODE		SRH 84
16:02:43.4		SRH 84	SCRATCH	File: @AF010838 Lib: #WPPSRH Vol: SYS400 Owner: SRH Fileclass:		SRH 84

Figure 10-1. Sample entries in a log file

Don't Log Passwords

If you are customizing the information that is logged to your log files, make sure that you keep passwords from being logged. Obviously, you wouldn't log valid passwords (entered during successful logins), but some people don't realize that it can be dangerous to log invalid passwords (entered during unsuccessful logins) as well. These passwords may simply be valid, but mistyped, passwords entered by authorized users. Someone looking over the logs could easily deduce what the real passwords are.

On the same principle, you may want to keep from logging account names or user IDs. Sometimes, users erroneously type their passwords instead of their user names or IDs. However, sometimes knowing what accounts are being attacked may help provide clues. If you do collect this information, be certain to protect it with great care.

Although it is often helpful to have the log files on-line, remember that someone who can successfully break into your system may also have the expertise to be able to change your log files—possibly eradicating any evidence of his entrance. The safest thing to do is to send all log file output to a hardcopy device, ideally one in a secure location on a different system from the one doing the logging. In addition to the standard log files, there are various programs—both commercial and public domain—that give you additional logging capabilities.

What do you look for in the log files? Here are some of the most obvious things to watch out for:

- Look for logins at different times or from different places from the usual. If all of your data-entry staff works from 9:00 a.m. to 5:00 p.m., and you start to see logins at midnight or on Sunday, something is fishy. If your staff rarely has any reason to log in remotely, and you start seeing logins from unfamiliar sites when nobody in the office is traveling, watch out.

- Watch for failed login attempts. We've already mentioned how such attempts can indicate that a cracker is looking for access. You may find a pattern of such attempts, culminating in some system damage.

- Be on the look-out for attempts to open files—or otherwise get access to resources—for which a user doesn't have authorization.

- Watch for attempts to change authorizations—either overall privileges (e.g., becoming the superuser on UNIX systems) or particular file protection on key files (many files are read-only or can be changed only by their creator).

NOTE

If you will potentially be using log files as evidence, the first thing you need to do is to make sure that they are reliable, complete, and tamper-proof. You must assure yourself-and, ultimately, the courts (as we describe in Chapter 11 and 12) that nobody can change an entry in the logs, remove an entry, or copy an old version or a log over the current one.

Be Careful from the Start

Here are some things you need to be careful about from the time you first realize that a computer crime has occurred. The more scrupulous you are about these procedures right from the start, the more likely you'll be to find and successfully prosecute the intruder.

Keep It Quiet—At First

When a crime is detected, it's important to keep the fact from becoming public, at least in the early stages. Make sure that only those people within your organization who need to know *do* know. This will keep the intruder from being alerted; your best chance of catching the intruder is early in the investigation. It may also keep employees and clients from panicking. During the early stages of an investigation, you don't know the extent of the crime—which files, if any, were compromised, which system programs might have been damaged, and whether any money or proprietary data were stolen. Make sure you know how and when to share the news with all those involved, however. Trying to keep computer intrusions a secret indefinitely isn't fair to those who use your system, and usually doesn't work anyway. When you do share the news, don't use email on the compromised system!

One good thing that may come out of a computer crime is that it will raise the awareness of everyone in your organization. So often, people think that it can't happen here. Because they've never seen any evidence that security policies matter, they are often reluctant to take them seriously and rarely do all they can to enforce security in the system. Once they see that it *can* happen, the staff may be much more vigilant.

Civil Litigation

Some computer crimes result in civil, as well as criminal, cases. For example, there have been several cases in which employees have stolen proprietary information from a company or have planted viruses that caused a substantial amount of damage to company programs and files. In such cases, the company can try to recover damages by suing the employee in civil court. In cases of this kind, the evidence gathered during the original investigation may end up being used during the civil process.

Insurance Claims

There have been a few cases in which claims have been filed with insurance companies for the recovery of losses caused by computer crimes. In such cases, the information gathered during the original investigation will have to be submitted to the insurance company. The main points of interest are the chronology of events, the identification of all suspects, and the total amount of the loss. The actions taken by the organization that suffered the loss—before, during, and after the crime—all may have an impact on the amount the insurance company may pay.

Write It Down

We've said it before and we'll say it again. Document everything that happens! Especially if the crime is an ongoing one, write down a description of what is going on. What did you discover? When? How do you think the perpetrator got into the site or the system? What did you and your team do? Who did you call and when? What did they say and do? Has this happened before? Do you have any idea who might have done it? Include every detail, but as we said before, keep all such documentation off the system that has been attacked. Otherwise, intruders may be able to watch your every move.

Keep careful track of what system files you examine. Print out the exact contents of the screen at the time you discovered evidence of a computer crime. If you actually catch an intruder on your system, and if your system gives you a way, record the entire session so you will have a record of everything the intruder did or tried to do. Print out any system logs or audit trails, as well as any other files in which you find evidence of intrusion. Whenever you print anything, sign and date the printout.

Remember that computer crime investigations can be complex and long term. You can't remember everything, and you need to be able to share information with the various people who may join the investigative team. Most importantly, computer crimes are difficult both to investigate (Chapter 11) and to prosecute (Chapter 12). The more raw information you can supply, the more likely the crime is to be solved and successfully prosecuted.

Figure 10-2 shows an excerpt from an activity report.

Routine entries

Date 1/12/95
From: Bart Jones
Installed gnutar in usr/local/bin; source is in /usr/source/local.

Date 4/8/95
From: Dorothy Marston
Modified /etc/fstab to mount dev dsk c0dLs3 on scratch.

Incident Entries

Date: 4/15/95 10:37 pm
From: Sam Roundtree
Noticed unusual login activity from a machine at Whatsamatta University.
Initiated planned incident response; attempted to contact Bart to evaluate
situation, but he was unavailable, so contacted Dorothy instead.

Date: 4/15/95 10:41 pm
From: Dorothy Marston
Logged in from home to investigate report from Sam. Crackers working
from Whatsamatta University seem to have broken into machine; not sure
how yet, or how far they ve gotten.
Called Sam to tell him to shut down network connection per response
plan, and to start contacting other members of response team, also per
plan, while I drive into work.

Date: 4/15/95 10:52 pm
From: Sam Roundtree
Disconnected from external net per response plan, on instructions from
Dorothy.

Date: 4/15/95 11:33 pm
From: Dorothy Marston
Arrived on site. Verified network disconnection and that other response
team members had been notified and were on their way. Made incident in
progress modifications to VP of engineering and CERT, per plan.
Beginning to analyze how attackers got in and what they ve done.

Figure 10-2. Sample entries in an activity report

Restoring the System

In planning how you will detect, investigate, and prosecute a computer crime,
don't forget that the business of the organization must continue, as much as
possible, without interruption.

How will the operations of the system—and the integrity of its data—be restored
after a computer crime has occurred? Computer downtime costs money, and the
organization needs to get the system back online as quickly as possible so users
and customers aren't further disrupted.

Planning how to restore system operation is an important part of contingency
planning. What will you do if the system itself is damaged? What if important files

have been lost? There are three particularly important aspects of contingency planning that may help you restore your system:

- Arrange for the use of other computer facilities or equipment in case of an emergency. Some organizations use disaster preparedness firms that keep emergency facilities ready at all times. If a disaster occurs, you will find computers, programs, and backup data waiting for you.

- Back up all program and data files so they will be available in case the original files are destroyed or compromised. Backups are vital to recovery. Back your data up frequently and keep the backups safely away from the main computing facility. (You don't want the same disaster to knock out both your original data and your backups in one fell swoop!) Keep your backups under lock and key, and consider encrypting them for extra security.

- Know how to check through the system for changes an intruder might have made. It's not always feasible to restore an entire system from backups. If you have some information about what an intruder might have done to your system, you stand a good chance of being able to recover piecemeal. (Of course, this won't always work, and you may have to restore portions of the system from backups. You'll have to make this determination based on your own site's activity and needs.) What should you check for? Look especially at any new accounts in the system, any changes in passwords, any changes in file protection, any new system programs, and any new programs with special privileges. Compare existing versions of programs with the original ones installed in your system to make sure they haven't been patched or tampered with.

11

Investigating a Computer Crime

The telephone rings, and it's your boss. You've just been assigned the responsibility for investigating a major computer crime. Maybe a computer-assisted fraud has cost a company millions of dollars in assets. Or maybe an electronic break-in has compromised proprietary information about the company's plans for a new product. Maybe it has even involved information critical to national defense.

Now what? Do you know what to do—and what not to do—when investigating a computer crime? Can you picture yourself on the witness stand, being cross-examined about your technical credentials? How will you explain to the court how you extracted important evidence from a reel of computer tape without damaging the integrity of the evidence or violating the suspect's right to privacy? Or how can you carefully dissect a computer virus and determine, based on the programming characteristics of the virus, that it could only have been written by the defendant? If you're like most investigators, you'd be a lot more comfortable investigating and testifying about the theft of more tangible assets.

This chapter won't make you an expert, but it does explore the major issues you'll need to contend with when you're investigating a computer crime. You may find more technical information in this chapter than you will personally need when conducting a computer crime investigation, but an awareness of this information will assist you in working more effectively with the experts you may call in to help with the investigation. It will also add to your credibility as a witness when the crime is eventually prosecuted.* For background information about preparing and executing search warrants in accordance with Fourth Amendment requirements, see, "Raiding the Computer Room: Fourth Amendment Considerations" by John Gales Sauls, reprinted in Appendix B.

Calling in Law Enforcement

Realize what you are doing when you call in law enforcement to investigate a computer crime at your site:

1. Get approval from upper management to call in law enforcement. Some organizations do not want law enforcement involved in all computer crime investigations. There are various reasons, including publicity, potential liability, and time involved. A major consideration may be the amount of time it might take to obtain search warrants and/or trap and trace orders. Check with your relevant federal, state, or local authorities for an estimate

2. Once law enforcement takes over a case, they do take over. Your own crisis management will very likely report to law enforcement.

3. The investigation will take time. You must be willing for your staff to invest the time necessary to help with explaining systems, procedures, assets, and losses to investigators.

4. If successful, the investigation will lead to prosecution. You'll need to allow additional time for court appearances.

Forming an Investigative Team

Computer crimes call for knowledge beyond the expertise of most investigators. For this reason, it's almost always a good idea to form an investigative team to carry out every computer crime investigation. The team approach is not unique to computer crime investigation; it is used in all major investigations. But it's more important here than in many types of investigations because computer crime investigations do demand special skills and expertise beyond that available to most untrained investigators. The typical management and team structure for a major case is illustrated in Figure 11–1.†

---

* For more detailed information about investigatory techniques, refer to the publications by Donn B. Parker and J.J. BloomBecker listed in Appendix A.
† Once law enforcement is brought into a case, that agency is in charge of the investigation. The supervisor running the case will usually be from the law enforcement agency, rather than from the victimized organization.

Dealing with the Media

These days, the media are very interested in computer crime. If you are involved in a high-profile investigation, you may find yourself on public display. Interest by television, print, and other media representatives may hinder your investigation by distracting people in the organization and by focusing undue attention on the case. Media attention may also affect witnesses, cause people to overreact, and generally stir people up. Stories about the coming of the Michaelangelo virus several years ago caused a virtual panic among many computer users, far beyond the actual impact of the virus itself. In spring of 1995, the announcement of the planned release of SATAN (Security Administrator Tool for Analyzing Networks), a program which some predicted would be as much a tool for crackers as for those seeking to thwart them, caused a similarly overwrought reaction. Media attention may also put both the victimized organization and the relevant prosecutor in a position where they must prosecute or be cast in a negative light.

If you can keep your case from getting the full treatment by the media, at least in the early stages, you'll be better off.

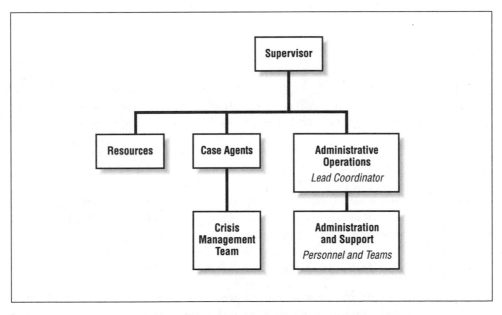

Figure 11-1. Organizational structure of a major case investigative team

Law enforcement (if called in) will work closely with the crisis management team set up by the organization that has been victimized by a computer crime. When forming the team and beginning investigations, be aware of the following:

- Communication among the different members of the team is vitally important.

- The communication process begins even before the major investigation kicks off; during this initial period, the team plans individual tasks and activities and determines how to coordinate those activities.

- The team will need to develop a written investigative plan that details all of the anticipated investigative and support activities.

- As time goes on, you may need to identify additional support personnel to help with the investigation; the type and number depend on the nature of the case.

How to Investigate

Although computer crime investigations have much in common with other major types of investigation, there are two major differences:

- You will search different types of records.

- You will be dealing with electronic media, equipment, and communications.

The following sections touch on some specific topics you'll need to explore in the early stages of an investigation.

Checking Records

The investigation begins with a careful check of all records associated with the case. These records include such information as computer system documentation, system logs, and background and operational information about the organization and its personnel.

If a suspect has already been identified, then you will also learn as much as you can about the suspect, the computer equipment that suspect used (or is using) to commit the crime, and the degree of his or her computer expertise. Telephone records may also prove to be valuable. (See information about the rules of evidence and admissibility later in this chapter.)

Interviewing Informants

Early in the investigation, you will want to interview all potential informants. Informants may be able to provide information about the methods used by the suspect and the frequency of his or her activities. They can help identify the equipment used to commit the crime and to identify co-conspirators and other associates.

Surveillance

Both physical and electronic surveillance of the suspect may help to validate information received from your informants. If telephone access codes were used during the crime, you may wish to use pen registers or dialed number recorders to help in gathering documentation. These devices may also be helpful in tracing intruders who have gained entry to computer systems via modems.

Bulletin Boards

If the suspect operates an electronic bulletin board system (BBS), you might want to gain access to that board. (Remember that you must operate within the provisions of the current statutes of the Electronic Communications Privacy Act.)[*] Such bulletin boards may contain unauthorized credit card information, manuals describing exploitable software vulnerabilities, and access code files.

Setting a Trap

We discussed in Chapter 10 the possibility that an organization that is being victimized might try to learn more about an intruder by "baiting a trap" for him. If the investigation warrants, you may consider doing even more. You might think about setting up an electronic sting operation—for example, an electronic bulletin board or a host computer that will interest the suspect. This is a tempting approach, but remember that it is both expensive and time intensive. It is also quite possible that experienced or highly focused perpetrators may not be fooled by the decoy—they might see right through you.

As we described in Chapter 10, you might also think about planting false information in computers that you know have been targeted by the suspect. If he or she is later found to be in possession of the planted information, you will have a solid way to establish an audit trail.

Be sure to check with legal authorities about the legality and admissibility of these activities.

Preparing a Search Warrant

The preparation of a search warrant for computer evidence is extremely important, as is the way in which you carry out the actual search. Because so few judges and juries are familiar with computer crime and evidence, the defense is in

---

[*] 18 USC, Chapter 119, Sections 2510/2511 et seq.

a good position to challenge such evidence on all fronts. (Chapter 12 discusses characteristics of this evidence, and Appendix D shows an actual search warrant.)

When you prepare a search warrant for the computer equipment and files you are interested in, be as specific as possible about what you expect to find at the scene. However, because often you won't know precisely what you can expect to find, your warrant will probably read something like this:

> "Any information in printed form or computer-readable media dealing with [you specify the category] subject matter."

As we mention in the section called "Getting Help from a Technical Adviser" in this chapter, a technical advisor who is familiar with the type of equipment and files you'll be examining can be of great help in preparing the warrant.

NOTE

The information in this section provides only general guidelines, which should not be construed as legal advice. Because most law enforcement agencies have their own specific guidelines, follow those whenever they are available.

Probable Cause

The Fourth Amendment to the United States Constitution concerns the right of citizens to be "secure in their persons, houses, papers and effects." It guards against unreasonable searches and seizures of property and persons. The U.S. Supreme Court has set guidelines for reasonable searches and seizures in the form of search warrants. Before a search warrant can be issued, you need to establish that:

1. There is probable cause that a crime has been committed.

2. There is probable cause that evidence exists of the crime.

3. There is probable cause to enter someone's home or business. You'll need to show that evidence is likely to exist in the particular place that investigators are seeking authorization to search.

The law enforcement officer, a local prosecutor (in most cases), and a judge all need to believe that there is probable cause.

For detailed information about each of these points, along with a discussion of cases supporting them, see "Raiding the Computer Room: Fourth Amendment Considerations," by John Gales Sauls, reprinted in Appendix B. Sauls's article also contains citations for particular cases. One quotation is from a search warrant issued in *United States* v. *Brien*, in which the courts ruled that, although the language is broad, it was appropriate because the firm being searched, Lloyd, Carr & Company, a commodities brokerage firm, was "solely and entirely a scheme to defraud." The search warrant authorized the seizure of Lloyd, Carr's bank statements, cash receipt books, option purchase records, sales material distributed to customers, employee compensation records, customer account records, sales training material, and customer lists.

Searching with Consent

Some searches are performed with the consent of the suspect organizations. If you are going to attempt to conduct a consent search, be sure to prepare, well in advance, a written document providing consent. Usually, such a document can't include all the evidence you expect to find. Instead, it should specify the overall scope of the consent. If the consent to search form is signed, then there is less chance that the search or the scope of the search will be challenged later in court. It is usually a good idea to have a search warrant in your possession as well. If the consent to search is not agreed to when you actually arrive at the site, you can execute the search warrant. This way, the search can still begin before suspects have time to destroy or tamper with evidence.

Respect Privacy

Be sure to respect issues of both proprietary data and privacy when you execute a search warrant. In some cases, victimized organizations may have client records on their systems; these records are considered to be proprietary information. The clients whose records are stored in the computer files may have a right to expect privacy with respect to these records. Try to get written permission from the victim company to search for evidence in their files. Be sure to recognize and respect the right to privacy of their clients as well.

What to Bring to the Scene

If you are getting ready to execute a search warrant of a suspect's premises, get the following materials ready so you'll be able to bring them with you for use during the search. As we've said, these are general guidelines; use your own law enforcement agency's specific guidelines.

1. Diskettes. These can be used for the storage of files copied from the computers being searched. They can also be used for temporary file storage. Make sure that you have the right size diskettes for the computers at the site

(bring a supply of each kind if you're not sure what you'll need) and that they have been formatted.

2. A supply of tape or disk media. Some computers have 9-track, cartridge, 4mm, or 8mm tape decks attached to them. You can use tapes for mass storage backup of the contents of a hard disk, as well as for the storage of individual programs and data files. In some cases, you may prefer to use other backup media, such as external hard disks or optical disks. (Tape backup programs often make optimized backups that fail to show deleted files and directories, which you may want to know about during your investigation.)

3. Plenty of evidence tape, adhesive labels, or other means of write-protecting the disks.

4. A set of utility computer programs for the target computers. These will be used to help retrieve and copy data files.

5. Adhesive color labels that can be used to identify and catalog evidence. Make sure that these labels look different from the evidence labels you're bringing along. Place one of these labels on each diskette you write on during the search; on it, list the files found on that diskette, along with the access commands used to write the files, the operating system name, and the information believed to be contained in the files.

6. Operation manuals and other necessary documentation for the target operating system and programming languages.

7. Extra form-feed paper for the printers.

8. Sterile operating system diskettes. Crackers often program their diskettes so that if the system is booted (turned on) by someone else, all evidence is destroyed.

9. Pen registers that can be used to down-load codes and numbers stored in the resident memory of the computer, modem, or programmable telephone.

10. Camera equipment you can use to videotape and photograph the scene.

11. A virus detection program. This will protect the system you're investigating from any possible contamination by tools you may be using.

12. A technical expert who can assist you in using all of the preceding tools and materials. Note that in many states, anyone accompanying law enforcement officers to a scene must be named in the search warrant. Check with your legal advisers about this point. Having advisers tag along, without prior approval, may jeopardize the case.

Executing a Search Warrant

Although there is no formula for exactly how a search and seizure must take place, there are some general guidelines. As we've said, view these steps as broad guidelines, not as specifics to follow in every situation; use your own law enforcement agency's specific guidelines.

Steps to Follow

In general, execution of a search warrant involves the following steps:[*]

1. Investigators must announce their intention to search. This is typically done before forcibly entering a site, but there are exceptions—for example, if there is reason to believe that the announcement would put people at risk or result in evidence being destroyed. (The latter is easy to do with computer equipment—just turn off the power, and a lot of information may be lost.)

2. Investigators must take control of the area being searched. Here, too, the extent to which people's work must be disrupted and their equipment seized depends on the particular case.

3. Investigators may search within the scope of the warrant. There are limitations of place (those places where an item might reasonably be concealed) and time (only until all items have been found or until all places have been explored). These limitations may be difficult to establish and follow when there are many thousands of computer files to examine.

4. Investigators must be careful not to cause damage during a search. Because computers can so easily be damaged, and data so readily lost, it is particularly important that technical advisers be present at a search of a computer facility.

5. Investigators may seize additional material under the "plain view" exception to search warrant requirements, as long as the item is obviously in view, is probably evidence of a crime, and is found while the investigators are searching for something within the scope of the warrant.

What to Collect

Although we supply a checklist here, the steps are only suggestions. Be aware that these steps may vary widely from case to case. Take the advice of your technical and legal advisors.

---

[*] For more information about these steps, see Appendix B. For detailed instructions, see the "Federal Guidelines on Searching and Seizing Computers."

> ## When Investigating . . .
>
> If you are investigating a case of hardware damage, make sure you identify both the components that have been damaged and the data that have been lost or compromised. Your cost estimates must go beyond just the hardware; be sure to include:
>
> - An estimate of the cost of the damaged hardware components
> - An estimate of the value of the information that has been lost
> - An estimate of the cost resulting from the loss of system availability
>
> In all computer crimes, the dollar cost of the loss is an important factor when considering whether to prosecute, to sue, or to make an insurance claim.

At the scene, be prepared to collect the following as evidence (assuming that it is listed in the warrant):

1. All hardware found at the scene.
2. All software found at the scene.
3. Computer diskettes, tape, and other media.
4. All documentation found at the scene.
5. All peripheral equipment including printers, modems, cables, etc.
6. Any discarded documentation, printouts, and printer ribbons. *Don't forget to check the trash containers during your search!*

At All Sites

When you serve the warrant, follow these guidelines:

Do Not:

- Touch the keyboard. (Although this is a good general guideline, there may be times when you must touch the keyboard. For example, in networked environments, you may need to run programs that download needed data.)
- Disconnect the power.
- Change the computer's current state in any way.

Do:

- Videotape the scene to document the system configuration and the condition of the site when you arrive, as well as the condition of all of the equipment you see.

- Photograph the equipment serial numbers, model numbers, and wiring schemes.

- Label all evidence so that the cables and other equipment can be reassembled in the same exact configuration.

- Write-protect all diskettes at the scene and make sure that they are labeled as previously discussed.

If the equipment is turned off when you arrive, your technical advisor will probably suggest that it be disassembled and tagged as evidence. The system can be reassembled later at a secure location, using the videotapes and photographs to help you reassemble it in the same configuration in which it was found. The technical advisor can then help you inspect the equipment and the media to identify incriminating evidence.

Sites Using BBSs

If you are serving a warrant at a location where an electronic bulletin board is in operation, note the following:

1. Observe the monitor to determine whether any incriminating information is currently being transmitted or received by the caller.

2. If so, let the system run and attempt to determine the identity of those accessing the system.

3. If not, disconnect only the modem.

4. Locate and secure printouts and other documents containing incriminating information.

NOTE

Determine in advance if the BBS claims that it is acting as a publisher, and get appropriate legal advice. Those who disseminate information to the public have special protection under the Privacy Protection Act of 1980.[*]

Sites Using Auto Dialers

If a speed dialer, programmable telephone, or other type of auto-dialer is found, note the following:

---

[*] 42 USC., Chapter 21A, Section 2000aa.

Be Careful

In general, be very careful with the equipment and all associated materials. You must take due care both to preserve evidence and to preserve the integrity of the materials seized.

Suppose that you're wrong about the suspect's involvement in the crime. Or suppose that the computer is also used by uninvolved third parties. In both cases, you will want to restore the system and its data to their original condition. You do not want to be the cause of the same type of damage you are investigating!

If the equipment is off when you arrive, *do not turn it on.* The computer could be programmed to destroy all evidence if it is not operated in a certain way. Be especially careful if the equipment is turned on and in operation when you arrive at the scene. Be sure that you do the following:

- Copy verbatim everything displayed on any computer screens.

- Don't let any suspects approach the computer.

- *Don't touch anything* without understanding what you are doing. You must follow certain protocols to turn off the system safely. If you don't follow them, you could cause valuable evidence to be lost. Your technical adviser can help you.

- If you don't have a technician with you, telephone one. You might be able to get advice over the phone.

Sometimes investigators try to run programs at the site in order to get information about computer files and operation. Be very careful when doing this. Because such programs may make changes to the computer's hard disk or to files on floppies (for example, by changing the dates on files), evidence might be changed—and later ruled to be inadmissible. It is very important that you preserve the evidence in exactly the condition in which you found it. Before you run anything, make sure that your technical adviser approves of any programs run at the scene.

If you seize magnetic tapes or disks, be sure to store them in an area where the stable temperature is within a range of 50 to 80 degrees Fahrenheit, with little humidity (in the 35–50 percent range). Keep them away from magnetic fields at all times. If you are unsure about what magnetic fields may exist in the area, consider bringing equipment to test for them. Remember, in an emergency, a simple compass works better than nothing at all.

1. Do not disconnect the telephone or auto-dialer from its source.

2. Connect a dialed number recorder to the telephone or auto-dialer if you are allowed to do so. (Most such recorders are illegal; see "Tracing the Intruder" in Chapter 10 for information, and consult your legal advisor. To do this, you must have obtained a court order.[*]

3. Place an outgoing call through each auto-dialer or telephone number storage port and obtain a printed record of the stored telephone number or telephone access code in resident memory.

4. After completing number 3 on this list, disconnect the telephone or auto-dialer and seize it as evidence.

Can't Move It?

What if it is physically impossible to move the evidence? You may find a mainframe computer, many rooms full of peripheral equipment, and thousands of reels of computer tape. In such a case, you may need to secure the equipment where it is, either with the consent of the parties involved or with a court order. This means placing a 24-hour guard at the location to safeguard the evidence.

Getting Help from a Technical Adviser

As we've mentioned a number of times, it's very important to enlist a technical adviser early in the investigation. Someone familiar with the computer equipment and the operating system of the type you will be searching can help with the following:

- Formulate the actual search warrant.

- Protect the equipment during the search and seizure.

- Answer questions during the trial.

Your technical adviser can help to ensure that the warrant itemizes all pertinent hardware and components. This advice can also help prevent you from filing for a warrant that is later determined to be overly broad—such a warrant might result in having crucial evidence excluded from trial. Remember that computers may be used for a great many things; not everything connected with your suspect's computer may be related to your particular investigation.

If you are planning to seize a computer and/or computer equipment when you execute a search warrant, it is all the more important to have a technical advisor accompany the investigators when the warrant is served. (Remember to identify

---

[*] Under 18 USC, Chapter 206, Section 3121 et seq.

this person in the search warrant.) The adviser can make sure that nobody touches the computer, the peripheral equipment, or the power source. If a technical specialist is not available, try to have one on call who can provide appropriate advice over the telephone.

The technical expert can also advise you on how to transport and store the evidence. Computer evidence is quite fragile. For example, certain types of computer media must be stored at regulated temperatures and humidity. Extra care must be taken not to touch certain areas of the media and not to fold, bend, or apply pressure to it. Be extremely careful not to expose magnetic media to magnetic fields. If the field is sufficiently strong, the magnets will erase all the information on the seized media.

As we've mentioned before, most judges are still unfamiliar with computer crime cases. It may be helpful to have your technical adviser also be present at the trial, in case the judge has questions regarding the search.

Auditing Tools

There are a number of different audit tools and utilities that your technical advisers may use during the investigation. We include a few examples here so you will better understand what your technical advisers are doing during this phase of the investigation.

Test Data Method
> Modifies the processing accuracy of the computer application systems. It does this by executing these systems with specially prepared sets of input data that produce preestablished results, and then comparing these results.

Integrated Test Facility (ITF)
> Reviews those functions of automated applications that are internal to the computer. Internal auditors' test data are used to compare the ITF processing results to precalculated test results.

Parallel Simulation
> Processes "live" data files and simulates normal computer application processing. These programs include only the application, logic, calculations, and controls that are relevant to specific audit objectives. This technique is not as complex as other audit methods.

Snapshot
> Takes a "picture" of the parts of a computer memory that contain the data elements in a computerized decision-making process at the time the decision is made. The results of the snapshot are printed in a report format for reconstructing the decision-making process.

Mapping

> Assesses the extent of the system testing and identifies specific program logic that has not been tested. Mapping is performed by a program measurement tool that analyzes a computer program during execution to indicate whether program statements have been executed.

Code Comparison

> Compares two copies, made at different times, of the program coding for a particular application. The objective of the technique is to identify or verify changes in the program.

Checksums

> Provides a numerical value to the execution module that can be compared later to suspect modules. Checksums can be run on data as well. Several algorithms for computing checksums exist in the public domain.

Guidelines for Handling Evidence

The guidelines included here have been prepared by the FBI Laboratory.[*] Although they are specifically aimed at preserving evidence that is being examined by that laboratory, the advice is helpful for anyone who is investigating a computer crime and seizing equipment. Remember that these steps are only guidelines; use your own law enforcement agency's guidelines.

Computer Analysis and Response Team (CART)

The FBI laboratory has established a Computer Analysis and Response Team (CART) at FBI headquarters in Washington, DC. The CART has a full range of hardware available, as well as special software for forensic examinations of computer-related evidence. The CART is staffed by experienced computer professionals who are sensitive to the particular needs of the law enforcement community. This service is available to any law enforcement agency that is authorized to submit evidence to the FBI for forensic examination.

---

[*] These guidelines are excerpted from the paper, "Computer Analysis and Response Team (CART): The Microcomputer as Evidence," by Michael G. Noblett of the Federal Bureau of Investigation. It is reprinted from the *FBI Crime Laboratory Digest*, Volume 19, Number 1, January, 1992. That paper is included in Appendix C of this book.

Guidelines for Preserving and Submitting Computer Evidence

Depending upon the overall investigation, the physical machine might not actually be part of the evidence. Instead, investigators often make an image copy of the hard disk and conduct their investigations on that copy.

NOTE

There are several references in these lists to wrapping equipment or media in plastic. Before you do this, make sure that you have powered down all equipment and let it return to room temperature. Also, be sure that you use anti-static plastic.

I. HARDWARE

A. PC/central processing unit (CPU)

  1. Determine if the system has an internal hard drive. If possible, secure the hard drive read/write heads with the appropriate software command. Do not remove the internal hard drive from the computer.

  2. Secure the read/write heads in the floppy drives with a blank floppy diskette.

  3. Label the cables and ports.

  4. Initial and date the CPU as required by your department's chain of custody procedures.

  5. Wrap the hardware in plastic and box for shipment to the laboratory.

B.. Monitor

  1. Label the cables.

  2. Initial and date the monitor as required by your department's chain of custody procedures.

  3. Wrap the monitor in plastic and box for shipment to the laboratory.

C. Keyboard

  1. Label the cables.

  2. Initial and date the keyboard as required by your department's chain of custody procedures.

  3. Wrap the keyboard in plastic and box for shipment to the laboratory.

D. External/removable hard drives

  1. Secure the hard drive read/write heads, if possible. Some are secured by software commands; others are secured automatically.

  2. Label the cables.

3. Initial and date the hard drive as required by your department's chain of custody procedures.

4. Wrap the hard drive in plastic and box for shipment to the laboratory.

E. External floppy diskette drives

1. Remove the floppy diskette(s) from the drive(s).

2. Secure the read/write heads with a blank floppy diskette, if possible.

3. Label the cables.

4. Initial and date the floppy diskette drive as required by your department's chain of custody procedures.

5. Wrap the floppy diskette drive in plastic and box for shipment to the laboratory.

F. External tape drive

1. Note and record the DIP (Dual In-Line) switch settings.

2. Remove the tape cartridge from drive.

3. Label the cables.

4. Initial and date the tape drive as required by your department's chain of custody procedures.

5. Wrap the tape drive in plastic and box for shipment to the laboratory.

G. Printers/plotters

1. Note and record the DIP switch settings.

2. Remove the ribbon. Initial and date the ribbon canister. (Some computer ribbons may be readable and could provide the most recent text printed on the device.)

3. Label the cables.

4. Initial and date the printer/plotter as required by your department's chain of custody procedures.

5. Wrap the printer/plotter in plastic and box for shipment to the laboratory.

H. Modems/acoustic couplers

1. Disconnect from the telephone.

2. Label the cables and ports.

3. Initial and date the modem/acoustic coupler as required by your department's chain of custody procedures.

4. Wrap the modem/acoustic coupler in plastic and box for shipment to the laboratory.

I.   Cables

1. Label both ends of each cable, describing the connection to PC, printer, etc.

2. Place cables in an appropriate evidence container.

3. Box the cables for shipment to the laboratory.

II. MAGNETIC MEDIA

A.   Floppy diskettes

1. Keep the diskettes away from magnetic fields.

2. Initial and date using a *felt-tip pen* as required by your department's chain of custody procedures.

3. Place the diskettes in an appropriate evidence container. *Do not* use plastic envelopes because of the risk of static electric discharge.

4. Label the outside of the shipment container "DO NOT X-RAY" to warn that evidence should be kept away from magnetic fields. Ship to the laboratory.

III. DOCUMENTATION

A.   Manuals/hand-written notes, etc.

1. Handle the item(s) with gloves to preserve for latent fingerprint examination.

2. Initial and date all loose sheets, pads, manuals, and other paper documents as required by your department's chain of custody procedures.

3. Place the item(s) in an appropriate evidence container.

4. Ship to the laboratory.

B.   Printouts/listings

1. Handle the items with gloves to preserve for latent fingerprint examination.

2. Initial and date the item(s) as required by your department's chain of custody procedures.

3. Place the Item(s) in appropriate evidence container.

4. Ship to the laboratory.

Guidelines for Examining Computer Evidence

Consider recording information found on floppy and hard disks both at the beginning and the end of the investigation. This way, you can demonstrate that you have not damaged the evidence.

I.   RECEIPT OF EVIDENCE

A.   Log evidence into appropriate evidence control system and assign to an examiner.

1. Use a unique numbering system to record the date and time received.

2. Identify the examiner.

3. Prepare documentation for chain of custody from evidence control to the examiner.

B. Transfer evidence to examiner.

1. Determine if other expert analyses such as accounting, drug record analysis, gambling analysis, latent fingerprint examination, and so on are necessary.

2. Prepare chain of custody documentation for other experts as necessary for complete examination.

3. Determine that all pieces of equipment listed as having been submitted are actually present.

4. Mark and initial each piece of evidence as required by your laboratory system and prepare work papers for notes.

II. EXAMINATION OF EVIDENCE

When you boot a system, do not use the software on the system being examined, or you will risk destroying evidence. Use your own system disk to examine the suspect files.

A. Determine if the submitted system is operational.

1. Review submitting communication to determine if the system was operational at the time of seizure.

2. Take the logical steps to render the system operational.

B. Floppy diskettes.

1. Write-protect all diskettes.

2. Identify the computer to be used for examination.

3. Convert the operating system if necessary.

4. Create directory/subdirectory listings.

5. Check for hidden and deleted files using appropriate commercial or custom software.

6. Display and print files.

C. Hard disk systems.

1. *Write-protect hard disk using appropriate software.*

2. Create directory/subdirectory listings and partition information.

3. Check for hidden and deleted files, deleted directories, and other hidden information using appropriate commercial or custom software.

4. Display and print files.

III. REPORTING RESULTS

A. Prepare the report, documenting what you did and the results.

B. Send the printouts and report to the contributor or subject matter expert for additional analysis.

C. Repack the computer and all disks.

D. Return the evidence to the contributor.

NOTE

Be aware that certain computer equipment is battery-powered. Batteries on certain types of battery-powered information carriers, such as PDA (Personal Digital Assistant) and CMOS Complementary Metal Oxide Semiconductor) equipment may wear out if a case takes several years to reach the courts. This situation could result in your having difficulty accessing the system or obtaining the stored information.

12

Prosecuting a Computer Crime

Prosecuting computer crimes is usually more complex and demanding than prosecuting most other types of crimes. It requires special technical preparation and a greater dependence on expert witness testimony. In a computer crime, the prosecution must be prepared to explain a highly complex series of technical acts to a judge and jury who may have little knowledge of computers and how they operate. Witnesses may need to explain why losses of intangibles—proprietary data and computer availability, for example—are as serious as losses of tangible stolen goods (and often more so). The more complex the crime, the harder it will be to explain the crime and its repercussions.

The prosecution of computer crimes is a relatively new challenge to both investigators and prosecutors. There will undoubtedly be new challenges as more cases are presented at trial and as defense attorneys develop new strategies to protect the rights of their clients. This chapter describes the major issues that can help or hinder the prosecution of computer crimes.

Judges and Juries

Some judges and members of juries may have a good deal of knowledge of computer technology, whereas others may know nothing at all. When preparing for a computer crime trial, a prosecutor will have to assume that the judge and jury have no knowledge of computer technology and be prepared to explain all of the events in the simplest of terms. The prosecutor, the expert witnesses, and the technical staff who are testifying at the trial must present their testimony in terms that everyone in the courtroom understands. Visual aids, simple analogies, and other innovative ways to bring the crime into focus can illustrate the crime and show how it was committed, as we describe later in this chapter under "Testifying in Computer Crime Cases."

Judges and juries may also vary in their attitudes toward computer crime. Some may take such crimes seriously. Others, seeing only that buildings were not destroyed and computers were not stolen, may greatly underestimate the damage a computer crime can do. In some cases, a little knowledge of computers, but not enough to make a solid decision, proves to be dangerous for both judge and jury. Sometimes, a judge or a juror incorrectly interprets the evidence presented and, as a result, reaches an erroneous conclusion.

Consider the case of Robert T. Morris, convicted of planting the worm in the Internet in 1988. The worm is said to have caused no tangible damage—that is, no data were stolen or damaged. However, the computer centers affected by the worm spent many millions in lost time—the time spent when the worm so clogged their systems that no other work could be done, and the time spent checking and restoring system operation. The defendant in this case admitted planting the worm but said he did it without malice. He was sentenced to probation and no prison time. How many other multi-million dollar crime convictions result in probation?

Evidence in Computer Crime Cases

In computer crime cases, you will have to contend with a variety of issues surrounding the admissibility of computer files and other records as evidence. You will find that even the definitions of what computers are and what they do differ widely from statute to statute. This section touches on some of the basic issues you will need to confront. For detailed information, it is best to obtain a legal opinion.

Don't let this section scare you. With the increase in computer crimes over the past few years, the courts are becoming more knowledgeable about the evidence that is likely to be presented in such cases.

The Hearsay Problem

Under the Federal Rules of Evidence, all business records, including computer records, are considered to be "hearsay" because there is no firsthand proof that they are accurate, reliable, and trustworthy. In general, hearsay evidence is not admissible in court. However, there are some well-established exceptions to the hearsay rule for business records. To be admissible as business records, computer records must satisfy several criteria:

- They must be produced, maintained, and used in the general course of business.

- They must be authenticated—that is, they must be shown, by qualified witnesses, to be reliable.

- They must meet the "best evidence rule"; that is, what is produced must be the best evidence available (not simply a copy of it, if the original is also available).

In addition, the investigators themselves must have the necessary expertise to testify about the investigation and the evidence collected. You can count on the fact that in a computer crime trial, the defense will do everything possible to mount attacks based on these issues.

Produced in the Regular Course of Business

To be admissible as evidence, computer records must generally be shown to have been produced during the regular course of doing business. Logs of system activity are a good example of this rule. If the system logs you introduce into evidence are those produced, day in and day out, by your system, they're likely to be admissible. Logs are much less likely to be accepted as evidence if you have produced them solely so the prosecution can demonstrate that a crime has taken place. The more you can show that the victimized organization itself uses the logs in the course of doing business, the better. Doing so demonstrates the organization's own trust in the records produced and the software that produced them.

A special problem occurs if a computer printout was not generated in the regular course of business but was printed solely for use in the trial. This does not completely preclude its admissibility. However, in accordance with custody of evidence requirements, you must be prepared to show that the system from which the printout came was secured from the initial stages of the investigation and/or that the medium from which it was printed was collected and maintained in accordance with these requirements. Be prepared for the fact that the defense is very likely to challenge the admissibility of computer records, particularly any produced especially for the prosecution.

Authentication of Evidence

To show that any written statement is authentic, you must introduce enough evidence to sustain a finding that the written statement is in fact what it claims to be (or you must establish this finding through other means). Such authentication is all the more vital when you are introducing computer records of any kind as evidence. When presenting computer files, logs, printouts, or other records, you will have to include testimony that the records are accurate representations of the data found in the computer and that they have not been altered in any way.

To avoid challenges by the defense to evidence in a computer crime case, don't make any extravagant claims. It is best to claim simply that the item was generated on a certain computer at a specific date and time. Do not make any claims that you cannot support absolutely; for example, do not attempt to claim that the document was originally prepared by a specific individual or that its configuration means that it could only have been originally produced by a certain individual or computer.

In general, the more accurate, complete, and established your evidence, the more likely that it will be admitted. As we've mentioned, log files produced during normal operation (as opposed to log files generated specifically to show that a crime has been committed) are more likely to be admitted. Similarly, the following are likely to be considered authentic:

- Files or messages that have been date stamped (with a date corresponding to the date of the offense, not some time after that date)

- Files or messages that contain digital signatures or checksum features

- Files or messages that were generated from commercial software rather than from public domain software

Best Evidence

To be admissible, you must be able to show that what is produced as evidence is the best evidence available. The "best evidence" rule states that you cannot introduce a photocopy of a document if the original of the document is also available. The Federal Rules of Evidence provide liberal exceptions to the best evidence rule, however, and you should check with your legal advisor for details. For example, for computer data, a printout of a disk copy is generally considered to be as good as a printout of the original, as long as the copying process is carefully explained.[*]

Nevertheless, you must expect witnesses for the defense to challenge the admissibility of documentary evidence. For example, they are likely to describe "computer errors" that lead to random or misleading results; they will probably question the copying procedures, point out how easily log files can be forged and file dates changed, and dispute the reliability of the software that was used to produce the computer files presented as evidence. You will have the best chance of winning your case if you use highly qualified experts who can testify to the

---

[*] For example, under the Federal Rules of Evidence, a duplicate is generally admissible to the same extent as an original. See Federal Rules of Evidence 1003.

truthfulness and validity of the evidence you are submitting and any procedures you performed on the evidence.

Reliability of Witnesses

Another aspect of determining whether computer records are an exception to the hearsay rule is whether a trusted witness (a "custodian" of the records) can testify that the records are reliable. Of course, the defense is likely to suggest that the experts interpreting the printouts in fact designed a program to give them the results they wanted.

In a computer fraud case, for example, experts may design audit programs to trace the fraud and to determine the amount of loss. If the defense successfully challenges the accuracy of these programs, it may be difficult to prove that a crime was even committed. For best results in court, use standardized programs and obviously qualified experts. Both will minimize the impact of potential defense objections.

Exclusionary Rule

Evidence must be gathered by law enforcement officers in accordance with court guidelines governing search and seizure. Otherwise, it will be excluded. (See the guidelines in Chapter 11 for a summary.)

Chain of Possession

For evidence to be admitted in court, the prosecution has to be able to show who obtained it, who secured it, and who has had control over it from the time it was first obtained.

Discovery

Before a case goes to court, the prosecution (but not the defense) must provide all reports, information on evidence, lists of potential witnesses, any criminal history of the witnesses—any information except how the prosecution is going to present the case in court. The defense has the right to see all of this information.

Protective Orders

A protective order can limit who has access to evidence, who can copy documents, and what the disposition is for them. Such orders are issued mainly in an effort to protect proprietary or trade secret documents seized or used as evidence.

Use of Documentation

Don't assume that the documentation associated with a computer program accurately reflects the actual program that was in operation at the time of the crime. Such documentation is unlikely to help your case in court because the defense can so easily attack it. By their nature, computer programmers are more concerned with developing programs than with writing documentation to explain those programs to others. The documentation, if it is written at all, may be full of inaccuracies and errors. In most system development projects, accurate documentation is of pretty low priority; it is written only after the programming itself is complete.

Proprietary Rights

Sometimes, to establish the magnitude of a loss brought about by a computer crime, you will need to establish proprietary rights or ownership of computer programs. This is not an easy matter. The courts will first look at whether the software has been appropriately labeled as being covered by copyright, patent, and trade secret law. Although commercial software is typically labeled properly, many proprietary packages are not.

How does a computer program or a set of data qualify as a trade secret? The first step in determining if adequate protection has been applied is to identify all copies, representations, forms, locations, and custodians of such assets. In one case (*Ward* v. *California*, 1972), the following safeguards and controls were accepted by the courts as adequate to establish that the information qualified as a trade secret:

1. Secret accounting number needed for terminal access

2. Secret site code number needed for terminal access

3. Unlisted telephone number used to access the computer

4. Secret file name under which the computer program was stored

5. Restricted use of the program by others; no copies of the program were given out

6. Awareness among data-processing employees of the proprietary nature of the program

In this particular case, the court accepted these criteria to establish that the information qualified as a trade secret in this case. Other courts may require more or fewer safeguards to reach the same conclusion.

Testifying in Computer Crime Cases

Testifying about a highly technical case before a nontechnical judge and jury can be a challenge. You want to explain without appearing to be condescending. You want to shed light on the events without boring your audience. In general, try to present the facts of the crime and all the associated evidence in as clear, concise, nontechnical, and unthreatening manner as possible. Remember television's Mr. Wizard? He could explain, in the simplest possible terms, complicated experiments one step at a time. When you are preparing to present technical evidence at a computer crime trial, try to emulate Mr. Wizard.

The best testimony includes more than the sound of your voice. When possible, use visual aids extensively. Here are some examples:

- Prepare investigative flowcharts that illustrate all of the technical support provided during the investigation. These help the judge and jury understand why you took each step, from start to finish.

- Use charts illustrating the cost of lost computer and personnel time, the importance of data that may have been compromised, and other losses resulting from the crime. Such information will help the court to understand the seriousness of the offense. These may counter the feeling that because the crime did not involve tangible losses in property, it must not have amounted to much.

- Use illustrations showing the connections across networks from the perpetrator's location to the scene of the crime. They make it clear how much planning and how much interstate and sometimes intercountry traffic took place.

Avoid the use of technical terms and computer jargon when you testify. Use analogies to help ensure that the court knows what you are talking about. Table 12–1 shows a list of examples of analogies that could be used. (See also the glossary at the back of this book for explanations of technical terms.)

Table 12-1. Computer Terms and Their Counterparts

Computer Term	Use or Compare to This Term
Software	Computer programs
Firmware	Computer programs in hardware devices
Bits	Binary digits
Bugs	Computer program errors

Table 12-1. Computer Terms and Their Counterparts (Continued)

Computer Term	Use or Compare to This Term
Magnetic tape and tape drives	Cassette and reel-to-reel audio recordings
Magnetic disk	Phonograph record
Optical disk	Compact disc (CD)
Computer printer and output listings	Printing adding machine, typewriter
Computer terminal and printer	Typewriter
Computer terminal with display	Television or monitor

Remember the KISS formula: Keep It Simple, Stupid. The better the formula is applied, the more easily the judge and jury will understand the scope and consequences of the crime.

After the Prosecution

If you find yourself involved in a major computer crime investigation and prosecution, you may be breaking new ground and setting future precedents. Don't let your hard-won knowledge go to waste. Use it to improve your future performance and the performance of other investigators and teams. As soon as possible after the case is closed, gather the entire investigation and prosecution team together to discuss the following:

1. What did we do right in this case?

2. Where could we have done things differently?

3. What lessons were learned?

4. If we were going to advise someone else who is about to begin this type of investigation, what would we suggest to that person?

Now, write it down. Document what happened in the investigation. You'll be doing the entire law enforcement and computing communities a great service.

Computer
Crime Laws

This part of the book lists the text of the major U.S. federal laws most often used to prosecute computer crime, as well as the relevant state laws and a number of laws from other countries. These statutes were current at the time this book went to press. However, because the area of computer crime law is a dynamic one, be sure to check with your legal advisor for up-to-date statutes and interpretations.

U.S. FEDERAL STATUTES

TITLE 15 - COMMERCE AND TRADE

CHAPTER 41 - CONSUMER CREDIT PROTECTION
SUBCHAPTER I - CONSUMER CREDIT COST DISCLOSURE
PART B - CREDIT TRANSACTIONS

Sec. 1644. Fraudulent use of credit cards; penalties

(a) Use, attempt or conspiracy to use card in transaction affecting interstate or foreign commerce

Whoever knowingly in a transaction affecting interstate or foreign commerce, uses or attempts or conspires to use any counterfeit, fictitious, altered, forged, lost, stolen, or fraudulently obtained credit card to obtain money, goods, services, or anything else of value which within any one-year period has a value aggregating $1,000 or more; or

(b) Transporting, attempting or conspiring to transport card in interstate commerce

Whoever, with unlawful or fraudulent intent, transports or attempts or conspires to transport in interstate or foreign commerce a counterfeit, fictitious, altered, forged, lost, stolen, or fraudulently obtained credit card knowing the same to be counterfeit, fictitious, altered, forged, lost, stolen, or fraudulently obtained; or

(c) Use of interstate commerce to sell or transport card

Whoever, with unlawful or fraudulent intent, uses any instrumentality of interstate or foreign commerce to sell or transport a counterfeit, fictitious, altered, forged, lost, stolen, or fraudulently obtained credit card knowing the same to be counterfeit, fictitious, altered, forged, lost, stolen, or fraudulently obtained; or

(d) Receipt, concealment, etc., of goods obtained by use of card

Whoever knowingly receives, conceals, uses, or transports money, goods, services, or anything else of value (except tickets for interstate or foreign transportation) which (1) within any one-year period has a value aggregating $1,000 or more, (2) has moved in or is part of, or which constitutes interstate or foreign commerce, and (3) has been obtained with a counterfeit, fictitious, altered, forged, lost, stolen, or fraudulently obtained credit card; or

(e) Receipt, concealment, etc., of tickets for interstate or foreign transportation obtained by use of card

Whoever knowingly receives, conceals, uses, sells, or transports in interstate or foreign commerce one or more tickets for interstate or foreign transportation, which (1) within any one-year period have a value aggregating $500 or more, and (2) have been purchased or obtained with one or more counterfeit, fictitious, altered,

forged, lost, stolen, or fraudulently obtained credit cards; or

(f) Furnishing of money, etc., through use of card

Whoever in a transaction affecting interstate or foreign commerce furnishes money, property, services, or anything else of value, which within any one-year period has a value aggregating $1,000 or more, through the use of any counterfeit, fictitious, altered, forged, lost, stolen, or fraudulently obtained credit card knowing the same to be counterfeit, fictitious, altered, forged, lost, stolen, or fraudulently obtained - shall be fined not more than $10,000 or imprisoned not more than ten years, or both.

TITLE 17 - COPYRIGHTS

CHAPTER 1 - SUBJECT MATTER AND SCOPE OF COPYRIGHT

Sec. 101. Definitions

Except as otherwise provided in this title, as used in this title, the following terms and their variant forms mean the following:

An "anonymous work" is a work on the copies or phonorecords of which no natural person is identified as author.

An "architectural work" is the design of a building as embodied in any tangible medium of expression, including a building, architectural plans, or drawings. The work includes the overall form as well as the arrangement and composition of spaces and elements in the design, but does not include individual standard features.

"Audiovisual works" are works that consist of a series of related images which are intrinsically intended to be shown by the use of machines, or devices such as projectors, viewers, or electronic equipment, together with accompanying sounds, if any, regardless of the nature of the material objects, such as films or tapes, in which the works are embodied.

The "Berne Convention" is the Convention for the Protection of Literary and Artistic Works, signed at Berne, Switzerland, on September 9, 1886, and all acts, protocols, and revisions thereto.

A work is a "Berne Convention work" if -

(1) in the case of an unpublished work, one or more of the authors is a national of a nation adhering to the Berne Convention, or in the case of a published work, one or more of the authors is a national of a nation adhering to the Berne Convention on the date of first publication;

(2) the work was first published in a nation adhering to the Berne Convention, or was simultaneously first published in a nation adhering to the Berne Convention and in a foreign nation that does not adhere to the Berne Convention;

(3) in the case of an audiovisual work -

(A) if one or more of the authors is a legal entity, that author has its headquarters in a nation adhering to the Berne Convention; or

(B) if one or more of the authors is an individual, that author is domiciled, or has his or her habitual residence in, a nation adhering to the Berne Convention;

(4) in the case of a pictorial, graphic, or sculptural work that is incorporated in a building or other structure, the building or structure is located in a nation adhering to the Berne Convention; or

(5) in the case of an architectural work embodied in a building, such building is erected in a country adhering to the Berne Convention.

For purposes of paragraph (1), an author who is domiciled in or has his or her habitual residence in, a nation adhering to the Berne Convention is considered to be a national of that nation.

For purposes of paragraph (2), a work is considered to have been simultaneously published in two or more nations if its dates of publication are within 30 days of one another.

The "best edition" of a work is the edition, published in the United States at any time before the date of deposit, that the Library of Congress determines to be most suitable for its purposes.

A person's "children" are that person's immediate offspring, whether legitimate or not, and any children legally adopted by that person.

A "collective work" is a work, such as a periodical issue, anthology, or encyclopedia, in which a number of contributions, constituting separate and independent works in themselves, are assembled into a collective whole.

A "compilation" is a work formed by the collection and assembling of preexisting materials or of data that are selected, coordinated, or arranged in such a way that the resulting work as a whole constitutes an original work of authorship. The term "compilation" includes collective works.

"Copies" are material objects, other than phonorecords, in which a work is fixed by any method now known or later developed, and from which the work can be perceived, reproduced, or otherwise communicated, either directly or with the aid of a machine or device. The term "copies" includes the material object, other than a phonorecord, in which the work is first fixed.

"Copyright owner", with respect to any one of the exclusive rights comprised in a copyright, refers to the owner of that particular right.

The "country of origin" of a Berne Convention work, for purposes of section 411, is the United States if -

(1) in the case of a published work, the work is first published -

(A) in the United States;

(B) simultaneously in the United States and another nation or nations adhering to the Berne Convention, whose law grants a term of copyright protection that is the same as or longer than the term provided in the United States;

C) simultaneously in the United States and a foreign nation that does not adhere to the Berne Convention; or

(D) in a foreign nation that does not adhere to the Berne Convention, and all of the authors of the work are nationals, domiciliaries, or habitual residents of, or in the case of an audiovisual work legal entities with headquarters in, the United States;

(2) in the case of an unpublished work, all the authors of the work are nationals, domiciliaries, or habitual residents of the United States, or, in the case of an unpublished audiovisual work, all the authors are legal entities with headquarters in the United States; or

(3) in the case of a pictorial, graphic, or sculptural work incorporated in a building or structure, the building or structure is located in the United States.

For the purposes of section 411, the "country of origin" of any other Berne Convention work is not the United States.

A work is "created" when it is fixed in a copy or phonorecord for the first time; where a work is prepared over a period of time, the portion of it that has been fixed at any particular time constitutes the work as of that time, and where the work has been prepared in different versions, each version constitutes a separate work.

A "derivative work" is a work based upon one or more preexisting works, such as a translation, musical arrangement, dramatization, fictionalization, motion picture version, sound recording, art reproduction, abridgment, condensation, or any other form in which a work may be recast, transformed, or adapted. A work consisting of editorial revisions, annotations, elaborations, or other modifications which, as a whole, represent an original work of authorship, is a "derivative work".

A "device", "machine", or "process" is one now known or later developed.

To "display" a work means to show a copy of it, either directly or by means of a film, slide, television image, or any other device or process or, in the case of a motion picture or other audiovisual work, to show individual images nonsequentially.

A work is "fixed" in a tangible medium of expression when its embodiment in a copy or phonorecord, by or under the authority of the author, is sufficiently permanent or stable to permit it to be perceived, reproduced, or otherwise communicated for a period of more than transitory duration. A work consisting of sounds, images, or both, that are being transmitted, is "fixed" for purposes of this title if a fixation of the work is being made simultaneously with its transmission.

The terms "including" and "such as" are illustrative and not limitative.

A "joint work" is a work prepared by two or more authors with the intention that their contributions be merged into inseparable or interdependent parts of a unitary whole.

"Literary works" are works, other than audiovisual works, expressed in words, numbers, or other verbal or numerical symbols or indicia, regardless of the nature of the material objects, such as books, periodicals, manuscripts, phonorecords, film, tapes, disks, or cards, in which they are embodied.

"Motion pictures" are audiovisual works consisting of a series of related images which, when shown in succession, impart an impression of motion, together with accompanying sounds, if any.

To "perform" a work means to recite, render, play, dance, or act it, either directly or by means of any device or process or, in the case of a motion picture or other audiovisual work, to show its images in any sequence or to make the sounds accompanying it audible.

"Phonorecords" are material objects in which sounds, other than those accompanying a motion picture or other audiovisual work, are fixed by any method now known or later developed, and from which the sounds can be perceived, reproduced, or otherwise communicated, either directly or with the aid of a machine or device. The term "phonorecords" includes the material object in which the sounds are first fixed.

"Pictorial, graphic, and sculptural works" include two-dimensional and three-dimensional works of fine, graphic, and applied art, photographs, prints and art reproductions, maps, globes, charts, diagrams, models, and technical drawings, including architectural plans. Such works shall include works of artistic craftsmanship insofar as their form but not their mechanical or utilitarian aspects are concerned; the design of a useful article, as defined in this section, shall be considered a pictorial, graphic, or sculptural work only if, and only to the extent that, such design incorporates pictorial, graphic, or sculptural features that can be identified separately from, and are capable of existing independently of, the utilitarian aspects of the article.

A "pseudonymous work" is a work on the copies or phonorecords of which the author is identified under a fictitious name.

"Publication" is the distribution of copies or phonorecords of a work to the public by sale or other transfer of ownership, or by rental, lease, or lending. The offering to distribute copies or phonorecords to a group of persons for purposes of further distribution, public performance, or public display, constitutes publication. A public performance or display of a work does not of itself constitute publication.

"Registration", for purposes of sections 205(c)(2), 405, 406, 410(d), 411, 412, and 506(e), means a registration of a claim in the original or the renewed and extended term of copyright.

To perform or display a work "publicly" means -

(1) to perform or display it at a place open to the public or at any place where a substantial number of persons outside of a normal circle of a family and its social acquaintances is gathered; or

(2) to transmit or otherwise communicate a performance or display of the work to a place specified by clause (1) or to the public, by means of any device or process, whether the members of the public capable of receiving the performance or display receive it in the same place or in separate places and at the same time or at different times.

"Sound recordings" are works that result from the fixation of a series of musical, spoken, or other sounds, but not including the sounds accompanying a motion picture or other audiovisual work, regardless of the nature of the material objects, such as disks, tapes, or other phonorecords, in which they are embodied.

"State" includes the District of Columbia and the Commonwealth of Puerto Rico, and any territories to which this title is made applicable by an Act of Congress.

A "transfer of copyright ownership" is an assignment, mortgage, exclusive license, or any other conveyance, alienation, or hypothecation of a copyright or of any of the exclusive rights comprised in a copyright, whether or not it is limited in time or place of effect, but not including a nonexclusive license.

A "transmission program" is a body of material that, as an aggregate, has been produced for the sole purpose of transmission to the public in sequence and as a unit.

To "transmit" a performance or display is to communicate it by any device or process whereby images or sounds are received beyond the place from which they are sent.

The "United States", when used in a geographical sense, comprises the several States, the District of Columbia and the Commonwealth of Puerto Rico, and the organized territories under the jurisdiction of the United States Government.

A "useful article" is an article having an intrinsic utilitarian function that is not merely to portray the appearance of the article or to convey information. An article that is normally a part of a useful article is considered a "useful article".

The author's "widow" or "widower" is the author's surviving spouse under the law of the author's domicile at the time of his or her death, whether or not the spouse has later remarried.

A "work of visual art" is -

(1) a painting, drawing, print, or sculpture, existing in a single copy, in a limited edition of 200 copies or fewer that are signed and consecutively numbered by the author, or, in the case of a sculpture, in multiple cast, carved, or fabricated sculptures of 200 or fewer that are consecutively numbered by the author and bear the signature or other identifying mark of the author; or

(2) a still photographic image produced for exhibition purposes only, existing in a single copy that is signed by the author, or in a limited edition of 200 copies or fewer that are signed and consecutively numbered by the author.

A work of visual art does not include -

(A)(i) any poster, map, globe, chart, technical drawing, diagram, model, applied art, motion picture or other audiovisual work, book, magazine, newspaper, periodical, data base, electronic information service, electronic publication, or similar publication;

(ii) any merchandising item or advertising, promotional, descriptive, covering, or packaging material or container;

(iii) any portion or part of any item described in clause (i) or (ii);

(B) any work made for hire; or

(C) any work not subject to copyright protection under this title.

A "work of the United States Government" is a work prepared by an officer or employee of the United States Government as part of that person's official duties.

A "work made for hire" is -

(1) a work prepared by an employee within the scope of his or her employment; or

(2) a work specially ordered or commissioned for use as a contribution to a collective work, as a part of a motion picture or other audiovisual work, as a translation, as a supplementary work, as a compilation, as an instructional text, as a test, as answer material for a test, or as an atlas, if the parties expressly agree in a written instrument signed by them that the work shall be considered a work made for hire.

For the purpose of the foregoing sentence, a "supplementary work" is a work prepared for publication as a secondary adjunct to a work by another author for the purpose of introducing, concluding, illustrating, explaining, revising, commenting upon, or assisting in the use of the other work, such as forewords, afterwords, pictorial illustrations, maps, charts, tables, editorial notes, musical arrangements, answer material for tests, bibliographies, appendixes, and indexes, and an "instructional text" is a literary, pictorial, or graphic work prepared for publication and with the purpose of use in systematic instructional activities.

A "computer program" is a set of statements or instructions to be used directly or indirectly in a computer in order to bring about a certain result.

Sec. 102. Subject matter of copyright: In general

(a) Copyright protection subsists, in accordance with this title, in original works of authorship fixed in any tangible medium of expression, now known or later developed, from which they can be perceived, reproduced, or otherwise communicated, either directly or with the aid of a machine or device. Works of authorship include the following categories:

(1) literary works;

(2) musical works, including any accompanying words;

(3) dramatic works, including any accompanying music;

(4) pantomimes and choreographic works;

(5) pictorial, graphic, and sculptural works;

(6) motion pictures and other audiovisual works;

(7) sound recordings; and

(8) architectural works.

(b) In no case does copyright protection for an original work of authorship extend to any idea, procedure, process, system, method of operation, concept, principle, or discovery, regardless of the form in which it is described, explained, illustrated, or embodied in such work.

Sec. 117. Limitations on exclusive rights: Computer programs

Notwithstanding the provisions of section 106, it is not an infringement for the owner of a copy of a computer program to make or authorize the making of another copy or adaptation of that computer program provided:

(1) that such a new copy or adaptation is created as an essential step in the utilization of the computer program in conjunction with a machine and that it is used in no other manner, or

(2) that such new copy or adaptation is for archival purposes only and that all archival copies are destroyed in the event that continued possession of the computer program should cease to be rightful.

Any exact copies prepared in accordance with the provisions of this section may be leased, sold, or otherwise transferred, along with the copy from which such copies were prepared, only as part of the lease, sale, or other transfer of all rights in the program.

Adaptations so prepared may be transferred only with the authorization of the copyright owner.

CHAPTER 5 - COPYRIGHT INFRINGEMENT AND REMEDIES

Sec. 501. Infringement of copyright

(a) Anyone who violates any of the exclusive rights of the copyright owner as provided by sections 106 through 118 or of the author as provided in section 106A(a), or who imports copies or phonorecords into the United States in violation of section 602, is an infringer of the copyright or right of the author, as the case may be. For purposes of this chapter (other than section 506), any reference to copyright shall be deemed to include the rights conferred by section 106A(a). As used in this subsection, the term "anyone" includes any State, any instrumentality of a State, and any officer or employee of a State or instrumentality of a State acting in his or her official capacity. Any State, and any such instrumentality, officer, or employee, shall be subject to the provisions of this title in the same manner and to the same extent as any nongovernmental entity.

(b) The legal or beneficial owner of an exclusive right under a copyright is entitled, subject to the requirements of section 411, to institute an action for any infringement of that particular right committed while he or she is the owner of it. The court may require such owner to serve written notice of the action with a copy of the complaint upon any person shown, by the records of the Copyright Office or otherwise, to have or claim an interest in the copyright, and shall require that such notice be served upon any person whose interest is likely to be affected by a decision in the case. The court may require the joinder, and shall permit the intervention, of any person having or claiming an interest in the copyright.

(c) For any secondary transmission by a cable system that embodies a performance or a display of a work which is actionable as an act of infringement under subsection (c) of section 111, a television broadcast station holding a copyright or other license to transmit or perform the same version of that work shall, for purposes of subsection (b) of this section, be treated as a legal or

beneficial owner if such secondary transmission occurs within the local service area of that television station.

(d) For any secondary transmission by a cable system that is actionable as an act of infringement pursuant to section 111(c)(3), the following shall also have standing to sue: (i) the primary transmitter whose transmission has been altered by the cable system; and (ii) any broadcast station within whose local service area the secondary transmission occurs.

(e) With respect to any secondary transmission that is made by a satellite carrier of a primary transmission embodying the performance or display of a work and is actionable as an act of infringement under section 119(a)(5), a network station holding a copyright or other license to transmit or perform the same version of that work shall, for purposes of subsection (b) of this section, be treated as a legal or beneficial owner if such secondary transmission occurs within the local service area of that station.

TITLE 18 - CRIMES AND CRIMINAL PROCEDURE

PART I - CRIMES
CHAPTER 5 - ARSON

Sec. 81. Arson within special maritime and territorial jurisdiction

Whoever, within the special maritime and territorial jurisdiction of the United States, willfully and maliciously sets fire to or burns, or attempts to set fire to or burn any building, structure or vessel, any machinery or building materials or supplies, military or naval stores, munitions of war, or any structural aids or appliances for navigation or shipping, shall be fined not more than $1,000 or imprisoned not more than five years, or both.

If the building be a dwelling or if the life of any person be placed in jeopardy, he shall be fined not more than $5,000 or imprisoned not more than twenty years, or both.

TITLE 18 - CRIMES AND CRIMINAL PROCEDURE

PART I - CRIMES
CHAPTER 31 - EMBEZZLEMENT AND THEFT

Sec. 641. Public money, property or records

Whoever embezzles, steals, purloins, or knowingly converts to his use or the use of another, or without authority, sells, conveys or disposes of any record, voucher, money, or thing of value of the United States or of any department or agency thereof, or any property made or being made under contract for the United States or any department or agency thereof; or

Whoever receives, conceals, or retains the same with intent to convert it to his use or gain, knowing it to have been embezzled, stolen, purloined or converted -

Shall be fined not more than $10,000 or imprisoned not more than ten years, or both; but if the value of such property does not exceed the sum of $100, he shall be fined not more than $1,000 or imprisoned not more than one year, or both.

The word "value" means face, par, or market value, or cost price, either wholesale or retail, whichever is greater.

Sec. 659. Interstate or foreign shipments by carrier; State prosecutions

Whoever embezzles, steals, or unlawfully takes, carries away, or conceals, or by fraud or deception obtains from any pipeline system, railroad car, wagon, motortruck, or other vehicle, or from any tank or storage facility, station, station house, platform or depot or from any steamboat, vessel, or wharf, or from any aircraft, air terminal, airport, aircraft terminal or air navigation facility with intent to convert to his own use any goods or chattels moving as or which are a part of or which constitute an interstate or foreign shipment of freight, express, or other property; or

Whoever buys or receives or has in his possession any such goods or chattels, knowing the same to have been embezzled or stolen; or

Whoever embezzles, steals, or unlawfully takes, carries away, or by fraud or deception obtains with intent to convert to his own use any baggage which shall have come into the possession of any common carrier for transportation in interstate or foreign commerce or breaks into, steals, takes, carries away, or conceals any of the contents of such baggage, or buys, receives, or has in his possession any such baggage or any article therefrom of whatever nature, knowing the same to have been embezzled or stolen; or

Whoever embezzles, steals, or unlawfully takes by any fraudulent device, scheme, or game, from any railroad car, bus, vehicle, steamboat, vessel, or aircraft operated by any common carrier moving in interstate or foreign commerce or from any passenger thereon any money, baggage, goods, or chattels, or whoever buys, receives, or has in his possession any such money, baggage, goods, or chattels, knowing the same to have been embezzled or stolen -

Shall in each case be fined not more than $5,000 or imprisoned not more than ten years, or both; but if the amount or value of such money, baggage, goods or chattels does not exceed $100, he shall be fined not more than $1,000 or imprisoned not more than one year, or both.

The offense shall be deemed to have been committed not only in the district where the violation first occurred, but also in any district in which the defendant may have taken or been in possession of the said money, baggage, goods, or chattels.

The carrying or transporting of any such money, freight, express, baggage, goods, or chattels in interstate or foreign commerce, knowing the same to have been stolen, shall constitute a separate offense and subject the offender to the penalties under this section for unlawful taking, and the offense shall be deemed to have been committed in any district into which such money, freight, express, baggage, goods, or chattels shall have been removed or into which the same shall have been brought by such offender.

To establish the interstate or foreign commerce character of any shipment in any prosecution under this section the waybill or other shipping document of such shipment shall be prima facie evidence of the place from which and to which such shipment was made. The removal of property from a pipeline system which extends interstate shall be prima facie evidence of the interstate character of the shipment of the property.

A judgment of conviction or acquittal on the merits under the laws of any State shall be a bar to any prosecution under this section for the same act or acts. Nothing contained in this section shall be construed as indicating an intent on the part of Congress to occupy the field in which provisions of this section operate to the exclusion of State laws on the same subject matter, nor shall any provision of this section be construed as invalidating any provision of State law unless such provision is inconsistent with any of the purposes of this section or any provision thereof.

TITLE 18 - CRIMES AND CRIMINAL PROCEDURE

PART I - CRIMES
CHAPTER 37 - ESPIONAGE AND CENSORSHIP

Sec. 793. Gathering, transmitting or losing defense information

(a) Whoever, for the purpose of obtaining information respecting the national defense with intent or reason to believe that the information is to be used to the injury of the United States, or to the advantage of any foreign nation, goes upon, enters, flies over, or otherwise obtains information concerning any vessel, aircraft, work of defense, navy yard, naval station, submarine base, fueling station, fort, battery, torpedo station, dockyard, canal, railroad, arsenal, camp, factory, mine, telegraph, telephone, wireless, or signal station, building, office, research laboratory or station or other place connected with the national defense owned or constructed, or in progress of construction by the United States or under the control of the United States, or of any of its officers, departments, or agencies, or within the exclusive jurisdiction of the United States, or any place in which any vessel, aircraft, arms, munitions, or other materials or instruments for use in time of war are being made, prepared, repaired, stored, or are the subject of research or development, under any contract or agreement with the United States, or any department or agency thereof, or with any person on behalf of the United States, or otherwise on behalf of the United States, or any prohibited place so designated by the President by proclamation in time of war or in case of national emergency in which anything for the use of the Army, Navy, or Air Force is being prepared or constructed or stored, information as to which prohibited place the President has determined would be prejudicial to the national defense; or

(b) Whoever, for the purpose aforesaid, and with like intent or reason to believe, copies, takes, makes, or obtains, or attempts to copy, take, make, or obtain, any sketch, photograph, photographic negative, blueprint, plan, map, model, instrument, appliance, document, writing, or note of anything connected with the national defense; or

(c) Whoever, for the purpose aforesaid, receives or obtains or agrees or attempts to receive or obtain from any person, or from any source whatever, any document, writing, code book, signal book, sketch, photograph, photographic negative, blueprint, plan, map, model, instrument, appliance, or note, of anything connected with the national defense, knowing or having reason to believe, at the time he receives or obtains, or agrees or attempts to receive or obtain it, that it has been or will be obtained, taken, made, or disposed of by any person contrary to the provisions of this chapter; or

(d) Whoever, lawfully having possession of, access to, control over, or being entrusted with any document, writing, code book, signal book, sketch, photograph, photographic negative, blueprint, plan, map, model, instrument, appliance, or note relating to the national defense, or information relating to the national defense which information the possessor has reason to believe could be used to the injury of the United States or to the advantage of any foreign nation, willfully communicates, delivers, transmits or causes to be communicated, delivered, or transmitted or attempts to communicate, deliver, transmit or cause to be communicated, delivered or transmitted the same to any person not entitled to receive it, or willfully retains the same and fails to deliver it on demand to the officer or employee of the United States entitled to receive it; or

(e) Whoever having unauthorized possession of, access to, or control over any document, writing, code book, signal book, sketch, photograph, photographic negative, blueprint, plan, map, model, instrument, appliance, or note relating to the national defense, or information relating to the national defense which information the possessor has reason to believe could be used to the injury of the United States or to the advantage of any foreign nation, willfully communicates, delivers, transmits or causes to be communicated, delivered, or transmitted, or attempts to communicate, deliver, transmit or cause to be communicated, delivered, or transmitted the same to any person not entitled to receive it, or willfully retains the same and fails to deliver it to the officer or employee of the United States entitled to receive it; or

(f) Whoever, being entrusted with or having lawful possession or control of any document, writing, code book, signal book, sketch, photograph, photographic negative, blueprint, plan, map, model, instrument, appliance, note, or information, relating to the national defense, (1) through gross negligence permits the same to be removed from its proper place of custody or delivered to anyone in violation of his trust, or to be lost, stolen, abstracted, or destroyed, or (2) having knowledge that the same has been illegally removed from its proper place of custody or delivered to anyone in violation of its trust, or lost, or stolen, abstracted, or destroyed, and fails to make prompt report of such loss, theft, abstraction, or destruction to his superior officer -

Shall be fined not more than $10,000 or imprisoned not more than ten years, or both.

(g) If two or more persons conspire to violate any of the foregoing provisions of this section, and one or more of such persons do any act to effect the object of the conspiracy, each of the parties to such conspiracy shall be subject to the punishment provided for the offense which is the object of such conspiracy.

(h)(1) Any person convicted of a violation of this section shall forfeit to the United States, irrespective of any provision of State law, any property constituting, or derived from, any proceeds the person obtained, directly or indirectly, from any foreign government, or any faction or party or military or naval force within a foreign country, whether recognized or unrecognized by the United States, as the result of such violation.

(2) The court, in imposing sentence on a defendant for a conviction of a violation of this section, shall order that the defendant forfeit to the United States all property described in paragraph (1) of this subsection.

(3) The provisions of subsections (b), (c), and (e) through (o) of section 413 of the Comprehensive Drug Abuse Prevention and Control Act of 1970 (21 U.S.C. 853(b), (c), and (e)-(o)) shall apply to -

(A) property subject to forfeiture under this subsection;

(B) any seizure or disposition of such property; and

(C) any administrative or judicial proceeding in relation to such property, if not inconsistent with this subsection.

(4) Notwithstanding section 524(c) of title 28, there shall be deposited in the Crime Victims Fund in the Treasury all amounts from the forfeiture of property under this subsection remaining after the payment of expenses for forfeiture and sale authorized by law.

Sec. 794. Gathering or delivering defense information to aid foreign government

(a) Whoever, with intent or reason to believe that it is to be used to the injury of the United States or to the advantage of a foreign nation, communicates, delivers, or transmits, or attempts to communicate, deliver, or transmit, to any foreign government, or to any faction or party or military or naval force within a foreign country, whether recognized or unrecognized by the United States, or to any representative, officer, agent, employee, subject, or citizen thereof, either directly or indirectly, any document, writing, code book, signal book, sketch, photograph, photographic negative, blueprint, plan, map, model, note, instrument, appliance, or information relating to the national defense, shall be punished by death or by imprisonment for any term of years or for life.

(b) Whoever, in time of war, with intent that the same shall be communicated to the enemy, collects, records, publishes, or communicates, or attempts to elicit any information with respect to the movement, numbers, description, condition, or disposition of any of the Armed Forces, ships, aircraft, or war materials of the United States, or with respect to the plans or conduct, or supposed plans or conduct of any naval or military operations, or with respect to any works or measures undertaken for or connected with, or intended for the fortification or defense of any place, or any other information relating to the public defense, which might be useful to the enemy, shall be punished by death or by imprisonment for any term of years or for life.

(c) If two or more persons conspire to violate this section, and one or more of such persons do any act to effect the object of the conspiracy, each of the parties to such conspiracy shall be subject to the punishment provided for the offense which is the object of such conspiracy.

(d)(1) Any person convicted of a violation of this section shall forfeit to the United States irrespective of any provision of State law -

(A) any property constituting, or derived from, any proceeds the person obtained, directly or indirectly, as the result of such violation, and

(B) any of the person's property used, or intended to be used, in any manner or part, to commit, or to facilitate the commission of, such violation.

(2) The court, in imposing sentence on a defendant for a conviction of a violation of this section, shall order that the defendant forfeit to the United States all property described in paragraph (1) of this subsection.

(3) The provisions of subsections (b), (c) and (e) through

(o) of section 413 of the Comprehensive Drug Abuse Prevention and Control Act of 1970 (21 U.S.C. 853(b), (c), and (e)-(o)) shall apply to -

(A) property subject to forfeiture under this subsection;

(B) any seizure or disposition of such property; and

(C) any administrative or judicial proceeding in relation to such property, if not inconsistent with this subsection.

(4) Notwithstanding section 524(c) of title 28, there shall be deposited in the Crime Victims Fund in the Treasury all amounts from the forfeiture of property under this subsection remaining after the payment of expenses for forfeiture and sale authorized by law.

TITLE 18 - CRIMES AND CRIMINAL PROCEDURE

PART I - CRIMES
CHAPTER 47 - FRAUD AND FALSE STATEMENTS

Sec. 1001. Statements or entries generally

> ED. NOTE: The following section was amended by the Violent Crimes Act of 1994—Title XXIX - Computer Crime, section 330016; those amendments are incorporated.

Whoever, in any matter within the jurisdiction of any department or agency of the United States knowingly and willfully falsifies, conceals or covers up by any trick, scheme, or device a material fact, or makes any false, fictitious or fraudulent statements or representations, or makes or uses any false writing or document knowing the same to contain any false, fictitious or fraudulent statement or entry, shall be fined under this title, or imprisoned not more than five years, or both.

Sec. 1029. Fraud and related activity in connection with access devices

> ED. NOTE: This section was amended by the Violent Crimes Act of 1994 (Title XXIX - Computer Crime, section 250007) and by the Communications Assistance for Law Enforcement Act (Public Law 103-414, popularly known as the Digital Telephony Bill); those amendments are incorporated.
>
> Note that those two sets of amendments each added separate paragraphs numbered (a)(5) and (a)(6), as well as separate paragraphs each numbered (e)(7). In this text, we have used the designations (5.1), (6.1), and (7.1) to refer to the paragraphs inserted by the Violent Crimes Act. Those numbered (5), (6), and (7) were inserted by the Communications Assistance for Law Enforcment Act. A technical amendment is expected to officially correct these discrepancies.

(a) Whoever -

(1) knowingly and with intent to defraud produces, uses, or traffics in one or more counterfeit access devices;

(2) knowingly and with intent to defraud traffics in or uses one or more unauthorized access de-

vices during any one-year period, and by such conduct obtains anything of value aggregating $1,000 or more during that period;

(3) knowingly and with intent to defraud possesses fifteen or more devices which are counterfeit or unauthorized access devices;

(4) knowingly, and with intent to defraud, produces, traffics in, has control or custody of, or possesses device-making equipment;

(5) knowingly and with intent to defraud uses, produces, traffics in, has control or custody of, or possesses a telecommunications instrument that has been modified or altered to obtain unauthorized use of telecommunications services; or

(6) knowingly and with intent to defraud uses, produces, traffics in, has control or custody of, or possesses—

(A) a scanning receiver; or

(B) hardware or software used for altering or modifying telecommunications instruments to obtain unauthorized access to telecommunications services; or

(5.1) knowingly and with intent to defraud effects transactions, with 1 or more access devices issued to another person or persons, to receive payment or any other thing of value during any 1-year period the aggregate value of which is equal to or greater than $1,000;

(6.1) without the authorization of the issuer of the access device, knowingly and with intent to defraud solicits a person for the purpose of

(A) offering an access device; or

(B) selling information regarding or an application to obtain an access device; or

(7) without the authorization of the credit card system member or its agent, knowingly and with intent to defraud causes or arranges for another person to present to the member or its agent, for payment, 1 or more evidences or records of transactions made by an access device; shall, if the offense affects interstate or foreign commerce, be punished as provided in subsection (c) of this section.

(b)(1) Whoever attempts to commit an offense under subsection (a) of this section shall be punished as provided in subsection (c) of this section.

(2) Whoever is a party to a conspiracy of two or more persons to commit an offense under subsection (a) of this section, if any of the parties engages in any conduct in furtherance of such offense, shall be fined an amount not greater than the amount provided as the maximum fine for such offense under subsection (c) of this section or imprisoned not longer than one-

half the period provided as the maximum imprisonment for such offense under subsection (c) of this section, or both.

(c) The punishment for an offense under subsection (a) or (b)(1) of this section is -

(1) a fine of not more than the greater of $10,000 or twice the value obtained by the offense or imprisonment for not more than ten years, or both, in the case of an offense under subsection

(a)(2), (3), (5.1), (6.1), or (7) of this conviction for another offense under either such subsection, or of this section which does not occur after a an attempt to commit an offense punishable under this paragraph;

(2) a fine of not more than the greater of $50,000 or twice the value obtained by the offense or imprisonment for not more than fifteen years, or both, in the case of an offense under subsection (a)(1), (4), (5a), or (6a) of this section which does not occur after a conviction for another offense under either such subsection, or an attempt to commit an offense punishable under this paragraph; and

(3) a fine of not more than the greater of $100,000 or twice the value obtained by the offense or imprisonment for not more than twenty years, or both, in the case of an offense under subsection (a) of this section which occurs after a conviction for another offense under such subsection, or an attempt to commit an offense punishable under this paragraph.

(d) The United States Secret Service shall, in addition to any other agency having such authority, have the authority to investigate offenses under this section. Such authority of the United States Secret Service shall be exercised in accordance with an agreement which shall be entered into by the Secretary of the Treasury and the Attorney General.

(e) As used in this section -

(1) the term "access device" means any card, plate, code, account number, electronic serial number, mobile identification number, personal identification number, or other telecommunications service, equipment, or instrument identifier, or other means of account access that can be used, alone or in conjunction with another access device, to obtain money, goods, services, or any other thing of value, or that can be used to initiate a transfer of funds (other than a transfer originated solely by paper instrument);

(2) the term "counterfeit access device" means any access device that is counterfeit, fictitious, altered, or forged, or an identifiable component of an access device or a counterfeit access device;

(3) the term "unauthorized access device" means any access device that is lost, stolen, expired, revoked, canceled, or obtained with intent to defraud;

(4) the term "produce" includes design, alter, authenticate, duplicate, or assemble; ·

(5) the term "traffic" means transfer, or otherwise dispose of, to another, or obtain control of with intent to transfer or dispose of;

(6) the term "device-making equipment" means any equipment, mechanism, or impression designed or primarily used for making an access device or a counterfeit access device;

(7) the term 'scanning receiver' means a device or apparatus that can be used to intercept a wire or electronic communication in violation of chapter 119.

(7.1) the term 'credit card system member' means a financial institution or other entity that is a member of a credit card system, including an entity, whether affiliated with or identical to the credit card issuer, that is the sole member of a credit card system.

(f) This section does not prohibit any lawfully authorized investigative, protective, or intelligence activity of a law enforcement agency of the United States, a State, or a political subdivision of a State, or of an intelligence agency of the United States, or any activity authorized under chapter 224 of this title. For purposes of this subsection, the term "State" includes a State of the United States, the District of Columbia, and any commonwealth, territory, or possession of the United States.

Sec. 1030. Fraud and related activity in connection with computers

> ED. NOTE: This section, enacted as the Computer Fraud and Abuse Act, was amended by the Computer Abuse Amendments Act of 1994—Title XXIX - Computer Crime, section 290001; those amendments are incorporated.

(a) Whoever -

(1) knowingly accesses a computer without authorization or exceeds authorized access, and by means of such conduct obtains information that has been determined by the United States Government pursuant to an Executive order or statute to require protection against unauthorized disclosure for reasons of national defense or foreign relations, or any restricted data, as defined in paragraph y. of section 11 of the Atomic Energy Act of 1954, with the intent or reason to believe that such information so obtained is to be used to the injury of the United States, or to the advantage of any foreign nation;

(2) intentionally accesses a computer without authorization or exceeds authorized access, and thereby obtains information contained in a financial record of a financial institution, or of a card issuer as defined in section 1602(n) of title 15, or contained in a file of a consumer reporting agency on a consumer, as such

terms are defined in the Fair Credit Reporting Act (15 U.S.C. 1681 et seq.);

(3) intentionally, without authorization to access any computer of a department or agency of the United States, accesses such a computer of that department or agency that is exclusively for the use of the Government of the United States or, in the case of a computer not exclusively for such use, is used by or for the Government of the United States and such conduct adversely affects the use of the Government's operation of such computer;

(4) knowingly and with intent to defraud, accesses a Federal interest computer without authorization, or exceeds authorized access, and by means of such conduct furthers the intended fraud and obtains anything of value, unless the object of the fraud and the thing obtained consists only of the use of the computer;

(5)(A) through means of a computer used in interstate commerce or communications, knowingly causes the transmission of a program, information, code, or command to a computer or computer system if-

(i) the person causing the transmission intends that such transmission will-

(I) damage, or cause damage to, a computer, computer system, network, information, data, or program; or

(II) withhold or deny, or cause the withholding or denial, of the use of a computer, computer services, system or network, information, data or program; and

(ii) the transmission of the harmful component of the program, information, code, or command-

(I) occurred without the authorization of the persons or entities who own or are responsible for the computer system receiving the program, information, code, or command; and

(II)(aa) causes loss or damage to one or more other persons of value aggregating $ 1,000 or more during any 1-year period; or

(bb) modifies or impairs, or potentially modifies or impairs, the medical examination, medical diagnosis, medical treatment, or medical care of one or more individuals; or

(B) through means of a computer used in interstate commerce or communication, knowingly causes the transmission of a program, information, code, or command to a computer or computer system-

(i) with reckless disregard of a substantial and unjustifiable risk that the transmission will-

(I) damage, or cause damage to, a computer, computer system, network, information, data or program; or

(II) withhold or deny or cause the withholding or denial of the use of a computer, computer services, system, network, information, data or program; and

(ii) if the transmission of the harmful component of the program, information, code, or command-

(I) occurred without the authorization of the persons or entities who own or are responsible for the computer system receiving the program, information, code, or command; and

(II)(aa) causes loss or damage to one or more other persons of a value aggregating $ 1,000 or more during any 1-year period; or

(bb) modifies or impairs, or potentially modifies or impairs, the medical examination, medical diagnosis, medical treatment, or medical care of one or more individuals;.

(6) knowingly and with intent to defraud traffics (as defined in section 1029) in any password or similar information through which a computer may be accessed without authorization, if -

(A) such trafficking affects interstate or foreign commerce; or

(B) such computer is used by or for the Government of the United States; shall be punished as provided in subsection (c) of this section.

(b) Whoever attempts to commit an offense under subsection (a) of this section shall be punished as provided in subsection (c) of this section.

(c) The punishment for an offense under subsection (a) or (b) of this section is -

(1)(A) a fine under this title or imprisonment for not more than ten years, or both, in the case of an offense under subsection (a)(1) of this section which does not occur after a conviction for another offense under such subsection, or an attempt to commit an offense punishable under this subparagraph; and

(B) a fine under this title or imprisonment for not more than twenty years, or both, in the case of an offense under subsection

(a)(1) of this section which occurs after a conviction for another offense under such subsection, or an attempt to commit an offense punishable under this subparagraph; and

(2)(A) a fine under this title or imprisonment for not more than one year, or both, in the case of an offense under subsection (a)(2), (a)(3) or (a)(6) of this sec-

tion which does not occur after a conviction for another offense under such subsection, or an attempt to commit an offense punishable under this subparagraph; and

(B) a fine under this title or imprisonment for not more than ten years, or both, in the case of an offense under subsection

(a)(2), (a)(3) or (a)(6) of this section which occurs after a conviction for another offense under such subsection, or an attempt to commit an offense punishable under this subparagraph;

(3)(A) a fine under this title or imprisonment for not more than five years, or both, in the case of an offense under subsection (a)(4) or (a)(5)(A) of this section which does not occur after a conviction for another offense under such subsection, or an attempt to commit an offense punishable under this subparagraph; and

(B) a fine under this title or imprisonment for not more than ten years, or both, in the case of an offense under subsection

(a)(4) or (a)(5) of this section which occurs after a conviction for another offense under such subsection, or an attempt to commit an offense punishable under this subparagraph; and

(4) a fine under this title or imprisonment for not more than 1 year, or both, in the case of an offense under subsection (a)(5)(B).

(d) The United States Secret Service shall, in addition to any other agency having such authority, have the authority to investigate offenses under this section. Such authority of the United States Secret Service shall be exercised in accordance with an agreement which shall be entered into by the Secretary of the Treasury and the Attorney General.

(e) As used in this section -

(1) the term "computer" means an electronic, magnetic, optical, electrochemical, or other high speed data processing device performing logical, arithmetic, or storage functions, and includes any data storage facility or communications facility directly related to or operating in conjunction with such device, but such term does not include an automated typewriter or typesetter, a portable hand held calculator, or other similar device;

(2) the term "Federal interest computer" means a computer -

(A) exclusively for the use of a financial institution or the United States Government, or, in the case of a computer not exclusively for such use, used by or for a financial institution or the United States Government and the conduct constituting the offense affects the use of the financial institution's operation or the Government's operation of such computer; or

(B) which is one of two or more computers used in committing the offense, not all of which are located in the same State;

(3) the term "State" includes the District of Columbia, the Commonwealth of Puerto Rico, and any other commonwealth, possession or territory of the United States;

(4) the term "financial institution" means -

(A) an institution, with deposits insured by the Federal Deposit Insurance Corporation;

(B) the Federal Reserve or a member of the Federal Reserve including any Federal Reserve Bank;

(C) a credit union with accounts insured by the National Credit Union Administration;

(D) a member of the Federal home loan bank system and any home loan bank;

(E) any institution of the Farm Credit System under the Farm Credit Act of 1971;

(F) a broker-dealer registered with the Securities and Exchange Commission pursuant to section 15 of the Securities Exchange Act of 1934;

(G) the Securities Investor Protection Corporation;

(H) a branch or agency of a foreign bank (as such terms are defined in paragraphs (1) and (3) of section 1(b) of the International Banking Act of 1978); and

(I) an organization operating under section 25 or section 25(a) of the Federal Reserve Act;

(5) the term "financial record" means information derived from any record held by a financial institution pertaining to a customer's relationship with the financial institution;

(6) the term "exceeds authorized access" means to access a computer with authorization and to use such access to obtain or alter information in the computer that the accesser is not entitled so to obtain or alter; and

(7) the term "department of the United States" means the legislative or judicial branch of the Government or one of the executive departments enumerated in section 101 of title 5.

(f) This section does not prohibit any lawfully authorized investigative, protective, or intelligence activity of a law enforcement agency of the United States, a State, or a political subdivision of a State, or of an intelligence agency of the United States.

(g) Any person who suffers damage or loss by reason of a violation of the section, other than a violation of subsection (a)(5)(B), may maintain a civil action against the violator to obtain compensatory damages and injunctive relief or other equitable relief. Damages for violations of any subsection other than subsection (a)(5)(A)(ii)(II)(bb) or

(a)(5)(B)(ii)(II)(bb) are limited to economic damages. No action may be brought under this subsection unless such action is begun within 2 years of the date of the act complained of or the date of the discovery of the damage.

(h) The Attorney General and the Secretary of the Treasury shall report to the Congress annually, during the first 3 years following the date of the enactment of this subsection, concerning investigations and prosecutions under section 1030(a)(5) of title 18, United States Code.

TITLE 18 - CRIMES AND CRIMINAL PROCEDURE

PART I - CRIMES
CHAPTER 63 - MAIL FRAUD

Sec. 1341. Frauds and swindles

Whoever, having devised or intending to devise any scheme or artifice to defraud, or for obtaining money or property by means of false or fraudulent pretenses, representations, or promises, or to sell, dispose of, loan, exchange, alter, give away, distribute, supply, or furnish or procure for unlawful use any counterfeit or spurious coin, obligation, security, or other article, or anything represented to be or intimated or held out to be such counterfeit or spurious article, for the purpose of executing such scheme or artifice or attempting so to do, places in any post office or authorized depository for mail matter, any matter or thing whatever to be sent or delivered by the Postal Service, or takes or receives therefrom, any such matter or thing, or knowingly causes to be delivered by mail according to the direction thereon, or at the place at which it is directed to be delivered by the person to whom it is addressed, any such matter or thing, shall be fined not more than $1,000 or imprisoned not more than five years, or both. If the violation affects a financial institution, such person shall be fined not more than $1,000,000 or imprisoned not more than 30 years, or both.

Sec. 1343. Fraud by wire, radio, or television

Whoever, having devised or intending to devise any scheme or artifice to defraud, or for obtaining money or property by means of false or fraudulent pretenses, representations, or promises, transmits or causes to be transmitted by means of wire, radio, or television communication in interstate or foreign commerce, any writings, signs, signals, pictures, or sounds for the purpose of executing such scheme or artifice, shall be fined not more than $1,000 or imprisoned not more than five years, or both. If the violation affects a financial institution, such person shall be fined not more than

$1,000,000 or imprisoned not more than 30 years, or both.

TITLE 18 - CRIMES AND CRIMINAL PROCEDURE

PART I - CRIMES

CHAPTER 65 - MALICIOUS MISCHIEF

Sec. 1361. Government property or contracts

Whoever willfully injures or commits any depredation against any property of the United States, or of any department or agency thereof, or any property which has been or is being manufactured or constructed for the United States, or any department or agency thereof, shall be punished as follows:

If the damage to such property exceeds the sum of $100, by a fine of not more than $10,000 or imprisonment for not more than ten years, or both; if the damage to such property does not exceed the sum of $100, by a fine of not more than $1,000 or by imprisonment for not more than one year, or both.

TITLE 18 - CRIMES AND CRIMINAL PROCEDURE

PART I - CRIMES

CHAPTER 101 - RECORDS AND REPORTS

Sec. 2071. Concealment, removal, or mutilation generally

(a) Whoever willfully and unlawfully conceals, removes, mutilates, obliterates, or destroys, or attempts to do so, or, with intent to do so takes and carries away any record, proceeding, map, book, paper, document, or other thing, filed or deposited with any clerk or officer of any court of the United States, or in any public office, or with any judicial or public officer of the United States, shall be fined not more than $2,000 or imprisoned not more than three years, or both.

(b) Whoever, having the custody of any such record, proceeding, map, book, document, paper, or other thing, willfully and unlawfully conceals, removes, mutilates, obliterates, falsifies, or destroys the same, shall be fined not more than $2,000 or imprisoned not more than three years, or both; and shall forfeit his office and be disqualified from holding any office under the United States. As used in this subsection, the term "office" does not include the office held by any person as a retired officer of the Armed Forces of the United States.

TITLE 18 - CRIMES AND CRIMINAL PROCEDURE

PART I - CRIMES

CHAPTER 105 - SABOTAGE

Sec. 2155. Destruction of national-defense materials, national-defense premises or national-defense utilities

(a) Whoever, with intent to injure, interfere with, or obstruct the national defense of the United States, willfully injures, destroys, contaminates or infects, or attempts to so injure, destroy, contaminate or infect any national-defense material, national-defense premises, or national-defense utilities, shall be fined not more than $10,000 or imprisoned not more than ten years, or both.

(b) If two or more persons conspire to violate this section, and one or more of such persons do any act to effect the object of the conspiracy, each of the parties to such conspiracy shall be punished as provided in subsection (a) of this section.

TITLE 18- CRIMES AND CRIMINAL PROCEDURES

PART I. CRIMES

CHAPTER 113. STOLEN PROPERTY

Sec. 2314. Transportation of stolen goods, securities, moneys, fraudulent State tax stamps, or articles used in counterfeiting

Whoever transports, transmits, or transfers in interstate or foreign commerce any goods, wares, merchandise, securities or money, of the value of $5,000 or more, knowing the same to have been stolen, converted or taken by fraud; or

Whoever, having devised or intending to devise any scheme or artifice to defraud, or for obtaining money or property by means of false or fraudulent pretenses, representations, or promises, transports or causes to be transported, or induces any person or persons to travel in, or to be transported in interstate or foreign commerce in the execution or concealment of a scheme or artifice to defraud that person or those persons of money or property having a value of $5,000 or more; or

Whoever, with unlawful or fraudulent intent, transports in interstate or foreign commerce any falsely made, forged, altered, or counterfeited securities or tax stamps, knowing the same to have been falsely made, forged, altered, or counterfeited; or

Whoever, with unlawful or fraudulent intent, transports in interstate or foreign commerce any traveler's check bearing a forged countersignature; or

Whoever, with unlawful or fraudulent intent, transports in interstate or foreign commerce, any tool, implement, or thing used or fitted to be used in falsely making, forging, altering, or counterfeiting any security or tax stamps, or any part thereof—

Shall be fined not more than $10,000 or imprisoned not more than ten years, or both.

This section shall not apply to any falsely made, forged, altered, counterfeited or spurious representation of an obligation or other security of the United States, or of an obligation, bond, certificate, security, treasury note, bill, promise to pay or bank note issued by any foreign government. This section also shall not apply to any falsely made, forged, altered, counterfeited, or spurious representation of any bank note or bill issued by a bank or corporation of any foreign country which is intended by the laws or usage of such country to circulate as money.

TITLE 18-CRIMES AND CRIMINAL PROCEDURE

PART I-CRIMES
CHAPTER 119-WIRE AND ELECTRONIC COMMUNICATIONS
INTERCEPTION AND INTERCEPTION OF ORAL
COMMUNICATIONS

> ED. NOTE: This section was amended by the Communications Assistance for Law Enforcement Act (Public Law 103-414, popularly known as the "Digital Telephony Bill"); those amendments are incorporated.

2510. Definitions

As used in this chapter—

(1) "wire communication" means any aural transfer made in whole or in part through the use of facilities for the transmission of communications by the aid of wire, cable, or other like connection between the point of origin and the point of reception (including the use of such connection in a switching station) furnished or operated by any person engaged in providing or operating such facilities for the transmission of interstate or foreign communications or communications affecting interstate or foreign commerce and such term includes any electronic storage of such communication;

(2) "oral communication" means any oral communication uttered by a person exhibiting an expectation that such communication is not subject to interception under circumstances justifying such expectation, but such term does not include any electronic communication;

(3) "State" means any State of the United States, the District of Columbia, the Commonwealth of Puerto Rico, and any territory or possession of the United States;

(4) "intercept" means the aural or other acquisition of the contents of any wire, electronic, or oral communication through the use of any electronic, mechanical, or other device.

(5) "electronic, mechanical, or other device" means any device or apparatus which can be used to intercept a wire, oral, or electronic communication other than—

(a) any telephone or telegraph instrument, equipment or facility, or any component thereof, (i) furnished to the subscriber or user by a provider of wire or electronic communication service in the ordinary course of its business and being used by the subscriber or user in the ordinary course of its business or furnished by such subscriber or user for connection to the facilities of such service and used in the ordinary course of its business; or (ii) being used by a provider of wire or electronic communication service in the ordinary course of its business, or by an investigative or law enforcement officer in the ordinary course of his duties;

(b) a hearing aid or similar device being used to correct subnormal hearing to not better than normal;

(6) "person" means any employee, or agent of the United States or any State or political subdivision thereof, and any individual, partnership, association, joint stock company, trust, or corporation;

(7) "Investigative or law enforcement officer" means any officer of the United States or of a State or political subdivision thereof, who is empowered by law to conduct investigations of or to make arrests for offenses enumerated in this chapter, and any attorney authorized by law to prosecute or participate in the prosecution of such offenses;

(8) "contents", when used with respect to any wire, oral, or electronic communication, includes any information concerning the substance, purport, or meaning of that communication;

(9) "Judge of competent jurisdiction" means—

(a) a judge of a United States district court or a United States court of appeals; and

(b) a judge of any court of general criminal jurisdiction of a State who is authorized by a statute of that State to enter orders authorizing interceptions of wire, oral, or electronic communications;

(10) "communication common carrier" shall have the same meaning which is given the term "common carrier" by section 153(h) of title 47 of the United States Code;

(11) "aggrieved person" means a person who was a party to any intercepted wire, oral, or electronic communication or a person against whom the interception was directed;

(12) "electronic communication" means any transfer of signs, signals, writing, images, sounds, data, or intelligence of any nature transmitted in whole or in part by a wire, radio, electromagnetic, photoelectronic or photooptical system that affects interstate or foreign commerce, but does not include—

(A) any wire or oral communication;

(B) any communication made through a tone-only paging device; or

(C) any communication from a tracking device (as defined in section 3117 of this title);

(13) "user" means any person or entity who—

(A) uses an electronic communication service; and

(B) is duly authorized by the provider of such service to engage in such use;

(14) "electronic communications system" means any wire, radio, electromagnetic, photooptical or photoelectronic facilities for the transmission of electronic communications, and any computer facilities or related electronic equipment for the electronic storage of such communications;

(15) "electronic communication service" means any service which provides to users thereof the ability to send or receive wire or electronic communications;

(16) "readily accessible to the general public" means, with respect to a radio communication, that such communication is not—

(A) scrambled or encrypted;

(B) transmitted using modulation techniques whose essential parameters have been withheld from the public with the intention of preserving the privacy of such communication;

(C) carried on a subcarrier or other signal subsidiary to a radio transmission;

(D) transmitted over a communication system provided by a common carrier, unless the communication is a tone only paging system communication;

(E) transmitted on frequencies allocated under part 25, subpart D, E, or F of part 74, or part 94 of the Rules of the Federal Communications Commission, unless, in the case of a communication transmitted on a frequency allocated under part 74 that is not exclusively allocated to broadcast auxiliary services, the communication is a two-way voice communication by radio; or

(F) an electronic communication;

(17) "electronic storage" means—

(A) any temporary, intermediate storage of a wire or electronic communication incidental to the electronic transmission thereof; and

(B) any storage of such communication by an electronic communication service for purposes of backup protection of such communication; and

(18) "aural transfer" means a transfer containing the human voice at any point between and including the point of origin and the point of reception.

Sec. 2511. Interception and disclosure of wire, oral, or electronic communications prohibited

(1) Except as otherwise specifically provided in this chapter any person who -

(a) intentionally intercepts, endeavors to intercept, or procures any other person to intercept or endeavor to intercept, any wire, oral, or electronic communication;

(b) intentionally uses, endeavors to use, or procures any other person to use or endeavor to use any electronic, mechanical, or other device to intercept any oral communication when -

(i) such device is affixed to, or otherwise transmits a signal through, a wire, cable, or other like connection used in wire communication; or

(ii) such device transmits communications by radio, or interferes with the transmission of such communication; or

(iii) such person knows, or has reason to know, that such device or any component thereof has been sent through the mail or transported in interstate or foreign commerce; or

(iv) such use or endeavor to use (A) takes place on the premises of any business or other commercial establishment the operations of which affect interstate or foreign commerce; or

(B) obtains or is for the purpose of obtaining information relating to the operations of any business or other commercial establishment the operations of which affect interstate or foreign commerce; or

(v) such person acts in the District of Columbia, the Commonwealth of Puerto Rico, or any territory or possession of the United States;

(c) intentionally discloses, or endeavors to disclose, to any other person the contents of any wire, oral, or electronic communication, knowing or having reason to know that the information was obtained through the interception of a wire, oral, or electronic communication in violation of this subsection; or

(d) intentionally uses, or endeavors to use, the contents of any wire, oral, or electronic communication, knowing or having reason to know that the information was obtained through the interception of a wire, oral, or electronic communication in violation of this subsection; or

(e)(i) intentionally discloses, or endeavors to disclose, to any other person the contents of any wire, oral, or electronic communication, intercepted by means authorized by sections 2511(2)(A)(ii), 2511(b)-(c), 2511(e), 2516, and 2518 of this subchapter,

(ii) knowing or having reason to know that the information was obtained through the interception of such a communication in connection with a criminal investigation,

(iii) having obtained or received the information in connection with a criminal investigation, and

(iv) with intent to improperly obstruct, impede, or interfere with a duly authorized criminal investigation, shall be punished as provided in subsection (4) or shall be subject to suit as provided in subsection (5).

(2)(a)(i) It shall not be unlawful under this chapter for an operator of a switchboard, or an officer, employee, or agent of a provider of wire or electronic communication service, whose facilities are used in the transmission of a wire or electronic communication, to intercept, disclose, or use that communication in the normal course of his employment while engaged in any activity which is a necessary incident to the rendition of his service or to the protection of the rights or property of the provider of that service, except that a provider of wire communication service to the public shall not utilize service observing or random monitoring except for mechanical or service quality control checks.

(ii) Notwithstanding any other law, providers of wire or electronic communication service, their officers, employees, and agents, landlords, custodians, or other persons, are authorized to provide information, facilities, or technical assistance to persons authorized by law to intercept wire, oral, or electronic communications or to conduct electronic surveillance, as defined in section 101 of the Foreign Intelligence Surveillance Act of 1978, if such provider, its officers, employees, or agents, landlord, custodian, or other specified person, has been provided with -

(A) a court order directing such assistance signed by the authorizing judge, or

(B) a certification in writing by a person specified in section 2518(7) of this title or the Attorney General of the United States that no warrant or court order is required by law, that all statutory requirements have been met, and that the specified assistance is required, setting forth the period of time during which the provision of the information, facilities, or technical assistance is authorized and specifying the information, facilities, or technical assistance required. No provider of wire or electronic communication service, officer, employee, or agent thereof, or landlord, custodian, or other specified person shall disclose the existence of any interception or surveillance or the device used to accomplish the interception or surveillance with respect to which the person has been furnished a court order or certification under this chapter, except as may otherwise be required by legal process and then only after prior notification to the Attorney General or to the principal prosecuting attorney of a State or any political subdivision of a State, as may be appropriate. Any such disclosure, shall render such person liable for the civil damages provided for in section 2520. No cause of action shall lie in any court against any provider of wire or electronic communication service, its officers, employees, or agents, landlord, custodian, or other specified person for providing information, facilities, or assistance in accordance with the terms of a court order or certification under this chapter.

(b) It shall not be unlawful under this chapter for an officer, employee, or agent of the Federal Communications Commission, in the normal course of his employment and in discharge of the monitoring responsibilities exercised by the Commission in the enforcement of chapter 5 of title 47 of the United States Code, to intercept a wire or electronic communication, or oral communication transmitted by radio, or to disclose or use the information thereby obtained.

(c) It shall not be unlawful under this chapter for a person acting under color of law to intercept a wire, oral, or electronic communication, where such person is a party to the communication or one of the parties to the communication has given prior consent to such interception.

(d) It shall not be unlawful under this chapter for a person not acting under color of law to intercept a wire, oral, or electronic communication where such person is a party to the communication or where one of the parties to the communication has given prior consent to such interception unless such communication is intercepted for the purpose of committing any criminal or tortious act in violation of the Constitution or laws of the United States or of any State.

(e) Notwithstanding any other provision of this title or section 705 or 706 of the Communications Act of 1934, it shall not be unlawful for an officer, employee, or agent of the United States in the normal course of his official duty to conduct electronic surveillance, as defined in section 101 of the Foreign Intelligence Surveillance Act of 1978, as authorized by that Act.

(f) Nothing contained in this chapter or chapter 121, or section 705 of the Communications Act of 1934, shall be deemed to affect the acquisition by the United States Government of foreign intelligence information from international or foreign communications, or foreign intelligence activities conducted in accordance with otherwise applicable Federal law involving a foreign electronic communications system, utilizing a means other than electronic surveillance as defined in section 101 of the Foreign Intelligence Surveillance Act of 1978, and procedures in this chapter or chapter 121 and the Foreign Intelligence Surveillance Act of 1978 shall be the exclusive means by which electronic surveillance, as defined in section 101 of such Act, and the interception of domestic wire and oral communications may be conducted.

(g) It shall not be unlawful under this chapter or chapter 121 of this title for any person -

(i) to intercept or access an electronic communication made through an electronic communication system that is configured so that such electronic communication is readily accessible to the general public;

(ii) to intercept any radio communication which is transmitted -

(I) by any station for the use of the general public, or that relates to ships, aircraft, vehicles, or persons in distress;

(II) by any governmental, law enforcement, civil defense, private land mobile, or public safety communications system, including police and fire, readily accessible to the general public;

(III) by a station operating on an authorized frequency within the bands allocated to the amateur, citizens band, or general mobile radio services; or

(IV) by any marine or aeronautical communications system;

(iii) to engage in any conduct which -

(I) is prohibited by section 633 of the Communications Act of 1934; or

(II) is excepted from the application of section 705(a) of the Communications Act of 1934 by section 705(b) of that Act;

(iv) to intercept any wire or electronic communication the transmission of which is causing harmful interference to any lawfully operating station or consumer electronic equipment, to the extent necessary to identify the source of such interference; or

(v) for other users of the same frequency to intercept any radio communication made through a system that utilizes frequencies monitored by individuals engaged in the provision or the use of such system, if such communication is not scrambled or encrypted.

(h) It shall not be unlawful under this chapter -

(i) to use a pen register or a trap and trace device (as those terms are defined for the purposes of chapter 206 (relating to pen registers and trap and trace devices) of this title); or

(ii) for a provider of electronic communication service to record the fact that a wire or electronic communication was initiated or completed in order to protect such provider, another provider furnishing service toward the completion of the wire or electronic communication, or a user of that service, from fraudulent, unlawful or abusive use of such service.

(3)(a) Except as provided in paragraph (b) of this subsection, a person or entity providing an electronic communication service to the public shall not intentionally divulge the contents of any communication (other than one to such person or entity, or an agent thereof) while in transmission on that service to any person or entity other than an addressee or intended recipient of such communication or an agent of such addressee or intended recipient.

(b) A person or entity providing electronic communication service to the public may divulge the contents of any such communication -

(i) as otherwise authorized in section 2511(2)(a) or 2517 of this title;

(ii) with the lawful consent of the originator or any addressee or intended recipient of such communication;

(iii) to a person employed or authorized, or whose facilities are used, to forward such communication to its destination; or

(iv) which were inadvertently obtained by the service provider and which appear to pertain to the commission of a crime, if such divulgence is made to a law enforcement agency.

(4)(a) Except as provided in paragraph (b) of this subsection or in subsection (5), whoever violates subsection (1) of this section shall be fined under this title or imprisoned not more than five years, or both.

(b) If the offense is a first offense under paragraph (a) of this subsection and is not for a tortious or illegal purpose or for purposes of direct or indirect commercial advantage or private commercial gain, and the wire or electronic communication with respect to which the offense under paragraph (a) is a radio communication that is not scrambled, encrypted, or transmitted using modulation techniques the essential parameters of which have been withheld from the public with the intention of preserving the privacy of such communication, then -

(i) if the communication is not the radio portion of a cellular telephone communication, a cordless telephone communication that is transmitted between the cordless telephone handset and the base unit, a public land mobile radio service communication or a paging service communication, and the conduct is not that described in subsection (5), the offender shall be fined under this title or imprisoned not more than one year, or both; and

(ii) if the communication is the radio portion of a cellular telephone communication, a cordless telephone communication that is transmitted between the cordless telephone handset and the base unit, a public land mobile radio service communication or a paging service communication, the offender shall be fined under this title.

(c) Conduct otherwise an offense under this subsection that consists of or relates to the interception of a satellite transmission that is not encrypted or scrambled and that is transmitted -

(i) to a broadcasting station for purposes of retransmission to the general public; or

(ii) as an audio subcarrier intended for redistribution to facilities open to the public, but not including data transmissions or telephone calls, is not an offense under this subsection unless the conduct is for the purposes of direct or indirect commercial advantage or private financial gain.

(5)(a)(i) If the communication is -

(A) a private satellite video communication that is not scrambled or encrypted and the conduct in violation of this chapter is the private viewing of that communication and is not for a tortious or illegal purpose or for purposes of direct or indirect commercial advantage or private commercial gain; or

(B) a radio communication that is transmitted on frequencies allocated under subpart D of part 74 of the rules of the Federal Communications Commission that is not scrambled or encrypted and the conduct in violation of this chapter is not for a tortious or illegal purpose or for purposes of direct or indirect commercial advantage or private commercial gain, then the person who engages in such conduct shall be subject to suit by the Federal Government in a court of competent jurisdiction.

(ii) In an action under this subsection -

(A) if the violation of this chapter is a first offense for the person under paragraph (a) of subsection (4) and such person has not been found liable in a civil action under section 2520 of this title, the Federal Government shall be entitled to appropriate injunctive relief; and

(B) if the violation of this chapter is a second or subsequent offense under paragraph (a) of subsection (4) or such person has been found liable in any prior civil action under section 2520, the person shall be subject to a mandatory $500 civil fine.

(b) The court may use any means within its authority to enforce an injunction issued under paragraph (ii)(A), and shall impose a civil fine of not less than $500 for each violation of such an injunction.

> ED. NOTE: The following section was added by the Communications Assistance for Law Enforcement Act (Public Law 103-414, popularly known as the "Digital Telephony Bill).

Sec. 2522. Enforcement of the Communications Assistance for Law Enforcement Act

(a) Enforcement by Court Issuing Surveillance Order: If a court authorizing an interception under this chapter, a State statute, or the Foreign Intelligence Surveillance Act of 1978 (50 U.S.C. 1801 et seq.) or authorizing use of a pen register or a trap and trace device under chapter 206 or a State statute finds that a telecommunications carrier has failed to comply with the requirements of the Communications Assistance for Law Enforcement Act, the court may, in accordance with section 108 of such Act, direct that the carrier comply forthwith and may direct that a provider of support services to the carrier or the manufacturer of the carrier's transmission or switching equipment furnish forthwith modifications necessary for the carrier to comply.

(b) Enforcement Upon Application by Attorney General: The Attorney General may, in a civil action in the appropriate United States district court, obtain an order, in accordance with section 108 of the Communications Assistance for Law Enforcement Act, directing that a telecommunications carrier, a manufacturer of telecommunications transmission or switching equipment, or a provider of telecommunications support services comply with such Act.

(c) Civil Penalty:

(1) In general: A court issuing an order under this section against a telecommunications carrier, a manufacturer of telecommunications transmission or switching equipment, or a provider of telecommunications support services may impose a civil penalty of up to $10,000 per day for each day in violation after the issuance of the order or after such future date as the court may specify.

(2) Considerations: In determining whether to impose a civil penalty and in determining its amount, the court shall take into account—

(A) the nature, circumstances, and extent of the violation;

(B) the violator's ability to pay, the violator's good faith efforts to comply in a timely manner, any effect on the violator's ability to continue to do business, the degree of culpability, and the length of any delay in undertaking efforts to comply; and

(C) such other matters as justice may require.

(d) Definitions: As used in this section, the terms defined in section 102 of the Communications Assistance for Law Enforcement Act have the meanings provided, respectively, in such section.

(e) Conforming Amendments:

(1) Section 2518(4) of title 18, United States Code, is amended by adding at the end the following new sentence:

Pursuant to section 2522 of this chapter, an order may also be issued to enforce the assistance capability and capacity requirements under the Communications Assistance for Law Enforcement Act.

(2) Section 3124 of such title is amended by adding at the end the following new subsection:

(f) Communications Assistance Enforcement Orders: Pursuant to section 2522, an order may be issued to enforce the assistance capability and capacity requirements under the Communications Assistance for Law Enforcement Act.

(3) The table of sections at the beginning of chapter 119 of title 18, United States Code, is amended by inserting after the item pertaining to section 2521 the following new item:

TITLE 18 - CRIMES AND CRIMINAL PROCEDURE

PART II - CRIMINAL PROCEDURE
CHAPTER 206 - PEN REGISTERS AND TRAP AND TRACE DEVICES

> ED. NOTE: This section was amended by the Communications Assistance for Law Enforcement Act (Public Law 103-414, popularly known as the "Digital Telephony Bill"); those amendments are incorporated.

Sec. 3121. General prohibition on pen register and trap and trace device use; exception

(a) In General. - Except as provided in this section, no person may install or use a pen register or a trap and trace device without first obtaining a court order under section 3123 of this title or under the Foreign Intelligence Surveillance Act of 1978 (50 U.S.C. 1801 et seq.).

(b) Exception. - The prohibition of subsection (a) does not apply with respect to the use of a pen register or a trap and trace device by a provider of electronic or wire communication service -

(1) relating to the operation, maintenance, and testing of a wire or electronic communication service or to the protection of the rights or property of such provider, or to the protection of users of that service from abuse of service or unlawful use of service; or

(2) to record the fact that a wire or electronic communication was initiated or completed in order to protect such provider, another provider furnishing service toward the completion of the wire communication, or a user of that service, from fraudulent, unlawful or abusive use of service; or (3) where the consent of the user of that service has been obtained.

(c) Limitation. - A government agency authorized to install and use a pen register under this chapter or under state law shall use technology reasonably available to it that restricts the recording or decoding of electronic or other impulses to the dialing and signaling information utilized in call processing.

(d) Penalty. - Whoever knowingly violates subsection (a) shall be fined under this title or imprisoned not more than one year, or both.

TITLE 42 THE PUBLIC HEALTH AND WELFARE

CHAPTER 21A - PRIVACY PROTECTION
SUBCHAPTER I - FIRST AMENDMENT PRIVACY PROTECTION- PART A - UNLAWFUL ACTS

Sec. 2000aa. Searches and seizures by government officers and employees in connection with investigation or prosecution of criminal offenses

> ED. NOTE: This section was enacted by Public Law 96-440, also known as the Privacy Protection Act of 1980.

(a) Work product materials

Notwithstanding any other law, it shall be unlawful for a government officer or employee, in connection with the investigation or prosecution of a criminal offense, to search for or seize any work product materials possessed by a person reasonably believed to have a purpose to disseminate to the public a newspaper, book, broadcast, or other similar form of public communication, in or affecting interstate or foreign commerce; but this provision shall not impair or affect the ability of any government officer or employee, pursuant to otherwise appliable law, to search for or seize such materials, if -

(1) there is probable cause to believe that the person possessing such materials has committed or is committing the criminal offense to which the materials relate: Provided, however, That a government officer or employee may not search for or seize such materials under the provisions of this paragraph if the offense to which the materials relate consists of the receipt, possession, communication, or withholding of such materials or the information contained therein (but such a search or seizure may be conducted under the provisions of this paragraph if the offense consists of the receipt, possession, or communication of information relating to the national defense, classified information, or restricted data under the provisions of section 793, 794, 797, or 798 of title 18, or section 2274, 2275, or 2277 of this title, or section 783 of title 50; or

(2) there is reason to believe that the immediate seizure of such materials is necessary to prevent the death of, or serious bodily injury to, a human being.

(b) Other documents

Notwithstanding any other law, it shall be unlawful for a government officer or employee, in connection with the investigation or prosecution of a criminal offense, to search for or seize documentary materials, other than work product materials, possessed by a person in connection with a purpose to disseminate to the public a newspaper, book, broadcast, or other similar form of public communication, in or affecting interstate or foreign commerce; but this provision shall not impair or affect the ability of any government officer or employee, pursuant to otherwise applicable law, to search for or seize such materials, if -

(1) there is probable cause to believe that the person possessing such materials has committed or is committing the criminal offense to which the materials relate: Provided, however, That a government officer or employee may not search for or seize such materials under the provisions of this paragraph if the offense to which the materials relate consists of the receipt, possession, communication, or withholding of such materials or the information contained therein (but such a search or seizure may be conducted under the provisions of this paragraph if the offense consists of the receipt, possession, or communication of information relating to the national defense, classified information, or restricted data under the provisions of section 793, 794, 797, or 798 of title 18, or section 2274, 2275, or 2277 of this title, or section 783 of title 50;

(2) there is reason to believe that the immediate seizure of such materials is necessary to prevent the death of, or serious bodily injury to, a human being;

(3) there is reason to believe that the giving of notice pursuant to a subpena duces tecum would result in the destruction, alteration, or concealment of such materials; or

(4) such materials have not been produced in response to a court order directing compliance with a subpena duces tecum, and -

(A) all appellate remedies have been exhausted; or

(B) there is reason to believe that the delay in an investigation or trial occasioned by further proceedings relating to the subpena would threaten the interests of justice.

(c) Objections to court ordered subpoenas; affidavits

In the event a search warrant is sought pursuant to paragraph (4)(B) of subsection (b) of this section, the person possessing the materials shall be afforded adequate opportunity to submit an affidavit setting forth the basis for any contention that the materials sought are not subject to seizure.

TITLE 47 - TELEGRAPHS, TELEPHONES, AND RADIOTELE-GRAPHS

CHAPTER 5 - WIRE OR RADIO COMMUNICATION
SUBCHAPTER II - COMMON CARRIERS

Sec. 226. Telephone operator services

(a) Definitions

As used in this section -

(1) The term "access code" means a sequence of numbers that, when dialed, connect the caller to the provider of operator services associated with that sequence.

(2) The term "aggregator" means any person that, in the ordinary course of its operations, makes telephones available to the public or to transient users of its premises, for interstate telephone calls using a provider of operator services.

(3) The term "call splashing" means the transfer of a telephone call from one provider of operator services to another such provider in such a manner that the subsequent provider is unable or unwilling to determine the location of the origination of the call and, because of such inability or unwillingness, is prevented from billing the call on the basis of such location.

(4) The term "consumer" means a person initiating any interstate telephone call using operator services.

(5) The term "equal access" has the meaning given that term in Appendix B of the Modification of Final Judgment entered August 24, 1982, in United States v. Western Electric, Civil Action No. 82-0192 (United States District Court, District of Columbia), as amended by the Court in its orders issued prior to October 17, 1990.

(6) The term "equal access code" means an access code that allows the public to obtain an equal access connection to the carrier associated with that code.

(7) The term "operator services" means any interstate telecommunications service initiated from an aggregator location that includes, as a component, any automatic or live assistance to a consumer to arrange for billing or completion, or both, of an interstate telephone call through a method other than -

(A) automatic completion with billing to the telephone from which the call originated; or

(B) completion through an access code used by the consumer, with billing to an account previously established with the carrier by the consumer.

(8) The term "presubscribed provider of operator services" means the interstate provider of operator services to which the consumer is connected when the consumer places a call using a provider of operator services without dialing an access code.

(9) The term "provider of operator services" means any common carrier that provides operator services or any other person determined by the Commission to be providing operator services.

(b) Requirements for providers of operator services

(1) In general

Beginning not later than 90 days after October 17, 1990, each provider of operator services shall, at a minimum -

(A) identify itself, audibly and distinctly, to the consumer at the beginning of each telephone call and before the consumer incurs any charge for the call;

(B) permit the consumer to terminate the telephone call at no charge before the call is connected;

(C) disclose immediately to the consumer, upon request and at no charge to the consumer -

(i) a quote of its rates or charges for the call;

(ii) the methods by which such rates or charges will be collected; and

(iii) the methods by which complaints concerning such rates, charges, or collection practices will be resolved;

(D) ensure, by contract or tariff, that each aggregator for which such provider is the presubscribed provider of operator services is in compliance with the requirements of subsection

(c) of this section and, if applicable, subsection (e)(1) of this section;

(E) withhold payment (on a location-by-location basis) of any compensation, including commissions, to aggregators if such provider reasonably believes that the aggregator (i) is blocking access by means of "950" or "800" numbers to interstate common carriers in violation of subsection (c)(1)(B) of this section or (ii) is blocking access to equal access codes in violation of rules the Commission may prescribe under subsection (e)(1) of this section;

(F) not bill for unanswered telephone calls in areas where equal access is available;

(G) not knowingly bill for unanswered telephone calls where equal access is not available;

(H) not engage in call splashing, unless the consumer requests to be transferred to another provider of operator services, the consumer is informed prior to incurring any charges that the rates for the call may not reflect the rates from the actual originating location of the call, and the consumer then consents to be transferred; and

(I) except as provided in subparagraph (H), not bill for a call that does not reflect the location of the origination of the call.

(2) Additional requirements for first 3 years

In addition to meeting the requirements of paragraph (1), during the 3-year period beginning on the date that is 90 days after October 17, 1990, each presubscribed provider of operator services shall identify itself audibly and distinctly to the consumer, not only as required in paragraph (1)(A), but also for a second time before connecting the call and before the consumer incurs any charge.

(c) Requirements for aggregators

(1) In general

Each aggregator, beginning not later than 90 days after October 17, 1990, shall -

(A) post on or near the telephone instrument, in plain view of consumers -

(i) the name, address, and toll-free telephone number of the provider of operator services;

(ii) a written disclosure that the rates for all operator-assisted calls are available on request, and that consumers have a right to obtain access to the interstate common carrier of their choice and may contact their preferred interstate common carriers for information on accessing that carrier's service using that telephone; and

(iii) the name and address of the enforcement division of the Common Carrier Bureau of the Commission, to which the consumer may direct complaints regarding operator services;

(B) ensure that each of its telephones presubscribed to a provider of operator services allows the consumer to use "800" and "950" access code numbers to obtain access to the provider of operator services desired by the consumer; and

(C) ensure that no charge by the aggregator to the consumer for using an "800" or "950" access code number, or any other access code number, is greater than the amount the aggregator charges for calls placed using the presubscribed provider of operator services.

(2) Effect of State law or regulation

The requirements of paragraph (1)(A) shall not apply to an aggregator in any case in which State law or State regulation requires the aggregator to take actions that are substantially the same as those required in paragraph (1)(A).

(d) General rulemaking required

(1) Rulemaking proceeding

The Commission shall conduct a rulemaking proceeding pursuant to this subchapter to prescribe regulations to -

(A) protect consumers from unfair and deceptive practices relating to their use of operator services to place interstate telephone calls; and

(B) ensure that consumers have the opportunity to make informed choices in making such calls.

(2) Deadlines

The Commission shall initiate the proceeding required under paragraph (1) within 60 days after October 17, 1990, and shall prescribe regulations pursuant to the proceeding not later than 210 days after October 17, 1990. Such regulations shall take effect not later than 45 days after the date the regulations are prescribed.

(3) Contents of regulations

The regulations prescribed under this section shall -

(A) contain provisions to implement each of the requirements of this section, other than the requirements established by the rulemaking under subsection (e) of this section on access and compensation; and

(B) contain such other provisions as the Commission determines necessary to carry out this section and the purposes and policies of this section.

(4) Additional requirements to be implemented by regulations

The regulations prescribed under this section shall, at a minimum -

(A) establish minimum standards for providers of operator services and aggregators to use in the routing and handling of emergency telephone calls; and

(B) establish a policy for requiring providers of operator services to make public information about recent changes in operator services and choices available to consumers in that market.

(e) Separate rulemaking on access and compensation

(1) Access

The Commission, within 9 months after October 17, 1990, shall require -

(A) that each aggregator ensure within a reasonable time that each of its telephones presubscribed to a provider of operator services allows the consumer to obtain access to the provider of operator services desired by the consumer through the use of an equal access code; or

(B) that all providers of operator services, within a reasonable time, make available to their customers a "950" or "800" access code number for use

in making operator services calls from anywhere in the United States; or

(C) that the requirements described under both subparagraphs (A) and (B) apply.

(2) Compensation

The Commission shall consider the need to prescribe compensation (other than advance payment by consumers) for owners of competitive public pay telephones for calls routed to providers of operator services that are other than the presubscribed provider of operator services for such telephones.

Within 9 months after October 17, 1990, the Commission shall reach a final decision on whether to prescribe such compensation.

(f) Technological capability of equipment

Any equipment and software manufactured or imported more than 18 months after October 17, 1990, and installed by any aggregator shall be technologically capable of providing consumers with access to interstate providers of operator services through the use of equal access codes.

(g) Fraud

In any proceeding to carry out the provisions of this section, the Commission shall require such actions or measures as are necessary to ensure that aggregators are not exposed to undue risk of fraud.

(h) Determinations of rate compliance

(1) Filing of informational tariff

(A) In general

Each provider of operator services shall file, within 90 days after October 17, 1990, and shall maintain, update regularly, and keep open for public inspection, an informational tariff specifying rates, terms, and conditions, and including commissions, surcharges, any fees which are collected from consumers, and reasonable estimates of the amount of traffic priced at each rate, with respect to calls for which operator services are provided. Any changes in such rates, terms, or conditions shall be filed no later than the first day on which the changed rates, terms, or conditions are in effect.

(B) Waiver authority

The Commission may, after 4 years following October 17, 1990, waive the requirements of this paragraph only if -

(i) the findings and conclusions of the Commission in the final report issued under paragraph (3)(B)(iii) state that the regulatory objectives specified in subsection (d)(1)(A) and (B) of this section have been achieved; and

(ii) the Commission determines that such waiver will not adversely affect the continued achievement of such regulatory objectives.

(2) Review of informational tariffs

If the rates and charges filed by any provider of operator services under paragraph (1) appear upon review by the Commission to be unjust or unreasonable, the Commission may require such provider of operator services to do either or both of the following:

(A) demonstrate that its rates and charges are just and reasonable, and

(B) announce that its rates are available on request at the beginning of each call.

(3) Proceeding required

(A) In general

Within 60 days after October 17, 1990, the Commission shall initiate a proceeding to determine whether the regulatory objectives specified in subsection (d)(1)(A) and (B) of this section are being achieved. The proceeding shall -

(i) monitor operator service rates;

(ii) determine the extent to which offerings made by providers of operator services are improvements, in terms of service quality, price, innovation, and other factors, over those available before the entry of new providers of operator services into the market;

(iii) report on (in the aggregate and by individual provider) operator service rates, incidence of service complaints, and service offerings;

(iv) consider the effect that commissions and surcharges, billing and validation costs, and other costs of doing business have on the overall rates charged to consumers; and

(v) monitor compliance with the provisions of this section, including the periodic placement of telephone calls from aggregator locations.

(B) Reports

(i) The Commission shall, during the pendency of such proceeding and not later than 5 months after its commencement, provide the Congress with an interim report on the Commission's activities and progress to date.

(ii) Not later than 11 months after the commencement of such proceeding, the Commission shall report to the Congress on its interim findings as a result of the proceeding.

(iii) Not later than 23 months after the commencement of such proceeding, the Commis-

sion shall submit a final report to the Congress on its findings and conclusions.

(4) Implementing regulations

(A) In general

Unless the Commission makes the determination described in subparagraph (B), the Commission shall, within 180 days after submission of the report required under paragraph (3)(B)(iii), complete a rulemaking proceeding pursuant to this subchapter to establish regulations for implementing the requirements of this subchapter (and paragraphs (1) and (2) of this subsection) that rates and charges for operator services be just and reasonable. Such regulations shall include limitations on the amount of commissions or any other compensation given to aggregators by providers of operator service.

(B) Limitation

The requirement of subparagraph (A) shall not apply if, on the basis of the proceeding under paragraph (3)(A), the

Commission makes (and includes in the report required by paragraph (3)(B)(iii)) a factual determination that market forces are securing rates and charges that are just and reasonable, as evidenced by rate levels, costs, complaints, service quality, and other relevant factors.

(i) Statutory construction

Nothing in this section shall be construed to alter the obligations, powers, or duties of common carriers or the Commission under the other sections of this chapter.

PUBLIC LAW 103-414

COMMUNICATIONS ASSISTANCE FOR LAW ENFORCEMENT ACT

ED. NOTE: Public Law 103-414, Communications Assistance for Law Enforcement Act (popularly known as the "Digital Telephony Bill") amends 18 USC Section 1029, Title 18, Part I Crimes, Chapter 47 - Fraud and false statements. It also amends 18 USC Sections 2510 and 2511, Part I -Crimes, Chapter 119 - Wire and electronic communications interception and interception or oral communications (known as the Electronic Communications Privacy Act).

TITLE I—INTERCEPTION OF DIGITAL AND OTHER COMMUNICATIONS

Sec. 101. Short Title.

This title may be cited as the 'Communications Assistance for Law Enforcement Act'.

Sec. 102. Definitions.

For purposes of this title—

(1) The terms defined in section 2510 of title 18, United States Code, have, respectively, the meanings stated in that section.

(2) The term 'call-identifying information' means dialing or signaling information that identifies the origin, direction, destination, or termination of each communication generated or received by a subscriber by means of any equipment, facility, or service of a telecommunications carrier.

(3) The term 'Commission' means the Federal Communications Commission.

(4) The term 'electronic messaging services' means software-based services that enable the sharing of data, images, sound, writing, or other information among computing devices controlled by the senders or recipients of the messages.

(5) The term 'government' means the government of the United States and any agency or instrumentality thereof, the District of Columbia, any commonwealth, territory, or possession of the United States, and any State or political subdivision thereof authorized by law to conduct electronic surveillance.

(6) The term 'information services'—

(A) means the offering of a capability for generating, acquiring, storing, transforming, processing, retrieving, utilizing, or making available information via telecommunications; and

(B) includes—

(i) a service that permits a customer to retrieve stored information from, or file information for storage in, information storage facilities;

(ii) electronic publishing; and

(iii) electronic messaging services; but

(C) does not include any capability for a telecommunications carrier's internal management, control, or operation of its telecommunications network.

(7) The term 'telecommunications support services' means a product, software, or service used by a telecommunications carrier for the internal signaling or switching functions of its telecommunications network.

(8) The term 'telecommunications carrier'—

(A) means a person or entity engaged in the transmission or switching of wire or electronic communications as a common carrier for hire; and

(B) includes—

(i) a person or entity engaged in providing commercial mobile service (as defined in section 332(d) of the Communications Act of 1934 (47 U.S.C. 332(d))); or

(ii) a person or entity engaged in providing wire or electronic communication switching or transmission service to the extent that the Commission finds that such service is a replacement for a substantial portion of the local telephone exchange service and that it is in the public interest to deem such a person or entity to be a telecommunications carrier for purposes of this title; but

(C) does not include—

(i) persons or entities insofar as they are engaged in providing information services; and

(ii) any class or category of telecommunications carriers that the Commission exempts by rule after consultation with the Attorney General.

Sec. 103. Assistance Capability Requirements.

(a) Capability Requirements: Except as provided in subsections

(b), (c), and (d) of this section and sections 108(a) and 109(b) and (d), a telecommunications carrier shall ensure that its equipment, facilities, or services that provide a customer or subscriber with the ability to originate, terminate, or direct communications are capable of—

(1) expeditiously isolating and enabling the government, pursuant to a court order or other lawful authorization, to intercept, to the exclusion of any other communications, all wire and electronic communications carried by the carrier within a service area to or from equipment, facilities, or services of a subscriber of such carrier concurrently with their transmission to or from the subscriber's equipment, facility, or service, or at such later time as may be acceptable to the government;

(2) expeditiously isolating and enabling the government, pursuant to a court order or other lawful authorization, to access call-identifying information that is reasonably available to the carrier—

(A) before, during, or immediately after the transmission of a wire or electronic communication (or at such later time as may be acceptable to the government); and

(B) in a manner that allows it to be associated with the communication to which it pertains, except that, with regard to information acquired solely pursuant to the authority for pen registers and trap and trace devices (as defined in section 3127 of title 18, United States Code), such call-identifying information shall not include any information that may disclose the physical location of the subscriber (except to the extent that the location may be determined from the telephone number);

(3) delivering intercepted communications and call-identifying information to the government, pur-

suant to a court order or other lawful authorization, in a format such that they may be transmitted by means of equipment, facilities, or services procured by the government to a location other than the premises of the carrier; and

(4) facilitating authorized communications interceptions and access to call-identifying information unobtrusively and with a minimum of interference with any subscriber's telecommunications service and in a manner that protects—

(A) the privacy and security of communications and call-identifying information not authorized to be intercepted; and

(B) information regarding the government's interception of communications and access to call-identifying information.

(b) Limitations:

(1) Design of features and systems configurations: This title does not authorize any law enforcement agency or officer—

(A) to require any specific design of equipment, facilities, services, features, or system configurations to be adopted by any provider of a wire or electronic communication service, any manufacturer of telecommunications equipment, or any provider of telecommunications support services; or

(B) to prohibit the adoption of any equipment, facility, service, or feature by any provider of a wire or electronic communication service, any manufacturer of telecommunications equipment, or any provider of telecommunications support services.

(2) Information services; private networks and interconnection services and facilities: The requirements of subsection (a) do not apply to—

(A) information services; or

(B) equipment, facilities, or services that support the transport or switching of communications for private networks or for the sole purpose of interconnecting telecommunications carriers.

(3) Encryption: A telecommunications carrier shall not be responsible for decrypting, or ensuring the government's ability to decrypt, any communication encrypted by a subscriber or customer, unless the encryption was provided by the carrier and the carrier possesses the information necessary to decrypt the communication.

(c) Emergency or Exigent Circumstances: In emergency or exigent circumstances (including those described in sections 2518 (7) or

(11)(b) and 3125 of title 18, United States Code, and section 1805(e) of title 50 of such Code), a carrier at its discretion may comply with subsection (a)(3) by allowing monitoring at its premises if that is the only means of accomplishing the interception or access.

(d) Mobile Service Assistance Requirements: A telecommunications carrier that is a provider of commercial mobile service (as defined in section 332(d) of the Communications Act of 1934) offering a feature or service that allows subscribers to redirect, hand off, or assign their wire or electronic communications to another service area or another service provider or to utilize facilities in another service area or of another service provider shall ensure that, when the carrier that had been providing assistance for the interception of wire or electronic communications or access to call-identifying information pursuant to a court order or lawful authorization no longer has access to the content of such communications or call-identifying information within the service area in which interception has been occurring as a result of the subscriber's use of such a feature or service, information is made available to the government (before, during, or immediately after the transfer of such communications) identifying the provider of a wire or electronic communication service that has acquired access to the communications.

Sec. 104. Notices of Capabity Requirements.

(a) Notices of Maximum and Actual Capacity Requirements:

(1) In general: Not later than 1 year after the date of enactment of this title, after consulting with State and local law enforcement agencies, telecommunications carriers, providers of telecommunications support services, and manufacturers of telecommunications equipment, and after notice and comment, the Attorney General shall publish in the Federal Register and provide to appropriate telecommunications industry associations and standard-setting organizations—

(A) notice of the actual number of communication interceptions, pen registers, and trap and trace devices, representing a portion of the maximum capacity set forth under subparagraph (B), that the Attorney General estimates that government agencies authorized to conduct electronic surveillance may conduct and use simultaneously by the date that is 4 years after the date of enactment of this title; and

(B) notice of the maximum capacity required to accommodate all of the communication interceptions, pen registers, and trap and trace devices that the Attorney General estimates that government agencies authorized to conduct electronic surveillance may conduct and use simultaneously after the date that is 4 years after the date of enactment of this title.

(2) Basis of notices: The notices issued under paragraph (1)—

(A) may be based upon the type of equipment, type of service, number of subscribers, type or size or carrier, nature of service area, or any other measure; and

(B) shall identify, to the maximum extent practicable, the capacity required at specific geographic locations.

(b) Compliance With Capacity Notices:

(1) Initial capacity: Within 3 years after the publication by the Attorney General of a notice of capacity requirements or within 4 years after the date of enactment of this title, whichever is longer, a telecommunications carrier shall, subject to subsection (e), ensure that its systems are capable of—

(A) accommodating simultaneously the number of interceptions, pen registers, and trap and trace devices set forth in the notice under subsection (a)(1)(A); and

(B) expanding to the maximum capacity set forth in the notice under subsection (a)(1)(B).

(2) Expansion to maximum capacity: After the date described in paragraph (1), a telecommunications carrier shall, subject to subsection (e), ensure that it can accommodate expeditiously any increase in the actual number of communication interceptions, pen registers, and trap and trace devices that authorized agencies may seek to conduct and use, up to the maximum capacity requirement set forth in the notice under subsection (a)(1)(B).

(c) Notices of Increased Maximum Capacity Requirements:

(1) Notice: The Attorney General shall periodically publish in the Federal Register, after notice and comment, notice of any necessary increases in the maximum capacity requirement set forth in the notice under subsection (a)(1)(B).

(2) Compliance: Within 3 years after notice of increased maximum capacity requirements is published under paragraph (1), or within such longer time period as the Attorney General may specify, a telecommunications carrier shall, subject to subsection (e), ensure that its systems are capable of expanding to the increased maximum capacity set forth in the notice.

(d) Carrier Statement: Within 180 days after the publication by the Attorney General of a notice of capacity requirements pursuant to subsection (a) or (c), a telecommunications carrier shall submit to the Attorney General a statement identifying any of its systems or services that do not have the capacity to accommodate simultaneously the number of interceptions, pen registers, and trap and trace devices set forth in the notice under such subsection.

(e) Reimbursement Required for Compliance: The Attorney General shall review the statements submitted under subsection (d) and may, subject to the availability of appropriations, agree to reimburse a telecommunications carrier for costs directly associated with modifications to attain such capacity requirement that are determined to be reasonable in accordance with section 109(e).

Until the Attorney General agrees to reimburse such carrier for such modification, such carrier shall be considered to be in compliance with the capacity notices under subsection (a) or (c).

Sec. 105. Systems Security and Integrity.

A telecommunications carrier shall ensure that any interception of communications or access to call-identifying information effected within its switching premises can be activated only in accordance with a court order or other lawful authorization and with the affirmative intervention of an individual officer or employee of the carrier acting in accordance with regulations prescribed by the Commission.

(a) Consultation: A telecommunications carrier shall consult, as necessary, in a timely fashion with manufacturers of its telecommunications transmission and switching equipment and its providers of telecommunications support services for the purpose of ensuring that current and planned equipment, facilities, and services comply with the capability requirements of section 103 and the capacity requirements identified by the Attorney General under section 104.

(b) Cooperation: Subject to sections 104(e), 108(a), and 109 (b) and (d), a manufacturer of telecommunications transmission or switching equipment and a provider of telecommunications support services shall, on a reasonably timely basis and at a reasonable charge, make available to the telecommunications carriers using its equipment, facilities, or services such features or modifications as are necessary to permit such carriers to comply with the capability requirements of section 103 and the capacity requirements identified by the Attorney General under section 104.

(a) Safe Harbor:

(1) Consultation: To ensure the efficient and industry-wide implementation of the assistance capability requirements under section 103, the Attorney General, in coordination with other Federal, State, and local law enforcement agencies, shall consult with appropriate associations and standard-setting organizations of the telecommunications industry, with representatives of users of telecommunications equipment, facilities, and services, and with State utility commissions.

(2) Compliance under accepted standards: A telecommunications carrier shall be found to be in compliance with the assistance capability requirements under section 103, and a manufacturer of telecommunications transmission or switching equipment or a provider of telecommunications support services shall be found to be in compliance with section

106, if the carrier, manufacturer, or support service provider is in compliance with publicly available technical requirements or standards adopted by an industry association or standard-setting organization, or by the Commission under subsection (b), to meet the requirements of section 103.

(3) Absence of standards: The absence of technical requirements or standards for implementing the assistance capability requirements of section 103 shall not—

(A) preclude a telecommunications carrier, manufacturer, or telecommunications support services provider from deploying a technology or service; or

(B) relieve a carrier, manufacturer, or telecommunications support services provider of the obligations imposed by section 103 or 106, as applicable.

(b) Commission Authority: If industry associations or standard-setting organizations fail to issue technical requirements or standards or if a Government agency or any other person believes that such requirements or standards are deficient, the agency or person may petition the Commission to establish, by rule, technical requirements or standards that—

(1) meet the assistance capability requirements of section 103 by cost-effective methods;

(2) protect the privacy and security of communications not authorized to be intercepted;

(3) minimize the cost of such compliance on residential ratepayers;

(4) serve the policy of the United States to encourage the provision of new technologies and services to the public; and

(5) provide a reasonable time and conditions for compliance with and the transition to any new standard, including defining the obligations of telecommunications carriers under section 103 during any transition period.

(c) Extension of Compliance Date for Equipment, Facilities, and Services:

(1) Petition: A telecommunications carrier proposing to install or deploy, or having installed or deployed, any equipment, facility, or service prior to the effective date of section 103 may petition the Commission for 1 or more extensions of the deadline for complying with the assistance capability requirements under section 103.

(2) Grounds for extension: The Commission may, after consultation with the Attorney General, grant an extension under this subsection, if the Commission determines that compliance with the assistance capability requirements under section 103 is not reasonably achievable through application of technology available within the compliance period.

(3) Length of extension: An extension under this subsection shall extend for no longer than the earlier of—

(A) the date determined by the Commission as necessary for the carrier to comply with the assistance capability requirements under section 103; or

(B) the date that is 2 years after the date on which the extension is granted.

(4) Applicability of extension: An extension under this subsection shall apply to only that part of the carrier's business on which the new equipment, facility, or service is used.

Sec. 108. Enforcement Orders.

(a) Grounds for Issuance: A court shall issue an order enforcing this title under section 2522 of title 18, United States Code, only if the court finds that—

(1) alternative technologies or capabilities or the facilities of another carrier are not reasonably available to law enforcement for implementing the interception of communications or access to call-identifying information; and

(2) compliance with the requirements of this title is reasonably achievable through the application of available technology to the equipment, facility, or service at issue or would have been reasonably achievable if timely action had been taken.

(b) Time for Compliance: Upon issuing an order enforcing this title, the court shall specify a reasonable time and conditions for complying with its order, considering the good faith efforts to comply in a timely manner, any effect on the carrier's, manufacturer's, or service provider's ability to continue to do business, the degree of culpability or delay in undertaking efforts to comply, and such other matters as justice may require.

(c) Limitations: An order enforcing this title may not—

(1) require a telecommunications carrier to meet the Government's demand for interception of communications and acquisition of call-identifying information to any extent in excess of the capacity for which the Attorney General has agreed to reimburse such carrier;

(2) require any telecommunications carrier to comply with assistance capability requirement of section 103 if the Commission has determined (pursuant to section 109(b)(1)) that compliance is not reasonably achievable, unless the Attorney General has agreed (pursuant to section 109(b)(2)) to pay the costs described in section 109(b)(2)(A); or

(3) require a telecommunications carrier to modify, for the purpose of complying with the assistance capability requirements of section 103, any equipment, facility, or service deployed on or before January 1, 1995, unless—

(A) the Attorney General has agreed to pay the telecommunications carrier for all reasonable costs directly associated with modifications necessary to bring the equipment, facility, or service into compliance with those requirements; or

(B) the equipment, facility, or service has been replaced or significantly upgraded or otherwise undergoes major modification.

(a) Equipment, Facilities, and Services Deployed on or Before January 1, 1995: The Attorney General may, subject to the availability of appropriations, agree to pay telecommunications carriers for all reasonable costs directly associated with the modifications performed by carriers in connection with equipment, facilities, and services installed or deployed on or before January 1, 1995, to establish the capabilities necessary to comply with section 103.

(b) Equipment, Facilities, and Services Deployed After January 1, 1995:

(1) Determinations of reasonably achievable: The Commission, on petition from a telecommunications carrier or any other interested person, and after notice to the Attorney General, shall determine whether compliance with the assistance capability requirements of section 103 is reasonably achievable with respect to any equipment, facility, or service installed or deployed after January 1, 1995. The Commission shall make such determination within 1 year after the date such petition is filed. In making such determination, the Commission shall determine whether compliance would impose significant difficulty or expense on the carrier or on the users of the carrier's systems and shall consider the following factors:

(A) The effect on public safety and national security.

(B) The effect on rates for basic residential telephone service.

(C) The need to protect the privacy and security of communications not authorized to be intercepted.

(D) The need to achieve the capability assistance requirements of section 103 by cost-effective methods.

(E) The effect on the nature and cost of the equipment, facility, or service at issue.

(F) The effect on the operation of the equipment, facility, or service at issue.

(G) The policy of the United States to encourage the provision of new technologies and services to the public.

(H) The financial resources of the telecommunications carrier.

(I) The effect on competition in the provision of telecommunications services.

(J) The extent to which the design and development of the equipment, facility, or service was initiated before January 1, 1995.

(K) Such other factors as the Commission determines are appropriate.

(2) Compensation: If compliance with the assistance capability requirements of section 103 is not reasonably achievable with respect to equipment, facilities, or services deployed after January 1, 1995—

(A) the Attorney General, on application of a telecommunications carrier, may agree, subject to the availability of appropriations, to pay the telecommunications carrier for the additional reasonable costs of making compliance with such assistance capability requirements reasonably achievable; and

(B) if the Attorney General does not agree to pay such costs, the telecommunications carrier shall be deemed to be in compliance with such capability requirements.

(c) Allocation of Funds for Payment: The Attorney General shall allocate funds appropriated to carry out this title in accordance with law enforcement priorities determined by the Attorney General.

(d) Failure To Make Payment With Respect To Equipment, Facilities, and Services Deployed on or Before January 1, 1995: If a carrier has requested payment in accordance with procedures promulgated pursuant to subsection (e), and the Attorney General has not agreed to pay the telecommunications carrier for all reasonable costs directly associated with modifications necessary to bring any equipment, facility, or service deployed on or before January 1, 1995, into compliance with the assistance capability requirements of section 103, such equipment, facility, or service shall be considered to be in compliance with the assistance capability requirements of section 103 until the equipment, facility, or service is replaced or significantly upgraded or otherwise undergoes major modification.

(e) Cost Control Regulations:

(1) In general: The Attorney General shall, after notice and comment, establish regulations necessary to effectuate timely and cost-efficient payment to telecommunications carriers under this title, under chapters 119 and 121 of title 18, United States Code, and under the Foreign Intelligence Surveillance Act of 1978 (50 U.S.C. 1801 et seq.).

(2) Contents of regulations: The Attorney General, after consultation with the Commission, shall prescribe regulations for purposes of determining reasonable costs under this title.

Such regulations shall seek to minimize the cost to the Federal Government and shall—

(A) permit recovery from the Federal Government of—

(i) the direct costs of developing the modifications described in subsection (a), of providing the capabilities requested under subsection (b)(2), or of providing the capacities requested under section 104(e), but only to the extent that such costs have not been recovered from any other governmental or nongovernmental entity;

(ii) the costs of training personnel in the use of such capabilities or capacities; and

(iii) the direct costs of deploying or installing such capabilities or capacities;

(B) in the case of any modification that may be used for any purpose other than lawfully authorized electronic surveillance by a law enforcement agency of a government, permit recovery of only the incremental cost of making the modification suitable for such law enforcement purposes; and

(C) maintain the confidentiality of trade secrets.

(3) Submission of claims: Such regulations shall require any telecommunications carrier that the Attorney General has agreed to pay for modifications pursuant to this section and that has installed or deployed such modification to submit to the Attorney General a claim for payment that contains or is accompanied by such information as the Attorney General may require.

Sec. 110. Authorization of Appropriations.

There are authorized to be appropriated to carry out this title a total of $500,000,000 for fiscal years 1995, 1996, 1997, and 1998.

Such sums are authorized to remain available until expended.

Sec. 111. Effective Date.

(a) In General: Except as provided in subsection (b), this title shall take effect on the date of enactment of this Act.

(b) Assistance Capability and Systems Security and Integrity Requirements: Sections 103 and 105 of this title shall take effect on the date that is 4 years after the date of enactment of this Act.

Sec. 112. Reports..

(a) Reports by the Attorney General:

(1) In general: On or before November 30, 1995, and on or before November 30 of each year thereafter, the Attorney General shall submit to Congress and make available to the public a report on the amounts paid during the preceding fiscal year to telecommunications carriers under sections 104(e) and 109.

(2) Contents: A report under paragraph (1) shall include—

(A) a detailed accounting of the amounts paid to each carrier and the equipment, facility, or service for which the amounts were paid; and

(B) projections of the amounts expected to be paid in the current fiscal year, the carriers to which payment is expected to be made, and the equipment, facilities, or services for which payment is expected to be made.

(b) Reports by the Comptroller General:

(1) Payments for modifications: On or before April 1, 1996, and every 2 years thereafter, the Comptroller General of the United States, after consultation with the Attorney General and the telecommunications industry, shall submit to the Congress a report—

(A) describing the type of equipment, facilities, and services that have been brought into compliance under this title; and

(B) reflecting its analysis of the reasonableness and cost-effectiveness of the payments made by the Attorney General to telecommunications carriers for modifications necessary to ensure compliance with this title.

(2) Compliance cost estimates: A report under paragraph (1) shall include the findings and conclusions of the Comptroller General on the costs to be incurred by telecommunications carriers to comply with the assistance capability requirements of section 103 after the effective date of such section 103, including projections of the amounts expected to be incurred and a description of the equipment, facilities, or services for which they are expected to be incurred.

TITLE II—AMENDMENTS TO TITLE 18, UNITED STATES CODE

(a) Court Orders Under Chapter 119: Chapter 119 of title 18, United States Code, is amended by inserting after section 2521 the following new section:

Sec. 2522. Enforcement of the Communications Assistance for Law Enforcement Act

(a) Enforcement by Court Issuing Surveillance Order: If a court authorizing an interception under this chapter, a State statute, or the Foreign Intelligence Surveillance Act of 1978 (50 U.S.C. 1801 et seq.) or authorizing use of a pen register or a trap and trace device under chapter 206 or a State statute finds that a telecommunications carrier has failed to comply with the requirements of the Communications Assistance for Law Enforcement Act, the court may, in accordance with section 108 of such Act, direct that the carrier comply forthwith and may direct that a provider of support services to the carrier or the manufacturer of the carrier's transmission or switching equipment furnish forthwith modifications necessary for the carrier to comply.

(b) Enforcement Upon Application by Attorney General: The

Attorney General may, in a civil action in the appropriate United States district court, obtain an order, in accordance with section 108 of the Communications Assistance for Law Enforcement Act, directing that a telecommunications carrier, a manufacturer of telecommunications transmission or switching equipment, or a provider of telecommunications support services comply with such Act.

(c) Civil Penalty:

(1) In general: A court issuing an order under this section against a telecommunications carrier, a manufacturer of telecommunications transmission or switching equipment, or a provider of telecommunications support services may impose a civil penalty of up to $10,000 per day for each day in violation after the issuance of the order or after such future date as the court may specify.

(2) Considerations: In determining whether to impose a civil penalty and in determining its amount, the court shall take into account—

(A) the nature, circumstances, and extent of the violation;

(B) the violator's ability to pay, the violator's good faith efforts to comply in a timely manner, any effect on the violator's ability to continue to do business, the degree of culpability, and the length of any delay in undertaking efforts to comply; and

(C) such other matters as justice may require.

(d) Definitions: As used in this section, the terms defined in section 102 of the Communications Assistance for Law Enforcement Act have the meanings provided, respectively, in such section.

(b) Conforming Amendments:

(1) Section 2518(4) of title 18, United States Code, is amended by adding at the end the following new sentence:

Pursuant to section 2522 of this chapter, an order may also be issued to enforce the assistance capability and capacity requirements under the Communications Assistance for Law Enforcement Act.

(2) Section 3124 of such title is amended by adding at the end the following new subsection:

(f) Communications Assistance Enforcement Orders: Pursuant to section 2522, an order may be issued to enforce the assistance capability and capacity requirements under the Communications Assistance for Law Enforcement Act.

(3) The table of sections at the beginning of chapter 119 of title 18, United States Code, is amended by inserting after the item pertaining to section 2521 the following new item:

2522. Enforcement of the Communications Assistance for Law Enforcement Act.

Sec. 202. Cordless Telephones.

(a) Definitions: Section 2510 of title 18, United States Code, is amended—

(1) in paragraph (1), by striking ', but such term does not include' and all that follows through 'base unit'; and

(2) in paragraph (12), by striking subparagraph (A) and redesignating subparagraphs (B), (C), and (D) as subparagraphs

(A), (B), and (C), respectively.

(b) Penalty: Section 2511 of title 18, United States Code, is amended—

(1) in subsection (4)(b)(i) by inserting 'a cordless telephone communication that is transmitted between the cordless telephone handset and the base unit,' after 'cellular telephone communication,'; and

(2) in subsection (4)(b)(ii) by inserting 'a cordless telephone communication that is transmitted between the cordless telephone handset and the base unit,' after 'cellular telephone communication,'.

Sec. 203. Radio-based data communications.

Section 2510(16) of title 18, United States Code, is amended—

(1) by striking 'or' at the end of subparagraph (D);

(2) by inserting 'or' at the end of subparagraph (E); and

(3) by inserting after subparagraph (E) the following new subparagraph:

(F) an electronic communication;'.

Section 2511(4)(b) of title 18, United States Code, is amended by striking 'or encrypted, then' and inserting ', encrypted, or transmitted using modulation techniques the essential parameters of which have been withheld from the public with the intention of preserving the privacy of such communication, then'.

Sec. 205. Technical Correction.

Section 2511(2)(a)(i) of title 18, United States Code, is amended by striking 'used in the transmission of a wire communication' and inserting 'used in the transmission of a wire or electronic communication'.

(a) Offense: Section 1029(a) of title 18, United States Code, is amended—

(1) by striking 'or' at the end of paragraph (3); and

(2) by inserting after paragraph (4) the following new paragraphs:

(5) knowingly and with intent to defraud uses, produces, traffics in, has control or custody of, or possesses a telecommunications instrument that has been modified or altered to obtain unauthorized use of telecommunications services; or

(6) knowingly and with intent to defraud uses, produces, traffics in, has control or custody of, or possesses—

(A) a scanning receiver; or

(B) hardware or software used for altering or modifying telecommunications instruments to obtain unauthorized access to telecommunications services,'

(b) Penalty: Section 1029(c)(2) of title 18, United States Code, is amended by striking '(a)(1) or (a)(4)' and inserting '(a) (1), (4), (5), or (6)'.

(c) Definitions: Section 1029(e) of title 18, United States Code, is amended—

(1) in paragraph (1) by inserting 'electronic serial number, mobile identification number, personal identification number, or other telecommunications service, equipment, or instrument identifier,' after 'account number,';

(2) by striking 'and' at the end of paragraph (5);

(3) by striking the period at the end of paragraph (6) and inserting '; and'; and

(4) by adding at the end the following new paragraph:

(7) the term 'scanning receiver' means a device or apparatus that can be used to intercept a wire or electronic communication in violation of chapter 119.'.

Sec. 207. Transactional Data.

(a) Disclosure of Records: Section 2703 of title 18, United States Code, is amended—

(1) in subsection (c)(1)—

(A) in subparagraph (B)—

(i) by striking clause (i); and

(ii) by redesignating clauses (ii), (iii), and (iv) as clauses (i), (ii), and (iii), respectively; and

(B) by adding at the end the following new subparagraph:

(C) 'A provider of electronic communication service or remote computing service shall disclose to a governmental entity the name, address, telephone toll billing records, telephone number or other subscriber number or identity, and length of service of a subscriber to or customer of such service and the types of services the subscriber or customer utilized, when the governmental entity uses an administrative subpoena authorized by a Federal or State statute or a Federal or State grand jury or trial subpoena or any means available under subparagraph (B).'; and

(2) by amending the first sentence of subsection (d) to read as follows: 'A court order for disclosure under subsection (b) or (c) may be issued by any court that is a court of competent jurisdiction described in section 3126(2)(A) and shall issue only if the governmental entity offers specific and articulable facts showing that there are reasonable grounds to believe that the contents of a wire or electronic communication, or the records or other information sought, are relevant and material to an ongoing criminal investigation.'.

(b) Pen Registers and Trap and Trace Devices: Section 3121 of title 18, United States Code, is amended—

(1) by redesignating subsection (c) as subsection (d); and

(2) by inserting after subsection (b) the following new subsection:

(c) Limitation: A government agency authorized to install and use a pen register under this chapter or under State law shall use technology reasonably available to it that restricts the recording or decoding of electronic or other impulses to the dialing and signaling information utilized in call processing.'.

Section 2516(1) of title 18, United States Code, is amended by inserting 'or acting Deputy Assistant Attorney General' after 'Deputy Assistant Attorney General'.

TITLE III—AMENDMENTS TO THE COMMUNICATIONS ACT OF 1934

Sec. 301. Compliance Cost Recovery.

Title II of the Communications Act of 1934 is amended by inserting after section 228 (47 U.S.C. 228) the following new section:

Sec. 229. Communications Asistance for Law Enforcement Act Compliance.

(a) In General: The Commission shall prescribe such rules as are necessary to implement the requirements of the Communications Assistance for Law En-forcement Act.

(b) Systems Security and Integrity: The rules pre-scribed pursuant to subsection (a) shall include rules to implement section 105 of the Communications Assis-tance for Law Enforcement Act that require common car-riers—

(1) to establish appropriate policies and pro-cedures for the supervision and control of its officers and employees—

(A) to require appropriate authoriza-tion to activate interception of communications or ac-cess to call-identifying information; and

(B) to prevent any such interception or access without such authorization;

(2) to maintain secure and accurate records of any interception or access with or without such autho-rization; and

(3) to submit to the Commission the policies and procedures adopted to comply with the require-ments established under paragraphs (1) and (2).

(c) Commission Review of Compliance: The Com-mission shall review the policies and procedures submit-ted under subsection (b)(3) and shall order a common carrier to modify any such policy or procedure that the Commission determines does not comply with Commis-sion regulations. The Commission shall conduct such in-vestigations as may be necessary to insure compliance by common carriers with the requirements of the regula-tions prescribed under this section.

(d) Penalties: For purposes of this Act, a violation by an officer or employee of any policy or procedure adopted by a common carrier pursuant to subsection (b), or of a rule prescribed by the Commission pursuant to subsection (a), shall be considered to be a violation by the carrier of a rule prescribed by the Commission pursuant to this Act.

(e) Cost Recovery for Communications Assistance for Law Enforcement Act Compliance:

(1) Petitions authorized: A common carrier may petition the Commission to adjust charges, practic-es, classifications, and regulations to recover costs ex-pended for making modifications to equipment, facilities, or services pursuant to the requirements of sec-tion 103 of the Communications Assistance for Law En-forcement Act.

(2) Commission authority: The Commission may grant, with or without modification, a petition un-der paragraph (1) if the Commission determines that such costs are reasonable and that permitting recovery is consistent with the public interest. The Commission

may, consistent with maintaining just and reasonable charges, practices, classifications, and regulations in con-nection with the provision of interstate or foreign com-munication by wire or radio by a common carrier, allow carriers to adjust such charges, practices, classifications, and regulations in order to carry out the purposes of this Act.

(3) Joint board: The Commission shall con-vene a Federal-State joint board to recommend appropri-ate changes to part 36 of the Commission's rules with respect to recovery of costs pursuant to charges, practic-es, classifications, and regulations under the jurisdiction of the Commission.'.

The schedule of application fees in section 8(g) of the Communications Act of 1934 (47 U.S.C. 158(g)) is amended by inserting under item 1 of the matter pertain-ing to common carrier services the following additional subitem:

d. Proceeding under section 109(b) of the Commu-nications Assistance for Law Enforcement Act5,000'.

Sec. 303. Clerical and Technical Amendments.

(a) Amendments to the Communications Act of 1934: The Communications Act of 1934 is amended—

(1) in section 4(f)(3), by striking 'overtime exceeds beyond' and inserting 'overtime extends be-yond';

(2) in section 5, by redesignating subsection (f) as subsection (e);

(3) in section 8(d)(2), by striking 'payment of a' and inserting 'payment of an';

(4) in the schedule contained in section 8(g), in item 7.f. under the heading 'equipment approval services/experimental radio' by striking 'Additional Charge' and inserting 'Additional Application Fee';

(5) in section 9(f)(1), by inserting before the second sentence the following:

'(2) Installment payments: ';

(6) in the schedule contained in section 9(g), in the item pertaining to interactive video data ser-vices under the private radio bureau, insert '95' after '47 C.F.R. Part';

(7) in section 220(a)—

(A) by inserting '(1)' after '(a)'; and

(B) by adding at the end the following new paragraph:

(2) The Commission shall, by rule, prescribe a uniform system of accounts for use by telephone com-panies. Such uniform system shall require that each com-mon carrier shall maintain a system of accounting methods, procedures, and techniques (including ac-

counts and supporting records and memoranda) which shall ensure a proper allocation of all costs to and among telecommunications services, facilities, and products (and to and among classes of such services, facilities, and products) which are developed, manufactured, or offered by such common carrier.';

(8) in section 220(b), by striking 'clasess' and inserting 'classes';

(9) in section 223(b)(3), by striking 'defendant restrict access' and inserting 'defendant restricted access';

(10) in section 226(d), by striking paragraph (2) and redesignating paragraphs (3) and (4) as paragraphs (2) and (3), respectively;

(11) in section 227(b)(2)(C), by striking 'paragraphs' and inserting 'paragraph';

(12) in section 227(e)(2), by striking 'national database' and inserting 'national database';

(13) in section 228(c), by redesignating the second paragraph

(2) and paragraphs (3) through (6) as paragraphs (3) through (7), respectively;

(14) in section 228(c)(6)(D), by striking 'conservation' and inserting 'conversation';

(15) in section 308(c), by striking 'May 24, 1921' and inserting 'May 27, 1921';

(16) in section 309(c)(2)(F), by striking 'section 325(b)' and inserting 'section 325(c)';

(17) in section 309(i)(4)(A), by striking 'Communications Technical Amendments Act of 1982' and inserting 'Communications Amendments Act of 1982';

(18) in section 331, by amending the heading of such section to read as follows:

'VERY HIGH FREQUENCY STATIONS AND AM RADIO STATIONS';

(19) in section 358, by striking '(a)';

(20) in part III of title III—

(A) by inserting before section 381 the following heading: 'VESSELS TRANSPORTING MORE THAN SIX PASSENGERS FOR HIRE REQUIRED TO BE EQUIPPED WITH RADIO TELEPHONE';

(B) by inserting before section 382 the following heading: 'VESSELS EXCEPTED FROM RADIO TELEPHONE REQUIREMENT';

(C) by inserting before section 383 the following heading: 'EXEMPTIONS BY COMMISSION';

(D) by inserting before section 384 the following heading: 'AUTHORITY OF COMMISSION; OP-

ERATIONS, INSTALLATIONS, AND ADDITIONAL EQUIPMENT';

(E) by inserting before section 385 the following heading: 'INSPECTIONS'; AND

(F) by inserting before section 386 the following heading: 'FORFEITURES';

(21) in section 410(c), by striking ', as referred to in sections 202(b) and 205(f) of the Interstate Commerce Act,';

(22) in section 613(b)(2), by inserting a comma after 'pole' and after 'line';

(23) in section 624(d)(2)(A), by inserting 'of' after 'viewing';

(24) in section 634(h)(1), by striking 'section 602(6)(A)' and inserting 'section 602(7)(A)';

(25) in section 705(d)(6), by striking 'subsection (d)' and inserting 'subsection (e)';

(26) in section 705(e)(3)(A), by striking 'paragraph (4) of subsection (d)' and inserting 'paragraph (4) of this subsection';

(27) in section 705, by redesignating subsections (f) and (g)

(as added by Public Law 100-667) as subsections (g) and (h); and

(28) in section 705(h) (as so redesignated), by striking 'subsection (f)' and inserting 'subsection (g)'.

(b) Amendments to the Communications Satellite Act of 1962: The Communications Satellite Act of 1962 is amended—

(1) in section 303(a)—

(A) by striking 'section 27(d)' and inserting 'section 327(d)';

(B) by striking 'sec. 29-911(d)' and inserting 'sec. 29-327(d)';

(C) by striking 'section 36' and inserting 'section 336'; and

(D) by striking 'sec. 29-916d' and inserting 'section 29-336(d)';

(2) in section 304(d), by striking 'paragraphs (1), (2), (3), (4), and (5) of section 310(a)' and inserting 'subsection (a) and paragraphs (1) through (4) of subsection (b) of section 310'; and

(3) in section 304(e)—

(A) by striking 'section 45(b)' and inserting 'section 345(b)'; and

(B) by striking 'sec. 29-920(b)' and inserting 'sec. 29-345(b)'; and

(4) in sections 502(b) and 503(a)(1), by striking 'the Communications Satellite Corporation' and inserting 'the communications satellite corporation established pursuant to title III of this Act'.

(c) Amendment to the Children's Television Act of 1990: Section 103(a) of the Children's Television Act of 1990 (47 U.S.C. 303b(a)) is amended by striking 'non-commerical' and inserting 'noncommercial'.

(d) Amendments to the Telecommunications Authorization Act of 1992: Section 205(1) of the Telecommunications Authorization Act of 1992 is amended—

(1) by inserting an open parenthesis before 'other than'; and

(2) by inserting a comma after 'stations)'.

(e) Conforming Amendment: Section 1253 of the Omnibus Budget Reconciliation Act of 1981 is repealed.

(f) Stylistic Consistency: The Communications Act of 1934 and the Communications Satellite Act of 1962 are amended so that the section designation and section heading of each section of such Acts shall be in the form and typeface of the section designation and heading of this section.

(a) Amendments to the Communications Act of 1934: The Communications Act of 1934 is amended—

(1) in section 7(b), by striking 'or twelve months after the date of the enactment of this section, if later' both places it appears;

(2) in section 212, by striking 'After sixty days from the enactment of this Act it shall' and inserting 'It shall';

(3) in section 213, by striking subsection (g) and redesignating subsection (h) as subsection (g);

(4) in section 214, by striking 'section 221 or 222' and inserting 'section 221';

(5) in section 220(b), by striking ', as soon as practicable,';

(6) by striking section 222;

(7) in section 224(b)(2), by striking 'Within 180 days from the date of enactment of this section the Commission' and inserting 'The Commission';

(8) in 226(e), by striking 'within 9 months after the date of enactment of this section,';

(9) in section 309(i)(4)(A), by striking 'The commission, not later than 180 days after the date of enactment of the Communications Technical Amendments Act of 1982, shall,' and inserting 'The Commission shall,';

(10) by striking section 328;

(11) in section 413, by striking ', within sixty days after the taking effect of this Act,';

(12) in section 624(d)(2)(B)—

(A) by striking out '(A)';

(B) by inserting 'of' after 'restrict the viewing'; and

(C) by striking subparagraph (B);

(13) by striking sections 702 and 703;

(14) in section 704—

(A) by striking subsections (b) and (d); and

(B) by redesignating subsection (c) as subsection (b);

(15) in section 705(g) (as redesignated by section 304(25)), by striking 'within 6 months after the date of enactment of the Satellite Home Viewer Act of 1988, the Federal Communications Commission' and inserting 'The Commission';

(16) in section 710(f)—

(A) by striking the first and second sentences; and

(B) in the third sentence, by striking 'Thereafter, the Commission' and inserting 'The Commission';

(17) in section 712(a), by striking ', within 120 days after the effective date of the Satellite Home Viewer Act of 1988,'; and

(18) by striking section 713.

(b) Amendments to the Communications Satellite Act of 1962: The Communications Satellite Act of 1962 is amended—

(1) in section 201(a)(1), by striking 'as expeditiously as possible,';

(2) by striking sections 301 and 302 and inserting the following:

Sec. 301. Creation of Corporation.

'There is authorized to be created a communications satellite corporation for profit which will not be an agency or establishment of the United States Government.

Sec. 302. Applicable Laws.

The corporation shall be subject to the provisions of this Act and, to the extent consistent with this Act, to the District of Columbia Business Corporation Act. The right to repeal, alter, or amend this Act at any time is expressly reserved.;

      (3) in section 304(a), by striking 'at a price not in excess of $100 for each share and';

      (4) in section 404—

            (A) by striking subsections (a) and (c); and

            (B) by redesignating subsection (b) as section 404;

      (5) in section 503—

            (A) by striking paragraph (2) of subsection (a); and

            (B) by redesignating paragraph (3) of subsection (a) as paragraph (2) of such subsection;

            (C) by striking subsection (b);

            (D) in subsection (g)—

                (i) by striking 'subsection (c)(3)' and inserting 'subsection (b)(3)'; and

                (ii) by striking the last sentence; and

            (E) by redesignating subsections (c) through (h) as subsections (b) through (g), respectively;

      (5) by striking sections 505, 506, and 507; and

      (6) by redesignating section 508 as section 505.

STATE STATUTES

ALABAMA STATUTES

TITLE 13A. CRIMINAL CODE
CHAPTER 8. OFFENSES INVOLVING THEFT.
ARTICLE 1. THEFT AND RELATED OFFENSES.

13A-8-10. Theft of services—Definition.

    (a) A person commits the crime of theft of services if:

      (1) He intentionally obtains services known by him to be available only for compensation by deception, threat, false token or other means to avoid payment for the services; or

      (2) Having control over the disposition of services of others to which he is not entitled, he knowingly diverts those services to his own benefit or to the benefit of another not entitled thereto.

    (b) "Services" includes but is not necessarily limited to labor, professional services, transportation, telephone or other public services, accommodation in motels, hotels, restaurants or elsewhere, admission to exhibitions, COMPUTER services and the supplying of equipment for use.

    (c) Where compensation for services is ordinarily paid immediately upon the rendering of them, as in the case of motels, hotels, restaurants and the like, absconding without payment or bona fide offer to pay is prima facie evidence under subsection (a) that the services were obtained by deception.

    (d) If services are obtained under subdivision (a) (1) from a hotel, motel, inn, restaurant or cafe, no prosecution can be commenced after 120 days from the time of the offense.

ARTICLE 5. ALABAMA COMPUTER CRIME ACT.

13A-8-100. Short title.

    This article may be cited as the Alabama COMPUTER CRIME Act.

13A-8-101. Definitions.

    When used in this chapter, the following terms shall have the following meanings, respectively, unless a different meaning clearly appears from the context:

    (1) Data. A representation of information, knowledge, facts, concepts, or instructions which are being prepared or have been prepared in a formalized manner, and is intended to be processed, is being processed, or has been processed in a COMPUTER system or COMPUTER network, and should be classified as intellectual property, and may be in any form, including COMPUTER printouts, magnetic storage media, punched cards, or stored internally in the memory of the COMPUTER.

    (2) Intellectual property. Data, including COMPUTER program.

    (3) COMPUTER program. An ordered set of data representing coded instructions or statements that, when executed by a COMPUTER, cause the COMPUTER to process data.

    (4) COMPUTER. An electronic magnetic, optical or other high speed data processing device or system which performs logical, arithmetic, and memory functions by manipulations of electronic magnetic or optical impulses, and includes all input, output, processing, storage, COMPUTER software, or communication facilities which are connected or related to the COMPUTER in a COMPUTER system or COMPUTER network.

    (5) COMPUTER software. A set of COMPUTER programs, procedures, and associated documentation concerned with the operation of a COMPUTER, COMPUTER system or COMPUTER network.

(6) COMPUTER system. A set of related, connected or unconnected, COMPUTER equipment, devices, or COMPUTER software.

(7) COMPUTER network. A set of related, remotely connected devices and communication facilities, including more than one COMPUTER system, with capability to transmit data among them through communication facilities.

(8) COMPUTER system services. The utilization of a COMPUTER, COMPUTER system, or COMPUTER network to assist an individual or entity with the performance of a particular lawful function which that individual or entity has been given the right, duty, and power, together with the responsibility, to perform.

(9) Property. Anything of value as defined by law, and includes financial instruments, information, including electronically produced data and COMPUTER software and COMPUTER programs in either machine or human readable form, and any other tangible or intangible items of value.

(10) Financial instrument. Includes any check, draft, warrant, money order, note, certificate of deposit, letter of credit, bill of exchange, credit or debit card, transaction authorization mechanism, marketable security, or any COMPUTER system representation thereof.

(11) Access. To instruct, communicate with, store data in, or retrieve data from a COMPUTER, COMPUTER system or COMPUTER network.

13A-8-102. Acts constituting offenses against intellectual property; punishment.

(a) Whoever willfully, knowingly, and without authorization or without reasonable grounds to believe that he has such authorization, attempts or achieves access, communication, examination, or modification of data, COMPUTER programs, or supporting documentation residing or existing internal or external to a COMPUTER, COMPUTER system, or COMPUTER network commits an offense against intellectual property.

(b) Whoever willfully, knowingly, and without authorization or without reasonable grounds to believe that he has such authorization, destroys data, COMPUTER programs, or supporting documentation residing or existing internal or external to a COMPUTER, COMPUTER system, or COMPUTER network commits an offense against intellectual property.

(c) Whoever willfully, knowingly, and without authorization or without reasonable grounds to believe that he has such authorization, discloses, uses, or takes data, COMPUTER programs, or supporting documentation residing or existing internal or external to a COMPUTER, COMPUTER system, or COMPUTER network commits an offense against intellectual property.

(d)(1) Except as otherwise provided in this subsection, an offense against intellectual property is a Class A misdemeanor, punishable as provided by law.

(2) If the offense is committed for the purpose of devising or executing any scheme or artifice to defraud or to obtain any property, then the offender is guilty of a Class C felony, punishable as provided by law.

(3) If the damage to such intellectual property is $2,500.00 or greater, or if there is an interruption or impairment of governmental operation or public communication, transportation, or supply of water, gas, or other public or utility service, then the offender is guilty of a Class B felony, punishable as provided by law.

(4) Whoever willfully, knowingly, and without authorization alters or removes data causing physical injury to any person who is not involved in said act shall be guilty of a Class A felony, punishable as provided by law.

13A-8-103. Acts constituting offense against COMPUTER equipment or supplies; punishment.

(a)(1) Whoever willfully, knowingly, and without authorization or without reasonable grounds to believe that he has such authorization, modifies equipment or supplies that are used or intended to be used in a COMPUTER, COMPUTER system, or COMPUTER network commits an offense against COMPUTER equipment or supplies.

(2)a. Except as provided in this subsection, an offense against COMPUTER equipment or supplies as provided in subdivision (a)(1) is a Class A misdemeanor, punishable as provided by law.

b. If the offense is committed for the purpose of devising or executing any scheme or artifice to defraud or to obtain any property, then the offender i s guilty of a Class C felony, punishable as provided by law.

(b)(1) Whoever willfully, knowingly, and without authorization or without reasonable grounds to believe that he has such authorization, destroys, uses, takes, injures, or damages equipment or supplies used or intended to be used in a COMPUTER, COMPUTER system, or COMPUTER network, or whoever willfully, knowingly, and without authorization or without reasonable grounds to believe that he has such authorization, destroys, injures, takes, or damages any COMPUTER, COMPUTER system, or COMPUTER network commits an offense against COMPUTER equipment and supplies.

(2)a. Except as provided in this subsection, an offense against COMPUTER equipment or supplies as provided in subdivision (b)(1) is a Class A misdemeanor, punishable as provided by law.

b. If the damage to such COMPUTER equipment or supplies or to the COMPUTER, COMPUT-

ER system, or COMPUTER network is $2,500.00 or greater, or if there is an interruption or impairment of governmental operation or public communication, transportation, or supply of water, gas, or other public utility service, then the offender is guilty of a Class B felony, punishable as provided by law.

ALASKA STATUTES

TITLE 11. CRIMINAL LAW
CHAPTER 46. OFFENSES AGAINST PROPERTY
ARTICLE 1. THEFT AND RELATED OFFENSES

SECTION 11.46.200. **Theft of services.**

(a) A person commits theft of services if

(1) the person obtains services, known by that person to be available onlyfor compensation, by deception, force, threat, or other means to avoid payment for the services;

(2) having control over the disposition of services of others to which the person is not entitled, the person knowingly diverts those services to the person's own benefit or to the benefit of another not entitled to them; or

(3) the person obtains the use of computer time, a computer system, a computer program, a computer network, or any part of a computer system or network, with reckless disregard that the use by that person is unauthorized.

(b) Absconding without paying for hotel, restaurant, or other services for which compensation is customarily paid immediately upon the receiving of them is prima facie evidence that the services were obtained by deception.

(c) A person may not be prosecuted under this section for theft of cable,microwave, subscription, or pay television or other telecommunications service if the service was obtained through the use of a device designed and used to intercept electromagnetic signals directly from a satellite, including a device commonly referred to as a home earth station.

ARTICLE 3. ARSON, CRIMINAL MISCHIEF, AND RELATED OFFENSES

11.46.484. **Criminal mischief in the third degree.**

(a) A person commits the crime of criminal mischief in the third degree if, having no right to do so or any reasonable ground to believe the person has such a right

(1) with intent to damage property of another, the person damages property of another in an amount of $50 or more but less than $500;

(2) the person drives, tows away, or takes the propelled vehicle of another;

(3) having custody of a propelled vehicle under a written agreement with the owner of the vehicle that includes an agreement to return the vehicle to the owner at a specified time, the person knowingly retains or withholds possession of the vehicle without the consent of the owner for so long a period beyond the time specified as to render the retention or possession of the vehicle an unreasonable deviation from the agreement;

(4) the person tampers with a fire protection device in a building that is a public place;

(5) the person knowingly accesses a computer, computer system, computer program, computer network, or part of a computer system or network;

(6) the person uses a device to descramble an electronic signal that has been scrambled to prevent unauthorized receipt or viewing of the signal unless the device is used only to descramble signals received directly from a satellite or unless the person owned the device before September 18, 1984; or

(7) the person knowingly removes, relocates, defaces, alters, obscures, shoots at, destroys, or otherwise tampers with an official traffic control device or damages the work upon a highway under construction.

(b) Except as provided in (c) of this section, criminal mischief in the third degree is a class A misdemeanor.

(c) A person convicted under (a)(2) of this section is guilty of a class C felony if, within the preceding seven years, the person was convicted under

(1) the provisions of (a)(2) of this section;

(2) former AS 28.35.010;

(3) the provisions of AS 11.46.482(a)(4);

(4) an offense involving the theft of a propelled vehicle under AS 11.46.120—11.46.140; or

(5) a law or ordinance of this or another jurisdiction with elements substantially similar to those of the offenses described in (1)—(4) of this subsection.

ARTICLE 6. GENERAL PROVISIONS

11.46.985. **Deceiving a machine.**

In a prosecution under this chapter for an offense that requires "deception" as an element, it is not a defense that the defendant deceived or attempted to deceive a machine. For purposes of this section, "machine" includes a vending machine, computer, turnstile, or automated teller machine.

11.46.990. Definitions.

In this chapter, unless the context requires otherwise,

(1) "access" means to instruct, communicate with, store data in, retrievedata from, or otherwise obtain the ability to use the resources of a computer, computer system, computer network, or any part of a computer system or network;

(2) "appropriate" or "appropriate property of another to oneself or a third person" means to

(A) exercise control over property of another, or to aid a third person toexercise control over property of another, permanently or for so extended a period or under such circumstances as to acquire the major portion of the economic value or benefit of the property; or

(B) dispose of the property of another for the benefit of oneself or a third person;

(3) "computer" means an electronic device that performs logical, arithmetic, and memory functions by the manipulation of electronic, optical or magnetic impulses, and includes all input, output, processing, storage, computer software, and communication facilities that are connected or related to a computer;

(4) "computer network" means an interconnection, including by microwave orother means of electronic or optical communication, of two or more computer systems, or between computers and remote terminals;

(5) "computer program" means an ordered set of instructions or statements,and related information that, when automatically executed in actual or modified form in a computer system, causes it to perform specified functions;

(6) "computer system" means a set of related computer equipment, devices and software;

(7) "data" includes a representation of information, knowledge, facts, concepts, or instructions, that is being prepared or has been prepared in a formalized manner and is used or intended for use in a computer, computer system, or computer network;

(8) "deprive" or "deprive another of property" means to

(A) withhold property of another or cause property of another to be withheld from that person permanently or for so extended a period or under such circumstances that the major portion of its economic value or benefit is lost to that person;

(B) dispose of the property in such a manner or under such circumstances as to make it unlikely that the owner will recover the property;

(C) retain the property of another with intent to restore it to that person only if that person pays a reward or other compensation for its return;

(D) sell, give, pledge, or otherwise transfer any interest in the property of another; or

(E) subject the property of another to the claim of a person other than the owner;

(9) "financial institution" means a bank, insurance company, credit union, building and loan association, investment trust, or other organization held out to the public as a place of deposit of funds or medium of savings or collective investment;

(10) "intent to defraud", when necessary to constitute an offense, is sufficiently established if an intent appears to defraud any person; "intent to defraud" means

(A) an intent to injure someone's interest which has value or an intent touse deception; or

(B) knowledge that the defendant is facilitating a fraud or injury to be perpetrated or inflicted by someone else;

(11) "obtain" means

(A) in relation to property, to bring about a transfer or a purported transfer of a legal interest in the property whether to the obtainer or another or to exert control over property of another; or

(B) in relation to a service, to secure performance of the service;

(12) "property of another" means property in which a person has an interest which the defendant is not privileged to infringe, whether or not the defendant also has an interest in the property and whether or not the person from whom the property was obtained or withheld also obtained the property unlawfully; "property of another" does not include property in the possession of the defendant in which another has only a security interest, even if legal title is in the secured party under a conditional sales contract or other security agreement; in the absence of a specific agreement to the contrary, the holder of a security interest in property is not privileged to infringe the debtor's right of possession without the consent of the debtor;

(13) "stolen property" means property of another that was obtained unlawfully.

ARTICLE 5. BUSINESS AND COMMERCIAL OFFENSES

11.46.740. Criminal use of computer.

(a) A person commits the offense of criminal use of a computer if, having no right to do so or any reasonable ground to believe the person has such a right, the person knowingly accesses or causes to be accessed a computer, computer system, computer program, computer network, or any part of a computer system or network, and as a result of that access

(1) obtains information concerning a person; or

(2) introduces false information into a computer, computer system, or computer network with the intent to damage or enhance the data record of a person.

(b) Criminal use of a computer is a class C felony.

ARTICLE 6. DEFINITIONS

11.81.900. Definitions.

(a) For purposes of this title, unless the context requires otherwise,

(1) a person acts "intentionally" with respect to a result described by a provision of law defining an offense when the person's conscious objective is to cause that result; when intentionally causing a particular result is an element of an offense, that intent need not be the person's only objective;

(2) a person acts "knowingly" with respect to conduct or to a circumstance described by a provision of law defining an offense when the person is aware that the conduct is of that nature or that the circumstance exists; when knowledge of the existence of a particular fact is an element of an offense, that knowledge is established if a person is aware of a substantial probability of its existence, unless the person actually believes it does not exist; a person who is unaware of conduct or a circumstance of which the person would have been aware had that person not been intoxicated acts knowingly with respect to that conduct or circumstance;

(3) a person acts "recklessly" with respect to a result or to a circumstance described by a provision of law defining an offense when the person is aware of and consciously disregards a substantial andunjustifiable risk that the result will occur or that the circumstance exists; the risk must be of such a nature and degree that disregard of it constitutes a gross deviation from the standard of conduct that a reasonable person would observe in the situation; a person who is unaware of a risk of which the person would have been aware had that person not been intoxicated acts recklessly with respect to that risk;

(4) a person acts with "criminal negligence" with respect to a result or to a circumstance described by a provision of law defining an offense when the person fails to perceive a substantial and unjustifiable risk that the result will occur or that the circumstance exists; the risk must be of such a nature and degree that the failure to perceive it constitutes a gross deviation from the standard of care that a reasonable person would observe in the situation.(b) In this title, unless otherwise specified or unless the context requires otherwise,

(1) "affirmative defense" means that

(A) some evidence must be admitted which places in issue the defense; and

(B) the defendant has the burden of establishing the defense by a preponderance of the evidence;

(2) "benefit" means a present or future gain or advantage to the beneficiary or to a third person pursuant to the desire or consent of the beneficiary;

(3) "building", in addition to its usual meaning, includes any propelled vehicle or structure adapted for overnight accommodation of persons or for carrying on business; when a building consists of separate units, including apartment units, offices, or rented rooms, each unit is considered a separate building;

(4) "cannabis" has the meaning ascribed to it in AS 11.71.900(10), (11), and (14);

(5) "conduct" means an act or omission and its accompanying mental state;

(6) "controlled substance" has the meaning ascribed to it in AS 11.71.900(4);

(7) "correctional facility" means premises, or a portion of premises, usedfor the confinement of persons under official detention;

(8) "credit card" means any instrument or device, whether known as a credit card, credit plate, courtesy card, or identification card or by any other name, issued with or without fee by an issuer for the use of the cardholder inobtaining property or services on credit;

(9) "crime" means an offense for which a sentence of imprisonment is authorized; a crime is either a felony or a misdemeanor;

(10) "culpable mental state" means "intentionally", "knowingly", "recklessly", or with "criminal negligence", as those terms are defined in (a) of this section;

(11) "dangerous instrument" means any deadly weapon or anything that, under the circumstances in which it is used, attempted to be used, or threatened to be used, is capable of causing death or serious physical injury;

(12) "deadly force" means force that the person uses with the intent of causing, or uses under circumstances that the person knows create a substantial risk of causing, death or serious physical injury; "deadly force" includes intentionally discharging or pointing a firearm in the direction of another person or in the direction in which another person is believed to be and intentionally placing another person in fear of imminent serious physical injury by means of a dangerous instrument;

(13) "deadly weapon" means any firearm, or anything designed for and capable of causing death or serious physical injury, including a knife, an axe, a club, metal knuckles, or an explosive;

(14) "deception" means to knowingly

(A) create or confirm another's false impression that the defendant does not believe to be true, including false impressions as to law or value and false impressions as to intention or other state of mind;

(B) fail to correct another's false impression that the defendant previously has created or confirmed;

(C) prevent another from acquiring information pertinent to the disposition of the property or service involved;

(D) sell or otherwise transfer or encumber property and fail to disclose a lien, adverse claim, or other legal impediment to the enjoyment of the property, whether or not that impediment is a matter of official record; or

(E) promise performance that the defendant does not intend to perform or knows will not be performed;

(15) "defense", other than an affirmative defense, means that

(A) some evidence must be admitted which places in issue the defense; and

(B) the state then has the burden of disproving the existence of the defense beyond a reasonable doubt;

(16) "drug" has the meaning ascribed to it in AS 11.71.900(9);

(17) "dwelling" means a building that is designed for use or is used as a person's permanent or temporary home or place of lodging;

(18) "explosive" means a chemical compound, mixture, or device that is commonly used or intended for the purpose of producing a chemical reaction resulting in a substantially instantaneous release of gas and heat, including dynamite, blasting powder, nitroglycerin, blasting caps, and nitrojelly, but excluding salable fireworks as defined in AS 18.72.050, black powder, smokeless powder, small arms ammunition, and small arms ammunition primers;

(19) "felony" means a crime for which a sentence of imprisonment for a term of more than one year is authorized;

(20) "fiduciary" means a trustee, guardian, executor, administrator, receiver, or any other person carrying on functions of trust on behalf of another person or organization;

(21) "firearm" means a weapon, including a pistol, revolver, rifle, or shotgun, whether loaded or unloaded, operable or inoperable, designed for discharging a shot capable of causing death or serious physical injury;

(22) "force" means any bodily impact, restraint, or confinement or the threat of imminent bodily impact, restraint, or confinement, "force" includes deadly and nondeadly force;

(23) "government" means the United States, any state or any municipality or other political subdivision within the United States or its territories; any department, agency, or subdivision of any of the foregoing; an agency carrying out the functions of government; or any corporation or agency formed under interstate compact or international treaty;

(24) "highway" means a public road, road right-of-way, street, alley, bridge, walk, trail, tunnel, path, or similar or related facility, as well as ferries and similar correlated facilities;

(25) "includes" means "includes but is not limited to";

(26) "incompetent person" means a person who is impaired by reason of mental illness or mental deficiency to the extent that the person lacks sufficient understanding or capacity to make or communicate responsible decisions concerning that person;

(27) "intoxicated" means intoxicated from the use of a drug or alcohol;

(28) "law" includes statutes and regulations;

(29) "leased" includes "rented";

(30) "metal knuckles" means a device that consists of finger rings or guards made of a hard substance and designed, made, or adapted for inflicting serious physical injury or death by striking a person;

(31) "misdemeanor" means a crime for which a sentence of imprisonment for a term of more than one year may not be imposed;

(32) "nondeadly force" means force other than deadly force;

(33) "offense" means conduct for which a sentence of imprisonment or fine is authorized; an offense is either a crime or a violation;

(34) "official detention" means custody, arrest, surrender in lieu of arrest, or confinement under an order of a court in a criminal or juvenile proceeding, other than an order of conditional bail release;

(35) "official proceeding" means a proceeding heard before a legislative, judicial, administrative, or other governmental body or official authorized to hear evidence under oath;

(36) "omission" means a failure to perform an act for which a duty of performance is imposed by law;

(37) "organization" means a legal entity, including a corporation, company, association, firm, partnership,

joint stock company, foundation, institution, government, society, union, club, church, or any other group of persons organized for any purpose;

(38) "peace officer" means a public servant vested by law with a duty to maintain public order or to make arrests, whether the duty extends to all offenses or is limited to a specific class of offenses or offenders;

(39) "person" means a natural person and, when appropriate, an organization, government, or governmental instrumentality;

(40) "physical injury" means a physical pain or an impairment of physical condition;

(41) "police dog" means a dog used in police work under the control of a peace officer;

(42) "possess" means having physical possession or the exercise of dominion or control over property;

(43) "premises" means real property and any building;

(44) "propelled vehicle" means a device upon which or by which a person or property is or may be transported, and which is self-propelled, including automobiles, vessels, airplanes, motorcycles, snow machines, all-terrain vehicles, sailboats, and construction equipment;

(45) "property" means an article, substance, or thing of value, including money, tangible and intangible personal property including data or information stored in a computer program, system, or network, real property, a credit card, a domestic pet or livestock regardless of value, choses-in-action, and evidence of debt or of contract; a commodity of a public utility such as gas, electricity, steam, or water constitutes property but the supplying of such a commodity to premises from an outside source by means of wires, pipes, conduits, or other equipment is considered a rendition of a service rather than a sale or delivery of property;

(46) "public place" means a place to which the public or a substantial group of persons has access and includes highways, transportation facilities, schools, places of amusement or business, parks, playgrounds, prisons, and hallways, lobbies, and other portions of apartment houses and hotels not constituting rooms or apartments designed for actual residence;

(47) "public record" means a document, paper, book, letter, drawing, map, plat, photo, photographic file, motion picture, film, microfilm, microphotograph, exhibit, magnetic or paper tape, punched card or other document of any other material, regardless of physical form or characteristic, developed or received under law or in connection with the transaction of official business and preserved or appropriate for preservation by any agency, municipality, or any body subject to the open meeting provision of AS 44.62.310, as evidence of the organization, function, policies, decisions, procedures, operations, or other activities of the state or municipality or because of the informational value in it; it also includes staff manuals and instructions to staff that affect the public;

(48) "public servant" means each of the following, whether compensated or not, but does not include jurors or witnesses:

(A) an officer or employee of the state, a municipality or other politicalsubdivision of the state, or a governmental instrumentality of the state, including legislators, members of the judiciary, and peace officers;

(B) a person who participates as an advisor, consultant, or assistant at the request or direction of the state, a municipality or other political subdivision of the state, or a governmental instrumentality;

(C) a person who serves as a member of the board or commission created by statute or by legislative, judicial, or administrative action by the state, a municipality or other political subdivision of the state, or a governmental instrumentality;

(D) a person nominated, elected, appointed, employed, or designated to act in a capacity defined in (A)—(C) of this paragraph, but who does not occupy the position;

(49) a "renunciation" is not "voluntary and complete" if it is substantially motivated, in whole or in part, by

(A) a belief that circumstances exist which increase the probability of detection or apprehension of the defendant or another participant in the criminal enterprise, or which render more difficult the accomplishment of the criminal purpose; or

(B) a decision to postpone the criminal conduct until another time or to transfer the criminal effort to another victim or another but similar objective;

(50) "serious physical injury" means

(A) physical injury caused by an act performed under circumstances that create a substantial risk of death; or

(B) physical injury that causes serious and protracted disfigurement, protracted impairment of health, protracted loss or impairment of the function of a body member or organ, or that unlawfully terminates a pregnancy;

(51) "services" includes labor, professional services, transportation, telephone or othercommunications service, entertainment, including cable, subscription, or pay television or other telecommunications service, the supplying of food, lodging, or other accommodations in hotels, restaurants, or elsewhere, admission to exhibitions, the use of a computer, computer time, a computer system, a computer program, a computer network, or

any part of a computer system or network, and the supplying of equipment for use;

(52) "sexual contact" means

(A) the defendant's

(i) knowingly touching, directly or through clothing, the victim's genitals, anus, or female breast; or

(ii) knowingly causing the victim to touch, directly or through clothing, the defendant's or victim's genitals, anus, or female breast;

(B) but "sexual contact" does not include acts

(i) that may reasonably be construed to be normal caretaker responsibilities for a child, interactions with a child, or affection for a child; or

(ii) performed for the purpose of administering a recognized and lawful form of treatment that is reasonably adapted to promoting the physical or mental health of the person being treated;

(53) "sexual penetration" means

(A) genital intercourse, cunnilingus, fellatio, anal intercourse, or an intrusion, however slight, of an object or any part of a person's body into the genital or anal opening of another person's body;

(B) but "sexual penetration" does not include acts performed for the purpose of administering a recognized and lawful form of treatment that is reasonably adapted to promoting the physical health of the person being treated;

(C) each party to any of the acts defined as "sexual penetration" is considered to be engaged in sexual penetration;

(54) "solicits" includes "commands";

(55) "threat" means a menace, however communicated, to engage in conduct described in AS 11.41.520(a)(1)—(7) but under AS 11.41.520(a)(1) includes all threats to inflict physical injury on anyone;

(56) "violation" is a noncriminal offense punishable only by a fine, but not by imprisonment or other penalty; conviction of a violation does not give rise to any disability or legal disadvantage based on conviction of a crime; a person charged with a violation is not entitled

(A) to a trial by jury; or

(B) to have a public defender or other counsel appointed at public expense to represent the person;

(57) "voluntary act" means a bodily movement performed consciously as a result of effort and determination, and includes the possession of property if the

defendant was aware of the physical possession or control for a sufficient period to have been able to terminate it.

ARIZONA STATUTES

TITLE 13. CRIMINAL CODE
.CHAPTER 23. ORGANIZED CRIME AND FRAUD

13-2301. Definitions

A. For the purposes of 13-2302 through 13-2304:

1. "Creditor" means any person making such an extension of credit or any person claiming by, under, or through any person making such an extension of credit.

2. "Debtor" means any person to whom such an extension of credit is made or any person who guarantees the repayment of an extension of credit, or in any manner undertakes to indemnify the creditor against loss resulting from the failure of any person to whom an extension is made to repay the same.

3. "Extortionate extension of credit" means any extension of credit with respect to which it is the understanding of the creditor and the debtor at the time such extension is made that delay in making repayment or failure to make repayment could result in the use of violence or other criminal means to cause harm to the person, reputation or property of any person.

4. "Extortionate means" means the use, or an express or implicit threat of use, of violence or other criminal means to cause harm to the person, reputation or property of any person.

5. "Repayment of any extension of credit" means the repayment, satisfaction or discharge in whole or in part of any debt or claim, acknowledged or disputed, valid or invalid, resulting from or in connection with that extension of credit.

6. "To collect an extension of credit" means to induce in any way any person to make repayment thereof.

7. "To extend credit" means to make or renew any loan or to enter into any agreement, tacit or express, whereby the repayment or satisfaction of any debt or claim, whether acknowledged or disputed, valid or invalid, and however arising, may or shall be deferred.

B. For the purposes of 13-2305 through 13-2307:

1. "Dealer in property" means a person who buys and sells property as a business.

2. "Stolen property" means property that has been the subject of any unlawful taking.

3. "Traffic" means to sell, transfer, distribute, dispense or otherwise dispose of stolen property to another person, or to buy, receive, possess or obtain control of stolen property, with intent to sell, transfer, distribute, dispense or otherwise dispose of to another person.

C. For the purposes of 13-2308:

1. "Combination" means persons who collaborate in carrying on or furthering the activities or purposes of a criminal syndicate even though such persons may not know each other's identity or membership in the combination changes from time to time or one or more members may stand in a wholesaler-retailer or other arm's length relationship with others as to activities or dealings between or among themselves in an illicit operation.

2. "Criminal syndicate" means any combination of persons or enterprises engaging, or having the purpose of engaging, on a continuing basis in conduct which violates any one or more provisions of any felony statute of this state.

D. For the purposes of 13-2312 through 13-2315, unless the context otherwise requires:

1. "Control", in relation to an enterprise, means the possession of sufficient means to permit substantial direction over the affairs of an enterprise and, in relation to property, means to acquire or possess.

2. "Enterprise" means any corporation, partnership, association, labor union, or other legal entity or any group of persons associated in fact although not a legal entity.

3. "Financial institution" means any business under the jurisdiction of the state banking department or a banking or securities regulatory agency of the United States or business under the jurisdiction of the securities division of the corporation commission, the real estate department or the department of insurance.

4. "Racketeering" means any act, including any preparatory or completed offense, committed for financial gain, which is chargeable or indictable under the laws of the state in which the act occurred and, if the act occurred in a state other than this state, would be chargeable or indictable under the laws of this state had the act occurred in this state and punishable by imprisonment for more than one year, regardless of whether such act is charged or indicted, involving:

(a) Homicide.

(b) Robbery.

(c) Kidnapping.

(d) Forgery.

(e) Theft.

(f) Bribery.

(g) Gambling.

(h) Usury.

(i) Extortion.

(j) Extortionate extensions of credit.

(k) Prohibited drugs, marijuana or other prohibited chemicals or substances.

(l) Trafficking in explosives, weapons or stolen property.

(m) Leading organized crime.

(n) Obstructing or hindering criminal investigations or prosecutions.

(o) Asserting false claims including, but not limited to, false claims asserted through fraud or arson.

(p) False statements or publications concerning land for sale or lease or sale of subdivided lands or sale and mortgaging of unsubdivided lands.

(q) Resale of realty with intent to defraud.

(r) Fraud in the purchase or sale of securities.

(s) Sale of unregistered securities or real property securities and transactions involving such securities by unregistered dealers or salesmen.

(t) A scheme or artifice to defraud.

(u) Obscenity.

(v) Child pornography.

(w) Prostitution.

(x) Restraint of trade or commerce in violation of s 34-252.

(y) Terrorism.

(z) Money laundering.

(aa) Obscene or indecent telephone communications to minors for commercial purposes.

5. "Records" means any book, paper, writing, record, COMPUTER program or other material.

E. For the purposes of 13-2316:

1. "Access" means to approach, instruct, communicate with, store data in, retrieve data from or otherwise make use of any resources of a COMPUTER, COMPUTER system or COMPUTER network.

2. "COMPUTER" means an electronic device which performs logic, arithmetic or memory functions

by the manipulations of electronic or magnetic impulses and includes all input, output, processing, storage, software or communication facilities which are connected or related to such a device in a system or network.

3. "COMPUTER network" means the interconnection of communication lines with a COMPUTER through remote terminals or a complex consisting of two or more interconnected COMPUTERS.

4. "COMPUTER program" means a series of instructions or statements, in a form acceptable to a COMPUTER, which permits the functioning of a COMPUTER system in a manner designed to provide appropriate products from such COMPUTER system.

5. "COMPUTER software" means a set of COMPUTER programs, procedures and associated documentation concerned with the operation of a COMPUTER system.

6. "COMPUTER system" means a set of related, connected or unconnected COMPUTER equipment, devices and softwares.

7. "Financial instrument" means any check, draft, money order, certificate of deposit, letter of credit, bill of exchange, credit card or marketable security or any other written instrument, as defined by s 13-2001, paragraph 7, which is transferable for value.

8. "Property" means financial instruments, information, including electronically produced data, COMPUTER software and programs in either machine or human readable form, and anything of value, tangible or intangible.

9. "Services" includes COMPUTER time, data processing and storage functions.

13-2316. COMPUTER fraud; classification

A. A person commits COMPUTER fraud in the first degree by accessing, altering, damaging or destroying without authorization any COMPUTER, COMPUTER system, COMPUTER network, or any part of such COMPUTER, system or network, with the intent to devise or execute any scheme or artifice to defraud or deceive, or control property or services by means of false or fraudulent pretenses, representations or promises.

B. A person commits COMPUTER fraud in the second degree by intentionally and without authorization accessing, altering, damaging or destroying any COMPUTER, COMPUTER system or COMPUTER network or any COMPUTER software, program or data contained in such COMPUTER, COMPUTER system or COMPUTER network.

C. COMPUTER fraud in the first degree is a class 3 felony. COMPUTER fraud in the second degree is a class 6 felony.

CHAPTER 30. EAVESDROPPING AND COMMUNICATIONS

13-3016. Government agency access to contents of stored electronic communications; backup preservation; delayed notice; violation; classification

A. The provisions of this section apply to electronic communications entrusted to a communication service provider or remote computing service solely for the purpose of transmission, storage or processing. Electronic communications in the possession of a person who is entitled to access the contents of such communications for any purpose other than transmission, storage or processing are ordinary business records, and may be obtained by subpoena or court order.

B. An agency of this state or its political subdivisions may require the disclosure by a provider of electronic communication services of the contents of an electronic communication that has been in electronic storage for one hundred eighty days or less only by obtaining a search warrant pursuant to chapter 38 of this title.

C. An agency of this state or its political subdivisions may require the disclosure by a provider of electronic communication services of the contents of an electronic communication that has been in electronic storage for more than one hundred eighty days:

1. Without notice to the subscriber or customer, by obtaining a search warrant issued pursuant to chapter 38 of this title.

2. With prior notice to the subscriber or customer, by subpoena, except that such notice may be delayed pursuant to subsection E.

3. With prior notice to the subscriber or customer if the agency obtains a court order on application and certification to the court that the information likely to be obtained is relevant to a legitimate law enforcement inquiry, except that such notice may be delayed pursuant to subsection E.

D. An agency of this state or its political subdivisions may require a provider of remote computing services to disclose the contents of any electronic communication that is held or maintained on that service on behalf of a subscriber or customer of the remote computing service solely for the purpose of providing storage or COMPUTER processing services to the subscriber or customer:

1. Without notice to the subscriber or customer, by obtaining a search warrant issued pursuant to chapter 38 of this title.

2. With prior notice to the subscriber or customer, by subpoena, except that such notice may be delayed pursuant to subsection E.

3. With prior notice to the subscriber or customer if the agency obtains a court order on application and certification to the court that the information likely to be obtained is relevant to a legitimate law enforce-

ment inquiry, except that such notice may be delayed pursuant to subsection E.

E. An agency acting pursuant to this section may include in its subpoena or court order a requirement that the service provider to whom the request is directed create a backup copy of the contents of the electronic communications sought in order to preserve those communications:

1. Without notifying the subscriber or customer, the provider shall:

(a) Create the backup copy as soon as practicable but in no event no later than two business days after receipt of the subpoena or order.

(b) Confirm to the requesting agency that the backup copy has been made.

(c) Promptly deliver the backup copy to the court issuing the subpoena or order.

2. The court shall seal and retain the backup copy or make such other provision as it deems necessary to ensure that the backup copy is preserved until resolution of any proceedings pursuant to this section.

3. Within three days after receipt of confirmation, the agency shall notify the subscriber or customer of the creation of the backup copy, except that notice may be delayed pursuant to this subsection.

4. Within fourteen days after notice by the agency, the subscriber or customer may challenge the agency's request by filing an application to quash the subpoena or vacate the court order and serving the requesting agency.

5. If after response by the agency and such further proceedings as the court may deem necessary, the court finds that the applicant is not the subscriber or customer for whom the communications sought by the agency are maintained by the provider, or that there is reason to believe that the communications sought are relevant to a legitimate law enforcement inquiry, the court shall deny the application and deliver the backup copy to the requesting agency. If the court finds that the applicant is the subscriber or customer for whom the communications sought by the agency are maintained, and that there is no reason to believe the communications sought are relevant to a legitimate law enforcement inquiry, the court shall grant the application and order the backup copy to be destroyed.

6. The court shall release the backup copy to the requesting agency no sooner than fourteen days after the agency's notice to the subscriber or customer if the subscriber or customer has not filed a challenge to the subpoena or court order.

7. The court shall not destroy the backup copy until the information requested is delivered or until the resolution of any proceedings arising from a challenge to the subpoena or order.

F. Notice to the subscriber or customer required by this section may be delayed for a period of not to exceed ninety days under any of the following circumstances:

1. If the applicant for a search warrant or court order pursuant to this section requests a delay of notification and the court finds that such delay is necessary to protect the safety of any person or to prevent flight from prosecution, tampering with evidence, intimidation of witnesses or jeopardizing an investigation.

2. If the investigator or prosecuting attorney proceeding by subpoena executes a written certification that there is reason to believe that notice to the subscriber or customer may result in danger to the safety of any person, flight from prosecution, tampering with evidence, intimidation of witnesses or jeopardizing an investigation. The agency shall retain a true copy of the certification.

3. If further delay of notification is necessary, extensions of up to ninety days each may be obtained by application to the court or certification pursuant to paragraphs 1 and 2 of this subsection.

4. Any agency acting pursuant to this section may apply for a court order directing the communication or computing service provider not to notify any other person of the existence of the subpoena, court order or warrant for such period as the court deems appropriate. The court shall grant the application if it finds that there is reason to believe that notice may cause an adverse result described in paragraphs 1 and 2 of this subsection. A person who violates an order issued pursuant to this subsection is guilty of a class 1 misdemeanor.

5. On the expiration of any period of delay under this section, the agency shall deliver to the subscriber or customer a copy of the process used and notice including:

(a) That information was requested from the service provider.

(b) The date on which the information was requested.

(c) That notification to the subscriber or customer was delayed.

(d) The identity of the court or agency ordering or certifying the delay.

(e) The provision of this section by which delay was obtained.

(f) That any challenge to the subpoena or order must be filed within fourteen days.

ARKANSAS STATUTES

TITLE 5. CRIMINAL OFFENSES
SUBTITLE 4. OFFENSES AGAINST PROPERTY
CHAPTER 41. COMPUTER-RELATED CRIMES

5-41-101. Purpose.

It is found and determined that computer-related crime poses a major problem for business and government; that losses for each incident of computer-related crime are potentially astronomical; that the opportunities for computer-related crime in business and government through the introduction of fraudulent records into a computer system, the unauthorized use of computers, the alteration or destruction of computerized information or files, and the stealing of financial instruments, data, and other assets are great; that computer-related crime has a direct effect on state commerce; and that, while various forms of computer-related crime might possibly be the subject of criminal charges based on other provisions of law, it is appropriate and desirable that a statute be enacted which deals directly with computer-related crime.

5-41-102. Definitions.

As used in this chapter, unless the context otherwise requires:

(1) "Access" means to instruct, communicate with, store data in, or retrieve data from a computer, computer system, or computer network;

(2) "Computer" means an electronic device that performs logical, arithmetic, and memory functions by manipulating electronic or magnetic impulses and includes all input, output, processing, storage, computer software, and communication facilities that are connected or related to that device in a system or a network;

(3) "Computer network" means the interconnection of communications lines with a computer through remote terminals or a complex consisting of two (2) or more interconnected computers;

(4) "Computer program" means a set of instructions, statements, or related data that, in actual or modified form, is capable of causing a computer or a computer system to perform specified functions;

(5) "Computer software" means one (1) or more computer programs, existing in any form, or any associated operational procedures, manuals, or other documentation;

(6) "Computer system" means a set of related, connected, or unconnected computers, other devices, and software;

(7) "Data" means any representation of information, knowledge, facts, concepts, or instructions which are being prepared or have been prepared and are intended to be processed or stored, are being processed or stored, or have been processed or stored in a computer, computer network, or computer system;

(8) "Financial instrument" includes, but is not limited to, any check, draft, warrant, money order, note, certificate of deposit, letter of credit, bill of exchange, credit or debit card, transaction authorization mechanism, marketable security, or any computer system representation thereof;

(9) "Property" includes, but is not limited to, financial instruments, data, computer programs, documents associated with computers and computer programs, or copies thereof, whether tangible or intangible, including both human and computer readable data, and data while in transit;

(10) "Services" includes, but is not limited to, the use of a computer, a computer system, a computer network, computer software, a computer program, or data.

5-41-103. Computer fraud.

(a) Any person commits computer fraud who intentionally accesses or causes to be accessed any computer, computer system, computer network, or any part thereof for the purpose of:

(1) Devising or executing any scheme or artifice to defraud or extort; or

(2) Obtaining money, property, or services with false or fraudulent intent, representations, or promises.

(b) Computer fraud is a Class D felony.

5-41-104. Computer trespass.

(a) Any person commits computer trespass who intentionally and without authorization accesses, alters, deletes, damages, destroys, or disrupts any computer, computer system, computer network, computer program, or data.

(b) Computer trespass is a Class C misdemeanor if it is a first violation which does not cause any loss or damage.

(c) Computer trespass is a Class B misdemeanor if:

(1) It is a second or subsequent violation which does not cause any loss or damage; or

(2) It is a violation which causes loss or damage of less than five hundred dollars ($500).

(d) Computer trespass is a Class A misdemeanor if it is a violation which causes loss or damage of five hundred dollars ($500) or more, but less than two thousand five hundred dollars ($2,500).

(e) Computer trespass is a Class D felony if it is a violation which causes loss or damage of two thousand five hundred dollars ($2,500) or more.

5-41-105. Venue of violations.

For the purpose of venue under this chapter, any violation of this chapter shall be considered to have been committed in any county:

(1) In which any act was performed in furtherance of any course of conduct which violated this chapter;

(2) In which any violator had control or possession of any proceeds of the violation or of any books, records, documents, property, financial instrument, computer software, computer program, data, or other material or objects which were used in furtherance of the violation;

(3) From which, to which, or through which any access to a computer or computer network was made whether by wires, electromagnetic waves, microwaves, or any other means of communication;

(4) In which any computer, computer system, or computer network is an object or an instrument of the violation is located at the time of the alleged violation.

5-41-106. Civil actions.

(a) Any person whose property or person is injured by reason of a violation of any provision of this chapter may sue therefor and recover for any damages sustained and the costs of suit. Without limiting the generality of the term, "damages" shall include loss of profits.

(b) At the request of any party to an action brought pursuant to this section, the court, in its discretion, may conduct all legal proceedings in such a way as to protect the secrecy and security of the computer, computer system, computer network, computer program, computer software, and data involved in order to prevent possible reoccurrence of the same or a similar act by another person and to protect any trade secrets of any party.

(c) No civil action under this section may be brought except within three (3) years from the date the alleged violation of this chapter is discovered or should have been discovered by the exercise of reasonable diligence.

5-41-107. Assistance of Attorney General.

If requested to do so by a prosecuting attorney, the Attorney General may assist the prosecuting attorney in the investigation or prosecution of an offense under this chapter or any other offense involving the use of a computer.

CALIFORNIA STATUTES

PART 1. OF CRIMES AND PUNISHMENTS
TITLE 13. OF CRIMES AGAINST PROPERTY
CHAPTER 5. LARCENY [THEFT]

499c. Trade secrets; theft; solicitation or bribery to acquire; punishment; defenses

(a) As used in this section:

(1) "Access" means to approach, a way or means of approaching, nearing, admittance to, including to instruct, communicate with, store information in, or retrieve information from a COMPUTER system or COMPUTER network.

(2) "Article" means any object, material, device or substance or copy thereof, including any writing, record, recording, drawing, sample, specimen, prototype, model, photograph, micro-organism, blueprint, map, or tangible representation of COMPUTER program or information, including both human and COMPUTER readable information and information while in transit.

(3) "Benefit" means gain or advantage, or anything regarded by the beneficiary as gain or advantage, including benefit to any other person or entity in whose welfare he is interested.

(4) "COMPUTER system" means a machine or collection of machines, one or more of which contain COMPUTER programs and information, that performs functions, including, but not limited to, logic, arithmetic, information storage and retrieval, communications, and control.

(5) "COMPUTER network" means an interconnection of two or more COMPUTER systems.

(6) "COMPUTER program" means an ordered set of instructions or statements, and related information that, when automatically executed in actual or modified form in a COMPUTER system, causes it to perform specified functions.

(7) "Copy" means any facsimile, replica, photograph or other reproduction of an article, and any note, drawing or sketch made of or from an article.

(8) "Representing" means describing, depicting, containing, constituting, reflecting or recording.

(9) "Trade secret" means the whole or any portion or phase of any scientific or technical information, design, process, procedure, formula, COMPUTER program or information stored in a COMPUTER, information in transit, or improvement which is secret and is not generally available to the public, and which gives one who uses it an advantage over competitors who do not know of or use the trade secret; and a trade secret shall be presumed to be secret when the owner thereof takes measures to prevent it from becoming available to

persons other than those selected by the owner to have access thereto for limited purposes.

(b) Every person is guilty of theft who, with intent to deprive or withhold from the owner thereof the control of a trade secret, or with an intent to appropriate a trade secret to his or her own use or to the use of another, does any of the following:

(1) Steals, takes, carries away, or uses without authorization a trade secret.

(2) Fraudulently appropriates any article representing a trade secret entrusted to him.

(3) Having unlawfully obtained access to the article, without authority makes or causes to be made a copy of any article representing a trade secret.

(4) Having obtained access to the article through a relationship of trust and confidence, without authority and in breach of the obligations created by such relationship makes or causes to be made, directly from and in the presence of the article, a copy of any article representing a trade secret.

(c) Every person who promises or offers or gives, or conspires to promise or offer to give, to any present or former agent, employee or servant of another a benefit as an inducement, bribe or reward for conveying, delivering or otherwise making available an article representing a trade secret owned by his or her present or former principal, employer or master, to any person not authorized by such owner to receive or acquire the same and every person who being a present or former agent, employee, or servant, solicits, accepts, receives or takes a benefit as an inducement, bribe or reward for conveying, delivering or otherwise making available an article representing a trade secret owned by his or her present or former principal, employer or master, to any person not authorized by such owner to receive or acquire the same is punishable by imprisonment in the state prison, or in a county jail not exceeding one year, or by fine not exceeding five thousand dollars ($5,000), or by both such fine and such imprisonment.

(d) In a prosecution for a violation of this section it shall be no defense that the person so charged, returned or intended to return the article.

TITLE 13. OF CRIMES AGAINST PROPERTY

502. Unauthorized access to computers, computer systems and computer data

(a) It is the intent of the Legislature in enacting this section to expand the degree of protection afforded to individuals, businesses, and governmental agencies from tampering, interference, damage, and unauthorized access to lawfully created computer data and computer systems. The Legislature finds and declares that the proliferation of COMPUTER technology has resulted in a concomitant proliferation of COMPUTER CRIME and oth-er forms of unauthorized access to COMPUTERS, COMPUTER systems, and COMPUTER data.

The Legislature further finds and declares that protection of the integrity of all types and forms of lawfully created computers, computer systems, and computer data is vital to the protection of the privacy of individuals as well as to the well-being of financial institutions, business concerns, governmental agencies, and others within this state that lawfully utilize those computers, computer systems, and data.

(b) For the purposes of this section, the following terms have the following meanings:

(1) "Access" means to gain entry to, instruct, or communicate with the logical, arithmetical, or memory function resources of a computer, computer system, or computer network.

(2) "Computer network" means any system which provides communications between one or more computer systems and input/output devices including, but not limited to, display terminals and printers connected by telecommunication facilities.

(3) "Computer program or software" means a set of instructions or statements, and related data, that when executed in actual or modified form, cause a computer, computer system, or computer network to perform specified functions.

(4) "Computer services" includes, but is not limited to, computer time, data processing, or storage functions, or other uses of a computer, computer system, or computer network.

(5) "Computer system" means a device or collection of devices, including support devices and excluding calculators which are not programmable and capable of being used in conjunction with external files, one or more of which contain computer programs, electronic instructions, input data, and output data, that performs functions including, but not limited to, logic, arithmetic, data storage and retrieval, communication, and control.

(6) "Data" means a representation of information, knowledge, facts, concepts, computer software, computer programs or instructions. Data may be in any form, in storage media, or as stored in the memory of the computer or in transit or presented on a display device.

(7) "Supporting documentation" includes, but is not limited to, all information, in any form, pertaining to the design, construction, classification, implementation, use, or modification of a computer, computer system, computer network, computer program, or computer software, which information is not generally available to the public and is necessary for the operation of a computer, computer system, computer network, computer program, or computer software.

(8) "Injury" means any alteration, deletion, damage, or destruction of a computer system, computer network, computer program, or data caused by the access.

(9) "Victim expenditure" means any expenditure reasonably and necessarily incurred by the owner or lessee to verify that a computer system, computer network, computer program, or data was or was not altered, deleted, damaged, or destroyed by the access.

(10) "Computer contaminant" means any set of computer instructions that are designed to modify, damage, destroy, record, or transmit information within a computer, computer system, or computer network without the intent or permission of the owner of the information. They include, but are not limited to, a group of computer instructions commonly called viruses or worms, which are self-replicating or self-propagating and are designed to contaminate other computer programs or computer data, consume computer resources, modify, destroy, record, or transmit data, or in some other fashion usurp the normal operation of the computer, computer system, or computer network.

(c) Except as provided in subdivision (h), any person who commits any of the following acts is guilty of a public offense:

(1) Knowingly accesses and without permission alters, damages, deletes, destroys, or otherwise uses any data, computer, computer system, or computer network in order to either (A) devise or execute any scheme or artifice to defraud, deceive, or extort, or (B) wrongfully control or obtain money, property, or data.

(2) Knowingly accesses and without permission takes, copies, or makes use of any data from a computer, computer system, or computer network, or takes or copies any supporting documentation, whether existing or residing internal or external to a computer, computer system, or computer network.

(3) Knowingly and without permission uses or causes to be used computer services.

(4) Knowingly accesses and without permission adds, alters, damages, deletes, or destroys any data, computer software, or computer programs which reside or exist internal or external to a computer, computer system, or computer network.

(5) Knowingly and without permission disrupts or causes the disruption of computer services or denies or causes the denial of computer services to an authorized user of a computer, computer system, or computer network.

(6) Knowingly and without permission provides or assists in providing a means of accessing a computer, computer system, or computer network in violation of this section.

(7) Knowingly and without permission accesses or causes to be accessed any computer, computer system, or computer network.

(8) Knowingly introduces any computer contaminant into any computer, computer system, or computer network.

(d) (1) Any person who violates any of the provisions of paragraph (1), (2),

(4), or (5) of subdivision (c) is punishable by a fine not exceeding ten thousand dollars ($10,000), or by imprisonment in the state prison for 16 months, or two or three years, or by both that fine and imprisonment, or by a fine not exceeding five thousand dollars ($5,000), or by imprisonment in the county jail not exceeding one year, or by both that fine and imprisonment.

(2) Any person who violates paragraph (3) of subdivision (c) is punishable as follows:

(A) For the first violation which does not result in injury, and where the value of the computer services used does not exceed four hundred dollars ($400), by a fine not exceeding five thousand dollars ($5,000), or by imprisonment in the county jail not exceeding one year, or by both that fine and imprisonment.

(B) For any violation which results in a victim expenditure in an amount greater than five thousand dollars ($5,000) or in an injury, or if the value of the computer services used exceeds four hundred dollars ($400), or for any second or subsequent violation, by a fine not exceeding ten thousand dollars ($10,000), or by imprisonment in the state prison for 16 months, or two or three years, or by both that fine and imprisonment, or by a fine not exceeding five thousand dollars ($5,000), or by imprisonment in the county jail not exceeding one year, or by both that fine and imprisonment.

(3) Any person who violates paragraph (6), (7), or (8) of subdivision (c) is punishable as follows:

(A) For a first violation which does not result in injury, an infraction punishable by a fine not exceeding two hundred fifty dollars ($250).

(B) For any violation which results in a victim expenditure in an amount not greater than five thousand dollars ($5,000), or for a second or subsequent violation, by a fine not exceeding five thousand dollars ($5,000), or by imprisonment in the county jail not exceeding one year, or by both that fine and imprisonment.

(C) For any violation which results in a victim expenditure in an amount greater than five thousand dollars ($5,000), by a fine not exceeding ten thousand dollars ($10,000), or by imprisonment in the state prison for 16 months, or two or three years, or by both that fine and imprisonment, or by a fine not exceeding five thousand dollars ($5,000), or by imprisonment in the county jail not exceeding one year, or by both that fine and imprisonment.

(e) (1) In addition to any other civil remedy available, the owner or lessee of the computer, computer system, computer network, computer program, or data may bring a civil action against any person convicted under this section for compensatory damages, including any expenditure reasonably and necessarily incurred by the owner or lessee to verify that a computer system, computer network, computer program, or data was or was not altered, damaged, or deleted by the access. For the purposes of actions authorized by this subdivision, the conduct of an unemancipated minor shall be imputed to the parent or legal guardian having control or custody of the minor, pursuant to the provisions of Section 1714.1 of the Civil Code.

(2) In any action brought pursuant to this subdivision the court may award reasonable attorney's fees to a prevailing party.

(3) A community college, state university, or academic institution accredited in this state is required to include COMPUTER-RELATED CRIMES as a specific violation of college or university student conduct policies and regulations that may subject a student to disciplinary sanctions up to and including dismis sal from the academic institution. This paragraph shall not apply to the University of California unless the Board of Regents adopts a resolution to that effect.

(f) This section shall not be construed to preclude the applicability of any other provision of the criminal law of this state which applies or may apply to any transaction, nor shall it make illegal any employee labor relations activities that are within the scope and protection of state or federal labor laws.

(g) Any computer, computer system, computer network, or any software or data, owned by the defendant, which is used during the commission of any public offense described in subdivision (c) or any computer, owned by the defendant, which is used as a repository for the storage of software or data illegally obtained in violation of subdivision (c) shall be subject to forfeiture , as specified in Section 502.01.

(h) (1) Subdivision (c) does not apply to any person who accesses his or her employer's computer system, computer network, computer program, or data when acting within the scope of his or her lawful employment.

(2) Paragraph (3) of subdivision (c) does not apply to any employee who accesses or uses his or her employer's computer system, computer network, computer program, or data when acting outside the scope of his or her lawful employment, so long as the employee's activities do not cause an injury, as defined in paragraph (8) of subdivision (b), to the employer or another, or so long as the value of supplies and computer services, as defined in paragraph

(4) of subdivision (b), which are used do not exceed an accumulated total of one hundred dollars ($100).

(i) No activity exempted from prosecution under paragraph (2) of subdivision

(h) which incidentally violates paragraph (2), (4), or (7) of subdivision (c) shall be prosecuted under those paragraphs.

(j) For purposes of bringing a civil or a criminal action under this section, a person who causes, by any means, the access of a computer, computer system, or computer network in one jurisdiction from another jurisdiction is deemed to have personally accessed the computer, computer system, or computer network in each jurisdiction.

(k) In determining the terms and conditions applicable to a person convicted of a violation of this section the court shall consider the following:

(1) The court shall consider prohibitions on access to and use of computers.

(2) Except as otherwise required by law, the court shall consider alternate sentencing, including community service, if the defendant shows remorse and recognition of the wrongdoing, and an inclination not to repeat the offense.

502.01. Forfeiture of property used in committing COMPUTER CRIMES; redemption of interests; application to minors; distribution of proceeds

(a) As used in this section:

(1) "Property subject to forfeiture" means any property of the defendant that is a computer, computer system, or computer network, and any software or data residing thereon, if the computer, computer system, or computer network was used in committing a violation of subdivision (c) of Section 502 or a violation of subdivision (b) of Section 502.7 or was used as a repository for the storage of software or data obtained in violation of those provisions. If the defendant is a minor, it also includes property of the parent or guardian of the defendant.

(2) "Sentencing court" means the court sentencing a person found guilty of violating subdivision (c) of Section 502 or a violation of subdivision (b) of Section 502.7 or, in the case of a minor found to be a person described in Section 602 of the Welfare and Institutions Code because of a violation of those provisions, the juvenile court.

(3) "Interest" means any property interest in the property subject to forfeiture.

(4) "Security interest" means an interest that is a lien, mortgage, security interest, or interest under a conditional sales contract.

(b) The sentencing court shall, upon petition by the prosecuting attorney, at any time following sentencing, or by agreement of all parties, at the time of sentencing, conduct a hearing to determine whether any property or property interest is subject to forfeiture under this section. At the forfeiture hearing, the prosecuting attorney shall have the burden of establishing, by a preponderance of the evidence, that the property or property interests are subject to forfeiture. The prosecuting attorney may retain seized property that may be subject to forfeiture until the sentencing hearing.

(c) Prior to the commencement of a forfeiture proceeding, the law enforcement agency seizing the property subject to forfeiture shall make an investigation as to any person other than the defendant who may have an interest in it. At least 30 days before the hearing to determine whether the property should be forfeited, the prosecuting agency shall send notice of the hearing to any person who may have an interest in the property that arose before the seizure.

A person claiming an interest in the property shall file a motion for the redemption of that interest at least 10 days before the hearing on forfeiture, and a copy of the motion to the prosecuting agency and to the probation department.

If a motion to redeem an interest has been filed, the sentencing court shall hold a hearing to identify all persons who possess valid interests in the property. No person shall hold a valid interest in the property if, by a preponderance of the evidence, the prosecuting agency shows that the person knew or should have known that the property was being used in violation of subdivision (c) of Section 502 or subdivision (b) of Section 502.7, and that the person did not take reasonable steps to prevent that use, or if the interest is a security interest, the person knew or should have known at the time that the security interest was created that the property would be used for such a violation.

(d) If the sentencing court finds that a person holds a valid interest in the property, the following provisions shall apply:

(1) The court shall determine the value of the property.

(2) The court shall determine the value of each valid interest in the property.

(3) If the value of the property is greater than the value of the interest, the holder of the interest shall be entitled to ownership of the property upon paying the court the difference between the value of the property and the value of the valid interest.

If the holder of the interest declines to pay the amount determined under paragraph (2), the court may order the property sold and designate the prosecutor or any other agency to sell the property. The designated agency shall be entitled to seize the property and the holder of the interest shall forward any documentation underlying the interest, including any ownership certificates for that property, to the designated agency. The designated agency shall sell the property and pay the owner of the interest the proceeds, up to the value of that interest.

(4) If the value of the property is less than the value of the interest, the designated agency shall sell the property and pay the owner of the interest the proceeds, up to the value of that interest.

(e) If the defendant was a minor at the time of the offense, this subdivision shall apply to property subject to forfeiture that is the property of the parent or guardian of the minor.

(1) The prosecuting agency shall notify the parent or guardian of the forfeiture hearing at least 30 days before the date set for the hearing.

(2) The computer shall not be subject to forfeiture if the parent or guardian files a signed statement with the court at least 10 days before the date set for the hearing that the minor shall not have access to any computer owned by the parent or guardian for two years after the date on which the minor is sentenced.

(3) If the minor is convicted of a violation of subdivision (c) of Section 502 or subdivision (b) of Section 502.7 within two years after the date on which the minor is sentenced, and the violation involves a computer owned by the parent or guardian, the original property subject to forfeiture, and the property involved in the new offense, shall be subject to forfeiture notwithstanding paragraph (2).

(f) If the defendant is found to have the only valid interest in the property subject to forfeiture, it shall be distributed as follows:

(1) First, to the victim, if the victim elects to take the property as full or partial restitution for injury, victim expenditures, or compensatory damages, as defined in paragraph (1) of subdivision (e) of Section 502. If the victim elects to receive the property under this paragraph, the value of the property shall be determined by the court and that amount shall be credited against the restitution owed by the defendant. The victim shall not be penalized for electing not to accept the forfeited property in lieu of full or partial restitution.

(2) Second, at the discretion of the court, to one or more of the following agencies or entities:

(A) The prosecuting agency.

(B) The public entity of which the prosecuting agency is a part.

(C) The public entity whose officers or employees conducted the investigation resulting in forfeiture.

(D) Other state and local public entities, including school districts.

(E) Nonprofit charitable organizations.

(g) If the property is to be sold, the court may designate the prosecuting agency or any other agency to sell the property at auction. The proceeds of the sale shall be distributed by the court as follows:

(1) To the bona fide or innocent purchaser or encumbrancer, conditional sales vendor, or mortgagee of the property up to the amount of his or her interest in the property, if the court orders a distribution to that person.

(2) The balance, if any, to be retained by the court, subject to the provisions for distribution under subdivision (f).

502.7. Obtaining telephone or telegraph services by fraud.

A person convicted of a violation of paragraph (1), (2), (4), or (5) of subdivision (c) of Section 502, or of a felony violation of paragraph (3), (6), (7), or (8) of subdivision (c) of Section 502, or a violation of subdivision (b) of Section 502.7 may be granted probation, but, except in unusual cases where the ends of justice would be better served by a shorter period, the period of probation shall not be less than three years and the following terms shall be imposed. During the period of probation, that person shall not accept employment where that person would use a computer connected by any means to any other computer, except upon approval of the court and notice to and opportunity to be heard by the prosecuting attorney, probation department, prospective employer, and the convicted person. Court approval shall not be given unless the court finds that the proposed employment would not pose a risk to the public.

1203.048. Property damage limitation; probation; conviction of COMPUTER CRIME

(a) Except in unusual cases where the interests of justice would best be served if the person is granted probation, probation shall not be granted to any person convicted of a violation of Section 502 or subdivision (b) of Section 502.7 involving the taking of or damage to property with a value exceeding one hundred thousand dollars ($100,000).

(b) The fact that the value of the property taken or damaged was an amount exceeding one hundred thousand dollars ($100,000) shall be alleged in the accusatory pleading, and either admitted by the defendant in open court, or found to be true by the jury trying the issue of guilt or by the court where guilt is established by plea of guilt or nolo contendere or by trial by the court sitting without a jury.

(c) When probation is granted, the court shall specify on the record and shall enter on the minutes the circumstances indicating that the interests of justice would best be served by such a disposition.

2702. Prisoners convicted of COMPUTER CRIMES; access to department COMPUTER system

No person imprisoned after conviction of a violation of Section 502 or of subdivision (b) of Section 502.7 shall be permitted to work on or have access to any computer system of the department.

(a) Any person who, knowingly, willfully, and with intent to defraud a person providing telephone or telegraph service, avoids or attempts to avoid, or aids, abets or causes another to avoid the lawful charge, in whole or in part, for telephone or telegraph service by any of the following means is guilty of a misdemeanor or a felony, as provided in subdivision (f):

(1) By charging the service to an existing telephone number or credit card number without the authority of the subscriber thereto or the lawful holder thereof.

(2) By charging the service to a nonexistent telephone number or credit card number, or to a number associated with telephone service which is suspended or terminated, or to a revoked or canceled (as distinguished from expired) credit card number, notice of the suspension, termination, revocation, or cancellation of the telephone service or credit card having been given to the subscriber thereto or the holder thereof .

(3) By use of a code, prearranged scheme, or other similar stratagem or device whereby the person, in effect, sends or receives information .

(4) By rearranging, tampering with, or making connection with telephone or telegraph facilities or equipment, whether physically, electrically, acoustically, inductively, or otherwise, or by using telephone or telegraph service with knowledge or reason to believe that the rearrangement, tampering, or connection existed at the time of the use .

(5) By using any other deception, false pretense, trick, scheme, device, or means.

(b) Any person who (1) makes, possesses, sells, gives, or otherwise transfers to another, or offers or advertises any instrument, apparatus, or device with intent to use it or with knowledge or reason to believe it is intended to be used to avoid any lawful telephone or telegraph toll charge or to conceal the existence or place of origin or destination of any telephone or telegraph message; or (2) sells, gives, or otherwise transfers to another or offers, or advertises plans or instructions for making or assembling an instrument, apparatus, or device described in paragraph (1) of this subdivision with knowledge or reason to believe that they may be used to make or assemble the instrument, apparatus, or device is guilty of a misdemeanor or a felony, as provided in subdivision (f).

(c) Any person who publishes the number or code of an existing, canceled, revoked, expired, or non-existent credit card, or the numbering or coding which is employed in the issuance of credit cards, with the intent that it be used or with knowledge or reason to believe that it will be used to avoid the payment of any lawful telephone or telegraph toll charge is guilty of a misdemeanor.

The provisions of subdivision (f) shall not apply to this subdivision. As used in this section, "publishes" means the communication of information to any one or more persons, either orally, in person or by telephone, radio, or television, or in a writing of any kind, including without limitation a letter or memorandum, circular or handbill, newspaper, or magazine article, or book.

(d) Subdivision (a) applies when the telephone or telegraph communication involved either originates or terminates, or both originates and terminates, in this state, or when the charges for service would have been billable, in normal course, by a person providing telephone or telegraph service in this state, but for the fact that the charge for service was avoided, or attempted to be avoided, by one or more of the means set forth in subdivision (a).

(e) Jurisdiction of an offense under this section is in the jurisdictional territory where the telephone call or telegram involved in the offense originates or where it terminates, or the jurisdictional territory to which the bill for the service is sent or would have been sent but for the fact that the service was obtained or attempted to be obtained by one or more of the means set forth in subdivision (a).

(f) If the total value of all telephone or telegraph services obtained in violation of this section aggregates over four hundred dollars ($400) within any period of twelve (12) consecutive months during the three years immediately prior to the time the indictment is found or the case is certified to the superior court, or prior to the time the information is filed, or if the defendant has previously been convicted of an offense in excess of four hundred dollars ($400) under this section or of an offense in excess of four hundred dollars ($400) under the laws of another state or of the United States which would have been an offense under this section if committed in this state, a person guilty of such offense is punishable by imprisonment in the county jail not exceeding one year, by a fine not exceeding one thousand dollars ($1,000), or both, or by imprisonment in the state prison, by a fine not exceeding ten thousand dollars ($10,000), or both.

(g) Any instrument, apparatus, device, plans, instructions, or written publication described in subdivision (b) or (c) may be seized under warrant or incident to a lawful arrest, and, upon the conviction of a person for a violation of subdivision (a), (b), or (c), the instrument, apparatus, device, plans, instructions, or written publication may be destroyed as contraband by the sheriff of the county in which the person was convicted or turned over to the person providing telephone or telegraph service in the territory in which it was seized.

(h) Any COMPUTER, COMPUTER system, COMPUTER network, or any software or data, owned by the defendant, which is used during the commission of any public offense described in this section or any COMPUTER, owned by the defendant, which is used as a repository for the storage of software or data illegally obtained in violation of this section shall be subject to forfeiture.

COLORADO STATUTES

TITLE 18. CRIMINAL CODE
ARTICLE 5.5. COMPUTER CRIME

18-5.5-101.Definitions

As used in this article, unless the context otherwise requires:

(1) "Authorization" means the express consent of a person which may include an employee's job description to use said person's computer, computer network, computer program, computer software, computer system, property, or services as those terms are defined in this section.

(2) "Computer" means an electronic device which performs logical, arithmetic, or memory functions by the manipulations of electronic or magnetic impulses, and includes all input, output, processing, storage, software, or communication facilities which are connected or related to such a device in a system or network.

(3) "Computer network" means the interconnection of communication lines (including microwave or other means of electronic communication) with a computer through remote terminals, or a complex consisting of two or more interconnected computers.

(4) "Computer program" means a series of instructions or statements, in a form acceptable to a computer, which permits the functioning of a computer system in a manner designed to provide appropriate products from such computer system.

(5) "Computer software" means computer programs, procedures, and associated documentation concerned with the operation of a computer system.

(6) "Computer system" means a set of related, connected or unconnected, computer equipment, devices, and software.

(7) "Financial instrument" means any check, draft, money order, certificate of deposit, letter of credit, bill of exchange, credit card, debit card, or marketable security.

(8) "Property" includes, but is not limited to, financial instruments, information, including electronically produced data, and computer software and programs in either machine or human readable form, and any other tangible or intangible item of value.

(9) "Services" includes, but is not limited to, computer time, data processing, and storage functions.

(10) To "use" means to instruct, communicate with, store data in, retrieve data from, or otherwise make use of any resources of a computer, computer system, or computer network.

18-5.5-102. Computer crime

(1) Any person who knowingly uses any computer, computer system, computer network, or any part thereof for the purpose of devising or executing any scheme or artifice to defraud; obtaining money, property, or services by means of false or fraudulent pretenses, representations, or promises; using the property or services of another without authorization; or committing theft commits computer crime.

(2) Any person who knowingly and without authorization uses, alters, damages, or destroys any computer, computer system, or computer network described in section 18-5.5-101 or any computer software, program, documentation, or data contained in such computer, computer system, or computer network commits computer crime.

(3) If the loss, damage, or thing of value taken in violation of this section is less than fifty dollars, computer crime is a class 3 misdemeanor; if fifty dollars or more but less than three hundred dollars, computer crime is a class 2 misdemeanor; if three hundred dollars or more but less than ten thousand dollars, computer crime is a class 5 felony; if ten thousand dollars or more, computer crime is a class 3 felony.

CONNECTICUT STATUTES

TITLE 53A. PENAL CODE
CHAPTER 952. PENAL CODE: OFFENSES
PART XXII. COMPUTER-RELATED OFFENSES

Sec. 53a-251. Computer crime.

(a) Defined. A person commits computer crime when he violates any of the provisions of this section.

(b) Unauthorized access to a computer system. (1) A person is guilty of the computer crime of unauthorized access to a computer system when, knowing that he is not authorized to do so, he accesses or causes to be accessed any computer system without authorization.

(2) It shall be an affirmative defense to a prosecution for unauthorized access to a computer system that: (A) The person reasonably believed that the owner of the computer system, or a person empowered to license access thereto, had authorized him to access; (B) the person reasonably believed that the owner of the computer system, or a person empowered to license access thereto, would have authorized him to access without payment of any consideration; or (C) the person reasonably could not have known that his access was unauthorized.

(c) Theft of computer services. A person is guilty of the computer crime of theft of computer services when he accesses or causes to be accessed or otherwise uses or causes to be used a computer system with the intent to obtain unauthorized computer services.

(d) Interruption of computer services. A person is guilty of the computer crime of interruption of computer services when he, without authorization, intentionally or recklessly disrupts or degrades or causes the disruption or degradation of computer services or denies or causes the denial of computer services to an authorized user of a computer system.

(e) Misuse of computer system information. A person is guilty of the computer crime of misuse of computer system information when: (1) As a result of his accessing or causing to be accessed a computer system, he intentionally makes or causes to be made an unauthorized display, use, disclosure or copy, in any form, of data residing in, communicated by or produced by a computer system; or

(2) he intentionally or recklessly and without authorization (A) alters, deletes, tampers with, damages, destroys or takes data intended for use by a computer system, whether residing within or external to a computer system, or (B) intercepts or adds data to data residing within a computer system; or (3) he knowingly receives or retains data obtained in violation of subdivision (1) or (2) of this subsection; or (4) he uses or discloses any data he knows or believes was obtained in violation of subdivision (1) or (2) of this subsection.

(f) Destruction of computer equipment. A person is guilty of the computer crime of destruction of computer equipment when he, without authorization, intentionally or recklessly tampers with, takes, transfers, conceals, alters, damages or destroys any equipment used in a computer system or intentionally or recklessly causes any of the foregoing to occur.

Sec. 53a-252. Computer crime in the first degree: Class B felony.

(a) A person is guilty of computer crime in the first degree when he commits computer crime as defined in section 53a-251 and the damage to or the value of the property or computer services exceeds ten thousand dollars.

(b) Computer crime in the first degree is a class B felony.

Sec. 53a-253. Computer crime in the second degree: Class C felony.

(a) A person is guilty of computer crime in the second degree when he commits computer crime as defined in section 53a-251 and the damage to or the value of the property or computer services exceeds five thousand dollars.

(b) Computer crime in the second degree is a class C felony.

Sec. 53a-254. Computer crime in the third degree: Class D felony.

(a) A person is guilty of computer crime in the third degree when he commits computer crime as defined in section 53a-251 and

(1) the damage to or the value of the property or computer services exceeds one thousand dollars or (2) he recklessly engages in conduct which creates a risk of serious physical injury to another person.

(b) Computer crime in the third degree is a class D felony.

Sec. 53a-255. Computer crime in the fourth degree: Class A misdemeanor.

(a) A person is guilty of computer crime in the fourth degree when he commits computer crime as defined in section 53a-251 and the damage to or the value of the property or computer services exceeds five hundred dollars.

(b) Computer crime in the fourth degree is a class A misdemeanor.

Sec. 53a-256. Computer crime in the fifth degree: Class B misdemeanor.

(a) A person is guilty of computer crime in the fifth degree when he commits computer crime as defined in section 53a-251 and the damage to or the value of the property or computer services, if any, is five hundred dollars or less.

(b) Computer crime in the fifth degree is a class B misdemeanor.

Sec. 53a-257. Alternative fine based on defendant's gain.

If a person has gained money, property or services or other consideration through the commission of any offense under section 53a-251, upon conviction thereof the court, in lieu of imposing a fine, may sentence the defendant to pay an amount, fixed by the court, not to exceed double the amount of the defendant's gain from the commission of such offense. In such case the court shall make a finding as to the amount of the defendant's gain from the offense and, if the record does not contain sufficient evidence to support such a finding, the court may conduct a hearing upon the issue.

For the purpose of this section, "gain" means the amount of money or the value of property or computer services or other consideration derived.

Sec. 53a-258. Determination of degree of crime.

Amounts included in violations of section 53a-251 committed pursuant to one scheme or course of conduct, whether from the same person or several persons, may be aggregated in determining the degree of the crime.

Sec. 53a-259. Value of property or computer services.

(a) For the purposes of this part and section 52-570b, the value of property or computer services shall be: (1) The market value of the property or computer services at the time of the violation; or

(2) if the property or computer services are unrecoverable, damaged or destroyed as a result of a violation of section 53a-251, the cost of reproducing or replacing the property or computer services at the time of the violation.

(b) When the value of the property or computer services or damage thereto cannot be satisfactorily ascertained, the value shall be deemed to be two hundred fifty dollars.

(c) Notwithstanding the provisions of this section, the value of private personal data shall be deemed to be one thousand five hundred dollars.

Sec. 53a-260. Location of offense.

(a) In any prosecution for a violation of section 53a-251, the offense shall be deemed to have been committed in the town in which the act occurred or in which the computer system or part thereof involved in the violation was located.

(b) In any prosecution for a violation of section 53a-251 based upon more than one act in violation thereof, the offense shall be deemed to have been committed in any of the towns in which any of the acts occurred or in which a computer system or part thereof involved in a violation was located.

Sec. 53a-261. Jurisdiction.

If any act performed in furtherance of the offenses set out in section 53a-251 occurs in this state or if any computer system or part thereof accessed in violation of section 53a-251 is located in this state, the offense shall be deemed to have occurred in this state.

Sec. 52-570b. Action for computer-related offenses.

(a) Any aggrieved person who has reason to believe that any other person has been engaged, is engaged or is about to engage in an alleged violation of any provision of section 53a-251 may bring an action against such person and may apply to the superior court for: (1) An order temporarily or permanently restraining and enjoining the commencement or continuance of such act or acts; (2) an order directing restitution; or (3) an order directing the appointment of a receiver. Subject to making due provisions for the rights of innocent persons, a receiver shall have the power to sue for, collect, receive and take into his possession any property which belongs to the person who is alleged to have violated any provision of section 53a-251 and which may have been derived by, been used in or aided in any manner such alleged violation. Such property shall include goods and chattels, rights and credits, moneys and effects, books, records, documents, papers, choses in action, bills, notes and property of every description including all computer system equipment and data, and including property with which such property has been commingled if it cannot be identified in kind because of such commingling. The receiver shall also have the power to sell, convey and assign all of the foregoing and hold and dispose of the proceeds thereof under the direction of the court. Any person who has suffered damages as a result of an alleged violation of any provision of section 53a-251, and submits proof to the satisfaction of the court that he has in fact been damaged, may participate with general creditors in the distribution of the assets to the extent he has sustained out-of-pocket losses.

The court shall have jurisdiction of all questions arising in such proceedings and may make such orders and judgments therein as may be required.

(b) The court may award the relief applied for or such other relief as it may deem appropriate in equity.

(c) Independent of or in conjunction with an action under subsection (a) of this section, any person who suffers any injury to person, business or property may bring an action for damages against a person who is alleged to have violated any provision of section 53a-251. The aggrieved person shall recover actual damages and damages for unjust enrichment not taken into account in computing damages for actual loss, and treble damages where there has been a showing of wilful and malicious conduct.

(d) Proof of pecuniary loss is not required to establish actual damages in connection with an alleged violation of subsection (e) of section 53a-251 arising from misuse of private personal data.

(e) In any civil action brought under this section, the court shall award to any aggrieved person who prevails, reasonable costs and reasonable attorney's fees.

(f) The filing of a criminal action against a person is not a prerequisite to the bringing of a civil action under this section against such person.

(g) A civil action may be brought under this section against the state or any political subdivision thereof and the defense of governmental immunity shall not be available in any such action.

The rights and liability of the state or any political subdivision thereof in each such action shall be coextensive with and shall equal the rights and liability of private persons in like circumstances.

(h) No civil action under this section may be brought but within three years from the date the alleged violation of section 53a-251 is discovered or should have been discovered by the exercise of reasonable diligence.

DELAWARE STATUTES

TITLE 11 CRIMES AND CRIMINAL PROCEDURE
PART I . DELAWARE CRIMINAL CODE
CHAPTER 5. SPECIFIC OFFENSES
SUBCHAPTER III. OFFENSES INVOLVING PROPERTY.
SUBPART A.. ARSON AND RELATED OFFENSES

931. **Definitions.**

As used in this subpart:

(1) "Access" means to instruct, communicate with, store data in or retrieve data from a computer, computer system or computer network.

(2) "Computer" means a programmable, electronic device capable of accepting and processing data.

(3) "Computer network" means:

    a. A set of related devices connected to a computer by communications facilities;

    b. A complex of 2 or more computers, including related devices, connected by communications facilities; or

    c. The communications transmission facilities and devices used to interconnect computational equipment, along with control mechanisms associated thereto.

(4) "Computer program" means a set of instructions, statements or related data that, in actual or modified form, is capable of causing a computer or computer system to perform specified functions.

(5) "Computer services" includes, but is not limited to, computer access, data processing and data storage.

(6) "Computer software" means 1 or more computer programs, existing in any form, or any associated operational procedures, manuals or other documentation.

(7) "Computer system" means a computer, its software, related equipment and communications facilities, if any, and includes computer networks.

(8) "Data" means information of any kind in any form, including computer software.

(9) "Person" means a natural person, corporation, trust, partnership, incorporated or unincorporated association and any other legal or governmental entity, including any state or municipal entity or public official.

(10) "Private personal data" means data concerning a natural person which a reasonable person would want to keep private and which is protectable under law.

(11) "Property" means anything of value, including data.

932. Unauthorized access.

A person is guilty of the computer crime of unauthorized access to a computer system when, knowing that he is not authorized to do so, he accesses or causes to be accessed any computer system without authorization.

933. Theft of computer services.

A person is guilty of the computer crime of theft of computer services when he accesses or causes to be accessed or otherwise uses or causes to be used a computer system with the intent to obtain unauthorized computer services, computer software or data.

934. Interruption of computer services.

A person is guilty of the computer crime of interruption of computer services when that person, without authorization, intentionally or recklessly disrupts or degrades or causes the disruption or degradation of computer services or denies or causes the denial of computer services to an authorized user of a computer system.

935. Misuse of computer system information.

A person is guilty of the computer crime of misuse of computer system information when:

(1) As a result of his accessing or causing to be accessed a computer system, he intentionally makes or causes to be made an unauthorized display, use, disclosure or copy, in any form, of data residing in, communicated by or produced by a computer system;

(2) That person intentionally or recklessly and without authorization:

a. Alters, deletes, tampers with, damages, destroys or takes data intended for use by a computer system, whether residing within or external to a computer system; or

b. Interrupts or adds data to data residing within a computer system;

(3) That person knowingly receives or retains data obtained in violation of subdivision (1) or (2) of this section; or

(4) That person uses or discloses any data which that person knows or believes was obtained in violation of subdivision (1) or (2) of this section.

936. Destruction of computer equipment.

A person is guilty of the computer crime of destruction of computer equipment when that person, without authorization, intentionally or recklessly tampers with, takes, transfers, conceals, alters, damages or destroys any equipment used in a computer system or intentionally or recklessly causes any of the foregoing to occur.

937. Penalties [Amendment effective with respect to crimes committed June 30, 1990, or thereafter].

(a) A person committing any of the crimes described in 932-936 of this title is guilty in the first degree when the damage to or the value of the property or computer services affected exceeds $10,000.

Computer crime in the first degree is a class D felony.

(b) A person committing any of the crimes described in 932-936 of this title is guilty in the second degree when the damage to or the value of the property or computer services affected exceeds $5,000.

Computer crime in the second degree is a class E felony.

(c) A person committing any of the crimes described in 932-936 of this title is guilty in the third degree when:

(1) The damage to or the value of the property or computer services affected exceeds $1,000; or

(2) That person engages in conduct which creates a risk of serious physical injury to another person.

Computer crime in the third degree is a class F felony.

(d) A person committing any of the crimes described in 932-936 of this title is guilty in the fourth degree when the damage to or the value of the property or computer services affected exceeds $500.

Computer crime in the fourth degree is a class G felony.

(e) A person committing any of the crimes described in 932-936 of this title is guilty in the fifth degree when the damage to or the value of the property or computer services, if any, is $500 or less.

Computer crime in the fifth degree is a class A misdemeanor.

(f) Any person gaining money, property services or other consideration through the commission of any offense under this subpart, upon conviction, in lieu of having a fine imposed, may be sentenced by the court to pay an amount, fixed by the court, not to exceed double the amount of the defendant's gain from the commission of such offense. In such case, the court shall make a finding as to the amount of the defendant's gain from the offense and, if the record does not contain sufficient evidence to support such a finding, the court may conduct a hearing upon the issue. For the purpose of this section, "gain" means the amount of money or the value of property or computer services or other consideration derived.

(g) Amounts included in violations of this subpart committed pursuant to 1 scheme or course of conduct, whether from the same person or several persons, may be aggregated in determining the degree of the crime.

(h) For the purposes of this subpart, the value of property or computer services shall be:

(1) The market value of the property or computer services at the time of the violation; or

(2) If the property or computer services are unrecoverable, damaged or destroyed as a result of a violation of this subpart, the cost of reproducing or replacing the property or computer services at the time of the violation.

When the value of the property or computer services or damage thereto cannot be satisfactorily ascertained, the value shall be deemed to be $250.

(i) Notwithstanding this section, the value of private personal data shall be deemed to be $500.

938. Venue.

(a) In any prosecution for any violation of 932-936 of this title, the offense shall be deemed to have been committed in the place at which the act occurred or in which the computer system or part thereof involved in the violation was located.

(b) In any prosecution for any violation of 932-936 of this title based upon more than 1 act in violation thereof, the offense shall be deemed to have been committed in any of the places at which any of the acts occurred or in which a computer system or part thereof involved in a violation was located.

(c) If any act performed in furtherance of the offenses set out in 932-936 of this title occurs in this State or in any computer system or part thereof accessed in violation of 932-936 of this title is located in this State, the offense shall be deemed to have occurred in this State.

939. Remedies of aggrieved persons.

(a) Any aggrieved person who has reason to believe that any other person has been engaged, is engaged or is about to engage in an alleged violation of any provision of 932-936 of this title may bring an action against such person and may apply to the Court of Chan-

cery for: (i) An order temporarily or permanently restraining and enjoining the commencement or continuance of such act or acts; (ii) an order directing restitution; or (iii) an order directing the appointment of a receiver. Subject to making due provisions for the rights of innocent persons, a receiver shall have the power to sue for, collect, receive and take into his possession any property which belongs to the person who is alleged to have violated any provision of this subpart and which may have been derived by, been used in or aided in any manner such alleged violation. Such property shall include goods and chattels, rights and credits, moneys and effects, books, records, documents, papers, choses in action, bills, notes and property of every description including all computer system equipment and data, and including property with which such property has been commingled if it cannot be identified in kind because of such commingling. The receiver shall also have the power to sell, convey and assign all of the foregoing and hold and dispose of the proceeds thereof under the direction of the Court. Any person who has suffered damages as a result of an alleged violation of any provision of 932-936 of this title, and submits proof to the satisfaction of the Court that he has in fact been damaged, may participate with general creditors in the distribution of the assets to the extent he has sustained out-of-pocket losses. The Court shall have jurisdiction of all questions arising in such proceedings and may make such orders and judgments therein as may be required.

(b) The Court may award the relief applied for or such other relief as it may deem appropriate in equity.

(c) Independent of or in conjunction with an action under subsection (a) of this section, any person who suffers any injury to person, business or property may bring an action for damages against a person who is alleged to have violated any provision of 932-936 of this title. The aggrieved person shall recover actual damages and damages for unjust enrichment not taken into account in computing damages for actual loss and treble damages where there has been a showing of wilful and malicious conduct.

(d) Proof of pecuniary loss is not required to establish actual damages in connection with an alleged violation of 935 of this title arising from misuse of private personal data.

(e) In any civil action brought under this section, the Court shall award to any aggrieved person who prevails reasonable costs and reasonable attorney's fees.

(f) The filing of a criminal action against a person is not a prerequisite to the bringing of a civil action under this section against such person.

(g) No civil action under this section may be brought but within 3 years from the date the alleged violation of 932-936 of this title is discovered or should have been discovered by the exercise of reasonable diligence.

FLORIDA STATUTES

TITLE XLVI CRIMES
CHAPTER 815 COMPUTER-RELATED CRIMES

815.01 Short title

The provisions of this act shall be known and may be cited as the "Florida Computer Crimes Act."

815.02 Legislative intent

The Legislature finds and declares that:

(1) Computer-related crime is a growing problem in government as well as in the private sector.

(2) Computer-related crime occurs at great cost to the public since losses for each incident of computer crime tend to be far greater than the losses associated with each incident of other white collar crime.

(3) The opportunities for computer-related crimes in financial institutions, government programs, government records, and other business enterprises through the introduction of fraudulent records into a computer system, the unauthorized use of computer facilities, the alteration or destruction of computerized information or files, and the stealing of financial instruments, data, and other assets are great.

(4) While various forms of computer crime might possibly be the subject of criminal charges based on other provisions of law, it is appropriate and desirable that a supplemental and additional statute be provided which proscribes various forms of computer abuse.

815.03 Definitions

As used in this chapter, unless the context clearly indicates otherwise:

(1) "Intellectual property" means data, including programs.

(2) "Computer program" means an ordered set of data representing coded instructions or statements that when executed by a computer cause the computer to process data.

(3) "Computer" means an internally programmed, automatic device that performs data processing.

(4) "Computer software" means a set of computer programs, procedures, and associated documentation concerned with the operation of a computer system.

(5) "Computer system" means a set of related, connected or unconnected, computer equipment, devices, or computer software.

(6) "Computer network" means a set of related, remotely connected devices and communication facilities including more than one computer system with capability to transmit data among them through communication facilities.

(7) "Computer system services" means providing a computer system or computer network to perform useful work.

(8) "Property" means anything of value as defined in 812.011 and includes, but is not limited to, financial instruments, information, including electronically produced data and computer software and programs in either machine-readable or human-readable form, and any other tangible or intangible item of value.

(9) "Financial instrument" means any check, draft, money order, certificate of deposit, letter of credit, bill of exchange, credit card, or marketable security.

(10) "Access" means to approach, instruct, communicate with, store data in, retrieve data from, or otherwise make use of any resources of a computer, computer system, or computer network.

815.04 Offenses against intellectual property

(1) Whoever willfully, knowingly, and without authorization modifies data, programs, or supporting documentation residing or existing internal or external to a computer, computer system, or computer network commits an offense against intellectual property.

(2) Whoever willfully, knowingly, and without authorization destroys data, programs, or supporting documentation residing or existing internal or external to a computer, computer system, or computer network commits an offense against intellectual property.

(3) Whoever willfully, knowingly, and withoutauthorization discloses or takes data, programs, or supporting documentation which is a trade secret as defined in 812.081 or is confidential as provided by law residing or existing internal or external to a computer, computer system, or computer network commits an offense against intellectual property.

(4)(a) Except as otherwise provided in this subsection, an offense against intellectual property is a felony of the third degree, punishable as provided in 775.082, 775.083, or 775.084.

(b) If the offense is committed for the purpose of devising or executing any scheme or artifice to defraud or to obtain any property, then the offender is guilty of a felony of the second degree, punishable as provided in 775.082, 775.083, or 775.084.

815.05 Offenses against computer equipment or supplies

(1)(a) Whoever willfully, knowingly, and without authorization modifies equipment or supplies used or intended to be used in a computer, computer system, or computer network commits an offense against computer equipment or supplies.

(b) 1. Except as provided in this paragraph, an offense against computer equipment or supplies as provided in paragraph (a) is a misdemeanor of the first degree, punishable as provided in s. 775.082, s. 775.083, or 775.084.

2. If the offense is committed for the purpose of devising or executing any scheme or artifice to defraud or to obtain any property, then the offender is guilty of a felony of the third degree, punishable as provided in 775.082, 775.083, or 775.084.

(2)(a) Whoever willfully, knowingly, and without authorization destroys, takes, injures, or damages equipment or supplies used or intended to be used in a computer, computer system, or computer network; or whoever willfully, knowingly, and without authorization destroys, injures, or damages any computer, computer system, or computer network commits an offense against computer equipment or supplies.

(b) 1. Except as provided in this paragraph, an offense against computer equipment or supplies as provided in paragraph (a) is a misdemeanor of the first degree, punishable as provided in 775.082, 775.083, or 775.084.

2. If the damage to suchcomputer equipment or supplies or to the computer, computer system, or computer network is greater than $200 but less than $1,000, then the offender is guilty of a felony of the third degree, punishable as provided in 775.082, 775.083, or 775.084.

3. If the damage to such computer equipment or supplies or to the computer, computer system, or computer network is $1,000 or greater, or if there is an interruption or impairment of governmental operation or public communication, transportation, or supply of water, gas, or other public service, then the offender is guilty of a felony of the second degree, punishable as provided ins. 775.082, 775.083, or 775.084.

815.06 Offenses against computer users

(1) Whoever willfully, knowingly, and without authorization accesses or causes to be accessed any computer, computer system, or computer network; or whoever willfully, knowingly, and without authorization denies or causes the denial of computer system services to an authorized user of such computer system services, which, in whole or part, is owned by, under contract to, or operated for, on behalf of, or in conjunction with another commits an offense against computer users.

(2)(a) Except as provided in this subsection, an offense against computer users is a felony of the third degree, punishable as provided in 775.082, 775.083, or 775.084.

(b) If the offense is committed for the purposes of devising or executing any scheme or artifice to defraud or to obtain any property, then the offender is guilty of a felony of the second degree, punishable as provided in 775.082, 775.083, or 775.084.

815.07 This chapter not exclusive

The provisions of this chapter shall not be construed to preclude the applicability of any other provision of the criminal law of this state which presently applies or may in the future apply to any transaction which violates this chapter, unless such provision is inconsistent with the terms of this chapter.

CHAPTER 847 OBSCENE LITERATURE; PROFANITY

847.0135 Computer pornography; penalties

(1) SHORT TITLE

This section shall be known and may be cited as the "Computer Pornography and Child Exploitation Prevention Act of 1986."

(2) COMPUTER PORNOGRAPHY

A person is guilty of a violation of this section if he knowingly compiles, enters into, or transmits by means of computer, or makes, prints, publishes, or reproduces by other computerized means, or knowingly causes or allows to be entered into or transmitted by means of computer, or buys, sells, receives, exchanges, or disseminates any notice, statement, or advertisement, or any minor's name, telephone number, place of residence, physical characteristics, or other descriptive or identifying information, for purposes of facilitating, encouraging, offering, or soliciting sexual conduct of or with any minor, or the visual depiction of such conduct.

(3) PENALTIES

Any person who violates the provisions of this section is guilty of a misdemeanor of the first degree, punishable as provided for in 775.082, 775.083, or 775.084.

GEORGIA STATUTES

TITLE 16. CRIMES AND OFFENSES
CHAPTER 9. FORGERY AND FRAUDULENT PRACTICES
ARTICLE 6. COMPUTER RELATED OFFENSES

16-9-90. Short title.

This article may be cited as the "Georgia Computer Systems Protection Act."

16-9-91. Legislative intent.

The General Assembly finds that:

(1) Computer related crime is a growing problem in the government and in the private sector;

(2) Such crime occurs at great cost to the public since losses for each incident of computer crime tend to be far greater than the losses associated with each incident of other white collar crime;

(3) The opportunities for computer related crimes in state programs and in other entities which operate

within the state through the introduction of fraudulent records into a computer system, unauthorized use of computer facilities, alteration or destruction of computerized information files, and stealing of financial instruments, data, or other assets are great;

(4) Computer related crime operations have a direct effect on state commerce; and

(5) The prosecution of persons engaged in computer related crime is difficult under current Georgia criminal statutes.

16-9-92. Definitions.

As used in this article, the term:

(1) "Access" means to approach, instruct, communicate with, store data in, retrieve data from, or otherwise make use of any resources of a computer, computer system, or computer network.

(2) "Computer" means an internally programmed, general-purpose, digital device that automatically processessubstantial data.

(3) "Computer network" means a set of two or more computer systems that automatically transmit data over communication circuits connecting them.

(4) "Computer program" means an ordered set of data that are coded instructions or statements that when executed by a computer cause the computer to process data.

(5) "Computer software" means a set of computer programs, procedures, and associated documentation concerned with the operation of a computer system.

(6) "Computer system" means a set of connected devices including a computer and possibly other devices such as data input, output, or storage devices, data communication circuits, and operating system computer programs that make the system capable of performing special-purpose data processing tasks for which it is specified.

(7) "Data" means a representation of information, knowledge, facts, concepts, or instructions which is being prepared or has been prepared in a formalized manner and is intended to be processed, is being processed, or has been processed in a computer system or computer network; which should be classified as intellectual property; and which may be in any form, including, but not limited to, computer printouts, magnetic storage media, punched cards, or stored internally in the memory of the computer.

(8) "Financial instruments" means any check, draft, money order, certificate of deposit, letter of credit, bill of exchange, credit card, or marketable security, or any computer system representation thereof.

(9) "Property" includes, but is not limited to, financial instruments, data, computer programs, documenta-

tion associated with data and computer systems and programs, all in machine-readable or human-readable form, and any other tangible or intangible item of value.

(10) "Services" includes, but is not limited to, providing a computer system to perform tasks.

16-9-93. Accessing of computers, etc., for fraudulent purposes; unauthorized access, alteration, destruction, etc., of computers, etc.

(a) Any person who knowingly and willfully, directly or indirectly, without authorization, accesses, causes to be accessed, or attempts to access any computer, computer system, computer network, or any part thereof which, in whole or in part, operates in commerce or is owned by, under contract to, or in conjunction with state, county, or local government or any branch, department, or agency thereof, any business, or any entity operating in or affecting commerce for the purpose of:

(1) Devising or executing any scheme or artifice to defraud; or

(2) Obtaining money, property, or services for themselves or another by means of false or fraudulent pretenses, representations, or promises, upon conviction thereof, shall be fined a sum of not more than two and one-half times the amount of the fraud or theft or imprisoned not more than 15 years, or both.

(b) Any person who intentionally and without authorization, directly or indirectly accesses, alters, damages, destroys, or attempts to damage or destroy any computer, computer system, or computer network, or any computer software, program, or data, upon conviction thereof, shall be fined not more than $50,000.00 or imprisoned not more than 15 years, or both.

16-9-94. Venue.

For the purpose of venue under this article, any violation of this article shall be considered to have been committed:

(1) In any county in which any act was performed in furtherance of any transaction which violated this article;

(2) In the county of the principal place of business in this state of the owner or lessee of a computer, computer system, computer network, or any part thereof;

(3) In any county in which any violator had control or possession of any proceeds of the violation or of any books, records, documents, property, financial instrument, computer software, computer program, or other material or objects which were used in furtherance of the violation; and

(4) In any county from which, to which, or through which any access to a computer or computer network was made, whether by wires, electromagnetic waves, microwaves, or any other means of communication.

16-9-95. Duty to report violations of this article; immunity from liability for making such report.

It is the duty of every business; partnership; college; university; person; state, county, or local governmental agency or department or branch thereof; corporation; or other business entity which has reasonable grounds to believe that a violation of this article has been committed to report promptly the suspected violation to law enforcement authorities. When acting in good faith, such business; partnership; college; university; person; state, county, or local governmental agency or department or branch thereof; corporation; or other business entity shall be immune from any civil liability for such reporting.

HAWAII STATUTES

DIVISION 5. CRIMES AND CRIMINAL PROCEEDINGS
TITLE 37. HAWAII PENAL CODE
CHAPTER 708. OFFENSES AGAINST PROPERTY RIGHTS
PART IX. COMPUTER CRIMES

708-890. Definition of terms in this part.

In this part, unless a different meaning plainly is required:

"Access" means to make use of any resources of a computer, computer system, or computer network.

"Computer" means an electronic device which performs logical, arithmetic, and memory functions by the manipulation of electronic or magnetic impulses and includes all input, output, processing, storage, software, or communication facilities which are connected or related to such a device in a computer system or computer network.

"Computer network" means the interconnection of communication lines with a computer through remote terminals or a complex consisting of two or more computers and includes interconnected remote terminals.

"Computer program" means a series of instructions or statements, in a form acceptable to a computer, which permits the functioning of a computer system in a manner designed to provide appropriate products from a computer system.

"Computer software" means a set of computer programs, procedures, or associated documentation concerned with the operation and function of a computer system.

"Computer system" means a set of related or interconnected computer equipment, devices, and software.

"Data" means a representation of information, knowledge, facts, concepts, or instructions, which are being prepared or have been prepared, in a formalized

manner, and are intended for use in a computer system or computer network.

"Financial instrument" includes, but is not limited to, any draft, warrant, money order, note, certificate of deposit, letter of credit, bill of exchange, credit or debit card, transaction authorization mechanism, marketable security, or any other computer system representation.

"Property" includes, but is not limited to, financial instruments, data, computer software, computer programs, documents associated with computer systems and computer programs, or copies, whether tangible or intangible, and data while in transit.

"Service" includes, but is not limited to, the use of the computer system, computer network, computer programs, computer software, or data prepared for computer use, data contained within a computer system, or data contained within a computer network.

708-891. Computer fraud in the first degree.

(1) A person commits the offense of computer fraud in the first degree if:

(a) He accesses or causes to be accessed any computer, computer system, computer network, or any of its parts with the intent to devise or execute any scheme or artifice to defraud;

(b) He accesses or causes to be accessed any computer, computer system, computer network, or any of its parts with the intent to obtain money, property, or services by means of embezzlement or false or fraudulent representations where the value of the money, property, or services exceeds $2,500; or

(c) He accesses or causes to be accessed any computer, computer system, computer network, or any of its parts with the intent to obtain unauthorized information concerning the credit information of another person or who introduces or causes to be introduced false information into that system or network with the intent to wrongfully damage or wrongfully enhance the credit rating of any person where the value of the damage or enhancement exceeds $2,500.

(2) Computer fraud in the first degree is a class C felony. In lieu of the statutory fine which may be imposed, any person who violates this section may be fined a sum of not more than two times the amount of the fraud.

708-892. Computer fraud in the second degree.

(1) A person commits the offense of computer fraud in the second degree if:

(a) He accesses or causes to be accessed any computer, computer system, computer network, or any of its parts with the intent to obtain money, property, or services by means of embezzlement or false or fraudulent representations, money, property, or services where the value of the money, property, or services exceeds $100 but is not more than $2,500; or

(b) He accesses or causes to be accessed any computer, computer system, computer network, or any of its parts with the intent to obtain unauthorized information concerning the credit information of another person or who introduces or causes to be introduced false information into that system or network with the intent to wrongfully damage or wrongfully enhance the credit rating of any person where the value of the damage or enhancement exceeds $100 but is not more than $2,500.

(2) Computer fraud in the second degree is a misdemeanor.

708-893. Computer fraud in the third degree.

(1) A person commits the offense of computer fraud in the third degree if:

(a) He accesses or causes to be accessed any computer, computer system, computer network, or any of its parts with the intent to obtain money, property, or services by means of embezzlement or false or fraudulent representations where the value of the money, property, or services is not more than $100; or

(b) He accesses or causes to be accessed any computer, computer system, computer network, or any of its parts with the intent to obtain unauthorized information concerning the credit information of another person or who introduces or causes to be introduced false information into that system or network with the intent to wrongfully damage or wrongfully enhance the credit rating of any person where the value of the damage or enhancement is not more than $100.

(2) Computer fraud in the third degree is a petty misdemeanor.

708-894. Unauthorized computer use in the first degree.

(1) A person commits the offense of unauthorized computer use in the first degree if heintentionally and without authorization accesses, alters, damages, or destroys any computer, computer system, computer network, computer program, or computer software, or any data stored therein, with a value exceeding $10,000.

(2) Unauthorized computer use in the first degree is a class C felony.

708-895. Unauthorized computer use in the second degree.

(1) A person commits the offense of unauthorized computer use in the second degree if he intentionally and without authorization accesses, alters, damages, or destroys any computer, computer system, computer network, computer program, or computer software, or any data stored therein, with a value exceeding $2,500 but not more than $10,000.

(2) Unauthorized computer use in the second degree is a misdemeanor.

708-896. Unauthorized computer use in the third degree.

(1) A person commits the offense of unauthorized computer use in the third degree if he intentionally and without authorization accesses, alters, damages, or destroys any computer, computer system, computer network, computer program, or computer software, or any data stored therein, with a value of not more than $2,500.

(2) Unauthorized computer use in the third degree is a petty misdemeanor.

IDAHO STATUTES

TITLE 18. CRIMES AND PUNISHMENTS
CHAPTER 22. COMPUTER CRIME

18-2201. Definitions.

As used in this chapter:

(1) To "access" means to instruct, communicate with, store data in, retrieve data from or otherwise make use of any resources of a computer, computer system, or computer network.

(2) "Computer" means, but is not limited to, an electronic device which performs logical, arithmetic, or memory functions by the manipulations of electronic or magnetic impulses, and includes all input, output, processing, storage, software, or communication facilities which are connected or related to such a device in a system or network.

(3) "Computer network" means, but is not limited to, the interconnection of communication lines (including microwave or other means of electronic communication) with a computer through remote terminals, or a complex consisting of two (2) or more interconnected computers.

(4) "Computer program" means, but is not limited to, a series of instructions or statements, in a form acceptable to a computer, which permits the functioning of a computer system in a manner designed to provide appropriate products from such computer system.

(5) "Computer software" means, but is not limited to, computer programs, procedures, and associated documentation concerned with the operation of a computer system.

(6) "Computer system" means, but is not limited to, a set of related, connected or unconnected, computer equipment, devices, and software.

(7) "Property" includes, but is not limited to, financial instruments, information, including electronically produced data, and computer software and programs in

either machine or human readable form, and any other tangible or intangible item of value.

(8) "Services" include, but are not limited to, computer time, data processing, and storage functions.

18-2202. Computer crime.

(1) Any person who knowingly accesses, attempts to access or uses, or attempts to use any computer, computer system, computer network, or any part thereof for the purpose of: devising or executing any scheme or artifice to defraud; obtaining money, property, or services by means of false or fraudulent pretenses, representations, or promises; or committing theft; commits computer crime.

(2) Any person who knowingly and without authorization alters, damages, or destroys any computer, computer system, or computer network described in section 18-2201, Idaho Code, or any computer software, program, documentation, or data contained in such computer, computer system, or computer network commits computer crime.

(3) Any person who knowingly and without authorization uses, accesses, or attempts to access any computer, computer system, or computer network described in section 18-2201, Idaho Code, or any computer software, program, documentation or data contained in such computer, computer system, or computer network, commits computer crime.

(4) A violation of the provisions of subsections (1) or (2) of this section shall be a felony. A violation of the provisions of subsection (3) of this section shall be a misdemeanor.

TITLE 48. MONOPOLIES AND TRADE PRACTICES
CHAPTER 8. IDAHO TRADE SECRETS ACT

48-801. Definitions.

As used in this chapter unless the context requires otherwise:

(1) "Improper means" include theft, bribery, misrepresentation, breach or inducement of a breach of a duty to maintain secrecy, or espionage through electronic or other means.

(2) "Misappropriation" means:

(a) Acquisition of a trade secret of another by a person who knows or has reason to know that the trade secret was acquired by improper means; or

(b) Disclosure or use of a trade secret of another without express or implied consent by a person who:

(A) Used improper means to acquire knowledge of the trade secret; or

(B) At the time of disclosure or use, knew or had reason to know that his knowledge of the trade secret was:

(i) Derived from or through a person who had utilized improper means to acquire it;

(ii) Acquired under circumstances giving rise to a duty to maintain its secrecy or limit its use; or

(iii) Derived from or through a person who owed a duty to the person seeking relief to maintain its secrecy or limit its use; or

(C) Before a material change of his position, knew or had reason to know that it was a trade secret and that knowledge of it had been acquired by accident or mistake.

(3) "Person" means a natural person, corporation, business trust, estate, trust, partnership, association, joint venture, government, governmental subdivision or agency, or any other legal or commercial entity.

(4) "Computer program" means information which is capable of causing a computer to perform logical operation(s) and:

(a) Is contained on any media or in any format;

(b) Is capable of being input, directly or indirectly, into a computer; and

(c) Has prominently displayed a notice of copyright, or other proprietary or confidential marking, either within or on the media containing the information.

(5) "Trade secret" means information, including a formula, pattern, compilation, program, computer program, device, method, technique, or process, that:

(a) Derives independent economic value, actual or potential, from not being generally known to, and not being readily ascertainable by proper means by, other persons who can obtain economic value from its disclosure or use; and

(b) Is the subject of efforts that are reasonable under the circumstances to maintain its secrecy.

ILLINOIS STATUTES

CHAPTER 38. CRIMINAL LAW AND PROCEDURE
DIVISION I. CRIMINAL CODE OF 1961
TITLE III. SPECIFIC OFFENSES
PART C. OFFENSES DIRECTED AGAINST PROPERTY
ARTICLE 15. DEFINITIONS

15-1. Property.

As used in this Part C, "property" means anything of value. Property includes real estate, money, commercial instruments, admission or transportation tickets, written instruments representing or embodying rights concerning anything of value, labor, or services, or otherwise of value to the owner; things growing on, affixed to, or found on land, or part of or affixed to any building; electricity, gas and water; birds, animals and fish, which ordinarily are kept in a state of confinement; food and drink; samples, cultures, microorganisms, specimens, records, recordings, documents, blueprints, drawings, maps, and whole or partial copies, descriptions, photographs, computerprograms or data, prototypes or models thereof, or any other articles, materials, devices, substances and whole or partial copies, descriptions, photographs, prototypes, or models thereof which constitute, represent, evidence, reflect or record a secret scientific, technical, merchandising, production or management information, design, process, procedure, formula, invention, or improvement.

15-2. Owner.

As used in this Part C, "owner" means a person, other than the offender, who has possession of or any other interest in the property involved, even though such interest or possession is unlawful, and without whose consent the offender has no authority to exert control over the property.

ARTICLE 16D. COMPUTER CRIME

16D-1. Short title.

This Article shall be known and may be cited as the "Computer Crime Prevention Law".

16D-2. Definitions

As used in this Article, unless the context otherwise indicates:

(a) "computer" means a device that accepts, processes, stores, retrieves or outputs data, and includes but is not limited to auxiliary storage and telecommunications devices connected to computers.

(b) "computer program" or "program" means a series of coded instructions or statements in a form acceptable to a computer which causes the computer to process data and supply the results of the data processing.

(c) "Data" means a representation of information, knowledge, facts, concepts or instructions, including program documentation, which is prepared in a formalized manner and is stored or processed in or transmitted by a computer.

Data shall be considered property and may be in any form including but not limited to printouts, magnetic or optical storage media, punch cards or data stored internally in the memory of the computer.

(d) In addition to its meaning as defined in Section 15-1 of this Code, "property" means:

(1) electronic impulses;

(2) electronically produced data;

(3) confidential, copyrighted or proprietary information;

(4) private identification codes or numbers which permit access to computer by authorized computer users or generate billings to consumers for purchase of goods and services, including but not limited to credit card transactions and telecommunications services or permit electronic fund transfers;

(5) software or programs in either machine or human readable form; or

(6) any other tangible or intangible item relating to a computer or any part thereof.

(e) "Access" means to use, instruct, communicate with, store data in, retrieve or intercept data from, or otherwise utilize any services of a computer.

(f) "Services" includes but is not limited to computer time, data manipulation or storage functions.

(g) "Vital services or operations" means those services or operations required to provide, operate, maintain, and repair network cabling, transmission, distribution, or computer facilities necessary to ensure or protect the public health, safety, or welfare. Public health, safety, or welfare include, but are not limited to, services provided by medical personnel or institutions, fire departments, emergency services agencies, national defense contractors, armed forces or militia personnel, private and public utility companies, or law enforcement agencies.

16D-3. Computer tampering

(a) A person commits the offense of computer tampering when he knowingly and without the authorization of a computer's owner, as defined in Section 15-2 of this Code, or in excess of the authority granted to him:

(1) Accesses or causes to be accessed a computeror any part thereof, or a program or data;

(2) Accesses or causes to be accessed a computer or any part thereof, or a program or data, and obtains data or services;

(3) Accesses or causes to be accessed a computer or any part thereof, or a program or data, and damages or destroys the computer or alters, deletes or removes a computer program or data;

(4) Inserts or attempts to insert a "program" into a computer or computer program knowing or having reason to believe that such "program" contains information or commands that will or may damage or destroy that computer, or any other computer subsequently accessing or being accessed by that computer, or that will or may alter, delete or remove a computer

program or data from that computer, or any other computer program or data in a computer subsequently accessing or being accessed by that computer, or that will or may cause loss to the users of that computer or the users of a computer which accesses or which is accessed by such "program".

(b) Sentence.

(1) A person who commits the offense of computer tampering as set forth in subsection (a)(1) of this Section shall be guilty of a Class B misdemeanor.

(2) A person who commits the offense of computer tampering as set forth in subsection (a)(2) of this Section shall be guilty of a Class A misdemeanor and a Class 4 felony for the second or subsequent offense.

(3) A person who commits the offense of computer tampering as set forth in subsection (a)(3) or subsection (a)(4) of this Section shall be guilty of a Class 4 felony and a Class 3 felony for the second or subsequent offense.

(c) Whoever suffers loss by reason of a violation of subsection (a)(4) of this Section may, in a civil action against the violator, obtain appropriate relief. In a civil action under this Section, the court may award to the prevailing party reasonable attorney's fees and other litigation expenses.

16D-4. Aggravated computer tampering

(a) A person commits aggravated computer tampering when he commits the offense of computer tampering as set forth in subsection (a)(3) of Section 16D-3 and he knowingly:

(1) causes disruption of or interference with vital services or operations of

State or local government or a public utility; or

(2) creates a strong probability of death or great bodily harm to one or more individuals.

(b) Sentence.

(1) A person who commits the offense of aggravated computer tampering as set forth in subsection (a)(1) of this Section shall be guilty of a Class 3 felony.

(2) A person who commits the offense of aggravated computer tampering as set forth in subsection (a)(2) of this Section shall be guilty of a Class 2 felony.

16D-5. Computer fraud

(a) A person commits the offense of computer fraud when he knowingly:

(1) Accesses or causes to be accessed a computer or any part thereof, or a program or data, for the purpose of devising or executing any scheme, artifice to defraud, or as part of a deception;

(2) Obtains use of, damages, or destroys a computer or any part thereof, or alters, deletes, or removes any program or data contained therein, in connection with any scheme, artifice to defraud, or as part of a deception; or

(3) Accesses or causes to be accessed a computer or any part thereof, or a program or data, and obtains money or control over any such money, property, or services of another in connection with any scheme, artifice to defraud, or as part of a deception.

(b) Sentence.

(1) A person who commits the offense of computer fraud as set forth in subsection (a)(1) of this Section shall be guilty of a Class 4 felony.

(2) A person who commits the offense of computer fraud as set forth in subsection (a)(2) of this Section shall be guilty of a Class 3 felony.

(3) A person who commits the offense of computer fraud as set forth in subsection (a)(3) of this Section shall:

(i) be guilty of a Class 4 felony if the value of the money, property or services is $1,000 or less; or

(ii) be guilty of a Class 3 felony if the value of the money, property or services is more than $1,000 but less than $50,000; or

(iii) be guilty of a Class 2 felony if the value of the money, property or services is $50,000 or more.

16D-6. Forfeiture

1. Any person who commits the offense of computer fraud as set forth in Section 16D-5 shall forfeit, according to the provisions of this Section, any monies, profits or proceeds, and any interest or property which the sentencing court determines he has acquired or maintained, directly or indirectly, in whole or in part, as a result of such offense. Such person shall also forfeit any interest in, security, claim against, or contractual right of any kind which affords him a source of influence over any enterprise which he has established, operated, controlled, conducted or participated in conducting, where his relationship to or connection with any such thing or activity directly or indirectly, in whole or in part, is traceable to any item or benefit which he has obtained or acquired through computer fraud. Proceedings instituted pursuant to this Section shall be subject to and conducted in accordance with the following procedures:

(a) The sentencing court shall, upon petition by the prosecuting agency, whether it is the Attorney General or a State's Attorney, at any time following sentencing, conduct a hearing to determine whether any property or property interest is subject to forfeiture under this Section. At the forfeiture hearing the People of the State of Illinois shall have the burden of establishing, by a preponderance of the evidence, that the property or property interests are subject to such forfeiture.

(b) In any action brought by the People of the State of Illinois under this Section, the circuit courts of Illinois shall have jurisdiction to enter such restraining orders, injunctions or prohibitions, or to take such other action in connection with any real, personal, or mixed property or other interest subject to forfeiture, as they shall consider proper.

(c) In any action brought by the People of the State of Illinois under this Section, wherein any restraining order, injunction or prohibition or any other action in connection with any property or interest subject to forfeiture under this Section is sought, the circuit court presiding over the trial of the person or persons charged with computer fraud shall first determine whether there is probable cause to believe that the person or persons so charged have committed the offense of computer fraud and whether the property or interest is subject to forfeiture pursuant to this Section. In order to make this determination, prior to entering any such order, the court shall conduct a hearing without a jury, where the People shall establish:

(1) probable cause that the person or persons so charged have committed the offense of computer fraud, and

(2) probable cause that any property or interest may be subject to forfeiture pursuant to this Section. Such hearing may be conducted simultaneously with a preliminary hearing if the prosecution is commenced by information or complaint, or by motion of the People at any stage in the proceedings. The court may enter a finding of probable cause at a preliminary hearing following the filing of an information charging the offense of computer fraud or the return of an indictment by a grand jury charging the offense of computer fraud as sufficient evidence of probable cause for purposes of this Section. Upon such a finding, the circuit court shall enter such restraining order, injunction or prohibition, or shall take such other action in connection with any such property or other interest subject to forfeiture under this Section, as is necessary to insure that such property is not removed from the jurisdiction of the court, concealed, destroyed or otherwise disposed of by the owner or holder of that property or interest prior to a forfeiture hearing under this Section. The Attorney General or State's Attorney shall file a certified copy of such restraining order, injunction or other prohibition with the recorder of deeds or registrar of titles of each county where any such property of the defendant may be located. No such injunction, restraining order or other prohibition shall affect the rights of any bona fide purchaser, mortgagee, judgment creditor or other lienholder arising prior to the date of such filing. The court may, at any time, upon verified petition by the defendant, conduct a hearing to release all or portions of any such property

or interest which the court previously determined to be subject to forfeiture or subject to any restraining order, injunction, prohibition or other action. The court may release such property to the defendant for good cause shown and within the sound discretion of the court.

(d) Upon conviction of a person under Section 16D-5, the court shall authorize the Attorney General to seize and sell all property or other interest declared forfeited under this Act, unless such property is required by law to be destroyed or is harmful to the public. The court may order the Attorney General to segregate funds from the proceeds of such sale sufficient: (1) to satisfy any order of restitution, as the court may deem appropriate; (2) to satisfy any legal right, title, or interest which the court deems superior to any right, title, or interest of the defendant at the time of the commission of the acts which gave rise to forfeiture under this Section; or (3) to satisfy any bona-fide purchaser for value of the right, title, or interest in the property who was without reasonable notice that the property was subject to forfeiture. Following the entry of an order of forfeiture, the Attorney General shall publish notice of the order and his intent to dispose of the property. Within the 30 days following such publication, any person may petition the court to adjudicate the validity of his alleged interest in the property. After the deduction of all requisite expenses of administration and sale, the Attorney General shall distribute th proceeds of such sale, along with any moneys forfeited or seized as follows:

(1) 50% shall be distributed to the unit of local government whose officers or employees conducted the investigation into computer fraud and caused the arrest or arrests and prosecution leading to the forfeiture. Amounts distributed to units of local government shall be used for training or enforcement purposes relating to detection, investigation or prosecution of financial crimes, including computer fraud. In the event, however, that the investigation, arrest or arrests and prosecution leading to the forfeiture were undertaken solely by a State agency, the portion provided hereunder shall be paid into the State Police Services Fund of the Illinois Department of State Police to be used for training or enforcement purposes relating to detection, investigation or prosecution of financial crimes, including computer fraud.

(2) 50% shall be distributed to the county in which the prosecution and petition for forfeiture resulting in the forfeiture was instituted by the State's Attorney, and deposited in a special fund in the county treasury and appropriated to the State's Attorney for use in training or enforcement purposes relating to detection, investigation or prosecution of financial crimes, including computer fraud. Where a prosecution and petition for forfeiture resulting in the forfeiture has been maintained by the Attorney General, 50% of the proceeds shall be paid into the Attorney General's Financial Crime Prevention Fund. Where the Attorney General and the State's Attorney have participated jointly in any

part of the proceedings, 25% of the proceeds forfeited shall be paid to the county in which the prosecution and petition for forfeiture resulting in the forfeiture occurred, and 25% shall be paid to the Attorney General's Financial Crime Prevention Fund to be used for the purposes as stated in this subsection.

2. Where any person commits a felony under any provision of this Code or another statute and the instrumentality used in the commission of the offense, or in connection with or in furtherance of a scheme or design to commit the offense, is a computer owned by the defendant or if the defendant is a minor, owned by his or her parents or legal guardian, the computer shall be subject to the provisions of this Section. However, in no case shall a computer, or any part thereof, be subject to the provisions of the Section if the computer accessed in the commission of the offense is owned or leased by the victim or an innocent third party at the time of the commission of the offense or if the rights of creditors, lienholders, or any person having a security interest in the computer at the time of the commission of the offense shall be adversely affected.

16D-7. Rebuttable presumption—Without authority

In the event that a person accesses or causes to be accessed a computer, which access requires a confidential or proprietary code which has not been issued to or authorized for use by that person, a rebuttable presumption exists that the computer was accessed without the authorization of its owner or in excess of the authority granted.

INDIANA STATUTES

TITLE 35 CRIMINAL LAW AND PROCEDURE
ARTICLE 43 OFFENSES AGAINST PROPERTY OFFENSES AGAINST PROPERTY
CHAPTER 1 ARSON—MISCHIEF

35-43-1-4. Computer tampering.

(a) As used in this section:

"Computer network" and "computer system" have the meanings set forth in IC 35-43-2-3.

"Computer program" means an ordered set of instructions or statements that, when executed by a computer, causes the computer to process data.

"Data" means a representation of information, facts, knowledge, concepts, or instructions that:

(1) May take any form, including computer printouts, magnetic storage media, punched cards, or stored memory;

(2) Has been prepared or is being prepared; and

(3) Has been processed, is being processed, or will be processed; in a computer system or computer network.

(b) A person who knowingly or intentionally alters or damages a computer program or data, which comprises a part of a computer system or computer network without the consent of the owner of the computer system or computer network commits computer tampering, a Class D felony. [P.L.35-1986, § 2.]

35-43-2-3. Computer trespass.

(a) As used in this section:

"Access" means to:

(1) Approach;

(2) Instruct;

(3) Communicate with;

(4) Store data in;

(5) Retrieve data from; or

(6) Make use of resources of; a computer, computer system, or computer network.

"Computer network" means the interconnection of communication lines with a computer through remote terminals or a complex consisting of two (2) or more interconnected computers.

"Computer system" means a set of related computer equipment, software, or hardware.

(b) A person who knowingly or intentionally accesses:

(1) A computer system;

(2) A computer network; or

(3) Any part of a computer system or computer network; without the consent of the owner of the computer system or computer network, or the consent of the owner's licensee, commits computer trespass, a Class A misdemeanor.

IOWA STATUTES

TITLE XXXV CRIMINAL LAW
CHAPTER 716A COMPUTER CRIME

716A.1 Definitions

As used in this chapter, unless the context otherwise requires:

1. "Access" means to instruct, communicate with, store data in, or retrieve data from a computer, computer system, or computer network.

2. "Computer" means an electronic device which performs logical, arithmetical, and memory functions by manipulations of electronic or magnetic impulses, and includes all input, output, processing, storage, computer software, and communication facilities which are connected or related to the computer in a computer system or computer network.

3. "Computer system" means related, connected or unconnected, computers or peripheral equipment.

4. "Computer network" means a set of related, remotely connected devices and communication facilities including two or more computers with capability to transmit data among them through communication facilities.

5. "Computer program" means an ordered set of instructions or statements that, when executed by a computer, causes the computer to process data.

6. "Computer software" means a set of computer programs, procedures, or associated documentation used in the operation of a computer.

7. "Data" means a representation of information, knowledge, facts, concepts or instructions that has been prepared or is being prepared in a formalized manner and has been processed, or is intended to be processed in a computer. Data may be in any form including, but not limited to, printouts, magnetic storage media, punched cards and as stored in the memory of a computer.

8. "Property" means anything of value as defined in section 702.14, including but not limited to computersand computer data, information, software, and programs.

9. "Services" means the use of a computer, computer system, or computer network and includes, but is not limited to, computer time, data processing, and storage functions.

10. "Loss of property" means the greatest of the following:

    a. The retail value of the property involved.

    b. The reasonable replacement or repair cost, whichever is less.

11. "Loss of services" means the reasonable value of the damage created by the unavailability or lack of utility of the property or services involved until repair or replacement can be effected.

716A.2 Unauthorized access

A person who knowingly and without authorization accesses a computer, computer system, or computer network commits a simple misdemeanor.

716A.3 Computer damage defined

A person commits computer damage when the person knowingly and without authorization damages or destroys a computer, computer system, computer network, computer software, computer program, or any other property as defined in section 716A.1, subsection 8, or knowingly and without authorization and with the intent to injure or defraud alters any computer, computer system, computer network, computer software, computer program, or any other property as defined in section 716A.1, subsection 8.

716A.4 Computer damage in the first degree

Computer damage is computer damage in the first degree when the damage results in a loss of property or services of more than five thousand dollars. Computer damage in the first degree is a class "C" felony.

716A.5 Computer damage in the second degree

Computer damage is computer damage in the second degree when the damage results in a loss of property or services of more than five hundred dollars but not more than five thousand dollars. Computer damage in the second degree is a class "D" felony.

716A.6 Computer damage in the third degree

Computer damage is computer damage in the third degree when the damage results in a loss of property or services of more than one hundred dollars but not more than five hundred dollars. Computer damage in the third degree is an aggravated misdemeanor.

716A.7 Computer damage in the fourth degree

Computer damage is computer damage in the fourth degree when the damage results in a loss of property or services of more than fifty dollars but not more than one hundred dollars. Computer damage in the fourth degree is a serious misdemeanor.

716A.8 Computer damage in the fifth degree

Computer damage is computer damage in the fifth degree when the damage results in a loss of property or services of not more than fifty dollars. Computer damage in the fifth degree is a simple misdemeanor.

716A.9 Computer theft defined

A person commits computer theft when the person knowingly and without authorization accesses or causes to be accessed a computer, computer system, or computer network, or any part thereof, for the purpose of obtaining services, information or property or knowingly and without authorization and with the intent to permanently deprive the owner of possession, takes, transfers, conceals or retains possession of a computer, computer system, or computer network or any computer software or program, or data contained in a computer, computer system, or computer network.

716A.10 Computer theft in the first degree

Computer theft is computer theft in the first degree when the theft involves or results in a loss of services or property of more than five thousand dollars. Computer theft in the first degree is a class "C" felony.

716A.11 Computer theft in the second degree

Computer theft is computer theft in the second degree when the theft involves or results in a loss of services or property of more than five hundred dollars but not more than five thousand dollars.Computer theft in the second degree is a class "D" felony.

716A.12 Computer theft in the third degree

Computer theft is computer theft in the third degree when the theft involves or results in a loss of services or property of more than one hundred dollars but not more than five hundred dollars. Computer theft in the third degree is an aggravated misdemeanor.

716A.13 Computer theft in the fourth degree

Computer theft is computer theft in the fourth degree when the theft involves or results in a loss of services or property of more than fifty dollars but not more than one hundred dollars. Computer theft in the fourth degree is a serious misdemeanor.

716A.14 Computer theft in the fifth degree

Computer theft is computer theft in the fifth degree when the theft involves or results in a loss of services or property of not more than fifty dollars. Computer theft in the fifth degree is a simple misdemeanor.

716A.15 Chapter not exclusive

This chapter does not preclude the applicability of any other provision of the law of this state which is not inconsistent with this chapter and which applies or may apply to an act or transaction in violation of this chapter.

716A.16 Printouts admissible as evidence

In a prosecution under this chapter, computer printouts shall be admitted as evidence of any computer software, program, or data contained in or taken from a computer, notwithstanding an applicable rule of evidence to the contrary.

KANSAS STATUTES

CHAPTER 21. CRIMES AND PUNISHMENTS
KANSAS CRIMINAL CODE
PART II. PROHIBITED CONDUCT
ARTICLE 37. CRIMES AGAINST PROPERTY

21-3704. Theft of services.

(1) Theft of services is obtaining services from another by deception, threat, coercion, stealth, tampering or use of false token or device.

(2) "Services" within the meaning of this section, includes, but is not limited to, labor, professional service, cable television service, public or municipal utility or transportation service, telephone service, entertainment and the supplying of equipment for use.

(3) "Tampering" within the meaning of this section, includes, but is not limited to:

(a) Making a connection of any wire, conduit or device, to any service or transmission line owned by a public or municipal utility, or by a cable television service provider;

(b) defacing, puncturing, removing, reversing or altering any meter or any connections, for the purpose of securing unauthorized or unmeasured electricity, natural gas, telephone service or cable television service;

(c) preventing any such meters from properly measuring or registering;

(d) knowingly taking, receiving, using or converting to such person's own use, or the use of another, any electricity or natural gas which has not been measured; or any telephone or cable television service which has not been authorized; or

(e) causing, procuring, permitting, aiding or abetting any person to do any of the preceding acts.

(4) In any prosecution under this section, the existence of any of the connections of meters, alterations or use of unauthorized or unmeasured electricity, natural gas, telephone service or cable television service, specified in subsection (3), shall be prima facie evidence of intent toviolate the provisions of this section by the person or persons using or receiving the direct benefits from the use of the electricity, natural gas, telephone service or cable television service passing through such connections or meters, or using the electricity, natural gas, telephone service or cable television service which has not been authorized or measured.

(5) Theft of services of the value of $50,000 or more is a class D felony. Theft of services of the value of at least $500 but less than $50,000 is a class E felony. Theft of services of the value of less than $500 is a class A misdemeanor.

21-3745. Theft of telecommunication services.

(1) Theft of telecommunication services is knowingly:

(a) Making or possessing any instrument, apparatus, equipment, or device designed, adapted, or which is used to conceal, or to assist another to conceal, from any supplier of telecommunication service or from any lawful authority the existence or place of origin or of destination of any telecommunication.

(b) Selling, giving, transporting or otherwise transferring to another or offering or advertising for sale, any instrument, apparatus, equipment, or device described in paragraph (a), or plans or instructions for making or assembling the same, under circumstances evincing an intent to use or employ such apparatus, equipment, or device, or to allow the same to be used or employed, for a purpose described in paragraph (a), or knowing or having reason to believe that the same is intended to be so used, or that the aforesaid plans or instructions are intended to be used for making or assembling such apparatus, equipment or device.

(c) Publishing plans or instructions for making or assembling or using any apparatus, equipment or device described in paragraph (a).

(d) Publishing the number or code of an existing, canceled, revoked or nonexistent telephone number, credit number or other credit device or method of numbering or coding which is employed in the issuance of telephone numbers, credit numbers or other credit devices under circumstances evincing an intent to have such telephone number, credit number, credit device or method of numbering or coding used to avoid the payment of a lawful charge for any telecommunication service, or knowing or having reason to believe that the same may be used to avoid the payment of any such charge.

(e) Obtaining or attempting to obtain credit for or to purchase or attempt to purchase any telecommunication service by the use of any false, fictitious or counterfeit telephone number, credit number or other credit device, or by the use of any telephone number, credit number or other credit device without the authority of the person to whom such number or device was issued, or by the use of any telephone number, credit number or other credit device knowing that such number or device has been revoked.

(f) Avoiding or attempting to avoid, or causing another to avoid, the lawful charges, in whole or in part, for any telecommunication service, by the use of any fraudulent scheme, device, means or method.

(2) As used in this section, the term "telecommunication service" means any telephone or telegraph service or the transmission of a message, signal or other communication by telephone or telegraph or over telephone or telegraph facilities.

(3) Any instrument, apparatus, device, plans or instructions or publications described in this section may be seized under warrant or incident to a lawful arrest, and, upon the conviction of a person for theft of telecommunication services, any such instrument, apparatus, device, plans, instructions or publication may be destroyed as contraband by the sheriff of the county in which such person was convicted or turned over to the person providing telecommunication services in the territory in which the same was seized.

(4) Theft of telecommunication services is a class A misdemeanor, except that on a second or subsequent conviction it shall be a class E felony if the telecommunication services obtained within any seven-day period are of the value of fifty dollars ($50) or more.

21-3755. Computer crime; unlawful computer access.

(1) As used in this section, the following words and phrases shall have the meanings respectively ascribed thereto:

(a) "Access" means to approach, instruct, communicate with, store data in, retrieve data from, or otherwise make use of any resources of a computer, computer system or computer network.

(b) "Computer" means an electronic device which performs work using programmed instruction and which has one or more of the capabilities of storage, logic, arithmetic or communication and includes all input, output, processing, storage, software or communication facilities which are connected or related to such a device in a system or network.

(c) "Computer network" means the interconnection of communication lines, including microwave or other means of electronic communication, with a computer through remote terminals, or a complex consisting of two or more interconnected computers.

(d) "Computer program" means a series of instructions or statements in a form acceptable to a computer which permits the functioning of a computer system in a manner designed to provide appropriate products from such computer system.

(e) "Computer software" means computer programs, procedures and associated documentation concerned with the operation of a computer system.

(f) "Computer system" means a set of related computer equipment or devices and computer software which may be connected or unconnected.

(g) "Financial instrument" means any check, draft, money order, certificate of deposit, letter of credit, bill of exchange, credit card, debit card or marketable security.

(h) "Property" includes, but is not limited to, financial instruments, information, electronically produced or stored data, supporting documentation and computer software in either machine or human readable form and any other tangible or intangible item of value.

(i) "Services" includes, but is not limited to, computer time, data processing and storage functions and other uses of a computer, computer system or computer network to perform useful work.

(j) "Supporting documentation" includes, but is not limited to, all documentation used in the construction, classification, implementation, use or modification of computer software, computer programs or data.

(2) Computer crime is:

(a) Willfully and without authorization gaining or attempting to gain access to and damaging, modifying, altering, destroying, copying, disclosing or taking possession of a computer, computer system, computer network or any other property;

(b) using a computer, computer system, computer network or any other property for the purpose of devising or executing a scheme or artifice with the intent to defraud or for the purpose of obtaining money, property, services or any other thing of value by means of false or fraudulent pretense or representation; or

(c) willfully exceeding the limits of authorization and damaging, modifying, altering, destroying, copying, disclosing or taking possession of a computer, computer system, computer network or any other property.

Computer crime which causes a loss of the value of less than $150 is a class A misdemeanor.

Computer crime which causes a loss of the value of $150 or more is a class E felony.

(3) In any prosecution for computer crime, it is a defense that the property or services were appropriated openly and avowedly under a claim of title made in good faith.

(4) Unlawful computer access is willfully, fraudulently and without authorization gaining or attempting to gain access to any computer, computer system, computer network or to any computer software, program, documentation, data or property contained in any computer, computer system or computer network. Unlawful computer access is a class A misdemeanor.

(5) This section shall be part of and supplemental to the Kansas criminal code.

KENTUCKY STATUTES

TITLE XL CRIMES AND PUNISHMENTS
CHAPTER 434 OFFENSES AGAINST PROPERTY BY FRAUD
SUBCHAPTER: UNLAWFUL ACCESS TO A COMPUTER

434.840 Definitions

For the purposes of KRS 434.845 and 434.850, the following words (including any form of the word) and terms shall have the following meanings:

(1) "Access" means to approach, instruct, communicate with, store data in, retrieve or intercept data from, or otherwise make use of any resources of, a computer, computer system, or computer network;

(2) "Computer" means a device that can perform substantial computation, including numerous arithmetic or logic operations, without intervention by a human operator during the processing of a job;

(3) "Computer network" means a set of two or more computer systems that transmit data over communication circuits connecting them;

(4) "Computer program" means an ordered set of data that are coded instructions or statements that when executed by a computer cause the computer to process data;

(5) "Computer software" means a set of computer programs, procedures, and associated documentation concerned with the operation of a computer, computer system, or computer network;

(6) "Computer system" means a set of connected devices including a computer and other devices including, but not limited to, one or more of the following: data input, output, or storage devices, data communication circuits, and operating system computer programs that make the system capable of performing data processing tasks;

(7) "Data" is a representation of information, knowledge, facts, concepts, or instructions which are being prepared or have been prepared in a formalized manner, and is intended to be stored or processed, or is being stored or processed, or has been stored or processed, in a computer, computer system or computer network;

(8) "Financial instruments" includes, but is not limited to, any check, cashier's check, draft, warrant, money order, certificate of deposit, negotiable instrument, letter of credit, bill of exchange, credit card, debit card, or marketable security, or any computer system representation thereof;

(9) "Intellectual property" includes data, which may be in any form including, but not limited to, computer printouts, magnetic storage media, punched cards, or may be stored internally in the memory of a computer;

(10) "To process" is to use a computer to put data through a systematic sequence of operations for the purpose of producing a specified result;

(11) "Property" includes, but is not limited to, intellectual property, financial instruments, data, computer programs, documentation associated with data, computers, computer systems and computer programs, all in machine-readable or human-readable form, and any tangible or intangible item of value; and

(12) "Services" includes, but is not limited to, the use of a computer, a computer system, a computer network, computer software, computer program, or data to perform tasks.

434.845 Unlawful access to a computer in the first degree

(1) A person is guilty of unlawful access to a computer in the first degree when he knowingly and willfully, directly or indirectly accesses, causes to be accessed, or attempts to access any computer software, computer program, data, computer, computer system, computer network, or any part thereof, for the purpose of:

(a) Devising or executing any scheme or artifice to defraud; or

(b) Obtaining money, property, or services for themselves or another by means of false or fraudulent pretenses, representations, or promises; or

(c) Altering, damaging, destroying, or attempting to alter, damage, or destroy, any computer, computer system, or computer network, or any computer software, program, or data.

(2) Accessing, attempting to access, or causing to be accessed any computer software, computer program, data, computer, computer system, computer network, or any part thereof, even though fraud, false or fraudulent pretenses, representations, or promises may have been involved in the access or attempt to access shall not constitute a violation of this section if the sole purpose of the access was to obtain information and not to commit any other act proscribed by this section.

(3) Unlawful access to a computer in the first degree is a Class C felony.

434.850 Unlawful access to a computer in the second degree

(1) A person is guilty of unlawful access to a computer in the second degree when he without authorization knowingly and willfully, directly or indirectly accesses, causes to be accessed, or attempts to access any computer software, computer program, data, computer, computer system, computer network, or any part thereof.

(2) Unlawful access to a computer in the second degree is a Class A misdemeanor.

434.855 Misuse of computer information

(1) A person is guilty of misuse of computer information when he:

(a) Receives, conceals, or uses, or aids another in doing so, any proceeds of a violation of KRS 434.845; or

(b) Receives, conceals, or uses or aids another in doing so, any books, records, documents, property, financial instrument, computer software, computer program, or other material, property, or objects, knowing the same to have been used in or obtained from a violation of KRS 434.845.

(2) Misuse of computer information is a Class C felony.

434.860 Venue

For the purpose of venue under the provisions of KRS 434.845, 434.850 or 434.855, any violation of KRS 434.845, 434.850 or 434.855 shall be considered to have been committed: in any county in which any act was performed in furtherance of any transaction violating KRS 434.845, 434.850 or 434.855; in any county in which any violator had control or possession of any proceeds of said violation or of any books, records, documents, property, financial instrument, computer software, computer program or other material, objects or items which were used in furtherance of said violation; and in any county from which, to which or through which any access to a computer, computer system, or computer network was made whether by wires, electromagnetic waves, microwaves or any other means of communication.

LOUISIANA STATUTES

TITLE 14. CRIMINAL LAW
CHAPTER 1. CRIMINAL CODE
PART III. OFFENSES AGAINST PROPERTY
SUBPART D. COMPUTER RELATED CRIME

73.1. Definitions

As used in this Subpart unless the context clearly indicates otherwise:

(1) "Access" means to program, to execute programs on, to communicate with, store data in, retrieve data from, or otherwise make use of any resources, including data or programs, of a computer, computer system, or computer network.

(2) "Computer" includes an electronic, magnetic, optical, or other high-speed data processing device or system performing logical, arithmetic, and storage functions, and includes any property, data storage facility, or communications facility directly related to or operating in conjunction with such device or system. "Computer" shall not include an automated typewriter or typesetter, a machine designed solely for word processing, or a portable hand-held calculator, nor shall "computer" include any other device which might contain components similar to those in computers but in which the components have the sole function of controlling the device for the single purpose for which the device is intended.

(3) "Computer network" means a set of related, remotely connected devices and communication facilities including at least one computer system with capability to transmit data through communication facilities.

(4) "Computer program" means an ordered set of data representing coded instructions or statements that

when executed by a computer cause the computer to process data.

(5) "Computer services" means providing access to or service or data from a computer, a computer system, or a computer network.

(6) "Computer software" means a set of computer programs, procedures, and associated documentation-concerned with operation of a computer system.

(7) "Computer system" means a set of functionally related, connected or unconnected, computer equipment, devices, or computer software.

(8) "Financial instrument" means any check, draft, money order, certificate of deposit, letter of credit, bill of exchange, access card as defined in R.S. 14:67.3, or marketable security.

(9) "Intellectual property" includes data, computer programs, computer software, trade secrets as defined in R.S. 51:1431(4), copyrighted materials, and confidential or proprietary information, in any form or medium, when such is stored in, produced by, or intended for use or storage with or in a computer, a computer system, or a computer network.

(10) "Proper means" include:

(a) Discovery by independent invention;

(b) Discovery by "reverse engineering", that is by starting with the known product and working backward to find the method by which it was developed. The acquisition of the known product must be by lawful means;

(c) Discovery under license or authority of the owner;

(d) Observation of the property in public use or on public display; or

(e) Discovery in published literature.

(11) "Property" means property as defined in R.S. 14:2(8) and shall specifically include but not be limited to financial instruments, electronically stored or produced data, and computer programs, whether in machine readable or human readable form.

73.2. Offenses against intellectual property

A. An offense against intellectual property is the intentional:

(1) Destruction, insertion, or modification, without consent, of intellectual property; or

(2) Disclosure, use, copying, taking, or accessing, without consent, of intellectual property.

B. (1) Whoever commits an offense against intellectual property shall be fined not more than five hundred dollars, or imprisoned for not more than six months, or both, for commission of the offense.

(2) However, when the damage or loss amounts to a value of five hundred dollars or more, the offender may be fined not more than ten thousand dollars, or imprisoned with or without hard labor, for not more than five years, or both.

C. The provisions of this Section shall not apply to disclosure, use, copying, taking, or accessing by proper means as defined in this Subpart.

73.3. Offenses against computer equipment or supplies

A. An offense against computer equipment or supplies is the intentional modification or destruction, without consent, of computer equipment or supplies used or intended to be used in a computer, computer system, or computer network.

B. (1) Whoever commits an offense against computer equipment or supplies shall be fined not more than five hundred dollars, or be imprisoned for not more than six months, or both.

(2) However, when the damage or loss amounts to a value of five hundred dollars or more, the offender may be fined not more than ten thousand dollars, or imprisoned with or without hard labor, for not more than five years, or both.

73.4. Offenses against computer users

A. An offense against computer users is the intentional denial to an authorized user, without consent, of the full and effective use of or access to a computer, a computer system, a computer network, or computer services.

B. (1) Whoever commits an offense against computer users shall be fined not more than five hundred dollars, or be imprisoned for not more than six months, or both, for commission of the offense.

(2) However, when the damage or loss amounts to a value of five hundred dollars or more, the offender may be fined not more than ten thousand dollars, or imprisoned with or without hard labor, for not more than five years, or both.

73.5. Computer fraud

A. Computer fraud is the accessing or causing to be accessed of any computer, computer system, computer network, or any part thereof with the intent to:

(1) Defraud; or

(2) Obtain money, property, or services by means of false or conduct, practices, or representations, or through the alteration, deletion, or insertion of programs or data.

B. Whoever commits computer fraud shall be fined not more than ten thousand dollars, or imprisoned with or without hard labor for not more than five years, or both.

MAINE STATUTES

TITLE 17-A. MAINE CRIMINAL CODE
PART 2. SUBSTANTIVE OFFENSES
CHAPTER 15. THEFT

357. Theft of services

1. A person is guilty of theft if he obtains services which he knows are available only for compensation by deception, threat, force or any other means designed to avoid the due payment therefor. As used in this section, "deception" has the same meaning as in section 354, and "threat" is deemed to occur under the circumstances described in section 355, subsection 2.

2. A person is guilty of theft if, having control over the disposition of services of another, to which he knows he is not entitled, he diverts such services to his own benefit, or to the benefit of some other person who he knows is not entitled thereto

3. As used in this section, "services" includes, but is not necessarily limited to, labor, professional service, public utility and transportation service, ski lift service, restaurant, hotel, motel, tourist cabin, rooming house and like accommodations, the supplying of equipment, tools, vehicles or trailers for temporary use, telephone, telegraph, cable television or computer service, gas, electricity, water or steam, admission to entertainment, exhibitions, sporting events or other events or services for which a charge is made.

4. Where compensation for service is ordinarily paid immediately upon the rendering of such service, as in the case of hotels, restaurants, ski lifts or sporting events and garages, nonpayment prior to use or enjoyment, refusal to pay or absconding without payment or offer to pay gives rise to a presumption that the service was obtained by deception.

MARYLAND STATUTES

ARTICLE 27. CRIMES AND PUNISHMENTS.
I CRIMES AND PUNISHMENTS
CREDIT CARD OFFENSES

145. Credit card offenses.

(a) Definitions.—For the purposes of this section:

(1) "Cardholder" means the person or organization named on the face of a credit card to whom or for whose benefit the credit card is issued by an issuer.

(2) "Credit card" means an instrument or device, whether known as a credit card, credit plate, or by any other name, issued by an issuer for the use of the cardholder in obtaining money, goods, services or anything else of value on credit. It includes a debit or access card or other device other than a check, draft or similar paper instrument used by the cardholder to effect a transfer of funds that is initiated through an electronic terminal, telephone, or computer, or magnetic tape ordering, instructing or authorizing a financial institution to debit or credit an account. It also includes a payment device number.

(3) "Issuer" means the business organization or financial institution which issues a credit card or its duly authorized agent.

(4) "Receives" or "receiving" means acquiring possession or control of a credit card.

(5) (i) "Payment device number" means any code, account number, or other means of account access, other than a check, draft, or similar paper instrument, that can be used to obtain money, goods, services, or anything of value, or to initiate a transfer of funds.

(ii) "Payment device number" does not include an encoded or truncated credit card number or payment device number.

(b) Fraud in procuring issuance.—A person who makes or causes to be made, either directly or indirectly, any false statement in writing, knowing it to be false and with the intent that it be relied on, respecting his identity or that of any other person, firm or corporation, for the purpose of procuring the issuance of a credit card, violates this section and is subject to the penalties set forth in subsection (h) (1) of this section.

(c) Credit card theft or forgery.—

(1) A person who takes a credit card from a person, or from the possession, custody or control of another without the cardholder's consent or who, with knowledge that it has been so taken, receives the credit card with intent to use it or to sell it or to transfer it to a person other than the issuer or the cardholder is guilty of credit card theft and is subject to the penalties set forth in subsection (h) (1) of this section.

(2) A person who receives a credit card that he knows to have been lost, mislaid, or delivered under a mistake as to the identity or address of the cardholder, and who retains possession with intent to use it or to sell it or to transfer it to a person other than the issuer or the cardholder is guilty of a credit card theft and is subject to the penalties set forth in subsection (h) (1) of this section.

(3) A person other than the issuer who sells a credit card or a person who buys a credit card from a person other than the issuer violates this section and is subject to the penalties set forth in subsection (h) (1) of this section.

(4) A person, other than the issuer who receives a credit card which he knows was taken or retained under circumstances which constitute credit card theft or a violation of subsection (b) of this section or paragraph (3) of this subsection violates this subsection

and is subject to the penalties set forth in subsection (h) (1) of this section.

(5) A person who, with intent to defraud a purported issuer, a person or organization providing money, goods, services or anything else of value, or any other person, falsely makes or falsely embosses a purported credit card, or utters such a credit card or possesses such a credit card with knowledge that such credit card has been falsely made or falsely embossed is guilty of credit card forgery and is subject to the penalties set forth in subsection (h) (2) of this section. A person "falsely makes" a credit card when he makes or draws, in whole or in part, a device or instrument which purports to be the credit card of a named issuer but which is not such a credit card because the issuer did not authorize themaking or drawing, or alters a credit card which was validly issued. A person "falsely embosses" a credit card when, without the authorization of the named issuer, he completes a credit card by adding any of the matter, other than the signature of the cardholder, which an issuer requires to appear on the credit card before it can be used by a cardholder.

(6) A person other than the cardholder or a person authorized by him who, with intent to defraud the issuer, or a person or organization providing money, goods, services or anything else of value, or any other person, signs a credit card is guilty of credit card forgery and is subject to the penalties set forth in subsection (h) (2) of this section.

(d) Obtaining money, etc., by theft, forgery or misrepresentation as to holder of credit card.—A person, who, with intent to defraud the issuer, a person or organization providing money, goods, services or anything else of value, or any other person, (i) uses for the purpose of obtaining money, goods, services or anything else of value a credit card obtained or retained in violation of subsection (c) of this section or a credit card which he knows is forged; or (ii) obtains money, goods, services or anything else of value by representing without the consent of the cardholder that he is the holder of a specified card or by representing that he is the holder of a card and such card has not in fact been issued, violates this subsection and is subject to the penalties set forth in subsection (h) (1) of this section, if the value of all money, goods, services and other things of value obtained in violation of this subsection does not exceed $300; and subject to the penalties set forth in subsection (h) (2) of this section if such value exceeds $300.

(e) Fraudulently furnishing money, etc., on stolen or forged credit card; fraudulently failing to furnish money, etc., as represented to issuer.—

(1) A person who is authorized by an issuer to furnish money, goods, services or anything else of value upon presentation of a credit card by the cardholder, or any agent or employee of such person, who, with intent to defraud the issuer or the cardholder, furnishes money, goods, services or anything else of value upon presentation of a credit card obtained or retained in violation of subsection (c) of this section or a credit card which he knows is forged violates this subsection and is subject to the penalties set forth in subsection (h) (1) of this section, if the value of all money, goods, services and other things of value furnished in violation of this subsection does not exceed $300 and is subject to the penalties set forth in subsection (h) (2) of this section if such value exceeds $300.

(2) A person who is authorized by an issuer tofurnish money, goods, services or anything else of value upon presentation of a credit card by the cardholder, or any agent or employee of such person, who, with intent to defraud the issuer or cardholder, fails to furnish money, goods, services or anything else of value which he represents in writing to the issuer that he has furnished violates this subsection and is subject to the penalties set forth in subsection (h) (1) of this section, if the difference between the value of all money, goods, services and anything else of value actually furnished and the value represented to the issuer to have been furnished does not exceed $300, and is subject to the penalties set forth in subsection (h) (2) of this section if such difference exceeds $300.

(f) Completing credit card without consent of issuer; possessing contrivance to reproduce credit card without consent.

A person other than the cardholder possessing an incomplete credit card, with intent to complete it without the consent of the issuer or a person possessing, with knowledge of its character, machinery, plates or any other contrivance designed to reproduce instruments purporting to be the credit cards of an issuer who has not consented to the preparation of such credit cards, violates this subsection and is subject to the penalties set forth in subsection (h) (2) of this section. A credit card is "incomplete" if part of the matter other than the name of the cardholder, which an issuer requires to appear on the credit card, before it can be used by a cardholder, has not yet been stamped, embossed, imprinted or written on it.

(g) Receiving money, etc., by stolen, forged or misrepresented credit card.—A person who receives money, goods, services or anything else of value obtained in violation of subsection (d) of this section, knowing or believing that it was so obtained violates this subsection and is subject to the penalties set forth in subsection (h) (1) of this section if the value of all money, goods, services and other things of value obtained in violation of this subsection does not exceed $300; and is subject to the penalties set forth in subsection (h) (2) of this section, if such value exceeds $300.

(h) Penalties.

(1) A person who is subject to the penalties of this subsection shall be guilty of a misdemeanor and

fined a sum not to exceed $500 or imprisoned not more than 18 months, or both.

(2) A person who is subject to the penalties of this subsection shall be guilty of a felony and fined a sum not to exceed $1,000 or imprisoned not more than 15 years, or both.

(i) Continuing course of conduct.

If a person commits a violation of this section pursuant to one scheme or continuing course of conduct, from the same or several sources, the conduct may be considered as one offense and the value of the money, goods, services, or anything else of value may be aggregated in determining if the offense is a felony or a misdemeanor.

(j) Applicability of other laws.

This section shall not be construed to preclude the applicability of any other provision of the criminal law of this State which presently applies or may in the future apply to any transaction which violates this section, unless such provision is inconsistent with the terms of this section.

(k) Severability.

If any provision of this section or its application to any person or circumstance is held invalid, the invalidity shall not affect other provisions or applications of the section which can be given effect without the invalid provision or application, and to this end the provisions of this section are declared to be severable. (1972, ch. 632; 1978, ch. 849, § 3; 1980, ch. 603; 1982, ch. 496; 1983, ch. 535; 1984, chs. 255, 747; 1985, ch. 10, § 1.)

146. Unauthorized access to computers prohibited.

(a) Definitions.

In this section the following words have the meanings indicated.

(1) (i) "Computer" means an electronic, magnetic, optical, organic, or other data processing device or system that performs logical, arithmetic, memory, or storage functions.

(ii) "Computer" includes any property, data storage facility, or communications facility that is directly related to or operated in conjunction with that device or system.

(iii) "Computer" does not include an automated typewriter or typesetter, or a portable calculator.

(2) "Computer control language" means any ordered statements that direct a computer to perform specific functions.

(3) "Computer data base" means a representation of information, knowledge, facts, concepts, or instructions that:

(i) Are being prepared or have been prepared in a formalized manner or are or have been produced by a computer, computer system, or computer network; and

(ii) Are intended for use in a computer, computer system, or computer network.

(4) "Computer network" means the interconnection of 1 or more computers through:

(i) The use of satellite, microwave, line, or other communication media; and

(ii) Terminals or a complex consisting of 2 or more interconnected computers whether or not the interconnection is continuously maintained.

(5) "Computer program" means an ordered set of instructions or statements that may interact with related data that, when executed in a computer system, causes the computer to perform specified functions.

(6) "Computer services" includes, but is not limited to, computer time, data processing, and storage functions.

(7) "Computer software" means computer programs, instructions, procedures, or associated documentation that is concerned with the operation of a computer system.

(8) "Computer system" means 1 or more connected or unconnected computers, peripheral devices, software, data, or programs.

(9) "Access" means to instruct, communicate with, store data in, retrieve data from, or otherwise make use of equipment including, but not limited to, computers and other data processing equipment or resources connected there with.

(b) Other applicable Code provisions.

This section does not preclude the applicability of any other provision of their Code.

(c) Illegal access.

(1) A person may not intentionally, willfully, and without authorization access, attempt to access, or cause access to a computer, computer network, computer software, computer control language, computer system, computer services, computer data base, or any part of these systems or services.

(2) A person may not intentionally, willfully, and without authorization access, attempt to access, or cause access to a computer, computer network, computer software, computer control language, computer sys-

tem, computer services, computer data base, or any part of these systems or services to:

(i) Cause the malfunction or interrupt the operation of a computer, computer network, computer software, computer control language, computer system, computer services, computer data base, or any part of these systems or services; or

(ii) Alter, damage, or destroy data or a computer program stored, maintained, or produced by a computer, computer network, computer system, computer services, computer data base, or any part of these systems or services.

(3) A person may not intentionally, willfully, and without authorization:

(i) Identify or attempt to identify any valid access codes; or

(ii) Distribute or publicize any valid access codes to any unauthorized person.

(d) Penalty.

(1) Any person who violates any provision of subsection (c) (1) of this section is guilty of a misdemeanor and on conviction is subject to a fine not exceeding $1,000 or imprisonment not exceeding 3 years or both.

(2) Any person who violates any provision of subsection (c) (2) or (c) (3) of this section is guilty of a misdemeanor and on conviction is subject to a fine not exceeding $5,000 or imprisonment not exceeding 5 years or both.

(e) Scope of offenses; jurisdiction.

(1) When illegal access to a computer, computer network, computer control language, computer system, computer services, computer software, computer data base, or any part of these systems or services is committed in violation of this section pursuant to 1 scheme or continuing course of conduct, the conduct may be considered as 1 offense.

(2) A court of competent jurisdiction in this State may try a person who allegedly violates any provision of subsection (c) of this section in any county in this State where:

(i) The person performs the act; or

(ii) The accessed computer is located.

I. CRIMES AND PUNISHMENTS
THEFT

340. Definitions.

In this subheading, the following words have the meanings indicated.

(a) "Coin machine" means a coin box, turnstile, vending machine, or other mechanical or electronic device or receptacle designed to receive a coin, or bill, or a token made to be received by the machine, and in return for the insertion or deposit thereof, automatically to offer, to provide, to assist in providing, or to permit the acquisition of some property or service.

(b) (1) "Deception" means knowingly to:

(i) Create or confirm in another an impression which is false and which the offender does not believe to be true;

(ii) Fail to correct a false impression which the offender previously has created or confirmed;

(iii) Prevent another from acquiring information pertinent to the disposition of the property involved;

(iv) Sell or otherwise transfer or encumber property, failing to disclose a lien, adverse claim, or other legal impediment to the enjoyment of the property, whether the impediment is or is not of value or is not a matter of official record;

(v) Insert or deposit a slug in a coin machine;

(vi) Remove, alter, or otherwise disfigure any label or price tag;

(vii) Promise performance which the offender does not intend to perform or knows will not be performed. The defendant's intention or knowledge that a promise would not be performed shall not be established by or inferred from the fact alone that the promise was not performed; or

(viii) Mispresent the value of a motor vehicle offered for sale by tampering with, interfering with, resetting or altering the odometer of any motor vehicle with the intent to change the number of miles indicated.

(2) "Deception" does not include puffing or false statements of immaterial facts and exaggerated representations unlikely to deceive ordinary persons.

(c) "Deprive" means to withhold property of another:

(1) Permanently; or

(2) For such a period as to appropriate a portion of its value; or

(3) With the purpose to restore it only upon payment of reward or other compensation; or

(4) To dispose of the property and use or deal with the property so as to make it unlikely that the owner will recover it.

(d) "Exerts control" includes but is not limited to the taking, carrying away, appropriating to one's own use or sale, conveyance, transfer of title to, interest in, or possession of property. The term "exerts control" does not include trespassing on the land of another or occupying without authorization the land of another.

(e) "Knowingly"—A person acts knowingly with respect to conduct or to a circumstance described by a statute defining an offense when he is aware of his conduct or that the circumstance exists. A person acts knowingly with respect to the result of conduct described by a statute defining an offense when he is practically certain that the result will be caused by his conduct. When knowledge of the existence of a particular fact is an element of an offense, that knowledge is established if a person is practically certain of its existence. Equivalent terms such as "knowing" or "with knowledge" have the same meaning.

(f) "Obtain" means:

(1) In relation to property, to bring about a transfer of interest or possession, whether to the offender or to another; and

(2) In relation to services, to secure the performance thereof.

(g) "Owner" means a person, other than the offender, who has possession of or any other interest in the property involved, even though that interest or possession is unlawful, and without whose consent the offender has no authority to exert control over the property.

(h) "Property" means anything of value, including but not limited to:

(1) Real estate;

(2) Money;

(3) Commercial instruments;

(4) Admission or transportation tickets;

(5) Written instruments representing or embodying rights concerning anything of value, or services, or anything otherwise of value to the owner;

(6) Things growing on or affixed to, or found on land, or part of or affixed to any building;

(7) Electricity, gas, and water;

(8) Birds, animals, and fish which ordinarily are kept in a state of confinement;

(9) Food and drink;

(10) Samples, cultures, micro-organisms, specimens;

(11) Records, recordings, documents, blueprints, drawings, maps, and whole or partial copies, descriptions, photographs, prototypes or models thereof; or any other articles, materials, devices, substances, and whole or partial copies, descriptions, photographs, prototypes, or models thereof which represent evidence, reflect or record secret scientific, technical, merchandising production or management information, designed process, procedure, formula, invention, trade secret, or improvement;

(12) Financial instruments, information, electronically produced data, computer software and programs in either machine or human readable form, and other tangible or intangible items of value.

(i) "Property of another" means real or personal property in which a person other than the offender has an interest which the offender does not have authority to defeat or impair, even though the offender himself may have an interest in the property.

(j) "Service" includes, but is not limited to:

(1) Labor or professional service;

(2) Telecommunication, public utility, toll facilities, or transportation service;

(3) Lodging, entertainment, or restaurant service; or

(4) The use of equipment (including, but not limited to, computers and other data processing equipment).

(k) "Slug" means an object or article which, by virtue of its size, shape, or any other quality, is capable of being inserted or deposited in a coin machine as an improper substitute for a coin, bill, or token required for the operation of the machine.

(l) (1) "Value" means the market value of the property or service at the time and place of the crime, or if the market value cannot be satisfactorily ascertained, the cost of the replacement of the property within a reasonable time after the crime.

(2) Whether or not they have been issued or delivered, certain written instruments, not including those having a readily ascertainable market value, shall be evaluated as follows:

(i) The value of an instrument constituting an evidence of debt, such as a check, draft, or promissory note, shall be determined as the amount due or collectible thereon or thereby, this figure ordinarily being the face amount of the indebtedness less any portion thereof which has been satisfied.

(ii) The value of any other instrument which creates, releases, discharges, or otherwise affects any valuable legal right, privilege, or obligation shall be determined as the amount of economic loss which the owner of the instrument might reasonably suffer by virtue of the loss of the instrument.

(3) The value of a trade secret which does not have a readily ascertainable market value shall be deemed any reasonable value representing the damage to the owner suffered by reason of losing an advantage over those who do not know of or use the trade secret.

(4) When it cannot be determined if the value of the property or service is more or less than $300 by the standards set forth in this subsection, its value shall be determined to be an amount less than $300.

(5) When theft is committed in violation of this subheading pursuant to one scheme or continuing course of conduct, whether from the same or several sources, the conduct may be considered as one offense and the value of the property or services aggregated in determining whether the theft is a felony or a misdemeanor. (1978, ch. 849, § 1; 1979, ch. 687, § 1; 1986, ch. 506; 1988, ch. 6, § 1.)

I. CRIMES AND PUNISHMENTS
COUNTERFEITING AND FORGERY

45A. False entry in public record; altering, defacing, destroying, removing or concealing public record; accessing public records.

(a) For the purposes of this section, the following words have the meanings indicated.

(1) "Public record" includes all official books, papers, or records whether kept on a manual or automated basis, which are created, received, or used by the State or any agency thereof, a bicounty or a multi-county agency, any county, municipality, or other political subdivision.

(2) "Access" means to instruct, communicate with, store data in, retrieve data from, or otherwise make use of equipment including, but not limited to, computers and other data processing equipment or resources connected therewith.

(b) It is unlawful for a person to do or attempt to do the following:

(1) Wilfully make a false entry in any public records;

(2) Except under proper authority, wilfully alter, deface, destroy, remove, or conceal any public record; or

(3) Except under proper authority, wilfully and intentionally access public records.

(c) Any person who violates this section is guilty of a misdemeanor and may be imprisoned up to 3 years or fined up to $1,000, or both. (1979, ch. 425; 1984, ch. 443.)

MASSACHUSETTS STATUTES

CHAPTER 233

Section 79K. Admissibility of Duplicate of Computer Data File or Program File.

A duplicate of a computer data file or program file shall be admissible as evidence as the original itself unless (1) a genuine question is raised as to the authenticity of the original or (2) in the circumstances it would be unfair to admit the duplicate in lieu of the original.

For the purposes of this section, if data is stored in a computer or similar device, any printout or other output readable by sight, shown to reflect the data accurately, shall be an original.

A "duplicate of a computer data file or program file" shall mean a file produced by the same impression as the original, or from the same matrix, or by mechanical or electronic recording, in the normal way such a duplicate is produced on a computer, or by other equivalent techniques that accurately reproduce the original.

CHAPTER 266

Section 33A. Fraudulent Obtaining of Commercial Computer Service; Penalty.

Whoever, with intent to defraud, obtains, or attempts to obtain, or aids or abets another in obtaining, any commercial computer service by false representation, false statement, unauthorized charging to the account of another, by installing or tampering with any facilities or equipment or by any other means, shall be punished by imprisonment in the house of correction for not more than two and one-half years or by a fine of not more than three thousand dollars, or both. As used in this section, the words "commercial computer service" shall mean the use of computers, computer systems, computer programs or computer networks, or the access to or copying of the data, where such use, access or copying is offered by the proprietor or operator of the computer, system, program, network or data to others on a subscription or other basis for monetary consideration.

CHAPTER 266

Section 120F. Unauthorized Accessing of Computer Systems; Penalty; Password Requirement as Notice

Whoever, without authorization, knowingly accesses a computer system by any means, or after gaining access to a computer system by any means knows that such access is not authorized and fails to terminate such access, shall be punished by imprisonment in the house of correction for not more than thirty days or by a fine of not more than one thousand dollars, or both.

The requirement of a password or other authentication to gain access shall constitute notice that access is limited to authorized users.

CHAPTER 266

Section 127. Malicious or Wanton Injuries to Real or Personal Property

Whoever destroys or injures the personal property, dwelling house or building of another in any manner or by any means not particularly described or mentioned in this chapter shall, if such destruction or injury is wilful and malicious, be punished by imprisonment in the state prison for not more than ten years or by a fine of three thousand dollars or three times the value of the property so destroyed or injured, whichever is greater and imprisonment in jail for not more than two and one-half years; or if such destruction or injury is wanton, shall be punished by a fine of fifteen hundred dollars, or three times the value of the property so destroyed or injured, whichever is greater, or by imprisonment for not more than two and one-half years; if the value of the property so destroyed or injured is not alleged to exceed two hundred and fifty dollars, the punishment shall be by a fine of three times the value of the damage or injury to such property or by imprisonment for not more than two and one-half months; provided, however, that where a fine is levied pursuant to the value of the property destroyed or injured, the court shall, after conviction, conduct an evidentiary hearing to ascertain the value of the property so destroyed or injured. The words "personal property", as used in this section, shall also include electronically processed or stored data, either tangible or intangible, and data while in transit.

CHAPTER 277

Section 58A 1/2.

The crimes described in sections thirty-three A and one hundred twenty F of chapter two hundred and sixty-six and section one hundred twenty-seven of chapter two hundred and sixty-six when the personal property involved is electronically processed or stored data, either tangible or intagible, and data while in transit, may be presecuted and punished, in any county where the defendent was physically located at the time of the violation, or where the electronic data was physically located at the time of the violation.

MICHIGAN STATUTES

CHAPTER 752. CRIMES AND OFFENSES
FRAUDULENT ACCESS TO COMPUTERS, COMPUTER SYSTEMS, AND COMPUTER NETWORKS

752.791. Meanings of words and phrases.

Sec. 1. For the purposes of this act, the words and phrases defined in sections 2 and 3 have the meanings ascribed to them in those sections. 752.792. Definitions; A to C.

Sec. 2. (1) "Access" means to approach, instruct, communicate with, store data in, retrieve data from, or otherwise use the resources of, a computer, computer system, or computer network.

(2) "Computer" means an electronic device which performs logical, arithmetic, and memory functions by the manipulations of electronic or magnetic impulses, and includes input, output, processing, storage, software, or communication facilities which are connected or related to a device in a system or network.

(3) "Computer network" means the interconnection of communication lines with a computer through remote terminals, or a complex consisting of 2 or more interconnected computers.

(4) "Computer program" means a series of instructions or statements, in a form acceptable to a computer, which permits the functioning of a computer system in a manner designed to provide appropriate products from the computer system.

(5) "Computer software" means a set of computer programs, procedures, and associated documentation concerned with the operation of a computer system.

(6) "Computer system" means a set of related, connected or unconnected, computer equipment, devices, and software.

752.793. Definitions; P to S.

Sec. 3. (1) "Property" includes financial instruments; information, including electronically produced data; computer software and programs in either machineor human readable form; and any other tangible or intangible item of value.

(2) "Services" includes computer time, data processing, and storage functions.

752.794. Prohibited access to computer, computer system, or computer network.

Sec. 4. A person shall not, for the purpose of devising or executing a scheme or artifice with intent to defraud or for the purpose of obtaining money, property, or a service by means of a false or fraudulent pretense, representation, or promise with intent to, gain access to or cause access to be made to a computer, computer system, or computer network.

752.795. Gaining access to, altering, damaging, or destroying computer, computer system or network, software program, or data.

Sec. 5. A person shall not intentionally and without authorization, gain access to, alter, damage, or destroy a computer, computer system, or computer network, or gain access to, alter, damage, or destroy a computer software program or data contained in a computer, computer system, or computer network.

752.796. Violations.

Sec. 6. A person shall not utilize a computer, computer system, or computer network to commit a violation of section 174 of Act No. 328 of the Public Acts of 1931, as amended, being section 750.174 of the Michigan Compiled Laws, section 279 of Act No. 328 of the Public Acts of 1931, being section 750.279 of the Michigan Compiled Laws, section 356 of Act No. 328 of the Public Acts of 1931, as amended, being section 750.356 of the Michigan Compiled Laws, or section 362 of Act No. 328 of the Public Acts of 1931, as amended, being section 750.362 of the Michigan Compiled Laws.

752.797. Penalties.

Sec. 7. A person who violates this act, if the violation involves $100.00 or less, is guilty of a misdemeanor. If the violation involves more than $100.00, the person is guilty of a felony, punishable by imprisonment for not more than 10 years, or a fine of not more than $5,000.00, or both.

MINNESOTA STATUTES

CRIMES, CRIMINALS
CHAPTER 609. CRIMINAL CODE
CRIMES AGAINST COMMERCE

609.87 Computer Crime Definitions.

Subdivision 1. Applicability. For purposes of sections 609.87 to 609.89, and section 609.891, the terms defined in this section have the meanings given them.

Subd. 2. Access. "Access" means to instruct, communicate with, store data in, or retrieve data from a COMPUTER, COMPUTER system, or COMPUTER network.

Subd. 3. COMPUTER. "COMPUTER" means an electronic device which performs logical, arithmetic or memory functions by the manipulations of signals, including but not limited to electronic or magnetic impulses.

Subd. 4. COMPUTER system. "COMPUTER system" means related, connected or unconnected, COMPUTERS and peripheral equipment.

Subd. 5. COMPUTER network. "COMPUTER network" means the interconnection of a communication system with a COMPUTER through a remote terminal, or with two or more interconnected COMPUTERS or COMPUTER systems, and includes private and public telecommunications networks.

Subd. 6. Property. "Property" includes, but is not limited to, electronically processed or produced data and information contained in a COMPUTER or COMPUTER software in either machine or human readable form.

Subd. 7. Services. "Services" includes but is not limited to, COMPUTER time, data processing, and storage functions.

Subd. 8. COMPUTER program. "COMPUTER program" means an instruction or statement or a series of instructions or statements, in a form acceptable to a COMPUTER, which directs the functioning of a COMPUTER system in a manner designed to provide appropriate products from the COMPUTER.

Subd. 9. COMPUTER software. "COMPUTER software" means a COMPUTER program or procedures, or associated documentation concerned with the operation of a COMPUTER.

Subd. 10. Loss. "Loss" means the greatest of the following:

(a) the retail market value of the property or services involved;

(b) the reasonable repair or replacement cost, whichever is less; or

(c) the reasonable value of the damage created by the unavailability or lack of utility of the property or services involved until repair or replacement can be effected.

Subd. 11. COMPUTER security system. "COMPUTER security system" means a software program or COMPUTER device that:

(1) is intended to protect the confidentiality and secrecy of data and information stored in or accessible through the COMPUTER system; and

(2) displays a conspicuous warning to a user that the user is entering a secure system or requires a person seeking access to knowingly respond by use of an authorized code to the program or device in order to gain access.

Subd. 12. Destructive COMPUTER program. "Destructive COMPUTER program" means a COMPUTER program that performs a destructive function or produces a destructive product. A program performs a destructive function if it degrades performance of the affected COMPUTER, associated peripherals or a COMPUTER program; disables the COMPUTER, associated peripherals or a COMPUTER program; or destroys or alters COMPUTER programs or data. A program produces a destructive product if it produces unauthorized data, including data that make COMPUTER memory space unavailable; results in the unauthorized alteration of data or COMPUTER programs; or produces a destructive COMPUTER program, including a self-replicating COMPUTER program.

609.88 Computer Damage.

Subdivision 1. Acts. Whoever does any of the following is guilty of COMPUTER damage and may be sentenced as provided in subdivision 2:

(a) Intentionally and without authorization damages or destroys any COMPUTER, COMPUTER system, COMPUTER network, COMPUTER software, or any other property specifically defined in section 609.87, subdivision 6;

(b) Intentionally and without authorization and with intent to injure or defraud alters any COMPUTER, COMPUTER system, COMPUTER network, COMPUTER software, or any other property specifically defined in section 609.87, subdivision 6; or

(c) Distributes a destructive COMPUTER program, without authorization and with intent to damage or destroy any COMPUTER, COMPUTER system, COMPUTER network, COMPUTER software, or any other property specifically defined in section 609.87, subdivision 6.

Subd. 2. Penalty. Whoever commits COMPUTER damage may be sentenced as follows:

(a) To imprisonment for not more than ten years or to payment of a fine of not more than $50,000, or both, if the damage, destruction or alteration results in a loss in excess of $2,500, to the owner, or the owner's agent, or lessee;

(b) To imprisonment for not more than five years or to payment of a fine of not more than $10,000, or both, if the damage, destruction or alteration results in a loss of more than $500, but not more than $2,500 to the owner, or the owner's agent or lessee; or

(c) In all other cases to imprisonment for not more than 90 days or to payment of a fine of not more than $700, or both.

609.89 Computer Theft.

Subdivision 1. Acts. Whoever does any of the following is guilty of COMPUTER theft and may be sentenced as provided in subdivision 2:

(a) Intentionally and without authorization or claim of right accesses or causes to be accessed any COMPUTER, COMPUTER system, COMPUTER network or any part thereof for the purpose of obtaining services or property; or

(b) Intentionally and without claim of right, and with intent to permanently deprive the owner of possession, takes, transfers, conceals or retains possession of any COMPUTER, COMPUTER system, or any COMPUTER software or data contained in a COMPUTER, COMPUTER system, or COMPUTER network.

Subd. 2. Penalty. Anyone who commits COMPUTER theft may be sentenced as follows:

(a) To imprisonment for not more than ten years or to payment of a fine of not more than $50,000, or both, if the loss to the owner, or the owner's agent, or lessee is in excess of $2,500; or

(b) To imprisonment for not more than five years or to payment of a fine of not more than $10,000, or both, if the loss to the owner, or the owner's agent, or lessee is more than $500 but not more than $2,500; or

(c) In all other cases to imprisonment for not more than 90 days or to payment of a fine of not more than $700, or both.

609.891 Unauthorized Computer Access.

Subdivision 1. CRIME. A person is guilty of unauthorized COMPUTER access if the person intentionally and without authority attempts to or does penetrate a COMPUTER security system.

Subd. 2. Felony. (a) A person who violates subdivision 1 in a manner that creates a grave risk of causing the death of a person is guilty of a felony and may be sentenced to a term of imprisonment of not more than ten years or to payment of a fine of not more than $20,000, or both.

(b) A person who is convicted of a second or subsequent gross misdemeanor violation of subdivision 1 is guilty of a felony and may be sentenced under paragraph (a).

Subd. 3. Gross misdemeanor. (a) A person who violates subdivision 1 in a manner that creates a risk to public health and safety is guilty of a gross misdemeanor and may be sentenced to imprisonment for a term of not more than one year or to payment of a fine of not more than $3,000, or both.

(b) A person who violates subdivision 1 in a manner that compromises the security of data that are protected under section 609.52, subdivision 2, clause (8), or are not public data as defined in section 13.02, subdivision 8a, is guilty of a gross misdemeanor and may be sentenced under paragraph (a).

(c) A person who is convicted of a second or subsequent misdemeanor violation of subdivision 1 within five years is guilty of a gross misdemeanor and may be sentenced under paragraph (a).

Subd. 4. Misdemeanor. A person who violates subdivision 1 is guilty of a misdemeanor and may be sentenced to imprisonment for a term of not more than 90 days or to payment of a fine of not more than $700, or both.

609.892 Definitions.

Subdivision 1. Applicability. The definitions in this section apply to Laws

1990, sections 1 and 6 to 8.

Subd. 2. Access device. "Access device" means a card, plate, code, account number, or other means of account access that can be used, alone or in conjunction with another access device, to obtain telecommunications service.

Subd. 3. Credit card number. "Credit card number" means the card number appearing on a credit card that is an identification card or plate issued to a person by a supplier of telecommunications service that permits the person to whom the card has been issued to obtain telecommunications service on credit.

The term includes the number or description of the card or plate even if the card or plate itself is not produced when obtaining telecommunications service.

Subd. 4. Telecommunications device. "Telecommunications device" means an instrument, apparatus, equipment mechanism, operating procedure, or code designed or adapted for a particular use and that is intended or can be used in violation of section 609.893. The term includes but is not limited to COMPUTER hardware, software, programs, electronic mail system, voice mail system, identification validation system, private branch exchange, or any other means of facilitating telecommunications service.

Subd. 5. Telecommunications provider. "Telecommunications provider" means a person, firm, association, or a corporation, private or municipal, owning, operating, or managing facilities used to provide telecommunications service.

Subd. 6. Telecommunications service. "Telecommunications service" means a service that, in exchange for a pecuniary consideration, provides or offers to provide transmission of messages, signals, facsimiles, or other communication between persons who are physically separated from each other by telephone, telegraph, cable, wire, fiber optic cable, or the projection of energy without physical connection. This term applies when the telecommunications service originates or ends or both originates and ends in this state.

Subd. 7. Telephone company. "Telephone company" means a telecommunications provider that provides local exchange telecommunications service.

CHAPTER 626A. PRIVACY OF COMMUNICATIONS

626A.27 Disclosure of Contents.

Subdivision 1. Prohibitions. Except as provided in subdivision 2:

(1) a person or entity providing an electronic communication service to the public must not knowingly divulge to a person or entity the contents of a communication while in electronic storage by that service; and

(2) a person or entity providing remote computing service to the public must not knowingly divulge to a

person or entity the contents of any communication that is carried or maintained on that service:

(i) on behalf of, and received by means of electronic transmission from, or created by means of COMPUTER processing of communications received by means of electronic transmission, from a subscriber or customer of the service; and

(ii) solely for the purpose of providing storage or COMPUTER processing services to the subscriber or customer, if the provider is not authorized to access the contents of any communications for purposes of providing any services other than storage or COMPUTER processing.

Subd. 2. Exceptions. A person or entity may divulge the contents of a communication:

(1) to an addressee or intended recipient of the communication or an agent of the addressee or intended recipient;

(2) as otherwise authorized in section 626A.02, subdivision 2, paragraph (a); 626A.05; or section 626A.28;

(3) with the lawful consent of the originator or an addressee or intended recipient of the communication, or the subscriber in the case of remote computing service;

(4) to a person employed or authorized or whose facilities are used to forward a communication to its destination;

(5) as may be necessarily incident to the rendition of the service or to the protection of the rights or property of the provider of that service; or

(6) to a law enforcement agency, if the contents:

(i) were inadvertently obtained by the service provider; and

(ii) appear to pertain to the commission of a CRIME.

MISSISSIPPI STATUTES

TITLE 97. CRIMES
CHAPTER 45. COMPUTER CRIMES

97-45-1. Definitions.

For the purposes of this chapter, the following words shall have the meanings ascribed herein unless the context clearly requires otherwise:

(a) "Access" means to program, to execute programs on, to communicate with, store data in, retrieve data from or otherwise make use of any resources, including data or programs, of a computer, computer system or computer network.

(b) "Computer" includes an electronic, magnetic, optical or other high-speed data processing device or system performing logical arithmetic and storage functions and includes any property, data storage facility or communications facility directly related to or operating in conjunction with such device or system. "Computer" shall not include an automated typewriter or typesetter, a machine designed solely for word processing which contains no data base intelligence or a portable hand-held calculator nor shall "computer" include any other device which contains components similar to those in computers but in which the components have the sole function of controlling the device for the single purpose for which the device is intended unless the thus controlled device is a processor of data or is a storage of intelligence in which case it too is included.

(c) "Computer network" means a set of related, remotely connected devices and communication facilities including at least one (1) computer system with the capability to transmit data through communication facilities.

(d) "Computer program" means an ordered set of data representing coded instructions or statements that when executed by a computer cause the computer to process data.

(e) "Computer software" means a set of computer programs, procedures and associated documentation concerned with operation of a computer system.

(f) "Computer system" means a set offunctionally related, connected or unconnected, computer equipment, devices or computer software.

(g) "Computer services" means providing access to or service or data from a computer, a computer system or a computer network and includes the actual data processing.

(h) "Financial instrument" means any check, draft, money order, certificate of deposit, letter of credit, bill of exchange, credit card as defined in Section 97-19-9(b), Mississippi Code of 1972, or marketable security.

(i) "Intellectual property" includes data, computer programs, computer software, trade secrets, copyrighted materials and confidential or proprietary information in any form or medium when such is stored in, produced by or intended for use or storage with or in a computer, a computer system or a computer network.

(j) "Property" means property as defined in Section 1-3-45, Mississippi Code of 1972, and shall specifically include, but not be limited to, financial instruments, electronically stored or produced data and computer programs, whether in machine readable or human readable form.

(k) "Proper means" includes:

(i) Discovery by independent invention;

(ii) Discovery by "reverse engineering"; that is, by starting with the known product and working backward to find the method by which it was developed. The acquisition of the known product must be by lawful means;

(iii) Discovery under license or authority of the owner;

(iv) Observation of the property in public use or on public display; or

(v) Discovery in published literature.

(l) "Use" means to make use of, to convert to one's service, to avail oneself of or to employ. In the context of this act, "use" includes to instruct, communicate with, store data in or retrieve data from, or otherwise utilize the logical arithmetic or memory functions of acomputer.

97-45-3. Computer fraud; penalties.

(1) Computer fraud is the accessing or causing to be accessed of any computer, computer system, computer network, or any part thereof with the intent to:

(a) Defraud; or

(b) Obtain money, property or services by means of false or fraudulent conduct, practices or representations; or through the false or fraudulent alteration, deletion or insertion of programs or data.

(2) Whoever commits the offense of computer fraud shall be punished, upon conviction, by a fine of not more than Ten Thousand Dollars ($10,000.00), or by imprisonment for not more than five (5) years, or by both such fine and imprisonment. However, when the damage or loss amounts to a value of One Hundred Dollars ($100.00) or more, the offender may be punished, upon conviction, by a fine of not more than Ten Thousand Dollars ($10,000.00), or imprisonment for not more than five (5) years, or by both such fine and imprisonment.

97-45-7. Offense against computer equipment; penalties.

(1) An offense against computer equipment or supplies is the intentional modification or destruction, without consent, of computer equipment or supplies used or intended to be used in a computer, computer system or computer network.

(2) Whoever commits an offense against computer equipment or supplies shall be punished, upon conviction, by a fine of not more than One Thousand Dollars ($1,000.00), or by imprisonment for not more than six months or both such fine and imprisonment. However, when the damage or loss amounts to a value of One Hundred Dollars ($100.00) or more, the offender may be punished, upon conviction, by a fine of not more than Ten Thousand Dollars ($10,000.00) or by imprison-

ment for not more than five (5) years, or by both such fine and imprisonment.

97-45-9. Offense against intellectual property; penalties.

(1) An offense against intellectual property is the intentional:

(a) Destruction, insertion or modification, without consent, of intellectual property; or

(b) Disclosure, use, copying, taking or accessing, without consent, of intellectual property.

(2) Whoever commits an offense against intellectual property shall be punished, upon conviction, by a fine of not more than One Thousand Dollars ($1,000.00), or by imprisonment for not more than six (6) months, or by both such fine and imprisonment. However, when the damage or loss amounts to a value of One Hundred Dollars ($100.00) or more, the offender may be punished, upon conviction, by a fine of not more than Ten Thousand Dollars ($10,000.00) or by imprisonment for not more than five (5) years, or by both such fine and imprisonment.

(3) The provisions of this section shall not apply to the disclosure, use, copying, taking, or accessing by proper means as defined in this chapter.

97-45-11. Venue.

For the purposes of venue under the provisions of this chapter, any violation of this chapter shall be considered to have been committed:

(a) In any county in which any act was performed in furtherance of any transaction violating this chapter; and

(b) In any county from which, to which or through which any access to a computer, computer system or computer network was made, whether by wire, electromagnetic waves, microwaves or any other means of communication.

97-45-13. Effect on other offenses.

The criminal offenses created by this chapter shall not be deemed to supersede, or repeal, any other criminal offense.

MISSOURI STATUTES

TITLE XXXVIII. CRIMES AND PUNISHMENT PEACE OFFICERS AND PUBLIC DEFENDERS
CHAPTER 569. ROBBERY, ARSON, BURGLARY AND RELATED OFFENSES

569.093. Definitions.

As used in sections 569.094 to 569.099 and in section 537.525, RSMo, the following terms mean:

(1) "Access", to instruct, communicate with, store data in, retrieve or extract data from, or otherwise make any use of any resources of, a computer, computer system, or computer network;

(2) "Computer", a functional unit that can perform substantial computation, including numerous arithmetic operations, logic operations, or data processing, without intervention by a human operator during a run;

(3) "Computer equipment", computers, terminals, data storage devices, and all other computer hardware associated with a computer system or network;

(4) "Computer network", a complex consisting of two or more interconnected computers or computer systems;

(5) "Computer program", a set of instructions, statements, or related data that directs or is intended to direct a computer to perform certain functions;

(6) "Computer software", a set of computer programs, procedures, and associated documentation pertaining to the operation of a computer system or computer network;

(7) "Computer system", a set of related, connected or unconnected, computer equipment, data, or software;

(8) "Damage", any alteration, deletion, or destruction of any part of a computer system or network;

(9) "Data", a representation of information, facts, knowledge, concepts, or instructions prepared in a formalized or other manner and intended for use in a computer or computer network. Data may be in any formincluding, but not limited to, printouts, microfiche, magnetic storage media, punched cards and as may be stored in the memory of a computer;

(10) "Property", anything of value as defined in subdivision (10) of section 570.010, RSMo, and includes, but is not limited to, financial instruments, information, including electronically produced data and computer software and programs in either machine or human readable form, and any other tangible or intangible item of value;

(11) "Services", the use of a computer, computer system, or computer network and includes, but is not limited to, computer time, data processing, andstorage or retrieval functions.

569.095. Tampering with computer data, penalties.

1. A person commits the crime of tampering with computer data if he knowingly and without authorization or without reasonable grounds to believe that he has such authorization:

(1) Modifies or destroys data or programs residing or existing internal to a computer, computer system, or computer network; or

(2) Modifies or destroys data or programs or supporting documentation residing or existing external to a computer, computer system, or computer network; or

(3) Discloses or takes data, programs, or supporting documentation, residing or existing internal or external to a computer, computer system, or computer network; or

(4) Discloses or takes a password, identifying code, personal identification number, or other confidential information about a computer system or network that is intended to or does control assess to the computer system or network;

(5) Accesses a computer, a computer system, or a computer network, and intentionally examines information about another person;

(6) Receives, retains, uses, or discloses any data he knows or believes was obtained in violation of this subsection.

2. Tampering with computer data is a class A misdemeanor, unless the offense is committed for the purpose of devising or executing any scheme or artifice to defraud or to obtain any property, the value of which is one hundred fifty dollars or more, in which case tampering with computer data is a class D felony.

569.097. Tampering with computer equipment, penalties.

1. A person commits the crime of tampering with computer equipment if he knowingly and without authorization or without reasonable grounds to believe that he has such authorization:

(1) Modifies, destroys, damages, or takes equipment or data storage devices used or intended to be used in a computer, computer system, or computer network; or

(2) Modifies, destroys, damages, or takes any computer, computer system, or computer network.

2. Tampering with computer equipment is a class A misdemeanor, unless:

(1) The offense is committed for the purpose of executing any scheme or artifice to defraud or obtain any property, the value of which is one hundred fifty dollars or more, in which case it is a class D felony; or

(2) The damage to such computer equipment or to the computer, computer system, or computer network is one hundred fifty dollars or more but less than one thousand dollars, in which case it is a class D felony; or

(3) The damage to such computer equipment or to the computer, computer system, or computer network is one thousand dollars or greater, in which case it is a class C felony.

569.099. Tampering with computer users, penalties.

1. A person commits the crime of tampering with computer users if he knowingly and without authorization or without reasonable grounds to believe that he has such authorization:

(1) Accesses or causes to be accessed any computer, computer system, or computer network; or

(2) Denies or causes the denial of computer system services to an authorized user of such computer system services, which, in whole or in part, is owned by, under contract to, or operated for, or on behalf of, or in conjunction with another.

2. The offense of tampering with computer users is a class A misdemeanor unless the offense is committed for the purpose of devising or executing any scheme or artifice to defraud or to obtain any property, the value of which is one hundred fifty dollars or more, in which case tampering with computer users is a class D felony.

MONTANA STATUTES

TITLE 45 CRIMES
CHAPTER 6 OFFENSES AGAINST PROPERTY
PART 3 THEFT AND RELATED OFFENSES

45-6-310. Definition—computer use

As used in 45-6-311, the term "obtain the use of" means to instruct, communicate with, store data in, retrieve data from, cause input to, cause output from, or otherwise make use of any resources of a computer, computer system, or computer network or to cause another to instruct, communicate with, store data in, retrieve data from, cause input to, cause output from, or otherwise make use of any resources of a computer, computer system, or computer network.

45-6-311. Unlawful use of a computer

(1) A person commits the offense of unlawful use of a computer if he knowingly or purposely:

(a) obtains the use of any computer, computer system, or computer network without consent of the owner;

(b) alters or destroys or causes another to alter or destroy a computer program or computer software without consent of the owner; or

(c) obtains the use of or alters or destroys a computer, computer system, computer network, or any part thereof as part of a deception for the purpose of obtaining money, property, or computer services from the owner of the computer, computer system, computer network, or part thereof or from any other person.

(2) A person convicted of the offense of unlawful use of a computer involving property not exceeding $300 in value shall be fined not to exceed $500 or be imprisoned in the county jail for a term not to exceed 6 months, or both. A person convicted of the offense of unlawful use of a computer involving property exceeding $300 in value shall be fined not more than 2 1/2 times the value of the property used, altered, destroyed, or obtained or be imprisoned in the state prison for a term not to exceed 10 years, or both.

NEBRASKA STATUTES

CHAPTER 28 CRIMES AND PUNISHMENTS
ARTICLE 13 MISCELLANEOUS OFFENSES COMPUTERS

28-1343. Terms, defined

For purposes of sections 28-1343 to 28-1348, unless the context otherwise requires:

(1) Access shall mean to instruct, communicate with, store data in, retrieve data from, or otherwise use the resources of a computer or computer network;.

(2) Computer shall mean a high-speed data processing device or system which performs logical, arithmetic, data storage and retrieval, communication, or control functions and includes any input, output, data storage, processing, or communication facilities directly related to or operating in conjunction with any such device or system;

(3) Computer network shall mean the interconnection of communication links with a computer or an interconnection of computers which communicate with each other;

(4) Computer program shall mean a set of instructions, statements, or related data that directs or is intended to direct the computer to perform certain specified functions;

(5) Data shall mean a representation of information, facts, knowledge, concepts, or instructions prepared in a formalized or other manner and intended for use in a computer or computer network;

(6) Property shall mean any tangible or intangible thing of value and shall include, but not be limited to, financial instruments, data, computer programs, information, computer-produced or stored data, supporting documentation, or data in transit, whether in human or computer readable form; and

(7) Services shall mean use of a computer or computer network including, but not limited to, data processing and storage functions, computer programs, or data.

28-1344. Unlawful acts; depriving or obtaining property or services; penalties

Any person who intentionally accesses or causes to be accessed, directly or indirectly, any computer or computer network without authorization or who, having accessed any computer or computer network with authorization, knowingly and intentionally exceeds the limits of such authorization shall be guilty of a Class IV felony if he or she intentionally: (1) Deprives another of property or services; or (2) obtains property or services of another, except that any person who obtains property or services or deprives another of property or services with a value of one thousand dollars or more by such conduct shall be guilty of a Class III felony.

28-1345. Unlawful acts; harming or disrupting operations; penalties

Any person who accesses or causes to be accessed any computer or computer network without authorization or who, having accessed any computer or computer network with authorization, knowingly and intentionally exceeds the limits of such authorization shall be guilty of a Class IV felony if he or she intentionally: (1) Alters, damages, deletes, or destroys any computer, computer network, computer program, data, or other property; or (2) disrupts the operation of any computer or computer network, except that any person who causes losses with a value of one thousand dollars or more by such conduct shall be guilty of a Class III felony.

28-1346. Unlawful acts; obtaining confidential public information; penalties

Any person who intentionally accesses or causes to be accessed any computer or computer network without authorization, or who, having accessed with authorization, knowingly and intentionally exceeds the limits of such authorization, and thereby obtains information filed by the public with the state or any political subdivision which is by statute required to be kept confidential shall be guilty of a Class II misdemeanor. For any second or subsequent offense under this section, such person shall be guilty of a Class I misdemeanor.

28-1347. Unlawful acts; access without authorization; exceeding authorization; penalties

Any person who intentionally accesses any computer, computer program, or data without authorization and with knowledge that such access was not authorized or who, having accessed any computer or computer network with authorization, knowingly and intentionally exceeds the limits of such authorization shall be guilty of a Class V misdemeanor. For any second or subsequent offense under this section, such person shall be guilty of a Class II misdemeanor.

28-1348. Sections; how construed

Sections 28-1343 to 28-1348 shall not be construed to preclude the applicability of any other provision of Chapter 28 which may apply to any transaction described in such sections.

NEVADA STATUTES

TITLE 15. CRIMES AND PUNISHMENTS
CHAPTER 205. CRIMES AGAINST PROPERTY. UNLAWFUL USE OF COMPUTERS

205.473. Definitions.

As used in NRS 205.473 to 205.477, inclusive, unless the context otherwise requires, the words and terms defined in NRS 205.4735 to 205.476, inclusive, have the meanings ascribed to them in those sections. (1983, p. 1203.)

205.4735. "Computer" defined.

"Computer" means an electronic device which performs logical, arithmetic and memory functions by manipulations of electronic or magnetic impulses and includes all equipment related to the computer in a system or network. (1983, p. 1203.)

205.474. "Data" defined.

"Data" means a representation in any form of information, knowledge, facts, concepts or instructions which is being prepared or has been formally prepared and is intended to be processed, is being processed or has been processed in a system or network. (1983, p. 1203.)

205.4745. "Network" defined.

"Network" means a set of related, remotely connected devices and facilities, including more than one system, with the capability to transmit data among them. (1983, p. 1203.)

205.475. "Program" defined.

"Program" means an ordered set of data representing coded instructions or statements which can be executed by a computer and cause the computer to perform one or more tasks. (1983, p. 1203.)

205.4755. "Property" defined.

"Property" means anything of value and includes a financial instrument, information, electronically produced data, program and any other tangible or intangible item of value. (1983, p. 1203.)

205.476. "System" defined.

"System" means a set of related equipment, whether or not connected, which is used with or for a computer.

205.4765. Unlawful use or destruction of computer, system or network.

1. Except as otherwise provided in subsection 4, a person who knowingly, willingly and without authorization:

    (a) Modifies;

    (b) Destroys;

    (c) Discloses;

    (d) Uses;

    (e) Takes;

    (f) Copies; or

    (g) Enters, data, a program or any supporting documents which exist inside or outside a computer, system or network is guilty of a misdemeanor.

2. Except as otherwise provided in subsection 4, a person who knowingly, willingly and without authorization:

    (a) Modifies;

    (b) Destroys;

    (c) Uses;

    (d) Takes; or

    (e) Damages, equipment or supplies that are used or intended to be used in a computer, system or network is guilty of a misdemeanor.

3. Except as otherwise provided in subsection 4, a person who knowingly, willingly and without authorization:

    (a) Destroys;

    (b) Damages; or

    (c) Takes, a computer, system or network is guilty of a misdemeanor.

4. If the violation of subsection 1, 2 or 3:

    (a) Was committed to devise or execute a scheme to defraud or illegally obtain property;

    (b) Caused damage in excess of $500; or

    (c) Caused an interruption or impairment of a public service, such as a governmental operation, system of public communication or transportation or supply of water, gas or electricity, the person shall be punished by imprisonment in the state prison for not less than 1 year nor more than 6 years, and may be further punished by a fine of not more than $100,000. (1983, p. 1203.)

205.477. Unlawful use or denial of use of computer, system or network.

1. Except as otherwise provided in subsection 3, a person who knowingly, willfully and without authorization denies or causes the denial of the use of a computer, system or network to a person who has the duty and right to use it is guilty of a misdemeanor.

2. Except as otherwise provided in subsection 3, a person who knowingly, willingly and without authoriza-

tion uses or causes the use of a computer, system or network to:

  (a) Obtain personal information about another person; or

  (b) Enter false information about another person to wrongfully damage or enhance that person's credit rating, is guilty of a misdemeanor.

  3. If the violation of subsection 1 or 2 was committed to devise or execute a scheme to defraud or illegally obtain property, the person shall be punished by imprisonment in the state prison for not less than 1 year nor more than 6 years, and may be further punished by a fine of not more than $100,000. (1983, p. 1204.)

NEW HAMPSHIRE STATUTES

TITLE LXII. CRIMINAL CODE
CHAPTER 638. FRAUD COMPUTER CRIME

638:16. Computer Crime; Definitions

For the purpose of this subdivision:

  I. "Access" means to instruct, communicate with, store data in, or retrieve data from a computer, computer system, or computer network.

  II. "Computer" means a programmable, electronic device capable of accepting and processing data.

  III. "Computer network" means (a) a set of related devices connected to a computer by communications facilities, or (b) a complex of 2 or more computers, including related devices, connected by communications facilities.

  IV. "Computer program" means a set of instructions, statements, or related data that, in actual or modified form, is capable of causing a computer or computer system to perform specified functions.

  V. "Computer services" includes, but is not limited to, computer access, data processing, and data storage.

  VI. "Computer software" means one or more computer programs, existing in any form, or any associated operational procedures, manuals, or other documentation.

  VII. "Computer system" means a computer, its software, related equipment, communications facilities, if any, and includes computer networks.

  VIII. "Data" means information of any kind in any form, including computer software.

  IX. "Person" means a natural person, corporation, trust, partnership, incorporated or unincorporated association, and any other legal or governmental entity, including any state or municipal entity or public official.

  X. "Property" means anything of value, including data.

638:17. Computer Related Offenses

  I. A person is guilty of the computer crime of unauthorized access to a computer system when, knowing that he is not authorized to do so, he knowingly accesses or causes to be accessed any computer system without authorization. It shall be an affirmative defense to a prosecution for unauthorized access to a computer system that:

  (a) The person reasonably believed that the owner of the computer system, or a person empowered to license access thereto, had authorized him to access; or

  (b) The person reasonably believed that the owner of the computer system, or a person empowered to license access thereto, would have authorized him to access without payment of any consideration; or

  (c) The person reasonably could not have known that his access was unauthorized.

  II. A person is guilty of the computer crime of theft of computer services when he knowingly accesses or causes to be accessed or otherwise uses or causes to be used a computer system with the purpose of obtaining unauthorized computer services.

  III. A person is guilty of the computer crime of interruption of computer services when he, without authorization, knowingly or recklessly disrupts or degrades or causes the disruption or degradation of computer services or denies or causes the denial of computer services to an authorized user of a computer system.

  IV. A person is guilty of the computer crime of misuse of computer system information when:

  (a) As a result of his accessing or causing to be accessed a computer system, he knowingly makes or causes to be made an unauthorized display, use, disclosure, or copy, in any form, of data residing in, communicated by, or produced by a computer system; or

  (b) He knowingly or recklessly and without authorization:

  (1) Alters, deletes, tampers with, damages, destroys, or takes data intended for use by a computer system, whether residing within or external to a computer system; or

  (2) Intercepts or adds to data residing within a computer system; or

  (c) He knowingly receives or retains data obtained in violation of subparagraph (a) or (b) of this paragraph; or

(d) He knowingly uses or discloses any data he knows or believes was obtained in violation of subparagraph (a) or (b) of this paragraph.

V. A person is guilty of the computer crime of destruction of computer equipment when he, without authorization, knowingly or recklessly tampers with, takes, transfers, conceals, alters, damages, or destroys any equipment used in a computer system or knowingly or recklessly causes any of the foregoing to occur.

638:18. Computer Crime Penalties

I. Computer crime constitutes a class A felony if the damage to or the value of the property or computer services exceeds $1,000.

II. Computer crime constitutes a class B felony if:

(a) The damage to or the value of the property or computer services exceeds $500; or

(b) The person recklessly engages in conduct which creates a risk of serious physical injury to another person.

III. Computer crime is a misdemeanor if the damage to or the value of the property or computer services, if any, is $500 or less.

IV. If a person has gained money, property, or services or other consideration through the commission of any offense under RSA 638:17, upon conviction thereof, the court, in addition to any sentence of imprisonment or other form of sentence authorized by RSA 651, may, in lieu of imposing a fine, sentence the defendant to pay an amount, fixed by the court, not to exceed double the amount of the defendant's gain from the commission of such offense. In such case, the court shall make a finding as to the amount of the defendant's gain from the offense and, if the record does not contain sufficient evidence to support such finding, the court may conduct a hearing upon the issue. For the purpose of this section, "gain" means the amount of money or the value of property or computer services or other consideration derived.

V. For the purposes of this section:

(a) The value of property or computer services shall be:

(1) The market value of the property or computer services at the time of the violation; or

(2) If the property or computer services are unrecoverable, damaged, or destroyed as a result of a violation of RSA 638:17 the cost of reproducing or replacing the property or computer services at the time of the violation.

(b) Amounts included in violations of RSA 638:17 committed pursuant to one scheme or course of conduct, whether from the same person or several persons, may be aggregated in determining the grade of the offense.

(c) When the value of the property or computer services or damage thereto cannot be satisfactorily ascertained, the value shall be deemed to be $250.

638:19. Venue

I. In any prosecution for a violation of RSA 638:17 the offense shall be deemed to have been committed in the town in which the act occurred or in which the computer system or part thereof involved in the violation was located.

II. In any prosecution for a violation of RSA 638:17 based upon more than one act in violation thereof, the offense shall be deemed to have been committed in any of the towns in which any of the acts occurred or in which a computer system or part thereof involved in a violation was located.

III. If any act performed in furtherance of the offenses prohibited by RSA 638:17 occurs in this state or if any computer system or part thereof accessed in violation of RSA 638:17 is located in this state, the offense shall be deemed to have occurred in this state.

NEW JERSEY STATUTES

TITLE 2A. ADMINISTRATION OF CIVIL AND CRIMINAL JUSTICE
SUBTITLE 6. SPECIFIC CIVIL ACTIONS
CHAPTER 38A COMPUTER SYSTEM

2A:38A-1. Definitions

As used in this act:

a. "Access" means to instruct, communicate with, store data in, retrieve data from, or otherwise make use of any resources of a computer, computer system, or computer network.

b. "Computer" means an electronic device or another similar device capable of executing a computer program, including arithmetic, logic, memory or input-output operations, by the manipulation of electronic or magnetic impulses and includes all computer equipment connected to such a device in a computer system or network.

c. "Computer equipment" means any equipment or devices, including all input, output, processing, storage, software, or communications facilities, intended to interface with the computer.

d. "Computer network" means the interconnection of communication lines, including microwave or other means of electronic communication, with a computer through remote terminals, or a complex consisting of two or more interconnected computers.

e. "Computer program" means a series of instructions or statements executable on a computer, which directs the computer system in a manner to produce a desired result.

f. "Computer software" means a set of computer programs, data, procedures, and associated documentation concerned with the operation of a computer system.

g. "Computer system" means a set of interconnected computer equipment intended to operate as a cohesive system.

h. "Data" means information, facts, concepts, or instructions prepared for use in a computer, computer system, or computer network.

i. "Data base" means a collection of data.

j. "Financial instrument" includes but is not limited to a check, draft, warrant, money order, note, certificate of deposit, letter of credit, bill of exchange, credit or debit card, transaction authorization mechanism, marketable security and any computer representation of these items.

k. "Property" includes but is not limited to financial instruments, information, data, and computer software, in either human readable or computer-readable form, copies or originals, and any other tangible or intangible item of value.

l. "Services" includes but is not limited to the use of a computer system, computer network, computer programs, data prepared for computer use and data contained within a computer system or computer network.

2A:38A-2. Value of property or services

For the purposes of this act, the value of any property or services, including the use of computer time, shall be their fair market value, if it is determined that a willing buyer and willing seller exist. Alternatively, value shall include but not be limited to the cost of generating or obtaining data and storing it within a computer or computer system.

2A:38A-3. Computer-related offenses; compensatory and punitive damages; costs and expenses

A person or enterprise damaged in business or property as a result of any of the following actions may sue the actor therefor in the Superior Court and may recover compensatory and punitive damages and the cost of the suit, including a reasonable attorney's fee, costs of investigation and litigation:

a. The purposeful or knowing, and unauthorized altering, damaging, taking or destruction of any data, data base, computer program, computer software or computer equipment existing internally or externally to a computer, computer system or computer network;

b. The purposeful or knowing, and unauthorized altering, damaging, taking or destroying of a computer, computer system or computer network;

c. The purposeful or knowing, and unauthorized accessing or attempt to access any computer, computer system or computer network;

d. The purposeful or knowing, and unauthorized altering, accessing, tampering with, obtaining, intercepting, damaging or destroying of a financial instrument; or

e. The purposeful or knowing accessing and reckless altering, damaging, destroying or obtaining of any data, data base, computer, computer program, computer software, computer equipment, computer system or computer network.

2A:38A-4. Value of loss; finding of fact

The value of damage, loss, property or income involved in any lawsuit shall be determined by the trier of fact.

2A:38A-5. Injunctions

In addition to any other action or proceeding authorized by law, the Attorney General, or a person or enterprise alleging injury or loss may bring an action in Superior Court to enjoin actions causing damage as described in this act or to enjoin any acts in furtherance thereof.

2A:38A-6. Venue of action

Actions brought under this act may be filed in the Superior Court of the county in which the computer which is accessed is located, or where the terminal used in the accessing is situated, or where the actual damage occurs.

TITLE 2C. THE NEW JERSEY CODE OF CRIMINAL JUSTICE SUBTITLE 2. DEFINITION OF SPECIFIC OFFENSES PART 2. OFFENSES AGAINST PROPERTY CHAPTER 20. THEFT AND RELATED OFFENSES

I. GENERAL PROVISIONS

2C:20-1. Definitions

In chapters 20 and 21, unless a different meaning plainly is required:

a. "Deprive" means: (1) to withhold or cause to be withheld property of another permanently or for so extended a period as to appropriate a substantial portion of its economic value, or with purpose to restore only upon payment of reward or other compensation; or (2) to dispose or cause disposal of the property so as to make it unlikely that the owner will recover it.

b. "Fiduciary" means an executor, general administrator of an intestate, administrator with the will annexed, substituted administrator, guardian, substituted guardian, trustee under any trust, express, implied, resulting or constructive, substituted trustee, executor, conservator, curator, receiver, trustee in bankruptcy, assignee for the benefit of creditors, partner, agent or officer of a corporation, public or private, temporary administrator, administrator, administrator pendente lite, administrator ad prosequendum, administrator ad litem or other person acting in a similar capacity.

c. "Financial institution" means a bank, insurance company, credit union, savings and loan association, investment trust or other organization held out to the public as a place of deposit of funds or medium of savings or collective investment.

d. "Government" means the United States, any state, county, municipality, or other political unit, or any department, agency or subdivision of any of the foregoing, or any corporation or other association carrying out the functions of government.

e. "Movable property" means property the location of which can be changed, including things growing on, affixed to, or found in land, and documents, although the rights represented thereby have no physical location. "Immovable property" is all other property.

f. "Obtain" means: (1) in relation to property, to bring about a transfer or purported transfer of a legal interest in the property, whether to the obtainer or another; or (2) in relation to labor or service, to secure performance thereof.

g. "Property" means anything of value, including real estate, tangible and intangible personal property, trade secrets, contract rights, chooses in action and other interests in or claims to wealth, admission or transportation tickets, captured or domestic animals, food and drink, electric, gas, steam or other power, financial instruments, information, data, and computer software, in either human readable or computer readable form, copies or originals.

h. "Property of another" includes property in which any person other than the actor has an interest which the actor is not privileged to infringe, regardless of the fact that the actor also has an interest in the property and regardless of the fact that the other person might be precluded from civil recovery because the property was used in an unlawful transaction or was subject to forfeiture as contraband. Property in possession of the actor shall not be deemed property of another who has only a security interest therein, even if legal title is in the creditor pursuant to a conditional sales contract or other security agreement.

i. "Trade secret" means the whole or any portion or phase of any scientific or technical information, design, process, procedure, formula or improvement which is secret and of value. A trade secret shall be presumed to be secret when the owner thereof takes measures to prevent it from becoming available to persons other than those selected by the owner to have access thereto for limited purposes.

j. "Dealer in property" means a person who buys and sells property as a business.

k. "Traffic" means:

(1) To sell, transfer, distribute, dispense or otherwise dispose of property to another person; or

(2) To buy, receive, possess, or obtain control of or use property, with intent to sell, transfer, distribute, dispense or otherwise dispose of such property to another person.

l. "Broken succession of title" means lack of regular documents of purchase and transfer by any seller except the manufacturer of the subject property, or possession of documents of purchase and transfer by any buyer without corresponding documents of sale and transfer in possession of seller, or possession of documents of sale and transfer by seller without corresponding documents of purchase and transfer in possession of any buyer.

m. "Person" includes any individual or entity or enterprise, as defined herein, holding or capable of holding a legal or beneficial interest in property.

n. "Anything of value" means any direct or indirect gain or advantage to any person.

o. "Interest in property which has been stolen" means title or right of possession to such property.

p. "Stolen property" means property that has been the subject of any unlawful taking.

q. "Enterprise" includes any individual, sold proprietorship, partnership, corporation, business trust, association, or other legal entity, and any union or group of individuals associated in fact, although not a legal entity, and it includes illicit as well as licit enterprises and governmental as well as other entities.

r. "Attorney General" includes the Attorney General of New Jersey, his assistants and deputies. The term shall also include a county prosecutor or his designated assistant prosecutor, if a county prosecutor is expressly authorized in writing by the Attorney General to carry out the powers conferred on the Attorney General by this chapter.

II. COMPUTER-RELATED CRIMES

2C:20-23. Definitions

As used in this act:

a. "Access" means to instruct, communicate with, store data in, retrieve data from, or otherwise make use of any resources of a computer, computer system, or computer network.

b. "Computer" means an electronic device or another similar device capable of executing a computer program, including arithmetic, logic, memory or input-output operations, by the manipulation of electronic or magnetic impulses and includes all computer equipment connected to such a device in a computer system or network.

c. "Computer equipment" means any equipment or devices, including all input, output, processing, storage, software, or communications facilities, intended to interface with the computer.

d. "Computer network" means the interconnection of communication lines, including microwave or other means of electronic communications, with a computer through remote terminals, or a complex consisting of two or more interconnected computers.

e. "Computer program" means a series of instructions or statements executable on a computer, which directs the computer system in a manner to produce a desired result.

f. "Computer software" means a set of computer programs, data, procedures, and associated documentation concerned with the operation of a computer system.

g. "Computer system" means a set of interconnected computer equipment intended to operate as a cohesive system.

h. "Data" means information, facts, concepts, or instructions prepared for use in a computer, computer system, or computer network.

i. "Data base" means a collection of data.

j. "Financial instrument" includes but is not limited to a check, draft, warrant, money order, note, certificate of deposit, letter of credit, bill of exchange, credit or debit card, transaction authorization mechanism, marketable security and any computer representation of these items.

k. "Services" includes but is not limited to the use of a computer system, computer network, computer programs, data prepared for computer use and data contained within a computer system or computer network.

2C:20-24. Value of property or services

For the purposes of this act, the value of any property or services, including the use of computer time, shall be their fair market value, if it is determined that a willing buyer and willing seller exist. Alternatively, value shall include but not be limited to the cost of generating or obtaining data and storing it within a computer or computer system.

2C:20-25. Computer-related theft

A person is guilty of theft if he purposely or knowingly and without authorization:

a. Alters, damages, takes or destroys any data, data base, computer program, computer software or

computer equipment existing internally or externally to a computer, computer system or computer network;

b. Alters, damages, takes or destroys a computer, computer system or computer network;

c. Accesses or attempts to access any computer, computer system or computer network for the purpose of executing a scheme to defraud, or to obtain services, property, or money, from the owner of a computer or any third party; or

d. Alters, tampers with, obtains, intercepts, damages or destroys a financial instrument.

2C:20-26. Property or services of $75,000 or more; degree of crime

a. Theft under section 4 of this act constitutes a crime of the second degree if the offense results in the altering, damaging, destruction or obtaining of property or services with a value of $75,000.00 or more. It shall also be a crime of the second degree if the offense results in a substantial interruption or impairment of public communication, transportation, supply of water, gas or power, or other public service.

b. A person is guilty of a crime of the third degree if he purposely or knowingly accesses and recklessly alters, damages, destroys or obtains any data, data base, computer, computer program, computer software, computer equipment, computer system or computer network with a value of $75,000.00 or more.

2C:20-27. Property or services between $500 and $75,000; degree of crime

a. Theft under section 4 of this act constitutes a crime of the third degree if the offense results in the altering, damaging, destruction, or obtaining of property or services with a value of at least $500.00 but less than $75,000.00.

b. A person is guilty of a crime of the fourth degree if he purposely or knowingly accesses and recklessly alters, damages, destroys or obtains any data, data base, computer, computer program, computer software, computer equipment, computer system or computer network with a value of at least $500.00 but less than $75,000.00.

2C:20-28. Property or services between $200 and $500; degree of crime

a. Theft under section 4 of this act constitutes a crime of the fourth degree if the offense results in the altering, damaging, destruction or obtaining of property or services with a value of more than $200.00 but less than $500.00.

b. A person is guilty of a disorderly persons offense if he purposely or knowingly accesses and recklessly alters, damages, destroys or obtains any data, data base, computer, computer program, computer software, computer equipment, computer system or computer network with a value of more than $200.00 but less than $500.00.

2C:20-29. Property or services of $200 or less; disorderly persons offense

a. Theft under section 4 of this act constitutes a disorderly persons offense when the offense results in the altering, damaging, destruction or obtaining of property or services with a value of $200.00 or less.

b. A person is guilty of a petty disorderly persons offense if he purposely or knowingly accesses and recklessly alters, damages, destroys or obtains any data, data base, computer, computer program, computer software, computer equipment, computer system or computer network with a value of $200.00 or less.

2C:20-30. Damage or wrongful access to computer system; no assessable damage; degree of crime

A person is guilty of a crime of the third degree if he purposely and without authorization accesses, alters, damages or destroys a computer system or any of its parts, where the accessing and altering cannot be assessed a monetary value or loss.

2C:20-31. Disclosure of data from wrongful access; no assessable damage; degree of crime

A person is guilty of a crime of the third degree if he purposely and without authorization accesses a computer system or any of its parts and directly or indirectly discloses or causes to be disclosed data, data base, computer software or computer programs, where the accessing and disclosing cannot be assessed a monetary value or loss.

2C:20-32. Wrongful access to computer; lack of damage or destruction; disorderly persons offense

A person is guilty of a disorderly persons offense if he purposely and without authorization accesses a computer or any of its parts and this action does not result in the altering, damaging or destruction of any property or services.

2C:20-33. Copy or alteration of program or software with value of $1,000 or less

The copying or altering of a computer program or computer software shall not constitute theft for the purposes of chapters 20 and 21 of Title 2C of the New Jersey Statutes or any offense under this act, if the computer program or computer software is of a retail value of $1,000.00 or less and is not copied for resale.

2C:20-34. Situs of offense

For the purpose of prosecution under this act, the situs of an offense of theft shall be the location of the computer which is accessed, or where the terminal used in the offense is situated, or where the actual damage occurs.

NEW MEXICO STATUTES

CHAPTER 15 ADMINISTRATION OF GOVERNMENT
ARTICLE 1 INFORMATION SYSTEMS

15-1-9. Records of state agencies; public records; copy fees; computer data bases; criminal penalty.

A. Except as otherwise provided by federal or state law, information contained in information systems data bases shall be a public record and shall be subject to disclosure in printed or typed format by the state agency which has inserted that information into the data base, in accordance with the Public Records Act [14-3-1 to 14-3-16, 14-3-18 NMSA 1978], upon the payment of a reasonable fee for the service.

B. The secretary shall recommend to the state commission of public records the procedures, schedules and technical standards for the retention of computer data bases.

C. The state agency which has inserted data in a data base, with the approval of the secretary, may authorize a copy to be made of a computer tape or other medium containing a computerized data base of a public record for any person if the person agrees:

(1) not to make unauthorized copies of the data base;

(2) not to use the data base for any political or commercial purpose unless the purpose and use is approved in writing by the secretary and the state agency that created the data base;

(3) not to use the data base for solicitation or advertisement when the data base contains the name, address or telephone number of any person unless such use is otherwise specifically authorized by law;

(4) not to allow access to the data base by any other person unless the use is approved in writing by the council and the state agency that created the data base; and

(5) to pay a royalty or other consideration to the state as may be agreed upon by the secretary and the state agency that created the data base.

D. If more than one state agency is responsible for the information inserted in the data base, a single state agency shall be designated by the secretary to carry out the responsibilities set forth in this section.

E. Subject to any confidentiality provisions of law, any state agency may permit another state agency access to all or any portion of a computerized data base created by a state agency.

F. If information contained in a data base is searched, manipulated or retrieved or a copy of the data base is made for any private or nonpublic use, a fee to be prescribed by rule of the secretary shall be charged by the state agency permitting access or use of the data base.

G. Except as authorized by law or rule of the secretary, any person who reveals to any unauthorized person information contained in a computer data base or who uses or permits the unauthorized use or access of any computer data base is guilty of a misdemeanor and upon conviction the court shall sentence such person to jail for a definite term not to exceed one year or to payment of a fine not to exceed five thousand dollars ($5,000) or both. Such person shall not be employed by the state for a period of five years after the date of conviction.

CHAPTER 30 CRIMINAL OFFENSES
ARTICLE 45 COMPUTER CRIMES

30-45-1. Short title.

This act [30-45-1 to 30-45-7 NMSA 1978] may be cited as the "Computer Crimes Act".

30-45-2. Definitions.

As used in the Computer Crimes Act [30-45-1 to 30-45-7 NMSA 1978]:

A. "access" means to program, execute programs on, intercept, instruct, communicate with, store data in, retrieve data from or otherwise make use of any computer resources, including data or programs of a computer, computer system, computer network or database;

B. "computer" includes an electronic, magnetic, optical or other high-speed data processing device or system performing logical, arithmetic or storage functions and includes any property, data storage facility or communications facility directly related to or operating in conjunction with such device or system. The term does not include an automated typewriter or typesetter or a single display machine in and of itself, designed and used solely within itself for word processing, or a portable hand-held calculator, or any other device which might contain components similar to those in computers but in which the components have the sole function of controlling the device for the single purpose for which the device is intended;

C. "computer network" means the interconnection of communication lines and circuits with a computer or a complex consisting of two or more interconnected computers;

D. "computer program" means a series of instructions or statements, in a form acceptable to a computer, which permits the functioning of a computer system in a manner designed to provide appropriate products from a computer system;

E. "computer property" includes a financial instrument, data, databases, computer software, computer programs, documents associated with computer systems and computer programs, or copies, whether tangible or intangible, and data while in transit;

F. "computer service" includes computer time, the use of the computer system, computer network, computer programs or data prepared for computer use, data contained within a computer network and data processing and other functions performed, in whole or in part, by the use of computers, computer systems, computer networks or computer software;

G. "computer software" means a set of computer programs, procedures and associated documentation concerned with the operation and function of a computer system;

H. "computer system" means a set of related or interconnected computer equipment, devices and software;

I. "data" means a representation of information, knowledge, facts, concepts or instructions which are prepared and are intended for use in a computer, computer system or computer network;

J. "database" means any data or other information classified, processed, transmitted, received, retrieved, originated, switched, stored, manifested, measured, detected, recorded, reproduced, handled or utilized by a computer, computer system, computer network or computer software; and

K. "financial instrument" includes any check, draft, warrant, money order, note, certificate of deposit, letter of credit, bill of exchange, credit or debit card, transaction, authorization mechanism, marketable security or any other computerized representation thereof.

30-45-3. Computer access with intent to defraud or embezzle.

Any person who knowingly and willfully accesses or causes to be accessed any computer, computer system, computer network or any part thereof with the intent to obtain, by means of embezzlement or false or fraudulent pretenses, representations or promises, money, property or anything of value, where:

A. the money, property or other thing has a value of one hundred dollars ($100) or less is guilty of a petty misdemeanor;

B. the money, property or other thing has a value of more than one hundred dollars ($100) but not more than two hundred fifty dollars ($250) is guilty of a misdemeanor and shall be sentenced pursuant to the provisions of Section 31-19-1 NMSA 1978;

C. the money, property or other thing has a value of more than two hundred fifty dollars ($250) but not more than two thousand five hundred dollars ($2,500) is guilty of a fourth degree felony and shall be sentenced pursuant to the provisions of Section 31-18-15 NMSA 1978;

D. the money, property or other thing has a value of more than two thousand five hundred dollars ($2,500) but not more than twenty thousand dollars ($20,000) is guilty of a third degree felony and shall be sentenced pursuant to the provisions of Section 31-18-15 NMSA 1978; or

E. the money, property or other thing has a value of more than twenty thousand dollars ($20,000) is guilty of a second degree felony and shall be sentenced pursuant to the provisions of Section 31-18-15 NMSA 1978.

30-45-4. Computer abuse.

Any person who knowingly, willfully and without authorization, or having obtained authorization:

A. directly or indirectly alters, changes, damages, disrupts or destroys any computer, computer network, computer property, computer service or computer system where:

(1) the damage to the computer property or computer service has a value of one hundred dollars ($100) or less is guilty of a petty misdemeanor;

(2) the damage to the computer property or computer service has a value of more than one hundred dollars ($100) but not more than two hundred fifty dollars ($250) is guilty of a misdemeanor and shall be sentenced pursuant to the provisions of Section 31-19-1 NMSA 1978;

(3) the damage to the computer property or computer service has a value of more than two hundred fifty dollars ($250) but not more than two thousand five hundred dollars ($2,500) is guilty of a fourth degree felony and shall be sentenced pursuant to the provisions of Section 31-18-15 NMSA 1978;

(4) the damage to the computer property or computer service has a value of more than two thousand five hundred dollars ($2,500) but not more than twenty thousand dollars ($20,000) is guilty of a third degree felony and shall be sentenced pursuant to the provisions of Section 31-18-15 NMSA 1978; or

(5) the damage to the computer property or computer service has a value of more than twenty thousand dollars ($20,000) is guilty of a second degree felony and shall be sentenced pursuant to the provisions of Section 31-18-15 NMSA 1978; or

B. directly or indirectly introduces or causes to be introduced data which the person knows to be false into a computer, computer system, computer network, computer software, computer program, database or any part thereof with the intent of harming the property or financial interests or rights of any person is guilty of a fourth degree felony and shall be sentenced pursuant to the provisions of Section 31-18-15 NMSA 1978.

30-45-5. Unauthorized computer use.

Any person who knowingly, willfully and without authorization, or having obtained authorization, uses the opportunity such authorization provides for purposes to which the authorization does not extend, directly or indirectly accesses, uses, takes, transfers, conceals, obtains, copies, or retains possession of any computer, computer network, computer property, computer service, computer system or any part thereof where:

A. the damage to the computer property or computer service has a value of one hundred dollars ($100) or less is guilty of a petty misdemeanor;

B. the damage to the computer property or computer service has a value of more than one hundred dollars ($100) but not more than two hundred fifty dollars ($250) is guilty of a misdemeanor and shall be sentenced pursuant to the provisions of Section 31-19-1 NMSA 1978;

C. the damage to the computer property or computer service has a value of more than two hundred fifty dollars ($250) but not more than two thousand five hundred dollars ($2,500) is guilty of a fourth degree felony and shall be sentenced pursuant to the provisions of Section 31-18-15 NMSA 1978;

D. the damage to the computer property or computer service has a value of more than two thousand five hundred dollars ($2,500) but not more than twenty thousand dollars ($20,000) is guilty of a third degree felony and shall be sentenced pursuant to the provisions of Section 31-18-15 NMSA 1978; or

E. the damage to the computer property or computer service has a value of more than twenty thousand dollars ($20,000) is guilty of a second degree felony and shall be sentenced pursuant to the provisions of Section 31-18-15 NMSA 1978.

30-45-6. Prosecution.

A. Prosecution pursuant to the Computer Crimes Act [30-45-1 to 30-45-7 NMSA 1978] shall not prevent any prosecutions pursuant to any other provisions of the law where such conduct also constitutes a violation of that other provision.

B. A person found guilty of violating any provision of the Computer Crimes Act shall, in addition to any other punishment, be ordered to make restitution for any financial loss sustained by anyone injured as the direct result of the commission of the crime. Restitution shall be imposed in addition to incarceration, forfeiture or fine, and not in lieu thereof, and may be made a condition of probation. The defendant's present and future ability to make such restitution shall be considered. In an extraordinary case, the court may determine that the interests of those injured and justice would not be served by ordering restitution. In such a case, the court shall make and enter specific written findings on the record substantiating the extraordinary circumstance presented upon which the court determined not to order restitution. In all other cases, the court shall determine the amount and method of restitution.

30-45-7. Forfeiture of property.

A. The following are subject to forfeiture:

(1) all computer property, equipment or products of any kind which have been used, manufactured, acquired or distributed in violation of the Computer Crimes Act [30-45-1 to 30-45-7 NMSA 1978];

(2) all materials, products and equipment of any kind which are used or intended for use in manufacturing, using, accessing, altering, disrupting, copying, concealing, destroying, transferring, delivering, importing or exporting any computer property or computer service in violation of the Computer Crimes Act;

(3) all books, records and research products and materials involving formulas, microfilm, tapes and data which are used or intended for use in violation of the Computer Crimes Act;

(4) all conveyances, including aircraft, vehicles or vessels, which are used or intended for use to transport or in any manner to facilitate the transportation of property described in Subsection A, B or C of this section for the purpose of violating the Computer Crimes Act;

(5) all property, real, personal or mixed, which has been used or intended for use, maintained or acquired in violation of the Computer Crimes Act; and

(6) all money or proceeds that constitute an instrumentality or derive from a violation of the Computer Crimes Act.

B. Notwithstanding the provisions of Paragraphs (1) through (6) of Subsection A of this section:

(1) no conveyance used by any person as a common carrier in the transaction of business as a common carrier is subject to forfeiture under this section unless it appears that the owner or other person in charge of the conveyance is a consenting party to a violation of the Computer Crimes Act;

(2) no conveyance, computer property, equipment or other material is subject to forfeiture under this section by reason of any act or omission established by the owner to have been committed or omitted without his knowledge or consent;

(3) a conveyance, computer property, equipment or other material is not subject to forfeiture for a violation of law the penalty for which is a misdemeanor or petty misdemeanor; and

(4) a forfeiture of a conveyance, computer property, equipment or material encumbered by a bona fide security interest shall be subject to the interest of a secured party if the secured party neither had knowledge of nor consented to the act or omission.

C. Property subject to forfeiture and disposal under the Computer Crimes Act may be seized by any law enforcement officer upon an order issued by the district court having jurisdiction.

D. Seizure without such an order may be made if:

(1) the seizure is incident to an arrest or search under a search warrant;

(2) the property subject to seizure had been the subject of a prior judgment in favor of the state in an injunction or forfeiture proceeding based upon the Computer Crimes Act; or

(3) the enforcement officer has probable cause to believe that the property, whether real, personal or mixed, was used or intended for use, maintained or acquired in violation of the Computer Crimes Act.

E. In the event of a seizure pursuant to Subsection C or Subsection D of this section, a proceeding under the Computer Crimes Act and the rules of civil procedure for the district courts shall be instituted promptly and not later than thirty days after seizure. The proceeding to forfeit property under the Computer Crimes Act is against the property and not against the owner or any other person. It is in rem wholly and not in personam. It is a civil case and not a criminal proceeding. The forfeiture proceeding is required, not to complete the forfeiture, but to prove the illegal use for which the forfeiture was suffered.

F. Except as otherwise specifically provided by law, whenever any property is forfeited to the state by reason of the violation of any law, the court by which the offender is convicted shall order the sale or other disposition of the property and the proceeds of any such sale as provided for in this section are subject to the court making due provisions for the rights of innocent persons and the legitimate rights to restitution on behalf of actual victims of the criminal acts.

G. Property taken or detained under this section shall not be subject to replevin but is deemed to be in the custody of the law enforcement agency seizing it subject only to the orders and decrees of the district court. When property is seized under the Computer Crimes Act, the enforcement officer may:

(1) place the property under seal;

(2) remove the property to a place designated by the law enforcement officer or by the district court; or

(3) require the law enforcement agency to take custody of the property and remove it to an appropriate location for disposition in accordance with law.

H. When property is forfeited under the Computer Crimes Act, the law enforcement agency seizing it shall:

(1) deliver custody of the property to the information systems council attached to the general services department. The council, based upon a plan, shall advertise and make available the forfeited property to stated agencies and political subdivisions of the state based upon a demonstrated need and plan of use for that property. The information systems council shall advertise and make the forfeited property available by bid for a minimum of one hundred twenty days and dispose of that property within another sixty days. All proceeds from the sale of forfeited property shall be deposited in the general fund; or

(2) where the court orders the property to be sold, the proceeds of the sale shall be paid into the general fund.

NEW YORK STATUTES

TITLE J OFFENSES INVOLVING THEFT
ARTICLE 155 LARCENY

155.00 Larceny; definitions of terms.

The following definitions are applicable to this title:

1. "Property" means any money, personal property, real property, computer data, computer program, thing in action, evidence of debt or contract, or any article, substance or thing of value, including any gas, steam, water or electricity, which is provided for a charge or compensation.

2. "Obtain" includes, but is not limited to, the bringing about of a transfer or purported transfer of property or of a legal interest therein, whether to the obtainer or another.

3. "Deprive." To "deprive" another of property means (a) to withhold it or cause it to be withheld from him permanently or for so extended a period or under such circumstances that the major portion of its economic value or benefit is lost to him, or (b) to dispose of the property in such manner or under such circumstances as to render it unlikely that an owner will recover such property.

4. "Appropriate." To "appropriate" property of another to oneself or a third person means (a) to exercise control over it, or to aid a third person to exercise control over it, permanently or for so extended a period or under such circumstances as to acquire the major portion of its economic value or benefit, or (b) to dispose of the property for the benefit of oneself or a third person.

5. "Owner." When property is taken, obtained or withheld by one person from another person, an "own-er" thereof means any person who has a right to possession thereof superior to that of the taker, obtainer or withholder.

A person who has obtained possession of property by theft or other illegal means shall be deemed to have a right of possession superior to that of a person who takes, obtains or withholds it from him by larcenous means.

A joint or common owner of property shall not be deemed to have a right of possession thereto superior to that of any other joint or common owner thereof.

In the absence of a specific agreement to the contrary, a person in lawful possession of property shall be deemed to have a right of possession superior to that of a person having only a security interest therein, even if legal title lies with the holder of the security interest pursuant to a conditional sale contract or other security agreement.

6. "Secret scientific material" means a sample, culture, micro-organism, specimen, record, recording, document, drawing or any other article, material, device or substance which constitutes, represents, evidences, reflects, or records a scientific or technical process, invention or formula or any part or phase thereof, and which is not, and is not intended to be, available to anyone other than the person or persons rightfully in possession thereof or selected persons having access thereto with his or their consent, and when it accords or may accord such rightful possessors an advantage over competitors or other persons who do not have knowledge or the benefit thereof.

7. "Credit card" means any instrument or article defined as a credit card in section five hundred eleven of the general business law.

7-a. "Debit card" means any instrument or article defined as a debit card in section five hundred eleven of the general business law.

8. "Service" includes, but is not limited to, labor, professional service, a computer service, transportation service, the supplying of hotel accommodations, restaurant services, entertainment, the supplying of equipment for use, and the supplying of commodities of a public utility nature such as gas, electricity, steam and water. A ticket or equivalent instrument which evidences a right to receive a service is not in itself service but constitutes property within the meaning of subdivision one.

9. "Cable television service" means any and all services provided by or through the facilities of any cable television system or closed circuit coaxial cable communications system, or any microwave or similar transmission service used in connection with any cable television system or other similar closed circuit coaxial cable communications system.

ARTICLE 156 OFFENSES INVOLVING COMPUTERS; DEFINITION OF TERMS

156.00 Offenses involving computers; definition of terms.

The following definitions are applicable to this chapter except where different meanings are expressly specified:

1. "Computer" means a device or group of devices which, by manipulation of electronic, magnetic, optical or electrochemical impulses, pursuant to a computer program, can automatically perform arithmetic, logical, storage or retrieval operations with or on computer data, and includes any connected or directly related device, equipment or facility which enables such computer to store, retrieve or communicate to or from a person, another computer or another device the results of computer operations, computer programs or computer data.

2. "Computer program" is property and means an ordered set of data representing coded instructions or statements that, when executed by computer, cause the computer to process data or direct the computer to perform one or more computer operations or both and may be in any form, including magnetic storage media, punched cards, or stored internally in the memory of the computer.

3. "Computer data" is property and means a representation of information, knowledge, facts, concepts or instructions which are being processed, or have been processed in a computer and may be in any form, including magnetic storage media, punched cards, or stored internally in the memory of the computer.

4. "Computer service" means any and all services provided by or through the facilities of any computer communication system allowing the input, output, examination, or transfer, of computer data or computer programs from one computer to another.

5. "Computer material" is property and means any computer data or computer program which:

(a) contains records of the medical history or medical treatment of an identified or readily identifiable individual or individuals. This term shall not apply to the gaining access to or duplication solely of the medical history or medical treatment records of a person by that person or by another specifically authorized by the person whose records are gained access to or duplicated;or

(b) contains records maintained by the state or any political subdivision thereof or any governmental instrumentality within the state which contains any information concerning a person, as defined in subdivision seven of section10.00 of this chapter, which because of name, number, symbol, mark or other identifier, can be used to identify the person and which is otherwise prohibited by law from being disclosed. This term shall not apply to the gaining access to or duplication solely of

records of a person by that person or by another specifically authorized by the person whose records are gained access to or duplicated; or

(c) is not and is not intended to be available to anyone other than the person or persons rightfully in possession thereof or selected persons having access thereto with his or their consent and which accords or may accord such rightful possessors an advantage over competitors or other persons who do not have knowledge or the benefit thereof.

6. "Uses a computer or computer service without authorization" means the use of a computer or computer service without the permission of, or in excess of the permission of, the owner or lessor or someone licensed or privileged by the owner or lessor after notice to that effect to the user of the computer or computer service has been given by:

(a) giving actual notice in writing or orally to the user; or

(b) prominently posting written notice adjacent to the computer being utilized by the user; or

(c) a notice that is displayed on, printed out on or announced by the computer being utilized by the user. Proof that the computer is programmed to automatically display, print or announce such notice or a notice prohibiting copying, reproduction or duplication shall be presumptive evidence that such notice was displayed, printed or announced.

7. "Felony" as used in this article means any felony defined in the laws of this state or any offense defined in the laws of any other jurisdiction for which a sentence to a term of imprisonment in excess of one year is authorized in this state.

156.05 Unauthorized use of a computer.

A person is guilty of unauthorized use of a computer when he knowingly uses or causes to be used a computer or computer service without authorization and the computer utilized is equipped or programmed with any device or coding system, a function of which is to prevent the unauthorized use of said computer or computer system.

Unauthorized use of a computer is a class A misdemeanor.

156.10 Computer trespass.

A person is guilty of computer trespass when he knowingly uses or causes to be used a computer or computer service without authorization and:

1. he does so with an intent to commit or attempt to commit or further the commission of any felony; or

2. he thereby knowingly gains access to computer material. Computer trespass is a class E felony.

156.20 Computer tampering in the second degree.

A person is guilty of computer tampering in the second degree when he uses or causes to be used a computer or computer service and having no right to do so he intentionally alters in any manner or destroys computer data or a computer program of another person.

Computer tampering in the second degree is a class A misdemeanor.

156.25 Computer tampering in the first degree.

A person is guilty of computer tampering in the first degree when he commits the crime of computer tampering in the second degree and:

1. he does so with an intent to commit or attempt to commit or further the commission of any felony; or

2. he has been previously convicted of any crime under this article or subdivision ten of section 165.15 of this chapter; or

3. he intentionally alters in any manner or destroys computer material; or

4. he intentionally alters in any manner or destroys computer data or a computer program in an amount exceeding one thousand dollars.

Computer tampering in the first degree is a class E felony.

156.30 Unlawful duplication of computer related material.

A person is guilty of unlawful duplication of computer related material when having no right to do so, he copies, reproduces or duplicates in any manner:

1. any computer data or computer program and thereby intentionally and wrongfully deprives or appropriates from an owner thereof an economic value or benefit in excess of two thousand five hundred dollars; or

2. any computer data or computer program with an intent to commit or attempt to commit or further the commission of any felony.

Unlawful duplication of computer related material is a class E felony.

156.35 Criminal possession of computer related material.

A person is guilty of criminal possession of computer related material when having no right to do so, he knowingly possesses, in any form, any copy, reproduction or duplicate of any computer data or computer program which was copied, reproduced or duplicated in violation of section 156.30 of this article, with intent to benefit himself or a person other than an owner thereof.

Criminal possession of computer related material is a class E felony.

156.50 Offenses involving computers; defenses.

In any prosecution:

1. under section 156.05 or 156.10 of this article, it shall be a defense that the defendant had reasonable grounds to believe that he had authorization to use the computer;

2. under section 156.20 or 156.25 of this article it shall be a defense that the defendant had reasonable grounds to believe that he had the right to alter in any manner or destroy the computer data or the computer program;

3. under section 156.30 of this article it shall be a defense that the defendant had reasonable grounds to believe that he had the right to copy, reproduce or duplicate in any manner the computer data or the computer program.

ARTICLE 165 OTHER OFFENSES RELATING TO THEFT

165.15 Theft of services.

A person is guilty of theft of services when:

1. He obtains or attempts to obtain a service, or induces or attempts to induce the supplier of a rendered service to agree to payment therefor on a credit basis, by the use of a credit card or debit card which he knows to be stolen.

2. With intent to avoid payment for restaurant services rendered, or for services rendered to him as a transient guest at a hotel, motel, inn, tourist cabin, rooming house or comparable establishment, he avoids or attempts to avoid such payment by unjustifiable failure or refusal to pay, by stealth, or by any misrepresentation of fact which he knows to be false. A person who fails or refuses to pay for such services is presumed to have intended to avoid payment therefor; or

3. With intent to obtain railroad, subway, bus, air, taxi or any other public transportation service without payment of the lawful charge therefor, or to avoid payment of the lawful charge for such transportation service which has been rendered to him, he obtains or attempts to obtain such service or avoids or attempts to avoid payment therefor by force, intimidation, stealth, deception or mechanical tampering, or by unjustifiable failure or refusal to pay; or

4. With intent to avoid payment by himself or another person of the lawful charge for any telecommunications service, including, without limitation, cable television service, or any gas, steam, sewer, water, electrical, telegraph or telephone service which is provided for a charge or compensation, he obtains or attempts to obtain such service for himself or another person or avoids or attempts to avoid payment therefor by himself

or another person by means of (a) tampering or making connection with the equipment of the supplier, whether by mechanical, electrical, acoustical or other means, or (b) offering for sale or otherwise making available, to anyone other than the provider of a telecommunications service for such service provider's own use in the provision of its service, any telecommunications decoder or descrambler, a principal function of which defeats a mechanism of electronic signal encryption, jamming or individually addressed switching imposed by the provider of any such telecommunications service to restrict the delivery of such service, or (c) any misrepresentation of fact which he knows to be false, or (d) any other artifice, trick, deception, code or device. For the purposes of this subdivision the telecommunications decoder or descrambler described in paragraph (b) above or the device described in paragraph (d) above shall not include any non-decoding and non-descrambling channel frequency converter or any television receiver type-accepted by the federal communications commission. In any prosecution under this subdivision, proof that telecommunications equipment, including, without limitation, any cable television converter, descrambler, or related equipment, has been tampered with or otherwise intentionally prevented from performing its functions of control of service delivery without the consent of the supplier of the service, or that telecommunications equipment, including, without limitation, any cable television converter, descrambler, receiver, or related equipment, has been connected to the equipment of the supplier of the service without the consent of the supplier of the service, shall be presumptive evidence that the resident to whom the service which is at the time being furnished by or through such equipment has, with intent to avoid payment by himself or another person for a prospective or already rendered service, created or caused to be created with reference to such equipment, the condition so existing. A person who tampers with such a device or equipment without the consent of the supplier of the service is presumed to do so with intent to avoid, or to enable another to avoid, payment for the service involved. In any prosecution under this subdivision, proof that any telecommunications decoder or descrambler, a principal function of which defeats a mechanism of electronic signal encryption, jamming or individually addressed switching imposed by the provider of any such telecommunications service to restrict the delivery of such service, has been offered for sale or otherwise made available by anyone other than the supplier of such service shall be presumptive evidence that the person offering such equipment for sale or otherwise making it available has, with intent to avoid payment by himself or another person of the lawful charge for such service, obtained or attempted to obtain such service for himself or another person or avoided or attempted to avoid payment therefor by himself or another person; or

5. With intent to avoid payment by himself or another person for a prospective or already rendered service the charge or compensation for which is measured by a meter or other mechanical device, he tampers with such device or with other equipment related thereto, or in any manner attempts to prevent the meter or device from performing its measuring function, without the consent of the supplier of the service. In any prosecution under this subdivision, proof that a meter or related equipment has been tampered with or otherwise intentionally prevented from performing its measuring function without the consent of the supplier of the service shall be presumptive evidence that the person to whom the service which is at the time being furnished by or through such meter or related equipment has, with intent to avoid payment by himself or another person for a prospective or already rendered service, created or caused to be created with reference to such meter or related equipment, the condition so existing. A person who tampers with such a device or equipment without the consent of the supplier of the service is presumed to do so with intent to avoid, or to enable another to avoid, payment for the service involved; or

6. He knowingly accepts or receives the use and benefit of service, including gas, steam or electricity service, which should pass through a meter but has been diverted therefrom, or which has been prevented from being correctly registered by a meter provided therefor, or which has been diverted from the pipes, wires or conductors of the supplier thereof. In any prosecution under this subdivision proof that service has been intentionally diverted from passing through a meter, or has been intentionally prevented from being correctly registered by a meter provided therefor, or has been intentionally diverted from the pipes, wires or conductors of the supplier thereof, shall be presumptive evidence that the person who accepts or receives the use and benefit of such service has done so with knowledge of the condition so existing; or

7. With intent to obtain, without the consent of the supplier thereof, gas, electricity, water, steam or telephone service, he tampers with any equipment designed to supply or to prevent the supply of such service either to the community in general or to particular premises; or

8. With intent to avoid payment of the lawful charge for admission to any theater or concert hall, or with intent to avoid payment of the lawful charge for admission to or use of a chair lift, gondola, rope-tow or similar mechanical device utilized in assisting skiers in transportation to a point of ski arrival or departure, he obtains or attempts to obtain such admission without payment of the lawful charge therefor.

9. Obtaining or having control over labor in the employ of another person, or of business, commercial or industrial equipment or facilities of another person, knowing that he is not entitled to the use thereof, and with intent to derive a commercial or other substantial benefit for himself or a third person, he uses or diverts to the use of himself or a third person such labor, equipment or facilities.

10. With intent to avoid payment by himself or another person of the lawful charge for use of any computer or computer service which is provided for a charge or compensation he uses, causes to be used or attempts to use a computer or computer service and avoids or attempts to avoid payment therefor. In any prosecution under this subdivision proof that a person overcame or attempted to overcome any device or coding system a function of which is to prevent the unauthorized use of said computer or computer service shall be presumptive evidence of an intent to avoid payment for the computer or computer service.

Theft of services is a class A misdemeanor, provided, however, that theft of cable television service as defined by the provisions of paragraphs (a), (c) and (d) of subdivision four of this section, and having a value not in excess of one hundred dollars by a person who has not been previously convicted of theft of services under subdivision four of this section is a violation, and provided further, however, that theft of services under subdivision eight of this section by a person who has not been previously convicted of theft of services under subdivision eight of this section is a violation.

TITLE K OFFENSES INVOLVING FRAUD
ARTICLE 170 FORGERY AND RELATED OFFENSES

170.00 Forgery; definitions of terms.

1. "Written instrument" means any instrument or article, including computer data or a computer program, containing written or printed matter or the equivalent thereof, used for the purpose of reciting, embodying, conveying or recording information, or constituting a symbol or evidence of value, right, privilege or identification, which is capable of being used to the advantage or disadvantage of some person.

2. "Complete written instrument" means one which purports to be a genuine written instrument fully drawn with respect to every essential feature thereof. An endorsement, attestation, acknowledgment or other similar signature or statement is deemed both a complete written instrument in itself and a part of the main instrument in which it is contained or to which it attaches.

3. "Incomplete written instrument" means one which contains some matter by way of content or authentication but which requires additional matter in order to render it a complete written instrument.

4. "Falsely make." A person "falsely makes" a written instrument when he makes or draws a complete written instrument in its entirety, or an incomplete written instrument, which purports to be an authentic creation of its ostensible maker or drawer, but which is not such either because the ostensible maker or drawer is fictitious or because, if real, he did not authorize the making or drawing thereof.

5. "Falsely complete." A person "falsely completes" a written instrument when, by adding, inserting or changing matter, he transforms an incomplete written instrument into a complete one, without the authority of anyone entitled to grant it, so that such complete instrument appears or purports to be in all respects an authentic creation of or fully authorized by its ostensible maker or drawer.

6. "Falsely alter." A person "falsely alters" a written instrument when, without the authority of anyone entitled to grant it, he changes a written instrument, whether it be in complete or incomplete form, by means of erasure, obliteration, deletion, insertion of new matter, transposition of matter, or in any other manner, so that such instrument in its thus altered form appears or purports to be in all respects an authentic creation of or fully authorized by its ostensible maker or drawer.

7. "Forged instrument" means a written instrument which has been falsely made, completed or altered.

TITLE N OFFENSES AGAINST PUBLIC ORDER, PUBLIC SENSIBILITIES AND THE RIGHT TO PRIVACY

ARTICLE 250 OFFENSES AGAINST THE RIGHT TO PRIVACY

250.30 Unlawfully obtaining communications information.

A person is guilty of unlawfully obtaining communications information when, knowing that he does not have the authorization of a telephone or telegraph corporation, he obtains or attempts to obtain, by deception, stealth or in any other manner, from such corporation or from any employee, officer or representative thereof:

1. Information concerning identification or location of any wires, cables, lines, terminals or other apparatus used in furnishing telephone or telegraph service; or

2. Information concerning a record of any communication passing over telephone or telegraph lines of any such corporation.

Unlawfully obtaining communications information is a class B misdemeanor.

NORTH CAROLINA STATUTES

CHAPTER 14. CRIMINAL LAW.
SUBCHAPTER XI. GENERAL POLICE REGULATIONS.
ARTICLE 60. COMPUTER-RELATED CRIME.

14-453. Definitions.

As used in this section, unless the context clearly requires otherwise, the following terms have the meanings specified:

(1) "Access" means to approach, instruct, communicate with, cause input, cause output, or otherwise make use of any resources of a computer, computer system or computer network.

(2) "Computer" means an internally programmed, automatic device that performs data processing.

(3) "Computer network" means the interconnection of communication systems with a computer through remote terminals, or a complex consisting of two or more interconnected computers.

(4) "Computer program" means an ordered set of data that are coded instructions or statements that when executed by a computer cause the computer to process data.

(5) "Computer software" means a set of computer programs, procedures and associated documentation concerned with the operation of a computer system.

(6) "Computer system" means a set of related, connected or unconnected computer equipment and devices.

(7) "Financial statement" includes but is not limited to any check, draft, money order, certificate of deposit, letter of credit, bill of exchange, credit card of [or] marketable security, or any electronic data processing representation thereof.

(8) "Property" includes but is not limited to, financial instruments, information, including electronically processed or produced data, and computer software and programs in either machine or human readable form, and any other tangible or intangible item of value.

(9) "Services" includes, but is not limited to, computer time, data processing and storage functions. (1979, c. 831, s. 1.)

14-454. Accessing computers.

(a) A person is guilty of a Class H felony if he willfully, directly or indirectly, accesses or causes to be accessed any computer, computer system, computer network, or any part thereof, for the purpose of:

(1) Devising or executing any scheme or artifice to defraud, unless the object of the scheme or artifice is to obtain educational testing material, a false educational testing score, or a false academic or vocational grade, or

(2) Obtaining property or services other than educational testing material, a false educational testing score, or a false academic or vocational grade for himself or another, by means of false or fraudulent pretenses, representations or promises.

(b) Any person who willfully and without authorization, directly or indirectly, accesses or causes to be accessed any computer, computer system, computer network, or any part thereof, for any purpose other than those set forth in subsection (a) above, is guilty of a misdemeanor. (1979, c. 831, s. 1; 1979, 2nd Sess., c. 1316, s. 19.)

14-455. Damaging computers and related materials.

(a) A person is guilty of a Class H felony if he willfully and without authorization alters, damages or destroys a computer, computer system, computer network, or any part thereof.

(b) A person is guilty of a misdemeanor if he willfully and without authorization alters, damages, or destroys any computer software, program or data residing or existing internal or external to a computer, computer system or computer network. (1979, c. 831, s. 1; 1979, 2nd Sess., c. 1316, s. 20.)

14-456. Denial of computer services to an authorized user.

Any person who willfully and without authorization denies or causes the denial of computer system services to an authorized user of such computer system services, is guilty of a misdemeanor. (1979, c. 831, s. 1.)

14-457. Extortion.

Any person who verbally or by a written or printed communication, maliciously threatens to commit an act described in G.S. 14-455 with the intent to extort money or any pecuniary advantage, or with the intent to compel any person to do or refrain from doing any act against his will, is guilty of a Class H felony. (1979, c. 831, s. 1; 1979, 2nd Sess., c. 1316, s. 21.)

626A. PRIVACY OF COMMUNICATIONS

626A.27 DISCLOSURE OF CONTENTS.

Subdivision 1. Prohibitions. Except as provided in subdivision 2:

(1) a person or entity providing an electronic communication service to the public must not knowingly divulge to a person or entity the contents of a communication while in electronic storage by that service; and

(2) a person or entity providing remote computing service to the public must not knowingly divulge to a person or entity the contents of any communication that is carried or maintained on that service:

(i) on behalf of, and received by means of electronic transmission from, or created by means of COMPUTER processing of communications received by means of electronic transmission, from a subscriber or customer of the service; and

(ii) solely for the purpose of providing storage or COMPUTER processing services to the subscriber or customer, if the provider is not authorized to access the contents of any communications for purposes of providing any services other than storage or COMPUTER processing.

Subd. 2. Exceptions. A person or entity may divulge the contents of a communication:

(1) to an addressee or intended recipient of the communication or an agent of the addressee or intended recipient;

(2) as otherwise authorized in section 626A.02, subdivision 2, paragraph

(a); 626A.05; or section 626A.28;

(3) with the lawful consent of the originator or an addressee or intended recipient of the communication, or the subscriber in the case of remote computing service;

(4) to a person employed or authorized or whose facilities are used to forward a communication to its destination;

(5) as may be necessarily incident to the rendition of the service or to the protection of the rights or property of the provider of that service; or

(6) to a law enforcement agency, if the contents:

(i) were inadvertently obtained by the service provider; and

(ii) appear to pertain to the commission of a CRIME.

NORTH DAKOTA STATUTES

CHAPTER 12.1-06.1-08

12.1.06.1-08. Computer fraud—Computer crime—Classification—Penalty.

1. A person commits computer fraud by gaining or attempting to gain access to, altering, damaging, modifying, copying, disclosing, taking possession of, or destroying any computer, computer system, computer network, or any part of such computer, system, or network, without authorization, and with the intent to devise or execute any scheme or artifice to defraud, deceive, prevent the authorized use of, or control property or services by means of false or fraudulent pretenses, representations, or promises. A person who commits computer fraud is guilty of a class C felony.

2. A person commits computer crime by intentionally and either in excess of authorization given or without authorization gaining or attempting to gain access to, altering, damaging, modifying, copying, disclosing, taking possession of, destroying, or preventing the authorized use of any computer, computer system, or computer network, or any computer software, program, or data contained in such computer, computer system, or computer network. A person who commits computer crime is guilty of a class A misdemeanor.

12.1-32-01. Classification of offenses—Penalties.

Offenses are divided into seven classes, hwhich are denominated and subject to maximum penalties, as follows:

1. Class AA felony, for which a maximum penalty of life imprisonment may be imposed. Notwithstanding the provisions of section 12-59-05, a person found guilty of a class AA felony shall not be eligible to have his sentence considered by the parole board for thirty years, less sentence reduction earned for good conduct, after his admission to the penitentiary.

2. Class A felony, for which a maximum penalty of twenty years' imprisonment, a fine of ten thousand dollars, or both, may be imposed.

3. Class B felony, for which a maximum penalty of ten years' imprisonment, a fine of ten thousand dollars, or both, may be imposed.

4. Class C felony, for which a maximum penalty of five years' imprisonment, a fine of five thousand dollars, or both, may be imposed.

5. Class A misdemeanor, for which a maximum penalty of one year's imprisonment, a fine of one thousand dollars, or both, may be imposed.

6. Class B misdemeanor, for which a maximum penalty of thirty days' imprisonment, a fine of five hundred dollars, or both, may be imposed.

7. Infraction, for which a maximum fine of five hundred dollars may be imposed. Any person convicted of an infraction who has, within one year prior to commission of the infraction of which he was convicted, been previously convicted of an offense classified as an infraction may be sentenced as though convicted of a class B misdemeanor.

OHIO STATUTES

TITLE XXIX CRIMES-PROCEDURE
CHAPTER 2913 THEFT AND FRAUD

2913.01 Definitions

As used in this chapter:

(A) "Deception" means knowingly deceiving another or causing another to be deceived by any false or misleading representation, by withholding information, by preventing another from acquiring information, or by any other conduct, act, or omission which creates, confirms, or perpetuates a false impression in another, including a false impression as to law, value, state of mind, or other objective or subjective fact.

(B) "Defraud" means to knowingly obtain, by deception, some benefit for oneself or another, or to knowingly cause, by deception, some detriment to another.

(C) "Deprive" means to:

(1) Withhold property of another permanently, or for such period as to appropriate a substantial por-

tion of its value or use, or with purpose to restore it only upon payment of a reward or other consideration;

(2) Dispose of property so as to make it unlikely that the owner will recover it;

(3) Accept, use, or appropriate money, property, or services, with purpose not to give proper consideration in return therefor, and without reasonable justification or excuse for not giving proper consideration.

(D) "Owner" means any person, other than the actor, who is the owner of, or who has possession or control of, or any license or interest in property or services, even though such ownership, possession, control, license, or interest is unlawful.

(E) "Services" include labor, personal services, professional services, public utility services, common carrier services, and food, drink, transportation, entertainment, and cable television services.

(F) "Writing" means any computer software, document, letter, memorandum, note, paper, plate, data, film, or other thing having in or upon it any written, typewritten, or printed matter, and also means any token, stamp, seal, credit card, badge, trademark, label, or other symbol of value, right, privilege, license, or identification.

(G) "Forge" means to fabricate or create, in whole or in part and by any means, any spurious writing, or to make, execute, alter, complete, reproduce, or otherwise purport to authenticate any writing, when such writing in fact is not authenticated thereby.

(H) "Utter" means to issue, publish, transfer, use, put or send into circulation, deliver, or display.

(I) "Coin machine" means any mechanical or electronic device designed to do both of the following:

(1) Receive a coin or bill, or token made for that purpose;

(2) In return for the insertion or deposit of a coin, bill, or token, automatically dispense property, provide a service, or grant a license.

(J) "Slug" means an object which, by virtue of its size, shape, composition, or other quality, is capable of being inserted or deposited in a coin machine as an improper substitute for a genuine coin, bill, or token made for that purpose.

(K) "Theft offense" means any of the following:

(1) A violation of section 2911.01, 2911.02, 2911.11, 2911.12, 2911.13, 2911.31, 2911.32, 2913.02, 2913.03, 2913.04, 2913.11, 2913.21, 2913.31, 2913.32, 2913.33, 2913.40, 2913.41, 2913.42, 2913.43, 2913.44, 2913.45, former section 2913.47 or 2913.48, or section 2913.51, 2913.81, 2915.05, 2915.06, or 2921.41 of the Revised Code;

(2) A violation of an existing or former municipal ordinance or law of this or any other state or the United States substantially equivalent to any section listed in division (K)(1) of this section;

(3) An offense under an existing or former municipal ordinance or law of this or any other state or the United States involving robbery, burglary, breaking and entering, theft, embezzlement, wrongful conversion, forgery, counterfeiting, deceit, or fraud;

(4) A conspiracy or attempt to commit, or complicity in committing any offense under division (K)(1), (2), or (3) of this section.

(L) "Computer services" includes, but is not limited to, the use of a computer system, computer network, computer program, data that is prepared for computer use, or data that is contained within a computer system or computer network.

(M) "Computer" means an electronic device that performs logical, arithmetic, and memory functions by the manipulation of electronic or magnetic impulses. "Computer" includes, but is not limited to, all input, output, processing, storage, computer program, or communication facilities that are connected, or related, in a computer system or network to such an electronic device.

(N) "Computer system" means a computer and related devices, whether connected or unconnected, including, but not limited to, data input, output, and storage devices, data communications links, and computer programs and data that make the system capable of performing specified special purpose data processing tasks.

(O) "Computer network" means a set of related and remotely connected computers and communication facilities that includes more than one computer system that has the capability to transmit among the connected computers and communication facilities through the use of computer facilities.

(P) "Computer program" means an ordered set of data representing coded instructions or statements that when executed by a computer cause the computer to process data.

(Q) "Computer software" means computer programs, procedures, and other documentation associated with the operation of a computer system.

(R) "Data" means a representation of information, knowledge, facts, concepts, or instructions that are being or have been prepared in a formalized manner and that are intended for use in a computer system or computer network.

(S) "Cable television service" means any services provided by or through the facilities of any cable television system or other similar closed circuit coaxial cable communications system, or any microwave or similar transmission service used in connection with any cable television system or other similar closed circuit coaxial cable communications system.

(T) "Gain access" means to approach, instruct, communicate with, store data in, retrieve data from, or otherwise make use of any resources of a computer, computer system, or computer network.

(U) "Credit card" includes, but is not limited to, a card, code, device, or other means of access to a customer's account for the purpose of obtaining money, property, labor, or services on credit, or for initiating an electronic fund transfer at a point-of-sale terminal, an automated teller machine, or a cash dispensing machine. "Electronic fund transfer" has the same meaning as in 92 Stat. 3728, 15 U.S.C.A. 1693a, as amended.

2913.04 Unauthorized use of property; unauthorized access to computer systems

(A) No person shall knowingly use or operate the property of another without the consent of the owner or person authorized to give consent.

(B) No person shall knowingly gain access to, attempt to gain access to, or cause access to be gained to any computer, computer system, or computer network without the consent of, or beyond the scope of the express or implied consent of, the owner of the computer, computer system, or computer network or other person authorized to give consent by the owner.

(C) The affirmative defenses contained in division (C) of section 2913.03 of the Revised Code are affirmative defenses to a charge under this section.

(D) Whoever violates this section is guilty of unauthorized use of property. If the offense involves a violation of division (A) of this section and does not involve any computer, computer system, computer network, computer software, or data, unauthorized use of property is a misdemeanor of the fourth degree. If the offense involves a violation of division (A) of this section and involves any computer, computer system, computer network, computer software, or data or if the offense involves a violation of division (B) of this section, unauthorized use of property is whichever of the following is applicable:

(1) If division (D)(2) or (3) of this section does not apply, a felony of the fourth degree;

(2) If division (D)(3) of this section does not apply and the offender previously has been convicted of a theft offense, a felony of the third degree;

(3) If the offense is committed for the purpose of devising or executing a scheme to defraud or to obtain property or services and the value of the property or services or the loss to the victim is one hundred thousand dollars or more, a felony of the second degree.

2913.42 Tampering with records

(A) No person, knowing he has no privilege to do so, and with purpose to defraud or knowing that he is facilitating a fraud, shall do any of the following:

(1) Falsify, destroy, remove, conceal, alter, deface, or mutilate any writing, data, or record;

(2) Utter any writing or record, knowing it to have been tampered with as provided in division (A)(1) of this section.

(B) No person, knowing he has no privilege to do so, shall falsify, destroy, remove, conceal, alter, deface, or mutilate any computer software or data.

(C)(1) Whoever violates this section is guilty of tampering with records.

(2) If the offense involves a violation of division (A) of this section and does not involve data, tampering with records is whichever of the following is applicable:

(a) If division (C)(2)(b) of this section does not apply, a misdemeanor of the first degree;

(b) If the writing or record is a will unrevoked at the time of the offense or a record kept by or belonging to a governmental agency, a felony of the fourth degree.

(3) If the offense involves a violation of division (A) of this section involving data, tampering with records is whichever of the following is applicable:

(a) If division (C)(3)(b) or (c) of this section does not apply, a felony of the fourth degree;

(b) If division (C)(3)(c) of this section does not apply and the writing or record is a record kept by or belonging to a governmental agency or the offender previously has been convicted of a theft offense, a felony of the third degree;

(c) If the value of the data involved in the offense or the loss to the victim is one hundred dollars or more, a felony of the second degree.

(4) If the offense involves a violation of division (B) of this section, tampering with records is whichever of the following is applicable:

(a) If division (C)(4)(b) or (c)of this section does not apply, a felony of the fourth degree;

(b) If division (C)(4)(c) of this section does not apply and the offender previously has been convicted of a theft offense, a felony of the third degree;

(c) If the offense is committed for the purpose of devising or executing a scheme to defraud or to obtain property or services and the value of the property or services or the loss to the victim is one hundred thousand dollars or more, a felony of the second degree.

2913.81 Denying access to a computer

(A) No person, without privilege to do so, shall knowingly deny or cause the denial of a computer system or computer services to an authorized user of a computer system or computer services that, in whole or in part, are owned by, under contract to, operated for, or operated in conjunction with another person.

(B) Whoever violates this section is guilty of denying access to a computer, a felony of the fourth degree. If the offender previously has been convicted of a theft offense, denying access to a computer is a felony of the third degree. If the offense is committed for the purpose of devising or executing a scheme to defraud or to obtain property or services and the value of the property or services or the loss to the victim is one hundred thousand dollars or more, denying access to a computer is a felony of the second degree.

OKLAHOMA STATUTES

TITLE 21. CRIMES AND PUNISHMENTS
PART VII. CRIMES AGAINST PROPERTY
CHAPTER 70. OTHER OFFENSES AGAINST PROPERTY RIGHTS
COMPUTER CRIMES ACT

1953. Prohibited acts

It shall be unlawful to:

1. Willfully, and without authorization, gain or attempt to gain access to and damage, modify, alter, destroy, copy, disclose or take possession of a computer, computer system, computer network or any other property as herein before defined. Any person who violates this paragraph shall be guilty of a felony and shall be punishable as provided in Section 5 of this act.

2. Use a computer, computer system, computer network or any other property as herein before defined for the purpose of devising or executing a scheme or artifice with the intent to defraud or for the purpose of obtaining money, property, services or other thing of value by means of a false or fraudulent pretense or representation. Any person who violates this paragraph shall be guilty of a felony and shall be punishable as provided in Section 5 of this act.

3. Willfully exceed the limits of authorization and damage, modify, alter, destroy, copy, disclose or take possession of a computer, computer system, computer network or any other property as herein before defined. Any person who violates this paragraph shall be guilty of a felony and shall be punishable as provided in Section 5 of this act.

4. Willfully and without authorization, gain or attempt to gain access to a computer, computer system,

computer network or any other property as herein before defined. Any person who violates this paragraph shall be guilty of a misdemeanor and shall be punishable as provided in Section 5 of this act.

1954. Certain acts as prima facie evidence of violation of act

Proof that any person has accessed, damaged, modified, altered, destroyed, caused to be accessed, copied, disclosed or taken possession of a computer, computer system, computer network or any other property as herein before defined, or has attempted to perform any of these enumerated acts without authorization or exceeding the limits of authorization, shall be prima facie evidence of the willful violation of this act.

1955. Penalties

A. Upon conviction of a felony under the provisions of the Oklahoma Computer Crimes Act, punishment shall be by a fine of not less than Five Thousand Dollars ($5,000.00) and not more than One Hundred Thousand Dollars ($100,000.00), or by confinement in the State Penitentiary for a term of not less than one (1) year nor more than ten (10) years, or by both such fine and imprisonment.

B. Upon conviction of a misdemeanor under the provisions of the Oklahoma Computer Crimes Act, punishment shall be by a fine of not more than Five Thousand Dollars ($5,000.00), or by imprisonment in the county jail not to exceed thirty (30) days, or by both such fine and imprisonment.

1956. Severability

The provisions of this act are severable and if any part or provision shall be held void the decision of the court so holding shall not affect or impair any of the remaining parts or provisions of this act.

OREGON STATUTES

TITLE 16. CRIMES AND PUNISHMENTS
CHAPTER 164. OFFENSES AGAINST PROPERTY
THEFT AND RELATED OFFENSES

164.125. Theft of services.

(1) A person commits the crime of theft of services if:

(a) With intent to avoid payment therefor, the person obtains services that are available only for compensation, by force, threat, deception or other means to avoid payment for the services; or

(b) Having control over the disposition of labor or of business, commercial or industrial equipment or facilities of another, the person uses or diverts to the use of the person or a third person such labor, equipment or facilities with intent to derive for the person or the third person a commercial benefit to which the person or the third person is not entitled.

(2) As used in this section, "services" includes, but is not limited to, labor, professional services, toll facilities, transportation, communications service, entertainment, the supplying of food, lodging or other accommodations in hotels, restaurants or elsewhere, the supplying of equipment for use, and the supplying of commodities of a public utility nature such as gas, electricity, steam and water. "Communication service" includes, but is not limited to, use of telephone, computer and cable television systems.

(3) Absconding without payment or offer to pay for hotel, restaurant or other services for which compensation is customarily paid immediately upon the receiving of them is prima facie evidence that the services were obtained with intent to avoid payment therefor. Obtaining the use of any communication system the use of which is available only for compensation, including but not limited to telephone, computer and cable television systems, or obtaining the use of any services of a public utility nature, without payment or offer to pay for such use is prima facie evidence that the obtaining of the use of such system or the use of such services was gained with intent to avoid payment therefor.

(4) Theft of services is:

(a) A Class C misdemeanor if the aggregate total value of services that are the subject of the theft is under $50;

(b) A Class A misdemeanor if the aggregate total value of services that are the subject of the theft is $50 or more but is under $500;

(c) A Class C felony if the aggregate total value of services that are the subject of the theft is $500 or more; and

(d) A Class B felony if the aggregate total value of services that are the subject of the theft is $10,000 or more.

CRIMINAL MISCHIEF AND RELATED OFFENSES

164.377. Computer crime.

(1) As used in this section:

(a) To "access" means to instruct, communicate with, store data in, retrieve data from or otherwise make use of any resources of a computer, computer system or computer network.

(b) "Computer" means, but is not limited to, an electronic device which performs logical, arithmetic or memory functions by the manipulations of electronic, magnetic or optical signals or impulses, and includes all input, output, processing, storage, software or communication facilities which are connected or related to such a device in a system or network.

(c) "Computer network" means, but is not limited to, the interconnection of communication lines, including microwave or other means of electronic communication, with a computer through remote terminals or a complex consisting of two or more interconnected computers.

(d) "Computer program" means, but is not limited to, a series of instructions or statements, in a form acceptable to a computer, which permits the functioning of a computer system in a manner designed to provide appropriate products from or usage of such computer system.

(e) "Computer software" means, but is not limited to, computer programs, procedures and associated documentation concerned with the operation of a computer system.

(f) "Computer system" means, but is not limited to, a set of related, connected or unconnected, computer equipment, devices and software.

(g) "Data" means a representation of information, knowledge, facts, concepts, computer software, computer programs or instructions. "Data" may be in any form, in storage media, or as stored in the memory of the computer, or in transit, or presented on a display device. "Data" includes, but is not limited to, computer or human readable forms of numbers, text, stored voice, graphics and images.

(h) "Property" includes, but is not limited to, financial instruments, information, including electronically produced data, and computer software and programs in either computer or human readable form, intellectual property and any other tangible or intangible item of value.

(i) "Proprietary information" includes any scientific, technical or commercial information including any design, process, procedure, list of customers, list of suppliers, customers' records or business code or improvement thereof that is known only to limited individuals within an organization and is used in a business that the organization conducts. The information must have actual or potential commercial value and give the user of the information an opportunity to obtain a business advantage over competitors who do not know or use the information.

(j) "Services" include, but are not limited to, computer time, data processing and storage functions.

(2) Any person commits computer crime who knowingly accesses, attempts to access or uses, or attempts to use, any computer, computer system, computer network or any part thereof for the purpose of:

(a) Devising or executing any scheme or artifice to defraud;

(b) Obtaining money, property or services by means of false or fraudulent pretenses, representations or promises; or

(c) Committing theft, including, but not limited to, theft of proprietary information.

(3) Any person who knowingly and without authorization alters, damages or destroys any computer, computer system, computer network, or any computer software, program, documentation or data contained in such computer, computer system or computer network, commits computer crime.

(4) Any person who knowingly and without authorization uses, accesses or attempts to access any computer, computer system, computer network, or any computer software, program, documentation or data contained in such computer, computer system or computer network, commits computer crime.

(5) A violation of the provisions of subsection (2) or (3) of this section shall be a Class C felony. A violation of the provisions of subsection (4) of this section shall be a Class A misdemeanor.

PENNSYLVANIA STATUTES

TITLE 18. CRIMES AND OFFENSES
PART II. DEFINITION OF SPECIFIC OFFENSES
ARTICLE C. OFFENSES AGAINST PROPERTY
CHAPTER 39. THEFT AND RELATED OFFENSE

3933. Unlawful use of computer

(A) OFFENSE DEFINED.—A person commits an offense if he:

(1) accesses, alters, damages or destroys any computer, computer system, computer network, computer software, computer program or database or any part thereof, with the intent to interrupt the normal functioning of an organization or to devise or execute any scheme or artifice to defraud or deceive or control property or services by means of false or fraudulent pretenses, representations or promises;

(2) intentionally and without authorization accesses, alters, interferes with the operation of, damages or destroys any computer, computer system, computer network, computer software, computer program or computer data base or any part thereof; or

(3) intentionally or knowingly and without authorization gives or publishes a password, identifying code, personal identification number or other confidential information about a computer, computer system, computer network or data base.

(B) GRADING.—An offense under subsection (a)(1) is a felony of the third degree. An offense under subsection (a)(2) or (3) is a misdemeanor of the first degree.

(C) DEFINITIONS.—As used in this section the following words and phrases shall have the meanings given to them in this subsection:

"ACCESS." To intercept, instruct, communicate with, store data in, retrieve data from or otherwise make use of any resources of a computer, computer system, computer network or data base.

"COMPUTER." An electronic, magnetic, optical, hydraulic, organic or other high speed data processing device or system which performs logic, arithmetic or memory functions and includes all input, output, processing, storage, software or communication facilities which are connected or related to the device in a system or network.

"COMPUTER NETWORK." The interconnection of two or more computers through the usage of satellite, microwave, line or other communication medium.

"COMPUTER PROGRAM." An ordered set of instructions or statements and related data that, when automatically executed in actual or modified form in a computer system, causes it to perform specified functions.

"COMPUTER SOFTWARE." A set of computer programs, procedures and associated documentation concerned with the operation of a computer system.

"COMPUTER SYSTEM." A set of related, connected or unconnected computer equipment, devices and software.

"DATA BASE." A representation of information, knowledge, facts, concepts or instructions which are being prepared or processed or have been prepared or processed in a formalized manner and are intended for use in a computer, computer system or computer network, including, but not limited to, computer printouts, magnetic storage media, punched cards or data stored internally in the memory of the computer.

"FINANCIAL INSTRUMENT." Includes, but is not limited to, any check, draft, warrant, money order, note, certificate of deposit, letter of credit, bill of exchange, credit or debit card, transaction authorization mechanism, marketable security or any computer system representation thereof.

"PROPERTY." Includes, but is not limited to, financial instruments, computer software and programs in either machine or human readable form, and anything of value, tangible or intangible.

"SERVICES." Includes, but is not limited to, computer time, data processing and storage functions.

RHODE ISLAND STATUTES

TITLE 11 CRIMINAL OFFENSES
CHAPTER 52 COMPUTER CRIME

11-52-1. Definitions.

As used in this chapter:

(A) "Access" means to approach, instruct, communicate with, store data in, enter data in, retrieve data from, or otherwise make use of any resources of, a computer, computer system, or computer network.

(B) "Computer" means an electronic device which performs logical, arithmetic, and memory functions by the manipulations of electronic or magnetic impulses, and includes all input, output, processing, storage, software, or communication facilities which are connected or related to such a device in a system or network.

(C) "Computer system" means a set of related, connected or unconnected, computer equipment, devices and software.

(D) "Computer network" means the interconnection of communication lines with a computer through remote terminals, or a complex consisting of two or more interconnected computers.

(E) "Property" includes, but is not limited to, financial instruments, information, including electronically produced data, and computer software and programs in either machine or human readable form, and any other tangible or intangible item of value.

(F) "Services" includes, but is not limited to, computer time, data processing, and storage functions.

(G) "Computer program" means a series of instructions or statements or related data that, in actual or modified form, is capable of causing a computer or a computer system to perform specified functions in a form acceptable to a computer, which permits the functioning of a computer system in a manner designed to provide appropriate products from such computer systems.

(H) "Computer software" means a set of computer programs, procedures, and associated documentation concerned with the operation of a computer system.

(I) "Data" means any representation of information, knowledge, facts, concepts, or instructions which are being prepared or have been prepared and are intended to be entered, processed or stored, are being entered, processed or stored or have been entered, processed or stored in a computer, computer system or computer network.

(J) "Source document" means an original document or record which forms the basis of every electronic entry put into a computer, computer system or computer network.

11-52-2. Access to computer for fraudulent purposes.

Whoever directly or indirectly accesses or causes to be accessed any computer, computer system, or computer network for the purpose of (1) devising or executing any scheme or artifice to defraud, (2) obtaining money, property, or services by means of false or fraudulent pretenses, representations, or promises, or (3) damaging, destroying, altering, deleting, or removing any program or data contained therein in connection with any scheme or artifice to defraud shall be guilty of a felony and shall be subject to the penalties set forth in 11-52-5.

11-52-3. Intentional access, alteration, damage or destruction.

Whoever intentionally and without authorization, directly or indirectly accesses, alters, damages, or destroys any computer, computer system, computer network, computer software, computer program or data contained in such computer, computer system, computer program or computer network shall be guilty of a felony and shall be subject to the penalties set forth in 11-52-5.

11-52-4. Computer theft.

Whoever, intentionally and without claim of right, and with intent to permanently deprive the owner of possession, takes, transfers, conceals or retains possession of any computer, computer system, computer network, computer software, computer program or data contained in such computer, computer system, computer program or computer network with a value in excess of five hundred dollars ($500) shall be guilty of a felony and shall be subject to the penalties set forth in § 11-52-5. If the value is five hundred dollars ($500) or less, then said person shall be guilty of a misdemeanor and may be punishable by imprisonment for a term not exceeding one (1) year, or by a fine of not more than one thousand dollars ($1,000), or both.

11-52-5. Penalties.

(A) Any person who is convicted of an offense which is classified as a felony under this chapter shall be fined not more than five thousand dollars ($5,000) or imprisoned for not more than five (5) years, or both.

(B) Any person who is convicted of an offense which is classified as a misdemeanor under this chapter shall be fined not more than five hundred dollars ($500) or imprisoned for not more than one (1) year, or both.

SOUTH CAROLINA STATUTES

TITLE 16. CRIMES AND OFFENSES
CHAPTER 16. COMPUTER CRIME ACT

16-16-10. Definitions.

For purposes of this chapter:

(a) "Computer" means an electronic device that performs logical, arithmetic, and memory functions by manipulating electronic or magnetic impulses, and includes all input, output, processing, storage, computer software, and communication facilities that are connected or related to a computer in a computer system or computer network but does not include any computer or other electronic device designed and manufactured for, and which is used exclusively for routine personal, family, or household purposes and which is not used to access, to communicate with, or to manipulate any other computer.

(b) "Computer network" means the interconnection of communications lines, or any other communications facilities, with a computer through remote terminals, or a system consisting of two or more interconnected computers.

(c) "Computer program" means a series of instructions or statements executable on a computer which directs the computer system in a manner to process data or perform other specified functions.

(d) "Computer software" means a set of computer programs, data, procedures, or associated documentation concerned with the operation of a computer system.

(e) "Computer system" means a set of related, connected or unconnected, computer equipment, devices, or software.

(f) "Property" means and includes, but is not limited to, financial instruments, data, computer software, documents associated with computer systems, and computer software, or copies thereof, whether tangible or intangible, including both human and computer system readable data, and data while in transit.

(g) "Services" means and includes, but is not limited to, the use of the computer system, computer network, computer programs, or data prepared for computer use, or data obtained within a computer system, or data contained within a computer network.

(h) "Data" means a representation of information, knowledge, facts, concepts, or instructions that has been prepared or is being prepared in a formalized manner and has been processed, is being processed, or is intended to be processed in a computer, computer system, or computer network. Data may be in any form including, but not limited to, computer printouts, magnetic storage media, punched cards, or as stored in the memory of the computer or in transit or displayed on a video device.

(i) "Access" means to instruct, communicate with, attempt to communicate with, store data in, retrieve data from, or otherwise make use of or attempt to make use of any resources of a computer, computer system, or computer network.

(j) "Computer hacking" means accessing all or part of a computer, computer system, or a computer network for the purpose of establishing contact only without the intent to defraud or commit any other crime after such contact is established and without the use of computer-related services except such services as may be incidental to establishing contact.

16-16-20. Offenses; penalties.

(1) It is unlawful for any person to willfully, knowingly, maliciously, and without authorization or for an unauthorized purpose to do any of the following:

(a) Directly or indirectly access or cause to be accessed any computer, computer system, or computer network for the purpose of (i) devising or executing any scheme or artifice to defraud, or (ii) obtaining money, property, or services by means of false or fraudulent pretenses, representations, promises, or (iii) committing any other crime.

(b) Alter, damage, destroy, or modify any computer, computer system, computer network, computer software, computer program, or data contained in such computer, computer system, computer program, or computer network.

(2) A person is guilty of computer crime in the first degree if the amount of gain directly or indirectly derived from the offense made unlawful by subsection (1) or the loss directly or indirectly suffered by the victim exceeds twenty-five thousand dollars. Computer crime in the first degree is a felony and, upon conviction thereof, a person must be punished by a fine of not more than one hundred twenty-five thousand dollars or imprisonment for not more than ten years, or both.

(3) (a) A person is guilty of computer crime in the second degree if the amount of gain directly or indirectly derived from the offense made unlawful by subsection (1) or the loss directly or indirectly suffered by the victim is greater than one thousand dollars but not more than twenty-five thousand dollars.

(b) A person is also guilty of computer crime in the second degree where (i) he interferes with, causes to be interfered with, denies or causes to be denied any computer service to any authorized user of such computer service for the purpose of devising or executing any scheme or artifice to defraud, or obtaining money, property, or services by means of false or fraudulent pretenses, representations, or promises, or committing any other felony; (ii) he deprives the owner of possession of, or takes, transfers, conceals, or retains possession of any computer, data, computer property, or computer-related property, including all parts of a computer, computer system, computer network, computer software, computer services, or information associated with a computer, whether in a tangible or intangible form; or (iii) the gain derived from the offense made unlawful by subsection (1) or loss suffered by the victim cannot reasonably be ascertained.

(c) Computer crime in the second degree is a felony and, upon conviction thereof, for a first offense, a person must be punished by a fine of not more than fifty thousand dollars or imprisonment for not more than three years, or both. Upon conviction for a second or subsequent offense, a person must be punished by a fine of not more than fifty thousand dollars or imprisonment for not more than seven years, or both.

(4) A person is guilty of computer crime in the third degree if the amount of gain directly or indirectly derived from the offense made unlawful by subsection (1) or the loss directly or indirectly suffered by the victim does not exceed one thousand dollars. A person is also guilty of computer crime in the third degree if he willfully, knowingly, and without authorization or for an unauthorized purpose engages in computer hacking. Computer crime in the third degree is a misdemeanor and, upon conviction thereof, for a first offense, a person must be punished by a fine of not more than two hundred dollars or imprisonment for not more than thirty days. Upon conviction for a second or subsequent offense, a person must be punished by a fine of not more than two thousand dollars or imprisonment for not more than two years, or both.

16-16-30. Venue.

For the purpose of venue under this chapter, any violation of this chapter shall be considered to have been committed in the county in which the violation took place; provided, that upon proper motion and the proper showing before a judge, venue may be transferred if justice would be better served by such transfer, to one of the following:

(1) In any county in which any act was performed in furtherance of any transaction which violated this chapter;

(2) In the county of the principal place of business in this State of the owner or lessee of a computer, computer system, computer network, or any part thereof which has been subject to the violation; or

(3) Any county in which any violator had control or possession of any proceeds of the violation or of any books, records, documents, property, financial instrument, computer software, computer program, or other material or objects which were used in the furtherance of the violation.

16-16-40. Applicability of other criminal law provisions.

The provisions of this chapter must not be construed to preclude the applicability of any other provision of the criminal law of this State, which presently applies or may in the future apply, to any transaction which violates this chapter.

SOUTH DAKOTA STATUTES

TITLE 43 PROPERTY
CHAPTER 43-43B COMPUTER PROGRAMS

43-43B-1. Unlawful uses of computer.

A person is guilty of unlawful use of a computer if he:

(1) Knowingly obtains the use of, or accesses, a computer system, or any part thereof, without the consent of the owner;

(2) Knowingly alters or destroys computer programs or data without the consent of the owner; or

(3) Knowingly obtains use of, alters, accesses or destroys a computer system, or any part thereof, as part of a deception for the purpose of obtaining money, property or services from the owner of a computer system or any third party; or

(4) Knowingly uses or discloses to another or attempts to use or disclose to another the numbers, codes, passwords or other means of access to a computer, computer program or computer system without the consent of the owner.

43-43B-2. Definition of terms.

Terms used in this chapter, unless the context requires otherwise, mean:

(1) "Computer," an internally programmed, general purpose digital device capable of automatically accepting data, processing data and supplying the results of the operation;

(2) "Computer system," a set of related, connected devices, including a computer and other devices, including but not limited to data input and output and storage devices, data communications links, and computer programs and data, that make the system capable of performing the special purpose data processing tasks for which it is specified;

(3) "Computer program," a series of coded instructions or statements in a form acceptable to a computer, which causes the computer to process data in order to achieve a certain result;

(4) "Access," to instruct, communicate with, store data in, retrieve data from a computer, computer system or computer network.

43-43B-3. Obtaining use, altering or destroying system, access and disclosure without consent—Value one thousand dollars or less.

A person convicted of a violation of subdivision (1), (2) or (4) of 43-43B-1 where the value of the use, alteration, destruction, access or disclosure is one thousand dollars or less is guilty of a Class 1 misdemeanor.

43-43B-4. Obtaining use, altering or destroying system, access and disclosure without consent—Value more than one thousand dollars.

A person convicted of a violation of subdivision (1), (2) or (4) of 43-43B-1 where the value of the use, alteration, destruction, access or disclosure is more than one thousand dollars is guilty of a Class 6 felony.

43-43B-5. Obtaining use, altering or destroying system as part of deception—Value one thousand dollars or less.

A person convicted of a violation of subdivision (3) of 43-43B-1 where the value of the money, property or services obtained is one thousand dollars or less is guilty of a Class 1 misdemeanor.

43-43B-6. Obtaining use, altering or destroying system as part of deception—Value more than one thousand dollars.

A person convicted of a violation of subdivision (3) of 43-43B-1 where the value of the money, property or services obtained is more than one thousand dollars shall be guilty of a Class 4 felony.

43-43B-7. Civil rights not affected.

The provisions of this chapter shall neither enlarge nor diminish the rights of parties in civil litigation.

43-43B-8. Venue for violations.

For the purpose of venue under the provisions of this chapter, any violation of this chapter shall be considered to have been committed: in any county in which any act was performed in furtherance of any transaction violating this chapter; in any county in which any violator had control or possession of any proceeds of said violation or of any books, records, documents, property, financial instrument, computer software, computer program or other material, objects or items which were used in any county from which, to which or through which any access to a computer, computer system or computer network was made whether by wires, electromagnetic waves, microwaves or any other means of communication.

TENNESSEE STATUTES

TITLE 39. CRIMINAL OFFENSES
CHAPTER 3. OFFENSES AGAINST PROPERTY
PART 14. COMPUTER OFFENSES

39-14-601. Definitions.—

The following definitions apply in this part, unless the context otherwise requires:

(1) "Access" means to approach, instruct, communicate with, store data in, retrieve or intercept data from, or otherwise make use of any resources of, a computer, computer system, or computer network;

(2) "Computer" means a device that can perform substantial computation, including numerous arithmetic or logic operations, without intervention by a human operator during the processing of a job;

(3) "Computer network" means a set of two (2) or more computer systems that transmit data over communication circuits connecting them.

(4) "Computer program" means an ordered set of data that are coded instructions or statements that, when executed by a computer, cause the computer to process data;

(5) "Computer software" means a set of computer programs, procedures, and associated documentation concerned with the operation of a computer, computer system, or computer network;

(6) "Computer system" means a set of connected devices including a computer and other devices including, but not limited to, one (1) or more of the following: data input, output, or storage devices, data communication circuits, and operating system computer programs that make the system capable of performing data processing tasks;

(7) "Data" is a representation of information, knowledge, facts, concepts, or instructions which is being prepared or has been prepared in a formalized manner, and is intended to be stored or processed, or is being stored or processed, or has been stored or processed, in a computer, computer system, or computer network;

(8) "Financial instruments" includes, but is not limited to, any check, cashier's check, draft, warrant, money order, certificate of deposit, negotiable instrument, letter of credit, bill of exchange, credit card, debit card, marketable security, or any computer system representation thereof;

(9) "Intellectual property" includes data, which may be in any form including, but not limited to, computer printouts, magnetic storage media, punched cards, or may be stored internally in the memory of a computer;

(10) "To process" is to use a computer to put data through a systematic sequence of operations for the purpose of producing a specified result;

(11) "Property" includes, but is not limited to, intellectual property, financial instruments, data, computer programs, documentation associated with data, computers, computer systems and computer programs, all in machine-readable or human-readable form, and any tangible or intangible item of value; and

(12) "Services" includes, but is not limited to, the use of a computer, a computer system, a computer network, computer software, computer program, or data to perform tasks.

39-14-602. Violations—Penalties.—

(a) Whoever knowingly, directly or indirectly, accesses, causes to be accessed, or attempts to access any computer software, computer program, data, computer, computer system, computer network, or any part thereof, for the purpose of obtaining money, property, or services for himself or another by means of false or fraudulent pretenses, representations, or promises violates this subsection and is subject to the penalties of 39-14-105.

(b) Whoever intentionally and without authorization, directly or indirectly: (1) accesses; or (2) alters, damages, destroys, or attempts to damage or destroy, any computer, computer system, computer network, computer software, program or data; violates this subsection.

(c) A violation of subdivision (b)(1) is a Class C misdemeanor.

(d) A violation of subdivision (b)(2) is punished as in Section 39-14-105.

(e) Whoever receives, conceals, uses, or aids another in receiving, concealing or using any proceeds resulting from a violation of either subsection (a) or subdivision (b)(2), knowing the same to be proceeds of such violation, or whoever receives, conceals, uses, or aids another in receiving, concealing or using, any books, records, documents, property, financial instrument, computer software, program, or other material, property, or objects, knowing the same to have been used in violating either subsection (a) or subdivision (b)(2) violates this subsection and is subject to the penalties of Section 39-14-105.

39-14-603. Venue.—

For the purposes of venue under the provisions of this part, any violation of this part shall be considered to have been committed:

(1) In any county in which any act was performed in furtherance of any transaction violating this part;

(2) In any county in which any violator had control or possession of any proceeds of the violation or of any books, records, documents, property, financial instrument, computer software, computer program or other material, objects or items which were used in furtherance of the violation; and

(3) In any county from which, to which or through which any access to a computer, computer system, or computer network was made, whether by wire, electromagnetic waves, microwaves, or any other means of communication.

TEXAS STATUTES

TITLE 7. OFFENSES AGAINST PROPERTY
CHAPTER 33. COMPUTER CRIMES

33.01. Definitions

In this chapter:

(1) "Communications common carrier" means a person who owns or operates a telephone system in this state that includes equipment or facilities for the conveyance, transmission, or reception of communications and who receives compensation from persons who use that system.

(2) "COMPUTER" means an electronic, magnetic, optical, electrochemical, or other high-speed data processing device that performs logical, arithmetic, or memory functions by the manipulations of electronic or magnetic impulses and includes all input, output, processing, storage, or communication facilities that are connected or related to the device.

(3) "COMPUTER network" means the interconnection of two or more COMPUTER systems by satellite, microwave, line, or other communication medium with the capability to transmit information among the COMPUTERS.

(4) "COMPUTER program" means an ordered set of data representing coded instructions or statements that when executed by a COMPUTER cause the COMPUTER to process data or perform specific functions.

(5) "COMPUTER security system" means the design, procedures, or other measures that the person responsible for the operation and use of a COMPUTER employs to restrict the use of the COMPUTER to particular persons or uses or that the owner or licensee of data stored or maintained by a COMPUTER in which the owner or licensee is entitled to store or maintain the data employs to restrict access to the data.

(6) "COMPUTER services" means the product of the use of a COMPUTER, the information stored in the COMPUTER, or the personnel supporting the COMPUTER, including COMPUTER time, data processing, and storage functions.

(7) "COMPUTER system" means any combination of a COMPUTER or COMPUTERS with the documentation, COMPUTER software, or physical facilities supporting the COMPUTER.

(8) "COMPUTER software" means a set of COMPUTER programs, procedures, and associated documentation related to the operation of a COMPUTER, COMPUTER system, or COMPUTER network.

(9) "COMPUTER virus" means an unwanted COMPUTER program or other set of instructions inserted into a COMPUTER's memory, operating system, or program

that is specifically constructed with the ability to replicate itself and to affect the other programs or files in the COMPUTER by attaching a copy of the unwanted program or other set of instructions to one or more COMPUTER programs or files.

(10) "Damage" includes partial or total alteration, damage, or erasure of stored data, or interruption of COMPUTER services.

(11) "Data" means a representation of information, knowledge, facts, concepts, or instructions that is being prepared or has been prepared in a formalized manner and is intended to be stored or processed, is being stored or processed, or has been stored or processed in a COMPUTER. Data may be embodied in any form, including but not limited to COMPUTER printouts, magnetic storage media, and punchcards, or may be stored internally in the memory of the COMPUTER.

(12) "Electric utility" has the meaning assigned by Subsection (c), Section 3, Public Utility Regulatory Act (Article 1446c, Vernon's Texas Civil Statutes).

33.02. Breach of COMPUTER Security

(a) A person commits an offense if the person:

(1) uses a COMPUTER without the effective consent of the owner of the COMPUTER or a person authorized to license access to the COMPUTER and the actor knows that there exists a COMPUTER security system intended to prevent him from making that use of the COMPUTER; or

(2) gains access to data stored or maintained by a COMPUTER without the effective consent of the owner or licensee of the data and the actor knows that there exists a COMPUTER security system intended to prevent him from gaining access to that data.

(b) A person commits an offense if the person intentionally or knowingly gives a password, identifying code, personal identification number, debit card number, bank account number, or other confidential information about a COMPUTER security system to another person without the effective consent of the person employing the COMPUTER security system to restrict the use of a COMPUTER or to restrict access to data stored or maintained by a COMPUTER.

(c) An offense under this section is a Class A misdemeanor.

33.03. Harmful Access

(a) A person commits an offense if the person intentionally or knowingly and without authorization from the owner of the COMPUTER or a person authorized to license access to the COMPUTER:

(1) damages, alters, or destroys a COMPUTER, COMPUTER program or software, COMPUTER system, data, or COMPUTER network;

(2) causes a COMPUTER to interrupt or impair a government operation, public communication, public transportation, or public service providing water or gas;

(3) uses a COMPUTER to:

(A) tamper with government, medical, or educational records; or

(B) receive or use records that were not intended for public dissemination to gain an advantage over business competitors;

(4) obtains information from or introduces false information into a COMPUTER system to damage or enhance the data or credit records of a person;

(5) causes a COMPUTER to remove, alter, erase, or copy a negotiable instrument; or

(6) inserts or introduces a COMPUTER virus into a COMPUTER program, COMPUTER network, or COMPUTER system.

(b) An offense under this section is a:

(1) felony of the second degree if the value of the loss or damage caused by the conduct is $20,000 or more;

(2) felony of the third degree if the value of the loss or damage caused by the conduct is $750 or more but less than $20,000; or

(3) Class A misdemeanor if the value of the loss or damage caused by the conduct is $200 or more but less than $750.

33.04. Defenses

It is an affirmative defense to prosecution under Sections 33.02 and 33.03 of this code that the actor was an officer, employee, or agent of a communications common carrier or electric utility and committed the proscribed act or acts in the course of employment while engaged in an activity that is a necessary incident to the rendition of service or to the protection of the rights or property of the communications common carrier or electric utility. s 33.05. Assistance by Attorney General

The attorney general, if requested to do so by a prosecuting attorney, may assist the prosecuting attorney in the investigation or prosecution of an offense under this chapter or of any other offense involving the use of a COMPUTER.

UTAH STATUTES

TITLE 76. CRIMINAL CODE
PART 7. COMPUTER CRIMES
CHAPTER 6. OFFENSES AGAINST PROPERTY

76-6-701. Computer Crimes Act—Short title.

This part is known as the "Utah Computer Crimes Act."

76-6-702. Computer Crimes Act—Definitions.

As used in this part:

(1) "Access" means to directly or indirectly use, attempt to use, instruct, communicate with, cause input to, cause output from, or otherwise make use of any resources of a computer, computer system, computer network, or any means of communication with any of them.

(2) "Computer" means any electronic device or communication facility with data processing ability.

(3) "Computer system" means a set of related, connected or unconnected, devices, software, or other related computer equipment.

(4) "Computer network" means the interconnection of communication or telecommunication lines between computers or computers and remote terminals.

(5) "Computer property" includes, but is not limited to, electronic impulses, electronically produced data, information, financial instruments, software, or programs, in either machine or human readable form, any other tangible or intangible item relating to a computer, computer system, computer network, and copies of any of them.

(6) "Services" include, but are not limited to, computer time, data manipulation, and storage functions.

(7) "Financial instrument" includes, but is not limited to, any check, draft, money order, certificate of deposit, letter of credit, bill of exchange, credit card, or marketable security.

(8) "Software" or "program" means a series of instructions or statements in a form acceptable to a computer, relating to the operations of the computer, or permitting the functioning of a computer system in a manner designed to provide results including, but not limited to, system control programs, application programs, or copies of any of them.

76-6-703. Computer crimes and penalties.

(1) A person who gains or attempts to gain access to and without authorization intentionally, and to the damage of another, alters, damages, destroys, discloses, or modifies any computer, computer network, computer property, computer system, program, or software is guilty of a felony of the third degree.

(2) A person who intentionally and without authorization uses a computer, computer network, computer property, or computer system to gain or attempt to gain access to any other computer, computer network, computer property, or computer system, program, or software, to the damage of another, and alters, damages, destroys, discloses, or modifies any of these, is guilty of a felony of the third degree.

(3) A person who uses or knowingly allows another person to use any computer, computer network, computer property, or computer system, program, or software to devise or execute any artifice or scheme to defraud or to obtain money, property, services, or other things of value by false pretenses, promises, or representations, is guilty of a felony of the second degree.

(4) A person who intentionally, and without authorization, interferes with or interrupts computer services to another authorized to receive the services is guilty of a class A misdemeanor.

(5) A person who intentionally and without authorization damages or destroys, in whole or in part, any computer, computer network, computer property, or computer system is guilty of a class A misdemeanor unless the amount of damage exceeds $1,000, in which case the person is guilty of a felony of the third degree.

76-6-704. Computer Crimes Act—Attorney general or county attorney to prosecute—Conduct violating other statutes.

(1) The attorney general or the county attorney shall prosecute suspected criminal violations of this part.

(2) Prosecution under this part does not prevent any prosecutions under any other law.

76-6-705. Reporting violations.

Every person, except those to whom a statutory or common law privilege applies, who has reason to believe that the provisions of Section 76-6-703 are being or have been violated shall report the suspected violation to the attorney general or to the county attorney of the county in which part or all of the violations occurred.

VERMONT STATUTES

NO KNOWN STATUTES.

VIRGINIA STATUTES

TITLE 18.2. CRIMES AND OFFENSES
CHAPTER 5. CRIMES AGAINST PROPERTY
ARTICLE 7.1. COMPUTER CRIMES

18.2-152.1. Short title.

This article shall be known and may be cited as the "Virginia Computer Crimes Act."

18.2-152.2. Definitions.

For purposes of this article:

"Computer" means an electronic, magnetic, optical, hydraulic or organic device or group of devices which, pursuant to a computer program, to human instruction, or to permanent instructions contained in the device or group of devices, can automatically perform computer operations with or on computer data and can communicate the results to another computer or to a person. The term "computer" includes any connected or directly related device, equipment, or facility which enables the computer to store, retrieve or communicate computer programs, computer data or the results of computer operations to or from a person, another computer or another device.

"Computer data" means any representation of information, knowledge, facts, concepts, or instructions which is being prepared or has been prepared and is intended to be processed, is being processed, or has been processed in a computer or computer network. "Computer data" may be in any form, whether readable only by a computer or only by a human or by either, including, but not limited to, computer printouts, magnetic storage media, punched cards, or stored internally in the memory of the computer.

"Computer network" means a set of related, remotely connected devices and any communications facilities including more than one computer with the capability to transmit data among them through the communications facilities.

"Computer operation" means arithmetic, logical, monitoring, storage or retrieval functions and any combination thereof, and includes, but is not limited to, communication with, storage of data to, or retrieval of data from any device or human hand manipulation of electronic or magnetic impulses. A "computer operation" for a particular computer may also be any function for which that computer was generally designed.

"Computer program" means an ordered set of data representing coded instructions or statements that, when executed by a computer, causes the computer to perform one or more computer operations.

"Computer services" includes computer time or services or data processing services or information or data stored in connection there with.

"Computer software" means a set of computer programs, procedures and associated documentation concerned with computer data or with the operation of a computer, computer program, or computer network.

"Financial instrument" includes, but is not limited to, any check, draft, warrant, money order, note, certificate of deposit, letter of credit, bill of exchange, credit or debit card, transaction authorization mechanism, marketable security, or any computerized representation thereof.

"Owner" means an owner or lessee of a computer or a computer network or an owner, lessee, or licensee of computer data, computer programs, or computer software.

"Person" shall include any individual, partnership, association, corporation or joint venture.

"Property" shall include:

1. Real property;

2. Computers and computer networks;

3. Financial instruments, computer data, computer programs, computer software and all other personal property regardless of whether they are:

    a. Tangible or intangible;

    b. In a format readable by humans or by a computer;

    c. In transit between computers or within a computer network or between any devices which comprise a computer; or

    d. Located on any paper or in any device on which it is stored by a computer or by a human; and

4. Computer services.

A person "uses" a computer or computer network when he:

1. Attempts to cause or causes a computer or computer network to perform or to stop performing computer operations;

2. Attempts to cause or causes the withholding or denial of the use of a computer, computer network, computer program, computer data or computer software to another user; or

3. Attempts to cause or causes another person to put false information into a computer.

A person is "without authority" when he has no right or permission of the owner to use a computer, or, he uses a computer in a manner exceeding such right or permission.

18.2-152.3. Computer fraud.

Any person who uses a computer or computer network without authority and with the intent to:

1. Obtain property or services by false pretenses;

2. Embezzle or commit larceny; or

3. Convert the property of another shall be guilty of the crime of computer fraud. If the value of the property or services obtained is $200 or more, the crime of computer fraud shall be punishable as a Class 5 felony. Where the value of the property or services obtained is less than $200, the crime of computer fraud shall be punishable as a Class 1 misdemeanor.

18.2-152.4. Computer trespass; penalty.

Any person who uses a computer or computer network without authority and with the intent to:

1. Temporarily or permanently remove computer data, computer programs, or computer software from a computer or computer network;

2. Cause a computer to malfunction regardless of how long the malfunction persists;

3. Alter or erase any computer data, computer programs, or computer software;

4. Effect the creation or alteration of a financial instrument or of an electronic transfer of funds;

5. Cause physical injury to the property of another; or

6. Make or cause to be made an unauthorized copy, in any form, including, but not limited to, any printed or electronic form of computer data, computer programs, or computer software residing in, communicated by, or produced by a computer or computer network shall be guilty of the crime of computer trespass, which shall be punishable as a Class 1 misdemeanor. If such act is done maliciously and the value of the property damaged is $2,500 or more, the offense shall be punishable as a Class 6 felony.

18.2-152.5. Computer invasion of privacy.

A. A person is guilty of the crime of computer invasion of privacy when he uses a computer or computer network and intentionally examines without authority any employment, salary, credit or any other financial or personal information relating to any other person. "Examination" under this section requires the offender to review the information relating to any other person after the time at which the offender knows or should know that he is without authority to view the information displayed.

B. The crime of computer invasion of privacy shall be punishable as a Class 3 misdemeanor.

18.2-152.6. Theft of computer services.

Any person who willfully uses a computer or computer network, with intent to obtain computer services without authority, shall be guilty of the crime of theft of computer services, which shall be punishable as a Class 1 misdemeanor.

18.2-152.7. Personal trespass by computer.

A. A person is guilty of the crime of personal trespass by computer when he uses a computer or computer network without authority and with the intent to cause physical injury to an individual.

B. If committed maliciously, the crime of personal trespass by computer shall be punishable as a Class 3 felony. If such act be done unlawfully but not maliciously, the crime of personal trespass by computer shall be punishable as a Class 1 misdemeanor.

18.2-152.8. Property capable of embezzlement.

For purposes of 18.2-111, personal property subject to embezzlement shall include:

1. Computers and computer networks;

2. Financial instruments, computer data, computer programs, computer software and all other personal property regardless of whether they are:

   a. Tangible or intangible;

   b. In a format readable by humans or by a computer;

   c. In transit between computers or within a computer network or between any devices which comprise a computer; or

   d. Located on any paper or in any device on which it is stored by a computer or by a human; and

3. Computer services.

18.2-152.9. Limitation of prosecution.

Notwithstanding the provisions of 19.2-8, prosecution of a crime which is punishable as a misdemeanor pursuant to this article must be commenced before the earlier of (i) five years after the commission of the last act in the course of conduct constituting a violation of this article or (ii) one year after the existence of the illegal act and the identity of the offender are discovered by the Commonwealth, by the owner, or by anyone else who is damaged by such violation.

18.2-152.10. Venue for prosecution.

For the purpose of venue under this article, any violation of this article shall be considered to have been committed in any county or city:

1. In which any act was performed in furtherance of any course of conduct which violated this article;

2. In which the owner has his principal place of business in the Commonwealth;

3. In which any offender had control or possession of any proceeds of the violation or of any books, records, documents, property, financial instrument, computer software, computer program, computer data, or other material or objects which were used in furtherance of the violation;

4. From which, to which, or through which any access to a computer or computer network was made whether by wires, electromagnetic waves, microwaves, or any other means of communication;

5. In which the offender resides; or

6. In which any computer which is an object or an instrument of the violation is located at the time of the alleged offense.

18.2-152.11. Article not exclusive.

The provisions of this article shall not be construed to preclude the applicability of any other provision of the criminal law of this Commonwealth which presently applies or may in the future apply to any transaction or course of conduct which violates this article, unless such provision is clearly inconsistent with the terms of this article.

18.2-152.12. Civil relief; damages.

A. Any person whose property or person is injured by reason of a violation of any provision of this article may sue therefor and recover for any damages sustained, and the costs of suit. Without limiting the generality of the term, "damages" shall include loss of profits.

B. At the request of any party to an action brought pursuant to this section, the court may, in its discretion, conduct all legal proceedings in such a way as to protect the secrecy and security of the computer, computer network, computer data, computer program and computer software involved in order to prevent possible recurrence of the same or a similar act by another person and to protect any trade secrets of any party.

C. The provisions of this article shall not be construed to limit any person's right to pursue any additional civil remedy otherwise allowed by law. D. A civil action under this section must be commenced before expiration of the time period prescribed in 8.01-40.1.

18.2-152.13. Severability.

If any provision or clause of this article or application thereof to any person or circumstances is held to be invalid, such invalidity shall not affect other provisions or applications of this article which can be given effect without the invalid provision or application, and to this end the provisions of this article are declared to be severable.

18.2-152.14. Computer as instrument of forgery.

The creation, alteration, or deletion of any computer data contained in any computer or computer network, which if done on a tangible document or instrument would constitute forgery under Article 1 18.2-168 et seq.) of Chapter 6 of this Title, will also be deemed to be forgery. The absence of a tangible writing directly created or altered by the offender shall not be a defense to any crime set forth in Article 1 18.2-168 et seq.) of Chapter 6 of this Title if a creation, alteration, or deletion of computer data was involved in lieu of a tangible document or instrument.

TITLE 8.01. CIVIL REMEDIES AND PROCEDURE
CHAPTER 3. ACTIONS
ARTICLE 3. INJURY TO PERSON
OR PROPERTY

8.01-40.1. Action for injury resulting from violation of Computer Crimes Act; limitations.

Any person whose property or person is injured by reason of a violation of the provisions of the Virginia Computer Crimes Act (18.2-152.1 et seq.) may sue and recover damages as provided in 18.2-152.12. An action shall be commenced before the earlier of (i) five years after the last act in the course of conduct constituting a violation of the Computer Crimes Act or (ii) two years after the plaintiff discovers or reasonably should have discovered the last act in the course of conduct constituting a violation of the Computer Crimes Act.

WASHINGTON STATUTES

TITLE 9A WASHINGTON CRIMINAL CODE
CHAPTER 9A.52 BURGLARY AND TRESPASS

9A.52.010 Definitions

The following definitions apply in this chapter:

(1) "Premises" includes any building, dwelling, structure used for commercial aquaculture, or any real property;

(2) "Enter". The word "enter" when constituting an element or part of a crime, shall include the entrance of the person, or the insertion of any part of his body, or any instrument or weapon held in his hand and used or intended to be used to threaten or intimidate a person or to detach or remove property;

(3) "Enters or remains unlawfully". A person "enters or remains unlawfully" in or upon premises when he is not then licensed, invited, or otherwise privileged to so enter or remain.

A license or privilege to enter or remain in a building which is only partly open to the public is not a license or privilege to enter or remain in that part of a building which is not open to the public. A person who enters or remains upon unimproved and apparently unused land, which is neither fenced nor otherwise enclosed in a manner designed to exclude intruders, does so with license and privilege unless notice against trespass is personally communicated to him by the owner of the land or some other authorized person, or unless notice is given by posting in a conspicuous manner. Land that is used for commercial aquaculture or for growing an agricultural crop or crops, other than timber, is not unimproved and apparently unused land if a crop or any other sign of cultivation is clearly visible or if notice is given by posting in a conspicuous manner. Similarily, a field fenced in any manner is not unimproved and apparently unused land;

(4) "Data" means a representation of information, knowledge, facts, concepts, or instructions that are being prepared in a formalized manner and are intended for use in a computer;

(5) "Computer program" means an ordered set of data representing coded instructions or statements that when executed by a computer cause the computer to process data;

(6) "Access" means to approach, instruct, communicate with, store data in, retrieve data from, or otherwise make use of any resources of a computer, directly or by electronic means.

CHAPTER 9A.48 ARSON, RECKLESS BURNING, AND MALICIOUS MISCHIEF

9A.48.100 Malicious mischief—"Physical damage" defined

For the purposes of RCW 9A.48.070 through 9A.48.090 inclusive:

(1) "Physical damage", in addition to its ordinary meaning, shall include the total or partial alteration, damage, obliteration, or erasure of records, information, data, computer programs, or their computer representations, which are recorded for use in computers or the impairment, interruption, or interference with the use of such records, information, data, or computer programs, or the impairment, interruption, or interference with the use of any computer or services provided by computers. "Physical damage" also includes any diminution in the value of any property as the consequence of an act;

(2) If more than one item of property is physically damaged as a result of a common scheme or plan by a person and the physical damage to the property would, when considered separately, constitute mischief in the third degree because of value, then the value of the damages may be aggregated in one count. If the sum of the value of all the physical damages exceeds two hundred fifty dollars, the defendant may be charged with

and convicted of malicious mischief in the second degree.

9A.52.120 Computer trespass in the second degree

(1) A person is guilty of computer trespass in the second degree if the person, without authorization, intentionally gains access to a computer system or electronic data base of another under circumstances not constituting the offense in the first degree.

(2) Computer trespass in the second degree is a gross misdemeanor.

9A.52.130 Computer trespass—Commission of other crime

A person who, in the commission of a computer trespass, commits any other crime may be punished for that other crime as well as for the computer trespass and may be prosecuted for each crime separately.

WEST VIRGINIA STATUTES

CHAPTER 61. CRIMES AND THEIR PUNISHMENT. ARTICLE 3C. WEST VIRGINIA COMPUTER CRIME AND ABUSE ACT

61-3C-1. Short title.

This act shall be known and may be cited as the "West Virginia Computer Crime and Abuse Act."

61-3C-2. Legislative findings.

The Legislature finds that:

(a) The computer and related industries play an essential role in the commerce and welfare of this state.

(b) Computer-related crime is a growing problem in business and government.

(c) Computer-related crime has a direct effect on state commerce and can result in serious economic and, in some cases, physical harm to the public.

(d) Because of the pervasiveness of computers in today's society, opportunities are great for computer related crimes through the introduction of false records into a computer or computer system, the unauthorized use of computers and computer facilities, the alteration and destruction of computers, computer programs and computer data, and the theft of computer resources, computer software and computer data.

(e) Because computers have now become an integral part of society, the Legislature recognizes the need to protect the rights of owners and legitimate users of computers and computer systems, as well as the privacy interest of the general public, from those who abuse computers and computer systems.

(f) While various forms of computer crime or abuse might possibly be the subject of criminal charges or civil suit based on other provisions of law, it is appropriate and desirable that a supplemental and additional statute be provided which specifically proscribes various forms of computer crime and abuse and provides criminal penalties and civil remedies therefor.

61-3C-3. Definitions.

As used in this article, unless the context clearly indicates otherwise:

(a) "Access" means to instruct, communicate with, store data in, retrieve data from, intercept data from, or otherwise make use of any computer, computer network, computer program, computer software, computer data or other computer resources.

(b) "Authorization" means the express or implied consent given by a person to another to access or use said person's computer, computer network, computer program, computer software, computer system, password, identifying code or personal identification number.

(c) "Computer" means an electronic, magnetic, optical, electrochemical, or other high speed data processing device performing logical, arithematic, or storage functions, and includes any data storage facility or communication facility directly related to or operating in conjunction with such device. The term "computer" includes any connected or directly related device, equipment or facility which enables the computer to store, retrieve or communicate computer programs, computer data or the results of computer operations to or from a person, another computer or another device, but such term does not include an automated typewriter or typesetter, a portable handheld calculator or other similar device.

(d) "Computer data" means any representation of knowledge, facts, concepts, instruction, or other information computed, classified, processed, transmitted, received, retrieved, originated, stored, manifested, measured, detected, recorded, reproduced, handled or utilized by a computer, computer network, computer program or computer software, and may be in any medium, including, but not limited to, computer printouts, microfilm, microfiche, magnetic storage media, optical storage media, punch paper tape or punch cards, or it may be stored internally in read-only memory or random access memory of a computer or any other peripheral device.

(e) "Computer network" means a set of connected devices and communication facilities, including more than one computer, with the capability to transmit computer data among them through such communication facilities.

(f) "Computer operations" means arithematic, logical, storage, display, monitoring or retrieval functions or any combination thereof, and includes, but is not limited to, communication with, storage of data in or to, or retrieval of data from any device and the human manual manipulation of electronic magnetic impulses. A "computer operation" for a particular computer shall also mean any function for which that computer was designed.

(g) "Computer program" means an ordered set of computer data representing instructions or statements, in a form readable by a computer, which controls, directs, or otherwise influences the functioning of a computer or computer network.

(h) "Computer software" means a set of computer programs, procedures and associated documentation concerned with computer data or with the operation of a computer, computer program, or computer network.

(i) "Computer services" means computer access time, computer data processing, or computer data storage, and the computer data processed or stored in connection therewith.

(j) "Computer supplies" means punchcards, paper tape, magnetic tape, magnetic disks or diskettes, optical disks or diskettes, disk or diskette packs, paper, microfilm, and any other tangible input, output or storage medium used in connection with a computer, computer network, computer data, computer software or computer program.

(k) "Computer resources" includes, but is not limited to, information retrieval; computer data processing, transmission and storage; and any other functions performed, in whole or in part, by the use of a computer, computer network, computer software, or computer program.

(l) "Owner" means any person who owns or leases or is a licensee of a computer, computer network, computer data, computer program, computer software, computer resources or computer supplies.

(m) "Person" means any natural person, general partnership, limited partnership, trust, association, corporation, joint venture, or any state, county or municipal government and any subdivision, branch, department or agency thereof.

(n) "Property" includes:

(1) Real property;

(2) Computers and computer networks;

(3) Financial instruments, computer data, computer programs, computer software and all other personal property regardless of whether they are;

(i) Tangible or intangible;

(ii) In a format readable by humans or by a computer;

(iii) In transit between computers or within a computer network or between any devices which comprise a computer; or

(iv) Located on any paper or in any device on which it is stored by a computer or by a human; and

(4) Computer services.

(o) "Value" means having any potential to provide any direct or indirect gain or advantage to any person.

(p) "Financial instrument" includes, but is not limited to, any check, draft, warrant, money order, note, certificate of deposit, letter of credit, bill of exchange, credit or debit card, transaction authorization mechanism, marketable security or any computerized representation thereof.

(q) "Value of property or computer services" shall be (1) the market value of the property or computer services at the time of a violation of this article; or (2) if the property or computer services are unrecoverable, damaged, or destroyed as a result of a violation of section three or four [61-3C-3 or 61-3C-4] of this article, the cost of reproducing or replacing the property or computer services at the time of the violation.

61-3C-4. Computer fraud; penalties.

Any person who, knowingly and willfully, directly or indirectly, accesses or causes to be accessed any computer, computer services or computer network for the purpose of (1) executing any scheme or artifice to defraud or (2) obtaining money, property or services by means of fraudulent pretenses, representations or promises shall be guilty of a felony, and, upon conviction thereof, shall be fined not more than ten thousand dollars or imprisoned in the penitentiary for not more than ten years, or both.

61-3C-5. Unauthorized access to computer services.

Any person who knowingly, willfully and without authorization, directly or indirectly, accesses or causes to be accessed a computer or computer network with the intent to obtain computer services shall be guilty of a misdemeanor, and, upon conviction thereof, shall be fined not less than two hundred dollars nor more than one thousand dollars or confined in the county jail not more than one year, or both.

61-3C-6. Unauthorized possession of computer data or programs.

(a) Any person who knowingly, willfully and without authorization possesses any computer data or computer program belonging to another and having a value of five thousand dollars or more shall be guilty of a felony, and, upon conviction thereof, shall be fined not more than ten thousand dollars or imprisoned in the penitentiary for not more than ten years, or both.

(b) Any person who knowingly, willfully and without authorization possesses any computer data or computer program belonging to another and having a value of less than five thousand dollars shall be guilty of a misdemeanor, and, upon conviction thereof, shall be fined

not more than one thousand dollars or confined in the county jail for not more than one year, or both.

61-3C-7. Alteration, destruction, etc., of computer equipment.

Any person who knowingly, willfully and without authorization, directly or indirectly, tampers with, deletes, alters, damages or destroys or attempts to tamper with, delete, alter, damage or destroy any computer, computer network, computer software, computer resources, computer program or computer data shall be guilty of a felony, and, upon conviction thereof, shall be fined not more than ten thousand dollars or confined in the penitentiary not more than ten years, or both, or, in the discretion of the court, be fined not less than two hundred nor more than one thousand dollars and confined in the county jail not more than one year.

61-3C-8. Disruption of computer services.

Any person who knowingly, willfully and without authorization, directly or indirectly, disrupts or degrades or causes the disruption or degradation of computer services or denies or causes the denial of computer services to an authorized recipient or user of such computer services, shall be guilty of a misdemeanor, and, upon conviction thereof, shall be fined not less than two hundred nor more than one thousand dollars or confined in the county jail not more than one year, or both.

61-3C-9. Unauthorized possession of computer information, etc.

Any person who knowingly, willfully and without authorization possesses any computer data, computer software, computer supplies or a computer program which he knows or reasonably should know was obtained in violation of any section of this article shall be guilty of a misdemeanor, and, upon conviction thereof, shall be fined not less than two hundred nor more than one thousand dollars or confined in the county jail for not more than one year, or both.

61-3C-10. Disclosure of computer security information.

Any person who knowingly, willfully and without authorization discloses a password, identifying code, personal identification number or other confidential information about a computer security system to another person shall be guilty of a misdemeanor, and, upon conviction thereof, shall be fined not more than five hundred dollars or confined in the county jail for not more than six months, or both.

61-3C-11. Obtaining confidential public information.

Any person who knowingly, willfully and without authorization accesses or causes to be accessed any computer or computer network and thereby obtains information filed by any person with the state or any county or municipality which is required by law to be kept confidential shall be guilty of a misdemeanor and, upon conviction thereof, shall be fined not more than five hundred dollars or confined in the county jail not more than six months, or both.

61-3C-12. Computer invasion of privacy.

Any person who knowingly, willfully and without authorization accesses a computer or computer network and examines any employment, salary, credit or any other financial or personal information relating to any other person, after the time at which the offender knows or reasonably should know that he is without authorization to view the information displayed, shall be guilty of a misdemeanor, and, upon conviction thereof, shall be fined not more than five hundred dollars or confined in the county jail for not more than six months, or both.

61-3C-13. Fraud and related activity in connection with access devices.

(a) As used in this section, the following terms shall have the following meanings:

(1) "Access device" means any card, plate, code, account number, or other means of account access that can be used, alone or in conjunction with another access device, to obtain money, goods, services, or any other thing of value, or that can be used to initiate a transfer of funds (other than a transfer originated solely by paper instrument);

(2) "Counterfeit access device" means any access device that is counterfeit, fictitious, altered, or forged, or an identifiable component of an access device or a counterfeit access device;

(3) "Unauthorized access device" means any access device that is lost, stolen, expired, revoked, canceled, or obtained without authority;

(4) "Produce" includes design, alter, authenticate, duplicate, or assemble;

(5) "Traffic" means transfer, or otherwise dispose of, to another, or obtain control of with intent to transfer or dispose of.

(b) Any person who knowingly and willfully possesses any counterfeit or unauthorized access device shall be guilty of a misdemeanor, and, upon conviction thereof, shall be fined not more than one thousand dollars or confined in the county jail for not more than six months, or both.

(c) Any person who knowingly, willfully and with intent to defraud possesses a counterfeit or unauthorized access device or who knowingly, willfully and with intent to defraud, uses, produces or traffics in any counterfeit or unauthorized access device shall be guilty of a felony, and, upon conviction thereof, shall be fined not more than ten thousand dollars or imprisoned in the penitentiary for not more than ten years, or both.

(d) This section shall not prohibit any lawfully authorized investigative or protective activity of any state, county or municipal law-enforcement agency.

61-3C-14. Endangering public safety.

Any person who accesses a computer or computer network and knowingly, willfully and without authorization (a) interrupts or impairs the providing of services by any private or public utility; (b) interrupts or impairs the providing of any medical services; (c) interrupts or impairs the providing of services by any state, county or local government agency, public carrier or public communication service; or otherwise endangers public safety shall be guilty of a felony, and, upon conviction thereof, shall be fined not more than fifty thousand dollars or imprisoned not more than twenty years, or both.

61-3C-15. Computer as instrument of forgery.

The creation, alteration or deletion of any computer data contained in any computer or computer network, which if done on a tangible document or instrument would constitute forgery under section five [§61-4-5], article four, chapter sixty-one of this code will also be deemed to be forgery. The absence of a tangible writing directly created or altered by the offender shall not be a defense to any crime set forth in section five, article four, chapter sixty-one if a creation, alteration or deletion of computer data was involved in lieu of a tangible document or instrument.

61-3C-16. Civil relief; damages.

(a) Any person whose property or person is injured by reason of a violation of any provision of this article may sue therefor in circuit court and may be entitled to recover for each violation:

(1) Compensatory damages;

(2) Punitive damages; and

(3) Such other relief, including injunctive relief, as the court may deem appropriate.

Without limiting the generality of the term, "damages" shall include loss of profits.

(b) At the request of any party to an action brought pursuant to this section, the court may, in its discretion, conduct all legal proceedings in such a manner as to protect the secrecy and security of the computer network, computer data, computer program or computer software involved in order to prevent any possible recurrence of the same or a similar act by another person or to protect any trade secret or confidential information of any person. For the purposes of this section "trade secret" means the whole or any portion or phase of any scientific or technological information, design, process, procedure or formula or improvement which is secret and of value. A trade secret shall be presumed to be secret when the owner thereof takes measures to prevent it from becoming available to persons other than those authorized by the owner to have access thereto for a limited purpose.

(c) The provisions of this section shall not be construed to limit any person's right to pursue any additional civil remedy otherwise allowed by law.

(d) A civil action under this section must be commenced before the earlier of: (1) Five years after the last act in the course of conduct constituting a violation of this article; or (2) two years after the plaintiff discovers or reasonably should have discovered the last act in the course of conduct constituting a violation of this article.

61-3C-17. Defenses to criminal prosecution.

(a) In any criminal prosecution under this article, it shall be a defense that:

(1) The defendant had reasonable grounds to believe that he had authority to access or could not have reasonably known he did not have authority to access the computer, computer network, computer data, computer program or computer software in question; or

(2) The defendant had reasonable grounds to believe that he had the right to alter or destroy the computer data, computer software or computer program in question; or

(3) The defendant had reasonable grounds to believe that he had the right to copy, reproduce, duplicate or disclose the computer data, computer program, computer security system information or computer software in question.

(b) Nothing in this section shall be construed to limit any defense available to a person charged with a violation of this article.

61-3C-18. Venue.

For the purpose of criminal and civil venue under this article, any violation of this article shall be considered to have been committed:

(1) In any county in which any act was performed in furtherance of any course of conduct which violates this article;

(2) In the county of the principal place of business in this state of the aggrieved owner of the computer, computer data, computer program, computer software or computer network, or any part thereof;

(3) In any county in which any violator had control or possession of any proceeds of the violation or any books, records, documentation, property, financial instrument, computer data, computer software, computer program, or other material or objects which were used in furtherance of or obtained as a result of the violation;

(4) In any county from which, to which, or through which any access to a computer or computer network was made, whether by wires, electromagnetic waves, microwaves or any other means of communication; and

(5) In the county in which the aggrieved owner or the defendant resides or either of them maintains a place of business.

61-3C-19. Prosecution under other criminal statutes not prohibited.

Criminal prosecution pursuant to this article shall not prevent prosecution pursuant to any other provision of law.

61-3C-20. Personal jurisdiction.

Any person who violates any provision of this article and, in doing so, accesses, permits access to, causes access to or attempts to access a computer, computer network, computer data, computer resources, computer software or computer program which is located, in whole or in part, within this state, or passes through this state in transit, shall be subject to criminal prosecution and punishment in this state and to the civil jurisdiction of the courts of this state.

61-3C-21. Severability.

If any provision of this article or the application thereof to any person or circumstance is held invalid, such invalidity shall not affect any other provisions or applications of this article which can be given effect without the invalid provision or application, and to that end the provisions of this article are declared to be severable.

WISCONSIN STATUTES

CHAPTER 943 CRIMES AGAINST PROPERTY
MISAPPROPRIATION

943.70 Computer crimes.

(1) DEFINITIONS. In this section:

(a) "Computer" means an electronic device that performs logical, arithmetic and memory functions by manipulating electronic or magnetic impulses, and includes all input, output, processing, storage, computer software and communication facilities that are connected or related to a computer in a computer system or computer network.

(b) "Computer network" means the interconnection of communication lines with a computer through remote terminals or a complex consisting of 2 or more interconnected computers.

(c) "Computer program" means an ordered set of instructions or statements that, when executed by a computer, causes the computer to process data.

(d) "Computer software" means a set of computer programs, procedures or associated documentation used in the operation of a computer system.

(dm) "Computer supplies" means a punch-cards, paper tape, magnetic tape, disk packs, diskettes and computer output, including paper and microfilm.

(e) "Computer system" means a set of related computer equipment, hardware or software.

(f) "Data" means a representation of information, knowledge, facts, concepts or instructions that has been prepared or is being prepared in a formalized manner and has been processed, is being processed or is intended to be processed in a computer system or computer network. Data may be in any form including computer printouts, magnetic storage media, punched cards and as stored in the memory of the computer. Data are property.

(g) "Financial instrument" includes any check, draft, warrant, money order, note, certificate of deposit, letter of credit, bill of exchange, credit or credit card, transaction authorization mechanism, marketable security and any computer representation of them.

(h) "Property" means anything of value, including but not limited to financial instruments, information, electronically produced data, computer software and computer programs.

(i) "Supporting documentation" means all documentation used in the computer system in the construction, clarification, implementation, use or modification of the software or data.

(2) OFFENSES AGAINST COMPUTER DATA AND PROGRAMS.

(a) Whoever willfully, knowingly and without authorization does any of the following may be penalized as provided in par. (b):

1. Modifies data, computer programs or supporting documentation.

2. Destroys data, computer programs or supporting documentation.

3. Accesses data, computer programs or supporting documentation.

4. Takes possession of data, computer programs or supporting documentation.

5. Copies data, computer programs or supporting documentation.

6. Discloses restricted access codes or other restricted access information to unauthorized persons.

(b) Whoever violates this subsection is guilty of:

1. A Class A misdemeanor unless subd. 2, 3 or 4 applies.

2. A Class E felony if the offense is committed to defraud or to obtain property.

3. A Class D felony if the damage is greater than $ 2,500 or if it causes an interruption or impairment of governmental operations or public communication, of transportation or of a supply of water, gas or other public service.

4. A Class C felony if the offense creates a substantial and unreasonable risk of death or great bodily harm to another.

(3) OFFENSES AGAINST COMPUTERS, COMPUTER EQUIPMENT OR SUPPLIES.

(a) Whoever willfully, knowingly and without authorization does any of the following may be penalized as provided in par. (b):

1. Modifies computer equipment or supplies that are used or intended to be used in a computer, computer system or computer network.

2. Destroys, uses, takes or damages a computer, computer system, computer network or equipment or supplies used or intended to be used in a computer, computer system or computer network.

(b) Whoever violates this subsection is guilty of:

1. A Class A misdemeanor unless subd. 2, 3 or 4 applies.

2. A Class E felony if the offense is committed to defraud or obtain property.

3. A Class D felony if the damage to the computer, computer system, computer network, equipment or supplies is greater than $2,500.

4. A Class C felony if the offense creates a substantial and unreasonable risk of death or great bodily harm to another.

(4) COMPUTER USE RESTRICTION. In addition to the other penalties provided for violation of this section, a judge may place restrictions on the offender's use of computers. The duration of any such restrictions may not exceed the maximum period for which the offender could have been imprisoned; except if the offense is punishable by forfeiture, the duration of the restrictions may not exceed 90 days.

(5) INJUNCTIVE RELIEF. Any aggrieved party may sue for injunctive relief under ch. 813 to compel compliance with this section. In addition, owners, lessors, users or manufacturers of computers, or associations or organizations representing any of those persons, may sue for injunctive relief to prevent or stop the disclosure of information which may enable another person to gain unauthorized access to data, computer programs or supporting documentation.

939.50(3) Penalties for felonies.

(a) For a Class A felony, life imprisonment.

(b) For a Class B felony, imprisonment not to exceed 20 years.

(c) For a Class C felony, a fine not to exceed $10,000 or imprisonment not to exceed 10 year, or both.

(d) For a Class D felony, a fine not to exceed $10,000 or imprisonment not to exceed 5 year, or both.

(e) For a Class E felony, a fine not to exceed $10,000 or imprisonment not to exceed 2 year, or both.

939.51(3) Penalties for misdemeanors.

(a) For a Class A misdemeanor, a fine not to exceed $10,000 or imprisonment not to exceed 9 months, or both.

(b) For a Class B misdemeanor, a fine not to exceed $1,000 or imprisonment not to exceed 90 days, or both.

(c) For a Class C misdemeanor, a fine not to exceed $500 or imprisonment not to exceed 30 days, or both.

WYOMING STATUTES

TITLE 6 CRIMES AND OFFENSES
CHAPTER 3 OFFENSES AGAINST PROPERTY
ARTICLE 5. COMPUTER CRIMES

6-3-501. Definitions.

(a) As used in this article:

(i) "Access" means to approach, instruct, communicate with, store data in, retrieve data from, or otherwise make use of any resources of a computer, computer system or computer network;

(ii) "Computer" means an internally programmed, automatic device which performs data processing;

(iii) "Computer network" means a set of related, remotely connected devices and communication facilities including more than one (1) computer system with capability to transmit data among them through communication facilities;

(iv) "Computer program" means an ordered set of data representing coded instructions or statements which when executed by a computer cause the computer to process data;

(v) "Computer software" means a set of computer programs, procedures and associated documentation concerned with the operation of a computer system;

(vi) "Computer system" means a set of related, connected or unconnected, computer equipment, devices or computer software;

(vii) "Computer system services" means providing a computer system or computer network to perform useful work;

(viii) "Financial instrument" means a check, draft, money order, certificate of deposit, letter of credit, bill of exchange, credit card or marketable security;

(ix) "Intellectual property" means data, including programs;

(x) "Property" includes financial instruments, information, electronically produced data, computer software and programs in machine-readable or human-readable form;

(xi) "Trade secret" means the whole or a portion or phase of a formula, pattern, device, combination of devices or compilation of information which is for use, or is used in the operation of a business and which provides the business an advantage or an opportunity to obtain an advantage over those who do not know or use it. "Trade secret" includes any scientific, technical or commercial information including any design, process, procedure, list of suppliers, list of customers, business code or improvement thereof. Irrespective of novelty, invention, patentability, the state of the prior art and the level of skill in the business, art or field to which the subject matter pertains, when the owner of a trade secret takes measures to prevent it from becoming available to persons other than those selected by the owner to have access to it for limited purposes, the trade secret is considered to be:

(A) Secret;

(B) Of value;

(C) For use or in use by the business; and

(D) Providing an advantage or an opportunity to obtain an advantage to the business over those who do not know or use it. (Laws 1982, ch. 75, 3.)

6-3-502. Crimes against intellectual property; penalties.

(a) A person commits a crime against intellectual property if he knowingly and without authorization:

(i) Modifies data, programs or supporting documentation residing or existing internal or external to a computer, computer system or computer network;

(ii) Destroys data, programs or supporting documentation residing or existing internal or external to a computer, computer system or computer network;

(iii) Discloses or takes data, programs, or supporting documentation having a value of more than seven hundred fifty dollars ($750.00) and which is a trade secret or is confidential, as provided by law, residing or existing internal or external to a computer, computer system or computer network.

(b) A crime against intellectual property is:

(i) A felony punishable by imprisonment for not more than three (3) years, a fine of not more than three thousand dollars ($3,000.00), or both, except as provided in paragraph (ii) of this subsection;

(ii) A felony punishable by imprisonment for not more than ten (10) years, a fine of not more than ten thousand dollars ($10,000.00), or both, if the crime is committed with the intention of devising or executing a scheme or artifice to defraud or to obtain property.

6-3-503. Crimes against computer equipment or supplies; interruption or impairment of governmental operations or public services; penalties.

(a) A person commits a crime against computer equipment or supplies if he knowingly and without authorization, modifies equipment or supplies used or intended to be used in a computer, computer system or computer network. A crime against computer equipment or supplies is:

(i) A misdemeanor punishable by imprisonment for not more than six (6) months, a fine of not more than seven hundred fifty dollars ($750.00), or both, except as provided in paragraph (ii) of this subsection;

(ii) A felony punishable by imprisonment for not more than ten (10) years, a fine of not more than ten thousand dollars ($10,000.00), or both, if the crime is committed with the intention of devising or executing a scheme or artifice to defraud or to obtain property.

(b) A person who knowingly and without authorization destroys, injures or damages a computer, computer system or computer network and thereby interrupts or impairs governmental operations or public communication, transportation or supplies of water, gas or other public service, is guilty of a felony punishable by imprisonment for not more than three (3) years, a fine of not more than three thousand dollars ($3,000.00), or both.

6-3-504. Crimes against computer users; penalties.

(a) A person commits a crime against computer users if he knowingly and without authorization:

(i) Accesses a computer, computer system or computer network;

(ii) Denies computer system services to an authorized user of the computer system services which, in whole or part, are owned by, under contract to, or operated for, on behalf of, or in conjunction with another.

(b) A crime against computer users is:

(i) A felony punishable by imprisonment for not more than three (3) years, a fine of not more than three thousand dollars ($3,000.00), or both except as provided in paragraph (ii) of this subsection;

(ii) A felony punishable by imprisonment for not more than ten (10) years, a fine of not more than ten thousand dollars ($10,000.00), or both, if the crime is committed with the intention of devising or executing a scheme or artifice to defraud or to obtain property.

6-3-505. This article not exclusive.

This article shall not preclude the application of any other provision of the criminal law of this state which applies, or may apply, to any violation of this article, unless the provision is inconsistent with this article.

INTERNATIONAL STATUTES

AUSTRALIAN STATUTES

AUSTRALIAN CRIMES ACT 1914 - PART VIA

Section 76A

(1) In this Part, unless the contrary intention appears: "carrier" means:

(a) a general carrier within the meaning of the Telecommunications Act 1991; or

(b) a mobile carrier within the meaning of that Act; or

(c) a person who supplies eligible services within the meaning of that Act under a class licence issued under section 209 of that Act; "Commonwealth" includes a public authority under the Commonwealth; "Commonwealth computer" means a computer, a computer, a computer system or a part of a computer system, owned, leased or operated by the Commonwealth; "data" includes information, a computer program or part of a computer program.

(2) In this Part:

(a) a reference to data stored in a computer includes a reference to data entered or copied into a computer; and

(b) a reference to data stored on behalf of the Commonwealth in the computer includes a reference to:

(i) data stored in the computer at the direction or request of the Commonwealth; and

(ii) data supplied by the Commonwealth that is stored n the computer under, or in the course of performing, a contract with the Commonwealth.

Section 76B

(1) A person who intentionally and without authority obtains access to:

(a) data stored in a Commonwealth computer; or

(b) data stored on behalf of the Commonwealth in a computer that is not a Commonwealth computer; is guilty of an offence.

Penalty: Imprisonment for 6 months

(2)A person who:

(a) with intent to defraud any person and without authority obtains access to data stored in a Commonwealth computer, or to data stored on behalf of the Commonwealth in a computer that is not a Commonwealth computer; or

(b) intentionally and without authority obtains access to data stored in a Commonwealth computer, or to data stored on behalf of the Commonwealth in a computer that is not a Commonwealth computer, being data that the person knows or ought reasonably to know relates to:

(i) the security, defence or international relations of Australia;

(ii) the existence or identity of a confidential source of information relating to the enforcement of a criminal law of the Commonwealth or of a State or Territory;

(iii) the enforcement of a law of the Commonwealth or of a State or Territory;

(iv) the protection of public safety;

(v) the personal affairs of any person;

(vi) trade Secrets;

(vii) records of a financial institution; or

(viii) commercial Information the disclosure of which could cause advantage or disadvantage to any person. is guilty of an offence

Penalty: Imprisonment for 2 years

(3)A person who:

(a) has intentionally and without authority obtained access to data stored in a Commonwealth computer, or to data stored on behalf of the Commonwealth in a computer that is not a Commonwealth computer;

(b) after examining part of that data, knows or ought reasonably to know that the part of the data which the person examined relates wholly or partly

to any of the matters referred to in paragraph (2) (b); and

(c) continues to examine that data; is guilty of an offence.

Penalty for a contravention of this subsection:

Imprisonment for 2 years

Section 76C

A person who intentionally and without authority or lawful excuse:

(a) destroys, erases or alters data stored in, or inserts data into a Commonwealth computer;

(b) interferes with, or interrupts or obstructs the lawful use of, a Commonwealth computer;

(c) destroys, erases, alters or adds data stored on behalf of the Commonwealth in a computer that is not a Commonwealth computer; or

(d) impedes or prevents access to, or impairs the usefulness or effectiveness of, data stored in a Commonwealth computer or data stored on behalf of the Commonwealth in a computer that is not a Commonwealth computer; is guilty of an offence.

Penalty: Imprisonment for 10 years

Section 76D

(1) A person who, by means of a facility operated or provided by the Commonwealth or by a carrier, intentionally and without authority obtains access to data stored in a computer, is guilty of an offence.

Penalty: Imprisonment for 6 months

(2)A person who:

(a) by means of a facility operated or provided by the Commonwealth or by a carrier, with intent to defraud any person and without authority obtains access to data stored in a computer; or

(b) by means of such a facility, intentionally and without authority obtains access to data stored in a computer, being data that the person knows or ought reasonably to know relates to:

(i) the security, defence or international relations of Australia;

(ii) the existence or identity of a confidential source of information relating to the enforcement of a criminal law of the Commonwealth or of a State or Territory;

(iii) the enforcement of a law of the Commonwealth or of a State or Territory;

(iv) the protection of public safety;

(v) the personal affairs of any person;

(vi) trade Secrets;

(vii) records of a financial institution; or

(viii) commercial Information the disclosure of which could cause advantage or disadvantage to any person. is guilty of an offence

Penalty: Imprisonment for 2 years

(3)A person who:

(a) by means of a facility operated or provided by the Commonwealth or by a carrier, has intentionally and without authority obtained access to data stored in a computer;

(b) after examining part of that data, knows or ought reasonably to know that the part of the data which the person examined relates wholly or partly to any of the matters referred to in paragraph (2) (b); and

(c) continues to examine that data; is guilty of an offence.

Penalty for a contravention of this subsection:

Imprisonment for 2 years

Section 76E

A person who, by means of a facility operated or provided by the Commonwealth or by a carrier, intentionally and without authority or lawful excuse:

(a) destroys, erases or alters data stored in, or inserts data into a computer;

(b) interferes with, or interrupts or obstructs the lawful use of, a computer;

(c) impedes or prevents access to, or impairs the usefulness or effectiveness of, data stored in a computer; is guilty of an offence.

Penalty: Imprisonment for 10 years

CANADIAN STATUTES

THE CANADIAN CRIMINAL CODE

301.2?

(1) Every one who fraudulently and without color of right

(a) obtains, directly or indirectly, any computer service,

(b) by means of an electromagnetic, acoustic, mechanical or other device, intercepts or causes to be intercepted, directly or indirectly, any function of a computer system, or

(c) causes to be used, directly or indirectly, a computer system with intent to commit an offence under paragraph (a) or (b) or an offence under section 387 in relation to data or a computer system is guilty of an indictable offence and is liable to imprisonment for a term not exceeding ten years, or is guilty of an offence punishable on summary conviction.

(2) In this section, "computer program" means data representing instructions or statements that, when executed in a computer system, causes the computer system to perform a function;

"computer service" includes data processing and the storage or retrieval of data;

"computer system" means a device that, or a group of interconnected or related devices one or more of which,

(a) contains computer programs or other data, and

(b) pursuant to computer programs,

(i) performs logic and control, and

(ii) may perform any other function;

"data" means representations of information or of concepts that are being prepared or have been prepared in a form suitable for use in a computer system;

"electromagnetic, acoustic, mechanical or other device" means any device or apparatus that is used or is capable of being used to intercept any function of a computer system, but does not include a hearing aid used to correct subnormal hearing of the user to not better than normal hearing;

"function" includes logic, control, arithmetic, deletion, storage and retrieval and communication or telecommunication to, from or within a computer system;

"intercept" includes listen to or record a function of a computer system, or acquire the substance, meaning or purport thereof.

387

(1.1) Every one commits mischief who wilfully

(a) destroys or alters data;

(b) renders data meaningless, useless or ineffective;

(c) obstructs, interrupts or interferes with the lawful use of data; or

(d) obstructs, interrupts or interferes with any person in the lawful use of data or denies access to data to any person who is entitled to access thereto.

(8) In this section, "data" has the same meaning as in section 301.2.

DUTCH STATUTES

DUTCH COMPUTER CRIME ACT
THE CRIMINAL CODE

Article 80 quinquies

Data shall mean any representation of any facts, ideas or instructions, in an agreed manner or otherwise, which are suitable for transfer, interpretation or processing by persons or automated equipment.

Article 80 sexies

Automated equipment shall mean equipment which is intended to store and process data by electronic means.

Article 98

1. Any person who intentionally supplies or puts at the disposal of a person or body not authorized to the cognizance thereof, any information in respect of which secrecy should be preserved in the interests of the State or its allies, or an object from which such information could be derived, or such data, and who know or may be reasonably expected to know that such information, such an object or such data are involved, shall be liable to a term of imprisorunent not exceeding six years or a fine of 100.000 guilders.

2. Any person who intentionally supplies or puts at the disposal of a person or body not authorized to the cognizance thereof, any information emanating from a prohibited place and relating to the security of the State or its allies, an object from which such information could be derived, or such data, and who knows or may be reasonably expected to know that such information, such an object or such data are involved, shall be liable to a term of imprisorunent not exceeding six years or a fine of 100.000 guilders.

Article 98a

1. Any person who intentionally discloses any information, objects or data as meant in article 98, or without being authorised to do so intentionally supplies it or puts it at the disposal of a foreign power, a person or body established abroad, or such a person or body that an danger exists that the information or the data will come to the knowledge of a foreign power or a person or body established abroad, and who knows or may be reasonably expected to know that such information, such an object or such data are involved, shall be liable to a term of imprisorunent not exceeding fifteen years or a fine of 100.000 guilders.

Article 98b

Any person who is to blame for any information, object or data as meant in article 98, being made public or put at the disposal of a person or body not authorized to the cognizance thereof, shall be liable to a term of imprisonment not exceeding one year or a fine of 10.000 guilders.

Article 98c

Any person who: a. without being authorised to so intentionally obtain or keep any information, object or data as meant in article 98, b. do a kind of action with the aim to obtain unauthorized any information, object or data as meant in article 98, shall be liable to a term of imprisoranent not exceeding six years or a fine of 100.000 guilders.

Article 138a

1. Any person who intentionally and unlawfully accesses an automated system for the storage or processing of data or part of such a system shall be liable as quilty of breach of computer peace, to a term of imprisonment not exceeding six months or a fine of 10.000 guilders if he: a. breaks through a security system, or b. obtains access by technical means using false signals or a false key or by assuming a false identity.

2. Breach of computer peace shall be punished by a term of imprisonment not exceeding four years or a fine of 25.000 guilders if the offender subsequently copies and records, for himself or another person, data stored in an automated system, to which he has gained unlawfully access.

3. Breach of computer peace committed through the telecommunications infrastructure shall be punished by a term of imprisonment not exceeding four years or a fine of 25.000 guilders if the offender subsequently: a. make use of the processing capacity of an automated system, with the aim of obtaining an unlawful advantage for himself, or b. gains access to the automated system of a third party by making use of the automated system which he has gained access.

Article 139a

1. Any person who uses a technical device intentionally to or to record a conversation conducted in a dwelling, an enclosed room or enclosed premises using an automated system shall be liable to a term of imprisonment not exceeding six months or a fine of 25.000 guilders, if he: a. eavesdrops to that conversation other than on the orders of a participant in that conversation, b. records that conversation other than on the orders of such a participant and without himself participating in it.

2. Any unauthorized person who uses a technical device intentionally to tap or to record data which is being transferred in a dwelling, enclosed place or premises by means of an automated system shall be liable to the same penalty.

3. Paragraphs 1 and 2 shall not apply to tapping or recording: a.telecommunications using the telecommunications infrastructure;

b. using a technical device which is not openly present on the authority of the person using the dwelling, enclosed place or enclosed premises, except in instances of obvious abuse; c. on the special joint order of the Prime Minister, the Minister of Justice and the Minister for Home Affairs collective, such order to be given to the Head of the Internal Security Office for a period of no more than three months at a time, in cases in which such action is required in the interests of the security of the State.

Article 139b

1. Any person who, with the aim of eavesdropping to or recording a conversation which is being conducted in a place other than a dwelling, an enclosed place or enclosed premises shall be liable to a term of imprisonment not exceeding three months or a fine of 10.000 guilders, if he secretly by means of a technical device: a. eavesdrops to that conversation other than on the orders of a participant in that conversation, b. records that conversation other than on the orders of such a participant and without himself participating in it.

2. Any unauthorised person who intentionally, secretly and by using a technical device taps or records data which is being transferred other than in a dwelling, enclosed place or premises by means of an automated system or teleconununications shall be liable to the same penalty.

3. Article 139a, paragraph 3 (a) and (c), shall apply mutatis mutandis to paragraphs 1 and 2 of this article. Article 139c, paragraph 2, shall apply mutatis mutandis to paragraph 2 of this article.

Article 139c

1. Any person who uses a technical device intentionally to tap or record data transferred by using the telecommunications infrastructure or terminal equipment connected thereto, which data is not intended for him alone, for him as well as others or for the person on whose orders he is acting, shall be liable to a term of imprisonment not exceeding one year or a fine of 25.000 guilders.

2. Paragraph 1 shall not apply to tapping or recording: a. data received via a radio-electric receiver, unless a special effort has been made or a prohibited receiver has been used in order to make reception possible; b. by or on the orders of the person entitled to use the the telecommunications connection, except in instances of obvious abuse; c. in the interests of the proper operation of the telecommunications infrastructure, in the interests of criminal procedure or, on the special joint orders of the Prime Minister, the Minister of Justice, the Minister for Home Affairs and the Minister of Transport and Public Works collective, to be given to the Head of the Internal Security Office for a period of no more than three months at a time, in cases in which such action is required in the interests of the security of the State.

Article 139d

Any person who ensures the presence of a technical device in a particular place with a view to its being used unlawfully to eavesdrop to, tap or record a conversation, telecommunications or any other form of data transfer by means of an automated system, shall be liable to a term of imprisorunent not exceeding six months or a fine of 25.000 guilders.

Article 139e

a. Any person who has an object at his disposal on which he knows or may reasonably be expected to know that data has been recorded which was obtained by unlawfully eavesdropping to, tapping or recording a conversation, telecommunications or other transfer of data using an automated system, or b. any person who intentionally makes known to another person data which he has obtained by unlawfully eavesdropping to, tapping or recording a conversation, telecommunications or other transfer of data using an automated system or, which he knows or may reasonably be expected to know has come to his knowledge as a result of such eavesdropping, tapping or recording, or c. any person who intentionally makes an object as defined under a. available to another person, shall be liable to a term of imprisorunent not exceeding six months or a fine of 25.000 guilders.

Article 161 sexies

Any person who intentionally destroys, damages or renders unserviceable any automated system for the storage or processing of data or any telecommunications installation, disrupts the operation or functioning of such a system or installation or renders ineffective any safety measures taken with regard to such a system or installation shall be liable to:

1. a term of imprisonment not exceeding six months or a fine of 100.000 guilders if the offence prevents or impedes the storage or processing of data for the general benefit or disrupts the telecommunications infrastructure;

2. a term of imprisonment not exceeding six years or a fine of 100.000 guilders if the offence may seriously endanger goods or the supply of services;

3. a term of imprisonment not exceeding nine years or a fine of 100.000 guilders if the offence may endanger the life of an other person;

4. a term of imprisonment not exceeding fifteen years or a fine of 100.000 guilders if the offence endangered the life of an other person resulting in death.

Article 161 septies

Any person who is to blame for any automated system for the storage or processing of data or any telecommunications installation being destroyed, damaged or rendered unserviceable, for any disruption being caused in the operation or functioning of such a system or installation or renders ineffective any safety measure taken with regard to such a system shall be liable to:

1. a term of imprisonment or detention not exceeding three months or a fine of 25.000 guilders if the offence prevents or impedes the storage or processing of data for the general benefit, disrupts the telecommunications infrastructure or seriously endangers goods or the supply of services;

2. a term of imprisonment or detention not exceeding six months or a fine of 25.000 guilders if the offence endangers the life of an other person;

3. a term of imprisonment or detention not exceeding one year or a fine of 25.000 guilders if the offence causes a person's death.

Article 232

1. Any person who intentionally counterfeits or falsifies a cheque card, credit card or cash card intended for use in making automated payments, with the aim of obtaining an advantage for himself or for another person, shall be liable to a term of imprisorunent not exceeding six years or a fine of 100.000 guilders, or both.

2. Any person who intentionally uses a falsified or counterfeit cheque card, credit card or cash card as if it were genuine and unfalsified shall be liable to the same penalty.

Article 273

1. Any person who intentionally: a. makes known details which he is obliged to keep secret concerning an enterprise engaged in trade, industry or services by which he is or has been employed, or b. makes known or uses for profit data obtained by a criminal offence from an automated system used by an enterprise engaged in trade, industry or services and which relates to that enterprise, if the data was not generally known at the time it was made known or used and any damage could arise as a result, shall be liable to a term of imprisonment not exceeding six months or a fine of 25.000 guilders.

2. Any person who makes such data known in the reasonably-based good faith that the public interest required it to be made known shall not be liable to any penalty.

3. Proceedings may be brought only if the board of the enterprise lodges a complaint.

Article 317

1. Any person who, with the aim of obtaining an unlawful advantage for himself or another person, compels any person by violence or threats of violence to surrender any property wholly or partially belonging to the latter or to a third party, to enter into an obligation or cancel a debt payable or to make available data with a monetary value in the marketplace, shall be guilty of extortion and liable to a term of imprisorunent not exceeding nine years or a fine of 100.000 guilders.

2. Any person who exercises compulsion as referred to in paragraph 1, by threatening that data stored by means of an automated system will be rendered unusable or inaccessible or will be destroyed shall be liable to the same penalty.

3. A term of imprisonment not exceeding twelve years or a fine of 100.000 guilders shall be imposed: a. if the offence is committed either in a dwelling or on enclosed premises containing the dwelling at an hour when people would normally be asleep, or on a public highway, or in a moving railway train;

b. if the offence is committed by two or more persons in collusion;

c. if the offender has gained access to the place of the offence by means of breaking and entering, climbing, the use of false keys, the use of a fake order, or by wearing a disguise;

d. if the offence has caused grievous bodily harm.

4. If as a consequence of the offence the victim dies, the offender shall be liable to a term of imprisonment not exceeding fifteen years or a fine of 100.000 guilders.

Article 318

1. Any person who, with the aim of obtaining an unlawful advantage for himself or another person, compels any person by threats of slander or libel or the making known of a secret to surrender any property wholly or partially belonging to the latter or to a third party, to enter into an obligation or cancel a debt payable or to make available data with a monetary value in the marketplace, shall be guilty of blackmail and liable to a term of imprisonment not exceeding three years or a fine of 100.000 guilders.

2. Proceedings may be brought only if the victim lodges a complaint.

Article 326

Any person who, with the aim of obtaining an unlawful advantage for himself or another person, compels any person either by adopting a false name or by acting in a false capacity, or by deception or a tissue of lies, to surrender any property, to make availabe any data with a monetary value in the marketplace or to enter into an obligation or cancel a debt payable, shall be guilty of fraud and liable to a term of imprisonment not exceeding three years or a fine of 100.000 guilders, or both.

Article 326c

1. Any person who employ technical devices or false signals to use a service offered to the public by means of telecommunications with the aim of not paying for it in full shall be liable to a term of imprisonment not exceeding three years or a fine of 100.000 guilders, or both.

2. Any person who intentionally uses an object or data obviously intended for the purposes of committing the offence referred to in paragraph 1, shall be liable to a term of imprisonment of one year or a fine of 10.000 guilders, if he: a. openly offers the object or data for distribution, b. has the object or data available for distribution or with a view to import into the Netherlands, or c. manufactures or keeps the object or data with a view to making a profit.

3. Any person who engages professionally or habitually in the offences referred to in paragraph 2, shall be liable to a term of imprisonment not exceeding three years or a fine of 100.000 guilders, or both.

Article 350a

1. Any person who intentionally and unlawfully changes, deletes, renders unserviceable or renders inaccessible any data which is stored, processed or transmitted by means of an automated system, or adds other data to them, shall be liable to a term of imprisonment not exceeding two years or a fine of 25.000 guilders.

2. Any person who commits the offence described in paragraph 1, by using the telecommunications infrastructure to gain unlawful access to an automated system and causes serious damage to the data shall be liable to a term of imprisonment not exceeding four years or a fine of 25.000 guilders.

3. Any person who intentionally or unlawfully makes available or distributes data which are intended to do damage by multiplying in an automated system shall be liable to a term of imprisonment not exceeding four years or a fine of 100.000 guilders.

4. Any person who undertakes the action described in paragraph 3, with a view to limiting the damage caused by the data shall not be liable to the penalty.

Article 350b

1. Any person who is to blame for data which are stored, processed or transferred in an automated system being unlawfully changed, deleted, or rendered unusable or inaccessible or for other data being added to them shall be liable to a term of imprisonment not exceeding one month or a fine of 5.000 guilders if the data are seriously damaged by such action.

2. Any person who is to blame for data which are intended to do damage by multiplying in an automated system being unlawfully made available or distributed shall be liable to a term of imprisonment not exceeding one month or a fine of 5.000 guilders.

Article 351

Any person who intentionally and unlawfully destroys, damages or renders unserviceable railway or electricity equipment, automated systems for the storage or processing of data or telecommunications installations, flood protection, water discharge, gas and water supply or sewerage works, in so far as they are used for the

general benefit, or installations for national defence, shall be liable to a term of imprisonment not exceeding three years or a fine of 25.000 guilders.

Article 374bis

Any public servant or any other person responsible for the supervision of or involved with the service provided by the telecommunications infrastructure who:

1. intentionally and unlawfully eavesdrops on, taps or records a transfer of data by means of this telecommunications infrastructure and which are not intended or not partly intended for him,

2. has in his possession an object from which he knows or may reasonably be expected to know data may be derived which was obtained through unlawfully eavesdropping to, tapping or recording such a transfer of data,

3. intentionally and unlawfully makes the content of such a transfer of data known to another person,

4. intentionally and unlawfully makes available to another person an object from which data concerning the contents of such a transfer of data may be derived, shall be liable to a term of imprisonment not exceeding one year and six months or a fine of 25.000 guilders.

Article 441

Any person who informs another person of the content or tenor of data which he may reasonably be expected to know was not intended for him or for him as well as others and which he has received by means of a radio-electric receiver of which he had charge or which he was using, when he may reasonably be expected to know that the said content or tenor will then be made public and it is indeed then made public, or who makes the content or tenor of such data public, keeps a note thereof or uses it in any way, shall be liable to a term of detention not exceeding three months or a fine of 10.000 guilders.

Article 441a

Any person who, without being solicited to do so, publicly or through the distribution of written material indicates that an object is obtainable or that he has such an object in stock and draws attention to the suitability of that object as a technical device for use in secretly eavesdropping to, tapping or recording conversations, telecommunications or other transfer of data using an automated system or as a component of such a technical device, shall be liable to a term of detention not exceeding two months or a fine of 10.000 guilders.

THE DUTCH CODE OF CRIMINAL PROCEDURE

Article 125f

In the event of an offender being caught in the act, in the case of an indictable offence for which a suspect may be remanded in custody or in the case of the offence as referred to in article 138a, any person who is employed by the concessionary as referred to in section 3, subsection 1, of the Telecommunications Act (Netherlands Bulletin of Acts, Orders and Decrees 1988, 520) shall provide the public prosecutor or, during the preliminary judicial investigation, the examining magistrate, with all information he requests with regard to any communication not intended for the public which is transmitted via the telecommunications infrastructure and in which it is suspected that the suspect may have participated.

Article 125g

During a preliminary judicial investigation the examining magistrate shall be empowered, if such is urgently required by the investigation and the investigation relates to an indictable offence for which a suspect may be remanded in custody, to order the tapping or recording by an investigating officer of any communication not intended for the public which is transmitted via the telecommunications infrastructure and in which it is suspected that the suspect may participate. An official report shall be drawn up of such tapping or recording within forty-eight hours.

Article 125h

The examining magistrate shall as soon as possible have destroyed in his presence official reports and other objects from which information may be derived which was obtained as a result of the information referred to in article 125f or by means of tapping or recording as referred to in article 125g and which are of no relevance to the investigation. An official report on their destruction shall be drawn up without delay.

Article 125i

1. During a preliminary judicial investigation the examining magistrate may order any person who may reasonably be expected to have access to certain data which may serve to reveal the truth, in so far as that data is stored, processed or transmitted by means of an automated system, to record that information, allow him access to it or bring it to the court registry within a time limit and in a manner to be determined in the examining magistrate's order.

2. Such an order may relate only to data: a. which reasonably may suspect that these data was entered by the suspect, was intended for the suspect, was used in the commission of the offence or in respect of which the offence was committed; b. that are in the suspect's possession; or c. which describes acts carried out by the suspect in relation to an automated system.

3. Such an order may be given verbally or in writing. In the latter case it shall be served.

Article 125j

1. In the event of a house search, at the stage where the house search is conducted, an investigation may be conducted in an automated system present elsewhere in order to find data which may reasonably serve to reveal the truth. Should such data be found, it may be recorded.

2. The investigation shall have no further access to such an automated system than that which the persons who are living or who usually work or stay at the place where the house search is conducted have with the permission of the rightful owner.

3. The house search shall extend to letters or other written material which do not form part of the object of the offence and did not serve in its commission only with the express permission of the court.

Article 125k

1. In so far as the interests of the investigation expressly require such action, any person who may reasonably be expected to know how the security system of an automated system works may be ordered in the course of a house search or in connection with the application of article 125j to provide access to the automated systems present or parts thereof. A person who receives such an order may comply by making his knowledge of the security system available.

2. Paragraph 1 of this article shall apply by analogy if encrypted data is found in an automated system. The order is directed to him of whom it may reasonably be supposed that he knows about the way of encryption of this data.

Article 125l

No investigation shall take place into data entered by or on behalf of persons entitled to exemption, except with their permission, in so far as they have an obligation to maintain secrecy. An investigation in an automated system in which such data is stored shall take place without their permission only in so far as it is possible to do so without violation of ecclesiastical, professional or official obligations of secrecy.

Article 125m

1. An order as referred to in articles 125l, paragraph 1, and 125k shall not be given to the suspect.

2. Should a house search or the application of one of the powers referred to in this part result in the recording of data stored using an automated system, a list of that data shall be given to the manager of the automated system.

Article 125n

1. Data recorded during a house search or as a result of the application of one of the powers referred to in this part shall be destroyed as soon as it is found to be of no further relevance to the investigation.

2. Its destruction shall be carried out by or on the orders of the person who recorded it. An official report shall be drawn up thereon and added to the documents in the case.

Article 552a, paragraph 1

1. Interested parties may complain in writing about seizure, the use of seized objects, failure to order the return of seized goods, examination or use of data stored using an automated system and recorded during a house search and the use of data as referred to in articles 125i and 125j.

Article 552n (summary)

1. If a request from the judicial authorities of a foreign state is founded on a treaty or convention and is admissible, the public prosecutor shall refer it to the examining magistrate if it concerns eavesdropping to, tapping or recording data which is transmitted via the telecommunications infrastructure and is not intended for the public.

2. Requests shall be submitted to the examining magistrate in the form of a written application setting out the response required of the examining magistrate.

Article 552o (summary)

1. If an application as referred to in article 552n, paragraph 2, is made in order to comply with a request from the judicial authorities of a foreign state which is founded on a treaty or convention and is admissible, it shall have the same consequences in law as an application for the institution of a preliminary judicial investigation as regards the powers of the examining magistrate in relation to the suspects, witnesses and experts to be examined by him and his powers to order the surrender or transfer of items of evidence, the entering and searching of property, the seizure of items of evidence and the tapping or recording of data which is transmitted via the telecommunications infrastructure and is not intended for the public.

2. Data may be tapped or recorded in accordance with paragraph 1 of this article if it would be liable to be tapped or recorded had the offence in question been committed in the Netherlands.

Article 552p (summary)

1. The examining magistrate shall return the request to the public prosecutor as soon as possible, enclosing the official reports of the examinations he has conducted and of any other action he has taken in the case.

2. If a court, taking into consideration the relevant treaty or convention, grants permission, items of evidence and data carriers containing data gathered using any power under the law of criminal procedure which have been seized by the examining magistrate shall be put at the disposal of the public prosecutor.

3. Unless it can be assumed that the persons lawfully entitled to the items of evidence which have been seized do not reside in the Netherlands, the permission referred to in the preceding paragraph may be granted only if it is agreed when the items are handed over to the foreign authorities that they shall be returned as soon as they are no longer needed for the purposes of criminal procedure.

4. If data carriers containing data gathered using any power under the law of criminal procedure are handed over to the foreign authorities conditions for the use thereof shall be agreed similar to those which might have been imposed by the examining magistrate.

Article 592

1. The state shall reimburse the person concerned for the costs of surrendering or transferring objects in accordance with an order issued by the examining magistrate or the public prosecutor; the reimbursement shall be charged to the budget of the examining magistrate or public prosecutor.

2. The person concerned can be reimbursed for the costs of complying with an order issued by the examining magistrate pursuant to article 125i; the reimbursement shall be charged to the budget of the examining magistrate. A lesser amount may be reimbursed if the person to whom the order was directed failed to keep and retain records as prescribed by the Civil Code.

3. The examining magistrate or the public prosecutor shall issue an enforcement order.

FRENCH STATUTES

90-1170

Law number 90-1170 published in the December 30, 1990 Journal Officiel.

ED. NOTE: The first 27 articles concern the encryption of information transmitted by radio or mail.

Art. 28. - "Cryptographic facilities" shall mean all facilities or services aimed at transforming, by means of secret arrangements, information or clear signals into information or signals unintelligible to third parties, or accomplishing the inverse operation, by hardware or software means conceived for that purpose. In order to preserve national defense interests and interior and exterior state security, the furnishing, export or use of cryptographic means or facilities are subject: a) to prior disclosure when the means or the facility has no purpose other than to authenticate a communication or to assure the integrity of the message transmitted;

b) to prior authorization from the Prime Minister in all other cases.

A decree from the State Council sets the conditions on which the disclosure is signed and given the aforesaid authorization. This decree may anticipate simplified regulations for declaration or authorization for certain types of material or facilities or for certain categories of users.

II. - Without prejudicing the application of customs codes, a fine of between 6000 and 500000 Francs or imprisonment of one to three months or both, will be imposed on whomsoever shall export a means of cryptology, furnish or cause to be furnished a cryptographic facility without the authorization cited in paragraph I of the preceding article. The court may, in addition, forbid the party from soliciting such authorization for a period of up to two years, or five years in the case of a second offense.

In case of conviction the court may also confiscate the cryptographic means.

III. - Besides the officers and agents of the judicial police and customs agents in exercise of their duties, agents qualified for such duty by the Prime Minister and sworn to conditions set by decree of the State Council may investigate and prosecute infractions of the intent of this article and the rules set for its application. Their charges are to be sent within five days to the attorney general. They may have access to the premises, sites or customary means of transport, require access to all professional documents and copy or collect, by warrant or on the spot, information and evidence.

92-1358

Decree number 92-1358 of December 28,1992 published in the Journal of December 30, 1992.

Order of December 28, 1992 concerning notification and petitions for authorization related to cryptographic means and facilities.

Art. 4 - Concerning the above declaration, the furnishing, export and use of services of any sort or cryptological facilities ... notably:

- The means, whether hardware or software, capable of assuring confidentiality of data in storage;

- The cryptographic facilities which assure confidentiality of part or all of a communication or of data in storage;

- The means and facilities of cryptographic analysis.

Art. 6 - Microprocessor cards which do not by themselves, that is to say without recourse to an external cryptographic device, assure confidentiality of communications benefit from declarations in force or authorizations obtained under title of the means and facilities in which they are used.

Art. 7 - Not considered as means of cryptography are means, whether hardware or software especially conceived to protect programs from illicit copying or use, even if they make use of methods or devices held secret, on condition that they do not permit ciphering either directly or indirectly by the program concerned.

Art. 9 - In the case of uncertainty on the part of the petitioner as to whether a means or facility belongs to the category of cryptographic means or facilities, the opinion of the central security service of information systems is to be sought.

GHANA STATUTES

GHANA COMPUTER CRIME LAW (PROPOSED)
COMPUTER CRIME LAW

ED. NOTE: Here is the text of a proposed computer crime law in Ghana. Please note that this law is only proposed. It has not yet been adopted.

In pursuance of the Provisional National Defense Council (Establishment) Proclamation 1981, this Law is hereby made:

1. Any person who, with intent to defraud,

(a) alters, damages, destroys or otherwise manipulates data or program stored in or used in connection with a computer, or

(b) obtains by any means, information stored in a computer and uses it to his advantage or to another person's advantage to the disadvantage of any other person, or

(c) uses a computer commits an offense.

Charge: Computer-related fraud.

ALTERNATIVE:

(1) A person commits an offense if that person obtains access to a computer program or data, whether stored in or used in connection with a computer or to a part of such program or data to erase or otherwise alter the program or data with the intention-

1. (a) of procuring an advantage for himself or another person: or

(b) of damaging another person's interests.

2. Any person who, by any means, without authority, wilfully destroys, damages, injures, alters or renders

ineffective data stored in or used in connection with a computer commits an offense.

Charge: Damaging Computer data.

3. Any person who, without authority, knowingly uses a computer commits and offense.

Charge: Unauthorized use of a computer.

4. Any person who, without authority, knowingly gains access to a computer, computer network, or any part thereof commits an offense.

Charge: Unauthorized access to a computer.

5. Any person who, knowingly and dishonestly introduces, records or stores, or causes to be recorded, stored or introduced into a computer or computer network by any means, false or misleading information as data commits an offense.

Charge: Insertion of false information as data.

ALTERNATIVE:

(5) A person commits an offense if, not having authority to obtain access to a computer program or data, whether stored in or used in connection with a computer, or to a part of such program or data, he obtains such unauthorized access and damages another person's interests by recklessly adding to, erasing or otherwise altering the program or the data.

6. Any person under a contractual or other duty to introduce, record or store authorised data into a computer network, who negligently or dishonestly fails to introduce, record or store, commits an offense.

Charge: Omission to introduce, record or store data.

ALTERNATIVE:

(6) Any person under a contractual or other duty to introduce, record or store data into a computer or computer network who negligently or dishonestly fails to introduce, record or store, commits an offense.

7. Any authorised person who willfully or intentionally allows information from a computer to get into the hands of an unauthorised person who uses such information to his advantage commits an offense.

Charge: Allowing unauthorised person to use computer data.

8. A person guilty of an offense under this Law shall be liable:-

(a) on summary conviction, to imprisonment for a term not exceeding two years or to a fine not exceeding the statutory maximum or both; or

(b) on conviction on indictment, to imprisonment for a term not exceeding ten years or to an unlimited fine, or both.

9. A court in Ghana shall have jurisdiction to entertain proceedings for an offense under this Law, if at the time the offense was committed:-

(a) the accused was in Ghana; or

(b) the program or the data in relation to which the offence was committed was stored in or used with a computer or computer network in Ghana.

10. In this Law, unless the context otherwise requires:-

"access" includes to log unto, instruct, store data or programs in, retrieve data or programs from, or otherwise communicate with a computer, or gain access to (whether directly or with the aid of any device) any data or program.

"computer" includes any device which is capable of performing logical, arithmetical, classifactory, mnemonic, storage or other like functions by means of optical, electronic or magnetic signals.

"Computer network" includes the interconnection of two or more computers, whether geographically separated or in close proximity or the interconnection of communication systems with a computer through terminals, whether remote or local.

"Computer program" includes an instruction or statement or series of instructions or statements capable of causing a computer to indicate, perform, or achieve any function.

"data" includes a representation in any form whether tangible or intangible that is capable of being stored in or retrieved by a computer.

GREAT BRITAIN STATUTES
COMPUTER CRIME ACT FROM GREAT BRITAIN

SECTION: Long title

TEXT:

An Act to make provision for securing computer material against unauthorised access or modification; and for connected purposes.

SECTION: 1 Unauthorised access to computer material

TEXT:

(1) A person is guilty of an offence if--

(a) he causes a computer to perform any function with intent to secure access to any program or data held in any computer;

(b) the access he intends to secure is unauthorised; and

(c) he knows at the time when he causes the computer to perform the function that that is the case.

(2) The intent a person has to have to commit an offence under this section need not be directed at--

(a) any particular program or data;

(b) a program or data of any particular kind; or

(c) a program or data held in any particular computer.

(3) A person guilty of an offence under this section shall be liable on summary conviction to imprisonment for a term not exceeding six months or to a fine not exceeding level 5 on the standard scale or to both.

SECTION: 2 Unauthorised access with intent to commit or facilitate commission of further offences

TEXT:

(1) A person is guilty of an offence under this section if he commits an offence under section 1 above ("the unauthorised access offence") with intent--

(a) to commit an offence to which this section applies; or

(b) to facilitate the commission of such an offence (whether by himself or by any other person); and the offence he intends to commit or facilitate is referred to below in this section as the further offence.

(2) This section applies to offences for which a person of twenty-one years of age or over (not previously convicted) may be sentenced to imprisonment for a term of five years (or, in England and Wales, might be so sentenced but for the restrictions imposed by section 33 of the Magistrates' Courts Act 1980).

(3) It is immaterial for the purposes of this section whether the further offence is to be committed on the same occasion as the unauthorised access offence or on any future occasion.

(4) A person may be guilty of an offence under this section even though the facts are such that the commission of the further offence is impossible.

(5) A person guilty of an offence under this section shall be liable--

(a) on summary conviction, to imprisonment for a term not exceeding six months or to a fine not exceeding the statutory maximum or to both; and

(b) on conviction on indictment, to imprisonment for a term not exceeding five years or to a fine or to both.

SECTION: 3 Unauthorised modification of computer material

TEXT:

(1) A person is guilty of an offence if--

(a) he does any act which causes an unauthorised modification of the contents of any computer; and

(b) at the time when he does the act he has the requisite intent and the requisite knowledge.

(2) For the purposes of subsection (1)(b) above the requisite intent is an intent to cause a modification of the contents of any computer and by so doing--

(a) to impair the operation of any computer;

(b) to prevent or hinder access to any program or data held in any computer; or

(c) to impair the operation of any such program or the reliability of any such data.

(3) The intent need not be directed at--

(a) any particular computer;

(b) any particular program or data or a program or data of any particular kind; or

(c) any particular modification or a modification of any particular kind.

(4) For the purposes of subsection (1)(b) above the requisite knowledge is knowledge that any modification he intends to cause is unauthorised.

(5) It is immaterial for the purposes of this section whether an unauthorised modification or any intended effect of it of a kind mentioned in subsection (2) above is, or is intended to be, permanent or merely temporary.

(6) For the purposes of the Criminal Damage Act 1971 a modification of the contents of a computer shall not be regarded as damaging any computer or computer storage medium unless its effect on that computer or computer storage medium impairs its physical condition.

(7) A person guilty of an offence under this section shall be liable--

(a) on summary conviction, to imprisonment for a term not exceeding six months or to a fine not exceeding the statutory maximum or to both; and

(b) on conviction on indictment, to imprisonment for a term not exceeding five years or to a fine or to both.

CROSS-HEADING: Jurisdiction

SECTION: 4 Territorial scope of offences under this Act

DATE-IN-FORCE: 29 August 1990

TEXT:

(1) Except as provided below in this section, it is immaterial for the purposes of any offence under section 1 or 3 above--

(a) whether any act or other event proof of which is required for conviction of the offence occurred in the home country concerned; or

(b) whether the accused was in the home country concerned at the time of any such act or event.

(2) Subject to subsection (3) below, in the case of such an offence at least one significant link with domestic jurisdiction must exist in the circumstances of the case for the offence to be committed.

(3) There is no need for any such link to exist for the commission of an offence under section 1 above to be established in proof of an allegation to that effect in proceedings for an offence under section 2 above.

(4) Subject to section 8 below, where--

(a) any such link does in fact exist in the case of an offence under section 1 above; and

(b) commission of that offence is alleged in the case of an offence under section 2 above;

section 2 above shall apply as if anything the accused intended to do or facilitate in any place outside the home country concerned which would be an offence to which section 2 applies if it took place in the home country concerned were the offence in question.

(5) This section is without prejudice to any jurisdiction exercisable by a court in Scotland apart from this section.

(6) References in this Act to the home country concerned are references--

(a) in the application of this Act to England and Wales, to England and Wales;

(b) in the application of this Act to Scotland, to Scotland; and

(c) in the application of this Act to Northern Ireland, to Northern Ireland.

CROSS-HEADING: Jurisdiction

SECTION: 5 Significant links with domestic jurisdiction

TEXT:

(1) The following provisions of this section apply for the interpretation of section 4 above.

(2) In relation to an offence under section 1, either of the following is a significant link with domestic jurisdiction--

(a) that the accused was in the home country concerned at the time when he did the act which caused the computer to perform the function; or

(b) that any computer containing any program or data to which the accused secured or intended to secure unauthorised access by doing that act was in the home country concerned at that time.

(3) In relation to an offence under section 3, either of the following is a significant link with domestic jurisdiction--

(a) that the accused was in the home country concerned at the time when he did the act which caused the unauthorised modification; or

(b) that the unauthorised modification took place in the home country concerned.

CROSS-HEADING: Jurisdiction

SECTION: 6 Territorial scope of inchoate offences related to offences under this Act

TEXT:

(1) On a charge of conspiracy to commit an offence under this Act the following questions are immaterial to the accused's guilt--

(a) the question where any person became a party to the conspiracy; and

(b) the question whether any act, omission or other event occured in the home country concerned.

(2) On a charge of attempting to commit an offence under section 3 above the following questions are immaterial to the accused's guilt--

(a) the question where the attempt was made; and

(b) the question whether it had an effect in the home country concerned.

(3) On a charge of incitement to commit an offence under this Act the question where the incitement took place is immaterial to the accused's guilt.

(4) This section does not extend to Scotland.

CROSS-HEADING: Jurisdiction

SECTION: 7 Territorial scope of inchoate offences related to offences under external law corresponding to offences under this Act

TEXT:

. . .

(4) Subject to section 8 below, if any act done by a person in England and Wales would amount to the offence of incitement to commit an offence under this Act

but for the fact that what he had in view would not be an offence triable in England and Wales--

(a) what he had in view shall be treated as an offence under this Act for the purposes of any charge of incitement brought in respect of that act; and

(b) any such charge shall accordingly be triable in England and Wales.

ANNOTATIONS:

1. Sub-ss (1), (2): amend the Criminal Law Act 1977,

1. Sub-s (3): amends the Criminal Attempts Act 1981,

CROSS-HEADING: Jurisdiction

SECTION: 8 Relevance of external law

TEXT:

(1) A person is guilty of an offence triable by virtue of section 4(4) above only if what he intended to do or facilitate would involve the commission of an offence under the law in force where the whole or any part of it was intended to take place.

(2) A person is guilty of an offence triable by virtue of section 1(1A) of the Criminal Law Act 1977 only if the pursuit of the agreed course of conduct would at some stage involve--

(a) an act or omission by one or more of the parties; or

(b) the happening of some other event;

constituting an offence under the law in force where the act, omission or other event was intended to take place.

(3) A person is guilty of an offence triable by virtue of section 1(1A) of the Criminal Attempts Act 1981 or by virtue of section 7(4) above only if what he had in view would involve the commission of an offence under the law in force where the whole or any part of it was intended to take place.

(4) Conduct punishable under the law in force in any place is an offence under that law for the purposes of this section, however it is described in that law.

(5) Subject to subsection (7) below, a condition specified in any of subsections (1) to (3) above shall be taken to be satisfied unless not later than rules of court may provide the defence serve on the prosecution a notice--

(a) stating that, on the facts as alleged with respect to the relevant conduct, the condition is not in their opinion satisfied;

(b) showing their grounds for that opinion; and

(c) requiring the prosecution to show that it is satisfied.

(6) In subsection (5) above "the relevant conduct" means--

(a) where the condition in subsection (1) above is in question, what the accused intended to do or facilitate;

(b) where the condition in subsection (2) above is in question, the agreed course of conduct; and

(c) where the condition in subsection (3) above is in question, what the accused had in view.

(7) The court, if it thinks fit, may permit the defence to require the prosecution to show that the condition is satisfied without the prior service of a notice under subsection (5) above. jurisdiction in Scotland permits the defence to require the prosecution to show that the condition is satisfied, it shall be competent for the prosecution for that purpose to examine any witness or to put in evidence any production not included in the lists lodged by it.

(8) In the Crown Court the question whether the condition is satisfied shall be decided by the judge alone.

(9) In the High Court of Justiciary and in the sheriff court the question whether the condition is satisfied shall be decided by the judge or, as the case may be, the sheriff alone.

CROSS-HEADING: Jurisdiction

SECTION: 9 British citizenship immaterial

TEXT:

(1) In any proceedings brought in England and Wales in respect of any offence to which this section applies it is immaterial to guilt whether or not the accused was a British citizen at the time of any act, omission or other event proof of which is required for conviction of the offence.

(2) This section applies to the following offences--

(a) any offence under this Act;

(b) conspiracy to commit an offence under this Act;

(c) any attempt to commit an offence under section 3 above; and

(d) incitement to commit an offence under this Act.

CROSS-HEADING: Miscellaneous and General

SECTION: 10 Saving for certain law enforcement powers

TEXT:

Section 1(1) above has effect without prejudice to the operation--

(a) in England and Wales of any enactment relating to powers of inspection, search or seizure; and

(b) in Scotland of any enactment or rule of law relating to powers of examination, search or seizure.

CROSS-HEADING: Miscellaneous

SECTION: 11 Proceedings for offences under section 1

TEXT:

(1) A magistrates' court shall have jurisiction to try an offence under section 1 above if--

(a) the accused was within its commission area at the time when he did the act which caused the computer to perform the function; or

(b) any computer containing any program or data to which the accused secured or intended to secure unauthorised access by doing that act was in its commission area at that time.

(2) Subject to subsection (3) below, proceedings for an offence under section 1 above may be brought within a period of six months from the date on which evidence sufficient in the opinion of the prosecutor to warrant the proceedings came to his knowledge.

(3) No such proceedings shall be brought by virtue of this section more than three years after the commission of the offence.

(4) For the purposes of this section, a certificate signed by or on behalf of the prosecutor and stating the date on which evidence sufficient in his opinion to warrant the proceedings came to his knowledge shall be conclusive evidence of that fact.

(5) A certificate stating that matter and purporting to be so signed shall be deemed to be so signed unless the contrary is proved.

(6) In this section "commission area" has the same meaning as in the Justices of the Peace Act 1979.

(7) This section does not extend to Scotland.

CROSS-HEADING: Miscellaneous and General

SECTION: 12 Conviction of an offence under section 1 in proceedings for an offence under section 2 or 3

TEXT:

(1) If on the trial on indictment of a person charged with--

(a) an offence under section 2 above; or

(b) an offence under section 3 above or any attempt to commit such an offence;

the jury find him not guilty of the offence charged, they may find him guilty of an offence under section 1 above if on the facts shown he could have been found guilty of that offence in proceedings for that offence brought before the expiry of any time limit under section 11 above applicable to such proceedings. relation to a person who is by virtue of this section convicted before it of an offence under section 1 above as a magistrates' court would have on convicting him of the offence.

(3) This section is without prejudice to section 6(3) of the Criminal Law Act 1967 (conviction of alternative indictable offence on trial on indictment).

(4) This section does not extend to Scotland.

CROSS-HEADING: Miscellaneous and General

SECTION: 13 Proceedings in Scotland

TEXT:

(1) A sheriff shall have jurisdiction in respect of an offence under section 1 or 2 above if--

(a) the accused was in the sheriffdom at the time when he did the act which caused the computer to perform the function; or

(b) any computer containing any program or data to which the accused secured or intended to secure unauthorised access by doing that act was in the sheriffdom at that time.

(2) A sheriff shall have jurisdiction in respect of an offence under section 3 above if--

(a) the accused was in the sheriffdom at the time when he did the act which caused the unauthorised modification; or

(b) the unauthorised modification took place in the sheriffdom.

(3) Subject to subsection (4) below, summary proceedings for an offence under section 1, 2 or 3 above may be commenced within a period of six months from the date on which evidence sufficient in the opinion of the procurator fiscal to warrant proceedings came to his knowledge.

(4) No such proceedings shall be commenced by virtue of this section more than three years after the commission of the offence.

(5) For the purposes of this section, a certificate signed by or on behalf of the procurator fiscal and stating the date on which evidence sufficient in his opinion to warrant the proceedings came to his knowledge shall be conclusive evidence of that fact.

(6) A certificate stating that matter and purporting to be so signed shall be deemed to be so signed unless the contrary is proved.

(7) Subsection (3) of section 331 of the Criminal Procedure apply for the purposes of this section as it applies for the purposes of that section.

(8) In proceedings in which a person is charged with an offence under section 2 or 3 above and is found not guilty or is acquitted of that charge, he may be found guilty of an offence under section 1 above if on the facts shown he could have been found guilty of that offence in proceedings for that offence commenced before the expiry of any time limit under this section applicable to such proceedings.

(9) Subsection (8) above shall apply whether or not an offence under section 1 above has been libelled in the complaint or indictment.

(10) A person found guilty of an offence under section 1 above by virtue of subsection (8) above shall be liable, in respect of that offence, only to the penalties set out in section 1.

(11) This section extends to Scotland only.

CROSS-HEADING: Miscellaneous and General

SECTION: 14 Search warrants for offences under section 1

TEXT:

(1) Where a circuit judge is satisfied by information on oath given by a constable that there are reasonable grounds for believing--

(a) that an offence under section 1 above has been or is about to be committed in any premises; and

(b) that evidence that such an offence has been or is about to be committed is in those premises; he may issue a warrant authorising a constable to enter and search the premises, using such reasonable force as is necessary.

(2) The power conferred by subsection (1) above does not extend to authorising a search for material of the kinds mentioned in section 9(2) of the Police and Criminal Evidence Act 1984 (privileged, excluded and special procedure material).

(3) A warrant under this section--

(a) may authorise persons to accompany any constable executing the warrant; and

(b) remains in force for twenty-eight days from the date of its issue.

(4) In exercising a warrant issued under this section a evidence that an offence under section 1 above has been or is about to be committed.

(5) In this section "premises" includes land, buildings, movable structures, vehicles, vessels, aircraft and hovercraft.

(6) This section does not extend to Scotland.

CROSS-HEADING: Miscellaneous and General

SECTION: 15 Extradition where Schedule 1 to the Extradition Act 1989 applies

TEXT:

The offences to which an Order in Council under section 2 of the Extradition Act 1870 can apply shall include--

(a) offences under section 2 or 3 above;

(b) any conspiracy to commit such an offence; and

(c) any attempt to commit an offence under section 3 above.

CROSS-HEADING: Miscellaneous and General

SECTION: 16 Application to Northern Ireland

TEXT:

(1) The following provisions of this section have effect for applying this Act in relation to Northern Ireland with the modifications there mentioned.

(2) In section 2(2)(b)--

(a) the reference to England and Wales shall be read as a reference to Northern Ireland; and

(b) the reference to section 33 of the Magistrates' Courts Act 1980 shall be read as a reference to Article 46(4) of the Magistrates' Courts (Northern Ireland) Order 1981.

(3) The reference in section 3(6) to the Criminal Damage Act 1971 shall be read as a reference to the Criminal Damage (Northern Ireland) Order 1977.

(4) Subsections (5) to (7) below apply in substitution for subsections (1) to (3) of section 7; and any reference in subsection (4) of that section to England and Wales shall be read as a reference to Northern Ireland.

(5) The following paragraphs shall be inserted after paragraph (1) of Article 9 of the Criminal Attempts and Conspiracy (Northern Ireland) Order 1983) (relevance of external law), if this paragraph applies to an agreement, this Part has effect in relation to it as it has effect in relation to an agreement falling within paragraph (1).

(1B) Paragraph (1A) applies to an agreement if--

(a) a party to it, or a party's agent, did anything in Northern Ireland in relation to it before its formation;

(b) a party to it became a party in Northern Ireland (by joining it either in person or through an agent); or

(c) a party to it, or a party's agent, did or omitted anything in Northern Ireland in pursuance of it; and the agreement would fall within paragraph (1) as an agreement relating to the commission of a computer misuse offence but for the fact that the offence would not be an offence triable in Northern Ireland if committed in accordance with the parties' intentions.".

(6) The following paragraph shall be inserted after paragraph (4) of that Article)

"(5) In the application of this Part to an agreement to which paragraph (1A) applies any reference to an offence shall be read as a reference to what would be the computer misuse offence in question but for the fact that it is not an offence triable in Northern Ireland.

(6) In this Article "computer misuse offence" means an offence under the Computer Misuse Act 1990.".

(7) The following paragraphs shall be inserted after Article 3(1) of that Order--

"(1A) Subject to section 8 of the Computer Misuse Act 1990 (relevance of external law), if this paragraph applies to an act, what the person doing it had in view shall be treated as an offence to which this Article applies.

(1B) Paragraph (1A) above applies to an act if--

(a) it is done in Northern Ireland; and

(b) it would fall within paragraph (1) as more than merely preparatory to the commission of an offence under section 3 of the Computer Misuse Act 1990 but for the fact that the offence, if completed, would not be an offence triable in Northern Ireland.".

(8) In section 8--

(a) the reference in subsection (2) to section 1(1A) of the Criminal Law Act 1977 shall be read as a reference to Article 9(1A)

(b) the reference in subsection (3) to section 1(1A) of the Criminal Attempts Act 1981 shall be read as a reference to Article 3(1A) of that Order.

(9) The references in sections 9(1) and 10 to England and Wales shall be read as references to Northern Ireland.

(10) In section 11, for subsection (1) there shall be substituted--

"(1) A magistrates' court for a county division in Northern Ireland may hear and determine a complaint charging an offence under section 1 above or conduct a preliminary investigation or preliminary inquiry into an offence under that section if--

(a) the accused was in that division at the time when he did the act which caused the computer to perform the function; or

(b) any computer containing any program or data to which the accused secured or intended to secure unauthorised access by doing that act was in that division at that time."; and subsection (6) shall be omitted.

(11) The reference in section 12(3) to section 6(3) of the Criminal Law Act 1967 shall be read as a reference to section 6(2) of the Criminal Law Act (Northern Ireland) 1967.

(12) In section 14--

(a) the reference in subsection (1) to a circuit judge shall be read as a reference to a county court judge; and

(b) the reference in subsection (2) to section 9(2) of the Police and Criminal Evidence Act 1984 shall be read as a reference to Article 11(2) of the Police and Criminal Evidence (Northern Ireland) Order 1989.

ANNOTATIONS:

Sub-ss (5)-(7): amend SI 1983 No 1120, arts 3, 9.

CROSS-HEADING: Miscellaneous and General

SECTION: 17 Interpretation

(1) The following provisions of this section apply for the interpretation of this Act.

(2) A person secures access to any program or data held in a computer if by causing a computer to perform any function he--

(a) alters or erases the program or data;

(b) copies or moves it to any storage medium other than that in which it is held or to a different location in the storage medium in which it is held;

(c) uses it; or

(d) has it output from the computer in which it is held (whether by having it displayed or in any other manner); and references to access to a program or data (and to an intent to secure such access) shall be read accordingly.

(3) For the purposes of subsection (2)(c) above a person uses a program if the function he causes the computer to perform--

(a) causes the program to be executed; or

(b) is itself a function of the program.

(4) For the purposes of subsection (2)(d) above--

(a) a program is output if the instructions of which it consists are output; and

(b) the form in which any such instructions or any other data is output (and in particular whether or not it represents a form in which, in the case of instructions, they are capable of being executed or, in the case of data, it is capable of being processed by a computer) is immaterial.

(5) Access of any kind by any person to any program or data held in a computer is unauthorised if--

(a) he is not himself entitled to control access of the kind in question to the program or data; and

(b) he does not have consent to access by him of the kind in question to the program or data from any person who is so entitled.

(6) References to any program or data held in a computer include references to any program or data held in any removable storage medium which is for the time being in the computer; and a computer is to be regarded as containing any program or data held in any such medium.

(7) A modification of the contents of any computer takes place if, by the operation of any function of the computer concerned or any other computer--

(a) any program or data held in the computer concerned is altered or erased; or

(b) any program or data is added to its contents; and any act which contributes towards causing such a modification shall be regarded as causing it.

(8) Such a modification is unauthorised if

(a) he is not himself entitled to determine whether the modification should be made; and

(b) he does not have consent to the modification from any person who is so entitled.

(9) References to the home country concerned shall be read in accordance with section 4(6) above.

(10) References to a program include references to part of a program.

CROSS-HEADING: Miscellaneous and General

SECTION: 18 Citation, commencement etc

(1) This Act may be cited as the Computer Misuse Act 1990.

(2) This Act shall come into force at the end of the period of two months beginning with the day on which it is passed.

(3) An offence is not committed under this Act unless every act or other event proof of which is required for conviction of the offence takes place after this Act comes into force.

Appendices

This part of the book contains a resource summary, two articles that expand on topics introduced in earlier chapters, and a sample search warrant.

Appendix A, *Resource Summary,* contains a listing of resources that may be helpful to you in preventing, investigating, and prosecuting computer crimes. It includes books, periodicals, and online resources relevant to computer crime.

Appendix B, *Raiding the Computer Room,* is an article by John Gales Sauls about seizing computer crime evidence and Fourth Amendment considerations.

Appendix C, *The Microcomputer as Evidence,* is an article originally entitled "Computer Analysis and Response Team (CART): The Microcomputer as Evidence," by Michael G. Noblett about examining computer crime evidence.

Appendix D, *A Sample Search Warrant,* is the text of an actual search warrant (only certain identifying information has been changed) used in the investigation of a computer crime at a university.

A

Resource Summary

Books

General Computer Security

Denning, Peter J., ed. *Computers Under Attack: Intruders, Worms, and Viruses.* Reading, MA: ACM Press, 1990.

Ferbrache, David. *The Pathology of Computer Viruses.* London, England: Springer-Verlag, 1992.

Fites, Philip E., Kratz, Martin P.J., and Brebner, Alan F. *Control and Security of Computer Information Systems.* Rockville, MD: Computer Science Press, 1989.

Garfinkel, Simson, and Spafford, Gene. *Practical UNIX Security,* Second Edition. Sebastopol, CA: O'Reilly & Associates, 1995.

Hoffman, Lance J. *Rogue Programs: Viruses, Worms, and Trojan Horses.* New York, NY: Van Nostrand Reinhold, 1990.

Nemeth, Evi, Snyder, Garth, Seebass, Scott, and Hein, Trent R. *UNIX System Administration Handbook,* Second Edition. Englewood Cliffs, NJ: Prentice-Hall, 1995.

Pfleeger, Charles F. *Security in Computing.* Englewood Cliffs, NJ: Prentice Hall, 1989.

Russell, Deborah, and Gangemi, G.T. Sr. *Computer Security Basics.* Sebastopol, CA: O'Reilly & Associates, 1991.

Stoll, Cliff. *The Cuckoo's Egg: Tracing a Spy Through the Maze of Computer Espionage.* New York, NY: Doubleday, 1989.

National Research Council, System Security Study Committee, et al. *Computers at Risk: Safe Computing in the Information Age.* Washington, DC: National Academy Press, 1991.

Wood, Charles Cresson, et al (Garcia, Abel A., ed). *Computer Security: A Comprehensive Controls Checklist.* New York, NY: Wiley Interscience, 1987.

Computer Crime

Arkin, S.S., et al. *Prevention and Prosecution of Computer and High Technology Crime.* New York, NY: Matthew Bender Books, 1989.

Best, Reba A. *Computer Crime, Abuse, Liability, and Security: A Comprehensive Bibliography, 1970–1984.* Jefferson, NC: McFarland, 1985.

BloomBecker, J.J. *Introduction to Computer Crime.* Santa Cruz, CA: National Center for Computer Crime Data, 1988. (Order from NCCCD: +1-408-475-4457.)

BloomBecker, J.J. *Spectacular Computer Crimes.* Homewood, IL: Dow Jones Irwin, 1990.

BloomBecker, J.J. (as Becker, Jay). *The Investigation of Computer Crime.* Columbus, OH: Battelle Law and Justice Center, 1992.

Conly, Catherine H. *Organizing for Computer Crime Investigation and Prosecution.* Washington, DC: U.S. Department of Justice, National Institutes of Justice, 1989.

Hafner, Katie and Markoff, John. *Cyberpunk: Outlaws and Hackers on the Computer Frontier.* New York, NY: Simon & Schuster, 1991.

McEwen, J. Thomas. *Dedicated Computer Crime Units.* Washington, DC: U.S. Department of Justice, National Institutes of Justice, 1989.

Parker, Donn B. *Computer Crime: Criminal Justice Resource Manual,* Second Edition. Washington, DC: U.S. Department of Justice, National Institutes of Justice, 1989. (Order from +1-800-851-3420.)

Power, Richard. *Current and Future Danger: A CSI Primer on Computer Crime and Information Warfare.* San Francisco, CA: Computer Security Institute, 1995.

Sieber, Ulrich, ed. *International Review of Penal Law: Computer Crime and Other Crimes against Information Technology.* Toulouse, France: 1992.

Cryptography

Denning, Dorothy E.R. *Cryptography and Data Security.* Reading, MA: Addison Wesley, 1983.

Hoffman, Lance J., *Building in Big Brother: The Cryptographic Policy Debate*, New York, NY: Springer-Verlag, 1995.

Garfinkel, Simson. *PGP: Pretty Good Privacy*, Sebastopol, CA: O'Reilly & Associates, 1995.

Schneier, Bruce. *Applied Cryptography*, New York, NY: John Wiley & Sons, 1994.

Simmons, G.J., ed. *Contemporary Cryptology: The Science of Information Integrity*. New York, NY: IEEE Press, 1992.

Network and Internet Security and Firewalls

Bellovin, Steve and Cheswick, Bill. *Firewalls and Internet Security*. Reading, MA: Addison-Wesley, 1994.

Chapman, D. Brent and Zwicky, Elizabeth D. *Building Internet Firewalls*, Sebastopol, CA: O'Reilly & Associates, 1995.

Kaufman, Charles, Perlman, Radia, and Speciner, Mike. *Network Security: Private Communications in a Public World*. Englewood Cliffs, NJ: Prentice-Hall, 1995.

Stallings, William. *Network and Internetwork Security*. Englewood Cliffs, NJ: Prentice Hall, 1995.

Periodicals

Computer Audit Update
Computer Fraud & Security Update
Computer Law & Security Report
Computers & Security
Elsevier Advanced Technology
Crown House, Linton Rd., Barking
Essex I611 8JU, England
Voice: +44-81-5945942
Fax: +44-81-5945942
Telex: 896950 APPSCI G
North American Distributor:
P.O. Box 882
New York, NY 10159
Voice: +1-212-989-5800

Computer Security, Auditing & Controls
57 Greylock Road
Box 81151
Wellesley Hills, MA 02181

Voice: +1-617-235-2895

Computing & Communications
(Law & Protection Report)
P.O. Box 5323
Madison, WI 53705
Voice: +1-608-271-6768

Computer Security Alert
Computer Security Institute
600 Harrison Street
San Francisco, CA 94107
Voice: +1-415-905-2626

FBI Law Enforcement Bulletin
Federal Bureau of Investigation
10th and Pennsylvania Avenue
Washington, DC 20535
Voice: +1-202-324-3000

Information Systems Security Journal
Auerbach Publications
31 St. James Street
Boston, MA 02116
Voice: +1-800-950-1216

Information Systems Security Monitor
U.S. Department of the Treasury
Bureau of the Public Debt
AIS Security Branch
200 3rd Street
Parkersburg, WV 26101
Voice: +1-304-480-6355
BBS: +1-304-480-6083

InfoSecurity News
498 Concord Street
Framingham, MA 01701
Voice: +1-508-879-9792

Journal of Computer Security
IOS Press
Van Diemenstraat 94
1013 CN Amsterdam, Netherlands
Fax: +31-20-620-3419

Police Chief
International Association of Chiefs of Police
110 North Glebe Road, Suite 200
Arlington, VA 22201-9900
Voice: +1-703-243-6500

Security Management
American Society for Industrial Security
1655 North Fort Meyer Drive, Suite 1200
Arlington, VA 22209
Voice: +1-703-522-5800

Virus Bulletin
Virus Bulletin CTD
Oxon, Engand
Voice: +44-235-555139
North American Distributor:
RG Software Systems
Voice: +1-602-423-8000

User Organizations

American Society for Industrial Security (ASIS)
1655 North Fort Meyer Drive, Suite 1200
Arlington, VA 22209
Voice: +1-703-522-5800

Association for Computing Machinery (ACM)
Special Interest Group (SIG) on Security, Audit, and Control
Special Interest Group (SIG) on Computers and Society
1515 Broadway
New York NY 10036
Voice: +1-212-869-7440

Center for Computer Law
1112 Ocean Drive
Manhattan Beach, CA 90266
Voice: +1-213-372-0198

Computer Security Institute (CSI)
600 Harrison Street
San Francisco, CA 94107
Voice: +1-415-905-2626

Financial Fraud Institute
Federal Law Enforcement Training Center
Department of the Treasury
Glynco, GA 31524
Voice: +1-912-267-2312

Information Systems Security Association (ISSA)
P.O. Box 9457
Newport Beach, CA 92658
Voice: +1-714-250-4772

Institute of Electrical and Electronics Engineers (IEEE)
Special Interest Groups (SIG) on Security and Privacy
1730 Massachusetts Avenue, N.W.
Washington D.C. 20036-1992
Voice: +1-202-785-2180

High Technology Crimes Investigation Association (HTCIA)
Silicon Valley Chapter (contact this chapter for referrals to the other chapters, including those in Northern California; Southern California; Austin, Texas, Portland, Oregon; Chicago, Illinois; New York, New York; New Mexico; in addition, chapters are forming in Arizona and the Netherlands)
Voice: +1-408-299-7401
Email jsmith@netcom.com

International Association of Chiefs of Police
110 North Glebe Road, Suite 200
Arlington, VA 22201-9900
Voice: +1-703-243-6500

National Center for Computer Crime Data (NCCCD)
1222 17th Avenue
Santa Cruz, CA 95062
Voice: 408-475-4457

USENIX Association
2560 9th Street #215
Berkeley, CA 94710
Voice: +1-510-528-8649
Email: office@usenix.org

Emergency Response Organizations

The Department of Justice, FBI, and U.S. Secret Service organizations listed below investigate violations of the federal laws described in Chapter 4 and listed in Part

IV of this book. The various response teams that comprise the Forum of Incident and Response Security Teams (FIRST) do not investigate computer crimes per se, but provide assistance when security incidents occur; they also provide research, information, and support that can often help those incidents from occurring or spreading.

Department of Justice (DOJ)

Criminal Division
General Litigation and Legal Advice Section
Computer Crime Unit
Department of Justice
Washington, DC 20001
Voice: +1-202-514-1026

Federal Bureau of Investigation (FBI)

National Computer Crimes Squad
Federal Bureau of Investigation
7799 Leesburg Pike
South Tower, Suite 200
Falls Church, VA 22043
Voice: +1-202-324-9164

U.S. Secret Service (USSS)

Financial Crimes Division
Electronic Crime Branch
U.S. Secret Service
Washington, DC 20001
Voice: +1-202-435-7700

Forum of Incident and Response Security Teams (FIRST)

FIRST Secretariat
Forum of Incident and Response Security Teams
National Institute of Standards and Technology
A-216 Technology Building
Gaithersburg, MD 20899-0001
Phone: +1-301-975-3359
Email: first-sec@first.org
FTP: *csrc.ncsl.nist.gov/pub/first/first-contacts*
WWW page: *http://www.first.org/first/team-info/first-contacts*

The Forum of Incident and Response Security Teams (FIRST) was established in March 1993. FIRST is a coalition that brings together a variety of computer security incident response teams from the public and private sectors, as well as from universities. FIRST's constituents comprise many response teams throughout the world. FIRST's goals are:

- To boost cooperation among information technology users in the effective prevention of, detection of, and recovery from computer security incidents

- To provide a means to alert and advise clients on potential threats and emerging incident situations

- To support and promote the actions and activities of participating incident response teams, including research and operational activities

- To simplify and encourage the sharing of security-related information, tools, and techniques

At the time this book went to press, FIRST consisted of the organizations that are listed below, along with a description of the constituencies served by each of the organizations. Check online for the most up-to-date list of members.

Constituency:	Air Force - U.S. Air Force
Response Team:)	AFCERT
Email:	afcert@afcert.csap.af.mil
Voice:	+1-800-854-0187, 24/7
FAX:	+1-210-977-3632

Constituency:	Apple Computer Worldwide R&D Community
Response Team:	Apple COmputer REsponse Squad:Apple CORES
Email:	lsefton@apple.com
Voice:	+1-408-974-5594
Emergency Phone:	+1-415-948-5394
FAX:	+1-408-974-4754

Constituency:	Australia - Internet .au domain
Response Team:	Security Emergency Response Team (SERT)
Email:	sert@sert.edu.au
Voice:	+61-7-365-4417
After Hours:	+61-7-365-4417
FAX:	+61-7-365-4477

Constituency:	All Boeing computing and communication assets for all Boeing Divisions headquartered in Seattle, Washington, with major out plant operations in Wichita, Kansas; Philadelphia, Pennsylvania; Huntsville, Alabama; Houston, Texas; Winnipeg, Canada; and worldwide customer interface offices

Response Team:	Boeing CERT (BCERT)
Email:	scogginl@maple.boeing.com
Voice:	+1-206-657-9403; 206-657-9377
After Hours:	+1-206-639-3292; 206-655-2222
FAX:	+1-206-657-9477

Constituency	Department of Defense-interest systems
Response Team:	DoD's ASSIST (Automated Systems Security Incident Support Team)
Email:	assist@assist.ims.disa.mil
Voice:	+1-703-756-7974, 9-5PM, EST
Emergency Phone:	+1-800-SKY-PAGE, pin #2133937 (pager)
FAX:	+1-703-756-7949

Constituency:	DFN-WiNet, German Internet Sites
Response Team:	DFN-CERT (Deutsches Forschungsnetz)
Email:	dfncert@cert.dfn.de
Telephone:	+49-40-54715-262
FAX:	+49-40-54715-241

Constituency:	Digital Equipment Corporation and Customers
Response Team:	SSRT (Software Security Response Team)
Email:	rich.boren@cxo.mts.dec.com
Voice:	+1-800-354-9000
Emergency Phone:	+1-719-592-4689
FAX:	+1-719-592-4121

Constituency:	DOW USA
Response Team:	DOW USA
Email:	whstewart@dow.com
Voice:	+1-517-636-8738
Emergency Phone:	+1-517-832-0029
FAX:	+1-517-638-7705

Constituency:	EDS and EDS customers worldwide
Response Team:	EDS-CEN (EDS Computer Emergency Network)
Email:	jcutle01@novell.trts01.eds.com
Voice:	+1-313-265-7514
Emergency Phone:	+1-313-455-5131
FAX:	+1-313-265-3432

Constituency:	Energy - U.S. Department of Energy sites and Energy Sciences Network (ESnet)
Response Team:	CIAC Computer Incident Advisory Capability)
Email:	ciac@llnl.gov
Voice:	+1-510-422-8193, 24/7
FAX:	+1-510-423-8002

Constituency: French Universities,Minister of Research and Education in France,CNRS, CEA,INRIA,CNES,INRA,IFREMER,EDF
Response Team: GIP RENATER
Email: rensvp@urec.fr
Voice: +33-44-27-26-12
FAX: +33-44-27-26-13

Constituency: GE Business
Response Team: General Electric Company
Email: sandstrom@geis.geis.com
Voice: +1-301-340-4848
Emergency Phone: +1-301-340-4700
FAX: +1-301-340-4059

Constituency: Germany - Southern Area
Response Team: Micro-BIT Virus Center
Email: ry15@rz.uni-karlsruhe.de
Voice: +49-721-37-64-22
Emergency Phone: +49-171-52-51-685
FAX: +49-721-32-55-0

Constituency: •   Internet
Response Team: CERT Coordination Center
Email: cert@cert.org
Voice: +1-412-268-7090, 24/7
FAX: +1-412-268-6989

Constituency: Motorola
Response Team   Motorola Computer Emergency Response Team (MCERT)
Email: mcert@mot.com
Voice: +1-708-576-0669
Emergency Phone: +1-708-576-1616
FAX: +1-708-576-2259

Constituency: MILNET
Response Team;   DDN (Defense Data Network)
Email: scc@nic.ddn.mil
Voice: +1-800-365-3642, 8-5PM, EST
Emergency Phone: +1-703-692-2714, 24/7
FAX: +1-703-692-5071

Constituency: NASA - NASA-wide
Response Team: NASA Automated Systems Incident Response Capability
Email: tencati@nssdca.gsfc.nasa.gov
Voice: +1-301-794-5201, 8-5PM, EST
After Hours: +1-759-7243, pin #5460866 (pager)
FAX: +1-301-513-1608

Constituency: NAVY - U.S. Department of the Navy
Response Team: NAVCIRT (Naval Computer Incident Response Team)
Email: navcirt@nosc.mil
Voice: +1-202-282-2601, 7-5PM, EST
Emergency Phone: +1-800-759-8255, pin #+1-2021306 (pager)
FAX: +1-202-282-0411-

Constituency: NORDUNET - Denmark
Response Team: Nordunet
Email: ber@sunet.se
Telephone: +46-8-790-6513
FAX: +46-8-24-11-79

Constituency: Penn State - The Pennsylvania State University
Response Team: Penn State
Email: krk5@psuvm.psu.edu
Voice: +1-814-863-9533, 8-5PM, EST
After Hours: +1-814-863-4357 or +1-814-237-8081
FAX: +1-814-865-3082

Constituency: Purdue University
Response Team: PCERT
Email: pcert@cs.purdue.edu
Voice: +1-317-494-3561
After Hours: +1-317-474-7094
FAX: +1-317-494-6440

Constituency: RARE membership
Response Team: Woolwich Centre for Computer Crime Research/CERT Task
                    Force
Email: woolwich@ex.ac.uk
Voice: +49-0392-263247
After Hours: +49-0392-436351
FAX: +49-0392-263247

Constituency: SBA/Small Business Community Nationwide
Response Team: SBA CERT
Email: bolden@first.org
Voice: +1-202-205-6708
After Hours: +1-202-205-6708
FAX: +1-202-205-7064

Constituency: SPAN-France
Response Team: SPAN France
Email: harvey%meudon.dnet@east.gsfc.nasa.gov
Voice: +33-1-4-507-2805
FAX: +33-1-4-507-2806

Constituency: Sprint - U.S. Sprint
Response Team: Sprint DNSU
Email: /PN=DATANETWORK.SECURITY/O=US.SPRINT/
                     ADMD=TELEMAIL /C=US/@sprint.com
Email: /PN=CORPINFO.SECURITY/O=US.SPRINT/ADMD=TELEMAIL
                     /C=US/@sprint.com
Voice: +1-703-689-7317, 8-5PM, EST
After Hours: +1-800-SKY-PAGE, pin #44260 (pager)
FAX: +1-703-689-7380

Constituency: Customers of Sun Microsystems
Response Team: Sun Microsystem's Customer Warning System (CWS)
Email: security-alert@sun.com
Voice: +1-415-688-9080
Emergency Phone: +1-415-688-9081
FAX: +1-415-688-9101

Constituency: SURFnet connect sites, Netherlands
Response Team: SURFnet Computer Emergency Response Team
Email: cert-nl@surfnet.nl
Voice: +31-30-310290
FAX: +31-30-340903

Constituency: TRW Network Area and System Administrators
Response Team: TRW's CERCUS (Computer Emergency Response Committee
                     for Unclassified Systems
Email: cercus@gumby.dsd.trw.com
Voice: +1-310-812-1839, 9-5PM, PST
Emergency Phone: +1-310-841-8943 (pager)
FAX: +1-310-813-4621

Constituency: UK - all government departments and agencies
Response Team: CCTA IT Security & Infrastructure Group
Email: sp305@ccta.uk
Voice: +44-71-217-3053
Emergency Phone: +44-71-217-3023
FAX: +44-71-217-3449

Constituency: Unisys Internal and External Users
Response Team: UCERT
Email: garb@dockmaster.ncsc.mil
Voice: +1-215-986-4038
Emergency Phone: +1-215-757-1862
FAX: +1-212-986-4409

Constituency:	Westinghouse Electric Corporation
Response Team	(W)CERT
Email:	Nicholson.M%wec@dialcom.tymnet.com
Voice:	+1-412-642-3097
Emergency Phone:	+1-412-642-3444
FAX:	+1-412-642-3871

Government Agencies

These two agencies are heavily involved in setting standards, evaluating systems, and distributing information about computer security.

National Institute of Standards and Technology (NIST)

National Institute of Standards and Technology
Gaithersburg, MD 20899
Voice: 301-975-2000

National Computer Security Center (NCSC)

National Computer Security Center
9800 Savage Road
Fort George G. Meade, MD 20755-6000
Voice: 301-688-6311

Electronic Resources

USENET

If your system has Internet access, you will be able to access the worldwide USENET news network. The main USENET newsgroups dedicated to computer security are listed below:

comp.risks	Discussions of the risks of technology
comp.security.announce	Announcements of computer security vulnerabilities (by CERT)
comp.virus	Discussions of computer viruses
comp.security.misc	Discussions of computer security issues
comp.security.unix	Discussions of UNIX computer security issues
alt.security	Discussions of computer security.

Although you can get a great deal of useful information from these newsgroups, be aware that sometimes they contain postings by people who have no real idea of what they are talking about, although they may sound authoritative. Some people even post misleading and incorrect information on purpose! In general, you should carefully cross-check any information you get from newsgroups before you rely on it.

Forum of Incident and Response Security Teams (FIRST)

FIRST maintains an electronic archive containing information about computer crime and other computer security issues. It is available via anonymous FTP at *first.org*. Most of the FIRST members also make their own information, programs, and documents available. Contact FIRST and its member organizations as shown above.

Computer Operations, Audit, and Security Technology (COAST)

The Internet's largest single archive of computer security-related tools, standards, documents, newsletters, and other information is the Computer Operations, Audit, and Security Technology (COAST) archive. Located at Purdue University, the COAST Laboratory is directed by Professor Eugene Spafford.

COAST Laboratory
Department of Computer Sciences
Purdue University
West Lafayette, IN 47907-1398
Voice: +1-317-494-6010
FTP: *coast.cs.purdue.edu/pub*
WWW page: *http://www.cs.purdue.edu/coast*

DOCKMASTER

DOCKMASTER is an electronic archive and email system used by federal government employees and contractors. It is connected to most computer networks. Contact DOCKMASTER at:

National Computer Security Center
Attn: C81 Accounts Administrator
9800 Savage Road
Fort George G. Meade, MD 20755-6000
Voice: +1-301-859-4360

Archives of Computer Crime Laws

There are two especially helpful sources of information on computer crime laws. The *thomas* archive contains U.S. Congressional bills and activities, with links to other electronic sources within the U.S. government. The *sulaw* archive contains many U.S. federal, state, and international laws, as well as articles, papers, and other information on computer security and computer crime. In addition, many states and countries now have their own World Wide Web pages. Contact your system administrator or Internet provider if you need help tracking them down.

FTP: *thomas.gov.edu*

WWW page: *http://www.thomas.gov.edu*

FTP:*sulaw.law.su.oz.au/pub/law*

B

Raiding the Computer Room

For several decades, electronic computing machines have been changing the world. Businesses now record their activities by computer. Law enforcement agencies maintain criminal records by computer, children are entertained by computer-driven electronic games, and authors process their words by computer. Even tasks such as medical diagnoses are being performed with the aid of computers.

In the last decade, the proliferation of low-cost "home computers" has facilitated the spread of computer power and knowledge to vast numbers of citizens. Thus, it should be no surprise that criminals have begun to use computers to commit crimes and to record the activities of their criminal enterprises. Consequently, law enforcement officers are finding it increasingly necessary to search for, examine, and seize computers and computerized records in successfully investigating and prosecuting many criminal acts.

While conducting investigations of computer-related crimes, officers must comply with an eighteenth century prohibition against "unreasonable searches and seizures"[1] and contend with twentieth century electronic technology. For example, investigators may at times find themselves searching for intangibles rather than familiar physical evidence, such as guns or stolen stock certificates. As one court has noted, the target of a search may be "records [that] exist as electronic impulses in the storage banks of a computer."[2] This new technology creates the possibility of a criminal armed with a home computer in Wisconsin contacting a computer in New York by telephone and illegally causing funds to

---

[1] U.S. Const. amend. IV.
[2] United States v. Hall, 583 F. Supp. 717, 718 (E.D. Va. 1984).

This appendix was originally published as a two-part article, "Raiding the Computer Room: Fourth Amendment Considerations," by John Gales Sauls, in the *FBI Law Enforcement Bulletin,* May and June, 1986.

be transferred electronically to a bank account in France. Regardless of these technological advances, search and seizure by law enforcement officers continues to be governed by the Fourth Amendment to the U.S. Constitution.[3]

This article will examine issues that arise when officers seek a warrant to search and seize a computer and the information it has processed. The first part of the article will address the application of the Fourth Amendment warrant requirement to computer-related searches, focusing on special problems officers may encounter in establishing probable cause to search and particularly describing the computer equipment to be seized. The second part will address the description of computer-processed information to satisfy the particularity requirement and then consider issues that may arise in the execution of a warrant authorizing the seizure of a computer and computer processed information.

Warrant Requirement

The Fourth Amendment protects the right of the people to be "secure in their persons, houses, papers and effects" against unreasonable government intrusion.[4] This protection extends to computers, which are effects, and to information processed by this electronic technology, which can be categorized as papers. The constitutional demand on the officer seeking to seize a person's computer or computerized information is that the seizure be reasonable.[5] The U.S. Supreme Court, in establishing guidelines for reasonable searches and seizures, has stated a preference that they be made pursuant to a judicially issued search warrant. The "Constitution requires that the deliberate, impartial judgment of a judicial officer be interposed between the citizen and the police searches conducted outside the judicial process, without prior approval by judge or magistrate, are per se unreasonable under the Fourth Amendment—subject only to a few specifically established and well delineated exceptions."[6] This requirement that a warrant be obtained prior to a search or seizure is applied with special strictness where business or residential premises, the places computers are most likely to be located, must be entered to perform the search.[7]

The Fourth Amendment sets forth certain procedural requirements that must be met if a valid warrant is to be issued. There must be a showing of probable cause supported by oath or affirmation, and the warrant must particularly describe the place to be searched and the persons or things to be seized.[8] In addition, the

---

[3] See Katz v. United States, 389 U.S. 347 (1967).
[4] U.S. Const. amend. IV.
[5] See Katz v. United States, 389 U.S. 347 (1967).
[6] Id. at 357.
[7] See Michigan v. Tyler, 436 U.S. 499 (1978).
[8] U.S. Const. amend. IV.

Supreme Court has held that the probable cause determination must be made by a neutral, detached magistrate. The requirements of oath or affirmation and of presentation to a neutral, detached magistrate raise no special problems where computer searches are concerned; however, the probable cause and particularity requirements pose unique problems where computers are the search target, and these issues merit discussion.

Probable Cause to Search

Central to the protections provided to citizens by the warrant requirement is the command that no warrants shall issue but upon probable cause.[9] This language has been interpreted to require that before a search warrant may be issued, the government must set forth facts that would cause a reasonable person to conclude that it is probably true that (1) a crime has been committed, (2) that evidence of that crime is in existence, and (3) that the evidence presently exists at the place to be searched.[10] Obviously, satisfying this requirement necessitates the collection and presentation of information, and law enforcement officers perform this task daily in regard to numerous crimes. Computer-related crimes present new challenges in the establishment of probable cause, though, because of the unfamiliar technology involved. Although a magistrate likely already understands how a murder may be committed with a gun, he may require considerable explanation before finding that an embezzlement was committed by means of a computer. The problem is largely an educational one.

Inasmuch as computers may be used in a wide variety of criminal endeavors, ranging from fraud to espionage, it is difficult to state concisely what is required to satisfy the probable cause requirement in a computer-related crime. In general, probable cause will be established just as it would in a case where no computer was involved, except that additional facts will have to be presented regarding the role of the computer in the criminal activity.

That a Crime Has Been Committed

The first hurdle in establishing probable cause to search is articulating facts to indicate that a crime probably has been committed. In determining what additional facts a magistrate will need to make such a finding where a computer is involved in the crime, it is helpful to examine the role played by the computer in the criminal activity. For example, when a computer is stolen, the crime is the same as any other theft, and the required factual showing, describing the computer as the

---

[9] U.S. Const. amend. IV.

[10] Zurcher v. Stanford Daily, 436 U.S. 547, 556-557 n. 6(1978), quoting Comment, 28 U. Chi. L. Rev. 664, 687 (1961).

object of the crime, would likewise be the same. When a computer is used as a tool to commit a crime, facts must be presented to show the crime was committed and to explain how the computer was used in the commission. Because computer systems are commonly installed so they may be used from distant locations by means of electronic communication over telephone lines, novel criminal opportunities have been created.[11] Valuable data may be transferred from one computer to another or modified to achieve advantage for the computer criminal.[12] Inasmuch as the means used to commit these crimes are unfamiliar, the officer must convince the magistrate that such a crime has been committed by detailing how it was committed.

An example of an officer successfully obtaining a search warrant in a case where new technology was being employed to commit the crime of fraud is found in the case of *Ottensmeyer* v.*Chesapeake & Potomac Telephone Co.*[13] Ottensmeyer, who ran a telephone answering service, decided to provide an alternative to his customers to normal, commercial long-distance telephone service. He found a strategically located town that enjoyed nontoll-calling service to a larger city on either side, despite the fact that a call from one of the larger cities to the other was a toll call. Ottensmeyer installed an electronic device in the small town that allowed a customer in one of the large cities to "patch" a call to the other large city through the device, thereby avoiding a toll call and defrauding the phone company of revenues to which it was entitled.

The investigator, a police officer who had special training in electronic technology and telecommunications, sought a warrant to search the premises where the "patching" device was located. In his affidavit, the officer "informed the judge of his experience in the electronic field and of his independent investigation and conclusions."[14] The officer articulated facts that explained how the scheme to defraud functioned, and drawing on his expertise, cited inferences he had drawn from the facts he had observed. The warrant was issued and the search performed.[15]

Obviously, an officer seeking to convince a magistrate that a novel crime has been committed should use care to ensure that the explanation of the mechanics of the crime is clear and easily understood. If the officer wishes the magistrate to consider the officer's interpretations of the facts he has observed, he must inform the magistrate in his affidavit of the experience and training that accredit these

---

[11] For a discussion of computer telecommunication crime, see Marbach, "Beware: Hackers at Play," *Newsweek*, September 5, 1983, p. 42.

[12] For an interesting discussion of computer crimes, see T. Whiteside, *Computer Capers* (Thomas Y. Crowell, 1978).

[13] 756 F.2d 986 (4th Cir. 1985).

[14] Id. at 990.

[15] Id. at 990, 991.

interpretations. Consideration of such inferences by a magistrate determining probable cause has been approved so long as the officer sets forth the training and experience upon which they are based.[16]

An officer seeking to establish probable cause where the crime is unusual or unfamiliar may also elect to use the services of an expert. An example of using information provided by experts in affidavits for search warrants is found in *United States v. Steerwell Leisure Corp.*, Inc.[17] Steerwell was charged with infringing upon the copyrights of a number of electronic video games, and the question of whether a crime had been committed turned on whether the games Steerwell was distributing were sufficiently similar to the copyrighted games to violate the copyright statute. The affidavits to support search warrants presented the magistrate with results of expert analysis in comparing the games distributed by the defendants with the copyright-protected games. In determining the validity of the warrants issued on those affidavits, the court concluded that the magistrate was entitled to accept the conclusions of the experts, but noted the "magistrate's determination of probable cause would be facilitated if the agents affidavits contained more details concerning the comparisons between protected games and intriguing games."[18]

The court also made reference to the importance of explaining to the magistrate how the crime was committed, in this case by duplication of the circuit boards that control the action of electronic games.[19] Again, the task of the officer includes providing sufficient technical details in layman's terms to familiarize the magistrate with the mechanics of an unusual crime.

That Evidence of the Crime Exists

The second hurdle for an officer seeking to establish probable cause to search is setting forth facts to convince a magistrate of the probability that evidence of the crime exists. When a computer is stolen, the stolen computer is evidence of the crime. If the theft is established factually, then the existence of the computer as evidence is likewise established. Similarly, when facts establish that a computer was used to commit a crime, the same facts establish that the computer used was an instrumentality of the crime. This was demonstrated in the Steerwell Leisure Corp. case where, if the magistrate found that the circuit boards in question violated the copyright laws, then the boards would also constitute evidence of that violation.[20]

---

[16] See, e.g., United States v. Ortiz, 422 U.S. 891 (1975). See also Johnson v. United States, 333 U.S. 10 (1948).

[17] 598 F.Supp. 171 (W.D. N.Y. 1984).

[18] Id. at 176.

[19] Id. at 177.

[20] Id.

When an investigator seeks to establish that computerized records of criminal activity are in existence, his task is essentially the same as establishing the existence of noncomputerized records. He must factually establish that records of the criminal activity have probably been created and retained. There is authority for the position that it is unnecessary to establish factually in the affidavit the physical form in which the records sought are expected to be found.[21] If the officer can establish factually the creation and retention of the records, he need not specify (or know) whether they are being maintained in written, magnetic, or some other form. In *United States v. Truglio*, audio cassettes were seized during the execution of a search warrant authorizing the seizure of "books, records, indices, movies regarding the interstate prostitution operation located at the King of the Road Health Club"[22] In approving seizure of the audio cassettes, the court noted that "it would have been more precise for the warrant to have specified 'written or electronic records,'" but then stated that "standards of pragmatism and commonsense must necessarily be adaptable to changing times and technological advances."[23] The court concluded by saying that "while decades ago it might have been difficult reasonably to infer that records existed in some form other than written, in the mid-1980's commonsense demands that we refrain from remaining so inflexible."[24]

That Evidence of the Crime Presently Exists at the Place to Be Searched

Finally, the investigator seeking to establish probable cause to search must factually establish the probability that the evidence sought is presently located at the place he is seeking authorization to search. Whether this requirement of recent information has been met is "determined by the circumstances of each case."[25] As stated by the U.S. Supreme Court, "The task of the issuing magistrate is simply to make a practical, commonsense decision whether, given all the circumstances set forth in the affidavit before him there is a fair probability that evidence of a crime will be found in a particular place."[26]

The requirement for recent information is easily satisfied when the investigator can set forth reliable information that the object sought has been recently observed at the proposed search site. When such facts are not available, other facts must be used to infer that the items to be seized are presently at the place to be searched. At times, having a computer or its records as the target of the search

---

[21] United States v. Truglio, 731 F.2d 1123 (4th Cir. 1984), cert. denied, 83 L. Ed.2d. 130 (1984).
[22] Id. at 1126.
[23] Id. at 1128.
[24] Id.
[25] Sgro v. United States, 287 U.S. 206 (1932).
[26] Illinois v. Gates, 462 U.S. 213, 238 (1983).

may simplify meeting this requirement. If a computer has been used to commit a crime telephonically, it is possible that it has also been set up to "answer" incoming calls, to allow other computer operators to call it using their computer terminals and a telephone. If such an operation exists, an incoming call will be answered with a tone called a "carrier."[27] When a particular phone is answered with a carrier, it seems reasonable for a magistrate who has been informed of the significance of the carrier to find that a computer and related equipment are probably present at the location of the telephone.

A somewhat analogous case involved a search warrant issued for the seizure of a "blue box," an electronic device used to create tones on the telephone system to facilitate the making of long-distance calls without being billed for the toll charges.[28] In this case, tones such as those produced by a blue box had been monitored by the telephone company on a particular telephone for a period of weeks, ending the day prior to the issuance of the warrant. This information was related to the magistrate in the affidavit. In upholding the validity of the resulting search warrant, the court concluded that "the affidavit set forth substantial information establishing clear probable cause to believe that a device emitting a 2600 cycle tone and Southwestern Bell multifrequency tones was being utilized at the residence."[29]

When computerized records are sought, the magistrate should consider that records, by their nature, are created to be kept for at least a minimum period of time, along with the other facts presented, in determining whether the records are presently at the place to be searched.[30] Although each case must be evaluated on its own facts, the U.S. Supreme Court and lower courts have held that under certain circumstances, it is reasonable to expect that records seen 3 months previously will still be present at that same location.[31]

Particularity

The Fourth Amendment commands that "no warrants shall issue except [those] particularly describing the place to be searched and the persons or things to be seized."[32] This provision requires that a warrant authorize only a search of a specific place for specific named items. Coupled with the probable cause requirement, this provision prevents general searches by ensuring that the warrant describes a discrete, defined place to be searched, describes only items connected

---

[27] See Fitzgerald and Eason, *Fundamentals of Data Communication*, pp. 42-433 (John Wiley & Sons, 1978).
[28] United States v. Harvey, 540 F.2d 1345 (8th Cir. 1976).
[29] Id. at 1354.
[30] United States v. McManus, 719 F.2d 1395 (6th Cir. 1983).
[31] Andresen v. Maryland, 427 U.S. 463, 478 n. 9 (1976).
[32] U.S. Const. amend IV.

with criminal activity for which probable cause has been established, and describes the items so definitely that it removes from an officer executing the warrant the discretion of determining which items are covered by the warrant and which are not.[33] It also provides a signal of when a search is at an end—that is, when all items named in the warrant have been located and seized or when all possible hiding places for items not located have been explored.[34] Since the "place to be searched" portion of the particularity requirement has no special impact on computer searches, it will not be discussed. However, the "things to be seized" portion of the requirement has a marked impact in seeking a warrant to authorize the seizure of a computer or information processed by a computer. This portion will be examined in regard to both the computer and the processed information.

Describing the Computer

The primary rule of particularity should be to make the description of the items to be seized as precise as the facts will allow. A court measuring the particularity of a description in a search warrant may consider what facts could reasonably be known by the investigator at the time application for the warrant was made, so long as the investigator includes all the facts known to him in the affidavit.[35] Consequently, the circumstances of each case can help determine whether a description is sufficiently particular. The nature of the item sought also is considered in determining the degree of particularity required. A less precise description is required of items that are contraband, such as controlled substances.[36] Conversely, greater particularity is demanded when the item sought is of a type in lawful use in substantial quantities.[37] Generally, when computer equipment is sought for seizure pursuant to a search warrant, a quite particular description will be required.

When a computer has been reported stolen, it is reasonable to expect that the owner will provide a detailed description of the stolen item. Therefore, if the object of the search is a stolen computer, a detailed description—including manufacturer, model number, and serial number, if known—will probably be required. This is especially true if the computer sought is a type commonly in lawful use. Care should be taken to ensure that all available descriptive information is included.

---

[33] See Marron v. United States, 275 U.S. 192 (1927). For a thorough discussion, see 2 W. LaFave, Search and Seizure 95-101 (1978).
[34] See 2 W. LaFave, Search and Seizure 162 (1978).
[35] Cf. Andresen v. Maryland, 427 U.S. 463 (1976).
[36] See, e.g., Steele v. United States, 267 U.S. 498 (1925).
[37] Supra note 35, at 99.

When computer equipment is sought because it was used as an instrumentality to commit a crime, the most precise description the facts will allow may be a more general one.[38] When a victim complains that his computer system has been accessed telephonically by an unknown person and a loss has resulted, it is likely that the investigator will only be able to determine generally what types of devices were used to accomplish the crime. He may, for example, learn that a computer terminal (a keyboard and display monitor) and a modem (a device that allows digitally encoded computer information to be transmitted over telephone lines) were necessary to perform the acts accomplished, but will have no information regarding the manufacturers of the equipment, model numbers, or serial numbers. If a telephone trace reveals the location from which the intruding call originated, the investigator may have probable cause to search. Under these circumstances, the general description of "a computer terminal and a modem of unknown make or model" may suffice.

An analogous case is *State* v. *Van Wert*,[39] where police had probable cause to believe Van Wert was using equipment to forge checks. A search warrant was issued authorizing the seizure of "check protectors and typewriters used in preparation of forged checks." The court approved use of this general language based upon the nature and information known concerning the crime, stating that greater particularity "was not needed in this case where defendant was under investigation for forgery rather than theft of a certain item."[40]

Similarly, the warrant in *United States v. Harvey* authorized the seizure of "a blue box," an electronic device that allows a caller to make long-distance calls without them being recorded for billing by the telephone company."[41] The agents executing this warrant ultimately seized audio cassette tapes that had tones such as those produced by a blue box recorded on them. The court noted that the affidavit clearly established that a device emitting blue box type-tones was being used at the place to be searched and then addressed the particularity question, observing that "neither the Southwestern Bell officials nor the FBI Agents knew the actual physical form which the device would take, and they assumed it would be in the form familiar to their research and experience"[42] The court, in approving the seizure, said, "The cassette tapes constituted 'an electronic device that allows a caller to make long distance phone calls without them being recorded for billing by the telephone company' and were thus properly seized as within the limitations of the warrant."[43]

---

[38] Id. at 104. See, e.g., Quigg v. Estelle, 492 F.2d 343 (9th Cir. 1974).
[39] 199 N.W.2d 514 (Minn. 1972).
[40] Id. at 515-516.
[41] Supra note 29, at 1353.
[42] Id. at 1354.
[43] Id.

Since computer systems are often comprised of a number of component parts,[44] an investigator applying for a warrant to seize a computer should ensure that the warrant describes all parts of the computer system that are probably present, as well as the various types of storage devices upon which the machine's operating instructions (computer programs) are maintained. It is prudent to consult an expert concerning the items to be listed. Equipment components will probably include a central processing unit, printers, terminals (keyboards and display screens), magnetic tape drives, and magnetic disc drives. Storage media will include magnetic tapes, magnetic discs, punched cards, and paper tapes. Computer printouts will also likely be present.[45] If information that has been processed is being sought, it is especially important to particularly describe the storage media. Consultation with an expert will increase the likelihood of a thorough listing of the items of evidence probably present, and provided the expert's education and experience are set forth in the affidavit, will give the magistrate a sound basis for concluding that the items sought are probably located at the place to be searched.

Describing Computer-Processed Information

Officers seeking to describe particular information that has been processed by a computer face two significant obstacles. The first obstacle is explaining in an affidavit for a search warrant that records being sought may be contained in sophisticated technological equipment—for example, digital computer systems store and process information in the form of electronic impulses.[46] For these purposes, this information is encoded into the binary number system, a "language" comprised only of the characters zero and one.[47] Since, for the officer seeking authority to search and seize and the court reviewing his applicationm, "information (either numbers or text) in binary form is useless unless it can be decoded,"[48] describing computerized information in its encoded form is not meaningful. Fortunately, therefore, for officers drafting search warrant applications, this first obstacle is easily overcome, since officers are not required to confront the technological realities of what occurs when information is transformed into an electronic record. They can simply state that the information sought may be in

---

[44] For a discussion of computer system components, see T. Schabeck, Computer Crime Investigation Manual, secs, 2.3-2.6 (Assets protection, 1980).

[45] An example of a detailed description of a computer system is: "One Alpha [Brand] Micro computer central processing unit, approximately four Alpha [Brand] Micro computer terminals, computer printers, and computer manuals, logs, printout files, operating instructions, including coded and handwritten notations, and computer storage materials, including magnetic tapes, magnetic discs, floppy discs, programs, and computer source documentation." Quoted from Voss v. Bergsgaard, 774 F.2d 402, 407 (1985) (warrant invalidated on other grounds).

[46] 14 Am. Jur. Proof of Facts 2d 183 (1977).

[47] ID. See also King v. State ex rel Murdock Acceptance Corporation, 222 So. 2d 393, 398 (1969)

[48] Id. at 184.

electronic or written form. It is the information itself that must be described with particularity, rarer than the form in which the information may be found. Thus, if what is sought is "a letter from John Jones to Bill Smith dated November 9, 1985, and concerning the ownership of 200 shares of IBM stock," the letter should be described in those specific terms. The descriptive problem regarding whether the letter should be found in the form of paper with writing on it or magnetic tape electronically inscribed with binary code is solved by using more general terms. Concluding the description of the letter and similar items with the statement that "the records sought are 'written or electronic'" should be sufficient to permit lawful seizures of the documents in either form, if the information sought is itself (as in the letter example) described with sufficient detail.[49] As previously noted, the storage media (magnetic discs, etc.) which could contain the information in electronic form should also be described as concisely as the facts known will allow.

The more difficult obstacle, then, is particularly describing the information that is the object of the search. Information, whether recorded in written or electronic form, is generally collected into documents. Documents are what officers usually describe in warrants authorizing the seizure of information. Because the particularity requirement is strictly applied where documents are concerned,[50] the descriptive task is often a demanding one. Nonetheless, courts reviewing applications for search warrants evaluate the particularity of the description of a document in light of the degree of precision the facts of a case will allow.[51] The officer must be as precise as possible in describing a document, consistent with the facts that are available to him. The detailed description is required whether the information is computerized or not.

For example, in the *United States v. Timpani,*[52] a search warrant authorizing the seizure of "any and all records relating to extortionate credit transactions (loan-sharking)"[53] was challenged as being insufficiently particular. In reviewing the warrant, the court noted that the warrant included a lengthy list of types of records (including "lists of loan customers, loan accounts, telephone numbers, address books"[54]) and that the warrant "provide[d] a standard for segregating the 'innocent' from the 'culpable' in the form of requiring a connection with [the] specific, identifiable crime [of loansharking]."[55] Approving the particularity of the

---

[49] See United States v. Truglio, 731 F.2d 1123 (4th Cir. 1984), cert. denied, 83 L.Ed.2d 130 (1984). See also United States v. Offices Known as 50 State Distrib., 708 F.2d 1371 (9th Cir. 1983), cert. denied, 79 L.Ed.2d 677 (1984).

[50] See Andresen v. Maryland, 427 U.S. 463 (1976).

[51] For a thorough discussion, see Rissler, "Documentary Search Warrants," *FBI Law Enforcement Bulletin,* vol. 49, No. 7, July 1980, pp. 27–31.

[52] 655 F.2d 1 (1st Cir. 1981).

[53] Id. at 4.

[54] Id.

[55] Id. at 5.

warrant, the court stated, "Most important, it is difficult to see how the search warrant could have been made more precise."[56]

The task of the officer is to describe the information sought with sufficient particularity to avoid a forbidden "general" warrant. If he is aware of specific documents sought, he should designate them by type (letter, memo, etc.), date, subject, author, and addressee, providing as much detail as possible. The earlier description of the letter regarding ownership of IBM stock is an example of this technique.

When only the general nature of the information sought is known, a highly detailed description is impossible. In such cases, officers must use great care to give a description that includes the information sought but limits the search as narrowly as possible. This is accomplished by use of a general description that is qualified by some standard that will enable the executing officers to separate the information to be seized from innocent information that may also be present. This qualifying standard is known as a *limiting phrase*.

The limiting phrase must be crafted based on the facts establishing probable cause to search. If the facts establish that the information sought comes from a particular time period, the phrase should limit the warrant to information of that time period. If the information sought is known to have been produced by a particular individual, the phrase should limit the description to material authored by that person. If the phrase combines several such factors, it is even more effective. As in *United States v. Timpani*, the phrase may restrict the description to particular criminal conduct. In that case, the limiting phrase was "records relating to extortionate credit transactions (loansharking)."[57] It is most important that the limiting phrase restrict the scope of the search so that it remains within the bounds of the probable cause set out in the affidavit. The warrant may not authorize the seizure of items for which probable cause to search has not been established. In upholding the description of items in the warrant in the *Timpani* case, the court noted that "each item is plausibly related to the crime—loansharking or gambling—that is specifically set out [in the affidavit]."[58] The description, even though the items to be seized were described in generic terms, did not exceed the probable cause because of the use of an appropriately narrow limiting phrase.

In Application of Lafayette Academy, Inc.,[59] a case involving a search for computerized information, the information sought was described in general terms with the inclusion of a limiting phrase, but the phrase was not made sufficiently

---

[56] Id.
[57] Id. at 4.
[58] Id. at 5.
[59] 610 F.2d 1 (1st Cir. 1979).

narrow. Lafayette Academy, Inc., was being investigated for fraudulent activities in connection with their participation in the Federally Insured Student Loan Program (FISLP). The warrant authorized seizure of "books, papers, rosters of students, letters, correspondence, documents, memoranda, contracts, agreements, ledgers, worksheets, books of account, student files, file jackets and contents, computer tapes/discs, computer operation manuals, computer tape logs, computer tape layouts, computer tape printouts, Office of Education (HEW) documents and forms ... which constitute evidence of the commission of violations of the laws of the United States, that is violations of 18 U.S.C. Sections 286, 287, 371, 1001, and 1014."[60] The probable cause in this case related to frauds pertaining to the FISLP. The court, in invalidating the search warrant, criticized the limiting phrase because it allowed seizure of items for crimes beyond the scope of the probable cause established. The court stated, "The warrant is framed to allow seizure of most every sort of book or paper at the described premises, limited only by the qualification that the seized item by evidence of violations of 'the laws of the United States, that is violations of 18 U.S.C. Sections 286, 287, 371, 1001, and 1014.' The cited statutes, however, penalize a very wide range of frauds and conspiracies. They are not limited to frauds pertaining to FISLP, and there is no indication from the warrant that the violations of federal law as to which evidence is being sought stem only or indeed at all from Lafayette's participation in FISLP. Thus, the warrant purports to authorize not just a search and seizure of FISLP-related records as the government contends but a general rummaging for evidence of any type of federal conspiracy or fraud."[61] The court continued that "the precise nature of the fraud and conspiracy offenses for evidence of which the search was authorized—fraud and conspiracy in the FISLP—needed to be stated in order to delimit the broad categories of documentary material and thus meet the particularity requirement."[62]

Occasionally, the nature of the probable cause will allow a very broad description. In *United States v. Brien,*[63] a search warrant was issued for the premises of Lloyd, Carr & Company, a commodities brokerage firm. The warrant authorized the seizure of "Lloyd, Carr's bank statements, cash receipt books, option purchase records, sales material distributed to customers, employee compensation records, customer account records, sales training material and customer lists."[64] Noting that the described items constituted most of the business records of the company, the court nonetheless upheld the warrant's particularity, since the affidavit's facts "warranted a strong belief that Lloyd, Carr's operation was, solely and entirely, a

---

[60] Id. at 3.
[61] Id.
[62] Id. at 3, 4.
[63] 617 F.2d 299 (1st Cir. 1980), cert. denied, 446 U.S. 919 (1980).
[64] Id. at 306.

scheme, to defraud."[65] Since the facts in the affidavit established that all of the records of the business probably were evidence of the crime being investigated, the scope of the description was sufficiently particular. In upholding the validity of the warrant, the court stated, "Where there is probable cause to find that there exists a pervasive scheme to defraud, all the business records of an enterprise may be seized, if they are, as here, accurately described so that the executing officers have no need to exercise their own judgment as to what should be seized."[66]

The items to be seized should be described as precisely as the facts will allow, and items for which probable cause to search has not been established should not be included. An innovative means of limiting the items described to those for which probable cause to search has been established is found in the case In Re Search Warrant Dated July 4, 1977, Etc.[67] Here, the scope of the description of items to be seized was limited to documents related to "the crimes which facts recited in the accompanying affidavit make out."[68] The court, in upholding the warrant, noted with approval the limiting phrase. As was done in this case, it is often desirable to incorporate the affidavit into the warrant by appropriate language and to attach the affidavit to the warrant. Officers preparing search warrants for computerized information should consider the use of this procedure.

Executing the Search Warrant

The protection of the Fourth Amendment does not end when an officer obtains a valid search warrant. The right of citizens to be free of "unreasonable searches and seizures" extends to the manner in which a search warrant is executed.[69] For the search to be lawful, it must be done in a reasonable manner.[70] The U.S. Supreme Court has recognized the flexibility of this standard, stating, "There is no formula for the determination of reasonableness. Each case is to be decided on its own facts and circumstances."[71] Perhaps because of the vagueness of this standard, certain statutes also regulate the action of officers executing search warrants.[72]

Generally, officers must give notice of their authority and purpose prior to entering premises to execute a search warrant.[73] Once inside, the actions taken to

---

[65] Id. at 308.
[66] Id. at 309, contra Voss v. Bergsgaard, 774 F.2d 402 (10th Cir. 1985).
[67] 667 F.2d 117 (D.C. Cir. 1981), cert. denied, 102 S.Ct. 1971 (1982).
[68] Id. at 141.
[69] Go-Bart Importing Company v. United States, 75 L.Ed. 374 (1931).
[70] Id.
[71] Id. at 382.
[72] An example is 18 U.S.C. 3109.
[73] Cf. Ker v. California, 374 U.S. 23 (1963) (concerning an entry to arrest). For a thorough discussion, see 2 W. LaFave, Search and Seizure, 122-140 (1978).

secure control of the premises and prevent destruction of evidence must be reasonable under the circumstances.[74] The search itself must be performed within the scope of the warrant,[75] and care must be taken to cause no unnecessary damage during the search.[76] Finally, only items named in the search warrant may be seized, subject to a limited exception, the "plain view" doctrine.[77] These aspects of execution will be examined as they relate to computer searches.

The Announcement Requirement

To protect the privacy interests of citizens and the safety of both occupants of premises and the officers making entry to execute a warrant, officers are generally required to knock and announce their identity and purpose before forcibly entering premises to perform a search.[78] This requirement is subject to certain exceptions that allow entry without notice under some circumstances.[79] The exceptions include situations where the announcement would jeopardize the safety of the officers or others and where it would likely result in the destruction of evidence.[80] This latter exception, destruction of evidence, becomes relevant in searching for computer-processed information.

Due to the manner in which it is processed and stored, computerized information is easily and quickly destroyed. As previously discussed, information is encoded into the binary number system for processing purposes. This encoded information may then be stored in the computer's internal memory or on magnetic or other external storage media.[81] Generally, the internal memory is used to store data that must be immediately accessible to perform the tasks for which the computer is presently being used. Because any power interruption will result in the loss of information stored in the computer's internal memory, important information is usually duplicated and stored on an external storage device, such as a magnetic tape or disc. Information that is in the computer's internal memory that has not been "backed up" by more permanent external storage may be destroyed in the instant it takes to flip a power interruption switch. Depending on the memory capacity of the computer, a considerable amount of information may be lost in this manner. Personal computers with internal storage capacities equal to 200 double-spaced typewritten pages are now common, and larger computers have

---

[74] See United States v. Offices Known as 50 State Distrib., supra note 50.
[75] Cf. Harris v. United States, 331 U.S. 145 (1947). For a thorough discussion, see 2 W. LaFave, Search and Seizure 160-163 (1978).
[76] See 2 W. LaFave, Search and Seizure 161 (1978).
[77] See Coolidge v. New Hampshire, 403 U.S. 443 (1971). For a thorough discussion, see 2 W. LaFave, Search and Seizure 163-184 (1978).
[78] Supra note 74.
[79] Id.
[80] Id.
[81] See generally 16 Am Jur. Proof of Facts 285-291 (1965).

much greater internal memory capacity. Information stored externally, especially if a magnetic storage medium is used, is likewise subject to rapid destruction. A device known as a *degausser* can instantly erase millions of data characters from a tape or disc.[82]

A pre-entry announcement is not required when officers know facts that cause them to reasonably believe that the making of an announcement will result in the destruction of evidence.[83] The ease and rapidity of destruction of the evidence sought is a factor courts will consider in determining whether a "no-knock" entry was reasonable.[84] Consequently, when officers know prior to execution of a warrant that information sought has been stored by computer and that persons with a motive to destroy the information are likely present at the place to be searched, an unannounced entry is likely reasonable.[85]

The announcement requirement is less stringently applied when warrants are executed against business premises.[86] Since computers are often located at businesses, this fact should also be considered in determining whether a pre-entry announcement is required.

Another alternative to the announced entry may exist when searching for processed data. When computerized information is the target of the search, technology may allow the execution of the search without any physical entry. If the computer is one where access is available to persons with remote terminals via telephone lines, it is possible that the information sought may be obtained by an expert who "breaks in" the system remotely, using his own terminal and telephone.[87] Also, the electronic operations of some computer systems may be observed from as far away as one-half mile if the proper equipment is used.[88] Presumably, where no physical entry takes place, no announcement is required. Such searches do, however, fall within the application of the Fourth Amendment and its attendant requirements,[89] and in most cases, a search warrant will be required for performing such a search.[90] Additionally, some sort of notice to the operator of the computer that a search has been performed is likely required.[91]

[82] D. Parker, *Fighting Computer Crime*, p. 42 (Charles Scribner's Sons, 1983).
[83] Supra note 74.
[84] Id.
[85] Id.
[86] See United States v. Francis, 646 F.2d 251, 258 (6th Cir. 1981), cert. denied, 70 L.Ed.2d 616 (1981).
[87] For a discussion of the ease with which an expert can gain access to a supposedly secure system, see T. Whiteside, Computer Capers, pp. 117-121 (1978).
[88] T. Schabeck, Computer Crime Investigation Manual, section 9.2.9 (Assets Protection, 1980).
[89] See Katz v. United States, 389 U.S. 347 (1967).
[90] Id.
[91] See Berger v. New York, 388 U.S. 41 (1967).

Controlling the Premises

The U.S. Supreme Court has noted the utility of officers who are executing a search warrant exercising "unquestioned command of the situation."[92] Consequently, officers executing a search warrant have the power to control access to the premises being searched and to control the movements of persons present to facilitate the search and to prevent the removal or destruction of evidence. Due to the previously noted ease of destruction of computerized information and the size and complexity of some computer facilities, the need likely will exist to quickly take control of a computer facility being searched. Actions taken to control the premises and prevent the destruction of evidence will be evaluated based upon the reasonableness of the actions under the circumstances.

An example of this analysis is found in *United States v. Offices Known as 50 State Distnb.*,[93] where a search warrant was executed on a building housing a large "boiler room" sales operation that was engaged in fraud and misrepresentation in selling its promotional merchandise. About 50 local and federal officers entered the premises to perform the search. At least 300 employees were present. The warrant authorized the seizure of almost all business records present. Upon entry, the officers required all persons present to remain at desks or in their assigned work areas. No one was permitted to go to the restroom without an escort. The court, in upholding the validity of the execution of the warrant, noted, "The breadth of the warrant rendered the execution of the warrant a most difficult task at best. Some control over the 300 employees was necessary for an orderly search."[94]

Searching within the Scope of the Warrant

The requirement of a particular description of the items to be seized limits the allowable scope of a search in two ways. First, it restricts the places where an officer may look. An officer may look only in places where the item sought might reasonably be concealed.[95] Second, it restricts the time of execution. An officer may only search under the authority of the warrant until all named items have been located or seized or until all possible places of concealment have been explored.[96] Failure to comply with either of these restrictions can result in an illegal, general search that violates the Fourth Amendment .

Investigators executing a search warrant must use care to insure that the search is restricted to places where the items to be seized may be concealed. This can be

---

[92] Michigan v. Summers, 452 U.S. 692, 703 (1981), citing 2 W. LaFave, Search and Seizure 150-151 (1978).
[93] See United States v. Offices Known as 50 State Distrib., supra note 50.
[94] Id. at 1376.
[95] Supra note 76.
[96] Id.

quite difficult where records are sought and a great number of files are present. Regardless of the difficulty, reasonable steps must be taken to ensure that the search is no broader than authorized by the warrant.

A sensible first step is to make sure that all searching officers are aware of what items are listed in the warrant. In upholding the execution of the warrant in In Re Search Warrant dated July 4, 1977 Etc., the court noted the procedure followed in that case, saying, "In preparation for the search the agents attended several meetings to discuss and familiarize themselves with the areas and documents described in the search warrant and accompanying affidavit. They were instructed to confine themselves to these areas and documents in their search. During the search each agent carried with him a copy of the search warrant and its 'Description of Property, and could contact one of three persons on the scene who carried the supporting affidavit."[97] In upholding a warrant execution in *United States v. Slocum*,[98] the court also noted a preexecution meeting.[99] Familiarizing the search team with the language of the warrant will increase the likelihood that a search will be performed in a manner a court will deem reasonable.

Once on the scene, the officers should continue to use care to restrict the search to the items listed in the warrant. A problem that frequently arises is that of sorting the items subject to seizure from those that are innocently possessed. This problem is especially common in cases where business records are the target of the search. In all cases, officers must restrict their search to places where the items named in the warrant are likely to be found and to limit the examination of innocent items to an extent no greater than that necessary to determine whether the item being examined is one of the items named in the warrant.[100] Again, the yardstick is reasonableness.

In many cases, a simple sorting process will be upheld as reasonable.[101] In *United States v. Slocum,* a warrant authorizing the seizure of business records related to illegal importation of tropical birds was executed. The U.S. Court of Appeals for the eleventh Circuit described the execution process as follows: The offices were a shambles and there was no apparent filing system; it was therefore concluded that it would be necessary to view each document to determine if it fell within the warrant. When an agent discovered a document that he or she believed covered by the warrant, the document was taken to one of four supervising agents who made the ultimate decision whether to seize the document."[102] The court

---

[97] Supra note 68, at 123.
[98] 708 F.2d 587 (11th Cir. 1983).
[99] Id. at 601.
[100] See generally 2 W. LaFave, Search and Seizure 173-178 (1978).
[101] See, e.g., In Re Search Warrant Dated July 4, 1977, Etc., supra note 68. See also United States v. Tamura, 694 F.2d 591 (9th Cir. 1982).
[102] 708 F.2d 587, 602 (11th Cir. 1983).

approved use of "a common sense standard"[103] in evaluating the reasonableness of the search method and noted that where a warrant authorizes the seizure of documents, "some perusal, generally fairly brief, was necessary in order for police to perceive the relevance of the documents to the crime."[104] The court cautioned, however, that "the perusal must cease at the point of which the warrant's inapplicability to each document is clear."[105]

In Re Search Warrant Dated July 4, 1977, Etc. also concerned the execution of a search warrant requiring the examination of a multitude of documents. Fifteen agents conducted a search that lasted 9 1/2 hours, during which they examined the contents of 93 file drawers, 14 desks, 3 bookshelves, and numerous boxes and piles of loose documents. The court described a systematic search where each document encountered was evaluated by search personnel to determine whether it fell within the description of items to be seized contained in the warrant. The U.S. Circuit Court of Appeals for the District of Columbia Circuit, in upholding the reasonableness of the search, noted that nothing in the record indicated a "general rummaging operation"[106] had taken place and that the agents involved in the search had been "...extensively briefed, instructed and supervised."[107]

Search for documents stored in electronic form by a computer will require use of the computer to view documents on a display screen or to print them by means of a printer. A sorting process similar to that employed in a search for "ink on paper" documents would seem reasonable under the circumstances. Such a sorting process was employed in *United States v. Harvey*.[108] There, an agent seeking, pursuant to a search warrant, an electronic device that produced telephone switching tones discovered some cassette audio tapes. He played about 12 of the tapes on a cassette player on the scene and determined that 2 contained recorded telephone switching tones. These tapes were seized. The U.S. Court of Appeals for the Eighth Circuit held these tapes were "properly seized as within the limitations of the warrant."[109] Use of computer equipment to examine computerized records should likewise be reasonable, since the records are otherwise incomprehensible to the searchers. Obviously, certain operational knowledge regarding the computer equipment will be required to perform this type of

---

[103] Id. at 604.
[104] Id.
[105] Id.
[106] Supra note 68, at 124.
[107] Id.
[108] United States v. Harvey, 540 F.2d 1345 (8th Cir. 1976).
[109] Id. at 1354.

search. Under these circumstances, expert assistance during the search may be essential.[110]

The sorting process, performed at the scene of the search, serves to prevent the seizure, and thus the denial of access and use by the owner, of innocent records. The mere fact that the sorting process is time consuming will not make a whole-sale seizure of records reasonable. Obviously, where a valid warrant authorizes the seizure of all business records, no sorting is required other than the elimination of nonbusiness records.[111] Otherwise, the reasonableness standard may require an arduous sorting process. Thus, where agents seized 11 cardboard boxes of computer printouts that were bound in 2000-page volumes, 34 file drawers of vouchers bound in 2000-page volumes, and 17 drawers of cancelled checks and hauled these records to another location where they sifted through them to extract the relevant documents (that were described in the search warrant) as a consequence of their determination that sorting at the site of the search would take a very long time, the seizure was held to be an unreasonable one.[112] Sorting at the scene of the search is generally required.

Certain characteristics of computerized record keeping may result in different treatment for computerized records.[113] First, the storage capacity of some computerized systems is such that review of all documents stored in the system could take a very long time. Second, unlike with paper files, the number of investigators who may assist in the search is limited by the number of computer terminals available for document display. Finally, where the records are stored magnetically, they may be quickly duplicated in their computerized form. Based on these considerations, it may be reasonable in some cases to duplicate the records quickly, leave copies for the use of the owner of the records, and seize the original records for later examination. The likely legal concern in this situation is that the innocent documents included in the records would be available for unrestrained viewing by investigators resulting in a postponed "general search." A potential control for this problem would be continuing judicial supervision of the sorting process.[114]

---

[110] An expert accompanied officers executing the search warrant in Ottensmeyer v. Chesapeake & Potomac Telephone Co., 756 F.2d 986 (4th Cir. 1985). Another case considering the role of an expert accompanying officers executing a search warrant is Forro Precision, Inc. v. International Business Machines Corp., 673 F.2d 1045 (9th Cir. 1982).

[111] See United States v. Brien, supra note 64.

[112] United States v. Tamura, supra note 102.

[113] See e.g., United States v. Tamura, supra note 102.

[114] Id. See also DeMassa v. Nunez, 747 F.2d 1283 (9th Cir. 1984) (special master appointed to supervise sorting of documents during search of attorney's office).

Finally, when all items named in a warrant have been located and seized, the warrant provides no authority to continue the search.[115] Absent other legal justification, the search must terminate .

Avoiding Damage During a Search

A further requirement for the reasonable execution of a warrant is that the officers take care to avoid unnecessary damage to the property being searched and seized. Since computers are complex and fragile,[116] considerable care must be exercised when one is seized. Expert assistance may be necessary to ensure a damage-free seizure.

The "Plain View" Doctrine

As previously noted, an officer executing a search warrant will frequently need to sort through information to determine what portion of it may be seized pursuant to the warrant. If, during the course of the process, the allowed limited perusal of information is sufficient to cause the officer to conclude that the information is probable evidence of a crime, he is not required to leave the document behind, even though it is not described in the warrant. He may seize it under the "plain view" exception to the warrant requirement provided that he is lawfully present (searching reasonably within the scope of the warrant), it is readily apparent that the document is evidence, and the discovery of the document is inadvertent (that is, the officer did not possess probable cause to search for the document prior to beginning the search he is presently engaged in).[117]

Conclusion

Since judicial guidance is still limited in the area, investigators seeking and executing search warrants authorizing the seizure of computers and computerized information are on untested ground. However, the legal standard by which such searches and seizures will be measured is the same as is applied to searches less concerned with modern technology. Careful adherence to established Fourth Amendment principles, coupled with the use of expert assistance when needed, will enhance the likelihood of obtaining computerized evidence that is judicially admissible.

---

[115] In addition to suppression of evidence, civil liability may result when a search continues after all items named in warrant have been seized. See Creamer v. Porter, 754 F.2d 1311 (5th Cir. 1985).
[116] For a discussion of the ways a computer may be physically damaged, see Fighting Computer Crime, supra note 82, pp. 41-42.
[117] Supra note 78.

C

The Microcomputer as Evidence

Introduction

Just as the business world increasingly relies on computers to perform day-to-day operations, the use of computers as criminal instruments or as devices to store data associated with criminal enterprises is rising. We were reminded of the potential for loss and the frailty of our computer systems when Robert T. Morris placed a program called a *worm** in an international network of computers and ground the entire system to a halt within hours (Burgess 1990; Markoff 1990). This act of computer fraud and abuse is well documented in both the law enforcement and legal communities. However, for every Robert Morris worm we face, the law enforcement community faces hundreds, perhaps thousands, of cases in which a computer is used incidentally in the crime. In these cases, records vital to the investigation or prosecution of a case are stored on the internal, or hard disk, drive of a computer.

If present trends continue, the use of computers in criminal activities will continue to rise. Likewise, the problems associated with them will continue to trouble investigators, prosecutors, and the computer specialist assigned to examine computer-related evidence. Criminals are using computers to store records regarding drug deals, money laundering, embezzlement, mail fraud, telemarketing fraud, prostitution, gambling matters, extortion, and a myriad of other criminal activities. In

---

* The Morris worm was a program which entered computers on the Internet network and replicated itself. This worm quickly overloaded the systems, making them slow down and ultimately crash. Morris was prosecuted under 18 U.S.C. Section 1030.

This appendix was originally published as an article entitled, "Computer Analysis and Response Team (CART): The Microcomputer as Evidence" by Michael G. Noblett of the Laboratory Division, Federal Bureau of Investigation, in the *FBI Crime Laboratory Digest*, Volume 19, No. 1, January 1992.

addition to simply storing records, they manipulate data, infiltrate the computers of financial institutions, illegally use telephone lines charged to unsuspecting businesses, and perform a host of other imaginative scams.

A growing segment of our population considers computers and the data stored within as nothing more than electronic paper. Most people feel very comfortable keeping their records (whether legal or illegal) in this electronic format. In order to reasonably address the legitimate law enforcement need for access to these devices and the information they contain, a structured approach to examining computer evidence is needed. The examination of computer evidence can furnish investigative and intelligence information to the law enforcement community and, at the same time, preserve the information for subsequent admission in the courts.

The following statistics are staggering and suggest that the law enforcement community must act quickly and decisively to meet the challenge presented by the computer:

- Over 4.7 million personal computers were sold in the United States in 1988, as compared with 386,500 in 1980 (Stites 1990).

- There are at least 400 connected networks nationally and internationally. One network alone, Internet, estimates that there could be more than 1 million users (Quarterman 1990).

- $500 million is lost annually through illegal use of telephone access codes (Marsa and Ray 1990).

- $1 trillion is moved electronically each week (Marsa and Ray 1990).

- Only 11 percent of computer crimes are reported (Stites 1990).

In the past few years, the FBI laboratory has seen a phenomenal increase in the submission of computer evidence. Consequently, the FBI laboratory established a Computer Analysis and Response Team (CART) at FBI headquarters in Washington, DC. This team is staffed by both sworn and nonsworn computer professionals with a wide range of experience and proficiency in the examination of computer-related evidence and a sensitivity to the particular needs of the law enforcement community. The CART has a full range of hardware available, as well as unique utility software for forensic examinations of this kind.

The CART's computer examination service is available for any law enforcement agency that is authorized to submit evidence to the FBI for forensic examination. Although there is no typical computer case, most fall into the category of white-collar crime, and the majority of the requests received by the FBI laboratory are for printouts of the information stored electronically in suspected computers. During the course of these examination, there are several recurring problems:

1. The preliminary examination is done locally.

When a computer used in criminal activities is seized, immediate action should be taken to protect the data stored on the computer's hard disk and associated floppy diskettes. The investigator often attempts to generate investigative and intelligence information on site. This approach is reasonable and should be encouraged. However, it is imperative that the computer be protected from the investigator's inadvertently altering the computer's hard disk or floppy diskette files. For instance, many computer systems update files to the current date each time they are retrieved. In order to preserve the evidence in its original condition, appropriate steps must be taken to insure that no dates are changed and no data are added to or deleted from the computer's hard disk or floppy diskettes. Specialized and commercially available software that protects the data on the computer hard disk and floppy diskettes can be purchased, and it should always be used before any examination.

The investigator should also consider that any individual that conducts any type of examination on the evidence may be called upon to testify about the procedures used and the accuracy of the results. Therefore, a documented policy and protocol should be established. This policy does not have to be extensive or detailed, but must be readily available to whomever is examining the evidence.

2. Supporting software is not seized with the computer.

When a computer is seized, all supporting software and documentation should be confiscated, if it is within the scope of the investigation. This simple action can eliminate numerous problems that may arise during the examination of the computer. It is logical but not necessarily correct to assume that the software that runs on the seized computer is identical to the software used in the investigator's office. This logic is reinforced if the software has the same name, such as Word-Perfect, Lotus, and so on. As commercial software is developed and marketed, new features are added and modifications are made to correct previously identified problems. The vendor then sells these new upgraded versions of the software; thus, the data seized may not be compatible with the particular version of the identical software in the investigator's office. It is advisable to confiscate all software, documentation, handwritten notes, such as instructions or passwords, and any other similar items found near the computer.

3. The entire computer system is not seized.

Many of the devices connected to a seized computer are probably standard pieces of equipment that can be found in any computer facility. However, it only takes one unique, nonstandard, or outdated component to render the entire system inoperable in a different office setting. For this reason, it is judicious to seize all the equipment connected to the computer. If it turns out that some of the equipment is not needed for the examination, it can be returned.

The FBI laboratory does not recommend that the hard disk drive located inside a computer be removed and submitted for examination. While this option would appear to satisfy the needs of a computer specialist in a well-equipped laboratory, the manner in which the rest of the computer is set up internally is often crucial to retrieving, displaying, and printing the data stored on the hard drive.

Because a decision such as whether or not to seize an entire computer system is based on technical considerations, it may be appropriate to employ an expert as a consultant in the execution of these types of search warrants. This is especially true if the entire computer system is not seized. The concerns regarding incompatibilities of computer systems should be stated in the supporting affidavit as justification if the entire computer system is to be confiscated.

4. Equipment is not properly packaged for shipment.

If a computer is shipped to the FBI laboratory or any other facility for examination, it must be packaged properly. A major reason the FBI laboratory is sometimes unable to conduct a requested examination quickly and efficiently is because a confiscated computer is damaged in shipment and must be repaired. Likewise, certain precautions must be exercised to ship computer floppy diskettes, magnetic tape, and other computer data recording devices. Due to the potential hazard of static electric discharge, these items should not be shipped in plastic evidence envelopes. The evidence should be appropriately labeled to avoid exposure to strong magnetic fields, such as those generated near X-ray machines.

Procedures for Submission and Examination of Computer Evidence

A set of guidelines [see the section in Chapter 11 called "Guidelines for Preserving and Submitting Computer Evidence"] has been prepared by the FBI laboratory that addresses the preservation and submission of computers and related evidence. Although these guidelines are not extensive, they can be used as a basic foundation to insure that evidence is preserved in its original condition for shipment to the FBI laboratory.

The list of computer equipment and materials represents typical items received by the FBI laboratory. New storage and peripheral devices are being marketed daily, and no listing could ever be both current and complete. As with all evidence submissions, common sense coupled with the investigator's knowledge and background will usually be enough to insure that the computer specialist is presented with materials suitable for examination.

After the evidence is preserved and submitted to the investigator's laboratory, the examination can proceed. At the FBI laboratory, the purpose of the examination is to make information contained in the storage media available to the investigator and prosecutor.

All types of evidence, including computer-related evidence, must be maintained so as to preserve the integrity of the evidence while it is in custody. In addition, documentation must be prepared which describes the chain of custody. It has been the experience of many laboratories that computer evidence is assigned for examination to computer specialists who work outside the scope of what is normally considered a forensic environment. These computer specialists are subject matter experts but don't necessarily have a knowledge of the special requirements and considerations for handling evidence. Consequently, it is imperative that each of the individuals assigned cases of this type is aware of these requirements and is provided appropriate training.

[The "Guidelines for Examining Computer Evidence" in Chapter 11 of this book] outline the basic procedures for the examination of computer evidence.

Conclusion

Clearly, the steadily increasing use of computers in society will soon impact every law enforcement investigative program. It is essential that law enforcement agencies be sufficiently educated and have the necessary procedures and guidelines in place to adequately manage the examination of computer-related evidence and records.

In addition to its traditional forensic examination services, the FBI laboratory's CART can provide on site field assistance to both FBI field offices and local police departments. Approval for this on site support is granted on a case-by-case basis, depending on the resources available and the needs of the requesting agency. Specific information regarding this service is available from the author.

References

Burgess, J. (1990). No jail time imposed in hacker case. Creator of "Virus" gets probation, fine, *Washington Post*, May 5, section 1, page A1.

Markoff, J. (1990). Computer intruder is put on probation and fined $10,000, *New York Times,* May 5, section 1, page 1, column 1.

Marsa, L., and Ray, D. (1990). Crime bytes back, *Omni*, August, 12:11:34–46+.

Quarterman, J.S. (1990). *The Matrix: Computer Networks and Conferencing Systems Worldwide*. Maynard, MA: Digital Press.

Stites, C.M. (1990). PCs—Personal computers or partners in crime? *Law and Order*, September, 39:9:161–165.

D

A Sample Search Warrant

SUPERIOR COURT

COUNTY JUDICIAL DISTRICT

AFFIDAVIT IN SUPPORT OF SEARCH WARRANT

JOHN C. SMITH, Sr. Criminal Investigator, County District Attorney's Office being sworn, says that on the basis of the information contained within this Affidavit and any attachments thereto, he has probable cause to believe and does believe that the property described below is lawfully seizable pursuant to Penal Code Section 1524, as indicated below, in that it:

( ) was stolen or embezzled;

(X) was used as the means of committing a felony;

( ) is possessed by a person with the intent to use same as a means of committing a public offense, or in the possession of another to whom he/she may have delivered same for the purpose of concealing or preventing its discovery;

(X) constitutes evidence tending to show that a felony has been committed or that a particular person has committed a felony; and that he has probable cause to believe and does believe that the described property is now located at, and will be found at, the location(s) set forth below and thus requests a warrant to search THE FOLLOWING FOUR (4) LOCATION(S):

Note: This is an actual search warrant used in an investigation of a computer crime at a university; only certain identifying information has been changed. Thanks to John Smith for the use of this material.

LOCATION A:

1. The three (3) electronic mail accounts, including the information from these accounts on the system backup tapes, belonging to Joe Suspect:

   #1 suspect@rome.univ.ede (Unix System);

   #2 suspect@univvm1.univuniv.edu (IBM system); and

   #3 guard@univvm1.univ.edu (IBM system).

   These accounts are on computers maintained and housed in the Computer Systems and Communications Department, University, ("CSC") Department, California, Any City University.

AND

2. The desk and work space of Joe Suspect at the Computer Information Center, Computer Systems and Computing Department,

FOR THE FOLLOWING PROPERTY:

1. Any and all documents and records, whether on paper or stored on magnetic media (including information stored within a computer) that contain any of the network electronic mail addresses, hertz@Rome.Univ.Edu, jeanc@college-ca.edu (Jean Clinton), or carol@college-ca.edu.

2. Any and all documents and records, whether on paper or stored on magnetic media which contain the code or computer instructions that are used for the automatic transfer of information or email from one account to another and directing the transfer of email to or from supect2nd@rome, hertz@rome, jeanc@college-ca, or carol@college-ca.

3. Any and all programs or computer instructions that would be used for the cracking, matching, or discovering encrypted passwords for computer accounts.

4. Any and all documents and records, whether on paper or stored on magnetic media which contain the code or computer instructions that create or operate a computer program commonly known as a "TROJAN HORSE", a shell or program that purports to have a valid purpose, but contains hidden in its code instructions that start another job such as automatically capturing a user's log-on identification and password and sends it to another location.

LOCATION B:

SUSPECT'S Apartment B, Drive, in the City of _____. This residence is a duplex type residence, that is painted gray and has a detached open carport. There are two street address number plaques attached to the front of the house. The plaque with ###B is nearest the corner of the west side, where there is a door that appears to be the front door for Apartment B. The premises to be searched also include any and all yards, outbuildings, storage areas, garages, carports, sheds, or mailboxes assigned to the described premises, including but not limited to those listed above.

LOCATION C:

The person of Joe Suspect and any personal effects such as but not limited to books, binders, backpacks, or briefcases where papers or computer disks may be carried.

LOCATION D:

A gray Ford bearing California license _____ registered to Joe Suspect, City of _____, wherever it may be located in the County.

STATEMENT OF PROBABLE CAUSE

Your affiant declares that the facts in support of issuance of his search warrant and court order are as follows:

Your affiant, John C. Smith, is a Senior Criminal Investigator (Peace Officer) employed by the County District Attorney's Office in County, California. Your affiant has been assigned to the High Technology Unit of that office since December 1989. He has been a California Peace Officer since June 1965. He is a member and past President of the High Technology Crime Prevention Association (HTCIA), and a member of the Santa Clara Valley Industrial Security Managers Association. He has been a Macintosh computer user since about 1986 and an IBM PC user since 1990 and owns both types of computers. He is a regular user of the Internet and has had classes on the Unix/Workstation operating environment. He has over 320 hours of training in the High Technology field. He has been involved in at least twenty (20) prior intrusion type cases and given several talks to computer professionals on investigating intrusions. He has conversed and worked with experts in federal law enforcement who have specialized in these cases, and who have considerable experience in investigating and interacting with persons who have illegally accessed computers.

Your affiant is currently investigating violations of California Penal Code Section 502 (Unlawful Access to Computer Systems).

Your affiant knows from training and experience that individuals who illegally access computers without authorization often do so from their own computer systems and maintain cracking or password matching programs which may include dictionary or word lists.

Your affiant knows that persons who illegally access computer services by fraudulent means maintain notes and ledgers which document the accesses that are valid, passwords which have been used or tried, and their written notes on how to bypass systems security measures installed. They also make notes of what systems are accessed, what files were downloaded or uploaded and who else they have been in contact with regarding the access codes being used.

Your affiant knows from training and experience that persons who have passwords on their computer system usually maintain a record of that password on a piece of paper, card, book, etc. so that it may be retrieved in case the persons fail to recall a password. Your affiant knows the above information may be in the form of hard copy printouts, paper notes, notes in a ledger, or files maintained on a computer system itself in the form of electronic media.

Your affiant knows from training and experience that a computer system used to communicate with other systems via modem and the telephone lines will be attached to a modem and a phone line that is installed in the residence.

On May 10, 1994, your affiant was contacted by Detective _____, University Police Department, and provided with police reports for case number 94- alleging a violation of California Penal Code Section 502, Computer Crime. Your affiant interviewed Dept Head, Associate Vice President, in charge of the Computer Systems and Computing (CSC) Department at AnyCity State University (Univ); Bill Sysop, Staff Systems Software Specialist, CSC; and Timothy J. Sysadmin, Network Systems Programmer, CSC. To the best of your affiant's knowledge, these three individuals are reliable and trustworthy citizens without involvement in criminal activity.

The following chronology of events prepared by your affiant after reading the police reports and interviewing the three individuals named above, was prepared for convenient review:

CHRONOLOGY OF EVENTS:

3-21-94 to 4-1-94 - Joe Suspect and Jason Student workers are suspended from their jobs at the Computer Information Center (CIC), CSC, Univ and are told not to use their network accounts for two weeks for verbally fighting and arguing via their electronic mail accounts on Univ's system and on America Online, a commercial system.

3-21-94 - A message is sent from "Patricia Hertz" to ten people, "From: Suspect!", stating the suspension and to send any email to hertz@.univ.edu.

4-12-94 - The email message to "Hello John", attached as Exhibit #1, accusing systems operators Sam Sysadmin and another employee of maintaining unauthorized files on the university system, was sent to the mailing list on another system maintained by Univ.

4-14-94 - Univ President Ferris receives an email message from jeanc@college-ca.edu regarding Univ computer administrators holding unauthorized files on the Univ system, attached as Exhibit #2.

4-15-94 - Dept Head assigns Bill Sysop to investigate this matter.

4-15-94 - Bill Sysop learns that there is no issued account to "Patricia Hertz", but he knows a Professor Hertz and contacts him. Professor Hertz states he was issued the account but does not use it.

- Bill Sysop checks logs on the IBM computer network and finds that (a) the message, Exhibit #2, sent to Univ President Ferris was received from jeanc@college-ca.edu on 4/14/94, at 17:49:14 hrs and that (b) suspect@univvm1.univ.edu sent a message to jeanc@college-ca.edu at 4/14/94 17:39:02 hrs, Exhibit #9.

4-27-94 - Univ Police report 94-#### was taken by Officer Laws. The suspect named was Joe Suspect.

- Sysadmin examines data in the broken "hertz account" obtained from the backup tapes of April 11, 1994, and observes a ".forward" file used by the Unix mail system to forward mail to another computer. The forwarding address listed was supect2nd@.univ.edu, Exhibit #11.

5-4-94 Front page article appears in Univ newspaper regarding unauthorized files on the Univ computer system.

*****

On 5-11-94 your affiant began his investigation by talking with Dept Head at his office at Univ. Dept Head related the following information:

In March 1994, Suspect and another student, Jason Student, were verbally fighting and arguing. This disagreement spilled into electronic mail. American OnLine sent a message to Supervisor and to Bill in the Computing Information Center, the supervisor of Suspect and Student, asking if something could be done to stop the bickering. Suspect and Student were then suspended from their jobs for two weeks by the Director of Information Services (a division of the CSC) after he investigated and concluded that they had behaved inappropriately. Supervisor also told Suspect and Student not to use their computer network accounts during their suspension.

The suspension was from March 21, 1994 to April 1, 1994. Sometime during this two weeks, Dept Head suspects that Joe Suspect hacked into the "hertz account". The "hertz account" belongs to Univ Professor Hertz who was assigned the account 2 yrs ago and has never used it. The Identifier that is printed when electronic mail is sent from the hertz account was changed from Professor to Patricia.

On 5-11-94 and 5-12-94, your affiant interviewed Bill Sysop, Staff Systems Software Specialist, Technical Services, Computer System and Computing Department, Univ, at the CSC. Sysop provided affiant with the following information:

The Computer Systems and Computing Department (CSC) is assigned the task of providing general academic and computing services and Administrative services to the University. Administrative services include student scheduling, records, grades, and other student information as well as purchasing and assorted administrative functions. The campus has an IP (Internet Protocol) type network that has both Unix and IBM computers attached to it. CSC has an Internet connection.

Sysop was assigned to investigate this matter by Dept Head after Ferris, the President of Univ, received an email message from a Jean Clinton dated 14 Apr 94, 17:49:13 PDT, stating in relevant part, "your university computer administrators are using the system as a holding area for unauthorized files." A copy of the messages is attached as Exhibit #2.

Sysop began his investigation by trying to find "Patricia Hertz". He asked the CIC (Computer Information Center) and learned there was no record of "Patricia Hertz". Sysop had worked with Professor Hertz, Univ, on prior occasions. Thinking it might be Patrick rather than Professor, Sysop phoned Professor Hertz, on April 15, 1994. Professor Hertz told Sysop that he did have a Unix account but that he did not use it. Professor Hertz told Sysop that he recalled being told that he needed a UNIX account to receive email and so about 2 years ago he signed up with Univ and was given a Unix account that was named hertz. He did not use the Unix account because he found he could use email facilities directly through the Unix Workstation he has on his desk.

On Friday April 15, 1994, Bill Sysop examined the SMTP (Mail Transfer) log for April 14, 1994, on the Univ IBM computer system, attached as Exhibit #9. He did this because Ferris's email account is on the IBM system. Sysop checked the log for the time that Ferris had received Exhibit #2 from Jean Clinton. Sysop then looked through the log and found that on 4/14/94, 17:39:02 hours, ten minutes before Exhibit #2 was sent, Suspect had been connected to jeanc@college-ca.edu. Your affiant has obtained a list of log-ins to the jeanc@college-ca account and verified this information. One of the log-ins was from 17:55 to 18:06 hours. The message to President Ferris from jeanc@college-ca was received at Univ at 18:05 hours.

Sysop knows Joe Suspect to be a paid Student Assistant at CIC, Computing Information Center, a division of CSC. CIC is assigned the task of providing computer support to the academic computing community at Univ and providing assistance to administrative computer users. Suspects' supervisor is _____ who reports to _____, Director of CIC. Sysop believes Suspect has worked there for about 2 years.

On May 12, 1994, your affiant interviewed Bill J. Sysadmin, Network Systems Programmer, CSC, at the computer center. Sysadmin maintains the Unix network. Sysadmin related the following information to your affiant:

The hertz account resides on a computer server called _____ which is the primary Unix server at Univ. Sysadmin made the printout labeled "Apr 17 23:27 1994 hertz.last Page 1.", attached as Exhibit #10. This printout, Exhibit #10, is a list of connections to the hertz account and shows that someone was connecting to the hertz account from a terminal server that houses the public modem pool. The entry, "csc-ts1.Univ.EDU", on the log indicates that the connection to hertz was most likely made through a dial-in telephone modem hooked to the terminal server.

The original message "Hello John" was sent to 1.BITNET, which distributed the message to a number of systems users. This message is attached as Exhibit #1. At that time there were 30 faculty members and students from the Univ campus on the mailing list to receive messages sent to the UnivSER account on UnivSER on the IBM system. This account serves as a general computer information source for asking questions and disseminating information regarding the computer system.

After seeing the message to President Ferris (Exhibit #2), Sysadmin opined that the hertz account had been broken into. His opinion was based on a number of factors. He recognized that the hertz account had a low user id number (meaning that it was an older account) and the wording of the message in Exhibit #1 caused him to infer the sender was a new user; also, the sender described him or herself as a student. Finally, faculty and staff are in one file system and students in another. The hertz account was a faculty account.

Sysadmin made a "last" printout that shows where the user logged in from and the date & time. A "last log" shows the account where the connection was made, the name of the computer or device where the connection came from, the date, the time, and the duration of the connection. On this "last log" printout, Exhibit #10, the log shows log-ins from College and a log-in from the Univ CIC, which is in the form of a network numerical address, IP address ###.##.##.##. This number shows up on the log since the computer at that location has not been given a name.

Sysadmin went to the backup tapes from April 11, 1994, for the server on the Unix system and recovered the home directory from the hertz account onto his (Sysadmin's) workstation. Sysadmin printed the stored mail messages recovered from the backup tape in the hertz account and gave your affiant the 56 pages that he printed. What appears to be the first message from the hertz account is attached as Exhibit #3. That message reads as follows:

> Date: Mon, 21 Mar 1994 15:11:36
> From: Patricia Hertz <hertz@.Univ.EDU>
> Subject: From Suspect!
> To: people <bart@>, (list of his friend's email addresses)
>
> Hello everybody,
>
> I'm sure you're wondering why I'm not using my account to mail this to all of you, well the reason is I got suspended for two weeks from work. Actually it was me and Jason Student that got suspended. It's a very long story, but suffice to say I got screwed royally on this one and as such, it is only right that I screw back.
>
> Student is toast.
>
> I'll send you all the gory details later.
>
> -Suspect

Another message that Sysadmin found in the hertz account deals with Trojan Horses, attached as Exhibit #4. This message is addressed as follows:

> Date: Tue, 22 Mar 1994 15:29:44 PST
> From: fly <cartert@.com>
> To: hertz@.univ.edu
> Subject: The Trojan Horse (For Suspect)

In this message, a "Trojan Horse Program" is discussed. fly states, "Here's what the code *might*(sic) look like", and describes what the code would be. Also in this message is a description of a Trojan Horse, which is a fake shell. That paragraph is as follows:

> When a user attempts to login on the Trojan Horse their login name and password are mailed to a specific user (defined in the code). The process then terminates and the user is left with the *REAL* login prompt. You now have a password and login for a specific user, in other words you have full access to their account.

How this happens is defined here:

When Sysadmin looked at the data in the broken hertz account, which he obtained from the backup tapes of April 11, 1994, he observed a ".forward" file used by the Unix mail system to forward mail to another computer. The forwarding address listed was supect2nd@.univ.edu. The file listing shows that the .forward file was last modified on April 6. On May 19, 1994, Sysadmin printed a copy of the .forward file from the hertz April 11 backup and gave it to your affiant. As indicated, this printout is attached as Exhibit #11.

Sysadmin told your affiant that he called the network system administrator at College-ca, College Sysadmin, and advised College Sysadmin that someone seemed to have broken into (the name of the primary Unix server for the .univ.edu system) from College's Network. Subsequently, College Sysadmin told Sysadmin that the "jeanc" and "carol" accounts had been broken into. College Sysadmin sent Sysadmin a list of log-ins to the computer "stargaze" at College-ca where the jeanc and carol accounts are located, (Exhibit #6). Roy College Sysadmin in his message of April 26, 1994 (Exhibit #6) states:

> The owner of the carol, account found that someone has tampered with her account. The user hertz@.univ.edu re-routed her e-mail using a .forward file. This has gone on about 2 weeks. She is understandably very upset and has lost some very important messages.

On May 15, 1994, your affiant spoke on the telephone with College's 2nd Sysop, who also serves as a systems administrator with College Sysadmin. Dr. College's 2nd Sysop said he was familiar with the situation with Univ. Dr. College's 2nd Sysop told affiant that Carol is a teacher at College. Mrs. Carol was using her child's name as a password; the password thus would have been on a standard word list or dictionary used by a cracker or password matching program.

Sysadmin made printouts from the "last" log for both accounts "hertz" and "suspect" from the Unix workstation named "homerun", which uses as a server. The printout for the supcct2nd account is attached as Exhibit #7 and the printout for hertz account is attached as Exhibit #8. Sysadmin found log entries on March 17 between 16:34 hours and 18:15 hours which appear to indicate that someone logged out of the supect2nd account and immediately into the hertz account. The following are entries of log-in and log-out time from the "last" logs if the two accounts:

supect2nd Mar 17 16:43 - 16:40

hertz Mar 17 16:40 - 16:52

supect2nd Mar 17 16:52 - 18:07

supect2nd Mar 17 18:07 - 18:09

hertz Mar 17 18:09 - 18:15

On May 19, 1994, your affiant talked with Bill Sysop and Sam Sysadmin at their office. They both informed affiant that it would be highly unusual for Joe Suspect to have his supect2nd account broken into without Suspect being aware of it and for Suspect not to make a report. Suspect's "vigil" account was set up to subscribe to various mailing lists dealing specifically with network security. Suspect is supposed to review any material that is received and distribute any relevant material to CIC employees. Sysadmin has never received any complaints from Suspect about problems with the Suspect account being compromised. Sysop told affiant that when he interviewed Suspect, he asked Suspect if he was having any problems with his (Suspect) IBM accounts. Suspect said he was not having any problems with his accounts.

On April 19, 1994, Sysadmin said he copied the contents of the supect2nd account from the backup tapes into his (Sysadmin's) workstation. Sysadmin also said that he had not looked at or examined the contents of that account until the legality of such examination can be determined.

Your affiant seeks permission to bring Bill Sysop and Sam Sysadmin along on the search to the four locations to assist with identifying the computer programs described in this affidavit that are to be searched and seized, and to have them operate the Univ computer system to search for the items listed in the Search Warrant. Sysop and Sysadmin will be acting under the direct supervision and control of your affiant or another peace officer assisting your affiant in the service of this warrant. Your affiant is aware that such a procedure was approved in People v. Superior Court (Moore) (1980) 104 Cal. App. 3d 1001.

Residence Information:

Joe Suspect told Officer Laws of the AnyCity State University Police Department that his home address is ### E. Street, AnyCity, California. Dept Head checked Payroll records and found that Suspect's address is listed as ###. E. Street, Apartment 2, AnyCity, California. Dept Head has also seen a business card for a business maintained by Joe Suspect that listed the same address.

Your affiant checked the California Department of Motor Vehicle records for the driver's license information on Joe Suspect based on the date of birth, 05-11-66, and driver's license number, C1111111, on the police report and found that Joe Suspect has a valid California Drivers License that expires on his birthday in 1997. This record states that his residence address is _____.

California DMV records checked by affiant also show that Joe Suspect is the registered owner of a Ford, license number Affiant drove by the residence and saw a gray Ford, California license number _____, in the carport of _____.

Computers:

Your affiant requests permission to search and seize any computer systems and magnetic media found at the scene.

Your affiant knows from his training and experience that computer systems commonly consist of central processing units (CPUs), hard disks, hard disk drives, floppy disk drives, tape drives, display screens, keyboards, printers, modems (used to communicate with other computers), electronic cables, cassette tapes, floppy disks, and other forms of magnetic media containing computer information.

Your affiant knows from his training and experience that such computers and magnetic media are used to store information. Your affiant believes, based on the information related above, that computers and magnetic media located at the place to be searched contain telephone numbers, access codes, and the software necessary to access such computer codes.

Your affiant knows from his training and experience that computer users will commonly keep computer hardware and software in their homes, garages, cars, carports, outbuildings, storage areas, and sheds assigned to their premises.

Your affiant requests permission to seize computer systems and magnetic media found at the scene without first conducting a detailed examination of each and every hard and floppy disk to determine if such systems and media contain the items requested by this affidavit. Computer users frequently collect a great deal of software on disks or other magnetic media. Searching that media within a reasonable amount of time to determine which material is relevant to this investigation would be difficult and could risk destruction of the evidence.

Your affiant may also need to examine at another location any computer(s) found at the scene because most hard disks contain so much data that an on-site inspection is impractical. The examination required to determine whether the hard disk contains the items requested by this affidavit could take days or weeks. Furthermore, there may be too many tapes and or disks to allow a thorough search of such disks within a reasonable time.

Finally, the computer and magnetic media is the best evidence available. Magnetic media is easily erased or destroyed. Leaving magnetic media behind may result in the loss of that magnetic media as evidence. Your affiant believes that it is better to seize the original evidence than to rely solely on copies which have not been authenticated in the presence of counsel for persons who could face criminal charges based on material found pursuant to this warrant.

Your affiant also seeks to seize documentation associated with the computer(s) found at the scene. Your affiant may need that documentation to search the computer. Moreover, that documentation may well contain information identifying the owner and/or user of that computer.

Occupancy:

Based on your affiant's training and experience, your affiant knows that occupants of dwellings usually receive correspondence addressed to the occupants at that particular dwelling. Such correspondence usually includes, but is not limited to, phone bills, utility bills, rental agreements, rent receipts, identification papers, canceled mail envelopes, and personal letters. Additionally, your affiant knows that other evidence of ownership and control of said dwellings can usually be found on the occupants of said dwellings and may include, but is not limited to, keys, rent receipts and photographic identification documents, with names and addresses on them. Your affiant seeks permission to seize those items.

Your affiant will not intercept electronic mail or examine electronic mail that has not been read and stored. To the best knowledge of your affiant, this Affidavit and Search Warrant complies with the requirements of Section 2703, of Title 18 United States Code dealing with the disclosure by a provider of electronic communications services of the contents of an electronic communication that is in electronic storage.

On the basis of the foregoing, your affiant believes that evidence of the commission of felony violations of California Penal Code section 502 will be found upon the premises and in the records heretofore described.

That based upon the above facts, your affiant prays that a search warrant be issued with respect to the above location for the seizure of said property, and that the same be held under Penal Code section 1536 and disposed of according to law.

AFFIANT John C. Smith

Criminal Investigator

Subscribed and sworn to before me

this 23rd day of January 1994.

JUDGE OF THE SUPERIOR COURT

Exhibits:

1. Message "Hello John", from Patricia Hertz, April 14, 1994.

2. Message to ferris@univ from jeanc@college-ca, April 14, 1994.

3. Message from Patricia Hertz, Subj: From Suspect, March 21, 1994, with Suspect explaining why he is using this account.

4. Message from fly <carter@.com>, to hertz@univ, Subj: THE TROJAN HORSE (for Suspect). March 22, 1994.

5. Dept Head's report/chronology of this event. April 20, 1994.

6. Message from Systemop@college-ca.edu, To: Sysadmin@isc.univ, Subj: last list. April 20, 1994.

7. "last" log from supect2nd (Unix) account showing activity on 3-17-94.

8. "last" log from hertz (Unix) account showing activity on 3-17-94.

9. SMTP, mail log, from IBM network showing message to jeanc@college-ca on April 14, 1994.

10. hertz@.univ "last" log showing connections and dates; this includes modem connections.

11. Copy of the "forward" file from the hertz@ account on the April 11 backup tape.

Glossary

acceptable level of risk A judicious and carefully considered assessment by the appropriate authority that a computing activity or network meets the minimum requirements of applicable security directives. The assessment should take into account the value of a site's assets; threats and vulnerabilities; countermeasures and their efficacy in compensating for vulnerabilities; and operational requirements.

access The ability and the means to approach, communicate with (input to or receive output from), or otherwise make use of any material or component in a computer system.

access code An identification number or a set of characters that is sometimes required to gain entry to a computer program or system. It is often desirable for individuals and companies to protect their valuable data or resources from unauthorized use. However, the computer has no way of knowing whether the person entering the password or code is legitimate or not; thus passwords should always be protected and changed often. Often synonymous with *password*.

access control The process of limiting access to the resources of a system only to authorized programs, processes, or other systems (in a network). Synonymous with controlled access and limited access.

accountability The principle that individuals using a facility or a computer system must be able to be identified. With accountability, violations or attempted violations of system security can be traced to individuals who can then be held responsible for their actions.

accuracy The principle that keeps information from being modified or otherwise corrupted either maliciously or accidentally. Accuracy protects against forgery or tampering. Usually synonymous with *integrity*.

asynchronous   When signals are sent to a computer at irregular intervals, they are described as asynchronous. When data are transmitted asynchronously, they are sent at irregular intervals by preceding each character with a start bit and following it with a stop bit. Asynchronous transmission allows a character to be sent at random after the preceding character has been sent, without regard to any timing device.

asynchronous attacks   Attacks that take advantage of dynamic system actions and the ability to manipulate the timing of those actions.

ATM (asynchronous transfer mode)   A new, high-speed form of networking that will support data communications, video, and voice communications on the same line. ATM will be used in both LANs and WANs more in the future.

attack   The act of trying to bypass security controls on a system. An attack may be active, resulting in the alteration of data, or passive, resulting in the release of data. The fact that an attack is made does not necessarily mean that it will succeed. The degree of success depends on the vulnerability of the system or activity and the effectiveness of existing countermeasures.

audit   To record independently and examine documents or system activity (e.g., logins and logouts, file accesses, security violations).

audit trail   A chronological record of system activities that is sufficient to enable the reconstruction, review, and examination of the sequence of environments and activities surrounding or leading to an operation, a procedure, or an event in a transaction from its inception to final results.

authentication   (1) The way a user proves to a system that he is who he claims to be; authentication is usually necessary before being given access to a system or its resources. (2) The verification of the integrity of data that have been stored, transmitted, or otherwise exposed to possible unauthorized modification.

authenticity   The principle that ensures that a message is received in exactly the same form in which it was sent.

authorization   The granting of rights to a user or a program. For example, certain users may be authorized to access certain files in a system, whereas only the system administrator may be authorized to export data or to change people's access rights.

automated information system   An assembly of computer hardware, software, and/or firmware configured to collect, create, communicate, compute, disseminate, process, store, and/or control data or information.

availability   The principle that ensures that computer systems and data are working and available to users. *Denial of service* is an attack on availability.

back door See *trap door*.

backup Copying of data to a medium from which the data can be restored if the original data are destroyed or compromised.

BBS (bulletin board system) A computer that operates with a program and either a network or a modem to allow other computers with similar connections to communicate with it, often on a round-the-clock basis. There are hundreds of MS-DOS and PC-related bulletin board systems in the United States offering a wealth of information and public domain software that can be downloaded; there are thousands of bulletin boards (usually known as "newsgroups") on the Internet dealing with every imaginable subject. Most BBSs fall into one of five distinct categories. The *general-interest BBS* caters to a large audience, with message bases devoted to several topics, a generous supply of public domain software, news, and entertainment. The *technical BBS* deals with questions about software, hardware, and programming. *System-specific* boards focus on some particular brand of computer system and contain compatibility tips and information on related issues. The *special-interest BBS* offers information on noncomputer subjects. Other boards exist primarily as sources for the many public domain programs available and contain massive libraries of files for downloading.

benign environment A nonhostile environment that may be protected from external hostile elements by physical, personnel, and procedural security countermeasures.

between-the-lines entry Access that an unauthorized user gets, typically by tapping the terminal that is inactive at the time, of a legitimate user. See *piggybacking*.

binary system The base 2 number system in which only the digits 1 and 0 are used is referred to as the binary system. The base 2 (or binary) system lets us express any number, if we have enough bits, as a combination of 1s and 0s.

bit Binary digit. In the binary (i.e., base 2) numeration system, either of the digits 0 or 1.

BITNET A worldwide academic and research network that connects many universities, colleges, and collaborating research centers. The name BITNET refers to the combined U.S. and Mexican constituencies, Canada, and EARN (the European Academic Research Network).

blue box devices Created by crackers and phone hackers ("phreakers") to break into the telephone system to make calls that bypass billing procedures. Other "color" boxes (e.g., black boxes) are also used in this way.

browsing The act of searching through storage to locate or acquire information without necessarily knowing of the existence or the format of the information being sought.

call back or dial back   A procedure for identifying a remote terminal. In a call back, the host system disconnects the caller and then dials the authorized telephone number of the remote terminal to reestablish the connection.

challenge-response   A type of authentication in which a user responds correctly (usually by performing some calculation based on the time and/or the user's secret key) to a challenge (usually a numeric, unpredictable one).

checksum   Numbers summed according to a particular set of rules and used to verify that transmitted data has not been modified during transmission.

ciphertext   In cryptography, the unintelligible text that results from encrypting original text.

cleartext   See **plaintext**.

communications security (COMSEC)   A type of security that protects telecommunications and ensures the authenticity of such telecommunications. Communications security measures include access controls, cryptographic methods, shielding of communications cabling, and firewalls.

compromise   A violation of the security policy of a system such that unauthorized disclosure of sensitive information may have occurred.

computer   An electronic device for performing high-speed arithmetic and logical operations. There are five key parts to a computer: the processor, the memory, the input/output, storage (disk or tape), and the software (programs). The four general classifications of computers are the microcomputer, the minicomputer, the mainframe, and the super-computer whose differences depend on the type of processor, size of memory, and the input/output devices utilized. Because of the rapid advances in computer technology, the boundaries between these classifications are not clearly defined.

computer abuse   The misuse, alteration, disruption, or destruction of data processing resources. The key aspect is that it is intentional and improper.

computer crime   Any violation of a computer crime statute.

computer fraud   Computer-related crimes involving deliberate misrepresentation, alteration, or disclosure of data in order to obtain something of value (usually for monetary gain). A computer system must have been involved in the perpetration or cover-up of the act or series of acts. A computer system might have been involved through improper manipulation of input data; output or results; applications programs; data files; computer operations; communications; or computer hardware, systems software, or firmware.

computer program   A series of statements instructing the computer to perform a task or process data. The program may be in a high-level source code form, which requires intermediate processing before the computer can execute it, or it may be in an object form that can be directly executed by the computer.

computer-related crime   Any illegal act for which knowledge of computer technology is involved for its investigation, perpetration, or prosecution.

computer security (COMPUSEC)   Measures taken to protect data that are being entered or stored in a computer system, including encryption of data files, the use of access controls on systems and files, and the assignment of security-critical functions only to certain individuals (e.g., the system or security administrator).

confidentiality   The principle that keeps information from being disclosed to anyone not authorized to access it. Synonymous with *secrecy.*

contingency plan   A plan for emergency response, backup operations, and postdisaster recovery maintained by an activity as a part of its security program that will ensure the availability of critical resources and facilitate the continuity of operations in an emergency situation. Synonymous with *disaster plan* and *emergency plan.*

controlled access   Synonymous with *access control.*

copy protection   Because it is a violation of law to make a copy of copyrighted software and pass it along to another person, many software developers devise methods to prevent or discourage this unauthorized duplication. Although copy protection has been implemented using various techniques, sometimes very sophisticated, there is often another program, called a *copy buster,* to unlock or override the copy protection scheme. As the copy protection schemes can often be broken and because they cause the purchaser unnecessary inconveniences when moving the programs to a new hard disk, by the late 1980s most copy protection had been removed from personal computer software.

copyright   The legal, exclusive right to the publication, production, or sale of the rights to a literary, dramatic, musical, or artistic work, or to the use of a commercial print or label, granted by law for a specified period of time to an author, artist, composer, programmer, and so on. A copyright is registered by depositing a copy of the work with the Copyright Office in Washington, DC. Note that U.S. copyright law has been changed several times in the last few decades: copyright coverage of any particular work may depend on when it was originally written. Current works are covered by copyright from the moment they are expressed in a fixed form (e.g., on paper or diskette). Registration is not required.

countermeasure   Any action, device, procedure, technique, or other measure that reduces the vulnerability of or threat to a system.

covert channel   A communications channel that allows two cooperating processes to transfer information in a manner that violates the system's security policy.

CPU   Every computer has a central processing unit. The CPU is the portion of a computer where instructions are fetched, decoded, and executed. The overall activity of the computer is controlled by the CPU. It consists essentially of an arithmetic and logic unit, a control unit, and an internal memory. The control of functions is exercised through the interpretation and execution of instructions. Today's CPUs for microcomputers are contained in chips small enough to easily fit in the palm of your hand.

cracker   A person who engages in computer and telecommunications intrusion.

cracking   The act of breaking into a computer system.

crash   A computer system or program is said to crash when it has become inoperable because of a malfunction in the equipment or the software. One of the most common reasons for a system crash is a fluctuation or loss of power supply. In most cases, when the system crashes because of a power fluctuation, rebooting the system will normally restore proper operations. However, one of the most dreaded types of crashes is the head crash. See also *head crash*.

CRT   Cathode ray tube. A device that presents data or graphics in visual form.

cryptography   The science and study of secret writing.

data   A representation of facts, concepts, or instructions suitable for communication, interpretation, or processing by humans or computers.

data diddling   Altering of data in an unauthorized manner before, during, or after input into a computer system.

data security   The protection of data from unauthorized (accidental or intentional) modification, destruction, or disclosure.

decryption   The transformation of encrypted text (called *ciphertext*) into original text (called *plaintext*).

denial of service   Any action or series of actions that prevent any part of a system from functioning in accordance with its intended purpose. This includes any action that causes unauthorized destruction, modification, or delay of service. Delay or partial denial is more often called *degradation of service*. Synonymous with *interdiction*.

dialed number recorder (DNR)   A device that records the telephone numbers of calls placed from a particular telephone. A DNR may help in tracing or documenting the actions of an intruder.

digital There are two main ways of doing things electronically: analog or digital. The digital method is to consider a circuit either on or off, a signal as either present or absent, with no levels in between. Electronic circuits using the digital mode are simple to design and (usually) less critical in operation. The all-or-nothing nature of digital circuits makes them more immune to drift and distortion, and their simplicity makes them easy to manufacture in large quantity. Digitizing is transforming a signal or piece of information into digital form.

disaster recovery See **contingency plan**.

dump A copy of the contents of storage locations in main memory at a specified point in time. A dump can be recorded on paper, to tape, or to a file to be used for debugging purposes.

dumpster diving Searching for access codes or other sensitive information in the trash. With the electronic version of dumpster diving, crackers may try to recover erased data from tapes or disks. Synonymous with *trashing*.

eavesdropping Listening in to voice or electronic data transmissions without authorization.

electronic mail (email) Electronic mail systems allow computer users to exchange information quickly and easily on a network of computers. The most sophisticated electronic mail systems provide a wide array of transfer functions for the exchange of documents, binary files, graphics, and even such data as voice messages and video images. There are three major types of email: network-based, for users on a single or multiple local area network; host email, which runs on mainframes and minicomputers as an important component of office automation; and public email, which is provided by communications-oriented companies and is accessible through telephone lines.

emanations Unintentional data-related or intelligence-bearing signals that, if intercepted and analyzed, disclose the information transmission received, handled, or otherwise processed by any information processing equipment. See *TEMPEST*.

emission security The protection resulting from all measures taken to deny unauthorized persons information of value that might be derived from interception and from an analysis of compromising emanations from systems.

encryption The transformation of original text (called *plaintext*) into unintelligible text (called *ciphertext*).

entrapment The deliberate planting of apparent flaws in a system for the purpose of detecting attempted penetrations.

erasure or degaussing   A process by which a signal recorded on magnetic media is removed. Erasure is accomplished in two ways: (1) by alternating current erasure, by which the information is destroyed by applying an alternating high and low magnetic field to the media; and (2) by direct current erasure, by which the media are saturated by applying a unidirectional magnetic field.

fault   A condition that causes a device or system component to fail to perform in a required manner.

fault tolerant   A fault-tolerant computer system is designed to provide continuous operation in the event of a failure. Such a system consists of redundant components and processes that are designed to immediately replace any failed component. Fault-tolerant computer systems are widely used in the finance industry for operations such as stock market transactions and online banking functions.

firewall   A hardware and/or software system that protects an internal system or network from the outside world (e.g., the Internet) or protects one part of a network from another. Often, firewalls screen all traffic, allowing some to pass through (that which is allowed by the site's security policy) and blocking the rest.

firmware   A computer program that is considered to be a part of a computer and not modifiable by the computer operating system. Typically embedded into microchips onboard the computer system components.

freeware   As a type of freely distributed software, freeware is a program placed in the public domain. It may be freely copied and passed on to others, with or without restrictions, but unlike user-supported software, each user is not expected to register with the author nor pay a usage fee. Often the author will include a request for comments on the value of the program.

gateway   A system that is attached to two systems, devices, or networks. Communications from one system or network to another are routed though the gateway. Security is typically concentrated at this gateway system. If a firewall is implemented for a system, it will often be on the gateway so it can screen or filter information that is not allowed to pass from one system or network to the other.

hacker   Someone who spends many hours with the computer, often successfully operating it by trial and error without first referring to the manual. A hacker is often a technical person in the computer field, such as an assembly language programmer or systems programmer. Today, the media have given the term a negative meaning. The news media have often used the term in a derogatory manner to refer to people who use their technical knowledge to gain unauthorized access and perform mischievous or destructive activity in computer systems and data banks. Members of the computing community often use the term *cracker* to refer to these criminals.

harassment In terms of computer security, using computer methods (e.g., email) to slander or bother someone.

head crash Disk contamination which may occur as a consequence of the read/ write heads colliding with the disk surface, resulting not only in lost data but also in damaged hardware.

identification The way a user tells the system who he is, usually by entering an account name or number.

impersonation Synonymous with *spoofing, mimicking*, and *masquerading*.

inference Legitimately viewing a number of small pieces of data, then putting them together to deduce some piece of nonobvious and secret data.

integrity See **accuracy**.

interdiction See **denial of service**.

internal security controls Hardware, firmware, and software features within a system that restrict access to resources (hardware, software, and data) to authorized subjects only (persons, programs, or devices).

Internet A worldwide set of interconnected TCP/IP networks. Originally, the ARPANET, the Internet includes, or has included (some have been absorbed by other networks) such networks as AARNet, CSNET, CSUNET, Cypress, the Terrestrial Wideband Network (part of the Defense Research Internet), ESnet, JUNET, Los Nettos, MILNET, NORDUnet, NSN, ONET, and NSFNET.

IP spoofing A method of masquerading in which an attacker forges the addresses on data packets sent over the Internet so they appear to be coming from inside a network in which systems trust each. IP stands for Internet Protocol

ISDN (integrated services digital networking) A service offered by an increasing number of phone companies. ISDN allows homes and businesses to share high-speed data communications along with voice communications on the same wires. It splits basic service into shared channels, each of which can be used for different calls.

leakage Unauthorized, covert removal or the obtaining of copies of data from a computer system. See also *covert and channel*.

limited access Synonymous with *access control*.

local area network (LAN) When two or more computers are linked together for the purpose of sharing information and/or peripheral devices they form a network. When the network is confined to a small geographically restricted area (up to a few miles), such as within the same building or perhaps on a college campus, it is referred to as a local area network. There are three types of data transmission media used on most of today's LANs: a twisted-pair of wires, coaxial cable, and the newest, fiber optical cable. There are also three basic types of LAN topologies in use today: the ring, the star, and the bus or line.

log   A recording (journal) of all environmental changes relative to the database. It may include copies of all transactions, before/after images of updated records, time and date stamps, user and terminal ID, security breaches, and so on. Logs also exist at the system and communications levels, recording significant events.

log file   A file that keeps track of system activity. If a system is attacked, the log files may contain evidence leading to the intruder or may help in restoring system operation.

login   The process of identifying oneself to, and having one's identity authenticated by, a computer system.

logic bomb   A resident computer program that triggers an unauthorized act when a certain event (e.g., a date) occurs.

luser   Slang for "losing user"; a naive or untrained computer user.

maintenance hook (exit)   Special instructions in software to allow easy maintenance and additional feature development. These are not clearly defined during access for design specification. Hooks frequently allow entry into the code at unusual points or without the usual checks, so they are a serious security risk if they are not removed prior to live implementation. Maintenance hooks are special types of trap doors.

malicious logic   Hardware, software, or firmware that is intentionally included in a system for an unauthorized purpose; e.g., a Trojan horse.

masquerading   Posing as an authorized user, usually in an attempt to gain access to a system. Synonymous with *spoofing, mimicking,* and *impersonation.*

microcomputer   In general, as a class of computers, the microcomputer is the smallest and least expensive. It is fully operational and uses microprocessors as its central processing units. Microcomputers are used in the home as personal computers; they are also widely used in businesses and schools.

mimicking   Synonymous with *spoofing, masquerading,* and *impersonation.*

minicomputer   A computer that is usually more powerful than a microcomputer and usually less powerful than a mainframe computer. Minicomputers are most often found in businesses and schools, and very rarely in the home. As computers become more and more powerful each year, the exact definitions of micros, minis, and mainframe computers continue to change. In 1959, Digital Equipment Corp. launched the minicomputer industry with the introduction of the PDP-1.

modem An acronym for MOdulator-DEModulator. It is a device that converts digital data from a computer or terminal into analog data that can be transmitted over telephone lines. On the receiving end, it then converts the analog data back to digital data. A modem handles the dialing and answering of a telephone call and generates the speed of the data transmission, which is measured in bits per second, or baud rates. Typical rates: 300, 1200, 2400, 9600, 19200, and higher. The telephone industry sometimes refers to a modem as a *dataset*.

need to know The principle stating that a user should have access only to the data he or she needs to perform a particular function.

network The interconnection of two or more computer systems or facilities that provide for the transfer or sharing of computer system resources. A typical network might consist of the central computer facilities, the remote terminals, PCs and workstations, the interconnecting communication links, the front end processor, and the telecommunications systems. A number of networks might be interconnected, providing connections to the Internet and to other global internetworks.

newsgroup See *BBS*.

off-the-shelf (OTS) A term designating commercial products that are ready for use without modification.

one-time password A nonreusable password, sometimes associated with smart cards. Because it's used only once, a one-time password is far more secure than a conventional one.

operating system (OS) Software that controls the execution of computer programs and that usually provides scheduling, debugging, input/output control, accounting, compilation, storage assignment, data management, and related services. An operating system is an integrated collection of service routines for supervising the sequencing and processing of programs by a computer. Operating systems control the allocation of resources to a user and their programs and play a central role in ensuring the secure operation of a computer system. Operating systems may perform debugging, input/output, accounting, resource allocation, compilation, storage assignment tasks, and other "system"-related functions. In a time-sharing environment, the operating system is a collection of programs remaining permanently in memory to provide overall coordination and control of the total operating system. It prevents users' programs from interfering with each other; each program is run for a certain length of time, and then the monitor switches control to another program in a rotating sequence. Switching is frequent enough so that all programs appear to run simultaneously. Another function of the time-sharing operating system is to process I/O commands.

operations security (OPSEC)   A type of security that prevents and detects security breaches. With operations security, an organization can deny to potential adversaries information about capabilities and intentions by identifying, controlling, and protecting evidence of the planning and execution of sensitive activities and operations.

packet   A group of data elements transmitted together that generally form part of a larger transmission made up of a number of packets. A packet also contains additional information such as packet number and error detecting codes. Packet switching is a method of communication that involves splitting a transmission into packets. Successive packets along a given channel can belong to different transmissions. A device used to create and unpack packets is called a PAD (packet assembler/disassembler). There is a different PAD for each protocol supported (i.e., X.25, TCP/IP, etc.).

packet-switching network (PSN)   A value-added network offering long distance computer communications allowing the user to access a remote computer, by dialing a local node, or access point. The PSNs use high-speed digital links, which can be land lines or satellite communications. They use synchronous communications, usually with the X.25 protocol. The routes are continually optimized, and successive packets of the same message need not necessarily follow the same path. The original ARPANET was a packet-switching network, as was Telenet (operated by General Telephone Co.) and TYMNET (operated by McDonnell-Douglas).

password   A protected word or string of characters that identifies or authenticates a user for access to a specific resource such as a facility, system, file, or record.

password sniffing   Sniffers are programs that monitor all traffic on a network, collecting a certain number of bytes from the beginning of each session, usually the part where the password is typed unencrypted on certain common Internet services such as FTP and Telnet.

pen register   A device that records the telephone numbers of calls received by a particular telephone. A pen register may help in tracing or documenting the actions of an intruder.

penetration   The successful act of bypassing the security mechanisms of a system.

penetration testing A type of security testing in which testers attempt to circumvent the security features of a system in an effort to identify system weaknesses.

personal identification number (PIN) An identifying code that a user enters to gain access to a system or application (e.g., a computer system, a door, an ATM machine).

personnel security A type of security that protects the people who work in an organization and protect computer equipment and data from these people and from those outside the organization. For example, personnel security establishes procedures ensuring that all personnel who have access to sensitive information have the required authority as well as appropriate clearances.

phreaking The act of employing technology to attack the public telephone system. Phreakers seek to place calls without being charged for them or charge them to others (fraud), penetrate phone company supervisory computers, and otherwise subvert or disrupt telephone operations. Many crackers are also phreakers: they seek ways to make repeated modem connections to computers they are attacking without being charged for those connections, and in a way that makes it difficult or impossible to trace their calls using conventional means.

physical security A type of security that protects the physical computer facility, computer equipment, and media from natural, environmental, and deliberate disasters. Physical security measures include locks and keys, devices such as surge protectors, and biometric controls.

piggybacking Using an authorized user to gain unauthorized access to a facility or a system. See also *between-the-lines entry*.

plaintext In cryptography, the original text that is encrypted. Synonymous with *cleartext*.

privileges Rights granted to a user or a program. For example, certain users might have privileges that allow them to access certain files in a system. Only the system administrator might have the privileges necessary to start up or reconfigure the system.

pseudo-flaw An apparent loophole deliberately implanted in an operating system program as a trap for intruders.

public domain In reference to software, public domain refers to one of the types of freely distributed programs. When the author or programmer of a piece of software retains no legal rights and has not attached a copyright notice, it is then referred to as "public domain." Some public domain programs have been copyrighted but do not request a fee for continued use. Anyone may use public domain software and freely pass it on to others.

race conditions   Races between processes operating on a system. Such conditions can be abused by skillful attackers.

repudiation   The denial by someone who did something in a system (e.g., sent a message) that he actually did perform that action.

reverse engineering   A process by which people take a computer chip or machine-code executable version of a program and figure out what the program or chip is doing.

RF (radio frequency)   A broad spectrum of electromagnetic radiation. RF radiation is used primarily for the purpose of communications.

risk   The possibility that a particular system vulnerability will be exploited.

risk analysis (or risk management)   The total process of identifying, controlling, and eliminating or minimizing uncertain events that may affect system resources. It includes risk analysis, cost/benefit analysis, selection, implementation and test, security evaluation of safeguards, and overall security review.

RJE (remote job entry).   Refers to the programs used to submit processing jobs from terminals.

salami technique   The process of secretly and repetitively slicing away tiny amounts of money (like the slices of a salami) in a way that is unlikely to be noticed (e.g., taking advantage of the rounding of decimals in bank interest calculations).

scanning   Running a program, often called a *war dialer* or a *demon dialer*, that tries a set of sequentially changing numbers (e.g., telephone numbers or passwords) to determine which ones respond positively; for example, with telephone numbers, the program would report those that successfully connect to modems. Synonymous with *war dialing*.

scavenging   Searching through object residue (e.g., discarded disks, tapes, or paper) to acquire sensitive data without authorization. Synonymous with *trashing* and *dumpster diving*.

security flaw   An error of commission or omission in a system that may allow protection mechanisms to be bypassed.

secrecy   See **confidentiality**.

security policy   The set of rules and practices that regulate how an organization manages, protects, and distributes sensitive equipment or information.

security safeguards The protective measures and controls that are prescribed to meet the security requirements specified for a system. Those safeguards may include but are not necessarily limited to: hardware and software security features, operating procedures, accountability procedures, access and distribution controls, management constraints, personnel security, and physical structures, areas, and devices. Also called *safeguards.*

session hijacking Taking over an authorized user's terminal session, either physically when the user leaves his terminal unattended or electronically when the intruder carefully connects to a just-disconnected communications line.

shareware Software that is distributed over bulletin boards for people to download. Unlike freeware, shareware is not public domain. Users who download and use shareware are expected to send a registration and fee to the shareware authors. In return, the user often gets an expanded or enhanced version of the shareware program.

shielding Buffering or putting a container of some kind around a piece of equipment (e.g., a computer, a disk drive or printer, a cable, or even an entire building) so emissions from the equipment cannot leak out and be decoded, leading to information compromise.

smart card An access card containing encoded information and sometimes a microprocessor and a user interface. The information on or generated by the card is used to authenticate the user so he or she can gain access to a facility or a system.

social engineering The process of gaining privileged information about a computer system by skillful lying, usually over a telephone. Some crackers are expert at social engineering, and use it to discover telephone numbers, account names, passwords, and other access information from legitimate users. Often, this is done by impersonating an authorized user or administrator, and asking for assistance.

software piracy Unauthorized copying of software, either commercial or otherwise controlled.

spoofing Synonymous with *impersonation, masquerading,* and *mimicking.*

superzapping Using a privileged system program, such as IBM's Superzap, to override ordinary security safeguards and controls.

tampering An unauthorized modification that alters the proper functioning of equipment or a system in a manner that degrades the security or functionality it provides.

technical attack   An attack that can be perpetrated by circumventing or nulli-fying hardware and software protection mechanisms, rather than by subverting system personnel or other users.

technical vulnerability   A hardware, firmware, communication, or software flaw that leaves a computer processing system open for potential exploitation, either externally or internally, thereby resulting in risk for the owner, user, or manager of the system.

TEMPEST   The study and control of spurious electronic signals emitted by elec-trical equipment. (TEMPEST is not an acronym.)

threat   Any circumstance or event with the potential to cause harm to the system or activity in the form of destruction, disclosure, modification of data, or denial of service. A threat is a potential for harm. Threats exist because of the very existence of the system or activity and not because of any specific weakness. For example, the threat of fire exists at all facilities, regardless of the amount of fire protection available.

threat agent   A method used to exploit a vulnerability in a system, operation, or facility.

threat analysis   The examination of all actions and events that might adversely affect a system or operation.

threat monitoring   The analysis, assessment, and review of audit trails and other data collected for the purpose of searching out system events that may constitute violations or attempted violations of system security.

timing attacks   Attacks that take advantage of the timing of computer processes and operations to get access.

traffic   The message flow across a network.

traffic analysis   Collection and analysis of information. Analysis of message characteristics (e.g., length, frequency, destination) can sometimes provide infor-mation to an eavesdropper.

trap and trace device   A generic term that may encompass pen registers, which record the telephone numbers received by a particular phone, and dialed number recorders, which record the telephone numbers dialed by a particular phone. Technically, a trap is placed on a telephone number in advance, while a trace is conducted while the call is in progress.

trap door   A hidden software or hardware mechanism that can be triggered to allow system protection mechanisms to be circumvented. It is activated in some innocent-appearing manner (e.g., a special "random" key sequence or transaction in an application at a terminal). Software developers often introduce trap doors in their code to enable them to reenter the system and perform certain functions. Synonymous with *back door.*

trashing See *dumpster diving.*

Trojan horse A computer program with an apparently or actually useful function that contains additional (hidden) functions that surreptitiously exploit the legitimate authorizations of the invoking process to the detriment of security or integrity.

tunneling Use of one data transfer method to carry data for another method.

USENET A worldwide news conferencing system. It is the largest BBS-like system in existence. Discussion lists in the USENET range from the highly technical, used in research and business, to the frivolous and nonsensical.

user A person or a process that accesses a computer system.

user ID A unique code or string of characters with which a particular user identifies himself or herself to a computer system.

UUCP A worldwide mail network based on the UNIX-to-UNIX Copy Program Protocol. It is usually telephone based.

validation The test activities associated with a product to ensure compliance of that product with its specified requirements. Validation is distinguished from verification testing in that verification is normally conducted by the developing activity, and validation is normally performed by an independent agency. The checking of data for correctness, or compliance with applicable standards, rules, and conventions.

virus A self-propagating program, which may be embedded in software or firmware. A virus spreads when the program containing it executes.

vulnerability A weakness in system security procedures, system design, implementation, internal controls, and so on that could be exploited to violate system security policy.

war dialing Synonymous with *scanning.*

warez Slang for pirated software traded in violation of copyright and license.

wide area network (WAN) When a network is a large-scale one that spans a large geographic area, usually larger than a single city or metropolitan area, it is referred to as a WAN. WANs are usually connected by leased, high-speed, long-distance data circuits, typically using a packet-switched technology. Contrast to *local area network (LAN).*

wiretapping Interception of communications signals with the intent to gain access to information transmitted over communications circuits.

worm A sometimes malicious stand-alone program that can propagate to other computers via networks.

Index

About the Authors

A nineteen-year career law enforcement officer, **David Icove** is presently employed by the Tennessee Valley Authority (TVA) Police-Public Safety Service, Risk and Emergency Management Division. Prior to coming to TVA in 1993, he served for nine years as an instructor in the Behavioral Science Unit at the FBI Academy in Quantico, Virginia. A coauthor of several textbooks on law enforcement and security-related subjects, Dr. Icove holds BS and MS degrees in Electrical Engineering and a Ph.D in Engineering Science and Mechanics from the University of Tennessee, and a BS in Fire Protection Engineering from the University of Maryland. He is a registered Professional Engineer in the states of Tennessee and Virginia.

Karl Seger is an Organizational Psychologist and President of Associated Corporate Consultants, Inc., a firm he founded in 1973. He has provided security consulting services across the United States, Central America and in Europe to multinational corporations, all branches of the U.S. military, the Department of Justice (FBI), the Department of the Treasury, and the Department of Energy. He conducts computer crime and security courses in the U.S. and in Germany and serves as the computer security instructor for the American Society for Industrial Security Assets Protection II Course. Dr. Seger is also the author of the *Antiterrorism Handbook* (Presidio Press, 1990).

William R. VonStorch is currently the head of the Foreign Counterintelligence Automated Data Processing Operations for the Naval Criminal Investigative Service. He has served more than 20 years in the United States Navy and Naval Reserves, specializing in areas of military intelligence and physical and personnel security. During the last 12 years his experience has been in the areas of counterintelligence, law enforcement, anti-terrorism, computer systems, and computer security. Bill also owns and operates a part-time computer consulting firm that specializes in various types of information management service. He co-developed the Computer-Assisted Security and Investigation Analysis Tool for use by the FBI to maintain information on malicious software, security-related incident information, critical elements of federal legislation, and vulnerabilities of computer systems, hardware, and software. He resides in Maryland.

Eugene H. Spafford is on the faculty of the Department of Computer Sciences at Purdue University. He is the founder and director of the Computer Operations, Audit, and Security Technology (COAST) Laboratory at Purdue, and is also associated with the Software Engineering Research Center (SERC) there. Professor Spafford is an active researcher in the areas of software testing and debugging, applied security, and professional computing issues. He was a participant in the effort to bring the Internet worm under control; his published analyses of that incident are considered the definitive explanations. He is the coauthor of *Practical UNIX Security* (O'Reilly & Associates, Second Edition, 1995), and has also coauthored a widely-praised book on computer viruses. He supervised the development of the first COPS and Tripwire security audit software packages, and he has been a frequently-invited speaker at computer ethics and computer security events around the world. He is on numerous editorial and advisory boards, and is active in many professional societies, including ACM, Usenix, IEEE (as a Senior Member), and the IEEE Computer Society. He is involved with several working groups with IFIP Technical Committee 11 on Security and Protection in Information Processing Systems.

Colophon

Our look is the result of reader comments, our own experimentation, and distribution channels.

Distinctive covers complement our distinctive approach to technical topics, breathing personality and life into potentially dry subjects. UNIX and its attendant programs can be unruly beasts. Nutshell Handbooks help you tame them.

The image on the cover of *Computer Crime: A Crimefighter's Handbook* is of a turn-of-the-century police officer, most likely from an American city. Hallmarks of American police uniforms of the time include the long coat, the truncheon (also called a nightstick or billy club) that he is carrying, and the copper helmet. It is from this helmet that the slang terms for U.S. police officers "copper," and its later abbreviated form, "cop," derives.

Edie Freedman designed the cover of this book, using a 19th-century engraving from the Dover Pictorial Archive. The cover layout was produced with Quark XPress 3.3 using the ITC Garamond font.

The inside layout was designed by Jennifer Niederst, with modifications by Nancy Priest, and implemented in FrameMaker 4.0 by Mike Sierra. The text and heading fonts are ITC Garamond Light and Garamond Book. The illustrations that appear in the book were created in Macromedia Freehand 5.0 by Chris Reilley. This colophon was written by Clairemarie Fisher O'Leary.

SYSTEM ADMINISTRATION

Books from O'Reilly & Associates, Inc.

Fall/Winter 1995-96

"Good reference books make a system administrator's job much easier. However, finding useful books about system administration is a challenge, and I'm constantly on the lookout. In general, I have found that almost anything published by O'Reilly & Associates is worth having if you are interested in the topic."

—*Dinah McNutt*, UNIX Review

INTERNET TOOLS

TCP/IP Network Administration

By Craig Hunt
1st Edition August 1992
502 pages, ISBN 0-937175-82-X

TCP/IP Network Administration is a complete guide to setting up and running a TCP/IP network for administrators of networks of systems or lone home systems that access the Internet. It starts with the fundamentals: what the protocols do and how they work, how to request a network address and a name (the forms needed are included in an appendix), and how to set up your network. Beyond basic setup, the book discusses how to configure important network applications, including sendmail, the r* commands, and some simple setups for NIS and NFS. There are also chapters on trouble-shooting and security. In addition, this book covers several important packages that are available from the Net (such as *gated*). Covers BSD and System V TCP/IP implementations.

"Whether you're putting a network together, trying to figure out why an existing one doesn't work, or wanting to understand the one you've got a little better, *TCP/IP Network Administration* is the definitive volume on the subject."
—Tom Yager, *Byte*

Networking Personal Computers with TCP/IP

By Craig Hunt
1st Edition July 1995
408 pages, ISBN 1-56592-123-2

If you're like most network administrators, you probably have several networking "islands": a TCP/IP-based network of UNIX systems (possibly connected to the Internet), plus a separate Netware or NetBIOS network for your PCs. Perhaps even separate Netware and NetBIOS networks in different departments, or at different sites. And you've probably dreaded the task of integrating those networks into one.

If that's your situation, you need this book! When done properly, integrating PCs onto a TCP/IP-based Internet is less threatening than it seems; long term, it gives you a much more flexible and extensible network. Craig Hunt, author of the classic *TCP/IP Network Administration*, tells you how to build a maintainable network that includes your PCs. Don't delay; as Craig points out, if you don't provide a network solution for your PC users, someone else will.

Covers: DOS, Windows, Windows for Workgroups, Windows NT, and Novell Netware; Chameleon (NetManage), PC/TCP (FTP Software), LAN WorkPlace (Novell), Super TCP, and Trumpet; Basic Network setup and configuration, with special attention given to email, network printing, and file sharing.

Managing Internet Information Services

By Cricket Liu, Jerry Peek, Russ Jones,
Bryan Buus & Adrian Nye
1st Edition December 1994
668 pages, ISBN 1-56592-062-7

This comprehensive guide describes how to set up information services and make them available over the Internet. It discusses why a company would want to offer Internet services, provides complete coverage of all popular services, and tells how to select which ones to provide. Most of the book describes how to set up Gopher, World Wide Web, FTP, and WAIS servers and email services.

"*Managing Internet Information Services* has long been needed in the Internet community, as well as in many organizations with IP-based networks. Although many on the Internet are quite savvy when it comes to administering these types of tools, *MIIS* will allow a much larger community to join in and perhaps provide more diverse information. This book will be a welcome addition to my Internet shelf."
—Robert H'obbes' Zakon, MITRE Corporation

Getting Connected: The Internet at 56K and HigherEstablishing a Presence on the Internet

By Kevin Dowd
1st Edition February 1996 (est.)
450 pages (est.), ISBN 1-56592-154-2

Everywhere you turn, the news is inescapable: The nation is hooking up to the Internet. Businesses publicizing their products; educators reaching out to rural communities; scientific researchers collaborating long-distance; consulting groups, church groups: Everybody's getting wired.

But getting your organization connected to the Internet is not as simple as requesting a telephone line. You have to learn about telecommunications technologies, the differences among networking hardware options, and internal networking issues. You need to figure out not only which Internet service provider is best for you, but which services you really need. You'll be faced with a series of technical decisions concerning network security, routing management, and email gateways. And, you'll want to know what's the best free software out there for rounding out your investment.

Getting Connected: Establishing a Presence on the Internet covers all of these issues and explains in detail everything you need to know to make informed decisions. And once you've set up your Internet connection, it helps you troubleshoot problems and introduces you to an array of Internet services, such as the World Wide Web. Tackles issues for the PC, Macintosh, and UNIX platforms.

DNS and BIND

By Paul Albitz & Cricket Liu
1st Edition October 1992
418 pages, ISBN 1-56592-010-4

DNS and BIND contains all you need to know about the Internet's Domain Name System (DNS) and the Berkeley Internet Name Domain (BIND), its UNIX implementation. The Domain Name System is the Internet's "phone book"; it's a database that tracks important information (in particular, names and addresses) for every computer on the Internet.
If you're a system administrator, this book will show you how to set up and maintain the DNS software on your network.

sendmail

By Bryan Costales, with Eric Allman & Neil Rickert
1st Edition November 1993
830 pages, ISBN 1-56592-056-2

This Nutshell Handbook® is far and away the most comprehensive book ever written on sendmail, the program that acts like a traffic cop in routing and delivering mail on UNIX-based networks. Although sendmail is used on almost every UNIX system, it's one of the last great uncharted territories—and most difficult utilities to learn—in UNIX system administration.
This book provides a complete sendmail tutorial, plus extensive reference material on every aspect of the program. It covers IDA sendmail, the latest version (V8) from Berkeley, and the standard versions available on most systems.

Using and Managing UUCP

By Tim O'Reilly, Dale Dougherty, Grace Todino & Ed Ravin
1st Edition March 1996 (est.)
350 pages (est.), ISBN 1-56592-153-4

Using and Managing UUCP describes, in one volume, this popular communications and file transfer program. UUCP is very attractive to computer users with limited resources, a small machine, and a dial-up connection. This book covers Taylor UUCP, the latest versions of HoneyDanBer UUCP, and the specific implementation details of UUCP versions shipped by major UNIX vendors.

Computer Crime

By David Icove, Karl Seger & William VonStorch
1st Edition August 1995
464 pages, ISBN 1-56592-086-4

Computer crime is a growing threat. Attacks on computers, networks, and data range from terrorist threats to financial crimes to pranks. *Computer Crime: A Crimefighters Handbook* is aimed at those who need to understand, investigate, and prosecute computer crimes of all kinds.

This book discusses computer crimes, criminals, and laws, and profiles the computer criminal (using techniques developed for the FBI and other law enforcement agencies). It outlines the the risks to computer systems and personnel, operational, physical, and communications measures that can be taken to prevent computer crimes. It also discusses how to plan for, investigate, and prosecute computer crimes, ranging from the supplies needed for criminal investigation, to the detection and audit tools used in investigation, to the presentation of evidence to a jury.

Contains a compendium of computer-related federal statutes, all statutes of individual states, a resource summary, and detailed papers on computer crime.

Computer Security Basics

By Deborah Russell & G.T. Gangemi Sr.
1st Edition July 1991
464 pages, ISBN 0-937175-71-4

There's a lot more consciousness of security today, but not a lot of understanding of what it means and how far it should go. This handbook describes complicated concepts, such as trusted systems, encryption, and mandatory access control, in simple terms. For example, most U.S. government equipment acquisitions now require "Orange Book" (Trusted Computer System Evaluation Criteria) certification. A lot of people have a vague feeling that they ought to know about the Orange Book, but few make the effort to track it down and read it. *Computer Security Basics* contains a more readable introduction to the Orange Book—why it exists, what it contains, and what the different security levels are all about—than any other book or government publication.

"A very well-rounded book, filled with concise, authoritative information…written with the user in mind, but still at a level to be an excellent professional reference."
—Mitch Wright, System Administrator, I-NET, Inc.

PGP: Pretty Good Privacy

By Simson Garfinkel
1st Edition December 1994
430 pages, ISBN 1-56592-098-8

PGP is a freely available encryption program that protects the privacy of files and electronic mail. It uses powerful public key cryptography and works on virtually every platform. This book is both a readable technical user's guide and a fascinating behind-the-scenes look at cryptography and privacy. It describes how to use PGP and provides background on cryptography, PGP's history, battles over public key cryptography patents and U.S. government export restrictions, and public debates about privacy and free speech.

"I even learned a few things about PGP from Simson's informative book."—Phil Zimmermann, Author of PGP

Building Internet Firewalls

By D. Brent Chapman & Elizabeth D. Zwicky
1st Edition September 1995
544 pages, ISBN 1-56592-124-0

Everyone is jumping on the Internet bandwagon, despite that fact that the security risks associated with connecting to the Net have never been greater. This book is a practical guide to building firewalls on the Internet. It describes a variety of firewall approaches and architectures and discusses how you can build packet filtering and proxying solutions at your site. It also contains a full discussion of how to configure Internetservices (e.g., FTP, SMTP, Telnet) to work with a firewall, as well as a complete list of resources, including the location of many publicly available firewall construction tools.

Practical UNIX and Internet Security, 2nd Edition

By Simson Garfinkel & Gene Spafford
2nd Edition February 1996 (est.)
800 pages (est.), ISBN 1-56592-148-8

A complete revision of the first edition, this new guide spells out the threats, system vulnerabilities, and counter-measures you can adopt to protect your UNIX system, network, and Internet connection. It's complete—covering both host and network security—and doesn't require that you be a programmer or a UNIX guru to use it. This edition contains hundreds of pages of new information on Internet security, including new security tools and approaches. Covers many platforms, both System V and Berkeley-based, including Sun, DEC, HP, IBM, SCO, NeXT, Linux, and other UNIX systems.

Essential System Administration

By Æleen Frisch
2nd Edition September 1995
788 pages, ISBN 1-56592-127-5

Essential System Administration takes an in-depth look at the fundamentals of UNIX system administration in a real-world, heterogeneous environment. Whether you are a beginner or an experienced administrator, you'll quickly be able to apply its principles and advice to your everyday problems.

The book approaches UNIX systems administration from the perspective of your job—the routine tasks and troubleshooting that make up your day. Whether you're dealing with frustrated users, convincing an uncomprehending management that you need new hardware, rebuilding the kernel, or simply adding new users, you'll find help in this book. You'll also learn about back up and restore and how to set up printers, secure your system, and perform many other systems administration tasks. But the book is not for full-time systems administrators alone. Linux users and others who administer their own systems will benefit from its practical, hands-on approach.

This second edition has been updated for the latest versions of all major UNIX platforms, including Sun OS 4.1, Solaris 2.3, AIX 4.1, Linux 1.1, Digital UNIX OSF/1, SCO UNIX version 3, HP/UX versions 9 and 10, and IRIX version 6. The entire book has been thoroughly reviewed and tested on all of the platforms covered. In addition, networking, electronic mail, security, and kernel configuration topics have been expanded.

Managing NFS and NIS

By Hal Stern
1st Edition June 1991
436 pages, ISBN 0-937175-75-7

Managing NFS and NIS is for system administrators who need to set up or manage a network filesystem installation. NFS (Network Filesystem) is probably running at any site that has two or more UNIX systems. NIS (Network Information System) is a distributed database used to manage a network of computers. The only practical book devoted entirely to these subjects, this guide is a "must-have" for anyone interested in UNIX networking.

Linux Network Administrator's Guide

By Olaf Kirch
1st Edition January 1995
370 pages, ISBN 1-56592-087-2

A UNIX-compatible operating system that runs on personal computers, Linux is a pinnacle within the free software movement. It is based on a kernel developed by Finnish student Linus Torvalds and is distributed on the Net or on low-cost disks, along with a complete set of UNIX libraries, popular free software utilities, and traditional layered products like NFS and the X Window System.

Networking is a fundamental part of Linux. Whether you want a simple UUCP connection or a full LAN with NFS and NIS, you are going to have to build a network.

Linux Network Administrator's Guide by Olaf Kirch is one of the most successful books to come from the Linux Documentation Project. It touches on all the essential networking software included with Linux, plus some hardware considerations. Topics include serial connections, UUCP, routing and DNS, mail and News, SLIP and PPP, NFS, and NIS.

System Performance Tuning

By Mike Loukides
1st Edition November 1990
336 pages, ISBN 0-937175-60-9

System Performance Tuning answers the fundamental question: How can I get my computer to do more work without buying more hardware? Some performance problems do require you to buy a bigger or faster computer, but many can be solved simply by making better use of the resources you already have.

termcap & terminfo

By John Strang, Linda Mui & Tim O'Reilly
3rd Edition April 1988
270 pages, ISBN 0-937175-22-6

For UNIX system administrators and programmers. This handbook provides information on writing and debugging terminal descriptions, as well as terminal initialization, for the two UNIX terminal databases.

The Computer User's Survival Guide

By Joan Stigliani
1st Edition October 1995
296 pages, ISBN 1-56592-030-9

The bad news: You can be hurt by working at a computer. The good news: Many of the factors that pose a risk are within your control. *The Computer User's Survival Guide* looks squarely at all the factors that affect your health on the job, including positioning, equipment, work habits, lighting, stress, radiation, and general health. It is not a book of gloom and doom. It is a guide to protecting yourself against health risks from your computer, while boosting your effectiveness and making your work more enjoyable.

This guide will teach you what's going on "under the skin" when your hands and arms spend much of the day mousing and typing, and what you can do to prevent overuse injuries. You'll learn various postures to help reduce stress; what you can do to prevent glare from modern office lighting; simple breathing techniques and stretches to keep your body well oxygenated and relaxed; and how to reduce eye strain. Also covers radiation issues and what electrical equipment is responsible for the most exposure.

The Future Does Not Compute

By Stephen L. Talbott
1st Edition May 1995
502 pages, ISBN 1-56592-085-6

This book explores the networked computer as an expression of the darker, dimly conscious side of the human being. What we have been imparting to the Net—or what the Net has been eliciting from us—is a half-submerged, barely intended logic, contaminated by wishes and tendencies we prefer not to acknowledge. The urgent necessity is for us to wake up to what is most fully human and unmachinelike in ourselves, rather than yield to an ever more strangling embrace with our machines. The author's thesis is sure to raise a controversy among the millions of users now adapting themselves to the Net.

Volume 8: X Window System Administrator's Guide

By Linda Mui & Eric Pearce
1st Edition October 1992
372 pages, ISBN 0-937175-83-8

As X moves out of the hacker's domain and into the "real world," users can't be expected to master all the ins and outs of setting up and administering their own X software. That will increasingly become the domain of system administrators. Even for experienced system administrators, X raises many issues, both because of subtle changes in the standard UNIX way of doing things and because X blurs the boundaries between different platforms. Under X, users can run applications across the network on systems with different resources (including fonts, colors, and screen size). Many of these issues are poorly understood, and the technology for dealing with them is in rapid flux.

This book is the first and only book devoted to the issues of system administration for X and X-based networks, written not just for UNIX system administrators, but for anyone faced with the job of administering X (including those running X on stand-alone workstations).

Note: The CD that used to be offered with this book is now sold separately, allowing system administrators to purchase the book and the CD-ROM in quantities they choose.

The X Companion CD for R6

By O'Reilly & Associates
1st Edition January 1995
(Includes CD-ROM plus 126-page guide)
ISBN 1-56592-084-8

The X CD-ROM contains precompiled binaries for X11, Release 6 (X11 R6) for Sun4, Solaris, HP-UX on the HP700, DEC Alpha, DEC ULTRIX, and IBM RS6000. It includes X11 R6 source code from the "core" and "contrib" directories and X11 R5 source code from the "core" directory. The CD also provides examples from O'Reilly and Associates X Window System series books and *The X Resource* journal.

The package includes a 126-page book describing the contents of the CD-ROM, how to install the R6 binaries, and how to build X11 for other platforms. The book also contains the X Consortium release notes for Release 6.

At Your Fingertips—
A COMPLETE GUIDE TO O'REILLY'S ONLINE SERVICES

O'Reilly & Associates offers extensive product and customer service information online. We invite you to come and explore our little neck-of-the-woods.

For product information and insight into new technologies, visit the O'Reilly Online Center

Most comprehensive among our online offerings is the O'Reilly Online Center. You'll find detailed information on all O'Reilly products, including titles, prices, tables of contents, indexes, author bios, software contents, and reviews. You can also view images of all our products. In addition, watch for informative articles that provide perspective on the technologies we write about. Interviews, excerpts, and bibliographies are also included.

After browsing online, it's easy to order, too by sending email to **order@ora.com**. The O'Reilly Online Center shows you how. Here's how to visit us online:

☞ Via the World Wide Web

If you are connected to the Internet, point your Web browser (e.g., **mosaic, netscape,** or **lynx**) to:

http://www.ora.com/

For the plaintext version, **telnet** to:
www.ora.com (login: **oraweb**)

☞ Via Gopher

If you have a Gopher program, connect your **gopher** to:
gopher.ora.com
Or, point your Web browser to:
gopher://gopher.ora.com/

Or, you can **telnet** to: **gopher.ora.com**
(login: **gopher**)

A convenient way to stay informed: email mailing lists

An easy way to learn of the latest projects and products from O'Reilly & Associates is to subscribe to our mailing lists. We have email announcements and discussions on various topics. Subscribers receive email as soon as the information breaks.

☞ To join a mailing list:

Send email to:
listproc@online.ora.com

Leave the message "subject" empty if possible.

If you know the name of the mailing list you want to subscribe to, put the following information on the first line of your message: **subscribe** "listname" "your name" **of** "your company."

For example: **subscribe ora-news Kris Webber of Fine Enterprises**

If you don't know the name of the mailing list, listproc will send you a listing of all the mailing lists. Put this word on the first line of the body: **lists**

To find out more about a particular list, send a message with this word as the first line of the body: **info** "listname"

For more information and help, send this message: **help**

For specific help, email to: **listmaster@online.ora.com**

The complete O'Reilly catalog is now available via email

You can now receive a text-only version of our complete catalog via email. It contains detailed information about all our products, so it's mighty big: over 200 kbytes, or 200,000 characters.

To get the whole catalog in one message, send an empty email message to: **catalog@online.ora.com**

If your email system can't handle large messages, you can get the catalog split into smaller messages. Send email to: **catalog-split@online.ora.com**

To receive a print catalog, send your snail mail address to: **catalog@ora.com**

Check out Web Review, our new publication on the Web

Web Review is our new magazine that offers fresh insights into the Web. The editorial mission of Web Review is to answer the question: How and where do you BEST spend your time online? Each issue contains reviews that look at the most interesting and creative sites on the Web. Visit us at **http://gnn.com/wr/**

Web Review is a product of the recently formed Songline Studios, a venture between O'Reilly and America Online.

Get the files you want with FTP

We have an archive of example files from our books, the covers of our books, and much more available by anonymous FTP.

`ftp` to:

`ftp.ora.com` (login: `anonymous` – use your email address as the password.)

Or, if you have a WWW browser, point it to:

`ftp://ftp.ora.com/`

FTPMAIL

The ftpmail service connects to O'Reilly's FTP server and sends the results (the files you want) by email. This service is for people who can't use FTP—but who can use email.

For help and examples, send an email message to:

`ftpmail@online.ora.com`
(In the message body, put the single word: `help`)

Helpful information is just an email message away

Many customer services are provided via email. Here are a few of the most popular and useful:

info@ora.com
> For general questions and information.

bookquestions@ora.com
> For technical questions, or corrections, concerning book contents.

order@ora.com
> To order books online and for ordering questions.

catalog@online.ora.com
> To receive an online copy of our catalog.

catalog@ora.com
> To receive a free copy of *ora.com*, our combination magazine and catalog. Please include your snail mail address.

international@ora.com
> Comments or questions about international ordering or distribution.

xresource@ora.com
> To order or inquire about *The X Resource* journal.

proposals@ora.com
> To submit book proposals.

O'Reilly & Associates, Inc.

103A Morris Street, Sebastopol, CA 95472
Inquiries: **707-829-0515, 800-998-9938**
Credit card orders: **800-889-8969** (Weekdays 6 A.M.- 5 P.M. PST)
FAX: **707-829-0104**

O'Reilly & Associates—
LISTING OF TITLES

INTERNET

CGI Scripting on the World Wide Web
(Winter '95-96 est.)
Connecting to the Internet:
An O'Reilly Buyer's Guide
Getting Connected (Winter '95-96 est.)
HTML Handbook (Winter '95-96 est.)
Smileys
The USENET Handbook
The Whole Internet User's
Guide & Catalog
The Whole Internet for Windows 95
Web Design for Designers
(Winter '95-96 est.)
The World Wide Web Journal
(Winter '95-96 est.)

SOFTWARE

Internet In A Box ™ Version 2.0
WebSite™ 1.1

WHAT YOU NEED TO KNOW SERIES

Bandits on the Information
Superhighway (Winter '95-96 est.)
Marketing on the Internet
(Winter '95-96 est.)
When You Can't Find Your
System Administrator
Using Email Effectively

HEALTH, CAREER & BUSINESS

Building a Successful Software Business
The Computer User's Survival Guide
Dictionary of Computer Terms
(Winter '95-96 est.)
The Future Does Not Compute
Love Your Job!
TWI Day Calendar - 1996

USING UNIX

BASICS

Learning GNU Emacs
Learning the bash Shell
Learning the Korn Shell
Learning the UNIX Operating System
Learning the vi Editor
MH & xmh: Email for Users &
Programmers
PGP: Pretty Good Privacy
SCO UNIX in a Nutshell
UNIX in a Nutshell: System V Edition
Using and Managing UUCP
(Spring '96 est.)
Using csh and tcsh

ADVANCED

Exploring Expect
The Frame Handbook
Learning Perl
Making TeX Work
Programming perl
Running Linux
Running Linux Companion CD-ROM
(Winter '95-96 est.)
sed & awk
UNIX Power Tools (with CD-ROM)

SYSTEM ADMINISTRATION

Building Internet Firewalls
Computer Crime:
A Crimefighter's Handbook
Computer Security Basics
DNS and BIND
Essential System Administration
Linux Network Administrator's Guide
Managing Internet Information Services
Managing NFS and NIS
Managing UUCP and Usenet
Networking Personal Computers
with TCP/IP
Practical UNIX and Internet Security
(Winter '95-96 est.)

sendmail
System Performance Tuning
TCP/IP Network Administration
termcap & terminfo
Volume 8 : X Window System
Administrator's Guide
The X Companion CD for R6

PROGRAMMING

Applying RCS and SCCS
C++: The Core Language
Checking C Programs with lint
DCE Security Programming
Distributing Applications Across DCE
and Windows NT
Encyclopedia of Graphics File Formats
Guide to Writing DCE Applications
High Performance Computing
lex & yacc
Managing Projects with make
Microsoft RPC Programming Guide
Migrating to Fortran 90
Multi-Platform Code Management
ORACLE Performance Tuning
ORACLE PL/SQL Programming
Porting UNIX Software
POSIX Programmer's Guide
POSIX.4: Programming for
the Real World
Power Programming with RPC
Practical C Programming
Practical C++ Programming
Programming with curses
Programming with GNU Software
(Winter '95-96 est.)
Programming with Pthreads
(Winter '95-96 est.)
Software Portability with imake
Understanding and Using COFF
Understanding DCE
Understanding Japanese Information
Processing
UNIX Systems Programming for SVR4
(Winter '95-96 est.)

BERKELEY 4.4 SOFTWARE DISTRIBUTION

4.4BSD System Manager's Manual
4.4BSD User's Reference Manual
4.4BSD User's Supplementary Docs.
4.4BSD Programmer's Reference Man.
4.4BSD Programmer's Supp. Docs.
4.4BSD-Lite CD Companion
4.4BSD-Lite CD Companion: Int. Ver.

X WINDOW SYSTEM

Volume 0: X Protocol Reference Manual
Volume 1: Xlib Programming Manual
Volume 2: Xlib Reference Manual
Volume 3: X Window System
User's Guide
Volume. 3M: X Window System
User's Guide, Motif Ed.
Volume. 4: X Toolkit Intrinsics
Programming Manual
Volume 4M: X Toolkit Intrinsics
Programming Manual, Motif Ed.
Volume 5: X Toolkit Intrinsics
Reference Manual
Volume 6A: Motif Programming Man.
Volume 6B: Motif Reference Manual
Volume 6C: Motif Tools
Volume 8 : X Window System
Administrator's Guide
Volume 9: X Window Window
Programming Extentions
(Winter '95-96 est.)
Programmer's Supplement for Release 6
The X Companion CD for R6
X User Tools (with CD-ROM)
The X Window System in a Nutshell

THE X RESOURCE

A QUARTERLY WORKING JOURNAL FOR X PROGRAMMERS

The X Resource: Issues 0 through 15

TRAVEL

Travelers' Tales France
Travelers' Tales Hong Kong (1/96 est.)
Travelers' Tales India
Travelers' Tales Mexico
Travelers' Tales Spain
Travelers' Tales Thailand
Travelers' Tales: A Woman's World

O'Reilly & Associates—
INTERNATIONAL DISTRIBUTORS

Customers outside North America can now order O'Reilly & Associates books through the following distributors. They offer our international customers faster order processing, more bookstores, increased representation at tradeshows worldwide, and the high-quality, responsive service our customers have come to expect.

EUROPE, MIDDLE EAST, AND AFRICA
(except Germany, Switzerland, and Austria)

INQUIRIES
International Thomson Publishing Europe
Berkshire House
168-173 High Holborn
London WC1V 7AA, United Kingdom
Telephone: 44-71-497-1422
Fax: 44-71-497-1426
Email: itpint@itps.co.uk

ORDERS
International Thomson Publishing Services, Ltd.
Cheriton House, North Way
Andover, Hampshire SP10 5BE, United Kingdom
Telephone: 44-264-342-832 (UK orders)
Telephone: 44-264-342-806 (outside UK)
Fax: 44-264-364418 (UK orders)
Fax: 44-264-342761 (outside UK)

GERMANY, SWITZERLAND, AND AUSTRIA

International Thomson Publishing GmbH
O'Reilly-International Thomson Verlag
Königswinterer Straße 418
53227 Bonn, Germany
Telephone: 49-228-97024 0
Fax: 49-228-441342
Email: anfragen@ora.de

ASIA *(except Japan)*
INQUIRIES
International Thomson Publishing Asia
221 Henderson Road
#08-03 Henderson Industrial Park
Singapore 0315
Telephone: 65-272-6496
Fax: 65-272-6498

ORDERS
Telephone: 65-268-7867
Fax: 65-268-6727

JAPAN
O'Reilly & Associates, Inc.
103A Morris Street
Sebastopol, CA 95472 U.S.A.
Telephone: 707-829-0515
Telephone: 800-998-9938 (U.S. & Canada)
Fax: 707-829-0104
Email: order@ora.com

AUSTRALIA
WoodsLane Pty. Ltd.
7/5 Vuko Place, Warriewood NSW 2102
P.O. Box 935, Mona Vale NSW 2103
Australia
Telephone: 02-970-5111
Fax: 02-970-5002
Email: woods@tmx.mhs.oz.au

NEW ZEALAND
WoodsLane New Zealand Ltd.
21 Cooks Street (P.O. Box 575)
Wanganui, New Zealand
Telephone: 64-6-347-6543
Fax: 64-6-345-4840
Email: woods@tmx.mhs.oz.au

THE AMERICAS
O'Reilly & Associates, Inc.
103A Morris Street
Sebastopol, CA 95472 U.S.A.
Telephone: 707-829-0515
Telephone: 800-998-9938 (U.S. & Canada)
Fax: 707-829-0104
Email: order@ora.com

TO ORDER: **800-889-8969** (CREDIT CARD ORDERS ONLY); **ORDER@ORA.COM**